W9-BVW-543

FREEDOM
NATIONAL

ALSO BY JAMES OAKES

The Radical and the Republican: Frederick Douglass,
Abraham Lincoln, and the Triumph of Antislavery Politics

Slavery and Freedom: An Interpretation of the Old South

The Ruling Race: A History of American Slaveholders

FREEDOM NATIONAL

The Destruction of Slavery in the United States, 1861–1865

JAMES OAKES

W. W. NORTON & COMPANY

NEW YORK • LONDON

LONGWOOD PUBLIC LIBRARY

Copyright © 2013 by James Oakes

All rights reserved
Printed in the United States of America
First Edition

For information about permission to reproduce selections from this book,
write to Permissions, W. W. Norton & Company, Inc.,
500 Fifth Avenue, New York, NY 10110

For information about special discounts for bulk purchases, please contact
W. W. Norton Special Sales at specialsales@wwnorton.com or 800-233-4830

Manufacturing by RR Donnelley, Harrisonburg, VA
Book design by Ellen Cipriano
Production manager: Anna Oler

Library of Congress Cataloging-in-Publication Data

Oakes, James.
 Freedom national : the destruction of slavery in the United States,
1861–1865 / James Oakes. — 1st ed.
     p. cm.
 Includes bibliographical references and index.
 ISBN 978-0-393-06531-2 (hardcover)
 1. Slaves—Emancipation—United States. 2. Slavery—United States—
History. 3. Antislavery movements—United States—History. 4. United
States. President (1861–1865 : Lincoln). Emancipation Proclamation.
5. United States—History—Civil War, 1861–1865. I. Title.
 E453.O13 2013
 973.7'14—dc23
                              2012035601

W. W. Norton & Company, Inc.
500 Fifth Avenue, New York, N.Y. 10110
www.wwnorton.com

W. W. Norton & Company Ltd.
Castle House, 75/76 Wells Street, London W1T 3QT

1 2 3 4 5 6 7 8 9 0

For

DEBORAH and DANIEL,

without whom, nothing

CONTENTS

Illustrations follow page 260.

PREFACE

O N M A R C H 2 4, 1 8 6 2, Illinois Republican Isaac Arnold introduced a bill in the House of Representatives that would "render freedom national, and slavery sectional."[1] Arnold's bill would go on to become the law that banned slavery from all of the western territories, but its title harkened back a decade to the first speech Charles Sumner delivered in Congress upon being elected senator from Massachusetts. In that speech, "Freedom National; Slavery Sectional," Sumner proposed a number of federal policies that he and most anti-slavery politicians believed would lead to the eventual destruction of slavery.[2] But the idea that *freedom* was *national* was much older than the policies Sumner specified. Its lineage could be traced to the famous *Somerset* decision issued by the Court of King's Bench in 1772 in which Lord Mansfield ruled that on English soil the law did not recognize a right of "property in man." *Somerset* was in turn a powerful reassertion of a venerable European ideal, the "freedom principle," which held that freedom was the natural condition of those residing within the realm—whether in France, Spain, or the Netherlands.[3] Isaac Arnold's bill was the lineal descendant of that tradition, and in it lay the origins of the Republican Party's antislavery policies during the Civil War.

Tracing the historical origins of a policy—or a war, or almost anything—always risks making it look as though the outcome were preordained. It's especially tempting to think of the destruction of slavery as inevitable, maybe even easy. Abolition in the United States came midway through the Age of Emancipation. The northern states had long since abolished slavery. The Haitian revolution had destroyed it from within, and the British Parliament had destroyed it in Jamaica and Barbados from without, as had the French and the Dutch in their own Caribbean empires. On the other hand, two of the largest slave societies in the Americas, Cuba and Brazil, abolished slavery only in the wake of the American Civil War. A century after the overthrow of New World slavery began, every plantation system in the hemisphere had done away with slave labor.[4] The trajectory is so clear, so relentless, as to make it seem as if the abolition of slavery in the United States had been determined by the irresistible forces of historical progress. Plenty of people talked that way in the middle of the nineteenth century. "Slavery is a hideous anachronism," one Republican congressman declared, "coming to us out of the barbarism and old dead night of the past.[5] The slaveholders were standing fast against the inexorable tide of human history. Their way of life was doomed, the argument went; the entire world was turning against slavery.

The assumption of slavery's inevitable demise shaped the way its opponents thought about how to end it. In 1787, delegates at the Constitutional Convention were willing to make compromises with slavery in part because they were certain the system was dying anyway. From classical political economists like Adam Smith, the Founders learned that slave economies were backward and inefficient, that in the long run slavery could never compete with the superior productivity, the sheer dynamism, of free labor. From moral philosophers they concluded that the progress of antislavery sentiment was steady and irreversible. In time everyone would come to see that slavery had to be abolished. Convinced that slavery was already doomed by the laws of political economy and the progress of morality, it was easy for the men in Philadelphia to conclude that nothing significant was sacrificed by compromising with slavery to create a new nation. How could they have foreseen that the protections for slavery they wrote into the Constitution would become one of the most formidable obstacles to abolition in the United States?[6]

It's also tempting to think that the only thing abolition required was the will to make it happen. If the abolitionists could persuade enough people to hate slavery, the end of slavery would surely follow. By the late eighteenth century, however, most people in the northern states already disliked slavery, and while the intensity of their dislike waxed and waned over the decades, the biggest problem abolitionists faced was not a proslavery public but a Constitution that protected slavery in the states where it already existed.[7] What could the federal government do to destroy slavery if everybody believed it was strictly a state matter, that the Constitution put it beyond the reach of federal intervention? How could there be any national antislavery politics if there was nothing the federal government could do about it? Answering such questions was the single greatest challenge for opponents of slavery. That challenge became more rather than less daunting as the explosive growth of the "Cotton Kingdom" after 1790 cemented the political power of the slaveholders and transformed the South into one of the largest slave societies in the history of the world.

Nevertheless, by 1860 antislavery lawyers and politicians had formulated two distinct scenarios for a national assault on slavery. One was federal pressure on states to abolish slavery themselves. Though nearly everyone agreed that the federal government could not directly abolish slavery in the states, Republicans endorsed a number of policies they believed would eventually force the southern states to destroy slavery on their own. The federal government would surround the South with free states, free territories, and free waters, building what they called a "cordon of freedom" around slavery, hemming it in until the system's own internal weaknesses forced the slave states one by one to abandon slavery. To these external pressures the Republicans would add a number of federal incentives—a gradual timetable, monetary compensation, and subsidies for the voluntary colonization of the freed slaves—all of them designed to speed up the process of state abolition, beginning in the slave states bordering on the North (Delaware, Maryland, Kentucky, and Missouri). This was a peacetime policy designed to put slavery on what Abraham Lincoln called a course of "ultimate extinction." But if there was a war or a rebellion, the Constitution empowered the federal government to implement a second policy, military emancipation, until peace and order were restored. Any educated person would have been familiar with the historical precedents, stretching back to antiquity, for emancipating enemy slaves in wartime. But the precedents had not produced a theory of military emancipation. The founding treatises on the laws of war had almost nothing to say about slavery. By 1863, however, when called on to defend the legality of the Emancipation Proclamation, antislavery lawyers deployed what amounted to an abolitionist theory of military emancipation. These two policies—state abolition and military emancipation— were widely proclaimed by Republicans throughout the secession crisis.

It was this unabashed Republican threat to slavery that provoked the South to secede from the Union in the immediate aftermath of Abraham Lincoln's election in November of 1860. Historians commonly dismiss secession as an outbreak of hysteria, irrationality, and paranoia. But events soon demonstrated that the Republican threat to slavery was far from imaginary. Before the first year of the war was out, both antislavery policies had been initiated. Based on the authority granted to it by the First Confiscation Act, the Lincoln administration began freeing slaves as a "military necessity" on August 8, 1861. Lincoln drafted his first proposals for state abolition a few months later.

It's important to bear in mind that military emancipation and state abolition were two different policies pursued by Republicans along parallel lines throughout the war. Military emancipation was always immediate; slaveholders were never compensated; it applied initially to the disloyal states; and it was implemented first, beginning in the summer of 1861. Gradual abolition applied to loyal slave states, which were beyond the reach of full-scale military emancipation. Lincoln first suggested gradual abolition for Delaware in late 1861, and it remained an option for loyal states as late as 1864. Yet all along, his administration was implementing immediate and uncompensated military emancipation in the seceded states. There was no shift from gradual abolition to immediate emancipation. On the contrary, immediate emancipation began in the rebel states months before Lincoln first proposed gradual abolition in the Border States.

Once initiated, the two policies were implemented more and more aggressively. As firm believers in the superior vitality and strength of free labor, Republicans originally assumed that slavery would crumble quickly under the pressure of war. But prescient observers like Frederick Douglass warned from the start that slavery was the "stomach" of the rebellion, and soon enough Republicans grasped the point. By early 1862 their confident predictions of slavery's swift demise gave way to the widespread recognition that slavery was actually a source of the rebellion's strength in the South. By July virtually all Republicans reached the conclusion that they would have to free all the slaves of all the rebels in the seceded states. With the Emancipation Proclamation, military emancipation reached its climax as the Lincoln administration for the first time ordered Union soldiers to entice slaves from their owners in the rebel states and to enlist blacks for "armed" service in the Union army. The proclamation also increased the pressure for state abolition because it led directly to the systematic recruitment of black soldiers from the loyal slave states, an escalation of the policy of forcing those states to abolish slavery on their own. Over the next few years both policies proved, in their own ways, successful. By 1865 military emancipation had freed hundreds of thousands of slaves, and six states had abolished slavery, ostensibly of their own accord but in fact under intense pressure from the federal government.

But it wasn't enough. There were four million slaves in 1860, and when the war ended no more than 15 percent of them had been emancipated. Slavery was still legal in nine of the fifteen slave states, including nearly all of the most densely populated plantation regions of the Deep South. An increasingly aggressive military emancipation, even when coupled with a more coercive approach to state abolition, could not fully destroy slavery. More disturbing still to Republicans was the distinct possibility that when the Union was restored, the southern states would reverse the results of the war and re-enslave those who had already been freed.

Once they realized that neither military emancipation nor state abolition would be sufficient, Lincoln and the Republicans turned to a third policy—a thirteenth amendment to the Constitution—as the only sure way to abolish slavery forever throughout the United States. Lincoln ran for reelection in 1864 on a platform pledged to rewriting the Constitution, but not until after he won could the Republicans muster the strength to push the amendment through Congress. And not until it was ratified in December of 1865 was slavery finally and irreversibly destroyed. In the end it took four years of brutal war, 750,000 deaths, and three different policies to bring slavery down.[8]

Freedom National is in part an attempt to demonstrate how much harder it was to destroy slavery than anyone first imagined.

IN TELLING THE STORY of how slavery was destroyed, I pay a good deal of attention to the broad antislavery movement, in particular the Republican Party that set out to abolish the institution. A generation ago few historians would have found this controversial. Between the late 1930s and the mid-1970s a number of scholars worked to reconstruct what the historian Dwight Lowell Dumond once called "the antislavery origins of the Civil War." They traced the emergence of political abolitionism in the 1830s and emphasized the continuities between the Liberty and Free Soil Parties of the 1840s and the Republican Party of the 1850s.[9] Since then a number of intellectual shifts have obscured those origins and continuities to the point where the claim that the Republicans intended to destroy slavery is more likely to be greeted with disbelief than assent.

As the antislavery origins of the Civil War receded from our intellectual horizons, there followed a revival of interpretations long associated with the so-called revisionists of the 1930s and 1940s. The Civil War is once again treated by some historians as an accident, by others as a tragic and unnecessary waste of life. It was brought on not by principled opponents who fundamentally disagreed about slavery, but by religious fanatics and moral terrorists who preferred demagogy to peace. If there was a principle at stake in the northern crusade, it was not antislavery but an ethically dubious nationalism aimed at the mere restoration of the Union. Abolitionism is once more consigned to a tiny, beleaguered minority, while the broad appeal of principled antislavery politics goes unexplained.[10] Persuaded that Republicans had no serious antislavery intentions, some historians have denounced the war as morally unjustified. These days most scholars agree that the

South seceded to protect slavery, but neo-revisionists commonly deny that the North was animated by any impulse to destroy it.

It would indeed be difficult to excuse so much bloodshed if it served no purpose other than the restoration of the Union, since that could have been accomplished easily had there been no fundamental disagreement over slavery. The real moral dilemma of the Civil War, however, arises from the fact that it *was* about slavery; the tragedy of the war lies not in its pointlessness, but in its necessity. There were plenty of hotheads who thought a war would be quick and clean. Nevertheless, by early 1861 most of the sober statesmen staring at one another across the Mason-Dixon Line understood that they had pretty much run out of options and were heading for a long and devastating war. As the struggle grew ever more deadly, Lincoln was tormented by the dilemma. He hated slavery and he hated the war. There was no easy way for him to balance the competing moral imperatives of ending the war quickly and destroying slavery completely. Sometimes he tried by suggesting a more gradual abolition in return for a more rapid end to the slaughter. I can't say whether I would have struck the same balance, but I am not inclined to judge Lincoln harshly for having done so. He was always less concerned with *how* slavery was abolished than with ensuring that it *was* abolished. By contrast, to deny that the war was about slavery—on the shaky ground that Republicans supposedly denied it, or the even shakier ground that slavery would have died out anyway—strikes me as an evasion of the moral dilemma of the Civil War, not a serious engagement with it.

Firmly convinced that slavery was the source of the rebellion, Republicans began attacking it almost as soon as the war began. Not having expected to find this, I did what comes naturally to any historian: I went back in time to find out where Republican antislavery policies came from. In my search for the antebellum origins of abolition I rediscovered the antislavery origins of the Civil War. Yet *Freedom National* should not be read as a full accounting of the war's origins. Such a book would require a much broader canvas than I attempt here—not least an account of the political economy of slavery, the development of a free labor society in the North, the evolution of party politics, the schisms within Protestant churches, and more attention to the international context within which both slavery and antislavery developed. *Freedom National* barely touches on these important matters. But it does, I hope, establish the critical role that political abolitionism played in the formulation of Republican antislavery policies and the coming of the Civil War.

Lincoln and the Republicans expected that slaves would run for their freedom if given the chance, and they constructed their antislavery policies on that expectation. They realized that they could not destroy slavery if they did not win the war, and they eventually concluded that they could not win the war unless they reversed decades of federal policy and enlisted tens of thousands of African Americans in the Union army. *Freedom National* therefore specifies in some detail precisely how federal policymakers came to rely on the "loyalty" of the slaves and with that, how important the legacy of slave resistance was to the destruction of slavery.

Nevertheless, I avoid the question of *who* freed the slaves because, framed that way, it tempts scholars to specify a single agent in a process that had many agents. I sometimes think that people in the 1860s understood this better than we do. Even before the war began, the slaves knew that Lincoln's election was of vital importance to their prospects for freedom, just as Republicans warned that the outbreak of civil war would provoke a wave of runaway slaves—maybe even a full-scale slave rebellion—that would ultimately destroy slavery. Everyone knew that an invading Union army posed a direct threat to slavery's survival. To rest the destruction of slavery on the shoulders of any single agent, or to deny the significance of any one of them, is to oversimplify the history of abolition. If Republicans stand out in *Freedom National*, it is not because "Republicans freed the slaves" but because this is a study of antislavery policy and Republicans were the policymakers

If my emphasis on the Republican Party can readily accommodate the role slaves played in slavery's downfall, so too does it fully acknowledge Abraham Lincoln's importance as president. I began this book as an admirer of Lincoln and I finish it with my admiration undiminished. But there's too much hyperbole in the way we talk about Lincoln. He was neither the Great Emancipator who bestrode his times and brought his people out of the darkness, nor was he in any way a reluctant emancipator held back by some visceral commitment to white supremacy. In the evolution of wartime antislavery policy, Lincoln was neither quicker nor slower than Republican legislators. Instead they seemed to move in tandem. Lincoln's swift endorsement of the "contraband" policy, his administration's aggressive implementation of the First Confiscation Act, and his Emancipation Proclamation all pushed Union antislavery policy beyond where Congress had left it. On the other hand, with the Confiscation Acts of 1861 and 1862, as with the abolition amendment in 1864, Congress moved a step beyond Lincoln's own policies up to that point. Neither was ever in the lead for long, and they were never very far apart.

More than ever I view Lincoln in much the same way that Frederick Douglass did in 1876. "Abraham Lincoln was at the head of a great movement," Douglass explained, "and was in living and earnest sympathy with that movement, which, in the nature of things, must go on until slavery should be utterly and forever abolished in the United States.["][11] *Freedom National* can be read as a history of that "great movement"—of the antislavery activists who struggled for decades to formulate the policies and build a political coalition that might one day be able to destroy slavery; of the fugitive slaves who became agents of slavery's destruction by escaping from their farms and plantations to the camps and fortresses of the Union army; and of those northern soldiers who moved into the slave states where they colluded with runaway slaves to undermine the slave system wherever they went. Radicals and runaways, Union soldiers black and white alike, have long since become familiar figures in the history of the "great movement" that destroyed slavery in the United States, and justifiably so.

But when Frederick Douglass spoke of the movement Lincoln led, he was also thinking of the Republican Party, and he would have been perplexed by the relatively inconspicuous place the party currently occupies in the stories we tell of slavery's destruction. "Men are important," he explained in 1880, "but parties are incomparably more important." By then Douglass was unapologetic about his own political allegiance. "I am a Republican," he declared before an enthusiastic audience of African Americans at Cooper Union, "a black Republican [applause,] dyed in the wool [Applause.] Of the Republican Party it may be said that it has been connected for the last 20 years with every reform. It came into existence to prevent the extension of slavery. [Applause.] It has done that. And it came into existence to save the country from slavery. It roused the spirit of the old master class in the South, and they rebelled. It met that rebellion and put it down, [applause,] beyond the possibility of resurrection. And it put down the cause of the rebellion and abolished forever the greatest reproach this Republic has ever known."[12]

Lincoln said in 1852 that under ordinary circumstances men "naturally divide into parties." The man "who is of neither party," he added, "cannot be of any consequence."[13] In the months after his election to the presidency, when supporters and opponents alike demanded a public statement that might defuse the secession crisis, Lincoln responded by declaring that he would never abandon the basic principles of the Republican Party. Asked to clarify his position on slavery, Lincoln said in late 1860 that "he was with his own party; that he had been elected by that party and intended to sustain his party in good faith."[14] There's nothing new in this: anyone who has spent some time studying Lincoln understands that he was, at bottom, a politician. But the party he headed in 1860 was an antislavery party. That's why most abolitionists were either Republicans or supporters of the Republican Party. That's why slaves across the South put so much hope in Lincoln's election. That's why the South seceded. Because when Lincoln took his oath of office in March of 1861, he and his party were committed to an array of policies aimed at the "ultimate extinction" of slavery.

This is not to say that there were no significant differences among Republicans. But most of those differences had to do with matters unrelated to slavery. The party was bitterly divided over the revenue bill to finance the war; it split over the Land-Grant College Act, the Pacific railroad bill, and homestead legislation. There were particularly sharp divisions over the government's power to confiscate real estate, and potentially disruptive tensions between Congress and the president over the reach of each other's war powers, nowhere more so than on the question of who was responsible for reconstruction policy. On bills and resolutions related to slavery, emancipation, and abolition, however, Republicans went out of their way to bury their differences and produced a remarkable string of unanimous or near-unanimous votes—all of them designed to undermine slavery, beginning in July of 1861 and lasting into 1865. Noah Brooks, the perceptive Washington reporter, noticed the pattern halfway through the war. President Lincoln "does not have the cordial and uniform support of his political friends," he observed. Among Republicans there was "an undercurrent of dissatisfaction" along with a "spirit of captious criticism" of their own party leader. It was nevertheless "true," Brooks added, "that upon all great questions, such as emancipation, confiscation, suspension of the writ of habeas corpus act, and other kindred measures, the administration party, *per se*, is a solid column."[15]

Party moderates and radicals worked hard to maintain their consensus against slavery throughout the Civil War. Though he never claimed to be an abolitionist, Lincoln viewed antislavery radicals as the indispensable base of the party, and most of them returned the favor by supporting him in 1860. Abolitionist criticism sometimes annoyed Lincoln, but more often when he spoke of the radicals he emphasized how close he was to them. He once said that the difference between himself and Charles Sumner was six weeks. During his presidency Lincoln met with leading abolitionists—Wendell Phillips, Frederick Douglass, William Lloyd Garrison, and several others—and in those conversations he generally stressed their shared hatred of slavery and their joint commitment to its destruction. No doubt there were differences between antislavery radicals and moderates, but they were differences of style more than substance, of strategy more than goals, differences *within* the "great movement" against slavery.

The determination among Republicans to maintain an antislavery consensus enabled the party to forge a unified opposition to any compromise with the opponents of emancipation. Republicans stood firm during the secession crisis, refusing to support any measures that represented a retreat from their fundamental antislavery policies. Through four years of war Republicans repeatedly swept aside every effort by northern Democrats to keep slavery out of the conflict. Border State leaders watched with increasing dismay as Republicans took advantage of what Lincoln called the "friction and abrasion" of war to undermine slavery even in the loyal slave states. The antislavery consensus began to crack in late 1863 and early 1864, as Republicans embarked on a frantic search for ways to ensure that when the war ended, slavery would be ended as well. But once the party settled on the Thirteenth Amendment, Republicans once again closed ranks against its opponents. Not until December in 1864 did the supermajority requirements of the amendment process force Republicans to trawl for votes among their congressional opponents, working to peel a handful of Democrats away from their party to support the amendment. But that was jawboning, not compromising.

Republicans never forgot that the fundamental conflict of mid-nineteenth-century America was not the squabbling between moderates and radicals within the antislavery movement, but the life and death struggle between those who hated slavery and were prepared to risk war rather than extend its life, and those who defended slavery and were willing to go to war to preserve it. As Lincoln himself explained in 1865, everyone knew that slavery was "somehow, the cause of the war." Where secessionists would "rend the Union, even by war," to "strengthen, perpetuate, and extend" the slave "interest," the Republicans would refuse to compromise on slavery and in so doing "would *accept* war" rather than let the Union perish.[16]

FREEDOM NATIONAL TRACES THE development of antislavery policy from its prewar origins to the ratification of the Thirteenth Amendment. It builds on the work of countless scholars who have charted the history of the antislavery movement, slave resistance, Lincoln's presidency, and emancipation. Yet what is new in this book stems less from any specific disagreements I might have with the work of others than from the implications of resuscitating the antislavery origins of the Civil War. Two of those implications seem worth highlighting.

A long and distinguished tradition of scholarship evaluates emancipation chiefly in terms of its consequences—the critical struggles over land and labor, the reconstruction of black family life, civil rights, political mobilization, issues that go to the very meaning of freedom in the United States after the Civil War. This book focuses instead on the development of antislavery policy, on the origins and implementation of abolition rather than the aftermath of slavery. It ends where many studies of emancipation begin.

Another tradition, equally distinguished, reconstructs the ideological origins of the antislavery movement—with its many roots in enlightenment philosophy, Christian evangelicalism, natural law, and the political cultures of the Whig and Democratic Parties. There's a lot of that sort of history in this book, especially in my reconstruction of the universe of constitutional assumptions within which the opponents of slavery operated as they formulated their policies. But my concern with antislavery constitutionalism is frankly utilitarian: I need to explain the ideas in order to explain the policies. You have to pay careful attention to what Republicans were saying about slavery to fully understand what they were doing, even to recognize that they were doing anything at all. You need to grasp what "freedom national" meant to appreciate what Republican policy was.

Reconstructing the history of antislavery policy has also compelled me to reconsider a popular assumption about the broader trajectory of the Civil War itself. Like most historians I always believed that the purpose of the war shifted "from Union to emancipation," but over the course of my research that familiar transition vanished like dust in the wind, and I have been unable to recover it. Republicans did not believe that the Constitution allowed them to wage a war for any "purpose" other than the restoration of the Union, but from the very beginning they insisted that slavery was the cause of the rebellion and emancipation an appropriate and ultimately indispensible means of suppressing it. It was the Democrats, not the Republicans, who insisted on keeping slavery out of the war, who hoped to restore the Union "as it was," who vehemently denied that the restoration of the Union required the destruction of slavery, and who tried to shift the discussion from slavery to race by demanding an answer to the question *What is to be done with the Negro?*[17] The real question, Republicans believed, was *What is to be done with slavery?* They never had to move from Union to emancipation because the two issues—liberty *and* union—were never separate for them. If there was a shift over the course of the war, it was the realization by Republicans that destroying slavery would be much harder than they had originally expected. Not until January 31, 1865, when the Thirteenth Amendment finally squeezed through the House of Representatives— with but a few votes to spare, and against overwhelming Democratic opposition—could Republicans be reasonably certain that slavery would be fully abolished.

What-if history is always a tricky business, but in this case Lincoln and the Republicans laid out the alternative scenario for us. They believed that if George B. McClellan, the Democratic candidate, were elected president in 1864, the Confederacy would still be defeated but slavery would survive the war. The mass emancipations of 1865 would not have happened. A President McClellan would not have required the defeated Confederate states to abolish slavery as a condition for readmission to the Union. There would have been no Thirteenth Amendment, and without it control over slavery would have reverted to the states where the slaveholders made it clear that even in defeat they would hold on to slavery forever if they could. If that happened there's no telling when, if ever, slavery would have ended in the United States. Who knows what would have happened to slavery in Cuba and Brazil? If the Republicans had not succeeded in making freedom national, we might not even be talking about an Age of Emancipation.

FREEDOM
NATIONAL

FREEDOM NATIONAL

NEBRASKA
TERRITORY

ILLINOIS

INDIAN

KANSAS

MISSOURI

St. Louis

KENTUCK

Fort Donels

Fort Henry

TENNESSEE

INDIAN
TERRITORY

Memphis

ARKANSAS

MISSISSIPPI

ALABAM

Vicksburg

TEXAS

Mobile

LOUISIANA

New Orleans

Gulf of Mexico

Border States (slave states that did not secede)
Confederate states
*The western counties of Virginia remained loyal
to the Union and were admitted as the state of
West Virginia in 1863.

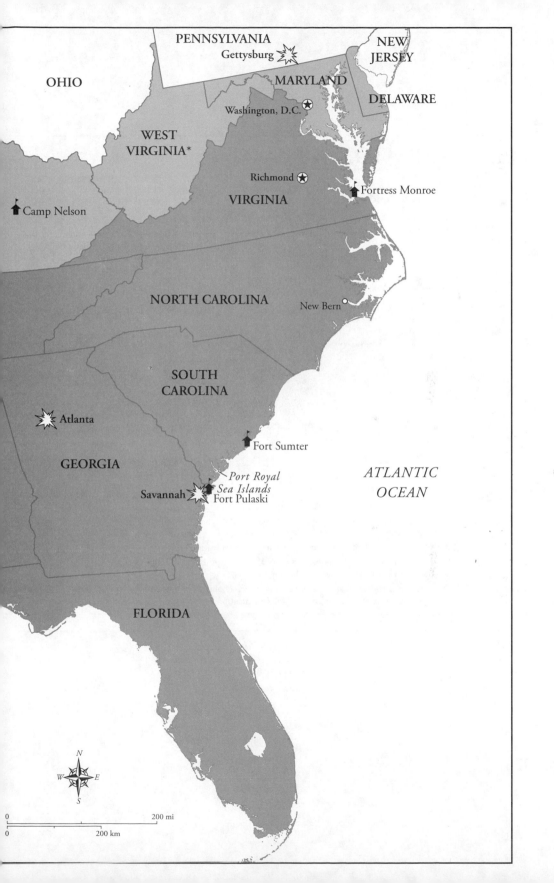

EMANCIPATION, 1861–1865

NEBRASKA TERRITORY

IOWA

PENNSYLVANIA

N.J.

OHIO

MD. DEL.

COLORADO TERRITORY

ILLINOIS

IND.

W. VA.

VIRGINIA

KANSAS

MISSOURI

KENTUCKY

NORTH CAROLINA

NEW MEXICO TERR.

INDIAN TERRITORY

ARKANSAS

TENNESSEE

SOUTH CAROLINA

GEORGIA

MISS.

ALABAMA

TEXAS

FLORIDA

LOUISIANA

Military Emancipation: areas where slaves were emancipated by occupying Union forces before the Emancipation Proclamation was signed.

Emancipation Proclamation: areas to which the Emancipation Proclamation applied.

State Abolition: states that abolished slavery after the signing of the Emancipation Proclamation but before the end of the war.

Thirteenth Amendment: states in which slavery was abolished on December 6, 1865, through the Thirteenth Amendment to the Constitution.

1   "ULTIMATE EXTINCTION"

A FEW WEEKS BEFORE ABRAHAM LINCOLN was inaugurated on March 4, 1861, the House of Representatives unanimously approved a resolution declaring that the federal government had no power to abolish slavery in any state. Lincoln had said the same thing many times before, and he reiterated the point in his inaugural address: "I have no purpose, directly or indirectly, to interfere with the institution of slavery in the States where it exists. I believe I have no lawful right to do so, and I have no inclination to do so." Lincoln went on to indicate that he would have "no objection" to a constitutional amendment that reaffirmed the existing ban on federal abolition of slavery in any state where it was already legal.[1] What clearer indication could there be that Lincoln and the Republicans were initially unwilling to make the Civil War into a struggle over slavery? But disavowals of the kind that Lincoln made had a long history within the antislavery movement. Abolitionists had been struggling for decades to develop an antislavery politics that could overcome one inescapable fact—that the U.S. Constitution recognized and protected slavery in the states where it already existed. Block out that history, and it is impossible to understand what the Republicans expected to do about slavery once Abraham Lincoln became president.

THE FEDERAL CONSENSUS

In 1787 the delegates at the Constitutional Convention in Philadelphia made a series of compromises that obliged the new national government to leave slavery untouched within the states. Charles Cotesworth Pinckney of South Carolina, one of a handful of slavery's forceful defenders in Philadelphia, had threatened to vote against the proposed Constitution if it "should fail to insert some security to the Southern states against an emancipation of the slaves." The specific passages in the Constitution dealing with slavery are well known. The federal government was prohibited from regulating the Atlantic slave trade for twenty-one years; the three-fifths clause counted 60 percent of the slave population for purposes of direct taxation and representation in Congress; and the fugitive slave clause gave masters a claim on runaways who escaped across state lines. In as many as a dozen other places the Constitution recognized slavery indirectly.[2]

Almost immediately Americans began to dispute the meaning of these various clauses, but there was general agreement that the Constitution gave Pinckney and the southern slaveholders what they most wanted: assurance that the federal government had no power to interfere with slavery in the states where it already existed. As one delegate explained to the Massachusetts ratifying convention, "[I]t is not in our power to do anything for or against those who are in slavery in the southern States." Elbridge Gerry, also of Massachusetts, "thought we had nothing to do with the conduct of the States as to Slavery."

Connecticut's Oliver Ellsworth agreed that under the new Constitution slavery was strictly a state institution. "The morality or wisdom of Slavery," he said, "are considerations belonging to the States themselves." This was as axiomatic in the South as it was in the North. During the Virginia ratification debates James Madison was "[s]truck with surprise" by anti-federalist claims that the proposed Constitution would empower the national government to abolish slavery in the states. "[T]here is not power to warrant it" in the Constitution, Madison insisted. "If there be, I know it not." Thomas Jefferson read the Constitution the same way. Shortly before the election in 1800 he allowed a spokesman in South Carolina to release a statement in his name affirming that "the Constitution has not empowered the federal legislature to touch in the remotest degree the question of the condition of property of slaves in any of the States, and that any attempt of that sort would be unconstitutional and a usurpation of rights Congress does not possess."[3]

For seventy-five years hardly anybody—North or South, proslavery or antislavery—doubted that the Constitution put slavery in the states beyond the reach of federal power. This was the federal consensus. No specific clause in the Constitution actually stated that slavery was strictly a state institution, beyond the ability of the federal government to interfere. And yet no other constitutional precept so profoundly shaped the contours of antislavery politics in the years between the founding of the nation and the Civil War.[4]

Even abolitionists agreed that the power to abolish slavery in any state resided solely within that state. Article II of the 1833 "Declaration of Sentiments" announcing the formation of the American Anti-Slavery Society stated unequivocally that "each State, in which Slavery exists, has, by the Constitution of the United States, the exclusive right to *legislate* in regard to its abolition in said State." William Lloyd Garrison wrote that, and he was not alone. In the blistering antislavery speech that Senator Thomas Morris of Ohio delivered in February of 1839—the speech that got him expelled from the Democratic Party—he acknowledged that "the Constitution left the subject of slavery entirely to the States." Joshua Giddings, who was nearly expelled from the Whig Party for *his* radical opposition to slavery, took a similar "state rights" position. With the adoption of the Constitution, Giddings argued, "slavery was made strictly a State institution." Slavery was a "strictly local" institution, the Liberty Party platform of 1844 announced, "its existence and continuance rest on no other support than State legislation." Four years later the Free Soil Party platform made the same declaration: slavery "depends on State laws alone, which cannot be repealed or modified by the Federal Government." The Free Soil platform would "therefore propose no interference by Congress with Slavery within the limits of any State." Because it was accepted even by abolitionists, the slaveholders clung to the federal consensus as the essential constitutional protection for slavery against a potentially powerful central government.[5]

But beginning in the 1830s antislavery activists invoked the same consensus as a means of restricting slavery, of confining its reach. Limiting slavery's scope was the point Supreme Court Justice John McLean was making in 1841 when he wrote in his explosive concurring opinion in *Groves v. Slaughter* that "[t]he power over Slavery belongs to the States respectively. It is local in its character, *and in its effects.*" The laws of slavery, McLean was saying, had no "effects" beyond the borders of the states that enacted them. McLean was undoubtedly influenced by his son-in-law, Salmon P. Chase, the prominent antislavery lawyer and later the most radical member of Lincoln's cabinet. In the late 1830s Chase began building an argument for restricting the constitutional reach of slavery to the states where it existed while enhancing the Constitution's power to spread freedom everywhere else. Slavery, Chase explained, "can have no existence beyond the territorial limits of the state which sanctions it." Other radicals made the same claim. Slavery was "a local institution, peculiar to the States and under the guardianship of State Rights," argued Charles Sumner, the closest thing to an abolitionist in the U.S. Senate. "It is impossible," Sumner added, "without violence, at once to the spirit and to the letter of the Constitution, to attribute to Congress any power to legislate, either for its abolition in the States or its support anywhere." Most antislavery radicals argued that the Constitution recognized slavery as a state institution, *but only as a state institution*.[6]

By 1861 Lincoln's inaugural promise not to interfere with slavery in the states was pro forma within the antislavery movement. In July of that year, for example, New Hampshire Senator John P. Hale, a fiery veteran of the antislavery crusade, declared that "from the earliest organization of anti-slavery societies in the eastern States, even of the most radical of them, as long ago as 1835, when they first started, twenty-six years ago, some of their first resolutions were to declare, in the strongest language they could command, their indisposition, and their want of power to interfere with slavery in the States. They disclaimed it, and have constantly done so from the first, even the most radical Abolitionists." This was a slight exaggeration. One small group of abolitionists—notably Alvan Stewart, Lysander Spooner, William Goodell, Gerrit Smith, and Frederick Douglass—theorized that the Constitution was an antislavery document that empowered the federal government to abolish slavery everywhere. Their interpretation of the Constitution, however, "has been made appreciable but to few minds," Douglass admitted.[7] When abolitionists pressed for national policies hostile to slavery, they almost always assumed that the federal government had no power to abolish slavery in the states where it existed. That was Lincoln's assumption as well. In promising to leave slavery alone in the states, he was saying something almost everybody believed, including most abolitionists.[8]

This raises the crucial question: If even slavery's opponents agreed that the Constitution prevented the federal government from "interfering" with slavery in the states, how then did abolitionists expect to get slavery abolished? We know a great deal about abolitionist ideals, the arguments they launched against slavery, the secular and religious principles that inspired them, the organizations they formed, the literature they circulated, the ties that bound them to a wider world of national and transnational reform movements, and the personal and sectarian squabbles that erupted among them. But we know very little about the practical policies that abolitionists formulated for destroying slavery. We know even less about how abolitionists hoped to overcome the great problem posed by the U.S. Constitution even though it was in many ways the most important problem the antislavery movement faced. What, they asked, could the federal government do to undermine slavery in light of the constitutional prohibition against federal interference with slavery in the states? How was it possible to abolish slavery when, by common consent, the Constitution protected it in the states where it already existed?

A viable antislavery politics was possible, most abolitionists concluded, because the Constitution did not speak with a single voice on the subject of slavery. It was not the unambiguously antislavery Constitution that Gerrit Smith and Frederick Douglass believed it to be, but neither was it the hopeless proslavery compact denounced by William Lloyd Garrison and Wendell Phillips. Most abolitionists understood that there had been a conflict raging over slavery in late-eighteenth-century America and that the conflict itself was reflected within, not swept away by, the Constitution. For example, the framers did not merely refuse to allow the word *slavery* into the document, they went out of their way to refer to slaves as "persons held in service" rather than as "property in man"—a deliberate choice that reflected the influence of antislavery jurisprudence at the time, a choice that would, moreover, become one of the core precepts of all antislavery politics. Similarly, the framers acknowledged that slaveholders had a right to recapture their runaway slaves, but the Constitution did not grant the *federal government* the power to enforce the right of reception. Precisely *who* was responsible for the capture and return of fugitive slaves would eventually become a major point of contention between the North and the South. Invoking the federal consensus, abolitionists argued that because slavery was strictly a state institution, enforcement of the fugitive slave clause was strictly a state responsibility. This reading of the Constitution would condition the North's response to slaves running for their freedom to Union lines during the Civil War. Most abolitionists acknowledged that there were proslavery elements in the Constitution that put very real limits on the scope of antislavery politics. But there were some things in the document that gave the opponents of slavery room for political maneuver.

Most important of all antislavery activists argued, the revolutionary generation had suffused the nation's founding documents with the bias toward freedom intrinsic to the "law of nations." One indication of the Founders' sensitivity to the law of nations is the fact that the Declaration of Independence was framed as a claim to recognition in the world of nations. The Constitution itself had a curiously dual character: it was a charter that created a new government for a sovereign nation, and it was a "treaty" among the constituent states. With an eye toward establishing their new nation's place in the "world of nations," the delegates in Philadelphia expressly incorporated the law of nations into the document. They also understood that the law of nations was based on the broad principles of natural law. This could not help but invest the Constitution with an antislavery element, for as antislavery politicians would later insist, a long tradition in Western culture held that slavery was incompatible with natural law. Hence in the eyes of slavery's opponents there were antislavery as well as proslavery features within the Constitution, and on its mixed message political abolitionists constructed a credible antislavery politics.[9]

By the time the Civil War broke out, the opponents of slavery had developed two distinct scenarios whereby the federal government could undermine slavery without actually violating the constitutional restriction on federal interference with slavery in the states. Under the first scenario the federal government would contain slavery within the southern states, steadily weakening it until the states eventually abolished slavery on their own. Under the second scenario the federal government would emancipate slaves in the process of suppressing a domestic insurrection. Until 1830 nobody had imagined destroying slavery by either of these means. By 1860 they were universally accepted within the Republican Party. But before that could happen, opponents of slavery had to overcome another constitutional obstacle: the natural right of property.

PROPERTY IN MAN

We call it "chattel slavery" because slaves were the legal property of their owners—human property to be sure, but property nonetheless. In the American South, slaves were personal property rather than real estate. "Moveables" is what Jefferson called them. This is what made slavery different from other forms of inequality such as patriarchy, serfdom, apprenticeship, and wage labor. Here the slaveholders were consistent. Their laws classified their slaves as property; they treated their slaves as property; and they defended slavery primarily as a right of property. It was no accident that the struggle over slavery so often came down to the right versus the wrong of "property in man." Abolitionists never doubted that it was immoral for one human being to own another as property, but before they could begin to formulate a federal policy aimed at the destruction of slavery, they had to develop a constitutionally viable argument for restricting the rights of property.[10]

This was no easy task, for although abolitionists hated the very idea of human property, they generally respected the rights of property. How could abolitionists attack slavery without undermining property rights? The answer they came up with was a straightforward but controversial adaptation of the federal consensus: slaves were property under state statutes, but they were not "property" under the Constitution. Instead the Constitution recognized slavery only as a servile status—"persons held in service"—not as a right of property. The distinction between slaves as *property* under state law but as *persons* under the Constitution rested on several premises: that the Constitution was imbued with the principles of natural law; that "property in man" was a violation of natural law; and that slavery could therefore exist only within the borders of those states in which "positive law" overruled the natural-law principles of the Constitution. This was the American version of the "freedom principle," with roots stretching deep into European history. It was imported into the colonies from England, where, on the eve of the American Revolution, Lord Mansfield ruled in the *Somerset* case that slavery was such a palpable violation of natural law that it required "positive" legislation creating slavery to overrule the presumption of freedom. English law recognized slavery as a servile status, not as a species of property.[11] In the United States *Somerset* became a benchmark for all subsequent efforts to end slavery by political means. By its careful reference to slaves as "persons held in service," abolitionists argued, the Constitution reflected the natural-law principle that condemned "property in man." Thus slavery was presumptively illegal wherever the Constitution was sovereign—in the territories, for example, on the high seas, or in Washington, D.C. This was the constitutional logic behind the familiar antislavery precept that freedom was national whereas slavery was local. It meant that there was no such thing as a constitutional right of property in slaves.

The logic of *Somerset* opened a legal pathway for the abolition of slavery in the northern states in the late eighteenth century. Although the earliest opponents of slavery took great care not to trample on the property rights of masters, they nevertheless narrowed the scope of property rights in ways that made it possible to attack slavery at the margins. They were willing to close down the slave *trade* on the theory that making it impossible to import a slave was different from taking slave property from someone who already had it. By freeing the children of slaves at the moment of birth—on the principle that everyone was "born free"—they would close off yet another source of new slaves without depriving masters of the slaves they already owned. "It is alleged," one New Jersey antislavery memorial read, "that to emancipate those now living" would violate the slaveholders' rights of property. "But as respects *those who may in future be* born this does not apply."[12] Emancipating states often required the children of slaves to work for their masters for a specified number of years—a form of compensation for the cost of raising the children and for some of the prospective losses from their labor as adults—but those same states then freed slaves once the master's claim of service had been duly acknowledged. Finally, the opponents of slavery would limit its expansion into new territories, once again reasoning that nobody's property rights were actually violated in the process.

The prevailing sensitivity to the slaveholders' rights of property meant that abolition before the Civil War was almost always gradual. Vermont was the first state to begin gradual abolition in its revolutionary constitution of 1777, which declared it illegal to hold any male in slavery "after he arrives to the age of twenty-one years; nor female, in like manner, after she arrives to the age of eighteen years." Gradual-abolition laws were subsequently passed in Pennsylvania in 1780, Rhode Island and Connecticut in 1784, New York in 1799, and New Jersey in 1804. Although there were variations from state to state in each case, freedom was promised to the children of slaves once they had served an apprenticeship.[13]

Gradual emancipation had less to do with racial prejudice or the fear of free blacks than with the widespread concern for the rights of property. It was the opponents of abolition who most frequently resorted to racial arguments, warning that blacks were unsuited to freedom in any form. By contrast, advocates of abolition tended to justify their support for gradual approaches by reference to their abiding respect for property. Jacob Morris, a strong promoter of abolition in New York, explained that his support for gradual, compensated emancipation grew out of his "sacred regard for the property of the Citizens." Slavery was "odious, and the practice of it in a free country much to be lamented," an anonymous Federalist writer explained in 1792, "but as the laws of society have tolerated the practice, it is but reasonable, that the abolitions should be effected in such a way, as not to interfere with the regard that is due to private property." By the late eighteenth century, slavery's opponents were already in the grip of a confounding paradox: the thing they hated most about slavery— property rights in human beings—was the thing that most inhibited their opposition to it.[14]

But the opponents of slavery found in the logic of *Somerset* a means of surmounting the legal obstacle presented by "property in man." Following Lord Mansfield's logic, the abolition statutes of early America redefined bondage as a servile status closer to indentured servitude than chattel slavery. In this sense the first emancipation was somewhat more immediate than the term *gradual abolition* suggests. Slavery immediately ceased to be a lifelong heritable condition. And by restricting the "property" element of the master-slave relationship to a claim of *service*, the opponents of slavery removed a barrier to state regulation of slavery. State governments found it much easier to restrict the terms of service than to take away property. New York provides the clearest case. Its legislature prohibited the sale of any slave out of state a full decade before it passed the general emancipation statute in 1799. Then, too, the 1799 statute immediately propelled far more emancipation than it formally required: it prompted many New York masters to enter into indenture agreements with their adult slaves, promising freedom in return

for several more years of loyal service. But that was only the beginning. Within a few years the legislature began altering the terms of the
master-slave relationship in significant ways. It legalized slave marriages, thereby prohibiting the masters from breaking up slave families. It gave slaves the right to own property, allowing them to
accumulate wealth on their own, independently of their owners.
Towns and cities began to close down slave auction houses, making it
hard for owners to sell slaves even within the state. Thereafter a master
who sold a slave out of state or who broke up a slave family had to
violate the law and risk punishment to do so. By 1810 thousands of
New York slaves had already been emancipated, but just as important
those still in bondage had been shifted from the legal category of personal property into an intermediate servile status, a status that afforded
them property rights, legally secure marriages, and specified terms for
the end of their services. To say that New York's 1799 emancipation
law "did not free a single slave" is to miss all that it did and to under-
estimate the achievement of those who struggled for its passage.[15]

And yet nothing about the "First Emancipation" implied that the
federal government had any authority to abolish slavery in a state.
Individual states could regulate slave property or redefine slavery as a
servile status, effectively abolishing slavery either immediately or
gradually. But the First Emancipation left undisturbed the prevailing
assumption that slaves could be defined as property under state law
and that states alone could abolish slavery within their borders. To be
sure, the new federal government was not completely paralyzed when
it came to regulating slavery beyond the borders of the slave states
themselves. The first Congress reenacted the Ordinance of 1787—
known as the Northwest Ordinance—declaring that in the federal
territories north of the Ohio River "[t]here shall be neither slavery nor
involuntary servitude . . . otherwise than in punishment of crimes
whereof the party shall have been duly convicted." The Northwest
Ordinance would go on to become a touchstone of antislavery poli-

tics, the statutory link between the abolitionists and the Founders, its very language eventually reproduced in the Thirteenth Amendment that would abolish slavery forever. In the short term the Northwest Ordinance, ambiguous and limited as it was, nevertheless established the principle that the federal government could regulate slavery in the territories. Opponents of slavery likewise moved quickly in 1807 to abolish the international slave trade at the earliest possible date. But northerners and southerners alike still insisted that slavery was strictly a state institution and the federal government had no power to regulate or interfere with it. The federal consensus was still understood as a restriction on the federal government rather than a restriction on slavery's reach.[16]

The weakness of antislavery constitutionalism was exposed in 1820 during the contentious congressional debates over the admission of Missouri as a slave state. Rufus King and a small coterie of northern congressmen pushed the federal consensus toward an antislavery conclusion, claiming that because slavery was strictly a state institution, it followed that property in slaves was a state and not a federal right.[17] If slave ownership *had* been constitutionally protected as a right of property, they argued, the federal government would have had no authority to close down the slave trade and ban slavery from the territories. "[I]s the power of holding slaves a federal right?" Congressman John W. Taylor of New York asked. His answer was a resounding *no*. How could it be? The laws of New Hampshire and Georgia treat slavery in "diametrically opposite" ways, Taylor reasoned, and by extension federal law did not automatically recognize slavery the way the southern states did. Federal law was based solely on the Constitution, the preamble of which embodied the antislavery principles of fundamental human equality spelled out in the Declaration of Independence. For Taylor this meant there was no such thing as a federal, or constitutional, right of property in slaves. In 1820, however, such arguments were too radical even for northern congressmen who professed to hate slavery. Southern congressmen rallied in unison around the inviolable rights of property, protected by the Constitution, and in the face of those arguments most northern legislators backed down. Two decades later the reasoning that shocked Taylor's contemporaries was rapidly becoming commonplace thanks to a revived antislavery movement that was grappling with the issue of southern slaves who claimed freedom in northern states.[18]

A crucial turning point came in 1836 when Massachusetts abolitionists took up the case of a six-year-old slave girl named Med, whose Louisiana mistress took her to Boston during an extended visit with the mistress's father, Thomas Aves. Antislavery lawyers, in this case Ellis Gray Loring, sued Aves on the grounds that Med was free under Massachusetts law—not because any statute declared her free, but on the *Somerset* principle that the state had adopted no "municipal" law that could legitimately deprive the girl of her freedom. Under the recognized principle of interstate comity, the court could have ruled that Massachusetts had an obligation to respect the Louisiana law that did, in fact, enslave Med. But instead Chief Justice Lemuel Shaw argued that the principles of comity "apply only to those commodities which are everywhere, and by all nations treated and deemed subject of property." Slaves were emphatically not recognized as "property" everywhere, Shaw noted, and they were not so recognized in Massachusetts. Indeed, if slaves were to be recognized as a constitutionally protected form of property, it would be impossible for any state to exclude slavery from within its borders because under ordinary circumstances "the right of property follows the person." Med was free, Shaw ruled, because she was not "property" under Massachusetts law. The case, *Commonwealth v. Aves*, established the single most important premise on which all antislavery politics would soon be built. There was no such thing as a constitutional right of property in slaves.[19]

SLAVERY LOCAL

Matilda Lawrence was owned by, and was quite possibly the daughter of, a Missouri planter named Larkin Lawrence. Her mother was a slave, half black, who died when Matilda was sixteen. She was raised in her owner's house and succeeded her mother as the family's house-keeper. Somewhere along the way Matilda Lawrence learned to read. But she lived an isolated existence, shunned by white society and yet forbidden to associate with blacks. In 1836 Matilda's owner took her with him to spend a year in New York, where he told people she was his daughter. No one suspected. Intelligent, well mannered, and beau-tiful, Matilda was widely accepted as the daughter of a southern gen-tleman. She began to dread the thought of returning to Missouri, where she faced the prospect of being sold once her ailing owner died. She asked him for her freedom papers. Alarmed by Matilda's request, Larkin Lawrence quickly packed up and set out on the return journey to Missouri. When they reached Cincinnati, Matilda asked once more for her freedom papers, and again her owner refused her request. She responded with promises of fidelity, but as soon as she got the chance Matilda left the hotel and made her way to the home of a black barber, who concealed the fugitive until her master left town a few days later.[20]

Once she was safe, Matilda took a job as a housekeeper in the home of James Gillespie Birney, himself a former slaveholder who had freed his slaves, moved to Ohio, and become active in the abolitionist movement. Birney's wife had recently had a difficult childbirth, and she hired Matilda to help out around the house. It was unclear what Matilda Lawrence told the Birneys and how much they knew about her past. She had clearly been educated, and at least at the beginning she told the Birneys nothing about her real background other than the fact that she had been born in Missouri. "We thought her white," Birney's son later recalled.[21]

What none of them knew was that before Larkin Lawrence left Cincinnati, he had hired a well-known slave-catcher named John W. Riley to find Matilda and return her to slavery in Missouri. For months Riley and his men secretly kept watch on the Birney house, until, on March 10, 1837, they seized Matilda and took her into custody on a warrant issued by an Ohio state court. Birney himself was legally liable for harboring a runaway in violation of the Fugitive Slave Act of 1793. Birney immediately employed a young attorney named Salmon Chase to take the *Matilda* case. Chase had not been active in antislavery circles, but a year earlier he had successfully defended Birney in a suit against an anti-abolition mob that had attacked Birney's radical newspaper, *The Philanthropist*. That experience had led Chase to think for the first time about the conflict between state and federal law regarding slavery. At Birney's request Chase quickly applied for a writ of habeas corpus so that Matilda could have her day in court.[22]

As important as the case was for Matilda—she was, after all, fighting for her freedom—it quickly became a turning point in the history of antislavery politics. Birney had been sued for harboring a fugitive slave in his home, allegedly violating the owner's property rights. But according to Chase it was "impossible, in Ohio, to commit the offense of harboring, or secreting a person *being the property* of another person," for the simple reason "that the relation of owner and property, as existing between person and person, has, or can have, no existence in this state." Ohio law did not recognize slaves as property but as persons held to service; slavery was a servile status, not a right of property. On this matter, Chase concluded, the laws of Ohio were "in full harmony with every provision of the constitution of the United States." Chase was discerning *Somerset* within the Constitution, the text of which "contains no recognition whatever, of any right of property in man." On the contrary, the Constitution left "this whole matter of property in human beings, precisely where the articles of confederation left it, with the states." Slavery was local; it had no claims beyond the borders of the specific states that created it. "Wherever it exists at all, it exists only by virtue of positive law," Chase explained. "The right to hold a man as a slave is a naked legal right. It is a right which, in its own nature, can have no existence beyond the territorial limits of the state which sanctions it, except in other states whose positive law recognizes and protects it."[23]

Chase's reasoning did not save Matilda Lawrence. It is hard to imagine a state court in the 1830s declaring the fugitive slave law of 1793 unconstitutional. There were arguments Chase might have made that were more likely to have won Lawrence her freedom, but with only one day to prepare, he had come into court armed only with propositions designed to clear the constitutional ground on which to build a national antislavery politics. Not surprisingly, the court ruled quickly in favor of the slave owner. In short order Matilda Lawrence was put on a boat bound for St. Louis, where she was most likely sold back into slavery, her ultimate fate unknown.[24]

Chase was not the only antislavery activist arguing that the Constitution protected slavery in only the most limited ways. The year after Chase argued the *Matilda* case before the Ohio court, a brilliant abolitionist named Theodore Dwight Weld extended the reasoning in an influential pamphlet titled *The Power of Congress over the District of Columbia*. On the face of it Weld was making a relatively narrow plea for congressional abolition of slavery in the nation's capital. In fact he was laying down a broad set of principles that implied extensive federal power to regulate slavery. Weld began by making a sharp distinction between state laws that created slavery within their own borders, and the Constitution, which was based on the antislavery principles of universal law, natural law, and common law. The Founders hated slavery, Weld argued, and assumed that over time "the moral sense of the nation," acting through legislatures, schools, and abolition societies, would create "a power of opinion that would abolish the system throughout the nation." The men who wrote the Constitution expressed this moral conviction by recognizing slaves only as "persons," never as "property."[25]

Weld's essay moved from the specific to the general, making ever larger claims as it proceeded. He began with the plausible assertion that in vesting Congress with sovereignty over Washington, D.C., the Constitution necessarily granted the legislative body the power to abolish slavery in the nation's capital. Weld then went on to argue that the Constitution did not recognize a right of property in slaves *anywhere*. Although the right of property was a fundamental principle of universal law, "property in slaves is, by general consent, an *exception*." The Constitution reflected the familiar precept that the rights of property originate in self-ownership. By the consent of the entire civilized world "slaves are not '*property*,' but *self-proprietors*." To own a slave as property was not a *natural* but a merely *legal* right, created "only by *positive legislative acts*, forcibly setting aside the law of nature, the common law, and the principles of universal justice and right between man and man." Beyond the limits of such states, wherever the Constitution was sovereign, the right of self-ownership prevailed. By Weld's reasoning, slavery itself was an assault on property rights, a form of theft, in which the individual's inalienable claim of ownership to his or her self was forcibly violated. Abolition, then, was not the denial but the restoration of property rights. "Instead of *taking* 'private property,' Congress, by abolishing slavery, would say '*private property* shall not *be* taken; and those who have been robbed of it already, shall be kept out of it no longer; and since every man's right to his own body is *paramount*, he shall be protected in it.'" This was bourgeois radicalism preparing the ground for bourgeois revolution.[26]

By 1838 radical opponents of slavery were routinely dismissing the idea of a constitutional right of property in slaves. New York's William Leggett was typical. The Constitution, he declared, "nowhere gives any countenance to the idea that slaves are considered *property* in the meaning of the term as used in the fifth article of the amendments." Ohio's Thomas Morris affirmed the point made by Weld—that slavery itself was a violation of the "property" rights that all human beings have in themselves. "To free a slave," Morris argued, is to take what had originally been stolen—property in one's self—"and bestow it upon its rightful owner."[27]

Opponents of slavery were gratified by the publication in 1840 of James Madison's notes from the Constitutional Convention, which they believed supported their antislavery constitutionalism. They pointed to a crucial exchange at the Philadelphia convention in which Roger Sherman objected to a proposed tax on slave imports "because it implied that they were *property*." When other delegates pointed out that the tax was designed to discourage the importation of slaves, Sherman said he would forgo the revenue rather than accede to wording that so much as hinted at the legitimacy of human property. James Madison agreed. He thought it "wrong to admit in the Constitution the idea that there could be property in men." A tax on slave imports could not be justified, he said, because "slaves are not like merchandise, consumed, & c." This exchange quickly became a staple of every extended argument against slavery as a constitutional right of property. Perhaps with Madison's *Notes* in mind, former president and now congressman John Quincy Adams argued before the U.S. Supreme Court on February 24, 1841, that "the Constitution of the United States recognizes the slaves, held within some of the States of the Union, only in their capacity of *persons*—*persons* held to labor or service in a State under the laws thereof—persons constituting elements of representation in the popular branch of the National Legislature—*persons*, the migration or importation of whom should not be prohibited by Congress prior to the year 1808. The Constitution no where recognizes them as property. The words *slave* and *slavery* are studiously excluded from the Constitution. Circumlocutions are the fig-leaves under which these parts of the body politic are decently concealed. Slaves, therefore, in the Constitution of the United States are recognized only as *persons*, enjoying rights and held to the performance of duties."[28]

A few weeks later, while Adams was there in the courtroom, one of the justices, John McLean, practically quoted the former president verbatim in a controversial concurring opinion in the case of *Groves v. Slaughter*. The high court had been asked to decide whether a state that restricted the importation of slaves (in this case Mississippi) violated the commerce clause of the Constitution, which granted Congress the power to regulate interstate trade. In a seemingly straightforward decision the court ruled that Congress had no power to interfere with slavery in the states. McLean voted with the majority, but his concurring opinion was anything but straightforward. He rested his decision on the fact that the commerce clause gave Congress the power to regulate *property*, whereas the "Constitution treats slaves as persons." *States* may treat slaves "as merchandise," McLean wrote, but "that cannot divest them of the leading and controlling quality of persons, by which they are designated in the Constitution." Slaves were property only where state law made them so; where the Constitution was sovereign, slaves were persons. "The character of property is given them by local law . . . , but the Constitution acts upon slaves as persons, and not as property." McLean concluded that federal authorities could not interfere with the interstate slave trade because the commerce clause gave Congress the power to regulate the flow of "merchandise," not "persons," across state lines.[29]

At the time McLean issued his opinion, abolitionists were petitioning Congress to ban the interstate slave trade, but the court's ruling in *Groves* made that impossible. Yet antislavery radicals were thrilled by the decision because McLean's reasoning represented a potentially much larger victory. The decision itself "renders it no longer advisable to petition Congress to abolish the inter-state slave trade," an abolitionist newspaper explained. "At the same time," the editors added, "the grounds for the decision will show that the cause of emancipation has gained much more than it has lost.—Let the principle that 'the constitution regards slaves only as persons, and not as property,' be fully carried out in all departments of the Federal Government, with the other principle, that slavery is the mere creature of local law, and can have no force beyond the boundaries of the state that creates it; and the various complicated entanglements in which the free states have felt themselves bound to its support, will entirely disappear."[30] *Groves* was a tactical loss but a strategic victory for antislavery constitutionalism. From the pen of a sitting justice on the U.S. Supreme Court came the unambiguous assertion that the Constitution recognized slaves only as persons and not as property. Radical antislavery doctrine was migrating into the mainstream.

William H. Seward's career reflected that same migration. As governor of New York in the early 1840s Seward had declared that under no constitution or body of laws was it possible for any human being to "be converted into chattel or a thing in which another being like himself can have property." By 1850, now a senator from New York, Seward invoked the same argument on the floor of Congress in response to southern congressmen who claimed that the "Constitution recognizes property in slaves." It wasn't true, Seward declared. "I deny that the Constitution recognizes property in man." In the few cases where the document recognizes slaves, it does so "not as slaves, much less as chattels, but as *persons*." If the Founders had recognized slaves as property, Seward added, the Constitution itself would be "repugnant to the law of nature and nations." Seward thereby linked the law of nations to the law of nature, which was "repugnant" to slavery—and he was not the only politician saying such things. "Slavery is admitted, on all hands, to be contrary to natural right," Chase declared. And since the Constitution was a natural-law document, slavery must therefore be incompatible with constitutional law. By the 1850s mainstream antislavery politicians were making similar claims. "What *natural* right requires Kansas and Nebraska to be opened to Slavery?" Abraham Lincoln asked in 1854. "Is not slavery universally granted to be, in the abstract, a gross outrage upon the law of nature?"[31]

For decades opponents of slavery had been paralyzed by the fact that, like it or not, the Constitution protected slavery as a fundamental right of property. This made it all but impossible to develop a national antislavery politics. But in denying the existence of a right of property in slaves, and by locating the law of nations—and with the natural-law rejection of slavery—within the nation's founding charter, the opponents of slavery opened the constitutional door to much more aggressive federal attacks on slavery. They could repudiate "gradualism"—the vague hope that someday, somehow, slavery would disappear—and instead devise federal policies, to be implemented immediately, that would bring about the ultimate extinction of slavery. They fully conceded that the federal government could not abolish slavery in the states where it existed, but they found ingenious ways to work around that restriction by making "freedom" the national policy of the United States.

"FREEDOM NATIONAL"

The *Creole* sailed out of Hampton Roads, Virginia, on October 25, 1841, packed with 135 blacks destined for the slave markets of New Orleans. Two weeks later, as the ship approached the Bahamas, about twenty of the slaves seized control, wounded the captain and several of the crew, killed another crew member, and "with great coolness and presence of mind," destroyed the documents proving their enslavement and ordered the rest of the crew to sail them into port at

Nassau. When the ship reached the island, then known as New Providence, the American consul demanded that the slaves be arrested and sent on their way to Louisiana. Instead the British government freed the slaves, including those who had been identified as "insurrectionists." The U.S. government responded with outrage, demanding reparations for the "property" improperly confiscated by the English government. Secretary of State Daniel Webster insisted that the slaves were "recognized as property by the Constitution of the United States in those States in which slavery exists." Webster's dispatch thus raised the very issue that abolitionists were pressing: Were the rights of property in slaves *constitutional*? If so, slave property was protected beyond the borders of the slave states. But if slave property was merely "municipal," grounded in local laws only, wasn't the property claim in slaves restricted to the locality itself?[32]

The *Creole* rebellion presented abolitionists with an opportunity to apply their emerging constitutional theories. If the right to own slaves was merely "a naked legal right," as Chase had argued in the *Matilda* case, that right "can have no existence beyond the territorial limits of the state which sanctions it, except in other states whose positive law recognizes and protects it." Otherwise the right to slave property "vanishes when the master and the slave meet together in a state where positive law interdicts slavery. The moment the slave comes within such a state, he acquires a legal right to freedom."[33] To Chase this meant that Matilda Lawrence had every right to claim her freedom the moment she set foot on Ohio soil. The same principle surely applied to the slaves on board the *Creole*. Were they not free the moment the ship left the territorial waters of Virginia and local slave laws no longer reached them? On the high seas the law of nations prevailed, and with it the natural law of freedom.

If there was scandal in the diplomatic crisis surrounding the *Creole* uprising, abolitionists declared, it was not the justifiable rebellion of the slaves but the inexcusable reaction of the U.S. government as reflected in Webster's dispatch. If slavery was a merely local, or "municipal" institution, the abolitionist lawyer William Jay wondered, why then was "the Federal Government, putting forth and pledging all its powers to protect slavery—not within the United States . . . but on the high seas, and even in the harbor of a nation, that does not acknowledge slavery." Commenting on the *Creole* case, Charles Sumner explained that slavery "is not a national institution; nor is it one recognized by the law of nations. It is peculiar to certain States. It draws its vitality from the legislation of those States. Now, this legislation is of course limited to those States. It is not extraterritorial in its influence."[34]

In his dispatch Webster claimed that slaves remained slaves even on a ship carrying them from Virginia to Louisiana, so that when the ship arrived in port at Nassau the American consul had every right to claim them as the property of U.S. citizens. Sumner argued that the slaves "became *free* men when taken, by the voluntary act of their owners, beyond the jurisdiction of the Slave States." Jay pointed out that the slaves had in fact rebelled on board the ship, thereby emancipating themselves, and that when they arrived in the Bahamas they were already free. In rebelling, the slaves had reclaimed their natural right to freedom. The *Creole* slaves were, in Jay's words, "self-emancipated." What the American consul was therefore demanding was the re-enslavement of free blacks. Sumner and Jay were pushing antislavery constitutionalism onto legal terrain that would have major consequences for the history of slavery's destruction.[35]

Reverberations from the *Creole* rebellion were felt on the floor of the House of Representatives. Congressman Joshua Giddings, an antislavery radical from Ohio, introduced a series of resolutions that reflected the emerging abolitionist principle that slavery was a merely local institution and that beyond the borders of the slave states—on the high seas, for example—freedom prevailed. These were the Giddings resolutions, and there were nine of them. They began by acknowledging the familiar federal consensus, that any individual state of the Union "exercised full and exclusive jurisdiction over the subject of slavery within its own territory." But slavery, "being an abridgement of the natural rights of man, can exist only by force of positive *municipal law*, and is necessarily confined to the territorial jurisdiction of the power creating it." Thus slavery could not exist beyond the reach of the "municipal" law that created it, for where there was no such law there was no slavery, only the natural right of freedom. Accordingly, when an American ship leaves the territorial waters of the states, it comes under the rule of law governing all Americans. When the *Creole* left Virginia, Giddings declared, the slave laws of Virginia ceased to operate on it. The slaves on board were thereby restored to "their natural rights of personal liberty." In claiming their freedom, even through insurrection, they violated no U.S. laws. Accordingly, all efforts to re-enslave the passengers aboard the *Creole* were "unauthorized" by the Constitution. This was the same principle Republican policymakers would invoke a generation later when slaves "rebelled" against their masters by running to Union lines during the Civil War: they had emancipated themselves, recovered their natural right to freedom, and could never be re-enslaved.[36]

Giddings's fellow congressmen immediately voted by more than a two-to-one margin to table his nine resolutions and then censured him for introducing such scandalous ideas into the House of Representatives. But the fifty-three votes cast in favor of the resolutions was another indication that abolitionist precepts were penetrating into the political mainstream. Giddings lost the vote, but there was vindication to be had. Having been censured by his colleagues, Giddings resigned from Congress and went back to Ohio, where he ran for reelection and was returned to the House of Representatives by a landslide vote. Giddings had made his point: abolitionist constitutional principles were no longer the preserve of a handful of radical pamphleteers.

CHASE, WELD, GIDDINGS, SUMNER, and others were building a case for cordoning slavery off, restricting it to the states where it existed and barring it from all influence on national policy. They would *denationalize* slavery. To a generation of Americans accustomed to Jacksonian arguments for the separation of church and state, or the separation of banking from the state, radical demands for the complete separation of slavery from the state made perfect sense. Yet those men were not merely theoreticians. They were also practical politicians, and to succeed they needed to do more than develop the principles that could justify antislavery policies. They needed to build the political organizations that could put such policies into practice. Before they could implement antislavery policies, they needed an antislavery party.

In 1839 political abolitionists, particularly in western New York, proposed the creation of a third party devoted exclusively to the abolition of slavery. The following year, what became known as the Liberty Party fielded its first presidential candidate, James Gillespie Birney, the man whom Chase had defended in the *Matilda* case. Launching a presidential campaign was a controversial move among political abolitionists, even in Birney's home state of Ohio. Within the Liberty Party itself differences developed between those who believed the Constitution was an antislavery document that empowered the federal government to abolish slavery in the states and those who believed that, like it or not, the Constitution protected slavery in the states where it already existed. The creation of the Liberty Party also completed the rupture between political abolitionists and the perfectionist strand of the movement led by William Lloyd Garrison and his followers, a rupture that by the 1850s would reduce the Garrisonians to relatively marginal figures within the broader antislavery movement.[37]

The founding principle of the Liberty Party was that the Constitution did not recognize slaves as property, therefore "all attempts to hold men as property within the limits of exclusive national jurisdiction, ought to be prohibited by law." If slaves were persons rather than property, the Constitution, "which declares that no person shall be deprived of life, liberty, or property, without due process of law," was incompatible with slavery. Only state law could override the Constitution by establishing slavery, but slavery remained "strictly local" and had no existence beyond the borders of the states that created it. The Liberty Party called for "the absolute and unqualified divorce of the General Government from Slavery." This did not mean that the federal government should sit by and do nothing about slavery. On the contrary, the Constitution obliged Congress to do everything it could—short of outright abolition in the slave states—to make freedom "national." The federal government had "shamefully violated" that obligation when it opened Louisiana and Florida to slavery, allowed slavery into the nation's capital, protected slavery on the high seas, allowed the coastwise slave trade to continue, and granted new slave states entrance to the Union. None of this should have been allowed to happen because "the General Government has, under the Constitution, no power to establish or continue slavery anywhere." That the federal government has allowed such violations of its own fundamental charter was due to the baneful influence of a "slave power" on national policy.[38]

Without quite saying so, the Liberty Party platform pushed the logic of antislavery constitutionalism close to the radical proposition that the Constitution was unambiguously hostile to slavery. This was the direction William Goodell, Gerrit Smith, Alvan Stewart, and a handful of other radicals were moving in the 1830s and 1840s, and there is some evidence that at the local level their version of antislavery constitutionalism was making headway within the Liberty Party.[39] But the platform stopped short of declaring that Congress had the power to abolish slavery in the states, no doubt because party leaders were divided on the issue. Chase in particular was convinced that it was both constitutionally incorrect and politically suicidal for an anti-slavery party to deny that the Constitution protected slavery in the states where it already existed. A viable antislavery politics, Chase and others believed, had to acknowledge that the Founders in Philadelphia had compromised with slavery for the sake of the Union, and in so doing had left the abolition of slavery *in* the states *to* the states. That the Liberty Party would not acknowledge as much was, in Chase's mind, the chief reason for its failure to attract a wider constituency. Though it scored some successes in local elections, the Liberty Party never gained nationwide electoral traction. In 1848 it was eclipsed by the Free Soil Party.

Free Soilers were clear where the Liberty Party had been ambiguous: the state laws creating slavery "cannot be repealed or modified by the Federal Government." Otherwise the constitutional premises of the Free Soil Party were identical to those of its predecessor—hardly a surprise since it was Salmon Chase who wrote the party platform. It would "rescue" the federal government from the control of the "Slave Power" and "*return*" national policy to the antislavery principles of the Founders. States could establish slavery within their borders, but the Constitution strictly forbade the federal government from supporting slavery in any way. "Congress has no more power to make a SLAVE than to make a KING." Demanding a strict separation of slavery from the national state, the 1848 Free Soil platform held that it was the "duty" of the federal government to "relieve itself from all responsibility for the existence or continuance of slavery" wherever it was sovereign. Freedom was national, and unqualified support for freedom should therefore be the national policy, tilted in favor of free labor and against slave labor. "No more Slave States," Free Soilers declared, "and no more Slave Territory. Let the soil of our extensive domains be kept free." The party's rallying cry had broad appeal: "Free Soil, Free Labor, Free Speech, Free Men."[40]

The Free Soil Party made an impressive showing in the 1848 presidential election, but it was still very much a minority party, explicitly positioning itself in opposition to the two major parties—the Whigs and the Democrats, both of which remained committed to keeping slavery out of national politics altogether. Over the next several years Free Soil leaders emphasized "fusion" with one of the two major parties. Chase put his hopes on the Democrats; others thought fusion with the Whigs was a better bet. Fusion achieved some successes at the state and local levels. It got Chase elected to the Senate from Ohio and Sumner from Massachusetts. But the Compromise of 1850 dampened antislavery sentiment. Far from committing themselves to fusion with the antislavery forces, the Whig and Democratic Parties became more adamant than ever that the slavery issue should be thoroughly excluded from national politics.[41]

Nevertheless the congressional debate over the compromise measures suggested that antislavery constitutionalism had penetrated still further into the political mainstream. On March 11, 1850, New York Senator William Seward, a prominent northern Whig, delivered the famous speech declaring that there was a "higher law" than the Constitution. Though it immediately earned him a reputation as a radical, Seward's crucial point was that the "higher" antislavery principles of natural law were already embedded within the Constitution—by then a standard theme among political abolitionists. The "blessings of liberty" were prescribed by the laws of nature, Seward argued, but promised in the Constitution's preamble. Slavery stood condemned under the law of nations, which the Founders had incorporated into the Constitution through the war powers and treaty-making clauses. Slavery was but a "temporary, accidental, partial, and incongruous" presence in the Constitution, Seward argued. "Freedom on the contrary, is a perpetual, organic, universal one." Denounced by conservatives as a revolutionary call to overturn the Constitution, Seward's "higher law" speech in fact ended with a worshipful paean to the nation's founding charter.[42]

Seward was not subjecting his fellow senators to a lesson in abstract political philosophy. He was arguing for a national policy in opposition to slavery and in defense of Free Soil. The antislavery precepts of the Constitution virtually required the federal government to protect freedom and undermine slavery in all areas of the "public domain," the territories held by the people of the United States. Congress could, within the Constitution, "impose *conditions*" for the admission of new states that were consistent with national principles. Under the "treaty-making power" (the law of nations) the federal government could restrict slave "property" and instead guarantee the "*personal right*" of freedom. Seward therefore opposed any of the "compromise" measures that would allow any more slave states to enter the Union. Nothing in Seward's speech was out of line with the principles and policies of the Liberty and Free Soil Parties.[43]

Yet Seward added an important element to antislavery politics—the conviction that the demise of slavery was inevitable. This was always implicit in the theory, nursed by enlightened opponents of slavery since the eighteenth century, that slavery was a source of weakness and instability. Economically, politically, socially, and militarily—slavery was said to be so debilitating that left to its own devices, it would die a natural death. The only thing preventing slavery from meeting its appointed destiny was the Slave Power, twisting the meaning of the Constitution to wring from the federal government policies that protected slavery and prolonged its life. In the 1840s, Liberty Party agitators and Free Soilers argued that slavery was bound to disappear once the "Slave Power" was overthrown. Republicans in the 1850s inherited that same conviction. Install antislavery men in the seats of federal power and slavery would "in some way or other work its own extinction."[44]

Seward took this popular theory of slavery's intrinsic weakness to its logical conclusion by declaring that abolition was "inevitable." To his mind, merely restricting slavery's expansion was tantamount to a sentence of death, albeit a gradual and virtually painless one. To be sure, the federal government lacked the authority to implement the "immediate and unconditional abolition of slavery." Under the Constitution, Seward conceded, only "the people of the slave states, could abolish it." Yet Seward was openly, even naively, optimistic that with the right federal policies in place the slave states would eventually feel compelled to abolish slavery on their own. "Under the steady, peaceful action of moral, social and political causes," Seward explained, slavery would "be removed by gradual voluntary effort, and with compensation." Notwithstanding all the talk of secession in 1850, he foresaw neither the dissolution of the Union nor the violent abolition that dissolution would bring. But he was certain that slavery was doomed. "I feel assured that slavery must give way, and will give way," he concluded. Stripped of the protective cover of the Slave Power and denied access to fresh western soils, slavery could never compete with the superior advantages of free labor. Under "the ripening influences of economy," Seward declared, "emancipation is inevitable, and is near."[45] A ban on slavery in the western territories was not the goal; it was the first step on the road to its ultimate extinction.

Seward did not propose to step back and wait for the inevitable to happen, however. On the contrary, he steadfastly opposed any policies that might "fortify" slavery, and supported those that "check its extension and abate its strength, [and] tend to its peaceful extirpation." Already in 1850 the southerners were asking for "guaranties" that the federal government would seek out and return fugitive slaves in the northern states. "That guaranty you cannot have," Seward declared. Nor would he offer "a guaranty against the abolition of slavery in the District of Columbia." He would give slavery no berth in the western territories. In all of these ways Seward would smother the ambitions of the Slave Power. But beyond merely frustrating slavery's whims, Seward would activate the federal government to move against slavery by every constitutional means at its disposal. There is "no reasonable limit to which I am not willing to go in applying the national treasures to effect the peaceful, voluntary removal of slavery," Seward declared, suggesting that the federal government could, within the Constitution, purchase slaves from individual masters and then emancipate them. Congress could not "usurp power to abolish slavery in the slave states," Seward readily admitted, but that did not mean that Congress was powerless to promote slavery's ultimate extinction.[46]

The previous generation of mainstream politicians, willing to wait passively until slavery gradually disappeared and deferring to the protection the Constitution afforded slavery, had opposed the very idea of a national antislavery politics. But by the 1850s Seward and likeminded politicians were arguing that although the federal government could not directly abolish slavery in the states where it existed, the Constitution nevertheless severely circumscribed the reach of slavery, restricted it to the states where it existed, and empowered the federal government to act aggressively against slavery everywhere else. "Immediate" abolitionism had opened a space for a truly national antislavery politics by developing a specific set of federal policies—policies that would be implemented immediately though designed to bring about the ultimate extinction of slavery. Charles Sumner spelled out those policies in his first major antislavery speech as a member of the U.S. Senate, "Freedom National; Slavery Sectional," delivered on August 26, 1852:

> In all national territories Slavery will be impossible. On the high seas, under the national flag, Slavery will be impossible. In the District of Columbia Slavery will instantly cease. . . . Congress can give no sanction to Slavery in the admission of

new Slave States. Nowhere under the Constitution, can the Nation, by legislation or otherwise, support Slavery, hunt slaves, or hold property in man.[47]

This was a prescription for building a "cordon of freedom" around the states where slavery already existed. Confined within those limits, slavery would eventually shrivel and die. The policies would be implemented immediately, but abolition itself would be gradual as the slave states succumbed to the pressure from the federal government. Wherever the federal government was sovereign—on the high seas, in the western territories, and in the nation's capital—slavery would be abolished by the national government. Federal officials would not be compelled to hunt down and re-enslave a species of "property" that existed only under the law of the southern states. Sumner and his fellow radicals wanted to repeal the Fugitive Slave Act of 1850; antislavery moderates wanted it revised to restore the right of states to protect their own citizens. But by 1860 most Republicans agreed that enforcement of the fugitive slave clause of the Constitution should be returned to the states.[48] They also agreed with Sumner that no new slave states should be admitted to the Union. That way the Slave Power's influence on federal policy would be steadily diminished and ultimately destroyed.

Such was the first scenario for abolition to emerge from antislavery politics. It was based on several crucial premises: that slavery had no legal existence outside the states that sanctioned it; that because the Constitution recognized slaves only as *persons*, there was no such thing as a constitutional right of property in slaves; that the federal government was therefore free—maybe even obliged—to attack slavery wherever the Constitution was sovereign; and that slavery was so weak that it would ultimately succumb to the pressure of federal antislavery policies. What had already happened in the North would eventually happen in the South: the slave states themselves would realize that slavery was holding them back economically, disrupting the social order, and promoting political instability. With a strong nudge from the federal government, the states would then abolish slavery on their own.

The opponents of slavery also had a second scenario for a federal attack on slavery, one that rested on many of the same premises but that would also, under certain circumstances, empower the federal government to enter the southern states and actually emancipate slaves.

EMANCIPATION AS A MILITARY NECESSITY

In 1839, shortly after the slave ship *La Amistad* sailed from Havana on its way to the Cuban town of Puerto Principe, some of the fifty-three slaves on board rose in rebellion, murdering the captain and his cook. Two crewmen escaped in a boat and made their way back to Havana, but the two Spanish traders who had purchased the slaves, Pedro Montez and José Ruiz, could not get away. The leader of the rebels, whom his captors named Joseph Cinqué, ordered the two traders to sail the *Amistad* back to his home among the Mende people of West Africa, in Sierra Leone. Not knowing how to sail a ship, Cinqué and the rebels were forced to rely on the two Spaniards who had purchased them. During the day Montez and Ruiz complied, but by night they shifted course and sailed the boat in a northwesterly direction. The *Amistad* ended up not on the West African coast but on the north shore of Long Island, in New York. There Cinqué and the rebels were arrested and taken to Connecticut for trial.[49]

Abolitionists immediately recognized the significance of the case and arranged for attorneys to represent the rebellious slaves. They were acquitted twice, in both district and circuit courts, but the administration of President Martin Van Buren, anxious to establish its bona fides with proslavery southerners, repeatedly appealed the decisions, hoping for a conviction that would allow the government to send the captive Africans to slavery in Cuba. Prejudging the outcome, the secretary of state gave assurances to both Cuban and Spanish officials that the slave traders—Montez and Ruiz—would be vindicated and their slave "property" returned to them. Once again the federal government was siding with slave owners in a case of slave rebellion on the high seas. Officials appealed every decision to free the slaves, and in 1841 the case reached the U.S. Supreme Court, where the rebels were defended by John Quincy Adams.

Adams's extended oral argument—it took two full days to deliver—was a précis of antislavery constitutionalism. Pointing dramatically to a copy of the Declaration of Independence hanging in the courtroom, Adams told the justices that he knew of "no law" that "reaches my clients . . . but the law of nature and of Nature's God." On the high seas there was no "municipal" or "positive" law of slavery, only the law of nations. Hence the Africans were wrongly arrested "as property, and salvage claimed upon them." The secretary of state had gone so far as to declare that the Africans were "Spanish property." But Adams dismissed the idea, declaring that the Constitution consistently "represented" slaves as persons and never as property. As persons under the Constitution and as human beings under the laws of nature, Adams argued, the *Amistad* slaves had reclaimed their inherent right to freedom by rebelling against their captors. Invoking the term that was becoming popular among abolitionists, Adams declared that the Africans aboard the *Amistad* were "self-emancipated." He denounced the Van Buren administration for sympathizing with the two Spanish "slave dealers" and for assuming that "all the right" was "on their side and all the wrong on the side of their surviving self-emancipated victims." By their rebellion aboard the *Amistad*. Adams declared, the Africans had "restored themselves to freedom."[50]

This was not entirely new reasoning for Adams. Under the Treaty of Paris, which ended the American Revolution, and a decade later under the terms of the Jay Treaty, the United States was forced to accept—over the vehement objections of southern slaveholders—that the British would not compensate Americans for slaves liberated in wartime. Later, as secretary of state, Adams himself had demanded reparations for the slaves liberated by the British during the War of 1812. But by 1820, when a dispute over the requirements of the Treaty of Ghent could be settled only by arbitration, Adams conceded that the British did not owe compensation for slaves they emancipated during the war. The dispute centered on when the war actually ended; the British would owe compensation only for slaves freed after that date. By the time he returned to Congress in the 1830s, Adams not only was aware of the historical precedents for wartime emancipation, but also invoked those precedents as a threat. His warning was prompted by the "gag rule" that Congress imposed on itself to prevent the reception of antislavery petitions. Adams led the opposition to the rule. Initially his defense of the petitioners reflected his deeply conservative impulses: superiors had an obligation to acknowledge the petitions sent up by their inferiors. That would change. Adams's courageous stance attracted the attention and ultimately the friendship of leading abolitionists and antislavery radicals, among them Weld and Giddings. The gag-rule debates dragged on for years, and by the early 1840s Adams was so closely aligned with the antislavery movement that abolitionists solicited him to argue the *Amistad* case before the Supreme Court, and by then Adams was willing to do so. His impeccable conservative credentials no doubt made Adams's support for antislavery petitioners all the more impressive, but by the 1840s abolitionists were attracted to him primarily for his defense of military emancipation.[51]

During the congressional debates over the gag rule, Adams argued that under certain circumstances the federal government had the power to emancipate slaves in the southern states. Emancipation of the ene-my's slaves in time of war was widely accepted under the law of nations, Adams argued, and it was just as widely understood that the Constitu-tion incorporated the law of nations within itself as part of the war powers. "This power is tremendous," Adams declared, and "it is strictly constitutional." Suppose Congress was called on to raise an army and allocate the funds necessary "to suppress a servile insurrection," he spec-ulated, "would they have no authority to interfere with the institution of slavery?" Suppose as well that the terms of the peace treaty ending a civil war required "the master of a slave to recognize his emancipation." In such a case, Adams asked, would Congress "have no authority to interfere with the institution of slavery, in any way?" Adams did not deny that in ordinary times, in times of peace, Congress had no author-ity to interfere with slavery in the state where it already existed. But in times of war the laws of war applied, and under the laws of war Con-gress would have the power to "interfere" with slavery by emancipating slaves. This was emancipation as a military necessity.[52]

No one doubted that the Founders had incorporated the law of nations—which included the laws of war—into the Constitution they drafted in Philadelphia. There was not much agreement, though, about what the "laws of war" actually allowed the government to do. The standard treatises of Grotius, Pufendorf, and Vattel said nothing about slavery and emancipation. Their American interpreters—Henry Wheaton and Henry Halleck, for example—were likewise silent on the matter. Those claiming that the government could emancipate slaves as a military necessity in time of war were unable to cite a repu-table authority on the law of nations. Nevertheless, prominent legal theorists, notably Joseph Story, generally agreed that the laws of war invested governments with extraordinary powers, and that the extent of those powers was to be found not in statutes or constitutions but in customary practices. What supporters of military emancipation could not find in theory they found instead in history.

Precedent after precedent demonstrated that emancipating an ene-my's slaves was widely accepted as a legitimate weapon for suppressing rebellions, prosecuting wars, and securing military victory. The Brit-ish had done it to the Americans, twice, first during the War of Independence and then in the War of 1812. On both occasions the British offered freedom to American slaves; on both occasions thou-sands of slaves ran for freedom to British lines; on both occasions the Americans—not least of them John Quincy Adams—demanded that the slaves be returned when the fighting stopped; and on both occa-sions the British refused to re-enslave those they had emancipated. A generation later Adams was citing historical examples as evidence that wartime emancipation was customary practice and as such valid under international law. Some of his most telling examples were homegrown. Even as southern congressmen were denouncing the very idea of military emancipation, U.S. generals in Florida were offering freedom to runaway slaves who abandoned their Seminole protectors and returned to American lines. When the Second Seminole War officially ended in August of 1842, the U.S. government honored the military emancipations, freeing hundreds of slaves and refusing to compensate their outraged owners. Adams likewise cited the recent wars of independence in Latin America. In 1814 General Pablo Morillo offered freedom to slaves who enlisted in the royal army and helped suppress the independence movement. A year later Simón Bolívar responded with an emancipation edict of his own, offering freedom to slaves and their families who joined in the rebellion against Spanish rule. There was nothing new in any of this. Arming slaves and emancipating them for their service was a venerable tradi-tion, as familiar to the Greek and Roman empires of antiquity as it was to the Spanish, French, and British empires of the early modern Atlantic. Throughout human history, warfare has been one of the most common sources of manumission.[53]

What made John Quincy Adams's recitation of the precedents so shocking was the constitutional argument he used to justify them. Amid the ongoing debates over the gag rule, for example, even Joshua Giddings included among his resolutions one that recognized that the states had the "exclusive right of consultation on the subject of slavery." It was a measure of how thoroughly radicalized Adams had become that he declared his opposition to Giddings's otherwise standard disclaimer: the federal government would refrain from interfering with slavery in the states only so long as the states themselves were "able to sustain their institutions." But if a rebellion were to break out in the slave states, Adams warned, "and two hostile armies are set in martial array, the commanders of both armies have power to emancipate all the slaves in the invaded territory.[54]

Adams's influence on the antislavery movement can scarcely be exaggerated. After 1836, when he first broached the argument, variations on the theme of military emancipation quickly made their way into abolitionist writings and eventually into antislavery politics. In 1838 Weld—who would later work closely with Adams in Washington—argued that Article I, Section 8, of the Constitution, which authorized Congress to suppress domestic insurrections, could be used "as well to protect blacks against whites, as whites against blacks." In providing "for the common defence," Weld added, Congress "would have the power to destroy slaves as *property* . . . while it legalized their existence as *persons*" by arming them, out of "*necessity*," in the national interest. The Liberty Party platform echoed Weld's argument when it declared that in authorizing Congress "to suppress insurrection," the Constitution "does not make it the duty of the Government to maintain slavery." On the contrary, "[w]hen freemen unsheath the sword," the platform announced, "it should strike for *Liberty*, not for Despotism." By 1850 even William Seward broached the possibility of military emancipation in his "higher law" speech. He fully expected slavery to die gradually, but if the slave states rebelled against the Union by seceding, it would lead to "scenes of perpetual border warfare, aggravated by interminable horrors of servile insurrection." The prospect of peaceful, gradual, compensated emancipation would vanish. Instead civil wars would ensue, "bringing on violent but complete and immediate emancipation." Freedom "follows the sword," Seward declared, and in the great confrontation between liberty and slavery there can be only one outcome: slavery must yield "to the progress of emancipation."[55]

Seward's words once again mark the migration into the political mainstream of the second abolitionist scenario for a federal attack on slavery—military emancipation as a means of suppressing domestic insurrection. Its advocates did not repudiate the federal consensus. They still acknowledged that the U.S. government had no power to interfere with slavery in the states where it already existed, at least not in peacetime. But in wartime, if the Union was called on to defend itself against domestic insurrection, the rules that normally restrained Congress gave way to the "necessity" of national self-preservation. Slavery's opponents argued that military emancipation was fully constitutional because it was the accepted practice under the laws of war, laws which were themselves embedded within the Constitution.

Unlike the proposal to promote state abolition through federal containment—which was developed by antislavery radicals beginning in the late 1830s—military emancipation had its origins in the respectable northern elite. To many an American eye, John Quincy Adams was the very essence of New England conservatism. In developing his own thoughts about slavery and the war powers, Adams himself was influenced by Joseph Story, another bastion of the northeastern legal establishment. As a sitting justice of the U.S. Supreme Court, as a professor at the Harvard Law School, and as a prolific legal theorist, Story did as much as anyone to develop and broadcast the proposition that the law of nations not only was an integral part of the Constitution but also invested the federal government with extraordinary powers to suppress insurrection and restore domestic tranquility. Yet despite its respectable pedigree, radicals were quick to appropriate the concept of military emancipation, and in the end the lines of influence between abolitionism and conservatism ran in both directions.

Sensing a potential convert, Giddings and Weld huddled together with Adams at a boardinghouse in Washington, nudging him toward the abolitionist constitutionalism that was so strikingly apparent in the *Amistad* brief. Story had incorporated an expansive version of the *Somerset* principle in an influential treatise on the conflict of laws. "Suppose a person to be a slave in his own country," Story asked, "is he upon his removal to a foreign country, where slavery is not tolerated, to be still deemed a slave?" Certainly not in England, Story answered. "[A]s soon as a slave lands in England, he becomes *ipso facto* a freeman." More important, the same rule applies under the U.S. Constitution. "[F]oreign slaves would no longer be deemed such after their removal thither." By this reasoning the *Amistad* captives were free as soon as they set foot on American soil, precisely as Adams claimed. Story himself had been too busy with his work on the Supreme Court to proofread the galleys for his treatise, so he assigned the task to his brilliant young protégé at the Harvard Law School, Charles Sumner. And it was Sumner who, upon hearing of the attack on Fort Sumter, marched from the Senate to the Executive Mansion waving copies of Adams's speeches in President Lincoln's face. Throughout the Civil War, in all of the numerous congressional debates over the constitutionality of military emancipation, one Republican speech after another invoked the authority of the canonical theorists of the law of nations. But more than Grotius and Vattel, John Quincy Adams was the name that came most often to Republican lips. He taught them that even though the federal government could not *abolish* slavery in a state, it could *emancipate* the slaves in any state that was in rebellion against the United States.[56]

• • •

By 1860 antislavery politicians had developed two very different scenarios for a federal assault on slavery. In peacetime the federal government would "cordon" off the states where slavery already existed, gradually compelling them to abolish slavery on their own. War and rebellion would unleash the second scenario, allowing the federal government to emancipate slaves immediately and unconditionally. Gradual abolition and military emancipation were two different policies, and during the Civil War the Union government would pursue both of them simultaneously. Each had distinctive limitations. Containment would free no slaves immediately, but it would, if successful, lead ultimately to slavery's complete abolition, whereas military emancipation would free slaves immediately, as individuals, without actually abolishing slavery anywhere. If containment was a painfully slow road to state abolition, the long history of slave societies at war made it clear that military emancipation was not designed to abolish slavery and rarely did so.

FREEDOM NATIONAL VS. SLAVERY NATIONAL

In the late 1850s the two major political parties vying for control of the federal government swore their allegiance to the federal consensus. The Democratic Party declared that "Congress has no power under the Constitution, to interfere with or control the domestic institutions of the several States." Republicans agreed that "the right of each state to order and control its own domestic institutions according to its own judgment exclusively, is essential to that balance of powers on which the perfection and endurance of our political fabric depends." Yet from this shared premise Democrats and Republicans drew profoundly different conclusions about the relationship between slavery and the federal government.[57]

Democrats argued—in their 1856 platform at least—that the

Constitution left the subject of slavery so completely to states and localities that the federal government was quite literally paralyzed. The "slavery question" was not even a fit subject for discussion in the national political arena. Democrats reduced their policy to an italicized proposition: *"Non-Interference by Congress with Slavery in State and Territory, or in the District of Columbia."* The contrast with Republicans was stark. Having absorbed the fundamental precepts of antislavery politics, they insisted that the Constitution *restricted* slavery to the states while committing the federal government to policies that would expand freedom everywhere it could. The guiding principle of federal policy, Republicans declared, was the "self-evident truth, that all men are endowed with the inalienable right to life, liberty, and the pursuit of happiness." Hence the "primary object" of the national government was to secure those rights "to all persons under its exclusive jurisdiction." Democrats denounced Republicans for promoting a purely "sectional" politics, but Republicans assumed that slavery itself was an exclusively "sectional" interest, that the Constitution made freedom *national*, and that antislavery was therefore the only truly national politics.[58]

Watching the emergence of the Republicans with increasing horror, more and more southerners concluded that the Democratic Party policy of "Non-Interference" was no longer adequate for the defense of slavery. Slaveholders started from the premise that their slaves were property, that owning slaves was a fundamental property right protected by the Constitution, and that the federal government had an obligation to protect that right wherever the Constitution applied. It was no longer enough to allow voters in the territories to decide for themselves whether to protect slave property, without the "intervention" of the federal government. That was the position long taken by the Democratic Party, and it remained the position of most northern Democrats. But as the prominent Mississippi Democrat Jefferson Davis explained, once Republicans began questioning the existence of a right of property in slaves, the Democratic Party would have to move beyond its policy of "non-intervention by the Federal Government in relation to slave property." This, Davis said, was "an evasion of the obligation to give equal protection to all kinds of property." We of the South "will never have obtained all our rights," Davis told a crowd at Jackson, Mississippi, in 1857, "until the legislation of congress shall amply protect slaves as it does all other property." The federal government had a positive "duty" to afford the same protection to slave property "as for other species of property."[59]

Davis, like most southern politicians, effectively reversed the Republican Party position by making slavery national and freedom merely local. Slaves were a constitutionally protected species of property, and wherever the Constitution was sovereign the federal government had an obligation to protect the property rights of slaveholders. That meant strict federal enforcement of the fugitive slave clause in the northern states, federal protection of slavery in the territories, federal support for slavery on the high seas, and federal maintenance of slavery in Washington, D.C. As they had done since the 1780s, southern slaveholders flatly denied the right of belligerents to emancipate slaves as a military necessity in wartime. Slavery national was soon written into the Constitution by the chief justice of the U.S. Supreme Court, Roger B. Taney. Reacting against the impressive showing of the Republicans in the 1856 presidential election, Taney engaged the debate over slave property in his controversial decision in *Dred Scott v. Sandford* in early 1857. The "right of property in a slave," Taney ruled, "is distinctly and expressly affirmed in the Constitution." The Constitution "makes no distinction between that description of property [slaves] and other property owned by a citizen." Taney had declared unconstitutional the most important premises of antislavery politics— that slave "property" was different from other forms of property, that under the Constitution slaves were persons rather than property, that there was no such thing as a constitutional right of property in slaves.[60]

But rather than abandon those premises, Republicans grew bolder in their rejection of a constitutional right of "property in man." Abraham Lincoln came relatively late to the conclusion, but when he reached it his assault on the right of property in slaves was unflinching. Because he had always hated slavery, Lincoln had no trouble questioning the morality of holding humans as property. Those who argue "that slave property and horse and hog property are alike to be allowed to go into the Territories, upon principles of equality," Lincoln argued, are "reasoning truly as if there is no difference between them as property." But if there is a difference, "if the one is property, held rightfully, and the other is wrong, then there is no equality between right and wrong." Like most abolitionists Lincoln thought the very idea of human property was immoral, but was it unconstitutional? Lincoln never denied that slaves were classified as "property" under the laws of the states in which slavery existed, but he did deny that state laws endowed slavery with the constitutional protection of fundamental property rights. The "right of property in negroes," he insisted, is "confined to those states where it is established by local law." *Dred Scott* was therefore wrongly decided. There is no constitutional right to slave property beyond the limits of the states where slavery was legal.[61]

Lincoln warmed to this conclusion over the course of his famous 1858 debates with Illinois Senator Stephen A. Douglas. At the first debate Lincoln scoffed at the idea of "*property*, so-called" in slaves. In the third debate he speculated that "if" he were to withhold legislative support for the *Dred Scott* decision, it "would be because I deny that this decision properly construes the Constitution." By the time he reached Galesburg for the fifth debate, Lincoln dropped the conditional tense and declared that "the right of property in a slave *is not* distinctly and expressly affirmed in the Constitution." But it was not until the final debate, at Alton, that Lincoln flatly denied that such a right existed. "I do not believe it is a constitutional right to hold slaves in a territory of the United States," he said. In the spring of 1859 Lincoln praised Thomas Jefferson for having elevated the "rights of persons" over the "rights of property." The same phrasing began to seep into his speeches. He supported the rights of property, he said, but whenever they came into conflict with the rights of persons, he would not hesitate to favor persons over property.[62]

In late 1859, following the tradition of a long line of antislavery constitutionalists, Lincoln went to the library to study the history of slavery and the Founders. He had been invited to New York to give a political lecture, and there, in February of 1860, he would present the results of his research in a speech that came to be known as the Cooper Union address. The burden of the speech was simple: Lincoln would prove that there was no such thing as a constitutional right of property in slaves. He pointed out that the Founders had deliberately excised from the Constitution any wording that might have suggested that human beings could be property. He reeled off a concise historical narrative showing that many of the same men who wrote the Constitution went on to support various laws aimed at restricting slavery's expansion. To those who had struggled for decades to formulate a politically viable antislavery constitutionalism, the logic and the evidence of Lincoln's Cooper Union address would have seemed both familiar and gratifying. What distinguished the speech was not its content but the man who wrote it and the circumstances surrounding its delivery.[63]

Lincoln was in New York presenting himself to leading Republicans as a candidate for the party's 1860 presidential nomination. That the Cooper Union address was much more than a history lesson was made clear in the way Lincoln shifted from his research into the past to its immediate significance, from history to politics. The setup was embedded in a series of lengthy footnotes in which Lincoln quoted a host of contemporary southerners claiming that any attempt to restrict slavery's expansion amounted to an unconstitutional assault

on their fundamental right to property in slaves. When you southerners "make these declarations," Lincoln said, "you have a specific and
well-understood allusion to an assumed Constitutional right of yours."
By that presumed right, he went on, you would carry your slaves into
the western territories and keep them there as your property. "But no
such right is specifically written into the Constitution," Lincoln
declared. "The instrument is literally silent about any such right." Lincoln then unveiled his own variation of the argument that Weld and
Chase and Giddings had done so much to develop. The words *slave* and
slavery appear nowhere in the Constitution, he pointed out. The word
property appears nowhere in connection to slavery. And "wherever in
that instrument the slave is alluded to, he is called a 'person.'" No matter how loudly or how often the southerners asserted their constitutional right to property in slaves, Lincoln told his New York audience,
do not believe it. "We deny," Lincoln said, that a right of property in
slaves "has any existence in the Constitution, even by implication."[64]

Lincoln's conclusion was the conclusion of his party in 1860. "We
deny" the right of property in slaves. Even in its short history, though,
the Republican Party had not always denied it. The 1856 Republican
platform contained no reference to the subject. But a lot had happened
since then. The Supreme Court had ruled that a right of property in
slaves was "expressly" affirmed in the Constitution. Southern Democrats demanded that their party do the same thing that Taney did—
expressly affirm a constitutional right of property in slaves. When
northern Democrats refused, southern Democrats walked out of the
1860 convention and formed their own party, dedicated to the proposition that "all citizens of the United States have an equal right to settle
with their property in the Territory, without their rights, either of
person or property, being destroyed or impaired by Congressional or
Territorial legislation." On the principle that slavery was national, not
even a territorial legislature could ban slavery because territories were
creatures of the federal government and were therefore obliged to

respect the constitutional right of property in slaves. The Republicans would have none of it. The Democrats had demonstrated their "measureless subserviency" to the southern slaveholders by making slavery national instead of freedom, by enforcing slavery "everywhere, on land and sea," and by "construing the personal relations between master and servant to involve an unqualified property in persons."[65]

"My doctrine was that of the Republican Party," New York Congressman Alexander Diven recalled two years later. Its "corner-stone," he said, was "that the Constitution recognized slavery nowhere." Slavery existed "simply and purely as a State institution." Beyond the borders of a state, where the Constitution was sovereign, a different rule applied. When "Congress acquired supremacy over any territory whatever, by virtue of the acquisition slavery did not go there under the Constitution." This was the difference between northern Republicans and southern secessionists. The latter believed that slave ownership was a fundamental right of property, and that the right of property followed the owner wherever the Constitution reached, except in those states that expressly abolished slavery within their borders. Proslavery constitutionalism deemed slavery national and freedom merely local. Republicans believed, on the contrary, "that the Constitution did not carry slavery anywhere." This was antislavery constitutionalism, the platform on which Abraham Lincoln ran for president, and on which he won. The issues at hand were varied yet familiar: the status of slaves brought to or escaping into the northern states, the status of slaves who rebelled on the high seas, and above all the status of slaves carried into the territories. But the principle at stake in each case was the status of slave property under the Constitution. "The grievance is not about the Territories. That is not it," Senator Louis Wigfall of Texas admitted. "It is the denial that slaves are property, and the Declaration that the Federal Government has a right to settle that question."[66]

2   "DISUNION IS ABOLITION"

IT WAS LATE DECEMBER of 1860, just before Christmas and only a few days after South Carolina seceded. The Union was beginning to fall apart, and a Republican newspaper in Massachusetts took a few moments to consider what it all meant. The crisis would be "decisive as to the supremacy of slavery," the editors predicted. If the South stays within the Union, slavery "will live longer and die more gradually and quietly." But if the southern states persist in their effort to leave the Union, slavery's "life will be one of constant peril and strife, and, like all great criminals, it will be pretty certain to come to a violent and bloody end."[1] Here in brief were the two options Republicans offered the slave states during the secession winter of 1860–61: peace, and with it a program of gradual abolition; or war, accompanied by an immediate but brutal military emancipation. Whichever way events turned, whether the South chose war or peace, slavery was finished. That, at least, is what Republicans were saying.

Even those who disagreed with Republicans understood that the fate of slavery hung in the balance during the winter of 1860–61. If that much was not already clear after the 1860 elections, it became undeniable over the ensuing months. Between Abraham Lincoln's victory in November and his inauguration in March of 1861, northerners and southerners of every political stripe registered their opinions in a nationwide discussion of emancipation and abolition. Their exchanges were embedded within the much larger series of debates over the legality of secession, the perpetuity of the Union, and the sovereignty of states—not to mention the relentless flow of contentious verbiage prompted by immediate events such as President James Buchanan's December message to Congress, the secession of South Carolina, and the various proposals for sectional compromise. Nevertheless, embedded within this mass of conflicting opinions was a blunt and revealing debate over the fate of slavery in the United States.

Throughout that debate Republicans spoke with such confidence of slavery's impending demise—in language that predicted, threatened, or merely warned of the inevitable cataclysm to come—as to make the outcome of the crisis seem a foregone conclusion. In the immediate aftermath of electoral victory in November, the Republicans assumed that they would be able to squeeze slavery to death—gradually but inexorably. Once the Deep South states seceded from the Union, however, Republicans argued that slavery would be destroyed in the rebellious states quickly but violently. Republicans were not very clear about how military emancipation would happen. They had not planned for war. So while they issued broad threats and painted vast scenarios, they had drafted no legislation, and of course issued no presidential orders. All of that would come, and come quickly, once the war began. It is enough to note that by the time Lincoln was inaugurated, virtually all Republicans believed that secession meant war and war meant immediate emancipation.

To be sure, the Republican Party in 1860 was a jerry-built contraption pasted together from discordant elements. Former Whigs and former Democrats still distrusted one another and still disagreed over such issues as the protective tariff, banking, and immigration. Nor did Republicans agree on issues of racial equality and discrimination. During his presidency Lincoln would often lock horns with his fellow Republicans in Congress over the relative powers of the executive and legislative branches of government. Yet throughout the war the differences dividing Democrats from Republicans were always more pronounced than the issues separating different factions within the Republican Party itself. And on the matters of emancipation and abolition—arguably the most significant of all—Republicans spoke with near unanimity from the beginning to the end of the Civil War. It is possible to speak with some precision of a "Republican" position in the secession-winter debates over slavery.[2]

FOR MONTHS, EVEN BEFORE the 1860 elections, Republicans across the North were giddily predicting the destruction of slavery in the South. With Abraham Lincoln as president and with wider Republican margins in Congress, the long reign of the Slave Power would be over. Although prohibited by the Constitution from interfering directly with slavery in the states where it already existed, the federal government would nevertheless do all it could to put slavery out of existence by interfering with it indirectly. At the very least, slavery would be banned from all the western territories, and no new slave states would be admitted to the Union. With the addition of each new free state, the already weakened power of the slaveholding oligarchy would diminish still further. Congress would abolish slavery in Washington, D.C., and repeal the despised Fugitive Slave Act of 1850. New appointments to the Supreme Court would transform America's highest judicial tribunal, shifting it from a proslavery to an antislavery bias. Most Republicans endorsed these policies in one form or another. A number of Republicans also proposed that the federal government purchase and then emancipate all the slaves in the Border States. The most radical Republicans went even further. They would restore "free speech" to the South, which could only mean that postmasters would no longer interrupt the flow of abolitionist propaganda into the slave states. Others would regulate the domestic slave trade by taxing every slave sold across state lines and outlawing the coastwise trade entirely.

Even shorn of its more radical elements, the basic Republican goal remained the same: Pressed down into the Gulf States, denied access to fresh western soils, and deprived of the life-giving support of federal power, slavery even in the cotton South would eventually become unprofitable, maybe even dangerous. Slavery's intrinsic weaknesses would become steadily more apparent. The blight of economic backwardness would spread across the South, its arrogant aristocracy would become ever more disdainful of democracy, and the slaves would become increasingly restless and insurrectionary. A homegrown antislavery movement would spring up within the slave states. It might take awhile, although most Republicans expected that abolition, accelerating over time, would be accomplished within a generation. But however long it took, and by whatever particular means, the destruction of slavery was inscribed in the Republican electoral victory in November of 1860.[3]

Lincoln had repeatedly vowed to put slavery on "the course of ultimate extinction." But what did this mean? He once said, in an offhand remark, that if slavery were to be abolished in the "most peaceful" and "most gradual" way, it might take a hundred years, but in the very next breath he signaled his doubt that abolition would or even should take that long.[4] He was skeptical that slavery would be abolished peacefully, for example, having already spoken ominously of an impending crisis, a violent struggle that would end in the complete victory of either slavery or freedom. Nor did he expect it to take a century. When in November of 1861 Lincoln drafted two proposals for the abolition of slavery in Delaware—a model, Lincoln hoped, for all four of the Border States that remained loyal—he indicated that the process would be completed in as little as five years, no more than thirty, although his preference was for ten. But voluntary gradual abolition by the states was only one of the ways Lincoln expected to attack slavery. By 1860 he was committed to banning slavery from the territories, abolishing it in Washington, and admitting no new slave states into the Union. He said that if he were in Congress he would vote to overrule the *Dred Scott* decision. He hated the Fugitive Slave Act of 1850 and warned that if the slave states seceded from the Union the North would stop enforcing it altogether. Lincoln had embraced the Republican Party scenario for slavery's demise—self-destruction by means of containment, restriction of slavery to the states where it already existed and, paradoxically, forcing it to die a natural death. Ultimate extinction.

When Lincoln spoke of these things he was relatively circumspect. Many of his fellow Republicans were more overt, and some would have pushed the policy further, but it was the same basic policy. Shortly before the November elections a Republican newspaper in Chicago spelled out in dramatic detail what would happen to the slave states should the Republicans triumph at the polls. "We will surround them with a cordon of Free States, as with a wall of fire.—We will hem them in, on all sides, by free and happy communities. . . . Deprived of the aid of the general government and thrown upon itself for support, slavery must gradually die out." Southerners would get antislavery literature in the mail. Missouri and Delaware would soon become free states, and slavery, "confined to its present limits . . . will become unprofitable, and a pecuniary as well as a moral curse. Then emancipation societies will spring up in all the slave States, and the blessed work will go on, until the last slave is free." The child is now born, the editors proclaimed, "who will live to see the emancipation of the last slave upon the American Continent." All of this would happen within the limits prescribed by the Constitution. After the Republicans take power, the slave states will be allowed to "keep their barbarous system. . . . We will let them alone." But this was true only in the narrow sense that Congress would not directly abolish slavery in the states where it already existed. There was nothing to stop the federal government from surrounding the slave states with a cordon of freedom and slowly squeezing slavery to death.[5]

Many Republicans were persuaded that slavery was so politically untenable, socially unstable, and economically irrational that it was kept artificially alive only by steady infusions of federal support funneled to the slaveholders thanks to the viselike grip the Slave Power maintained over every branch of the federal government. Slavery was "seated in the President's chair, ruling in the Council chamber, judging on the bench of the Supreme Court, moving to and fro armed among Senators and representatives." Without the support of the Slave Power the slaves would have been restored to their natural condition of freedom long before. Republicans believed that with their electoral victory in November of 1860, the Slave Power would at last be overthrown. "The power of the slave interest is broken," Henry Ward Beecher announced just before Election Day, "the crisis is over." A few days after the Republican victory, Salmon Chase, who would soon begin serving as Lincoln's Treasury secretary, wrote that one of the "great objects" of his life, "the overthrow of the Slave Power, is now happily accomplished." So long as the Republicans implemented the policies to which the party was committed, Chase believed, slavery was doomed. Republicans may not have secured majority control of Congress, but they had overthrown the Slave Power, tilted the government toward freedom, and thereby sealed slavery's fate. William Seward, soon to become secretary of state, was never one to shy away from bold predictions, and he did not do so now: Lincoln's election, he flatly declared "is the downfall of slavery."[6]

It was certainly the downfall of circumspection, for Lincoln's election loosened a number of Republican tongues. Where they had once been vague about slavery's future, they were suddenly bold and specific. In January of 1861, for example, Horace Greeley, the Republican editor of the influential *New York Tribune*, published the details of a plan to have the federal government purchase—at four hundred dollars apiece—and then emancipate every slave in the states surrounding the cotton South: Delaware and Maryland, plus the westernmost slave states running southward from Missouri and Arkansas through Louisiana and Texas. The emancipated slaves would then be "colonized" somewhere outside the United States. "Rent by internal discords and jealousies," Greeley explained, "the seceding States will, one by one, abolish Slavery and return" to the Union. Before the year was out, Lincoln would be drafting statutes that nearly duplicated Greeley's plan, though without colonization.[7]

Northern Democrats warned that the Greeley proposal would "turn nearly a million negroes loose upon our borders to immigrate into Ohio to mix with the white population, and compete with the white laborers for a living." But there were no comparable objections among Republicans. On the contrary, they were soon floating the same proposal in Washington. On February 11, only a few weeks after Greeley published his plan, Congressman James B. McKean of New York introduced a resolution in the House of Representatives urging the appointment of a "select committee" of five members to determine if "it be practicable for the General Government to procure the emancipation of the slaves in some, or all, of the 'border states.'"[8]

These proposals rested on the premise that slaves were "property" only under state law, and that the moment the federal government took possession of the slaves, they were emancipated because the Constitution did not recognize the slaves as property. Paraphrasing Lincoln at Cooper Union, Republican editors at the *Hartford Evening Press* insisted that "if slaves were referred" to anywhere in the Constitution, "they were spoken of as 'persons' and not as 'property.'" They explained, "Mr. Madison, in the convention, 'thought it wrong to admit into the constitution the idea that there could be property in men,' and in that spirit was the instrument made. Slavery was left as they found it, sustained only by local, state legislation." A radical paper in Chicago made the same familiar point: the "framers were careful to avoid the introduction of a single word that should intimate the recognition of the right of property in man." The more conservative *Cincinnati Daily Commercial* denounced the *Dred Scott* decision on the same grounds. In "proclaiming that slaves are property under the Constitution," the Supreme Court issued a "monstrous decision."[9]

The Republican consensus that there was no right of property in slaves dampened the prospect of a meaningful sectional compromise. In his much-awaited annual message to Congress in December of 1860, President James Buchanan proposed a series of constitutional amendments, the first of which, echoing the *Dred Scott* decision, would grant "express recognition of the right of property in slaves" in the states where slavery already exists as well as in "all the common Territories" of the United States. This was slavery national—wherever the Constitution was sovereign, slavery was protected. Even Democratic papers conceded that no Republican could endorse Buchanan's proposed amendment. In fact the Republicans were outraged. "The Constitution does not chattelise human beings," the *Iowa State Register* declared, "and no system of terrorism that the South can inaugurate will drive the free States into an admission that it does." Republican editors across the North uniformly pronounced the Buchanan proposal dead on arrival. The basic difference between Abraham Lincoln and Jefferson Davis, a pro-southern editor in Philadelphia explained, is that "[o]ne protects slave property as it protects all other property. The other makes war upon slave property, as it does *not* upon any other property."[10]

If any one issue sent the slave states fleeing from the Union, this was it: the Republican Party had elected a president who did not believe there was a constitutional right of property in slaves. Secessionists went to great lengths refuting the Republican position. "Slaves are recognized both as property and as a basis of political power by the Federal compact," an Alabama secessionist wrote, "and special provisions are made by that instrument for their protection as property." The Republicans have already rendered meaningless "the fundamental principle of all good governments—the duty to protect the property of the citizen." No matter how artfully Lincoln tries to cover over his intentions, Congressman J. L. M. Curry of Alabama warned, the policy of his administration "is not to recognize the right of the Southern citizen to property in the labor of African slaves."[11]

Defenders of slavery insisted that the Constitution, far from stigmatizing slavery, singled it out for special protection. It counted three-fifths of the slave population for purposes of representation, boosting the power of the slave states in the House of Representatives and the Electoral College. The fugitive slave clause guaranteed that slaves escaping into free states would be returned to their masters. Congress was prohibited by the Constitution from outlawing the international slave trade for twenty-one years after ratification. State governments alone could determine what did or did not count as "property," and nowhere did the Constitution exempt any particular "species of property" from the fundamental rights of property. Congress has no power to "decide what shall or shall not be property," Curry explained. "The Constitution of the United States discriminates specially in favor of slave property; provides for its security, and for its representation in this body. It recognized property in slaves; and the Supreme Court has affirmed our right to emigrate to, and occupy with slaves, the common territory." There were few southerners in 1860 who doubted that the Constitution established a right of property in slaves.[12]

When the republic was formed, Jefferson Davis explained a few weeks after the war began, "the right of property in slaves was protected by law" in twelve out of the thirteen original states. "This property," he went on, was also "recognized in the Constitution," whereas Congress was given no power at all "to legislate" in any way that might prejudice "that species of property." A New Orleans editor put it succinctly: "The Constitution of the country recognizes slaves as property; the laws of Congress recognize slaves as property; the decisions of the Supreme Court recognize slaves as property." Such convictions were commonplace among secessionists. "It is not safe," one Georgia editor warned, "to trust eight hundred millions of dollars worth of negroes, in the hands of a power which says that we do not own the property, that the title under the Constitution is bad." It was not only hot-blooded secessionists who believed this. The northern states "should pass laws giving full protection to slave property in the Territories," a moderate newspaper in Gallatin, Tennessee, proposed, "and should recognize slave property as on the same footing as any other species of property." Only then could the disaster of disunion be averted. South Carolina leaders understood this, which is why, in their widely publicized "Declaration" of the causes for its secession, they proclaimed that "[t]he right of property in slaves was recognized" in the Constitution.[13]

If Republican constitutional principles were outrageous, the party's policy proposals were still more threatening. Secessionists warned that once in power the Republicans would implement plans designed to force the slave states to abolish slavery on their own. Historians often treat such rhetoric as though it was a species of hysteria, replete with fantasies of improbable Republican depredations, when in fact all the secessionists did was take Republicans at their word. Secessionist editorials often read like the mirror images of Republican editorials. The *Kentucky Statesman* warned readers that with control of Congress, Republicans would repeal the Fugitive Slave Act of 1850 and, in impudent defiance of the Supreme Court, prohibit slavery in all the western territories. And that was only the beginning. Republicans would block the admission of new slave states, abolish slavery in

Washington, and exclude it from all federal property—forts, dock-yards, and arsenals—within the South. Eventually Republicans would ban the interstate slave trade. If their party "shall succeed in attaining control of the government," the *Statesman* warned, "its history leaves no doubt that it will undertake to carry out these purposes."[14] And with that, the slave states would have no choice but to secede from the Union.

Secessionists waved aside all Republican promises not to "interfere" directly in the states where slavery already existed. "Where they cannot attack it in the States they will attack it at every other point they can reach," a Louisiana secessionist paper argued. "They will set fire to all the surrounding buildings in the hope that some spark may catch, and everything be destroyed in a general conflagration. They will undermine the pillars of the institution, and then wait quietly for the whole edifice to tumble." Lincoln's election would bring with it "no direct act of violence against negro property," the *Richmond Enquirer* pointed out. Instead the Republicans would go after slavery indirectly. "[U]nder the fostering hand of federal power," abolitionism would insidiously plant itself in the Border States, "converting them into free States, then into 'cities of refuge' for runaway negroes from the gulf States." The Republicans could accomplish all of this while technically adhering to their promises not to interfere directly with slavery in the southern states. "No act of violence may ever be committed, no servile war waged, and yet the ruin and degradation of Virginia will be as fully and as fatally accomplished as though bloodshed and rapine ravished the land." As Alabama's Congressman Curry correctly noted, Republican policies were designed to "*force* the abolition of slavery" by the southern states themselves. "Do you not call this interference?" North Carolina Congressman Zebulon B. Vance asked. "*You are interfering.*" And in so doing, he added, Republicans violate one of the oldest and plainest principles of justice and reason—that you cannot do indirectly what you are forbidden to do directly."[15]

Northern Democrats, like southern secessionists, roundly assailed Republican plans to squeeze slavery to death indirectly. Six weeks before the election, the *Daily Illinois State Register* denounced Lincoln for proposing "to legislate so that slavery must soon be extinguished." He would load the judiciary with antislavery judges, the editors warned. Others cautioned the slave states to remain within the Union, where they would be "protected from foreign invasion and domestic insurrection" and where their property rights were secure. If Republicans force the South to secede, the slaves would be "cajoled and coaxed into the North, where no owner could hope to recover them," a New York paper predicted, and if a war should come, northern "miscreants" would follow the Union forces into the South, where the slaves "would be kidnapped, excited and roused into rebellion."[16]

In the South avid secessionists and cautious cooperationists all read Republican plans the same way. The *Charleston Mercury*, the leading editorial voice of the South Carolina secession movement, predicted that once Republicans were "enthroned at Washington, in the Executive and Legislative departments of Government," the process of abolition would commence. First slavery would be systematically weakened in the Border States, so that Kentucky, Virginia, and Missouri would soon *"enter on the policy of making themselves Free States."* Surrounded by hostile free states, the *Mercury* warned, the "timid" in the cotton states would begin selling off their own slaves, but there would be no purchasers. The value of slave property would sink to nothing. Similar sentiments were echoed in New Orleans, where, a month before the election, the *Daily True Delta* conceded that Lincoln would not directly "overthrow" slavery or "conspire" against southern rights. But "so far as the south can be dwarfed, cramped and shut in from healthy intercourse with the world . . . , the abolition president will use the whole power of the country against it." Lincoln's election, then, would be "the death knell of the political and social prosperity of the south." No southerner will be represented in his cabinet; none would be appointed to diplomatic posts. Not another slave state would enter the Union, and indeed the nation would acquire no more territory at all unless it, too, was free of slavery. The New Orleans editors were skeptical about secession, whereas Charleston's were enthusiastic, but both recognized the identical threat to slavery coming from the Republican Party. For all its secessionist zeal, the *Charleston Mercury* was in some ways quite clearheaded. On the eve of the election it put the matter bluntly: "The issue before the country is the extinction of slavery." If the Republicans win, the only way to protect slavery would be to leave the Union. Which is precisely what the cotton states did.[17]

The secession movement began in South Carolina, within weeks after Lincoln's election, and by Christmas of 1860 the Palmetto State had declared its independence from the Union. The remaining states of the Deep South hardly needed South Carolina's coaxing. Beginning in early January and continuing into February, all the cotton states—Florida, Georgia, Alabama, Mississippi, Louisiana, and Texas—seceded from the Union. By February of 1861 they had come together to form a new government, the Confederate States of America, under an explicitly proslavery constitution, with an interim president, Jefferson Davis, a wealthy cotton planter from Mississippi. As they made their departures from the Union, each of the seceded states made it unmistakably clear that their action was prompted by the urgent need to protect the right of property in slaves from the impending assault of the Republicans who were about to take control of the federal government.[18]

The conflict over slavery had become irreconcilable. Secessionists argued that it was both naive and dangerous for any slaveholder to think that slavery could remain secure under the rule of Republicans, who denied that there was such a thing as a right of property in slaves. Disunion was the only way to protect slavery from the assaults that Republicans themselves were promising to deliver. What secessionists did not expect was the way disunion itself would fundamentally alter the terms of the debate over slavery's fate. With remarkable speed, secession drove Republicans from their emphasis on gradual abolition by means of federal containment to their second scenario, immediate emancipation as a military necessity.

SEWARD'S ALTERNATIVES

Curiously, Abraham Lincoln is the least useful Republican by which to gauge the shift in Republican discussions of slavery during the secession crisis. The last major speech he ever gave explaining his position on slavery was at Cooper Union in Manhattan, in February of 1860, as part of his bid for the Republican presidential nomination. After his New York appearance he toured New England giving different versions of the same speech. Then, in keeping with the electoral practices of his day, Lincoln went home to Springfield and stopped talking in public. Throughout the race for the nomination, through the fall presidential campaign, and then through the entire secession winter until his inauguration, Lincoln did not give a single major speech. He let leak private indications of where he stood on the legality of secession and the danger of compromising with secessionists on the territorial expansion of slavery, and he made a number of brief public statements to that effect while en route from Springfield to Washington for his inauguration. Otherwise Lincoln remained largely silent during some of the most turbulent months in American political history.[19]

Even in private correspondence Lincoln was reluctant to speak. Congressman John Gilmer of North Carolina addressed a series of questions to Lincoln in mid-December, questions that reflected the fears of many southern leaders that once in power the Republicans would move against slavery indirectly. Lincoln was "greatly disinclined" to answer the questions, but because he was considering Gilmer as a potential southern member of his cabinet, he felt compelled to respond. The result was an almost comical series of non-responses. Gilmer asked, for example, "whether as President you will favor the abolition of Slavery in the District of Columbia." To which Lincoln replied that he had "no thought of recommending the abolition of slavery in the District of Columbia" to Congress—which hardly answered the question he was asked. Lincoln gave the same type of response when Gilmer asked him whether he "would approve any law of Congress" regulating the domestic slave trade: Lincoln had "no thought" of recommending such a law to Congress. But what if Congress passed such a law, without the president's recommendation? Lincoln did not say. What if Congress passed a law "prohibiting the employment of Slaves in the Arsenals and Dock Yards" of the southern states? Well, Lincoln answered, that was "a thing I never thought of in my life, to my recollection, till I saw your letter." Would Lincoln use his influence to pressure northern states to repeal the laws they passed aimed at frustrating enforcement of the fugitive slave clause— the so-called personal liberty laws? "I really know very little of them," Lincoln answered, but if "any of them are in conflict with the fugitive slave clause, or any other part of the constitution, I certainly should be glad of their repeal." Needless to say, there were not many Republicans in 1860 who believed northern personal liberty laws were "in conflict" with the Constitution. Some questions Lincoln simply ignored. Would he, Gilmer asked, "enforce the fugitive slave law . . . favor its repeal . . . [or] suggest amendments impairing its efficiency?" Lincoln could hardly answer that one, as he was soon to propose such "amendments" in his inaugural address, so he passed over the question in silence. Likewise, to Gilmer's inquiry as to whether Lincoln would oppose the admission of any new slave states; Lincoln said nothing at all. When, however, Gilmer mentioned policies to which Republicans were pledged by virtue of their party's platform, Lincoln's answers were straightforward. "On the territorial question, I am inflexible," he wrote. It is hard to imagine that Gilmer would be satisfied by such evasive responses. Yet Lincoln was so concerned that they not leak out that he marked the letter "strictly confidential."[20] When pressed to speak out publicly during the secession crisis, Lincoln repeatedly said that he was a Republican, that his position was reflected in the Republican Party platform, and that he would take no stance that went against his party.

Given Lincoln's near-total silence, all eyes turned instead to another leading Republican politician of the day: Senator William Seward of New York. Long viewed as an ideological spokesman for his party, one of those who worked hardest to formulate and popularize its positions on slavery, Seward had been a favorite to win the Republican presidential nomination in 1860. Yet despite his loss to Lincoln, Seward was still recognized as one of the party's most important leaders. Lincoln's recent nomination of Seward to be his secretary of state did nothing to diminish Seward's stature. Many assumed that his was the public voice of the incoming administration. As a result, while Lincoln remained publicly silent, everyone waited expectantly for the major statement Seward was set to make in the Senate on January 12, 1861. It was a critical moment. Alabama and Florida had seceded the day before; Mississippi, two days before that. It was clear that Louisiana, Georgia, and Texas would soon secede as well. What would Seward have to say about this? Would he, like most of his fellow Republicans, stand his ground and refuse to compromise with the secessionists? Or would Seward offer the South concessions that would save the Union?

Even more than most Republicans, Seward was convinced that the mere election of Lincoln signaled the overthrow of the Slave Power and with it the inevitable destruction of slavery. Ten years earlier he had announced that emancipation was "inevitable." Now that the hour of slavery's demise was at hand, the only thing Republicans had to do was hold the Union together until Lincoln's inauguration. There would be no need for any "overt act" against slavery because slavery was doomed anyway. Leading Republican radicals, including Senator Charles Sumner and Salmon Chase, assumed the same conciliatory posture.[21] But conciliation was not the same thing as compromise. It could mean almost the reverse. Republicans in general, and Seward in particular, believed that slavery's fate was already sealed by their electoral victory. Convinced that slavery could be abolished peacefully, the conciliators urged fellow Republicans to speak as softly as possible—perhaps saying nothing at all. Why add fuel to the secessionist fire? As Chase wrote in late November of 1860, "[A]ll needless irritation should be carefully avoided." There was no need for war because the Slave Power had been dislodged and federal policy was about to shift in a dramatically antislavery direction. Charles Francis Adams, who along with Seward was a leading Republican supporter of conciliation, freely admitted that his moderate stance toward the South did not mean he was willing to compromise basic Republican principles. If anything, Adams and Seward were willing to conciliate because they were *not* willing to compromise.[22]

So fervently did Seward believe that war was unnecessary to destroy slavery that he made heroic but misleading efforts to cultivate unionists in the Upper South in a desperate attempt to limit the scope of secession to the Deep South. Inevitably his behavior raised suspicions among the "stiff-backs" in the Republican Party. Was Seward willing to offer the South a proposal that would allow slavery to expand into the territories? That was the line in the sand Republicans had drawn—no more expansion of slavery—yet only by abandoning that line was there any hope of avoiding war, if there was indeed any chance at all. Given Seward's desperate desire to avoid a war and his own driving ambition to take charge of the situation, some people thought he might cross the line and support an agreement that would allow slavery into some of the western territories. In fact he never did.

Not once—in Senate debates, in public speeches, or in private correspondence—did Seward so much as hint that he would support a settlement that would extend the Missouri Compromise line and allow slavery into the territories south of it. As Seward explained to his wife, he was trying "to gain time for the new administration to organize and for the frenzy of passion to subside. I am doing this," he added, "without making any compromise whatever, by forbearance, conciliation, magnanimity."[23]

Whatever he was telling Upper South unionists in private, in public Seward conceded nothing. The tone of his January 12 speech to the Senate was conciliatory, his prose was obscure, but his substance was unyielding. There was nothing to distinguish it from the speeches that had marked him as a radical ten years earlier. He would not concede that slaves were "property" under the Constitution, he would modify the Fugitive Slave Act of 1850, and he would suppress the southern rebellion by force. Secession was illegal and the Union indissoluble.[24] In short, Seward held fast to the standard Republican positions. But he also said more than that.

If it comes to war—if the North has to invade the South to enforce the law—the result, said Seward, would be slave rebellion. For although this was ostensibly a dispute over the disposition of the territories, it was at bottom a more fundamental conflict over "the relation of African slaves to the domestic population of the country." It was a struggle over slavery, and the slaves knew it, Seward warned. "Freedom is to them, as to all mankind, the chief object of desire." With a "flagrant civil war" raging all about them, can anyone expect that the slaves "will remain stupid and idle spectators?" Of course not, Seward argued. All of human history teaches us what the slaves will do in the midst of civil war. An "uprising" and "ferocious African slave population," numbering in the millions, would overwhelm the South, and the entire slave system would come crashing down.[25]

There were only two ways to abolish slavery, Seward explained.

The "American" way achieves abolition gradually by means of federal containment: close off access to the African slave trade, restrict slavery to the states where it already exists, and let it die a natural death. As slavery weakens, the slave states themselves will eventually realize that they must abolish slavery on their own. This was the peaceful resolution he and the Republicans hoped to pursue. But there was a second, "European" path by which "direct abolition" would be "effected, if need be, by compulsion." Seward was likely referring to the cases in which European nations had imposed abolition on their Caribbean colonies. In the United States the Constitution did not allow the federal government to emancipate slaves in the states—except in wartime when, Republicans believed, federal authorities could legally free slaves in an effort to suppress a rebellion. So long as the slave states remained within the Union, the United States would follow the "American" path. But if the South secedes, "if dissolution prevail," Seward asked, "what guarantee shall there be against the full development here of the fearful and uncompromising hostility to slavery which elsewhere pervades the world?"[26] Secession meant war, Seward warned, and war promised swift, violent military emancipation.

Such were the alternatives Seward and the Republicans were offering to the slave states: abandon any claim to a constitutional right of property in slaves and submit to a peaceful containment policy that would put slavery on the course of ultimate extinction, or leave the Union and face the prospect of immediate, violent military emancipation. Once a slave state left the Union, gradual abolition was no longer an option, except in the Border States that remained loyal. Secession will "hasten the downfall of American slavery at least one hundred years," the *Indianapolis Daily Journal* explained. Far from resolving the sectional crisis, an Iowa Republican declared in January of 1861, secession ensured that the "irrepressible conflict" would "gather fierceness and energy, and will continue until the last chain forged for the enslavement of men on this continent, will fall from the limbs of the bondman." The secessionists, the editor argued, are working "for the extinction of slavery" just as surely as they are "for the dismemberment of the Government." Secession will not protect slavery, Republicans warned. "Disunion, rather, is abolition," Salmon Chase explained, "and abolition through civil and servile war, which God forbid!"

Northern threats of military emancipation rose in tandem with secessionism in the Lower South. The very idea of secession is "utterly preposterous," one pro-Lincoln paper in Boston declared shortly after Lincoln's victory was announced. "The only results to the rebellious States would be a bloody strife confined entirely to their own territory, [and] the immediate and violent abolition of slavery." In December, days before South Carolina seceded, the *Indianapolis Daily Journal* found some cause for "satisfaction" among those who hated slavery: "The dissolution of the American Union seals the doom of American slavery." Secession will fail, a Republican editor in Springfield, Illinois, declared. "Universal Liberty is to be the eventual law of this land. Slave-holding traitors are only hastening the day when that law shall take effect." If the Union is destroyed, the Bloomington, Illinois, *Weekly Pantagraph* warned, "one may foresee that American slavery is destined to die a bloody death, and to come sooner and more suddenly to a tragical termination. It will not be in the power of man to avert it."[28] With secession Republicans promised a military emancipation that would abolish slavery more quickly—and with more bloodshed—than peaceful containment.

These were the loud editorial echoes of the constitutional principles developed by antislavery activists over several decades. As John Quincy Adams had long before warned, the constitutional protection of slavery would be nullified if the slave states rebelled, for then the federal government would be empowered to emancipate slaves as a means of suppressing a rebellion. In the very act of seceding, Republicans declared, the slave states forfeited any "rights" slavery had under the Constitution. Lincoln himself had hinted at this in September of 1859. Addressing southerners who were already threatening secession, he declared that if they "divided the Union" because Republicans refused to treat slavery the way secessionists demanded, northerners would "cease to be under obligations to do anything for you." In that case, Lincoln asked ominously, "how much better off do you think you will be?"[29]

By early 1861 Republicans everywhere were issuing similar threats, only more overtly. "Suppose the southern states go out of the Union to escape northern aversion to slavery." That would only "free" the North "from all the constitutional restraints that now limit its action." Until now the North has always been "willing to allow to slavery all the protection that the Constitution even by implication requires," the *Iowa State Register* argued. But "when the severance comes" the northern states "will see to it, that the curse of human bondage shall not pass beyond its present limits." An Indiana paper was even more emphatic that the North was constitutionally freed from slavery thanks to secession. "No more protection then," it declared, "no more fugitive slave laws, no more right of transit, no more suppressing of slave insurrections by Federal troops." By January of 1861, this was standard Republican rhetoric.[30]

Slavery, Republicans believed, was too feeble to survive on its own. Stripped of federal protection, slavery would collapse beneath its intrinsic weaknesses. It had always been propped up by the Slave Power, whose strength depended on its control of the presidency, Congress, and the courts. Slavery needed the steadying hand, the stabilizing force, of the national government. Without that protection the slave states would become international pariahs, subject to the unrestrained attacks of abolitionists foreign and domestic. "How long," one midwestern editor asked, "would the abnormal institution of slavery, already effete and staggering to its grave, live when brought under the crushing effects of these great influences? The logic of events is a stern and terrible thing."[31] Among the most "terrible" of the events that secession and war promised was slave rebellion.

"SLAVERY WILL GO OUT IN BLOOD"

Slaves so hated their bondage, Republicans argued, that a police state was required to maintain order in the South. An invading Union army would destroy that state apparatus, giving free rein to the pent-up insurrectionary instincts of four million slaves. As soon as the secession crisis erupted, Republicans began forecasting slave rebellion in the South as the inescapable consequence of war. The slave states, even joined together in a confederacy, "have not the means within themselves of keeping their negroes in subjection in such a contest." Secessionists must consider "the *negro element*," the *Worcester Palladium* warned. "God only knows what that element would accomplish, should it sweep over the land in the form of an ungovernable insurrection." It may be true that the slaves were "loyal and obsequious" to their masters under "ordinary circumstances," a pro-Lincoln paper in Kansas argued, but "we cannot escape the great facts which the history of this race reveals—that the black race perceive and deeply feel their wrongs, and when a fitting opportunity affords, will revenge them in the most implacable manner." It would be a sanguine business. Republicans warned that if southerners did not abandon their "treasonable operations," slavery would "go out in blood." If the South refuses to accept the results of a proper presidential election, "then indeed any one may foresee that American slavery is destined to die a bloody death." The Union invasion of the South would become the catalyst for slavery's internal collapse, opening the door to the possibility of slave rebellion.[32]

Republican conservatives shuddered at the prospect of brutal slave uprisings, even as they predicted them. Ohio Senator John Sherman, as conciliatory a Republican as there was during the secession crisis, insisted that southerners would "find no injury" coming from the Republicans "unless by their misrepresentation of us they stir up their slaves to insurrection." A few months later Edward Bates, Lincoln's conservative attorney general, was "convinced that flagrant Civil war in the Southern states would soon become a social war, and that could hardly fail to bring on a servile war." This was not something Bates wanted to happen, but the mere fact that he worried about it indicates how widely slave insurrection was being discussed among Republicans. Nor was Bates the only conservative to contemplate an insurrectionary emancipation. Days after the attack on Fort Sumter, George Templeton Strong, the conservative New Yorker, mused over the revolutionary potential of the slave population. "Very well," he wrote in his diary as he fumed over Jefferson Davis's declaration that privateers would be licensed to attack northern ships. "Then we shall have no scruples about retaliating on Southern property, which is peculiar for possessing a capacity for being invited to go away, and legs to take itself off, and arms wherewith to use such implements as may aid it in so doing."[33]

As the war commenced, a remarkable number of Republicans spoke—sometimes in horror, often with equanimity—of slave rebellion as the fate the slave states were bringing on themselves. No Republican argued that the North should invade the South with the intention of provoking slaves into rebellion. But that secession meant war, and that war meant slave rebellion, few Republicans disputed. The slaveholders were now faced with an impossible choice. If they remained within the Union, Republicans promised to abolish slavery gradually, but if they seceded from the Union, Republicans predicted a swift and brutal military emancipation. By the middle of January, Republican editors and politicians were falling into line declaring that, far from protecting slavery, secession in fact meant its swift and violent demise.

Cooperationists were quick to point out that if the southern states remained within the Union, the Republicans would not have the votes in Congress to implement their antislavery agenda. The Republicans had scored large victories in the northern states in the 1860 elections, enough to win the presidency, but not enough to control Congress—unless the slave states seceded. The southern states "have it in their power to stop the machinery of government" and thereby thwart the Republicans. Cooperationists had good reason to believe this. Ever since the 1790s a virtually unanimous southern congressional bloc, in coalition with a minority of northerners, had consistently beat back every antislavery proposal put forward by an effectively powerless majority of northern congressmen. The same would have been true had not so many slave states seceded. Lacking a Republican majority in Congress, one Kentucky editor explained in November of 1860, Lincoln "will be powerless . . . if the opposition to him is concentrated and well directed."[34] By January cooperationists were arguing that secession, far from preventing emancipation, would all but ensure it.

Echoing the Republicans, cooperationists warned that any state leaving the Union would forfeit all the protection the Constitution guaranteed to slavery. "The Constitution of the United States recognizes and protects slavery," a Louisville editor explained; it was the Constitution that had always kept the abolitionists at bay. "Take slavery out of the Constitution of the United States," and the entire South would find itself surrounded by "abolitionized" state and federal governments. On the other hand, if the Border States remain within the Union, "slavery will still be part of the Constitution" and thus "under its protection." The *Republican Banner* in Nashville agreed. Slavery "has depended mainly for its existence on the protection afforded by the Constitution. . . . But how will it be after the present government is dissolved, and the Northern States are absolved from their Constitutional obligations, and instead of being parties to the maintenance of slavery, as they are under the Constitution, become its open and avowed enemies . . . ? It is clear to be seen that the South will be greatly and fatally weakened" by secession, the editors concluded, "and the doom of slavery is irrevocably fixed."[35]

THE INAUGURAL ADDRESS AND
THE END OF COMPROMISE

Through the secession winter Lincoln stood firmly with his fellow Republicans in refusing to compromise on the fundamental issues— in particular the constitutional right of property in slaves on which every specific sectional dispute rested. Southern leaders uniformly dismissed the Republican alternative to war, gradual abolition along with a promise that the federal government would never directly abolish slavery in any state. Republicans just as uniformly rejected the proslavery alternative to war, the series of constitutional amendments and congressional resolutions offered by Kentucky Congressman John J. Crittenden in late 1860. The Crittenden compromise, as it has come to be known, would have recognized a constitutional right to slave property in the territories south of the old Missouri Compromise line, guaranteed the admission of new slave states organized south of the line, prevented Congress from abolishing slavery in Washington, and banned federal regulation of the domestic slave trade. Additional resolutions called for vigorous federal enforcement of the Fugitive Slave Act and the repeal of northern personal liberty laws. Taken together, these proposals would very nearly make slavery national. Each element presupposed the very thing Republicans most forcefully denied—that there was a constitutionally protected right of property in slaves. In effect, the Crittenden compromise called for the repudiation of every policy Republicans planned to implement in order to undermine slavery.

Most of the remaining compromise proposals were no more promising, and many were essentially meaningless. This was certainly true of the amendment to the Constitution, proposed by Ohio Republican Congressman Thomas Corwin in March of 1861, that would have preserved the existing ban on federal interference with slavery in the states where it currently existed. Everyone already agreed that the Constitution contained such a ban. The amendment did nothing more than reassert the familiar federal consensus. Indeed, the 1860 Republican Party platform explicitly affirmed the "inviolate" right of every state "to order and control its own domestic institutions according to its own judgment exclusively." An amendment saying what everyone already believed would have been superfluous. A number of congressional Republicans, recoiling against what felt like blackmail, voted against the Corwin amendment even though their own party platform endorsed it. Indeed, there is some evidence suggesting that Republicans endorsed the amendment knowing it was pointless but hoping to deflect charges that they were unwilling to compromise. Yet even in the unlikely event that the Corwin amendment had been ratified, it would have done nothing to thwart Republican antislavery policies. For that very reason neither the secessionists nor the cooperationists saw the Corwin amendment as a viable compromise proposal. It would not have forestalled the Civil War, and a war would render it meaningless. Any states that seceded from the Union would still forfeit whatever protection the Constitution might otherwise have afforded them, leaving them as vulnerable as ever to military emancipation. In short, the Corwin amendment changed nothing. Lincoln's lukewarm endorsement of it in his inaugural address was an empty gesture in a speech that stoutly reaffirmed the basic Republican positions.

What Lincoln's inaugural address actually revealed was how deeply the precepts of antislavery constitutionalism had penetrated into the political mainstream. He repeated the promise made by generations of antislavery activists—that he would not "interfere" with slavery in the states where it already existed—but he did not repudiate Republican plans to undermine slavery by means of containment. He would respect whatever "rights" the Constitution guaranteed to every state, knowing full well that a major source of conflict was the Republican claim that there was no such thing as a constitutional right of property in slaves. But the clearest indication of where Lincoln stood came in his extended remarks on the issue of fugitive slaves.[36]

Lincoln's first reference to the fugitive slave issue struck an eminently conservative tone. He quoted the entire fugitive slave clause of the Constitution and then noted that he, along with every member of Congress, was sworn to uphold the Constitution—"this provision as much as any other." Had he stopped there he might have eased the concerns of many a slaveholder. Instead, Lincoln went on to point out that there was "some difference of opinion whether this clause should be enforced by national or state authority." To say the least: southern leaders insisted that the federal government had to enforce the fugitive slave clause within the northern states. But most Republicans, starting from the premise that freedom was national, argued that the federal government had no business enforcing the fugitive slave clause, that slaveholders seeking to recapture fugitives should be obliged to press their case in state courts. By this reasoning the federal enforcement provisions of the Fugitive Slave Act of 1850 were illegitimate.[37]

Though Lincoln hated the 1850 law, he offered the South a substantive compromise proposal on fugitive slaves during the secession crisis. Unlike most antislavery politicians, Lincoln was willing to concede that the fugitive slave clause might be enforced by the federal government, but in return for that concession he demanded a federal personal liberty law guaranteeing accused blacks "the usual safeguards of liberty, securing free men against being surrendered as slaves." In addition, Lincoln wanted northern civilians exempted from any obligation to participate in the enforcement of the fugitive slave clause. These proposals would require a substantial revision of the Fugitive Slave Act of 1850, but they went against the views of Lincoln's own party. Seward warned Lincoln that most Republicans were "unwilling to give up their old opinion that the duty of executing the constitutional provisions concerning fugitives belongs to the States." Lincoln nevertheless revived the offer of federal enforcement in return for black citizenship in his inaugural address. In "any law upon this subject," Lincoln said, "ought not all the safeguards of liberty known in civilized and humane jurisprudence be introduced," in particular the "privileges and immunities of citizens" to which free blacks were entitled. Lincoln's proposal flatly contradicted the Supreme Court's ruling in *Dred Scott*, which denied that blacks were citizens. It could hardly have mollified the slaveholders that Lincoln urged everyone to obey the fugitive slave law, like all the other laws "which stand unrepealed," until such time as Congress acted to repeal it.[38]

In an obvious play on the wording of the *Dred Scott* decision—made all the more extraordinary by the fact that its author, Chief Justice Roger Taney, was sitting there listening—Lincoln distinguished between the rights everyone agreed to respect because they were "plainly written in the Constitution" and those over which there was serious disagreement because they were not plainly specified. Taney had ruled against Dred Scott's suit for freedom partly on the ground that the Constitution "expressly" recognized a right of property in slaves, something Lincoln had repeatedly disputed. Now, in his inaugural address, Lincoln argued that much of the political disagreement about slavery arose precisely from those questions on which the Constitution was silent. "Shall fugitives from labor be surrendered by national or by State authority?" Lincoln asked. "The Constitution does not expressly say. *May* Congress prohibit slavery in the territories? The Constitution," Lincoln answered, "does not expressly say." All of "our constitutional controversies," Lincoln explained, arise from disagreements over what the Constitution "does not expressly say" regarding the enforcement of the fugitive slave clause and slavery in the territories. Whenever such disagreements arise, "we divide upon them into majorities and minorities," and disputes over what the Constitution says are settled by means of democratic elections. Thereafter the minority must "acquiesce," or else "the government must cease." Secession thus amounted to a minority's refusal to acquiesce in the democratic legitimacy of majority rule. In this case the specific issues prompting the minority's rejection of democratic decision-making were the majority's views on the proper enforcement of the fugitive slave clause and the exclusion of slavery from the territories. These were the "real" ills that Lincoln freely admitted southerners faced by remaining within the Union.[39]

But there were even "greater" ills that Lincoln was "certain" would arise if the slave states left the Union. Continuing his attack on the *Dred Scott* decision, Lincoln doubled back yet again to the matter of fugitive slaves. In ordinary cases the people could rely on the Supreme Court to settle constitutional questions, Lincoln explained. But the Supreme Court cannot resolve "vital questions, affecting the whole people," otherwise "the people will have ceased, to be their own rulers." In the current crisis the vital question was clear: "One section of our country believes slavery is *right*, and ought to be extended, while the other believes it *wrong*, and ought not to be extended." Under the circumstances the laws regulating slavery could never be "perfectly" enforced because the supporters and opponents of slavery would never be able to agree on which laws should or should not be strictly applied. Lincoln cited two particular laws: the "fugitive slave clause of the Constitution, and the law for the suppression of the foreign slave trade." Both were about "as well enforced, perhaps, as any law can ever be in a community where the moral sense of the people imperfectly supports the law itself." So long as large numbers of southerners were willing to violate the ban on slave trading, the ban could only be imperfectly enforced. And so long as northerners were offended by the spectacle of slave-catchers in their midst, the fugitive slave clause would likewise be enforced "imperfectly." But what would happen if the South tried to secede from the Union? Lincoln asked. Then the circumstances of law enforcement would be changed. The South, he predicted, would reopen the Atlantic slave trade, and the commerce, "now imperfectly suppressed, would be ultimately revived without restriction." Meanwhile in the North, Lincoln added, "fugitive slaves, now only partially surrendered, *would not be surrendered at all.*" Having opened his discussion of fugitive slaves with a respectably conservative promise to abide by his oath of office and uphold the law, Lincoln steadily gravitated toward the more radical conclusion that if the South "separated" from the Union, neither the federal government nor the northern states would enforce the fugitive slave clause of the Constitution.[40]

In a speech often condemned for avoiding the issue of slavery, Lincoln actually referred to slavery repeatedly—citing it as the only cause of the sectional crisis, questioning the federal government's obligation to enforce the fugitive slave clause, reasserting the government's constitutional right to exclude slavery from the federal territories, and affirming the conviction that slavery was a moral wrong. If the inaugural address was Lincoln's attempt to avoid the subject of slavery, it was a miserable failure.

"AN ACTIVE WAR OF EMANCIPATION"

Perhaps because it reflected the familiar constitutional premises of the Republican Party, Lincoln's first inaugural address changed nothing. It brought none of the seceded states back into the Union, and it provoked no new wave of secessions in the Upper South. As an affirmation of Republican dogma, the speech provoked cries of outrage among northern Democrats. "There can no longer be any doubt that anti-slavery is the *corpus*, the strength, the visible life of the party which has now assumed the reins of government," the *Philadelphia Evening Journal* declared the next day.[41] If the new president carries out the "provisions and recommendations" of his speech, a Wisconsin Democrat declared, "blood will stain soil and color the waters of the entire continent." Nevertheless, the national argument over slavery's fate remained where it had stood for several months.

The attack on Fort Sumter had a more discernible effect. On April 12, 1861, heavily fortified Confederate batteries surrounding Charleston Harbor opened fire on the U.S. military installation at Fort Sumter, which was in the middle of the bay. There was no way the Union troops inside the fort could withstand the assault. With their inevitable surrender to the South, the war that everyone expected finally began. Lincoln immediately called up seventy-five thousand volunteers to suppress the rebellion. His action provoked four more slave states—Virginia, North Carolina, Tennessee, and Arkansas—to join the Confederacy, and with that the antislavery mood among northerners grew more defiant than ever. For the first time, a small but vocal minority of northern Democrats joined the Republican chorus in declaring that slavery was doomed. For many northerners the secession of the Upper South, especially Virginia, was the final act of treachery, prompting more threats of slave rebellion and renewed demands for emancipation. Many of these demands were now aimed at the new Republican president.

Lincoln could hardly have missed all the prophesying about slavery's doom among his fellow Republicans. His own cabinet members were predicting that secession would lead to slave rebellion and emancipation. And Lincoln's mailbox was rapidly filling up with letters from politicians and pundits across the Republican spectrum, all of them telling the new president the same thing. In late April the radical William Channing wrote to Lincoln "advising [the] abolition of Slavery by martial law as the surest way to conquer rebellious States

& preserve the border ones." Similar letters to Lincoln arrived from other states, and not only from radicals. "Had I the power," George Field wrote from Brooklyn in early May, "I would march an army forthwith to Richmond proclaiming every where *immunity* & protection to all *of any color* who would desert the Rebel standard." "The war must be carried into Africa," a Republican politician from New York wrote in May of 1861. "Take the occasion by the hand," one Pennsylvanian wrote, "*and make The bound of freedom wider yet.*" Lincoln's mercurial Illinois friend Orville H. Browning predicted that the time would come when the president would have to push the war "to the uttermost extremity," when "it will be necessary for you to march an army into the South, and proclaim freedom to the slaves." Browning's letters expressed the views of many northerners at the time. Slavery had caused the rebellion; suppressing the rebellion would therefore require the destruction of slavery.[42]

The "contest sounds the death-knell of slavery," an Indiana journal explained a few days after Fort Sumter was captured. And who "will mourn its loss?" Slavery has divided the country and hindered its progress for so long that "it would be truly a God's blessing to be rid of it. So every patriot feels in his heart of hearts." An independent newspaper in Paris, Maine, echoed the thought. We are in the midst of a revolution caused by the institution of slavery, the *Oxford Democrat* explained. Whatever happens, "the final abolition of slavery will be hastened by the movement." Slave insurrections will erupt across the South, "touched off by any John Brown or Nat Turner that has the courage to apply the fuse." The federal government has long been "the great protection of slavery in this country," but with the slave states gone from the Union that same government "will be the greatest agency that can be brought into existence to extinguish slavery in the United States." Southerners must understand, another paper in Roxbury, Massachusetts, explained, that "[t]he rule of the Slave power in America is at length ended." Slavery's "besotted arrogance has proved its ruin." It was May of 1861, the war had just begun, and already there was nothing remarkable about Republican declarations that the conflict could result only in the complete destruction of slavery.[43]

More surprising was the support for emancipation expressed by a small but growing number of northern Democrats, opening a rift within the party that would persist through the war. Before the firing on Fort Sumter, virtually all Democrats in the North blamed the crisis on the Republicans' relentless attacks on slavery, and most Democrats continued to make that claim. They often resorted to racist demagoguery, hoping to redefine the struggle over slavery as a struggle over racial equality. But most northern Democrats were also unionists, and with the attack on Fort Sumter some of them turned against the South and with it slavery. "With the first gun from the rebels in arms perished every sympathy at the North with slavery," a Democratic editor in Wisconsin explained. "The war cannot now end but with the total extinction of slavery, which was the cause of the war." Democrats in Columbus, Ohio, who had supported the pro-southern candidate John C. Breckinridge in the recent presidential election suddenly sounded like radical Republicans. "The South is doomed, and with it slavery," they declared. If poor whites join with slaves to overthrow the rule of the southern aristocracy, slavery may end quickly in a servile insurrection. "In your rebellious zeal you have sown the wind that you may reap the tornado, whose tracks will be blood, blood, blood."[44]

But if secession divided northern Democrats over slavery, it solidified the Republican commitment to slavery's destruction. Over the next several years Republicans would disagree among themselves about many things—the confiscation of rebel property, the power of the president versus Congress, and above all Reconstruction policy—but they did not disagree about slavery and abolition. Even before the war started, William Howard Russell, the perceptive reporter for the

London *Times*, could not find any Republicans in Washington who doubted that the war would end in the complete destruction of slavery. The reporter showed up at a state dinner held at the White House on March 28—halfway between inauguration day and the day of the attack on Fort Sumter. The affair was hosted by the president and the First Lady; Lincoln's cabinet members and leading Republican politicians were in attendance. As Russell worked the room, chatting with them and listening in on their conversations, he noticed a "uniform tendency" in the way they spoke. "They seemed to think," Russell reported, "that England was bound by her anti-slavery antecedents to discourage to the utmost any attempt of the South to establish its independence on a basis of slavery, and to assume that they were the representatives of an active war of emancipation."[45]

Russell viewed such talk among Republicans as arrogant bluster, and no doubt much of it was. The war had not yet begun. Until then all the Republicans could do was make predictions, issue warnings, and hurl threats. It was easy enough for Republicans to wrap themselves in the mantle of emancipation, threaten the South with slave rebellion, and predict the downfall of slavery. But scenarios were not the same as policies. It remained to be seen whether Republicans were prepared to act on their promises. Yet surely it matters that Republicans were contemplating slavery's destruction from the beginning. If it is too much to say that they went to war with clearly formulated plans about how to go about abolishing slavery, it is a more serious mistake to claim that Republicans were not talking openly about the destruction of slavery.

By the time Lincoln was inaugurated, Republicans had inherited from the antislavery movement two broad scenarios for a federal attack on slavery—a peacetime policy that would cordon off the slave states and gradually force them to abolish slavery on their own, and a wartime policy of immediate emancipation as a military necessity—both of which they repeatedly affirmed during the secession winter of

1860–61. Precisely how the two scenarios would be implemented nobody could really know, but that one or both would bring about the destruction of slavery the Republicans seemed certain. They blustered. They were arrogant—though scarcely more so than the secessionists, the northern Democrats, and not a few abolitionists. More important Republicans were naive about how easy it would be to destroy slavery. Yet they were anything but reluctant emancipators.

3

"FULFILLMENT OF THE PROPHECIES"

NESTLED WITHIN THE LARGER SECESSION debate over the fate of slavery was a smaller but equally fascinating dispute over what the slaves would do. On January 12, 1861, the same day that William Seward was warning his southern colleagues in the Senate that the slaves might take advantage of a civil war by rising in rebellion, a Democratic newspaper in Cleveland dismissed the forecast of slave insurrection as a "popular error" among Republicans. If there is a war, the editors predicted, "no class of beings will be less troublesome than these blacks. Docility is the leading feature of the race." The slaves "are more happy and contented than any other race of people on the earth." Left alone, the editor explained, a "pure blooded African . . . has no aspirations for liberty as we understand it."[1] Republicans started from a very different premise. They generally assumed that African Americans harbored the same instinctive desire for freedom that all human beings shared. "Whenever our armies march into the Southern states," Orville Browning wrote, "the negroes will, of course, flock to our standards—They will rise in rebellion, and strike a blow for emancipation from servitude, and to avenge the wrongs of ages. This," he declared, "is inevitable."[2]

What would the slaves do? The question was everywhere when the war began. Would they take advantage of the Union invasion by acting on their natural human desire for freedom, as Republicans predicted? Or were slaves so comfortably situated, were blacks so innately subservient, that they would, as northern and southern Democrats alike insisted, remain loyal to their masters?

OUTRAGED BY REPUBLICAN PREDICTIONS of servile insurrection, many slaveholders ostentatiously avowed their faith if not in the loyalty at least in the docility of their slaves. Traveling through the slave states in May of 1861, William Howard Russell found that "[n]one of the Southern gentlemen have the smallest apprehension of a servile insurrection. They use the universal formula 'Our Negroes are the happiest, most contented, and most comfortable people on the face of the earth.'"[3] On a plantation in South Carolina, Russell noticed that the "fidelity" of the slaves was "undoubted." The house, he observed, "breathes an air of security." The doors and windows were unlocked. There was a single gun on the premises. Here, as elsewhere, the planter had no "dread" of any of his slaves. Near Fort Pickens in Florida, Russell struck up a conversation with a slaveholder who had joined the Confederate army, leaving his wife and children "to the care of the niggers." Aren't you "afraid of the slaves rising?" Russell asked. "They're ignorant poor creatures, to be sure," the master answered, "but as yet they're faithful."[4] Russell heard the same thing in Alabama. "Not the smallest fear is entertained of the swarming black population."[5] Similar reports came in from farms and plantations across much of the South.[6]

But Russell was skeptical of all the talk of loyal slaves. He knew that insurrection panics had erupted across the South during the election campaign and the secession crisis, and he had read recent accounts of slaves murdering their masters—accounts that at the very least suggested more anxiety than the slaveholders were letting on.[7] "There is something suspicious in the constant never ending statement that 'we are not afraid of our slaves,'" Russell observed. He concluded that the slaveholders were relatively unconcerned because southern slave society had made itself into something close to an armed camp. "The curfew and the night patrol in the streets, the prisons and watch-houses, and the police regulations prove that strict supervision, at all events, is needed and necessary."[8] As long as the South was able to maintain this police system, Russell believed, it was not surprising that white southerners would feel secure in their own homes.

When the war began, the slaveholders' first instinct was not to lock down their plantations but to beef up the local militias, redouble the slave patrols, organize "home guards," and enforce the curfews. These were the official and semi-official institutions that maintained order within the plantation by sustaining the master's authority without. Sheriffs, justices of the peace, and local police were only one part of a much larger network of accomplices who upheld the security of southern slavery. It worked well enough. Slaves resisted in various ways but rarely rose in outright rebellion. They ran away all the time in the Old South, but only a tiny fraction of fugitives succeeded in escaping from slavery. It is not surprising that when the war began, so many slaveholders expressed confidence in the security of their system.[9]

And yet there were indications that the slaveholders were more anxious than they let on, at least to English reporters. They nervously read reports of disturbances among slaves, especially those nearby. Daniel Cobb, a slaveholder in southeastern Virginia, reported no disruption among his own slaves, but he peppered his diary with rumors of insurrectionary plots and tales of slaves who murdered their masters. He paid close attention to the stories about other peoples' slaves escaping to Union lines. In January of 1861, Cobb heard that a "Bachelor was taken by his servants from his bead at Midnight. Carried out of the house and beat to death with an ax." Outsiders may have been impressed by open windows and unlocked doors, but Cobb was upset by the news that on the farm where the ax murder took place, "the door was left unfastened by the house Boy." In March, Cobb reported that "People has several Negrows Runaway &c." In April he "hurd of several fires round that Could not be accounted for." By June, as Union forces had begun to establish bases in northern and eastern Virginia, Cobb heard reports of slaves in groups of ten or twenty who "has made there escape." Daniel Cobb was fifty—too old, he thought, to join the Confederate army. But he made his own contribution to the southern cause by helping to organize a local "Home Guard" to monitor "all misconduct of negrows and low life white people of the County and to keep the state of affair right." Yet despite all of this concern with security—or perhaps because of it—there was no disruption among Cobb's slaves through the first year, except in November when the Confederate government began impressing some of his slaves to work on local embankments.[10]

The slaveholders' anxiety revealed itself most clearly in their concerns about the ability of government to maintain order. They wrote pleading letters to state and local officials, and even to the new Confederate president. Less than two weeks after the capture of Fort Sumter, Charles Mitchell wrote to Jefferson Davis from Louisiana about the "great fear" of a northern invasion down the Mississippi River and the "sense of insecurity" that was already widespread. There was "a deep seated anxiety in regard to *negroes*," a widespread fear that a Yankee invasion would likely provoke a "panic" that could only "be ruinous to our cause."[11] A week later William H. Lee, of Bell's Landing, Alabama, wrote to Davis suggesting that the best way to thwart slave insurrection (and alleviate white fears) was for the Confederate government to order all black men "in the army and make them fite."[12] Barely a month after the war began, George Gayle of Dallas County, Alabama, was already worried that so many of the locals had joined the Confederate army that if any more enlisted, there would not be enough men left "to save ourselves from the horrors of insurrection."[13] The slaveholders knew that the security of slavery depended on the viability of their government.

This is what made an invading Union army so worrisome—not merely its capacity for physical destruction, or even its attractiveness to runaway slaves, but its profound threat to the civil authority in the South. Runaway slaves and insurrection panics were nothing new to southern slave society. This was different, however, because at stake was the South's ability to police the slave system in the face of an invading army. Union authorities claimed that northern invasion of the Confederacy was necessary to restore "civil authority" to those parts of the South where it had ceased to function properly—that is, loyally. Hence, the U.S. Army had to be sent in to fill the presumed void. This meant that whatever else the Union army was, it was not an extension of the slaveholders' authority. If the sectional conflict proved anything, it was that the slaveholders' power was ultimately political power.

The slaves could hardly remain unaware of this, if only because their masters were so often indiscreet. During the 1860 election campaign, observers noticed that the "colored population" of Georgia was "manifesting an unusual interest in politics, and the result of the Presidential election." In Macon "every political speech" attracted "a number of negroes" who "managed to linger around and hear what the orators say."[14] Thomas Johnson, a Virginia slave, recalled that in 1860 "there was great excitement in Richmond over the election of Mr. Abraham Lincoln as President of the United States. The slaves prayed to God for his success, and they prayed very especially the night before the election. We knew he was in sympathy with the abolition of Slavery. The election was the signal for a great conflict for which the Southern States were ready."[15] Further South, George Womble in Talbot County, Georgia, overheard his owner declare that "he was going to join the army and bring Abe Lincoln's head back for a soap dish. He also said that he would wade in blood up to his neck to keep the slaves from being freed."[16] In Montgomery, Alabama, the governor gave an impromptu speech "in which he dwelt on Southern Rights, Sumter, victory, and abolition-dom," while nearby "[t]here were a number of blacks listening."[17] The slaves have "been talking a great deal about Lincoln freeing the servants," a Mississippi mistress worried in her diary in May of 1861.[18] The slaveholders made no attempt to disguise the fact that they had seceded because Abraham Lincoln had been elected president. When he was a young slave in Georgia, Levi Branham recalled, one of his "young masters" told him about the 1860 election and said "that if Mr. Abe Lincoln was elected the negroes would be free. Then he asked me if I wanted to be free and I told him 'yes.'"[19] How could the slaves not know what was going on?

Aware of the significance of Lincoln's election, it did not take long before slaves realized that Union military installations in the Confederate states represented a kind of counter-state within the southern states, an alternative government inside the South but beyond the reach of the police powers of southern slave society. When the war began, Minerva Boyd recalled, "I thought & said the Union Armies would make us free."[20] Barely a week after Lincoln's inauguration, four runaway slaves, "entertaining the idea" that U.S. troops "were placed here to protect them and grant them their freedom," showed up at Fort Pickens in Florida, which was still under Union control. The war had not yet started, though, and there could be no "military emancipation" until there was a military conflict, so the officer in charge quickly returned the fugitives to the Pensacola city marshal to be sent back to their owners. "That same night four more made their appearance," but these runaways "were also turned over to the authority the next morning."[21] Union soldiers had long assumed that as agents of the federal government they were obliged to return runaway slaves to their owners. That policy was still in effect in the loyal Border States when the war began.

During the earliest months of fighting, many Union generals in the four slave states that remained loyal to the Union—Delaware, Maryland, Kentucky, and Missouri—took the position that the laws of those states, including the fugitive slave laws, were in full force and that the Union army was obliged to enforce them. On April 23, 1861, General Benjamin F. Butler, invoking the familiar understanding of slavery as a state institution, assured slaveholders in Maryland that "the forces under my command are not here in any way to interfere with or countenance any interference with the laws of the State." On the contrary, Butler declared, he stood ready to assist state authorities "in suppressing most promptly and effectively any insurrection against the laws of Maryland."[22]

Yet Butler's announcement that he would enforce state laws was ingeniously double-edged. When he arrived in Maryland there was an insurrection under way, but it was a secessionist insurrection. Confederate supporters had recently rioted in the streets of Baltimore, cutting the rail lines into Washington to prevent Union troops from protecting the capital and intimidating unionists into silence. Butler's promise to suppress "any" insurrection turned out to be more of a threat to disloyal whites than a reassurance to nervous slaveholders. Even so, Butler believed that slaveholders in loyal states were still protected by the Constitution. Not so in the seceded states.

Butler had arrived in Maryland with meager credentials as an opponent of slavery. Born and raised in New England, trained as a lawyer, he should have been a Whig. Instead, he was a lifelong Jackson Democrat who hated snobbery and viewed Whigs as the party of aristocracy. Unable to secure an appointment to West Point, Butler opted instead for a legal and political career. In his hometown of Lowell, Massachusetts, Butler fused his politics with his law practice by defending workers' rights against the local mill owners. Smart, energetic, and sarcastic—implacable in debate—Butler presented himself to voters as the enemy of corporations and the friend of working people. Butler was a Free Soil Democrat in 1848, and in the early 1850s he joined the new Free Soil political coalition of Massachusetts "Conscience Whigs" and independent Democrats. It was a fusion of convenience, however, embraced by Democrats as the only way of dislodging the entrenched Whig oligarchy of Massachusetts. Butler's own campaigns bore little of the imprint of the antislavery movement. In 1851 he ran for local office as a candidate of the new antislavery coalition on a "Ben Butler Ten Hour Ticket" that had nothing to say about slavery. It worked, in a manner of speaking. The Whig oligarchy was overthrown, and the Democrats in the legislature paid their dues by throwing their support to Charles Sumner, the fiery antislavery radical, who thereby became the junior senator from Massachusetts. That was as far as the fusion Democrats were willing to go, however. They passed a raft of legislation for the relief of debtors and workers, but they refused to support personal liberty laws and other antislavery measures. Predictably, the Free Soil–Democratic coalition in Massachusetts fell apart.[23]

Rather than embrace the new antislavery Republican Party, Butler went back to the Democrats. He campaigned for James Buchanan in 1856, endorsed the proslavery Lecompton Constitution for Kansas, supported the *Dred Scott* decision, and appealed to white workers with racial demagoguery. At his party's tumultuous 1860 presidential nominating convention in Charleston, South Carolina, Butler voted more than fifty times for Jefferson Davis and ended up supporting John Breckinridge, the proslavery Democrat. Butler even apologized for having once flirted with the Free Soil Party. The best that can be said of Butler's antislavery record is that it was unimpressive. Certainly there was little in it that foreshadowed the role Butler was soon to play in the history of slavery's destruction.[24]

Butler was outraged by a secession movement whose leaders included many of the same southerners he had recently worked with and supported. There is no treachery like the treachery of friends. By January of 1861, Butler was denouncing southern "traitors" and urging Massachusetts's antislavery Governor John Andrew to hasten military preparations for the coming war against southern rebellion. Butler had always attacked Republicans as the party of disunion, so he could claim a modicum of consistency in his sudden call to arms in defense of the Union. He swore his devotion to the Lincoln administration. But it was the attack on Fort Sumter that truly galvanized Butler. Ever since he was a young man he dreamt of a military career. Disappointed that that wasn't an option, he nevertheless became active in the local militia, and with the outbreak of war he pulled every political string he could grab to gain command of the Massachusetts militia. Governor Andrew obliged, and General Benjamin Butler was soon on his way to Washington to relieve the endangered capital.

Upon reaching his destination, Butler was given command of the new "Department of Annapolis" and sent to Maryland with vague instructions to secure the state against secessionist conspiracies. There he issued his bombastic decrees vowing to suppress any evidence of insurrection. Anxious for glory, Butler—against what he knew to be the wishes of the army's general-in-chief, Winfield Scott—decided to occupy the city of Baltimore and sweep out its nest of secessionists. By the time he got to the city the rioters had dispersed, but Butler declared victory and was hailed in the northern press as a general who got things done. Scott disliked political generals like Butler to begin with, and he was particularly infuriated by Butler's penchant for dramatic, unauthorized moves. Scott wanted to fire Butler but he was too popular for that. Instead, the unruly politico was kicked upstairs, promoted to major general and transferred to Fortress Monroe in the harbor we know as Hampton Roads, Virginia. Butler considered the transfer a "censure" and later recalled that he did not want to accept the commission, but Lincoln persuaded him to.[25] It turned out to be one of the most consequential military assignments of the war.

THE AREA AROUND FORTRESS MONROE was steeped in the history of American slavery. In 1619 a Dutch trading ship sailed through the channel separating Chesapeake Bay and Hampton Roads, then continued across the harbor and upriver to Jamestown, where the captain sold twenty slaves to the English settlers—the first of the half-million slaves that would be sold over the next two centuries in the colonies that eventually became the United States. By a fateful coincidence of American history, slavery began in 1619 at the same place it began to end in 1861.[26] In May of that year, in the same channel separating Chesapeake Bay from Hampton Roads, three slaves fled from their owner to the Union troops stationed at Fortress Monroe at the entrance to the harbor. They were the first of many slaves who over the next four years would help bring slavery down by running to Union lines and securing their freedom. Since the nation was founded, the laws of the United States, indeed the Constitution itself, mandated the return of fugitive slaves. But what did the Constitution mandate in a state that seceded from the Union? At Fortress Monroe, Benjamin Butler would answer that question.

Hampton village sat at the southern tip of the peninsula bounded by the York and James Rivers. It was linked by Hampton Bridge to Old Point Comfort, where Fortress Monroe stood guard over a strategically vital entrance to the harbor. By 1860 Hampton itself no longer thrived, but the impressive natural harbor sustained the economically and militarily important towns of Newport News, Norfolk, and Portsmouth. Seventy-five miles up the James River—which empties into Hampton Roads—stood the city of Richmond, the venerable old capital of the Commonwealth of Virginia, which in the spring of 1861 became the new capital of the recently established Confederate States of America.

Whoever occupied Fortress Monroe dominated one of the lifelines of the Confederacy. "The Fort occupies a commanding position," one Union private wrote in late April. "It controls the commerce of Norfolk, Richmond, Washington, and Baltimore. It is the key to Virginia and the border States." At the start of the war, northern forces had scrambled to ensure that the Union maintained control of the fortress along with the harbor and the town of Hampton. The South desperately wanted them back. But unlike Fort Sumter, farther south at the entrance to Charleston Harbor, southern forces were in no position to grab Fortress Monroe from the Yankees. By May there were twelve thousand Union troops stationed at the fortress, and the Confederate officer in charge of the peninsula, Colonel Benjamin Ewell, realized that he was powerless to control much less protect the nearby village of Hampton. "It is difficult to manage Hampton," Ewell confessed to his superiors in Richmond.[28] He would build the fortifications to protect the peninsula from Yankee invasion, but he could not save the town itself. The white citizens of Hampton had to either flee with their furniture and slaves or make their own peace with the Union army. Most whites fled.

Their slaves, however, balked. By 1860 there were nearly twenty-five hundred slaves in Elizabeth City County, and their distinctive history made them especially attentive to the prospect of freedom now dangling before them by a war over slavery. The tobacco economy had long since declined in the depleted sandy soil at the lower end of the peninsula. There were few large plantations. Instead, the slaves worked at a variety of occupations. Nearly one thousand of them were hired out by their owners to work as fishermen, oystermen, craftsmen, or laborers on the small farms that supplied the more prosperous towns around Hampton Roads. Compared to the relatively restricted experience of slaves living on isolated rice, sugar, and cotton plantations across much of the South, the slaves in and around Hampton lived more varied lives, they were freer to move about, they were subjected to fewer constraints by local whites, and they had close ties to Elizabeth City County's two hundred free blacks. The free blacks were in turn unusually literate, prosperous, and resourceful. More than most African Americans in the South, the slaves of Hampton were in a position to grasp at the possibility of freedom very early in the war.[29]

On Thursday evening, May 23, 1861, three slaves—Shepard Mallory, Frank Baker, and James Townsend—decided to take their chances by running for their freedom to the Union forces stationed at Fortress Monroe. Their owner, Charles Mallory—a Hampton lawyer from a distinguished Virginia family and now a Confederate colonel—had decided to take the three slaves to North Carolina "for the purpose of aiding the secession forces there." Two of the slaves had wives living in Hampton, one of them a free black woman, and between them they had several children in the area. Unwilling to leave their families behind, and fearful of being put to service for the Confederate army, the slaves commandeered a small boat and rowed from Sewall's Point to the fortress, where they asked for asylum.

General Butler arrived at Fortress Monroe the day before the fugitive slaves did. On Friday, the day after their arrival, Major John Cary of the Virginia Artillery showed up and demanded the return of Colonel Mallory's three runaways. By then Butler had investigated the matter and interviewed the three men. He had learned that the Confederates were employing blacks in the area to construct their batteries at Sewall's Point, "which it would be nearly or quite impossible to construct without their labor." He could hardly send the slaves back to assist the rebel cause. And besides, Butler concluded, he could use these able-bodied men in his own quartermaster department. So instead of sending the slaves back to their owner, Butler issued receipts for them that Colonel Mallory could redeem once the hostilities between the North and South had ended.

Butler was acting on impulse—the war had just begun and there was no formal antislavery policy in place. But if he was feeling his way, he was not flailing about blindly. On the contrary, Butler was guided by the familiar Republican warning that any state seceding from the Union would forfeit the protection slavery was afforded under the Constitution. Major Cary claimed that Butler was obliged by the Fugitive Slave Act of 1850 to return the slaves to their owners. That may or may not have been true in Maryland, where only weeks before Butler had offered to put down any insurrections—by secessionists as well as by slaves. But Maryland had not seceded, and it was still under the protection of the U.S. government. Virginia was different. On May 24, the day after the slaves escaped, Virginia voters ratified the ordinance of secession. As far as Butler was concerned, they had thereby forfeited federal protection of slavery. So when Cary insisted that the general was under a constitutional obligation to return the slaves to their rightful owner, Butler refused on the ground that "the fugitive-slave act did not affect a foreign country which," as Butler pointed out to Cary, "Virginia claimed to be." If, on the other hand, Colonel Mallory presented himself at Fortress Monroe and swore an oath of allegiance to the Union, Butler would "deliver the men up to him and endeavor to hire their services of him." Butler knew that Mallory would do no such thing.[30] The slaves, therefore, would remain with the Union army, Butler told Cary, their fate to be determined by policymakers in Washington.

In refusing to return the runaway slaves, Butler was following familiar precedents under the laws of war. Even if slaves were legally "property" according to the state laws of Virginia, one of Butler's soldiers explained, it was nonetheless true that under the law of nations "all the property of the enemy may be seized."[31] As Butler explained it, "[P]roperty of whatever nature, used or capable of being used for warlike purposes, and especially when being so used, may be captured and held either on sea or on shore as property contraband of war." But were slaves property, or were they persons? Butler doubted "whether there may be a property in human beings," but it hardly mattered because under the laws of war it was also legitimate to deprive enemies of their slaves' labor.[32] If the slaves were property, they could be confiscated. If they were "persons held in service," as most Republicans believed, their services could be appropriated. Either way, Butler felt justified in denying Mallory's request for the return of his slaves.

Major Cary reported the results of his interview with Butler to his superior officer, Colonel J. B. Magruder, on the evening of May 24. Butler, Cary wrote, "indicated his determination to take possession of anything which he might deem necessary for his use," and for that reason he has "refused to give up" Colonel Mallory's three slaves.[33] The next day, May 25, Butler sent a report of the incident to Washington asking for approval of his decision to retain the fugitives. He fully understood that this was "but an individual instance in a course of policy which may be required with regard to this species of property." Butler was asking for more than specific approval of an individual decision; he was also urging the government to issue a broader policy statement regarding slaves coming into Union lines from rebel owners. Should the Confederates "be allowed the use of this property against the United States," Butler asked, "and we not allowed its use in aid of the United States?"

On May 27, Butler wrote a second letter to General Winfield Scott, who commanded all the Union forces from Washington. This morning, Butler explained, Confederate batteries at Sewall's Point fired on some of Butler's troops. Those were the batteries recently constructed by slaves, a dozen of whom had by then escaped to Fortress Monroe. The number of runaway slaves was rapidly increasing, Butler noted, and he was happy to put the able-bodied men to work. But in the past few days a number of women and children had arrived, and this raised a serious question that had to be addressed. Butler could plausibly retain adult men on the grounds of military necessity: it deprived the Confederates of labor used to advance their own military needs while it enhanced the labor power of the Union army. Butler could likewise use the services of able-bodied women, who could earn their keep by sewing, cooking, and washing clothes for his men. But what about the children? Butler asked. "As a political question and a question of humanity can I receive the services of a father and mother and not take the children?" The humanitarian question was easy to answer: he could not break up slave families by returning children to their masters. But this was also a political question, Butler shrewdly pointed out, and the answer to that would have to come from Washington.[34]

Without waiting for a reply, Butler ordered one of his officers to see to it that "all able-bodied negroes within your lines" should be "taken" and put to work "in the trenches and on the works." Rations were to be provided for the workers as well as their families. He also ordered his officer to keep an accurate record of the slaves, the work they performed, the rations they received, as well as the names of their owners. The records were "for future use." At that point nobody knew what that future use might be.[35]

News of the events at Fortress Monroe spread quickly. On May 28, only one day after Butler sent his second request to Washington, reporters were publishing their own dispatches from Fortress Monroe telling of slaves running unsolicited to Union lines. On May 29, Lincoln's postmaster general, Montgomery Blair, wrote Butler a letter endorsing the general's decision not to return runaway slaves to their owners. But Blair was concerned that Butler's order reached too far. Only able-bodied men who had been used on Confederate fortifications should be held by Union forces, Blair argued. He was inclined to doubt the stories the slaves told, about the threat of being moved farther South. Blair was a fierce unionist who was eager to punish the secessionists, but he was also among the least inclined of Lincoln's cabinet members to push a rapid emancipation. By his own account, other officials in Washington—including General Scott—were a good deal more enthusiastic. President Lincoln, Blair reported, had never seen Scott so excited as he was by Butler's decision. "He called it Butler's fugitive slave law."[36]

Lincoln can hardly have been surprised by this turn of events. In an 1859 speech in Cincinnati, he had looked across the Ohio River to the slave state of Kentucky and warned southerners that if they seceded from the Union the federal government would no longer capture escaping slaves. What will you do then? Lincoln had asked. Do you really believe you would be better off "by leaving us here under no obligation whatever to return those specimens of your moveable property that come hither?"[37] In his inaugural address Lincoln had warned that if the slave states seceded from the Union, "fugitive slaves, now only partially surrendered, would not be surrendered at all."[38] A few months later, President Lincoln was passing along jokes about "Butler's fugitive slave law" and scheduling cabinet meetings to discuss the matter. The cabinet met on May 30, less than a week after the first slaves had taken their boat from Sewall's Point to Fortress Monroe. There are no transcripts or diary accounts of what went on at the meeting, but when it was over Simon Cameron, the secretary of war, telegraphed Butler to inform him that his contraband policy "is approved."

The May 30 instructions were the first of two major statements guiding administration policy toward slavery in the seceded states for the next year.[39] Union troops were not permitted to interfere with the ordinary operations of slavery in the rebellious states, Cameron wrote. But if a state declared itself in rebellion against the laws of the United States, and if any slaves in those states "come within your lines," Butler was to "refrain from surrendering" such slaves to their "alleged masters." In the meantime, Butler was to employ able-bodied slaves as he saw fit, keeping careful records and charging the expenses for the care of their families against the wages of the refugees. Postmaster General Blair had not succeeded in restricting the contraband policy only to able-bodied men. Instead, the cabinet endorsed Butler's broader decision to allow "able-bodied" men *and* women to work for wages for the Union army and to remain, along with their children, at the fortress.[40] It was a swift, unambiguous endorsement of Butler's decision.

The War Department's May 30 instructions introduced a distinction that would guide federal emancipation policy until Lincoln issued the Emancipation Proclamation sixteen months later. Slaves from the seceded states who entered Union lines voluntarily would not be returned to their owners, but Union soldiers were not to *entice* slaves away from peacefully functioning farms and plantations. This was understood almost immediately. "The slaves are running away from their masters in troops," the *New York Times* reported on May 31. "The soldiers have orders not to interfere with the rights of persons or property, and when the negroes run away they do it without solicitation from any of our forces."[41] Within months Union authorities would decide that slaves who escaped "without solicitation" would be emancipated, and what counted as "voluntary" arrival would expand dramatically, but the formal ban on enticement remained in place until January 1, 1863.

The administration's policy was soon expanded to the navy. In mid-July, Union naval squadrons on the Virginia coast picked up "six Negroes who had deserted from the shore during the night." The runaways claimed that their masters onshore, secessionists all, were preparing to put their slaves "in the front of the Battle," that is, to support the Confederate war. The slaves wanted no part of it and began scrambling to escape. They commandeered a small craft and rowed it out to a lighthouse, where they set the boat adrift and waited. Hearing their story, Commander O. S. Glisson decided not to return the runaways to their owners. Instead, like Butler, he wrote his superiors and asked for instructions. Flag Officer Silas Stringham endorsed Glisson's decision to retain the fugitives. "If negroes are to be used in this contest," he wrote, "I have no hesitation in saying, they should be used to preserve the Government not to destroy it." Stringham forwarded his endorsement, along with Glisson's note, to Lincoln's secretary of the navy, Gideon Welles, who in turn gave both officers his own endorsement. Under the circumstances, Welles wrote in late July, "no other course than that pursued by Commander Glisson could be adopted without violating every principle of humanity." To return the fugitives to their owners, Welles added, "would be impolitic as well as cruel."[42] Thus by mid-July of 1861 the administration's position was clear. Army and navy officers were under no obligation to return slaves escaping from any state that had seceded from the Union.

The decision to retain runaways did not mean that the slaves had been emancipated. The Welles and Cameron endorsements were enthusiastic, but they were also limited. "The question of their final disposition," Cameron wrote, "will be reserved for further determination."[43] Lincoln had already called a special session of Congress to convene on July 4, at which time the Republican majority would make that determination. For the next two months the final status of the fugitives would remain uncertain. Yet the direction of Union policy was already clear. Butler had justified his refusal to return escaping slaves as a matter of both policy and "humanity." Welles said that to return escaping slaves to their owners would be both "impolitic" and "cruel." This was the language Republicans would use throughout the war: emancipation, they said, was a matter of both justice and humanity. Butler's own language also foreshadowed the distinction Republicans would maintain between the status of slaves as "persons" and the confiscation of rebel property. The general was nothing if not respectful of property rights. "The rights of private property and of peaceable citizens must be respected," he wrote on May 26. Even when "the exigencies of service require that private property be taken for public use," Butler explained, "it must be done by proper officers, giving suitable vouchers therefore."[44] But did these rules apply to slaves? To be a slave was to be "property" under the laws of the slave states, but opponents of slavery objected to the very idea of "property in man" and believed that the Constitution recognized slaves only as "persons." The distinction put the opponents of slavery in something of a linguistic bind. Being property is what made slaves *slaves*. Even those who believed that "property in man" was both immoral and unconstitutional could not help speaking of slaves as "property" because, legally, that's what slaves were under the laws of the southern states. But this hardly meant that slavery's opponents thought of blacks as less than human. The dilemma was perfectly captured in the phrase *contraband of war*.

Butler did not refer to slaves as "contraband of war" in his earliest letters to Washington explaining his decision, but he probably used the phrase when he spoke to reporters on the scene because they began using it in their stories. It was instantly popular. Yet policymakers in Washington carefully avoided the term *contraband*. Over the entire course of the Civil War, none of the important laws, resolutions, or proclamations related to slavery used the term *contrabands*, possibly because the basic premise of antislavery politics was that slaves were *not* property, either morally or constitutionally. Yet *contrabands* quickly became the popular term of choice among civilians and within the military. This did not necessarily mean that those who referred to fugitive slaves as contraband thought of them as property. The first time Butler used the phrase *contraband of war* was in a July 30 letter to his superiors in Washington asking for clarification of the status of the runaways he had been authorized to hold. Yet in the very same paragraph in which he first used the phrase, Butler explicitly rejected the idea that they were property. No doubt the contrabands had previously been held as "property" under the laws of the slave states, Butler explained, but "we do not need and will not hold such property, and will assume no such ownership: has not, therefore, all proprietary relation ceased? Have they not become, thereupon, men, women, and children?" In Butler's mind, the moment the slaves became "contrabands" was the moment they *ceased* to be "property."[45]

OFFICIALS IN WASHINGTON WERE AWARE that the implications of the fugitive slave policy were broader than its immediate consequences, that there was more at stake than the fate of the runaways at Fortress Monroe. The same day that Secretary of War Cameron sent word that the administration had endorsed Butler's decision, he and Lincoln attended a military review at which Cameron gave a speech. "One remark made by Gen. Cameron had peculiar significance," the *New York Times* reported. "He said that the war would not close until the causes which produced the contest had been entirely removed."[46] He was talking about slavery, and the contraband policy was the first step in its removal.

A tacit alliance between escaping slaves and the Union army was being created with the approval of officials in Washington. Butler clearly took some delight in the situation and was happy to rely on runaway slaves to drive the opening wedge into Union policy. A different Union general, one less willing to attack the social basis of the southern rebellion, would have returned Colonel Mallory's slaves without hesitation. A different administration, one less hostile to slavery, might have overruled Butler and ordered him to return the runaways. In the states that seceded from the Union, slavery was already losing the protection it once had under the Constitution.

The policy did not necessarily apply to Delaware, Maryland, Kentucky, and Missouri—the four slave states that remained within the Union. There the federal government was still obliged by the Constitution to recognize slavery's legality. As Butler himself pointed out, once Virginia had claimed to be "a foreign country," it could no longer demand the return of fugitive slaves under the U.S. Constitution, whereas "in Maryland, a loyal state," Butler explained, "fugitives from service had been returned."[47] At the same time, the union commander in the Department of the West, General William S. Harney, declared that the Union army would no more contemplate the overthrow of slavery in another loyal slave state, Missouri, than it would imagine "the overthrow of any other kind of property."[48] For the moment, slavery in the Border States was still being protected by the federal government, although this would soon change.

Nor did all the officers in the Union army follow Butler's lead in the rebellious states. The administration had endorsed Butler's decision, but not until Congress spoke up in August would Union officials begin instructing their officers in the seceded states to implement the same policy. As Butler and the Lincoln administration were formulating his fugitive slave policy in eastern Virginia, George McClellan was promising the residents of western Virginia that he would not interfere with the "property" of local citizens, including their slaves, and vowed as well to "crush any attempt at insurrection" among the slaves. Strictly speaking, Butler and McClellan were not taking different positions—everyone was still promising not to "interfere" with the peaceful operation of slavery even in the seceded states. Yet William Howard Russell detected a significant difference. "The first step taken by McClellan in western Virginia was atrocious—he talked of slaves in a public document as property. Butler, at Monroe, had dealt with them in a very different spirit and had used them for State purposes under the name of contraband."[49] Like Butler, Russell understood that treating fugitive slaves as "contraband" was very different from treating them as "property."

Northerners had been watching to see what the slaves would do, and the slaves had been watching as well. A few days after the contraband policy was announced, a New Yorker visiting Fortress Monroe struck up a conversation with several of those who had recently escaped. The slaves had clearly been paying attention to national politics, at least since the elections of the previous November. One of them had heard that "the Northern gen'lmen were favorable to the colored population," and so "I thought I'd come over here." Another explained that his friends had "been expecting the Northern gentlemen down here ever since Massa Lincoln was elected."[50] When the "northern gentlemen" arrived, the slaves around Hampton Roads did exactly what antislavery northerners predicted they would do: they ran to Union lines to claim their freedom. As the *New York Times* declared, Butler's decision "is but the fulfillment of the prophecies of loss which would be entailed upon the Southern states, and especially Virginia, if secession was carried to a bloody issue."[51]

But prophecies are notoriously vague. Butler and Lincoln were not acting out their parts in a script that had already been written. The slaves of Hampton village guessed—hoped, really—that they would be protected if they ran to Union lines, and it was a reasonable hope. They were certainly not going to run to Confederate lines. And given their constitutional premises and their antislavery biases, it's hardly surprising that the Union general and the Republican president made the decisions they made. They were making those decisions as they went along, however, as the arrival of the runaway slaves demanded, and none of them knew what would happen next.

4

AUGUST 8, 1861:
EMANCIPATION BEGINS

THE "THREE PIONEER NEGROES" who had run to Fortress Monroe in search of freedom left behind an African American community anxious to learn of how they had been received by the Union army. "[I]f they were not sent back," those at home "would understand that they were among friends, and more would come the next day." Two days after the first contrabands had been welcomed, eight more slaves showed up at the fortress asking to speak to General Butler. The next day forty-seven more "came in one squad," including half a dozen families, followed later on by "a dozen good field hands." They kept coming, now in groups of twenty, thirty, or more. Word was spreading so rapidly among the slaves of Hampton that Union soldiers could only marvel at "the mysterious spiritual telegraph which runs through the slave population."[1]

By the end of July in 1861, some nine hundred slaves had come within Benjamin Butler's lines in and around Fortress Monroe. One-third of them were adult men. There were 175 women and thirty seniors. The rest were children and teenagers. Most of them lived across the harbor in the village of Hampton. They had escaped, according to Butler, "from marauding parties of rebels, who had been gathering up able-bodied blacks to aid them in constructing their batteries." Butler in turn put the men to work "throwing up intrenchments," working "zealously . . . under the gleam of the mid-day sun." The women also worked, "earning substantially their own subsistence," by taking in washing, marketing, and mending the clothing for Butler's own soldiers. The refugees made their homes in Hampton, and all seemed to be going well until late July, when most of Butler's troops were called away to defend Washington after the Union defeat at Bull Run. Without those troops Butler could no longer guarantee the safety of the blacks in Hampton. Confederate soldiers made it clear that they would shoot to kill any of the men who had given their services to the Union army; recaptured women would be sent back into a form of slavery "worse than Egyptian bondage."[2]

Butler explained all of this on July 30 in another one of his remarkable and, one suspects, faux naive letters to Secretary of War Simon Cameron. What, Butler asked, should he do with these people? More to the point, what was their "state and condition"? He was not a man to mince words. "Are these men, women, and children slaves?" Butler asked pointedly. "Are they free?" Are they persons, he wondered, "or are they property?" If they were property, they were abandoned property and he had, in effect, salvaged them. "But we, their salvors, do not need and will not hold such property." And if they are no longer property, have they not become "free, manumitted, sent forth from the hand that held them?" What difference does it make, Butler wondered, if these people fled from or were abandoned by their owners? More to the point, what difference did it make whether or not an escaped slave "had labored upon the rebel intrenchments?" A fugitive slave was still a fugitive slave. If they come into Union lines, no matter how and no matter what they had been doing, shouldn't they be emancipated?[3]

This wasn't a letter; it was a pamphlet. In the guise of a request to his superiors for instructions, Butler had written a defense of emancipation on the ground that the Union did not recognize slaves as "property" under the Constitution. Butler had to know that at the moment he wrote his request for instructions Congress was embroiled in a debate over a proposed confiscation bill that might, if passed, endorse the emancipation of slaves who had been used by their owners to support the rebellion. Butler was raising the same fundamental questions that Republicans in Congress were grappling with. Were fugitives to be recognized as persons, as the Constitution did and as all those opposed to slavery believed they should be, or as property, the way the laws of the slave states defined them? And if they were persons, could anyone in good conscience send them back into slavery? Before anyone in Washington could answer Butler's questions, Congress would have to clarify its policy.

That clarification would come after a protracted debate in the Senate and the House of Representatives recapitulating many of the themes of the secession-winter dispute over the fate of slavery and the purpose of the war. The divisions among the lawmakers were sharp and clear. There were radical and moderate factions within the Republican Party, but they were nearly uniform in their hatred of secession, their unshakable conviction that slavery was the cause of the war, and their willingness to undermine slavery to save the Union. Conservatives fell into two distinct groups—proslavery representatives mostly from the Border States, and northern Democrats—but they, too, shared certain premises. They were repelled by the war, but not because they were the party of peace. Rather, conservatives were held together by the conviction that the war had been caused by antislavery fanaticism rather than slavery itself. They were determined to leave slavery alone. Conservative opposition intensified as Republicans edged closer to "interfering" with slavery within the Confederacy. In the first congressional debates over confiscation, the sharpest lines were drawn between the antislavery Republicans and the proslavery conservatives.

Proslavery senators and representatives were a surprisingly vocal and persistent minority in Congress. Four slave states had remained in the Union, and several members representing loyal elements from other slave states—including Virginia and Tennessee—had also been seated. Southern representatives, in alliance with most northern Democrats, took a leading role in opposing every Republican effort to emancipate slaves. If conservatives could not muster the votes, they could certainly take the floor, argue their case, and repeatedly introduce resolutions and amendments condemning all Republican moves to link the struggle for the Union with the struggle against slavery. Despite their minority standing, conservatives tried desperately to thwart the Republicans' antislavery agenda and, by their mere presence, provoked a sustained debate over emancipation.

The strategy backfired. By their aggressive defense of slavery and their belligerent attacks on Lincoln and the Republicans, conservatives—in a repeat performance of the 1850s—forced moderates to acknowledge the crucial antislavery premises they shared with their more radical colleagues. Radicals, for example, openly embraced the prospect of an assault on slavery, but they insisted that the destruction of slavery was the effect rather than the goal of the war. Nevertheless, radicals warned, the longer the South persisted in making war on the Union, the more thorough emancipation would be. They predicted that slavery would collapse of its own accord because wherever the Union army went, slaves would run to their freedom. And once that began to happen, the northern people would scarcely tolerate turning their soldiers into slave-catchers for the traitors who made war on the Constitution. If emancipation was not the purpose of the war, radicals explained, it would surely to be the consequence.

It did not take much pressure to get moderate Republicans to say the same things. Their chief difference with the radicals lay in the tenor of their remarks rather than the substance of their positions. When pressed by conservatives, Republican moderates refused to repudiate emancipation as a likely consequence of a protracted war. Forced to choose between the destruction of the Union and the destruction of slavery, moderates argued, they would opt without question for slavery's destruction. Where radicals embraced the prospect of emancipation with enthusiasm, moderates were fully prepared to accept it—and even those who accepted it with reluctance often declared that emancipation was nonetheless a good thing. All Republicans, radical and moderate alike, argued that the official "purpose" of the war was the restoration of the Union, but all agreed that slavery had caused the war and all were prepared to free slaves as a means of ending it.

In several congressional votes on slavery taken during the summer of 1861, moderates and radicals voted the same way. Moderates were concerned about maintaining constitutional principles but were nevertheless prepared to accept emancipation as necessary to suppress the Confederacy. And yet it was the radicals who offered some of the most powerful arguments for the constitutional legitimacy of emancipation. As a result, Republicans voted almost unanimously in favor of the first federal law in American history designed to emancipate slaves in states where slavery was legal. By contrast, Democrats and Border State congressmen argued that federal emancipation in any form was illegal. They always voted against it.

NOT THE DUTY OF THE ARMY

As soon as the war began, Lincoln called the Thirty-Seventh Congress into special session, five months ahead of schedule, to convene on July 4, 1861. Only war measures were to be considered; all other business would be taken up in the normal session that would meet later, from December through July of 1862. One crucial consequence of Congress's decision to restrict the special session exclusively to war matters was that "military emancipation" was initiated in the summer of 1861, whereas the peacetime policy of gradual state abolition through containment was implemented later in the regular session of Congress. The most important business at hand in July of 1861 was the retrospective sanctioning of the president's unilateral decision, in the wake of the attack on Fort Sumter, to raise an army to suppress the southern rebellion. There was no doubt that Congress would authorize the expenditures and the military buildup necessary to sustain the war. Yet throughout the special session the fate of slavery also commanded the sustained attention of Congress, an indication that from the very beginning Republicans saw slavery as inseparable from the war.

The first issue to come up, only a few days after Congress convened, revealed a sharp Republican reaction against military commanders who were turning fugitive slaves away from Union lines. In the two months since Butler's fugitive slave policy had been approved, the Union army revealed deep internal divisions about how to handle slaves who ran to Union lines. Some soldiers refused to turn slaves away or send them back; others insisted on doing so. The outbreak of war had led to a reversal of the policy at Fort Pickens, where escaping slaves had been returned to their owners during the secession crisis. After the war began, however, Colonel Harvey Brown bluntly informed his superiors in Washington that he would "not send the negroes back as I shall never be voluntarily instrumental in returning a poor wretch to slavery." Rank-and-file soldiers sometimes evaded higher-ups who ordered the return of runaway slaves. A number of Ohio troops stationed at Camp Upton, Virginia, were accused of "practicing a little of the abolition system in protecting the runaway" whose owner came looking for him. Superiors ordered the commanding officer to return runaways to their rightful owners, but, strangely, nobody could find fugitives anywhere in the camp. Colonel Thomas Davies, in Alexandria, was sharply rebuked when he decided not to send slaves back to their owners. Davies "has been instructed," Colonel D. S. Miles explained, "to respect private property and to send back to the farm the negroes his troops brought away." If emancipation was to proceed along the lines Republicans had assumed, such internecine squabbles within the Union army would have to be resolved in favor of the soldiers who refused to return runaway slaves to their owners.[4]

From the Republicans' perspective the most disturbing news was the proclamation issued by General George McClellan, on May 26, "To the Union Men of Western Virginia." "Your homes, your families, & your property are safe under our protection," McClellan declared. He urged Virginians to disregard the warning of secessionist traitors that the Union army intended to interfere with "your slaves." The Union will do no such thing. "[N]ot only will we abstain from all such interference," McClellan wrote, "but we will on the contrary with an iron hand, crush any attempt at insurrection on their part."[5] Only a few days before McClellan issued his proclamation, Virginia's voters ratified the decision to leave the Union. To Republicans this meant that Virginia had forfeited any right to claim protection for slavery under the Constitution. But McClellan was a Democrat, and he would never reconcile himself to the Republican view that a war to restore the Union was inescapably a war over slavery's fate as well.

On July 8, a few days after Congress opened its special session, Lincoln told Illinois Senator Orville Browning that "the government neither should, nor would send back to bondage such as came to our armies." The very next day Illinois Congressman Owen Lovejoy introduced a resolution declaring that "it is no part of the duty of the sol-

diers of the United States to capture and return fugitive slaves."
Lovejoy wanted to put Congress on record in opposition to the
orders and proclamations of men like McClellan. He offered a resolution because a statute seemed unnecessary; in his mind, the U.S.
military had no legal authority to capture and return slaves. Lovejoy's resolution thereby raised, at the very outset of the war, the
explosive question of who was responsible for enforcing the fugitive
slave clause of the Constitution. Most Republicans believed that
states alone should be responsible. The Fugitive Slave Act of 1850,
which nearly all Republicans hated, created a special cadre of U.S.
commissioners to enforce the clause. As the Lovejoy resolution
affirmed, however, there was nothing in either the Constitution or
the 1850 statute authorizing American soldiers to capture or return
fugitive slaves. Border State congressmen scrambled to table the resolution, but after a brief flurry of parliamentary maneuvering, Lovejoy's wording was endorsed by a lopsided vote of 93 to 55. Though
the resolution never came up in the Senate, the overwhelming vote
in the House suggests that the outcome would have been the same.
Nearly all the Republicans supported it, while just about every
Democrat and Border State congressman voted against it.[6]

THE OBJECT OF THE WAR

Two days after the House endorsed the Lovejoy resolution, Clement
Vallandingham, the antiwar Democrat from Ohio, made the first of
many attempts to stop the emancipation juggernaut just as it was get-
ting started. Mimicking Lovejoy's language, Vallandingham pro-
posed an amendment to a military appropriations bill declaring that
U.S. military forces had no business "abolishing or interfering with
African slavery in any of the States." A week later, Senator Lazarus W.
Powell of Kentucky introduced a similar resolution, likewise declar-

ing that "no part of the Army or Navy of the United States shall be employed . . . in abolishing or interfering with slavery in any of the states."[7] Powell and Vallandingham were responding to widespread talk among Republican members of Congress suggesting that emancipation would be one of the inescapable consequences of a prolonged war. In offering their amendments, conservatives provoked an extensive congressional debate over emancipation weeks before any emancipation bill came up for discussion. At issue in the debate was nothing less than the purpose of the war.

The debate over the war's "object" or "purpose" had been simmering in the northern press for some months before Congress convened in July. Within weeks of the firing on Fort Sumter, editorials questioning "The Object of the War" began appearing in Democratic newspapers across the North. They were already protesting against Republican efforts to bind the "object" of the war—the restoration of the Union—to the destruction of slavery. On May 7, for example, Lincoln told his private secretary that "the central idea" of the war was "whether in a free government the minority have the right to break up that government whenever they choose." Nevertheless, Lincoln added, there was "one consideration" that may be used "in stay of such final judgment," and that consideration was slavery, the "vast and far reaching disturbing element" that had caused the war to begin with.[8]

By July, when the debate reached the floor of Congress, the administration's endorsement of Butler's contraband policy had been widely publicized. Democrats declared that Lincoln was behaving like a tyrant, that Republicans were prosecuting the war by unconstitutional means, and that the clearest indication of this was their willingness to let the army and navy "interfere" with slavery in the seceded states. In the House, for example, Democratic Representative Henry Burnett of Kentucky denounced Lincoln as "a despot" and asked his fellow congressman the question of the hour: "What are the objects of the war? Are they to maintain the Constitution and the Union? No, sir; that Constitution has already been discarded, set aside, suspended in its operation, trodden under foot" by the Republican president. Representative William Holman, an Indiana Democrat, quickly took up Burnett's question. "*What is the object of the war?*" Certainly not the abolition of slavery. He would fight to the death to restore the Union, but he would never countenance federal interference in southern slavery. "I am for prosecuting this war for the purpose of vindicating the Federal authority and putting down rebellion," Representative John McClernand, an Illinois Democrat, insisted, "and not for the purpose of subjugating the seceding States and holding them as conquered provinces; nor for the purpose of abolishing slavery." The Vallandingham-Powell resolutions expressed the views of Democrats and Border State congressmen who wanted to prevent the Union army from "interfering" with slavery.[9]

Republicans, however, believed that U.S. soldiers were perfectly within their rights to "interfere" with slavery in the seceded states. It was true that the Constitution did not allow the federal government to prosecute the war for the explicit *purpose* of destroying slavery in those states, but to Republicans that did not mean the federal government could not attack slavery as a means of suppressing the rebellion. On the contrary, they uniformly declared that although the abolition of slavery was not the *purpose* of the war, they would readily destroy slavery to save the Union because slavery was the cause of the war. If, "in the course of events, it shall appear that either slavery or the Government must perish," Senator James Dixon of Connecticut declared, "then the voice of a united people will declare, let slavery perish and let the Government live forever." This was not the overheated rhetoric of fire-breathing radicals, Dixon added. Rather, it was "the stern determination to which thousands have come, who have been considered heretofore men of moderate views"—men like Dixon himself. He spoke in neutral terms of the destruction of slavery, expressing neither disdain nor enthusiasm for it. Instead, he simply claimed that emancipation was something that was bound to happen as an inescapable consequence of the war. "Let me not be misunderstood," Dixon insisted. "The object of the struggle we are engaged in, on the part of the loyal States, is not the abolition of slavery; but if it shall prove a long continued contest, that may be its inevitable consequence."[10]

Mindful of the fact that the Constitution protected slavery in the states where it existed, Republicans were always careful to separate the "object" or "purpose" of the war—which was the suppression of the rebellion and the restoration of the Union—from the effect of the war—which was likely to be the destruction of slavery. "[A]lthough the abolition of slavery is not an object of the war," the pugnacious antislavery Senator John P. Hale of New Hampshire declared, the rebels "may, in their madness and folly and treason, make the abolition of slavery one of the results of the war. This is what I understand to be precisely the position of the Administration upon the subject of this war." James K. Lane, the Republican senator from Kansas, agreed. Despite having survived the attempt by the "slave oligarchy" to force slavery on his Kansas constituents, he and they had been willing to abide by all the constitutional guarantees of slavery wherever it existed. But in their boundless arrogance slaveholders had provoked all-out war whose "logical conclusion" was emancipation. Lane predicted "that the institution of slavery will not survive, in any State of this Union, the march of the Union armies." Slavery had been "the curse of the country" for as long as he could remember. "There is no crime that the devotees of slavery will not commit in maintaining or extending it." If the war destroys slavery, "I thank god that [it] is so."[11]

Republicans insisted not only that the rebellion had been caused by slavery but that war was forcing loyal northerners to choose between the survival of slavery and the survival of the Union. The loyal citizens of the North are prepared to sacrifice millions of dollars and thousands of lives to uphold the Union, radical Senator Samuel C. Pomeroy argued. If slavery is abolished as one of "the incidental results of this war . . . , I can only say that it is a year of sacrifices to us all." If the rebel states "are called upon to sacrifice that species of property," Pomeroy concluded, "it is only in harmony with the sacrifices that the loyal States of the Union are called upon to make." Senator Browning, one of the most conservative Republicans, was even more blunt. "[I]f our brethren of the South force upon us the distinct issue . . . , whether the Government shall go down to maintain the institutions of slavery, or whether slavery shall be obliterated to sustain the Constitution and the Government . . . then I am for the Government and against slavery." As another Republican had put it, "[I]f we force the country to the issue of choosing between the continuance of slavery and the perpetuation of the Government, then slavery must fall."[12]

What distinguished the moderate from the radical Republicans on slavery's fate—if there was any distinction at all—was the tendency among moderates to shed crocodile tears over the fact that they were being "forced" to confront the issue. For a radical like Lane, if "the institution of slavery perish, we will thank God." Moderates were more fatalistic. Dixon believed he was speaking for northerners who had long tolerated and "even guaranteed" the rights of slaveholders. But the northern people do not "love slavery as they love the Union," Dixon warned. "If either must be sacrificed," Dixon concluded, "they will have no question as to which it shall be." Here again was a difference of tone rather than substance. Moderates often declared that although they regretted the "necessity" of emancipation, they nevertheless welcomed it. Browning, for example, spoke warmly of "sweeping the last vestige of barbarism from the face of the continent." He viewed himself and his fellow unionists as "the conservators of the eternal principles of justice and freedom for the whole human family. . . . We do not desire this issue; we do not want this necessity; but we have no power to prevent it."[13] As far as Republicans were concerned, the rebellion was making slavery's destruction inevitable.

It was a measure of how widespread talk of slavery's demise was that this intense debate took place before any confiscation bill had been reported out of the Senate or House Judiciary Committees. By the time the bill was finally introduced, many of the terms of the debate had already been established. Opponents of emancipation claimed that because slave property could not be legally or constitutionally distinguished from any other form of property, slaves could be "confiscated" only from those who were duly convicted of treason. By that reasoning, the federal government would never be able to emancipate slaves. In contrast, supporters of emancipation defined slaves as "persons" rather than "property" and therefore not subject to the same constitutional restrictions on permanent confiscation. Moreover, they rested their case on the ground of "military necessity," and under the laws of war emancipation was constitutionally legitimate.

The Powell and Vallandingham resolutions, designed to disarm Republican support for military emancipation, went down to overwhelming defeat. Republicans voted, as usual almost unanimously, against any public statement declaring that the army and navy had no business "abolishing" or "interfering" with slavery in the seceded states. When the Senate at last voted on Powell's version of the resolution on July 18, only nine senators supported it; thirty voted against it. Congress thereby declared that although the destruction of slavery was not the purpose of the war, it was fully prepared to let the army "interfere" with slavery in the states that had seceded from the Union.[14]

TRUMBULL'S AMENDMENT

On July 20, two days after the Senate rejected Powell's resolution, Illinois Senator Lyman Trumbull, acting as chair of the Senate Judiciary Committee, reported a confiscation bill to the floor. The bill was brief. It included three short sections that taken together, established the legal procedures for confiscating the property of traitors. Section 1 stipulated that if the president declared an area to be in rebellion, the military could seize the property of active rebels within that area. Once the property was seized, the courts took over. Section 2 required either district or circuit courts to determine the guilt or innocence of any rebels whose property had been seized. Finally, Section 3 prescribed that the property of anyone found guilty of treason would be condemned by the court and sold, the proceeds of the sales going to the federal Treasury to defray the cost of the war. Nothing in the bill was applicable to slaves.[15]

Immediately upon introducing it, however, Trumbull offered two amendments to the committee's bill. The first, prepared at the direction of the committee, specified the jurisdiction of U.S. district or circuit courts in cases arising "in admiralty" from the confiscation of property. This, too, had nothing to do with slavery. But Trumbull's second amendment was his own, and it had nothing to do with property confiscation. Even the language was different. The first three sections of the bill dealt exclusively with "property," but Trumbull's second amendment referred only to "persons," and the persons concerned were masters and slaves. It declared that any "person"—the master—"claiming to be entitled to the labor of any other person"—the slave—and who allowed the slave's labor to be used in support of the rebellion,

> shall forfeit all right to such service or labor, and the person whose labor or service is thus claimed shall be henceforth discharged therefrom; any law to the contrary notwithstanding.[16]

This was not confiscation; it was emancipation—immediate and uncompensated—of some but not all slaves. Masters who allowed slaves to be used in support of the rebellion "forfeited" their slaves, and the slaves were "henceforth discharged" from service to the master.

Trumbull's wording was not accidental. At least since the *Somerset* case in the 1770s, the opponents of slavery insisted on the legal distinction between slaves as "property" and slaves as "persons." All of antislavery constitutionalism rested on the proposition that the framers had deliberately chosen to refer to slaves as "persons" rather than property. Trumbull's own language was taken almost verbatim from the fugitive slave clause of the Constitution. Under the terms spelled out in Article IV, Section 2, "No Person held to Service or Labour in one State, under the Laws thereof, escaping into another, shall, in Consequence of any Law or Regulation therein, be discharged from such Service or Labour." Trumbull was being scrupulous, not ironic, when he referred to slaves not as "property" but as "persons held in service."

Trumbull's amendment thus reflected a universal Republican conviction—derived from radical antislavery lawyers and spelled out by Lincoln in his Cooper Union address more than a year earlier—that slaves were not recognized as property under the Constitution and therefore could not be treated as such by Congress or the Union army. Commenting on Lincoln's understanding of the law a month after it was passed, Treasury Secretary Salmon Chase noted that "the slaves are not recognized as the property of rebels [and] are not recognized as the property of rebels when employed in hostility to the Union."[17] If Chase's rendering is accurate, Lincoln had gone beyond his argument at Cooper Union. There Lincoln denied a constitutional right of property in slaves, but he had not denied that slaves were property under the laws of the slave states. Now he was arguing that slaves were not the property of rebels, even in the slave states, maybe even rebellious masters in loyal slave states. Rebellion stripped rebels of any claim to slave property whatsoever. This was military emancipation, justified under the laws of war.

The emancipation debate was not the only point at which the status of slaves as "persons" rather than "property" arose. The issue came up in the same special session of Congress in July of 1861 when Thaddeus Stevens, the radical Republican congressman from Pennsylvania, proposed an amendment to a revenue bill imposing taxes on various forms of property, including "slaves." The Stevens bill was yet another way of getting at slavery indirectly without actually abolishing it in the states, yet it alarmed Owen Lovejoy, the abolitionist congressman from Illinois. If Congress planned to *tax* slaves as property, Lovejoy asked, was it not also obliged to *protect* slaves as property? Stevens insisted that he was proposing a "capitation tax" that in no way implied that slaves were property. Ohio Congressman John A. Bingham agreed. Slaves were "taxable persons," he said, not property. Bingham also claimed that Stevens's amendment, by specifying land, houses, and slaves, implicitly recognized the distinction between persons and property. Lovejoy was not persuaded. "This is not a personal tax," he explained. "It is on the valuation of these items of property." To Lovejoy's way of thinking, Bingham's argument was specious. He was proposing a tax based on the "valuation" of the slaves, which meant that they were "to be taxed—not as persons—but according to their valuations; just as horses or any other species of property is taxed."[18] It was a minor debate, interesting primarily because Republicans on all sides went out of their way to deny that slaves could be treated legally as property.

Conservatives responded to Trumbull's amendment by disputing the Republican distinction between persons and property. Slaves, they insisted, were protected as a right of property in exactly the same way as other forms of property. When "Congress undertakes to confiscate slave property," Kentucky Congressman Henry Burnett insisted, "that species of property should be upon the very same bases as well as all other property confiscated by the General Government." Senator John Carlile of Virginia did not doubt the government's power to confiscate the property of convicted traitors, but it could not single out slave property for special treatment. "I know no distinction of property," Carlile insisted.[19] If Burnett and Carlile were right, if slaves were property on the same "footing" as every other "species of property," Trumbull's amendment could not possibly be constitutional.

But to slavery's opponents the dual character of slaves as "property" under state law but "persons" under the Constitution was crucial. Slave emancipation was contained within a "confiscation" bill because under state law slaves were property, but the bill itself treated slaves as "persons held in service" because that's how slaves were recognized in the Constitution. In one sense the title of the law is misleading: it "confiscated" property, but it "emancipated" slaves. The distinction is clear even within the statute itself. Confiscated property was to be sold to pay for the war effort, and eventually real estate could be restored to the heirs of a convicted traitor. But because slaves were persons rather than property, nobody dared propose that they be confiscated and then sold, much less returned to their owners. Rather, masters "forfeited" their claim to the labor of "persons held in service," and those persons would be "discharged" from any further obligation to their masters. They were emancipated. Nor did emancipation require judicial proceedings, because the legal basis for it was not the law of treason.[20] Instead, emancipation was justified under the laws of war, and Trumbull was adamant that this made military emancipation fully constitutional because the laws of war were embedded within the Constitution. Years of effort by diligent abolitionist lawyers were now paying off.

Trumbull submitted the committee's bill along with his two amendments to the full Senate on Saturday, July 20, but discussion of the legislation was postponed until the following Monday.[21] The next day, while Congress was in Sunday recess, the first significant battle of the war took place twenty-five miles away.

"WE SHALL PROCLAIM FREEDOM WHEREVER WE GO"

Everyone knew the battle was coming. "[T]he expected pageantry in Virginia," Ohio Democrat Samuel Cox later recalled, "aroused the wildest excitement" among his fellow congressmen.[22] On that sweltering July morning several members of the House and Senate—including prominent radicals Benjamin Wade and Zachariah Chandler—rode out to witness the events near a crossroads at Manassas Junction. Approaching from the northeast, Union troops, led by General Irvin McDowell, reached a shallow river known as Bull Run. The Confederates, under General Pierre Beauregard, had taken up positions along the southwest side of the river. Both generals had the same idea. Each planned to cross the river in a flanking maneuver aimed at turning the enemy's left. But McDowell took the offensive first, crossing Bull Run early in the morning at Sudley's Ford, farther north than Beauregard had expected. Initially it looked as though McDowell's surprise move would work, but Beauregard quickly shifted his troops north to the scene of the battle. In the afternoon the tide turned in favor of the Confederates, who had taken up strong defensive positions atop Henry House Hill. The southerners were also aided by timely reinforcements rushed to the scene by General Joseph E. Johnston. All afternoon a confused series of attacks and counterattacks left the green Union troops dazed, and by 4:30 they began drifting into retreat. During another surge by the emboldened Confederates, shouting their soon-to-be-famous "rebel yell," the Yankee soldiers panicked.[23]

The congressmen at the scene looked on in horror. To Republican Albert Riddle of Maine it seemed as if "the very devil of panic and cowardice" had suddenly seized every Union soldier and officer on the battlefield. "No officer tried to rally the soldiers, or to do anything,"

Riddle explained, "except to spring and run." The congressmen shouted at the retreating Yankees; some pulled out revolvers and threatened to shoot the "cowards," but to no avail. Nothing could stop the mad scramble back to Washington, where the first to arrive were fugitive slaves.[24]

In the wake of their exhilarating victory, southerners predicted a swift Union capitulation, but William Howard Russell, who witnessed the battle and described the rout in vivid terms, was not persuaded. This "prick in the great northern balloon," Russell predicted, "will rouse the people to a sense of the nature of the conflict on which they have entered."[25] Russell was right. If anything, the Union defeat stiffened northern opposition to slavery. Soldiers returning from Manassas told of the "thousands of slaves" being used by Confederates to sustain their troops in battle, including reports of a small number of black sharpshooters among the rebels.[26] At the same time, rumors circulated that Confederate troops had desecrated the bodies of fallen Union soldiers or had abused Yankee prisoners. "We *must* soon begin treating the enemy with the hempen penalties of treason," a prominent New Yorker wrote in his diary. But there were other penalties to be inflicted besides swinging traitors from a rope. More Yankees than ever were prepared to undermine the rebellion by undermining slavery. Northerners were no longer calling "only for vengeance and righteous retribution," Frederick Douglass declared, but for "the destruction of the cause of their great national disaster. A cry has gone forth for the abolition of slavery." This was not merely the wishful thinking of a radical abolitionist. Mainstream politicians were saying the same thing. "We may commence the war without meaning to interfere with slavery," a former Rhode Island congressman declared, "but let us have one or two battles, and get our blood excited, and we shall not only not restore any more slaves, but shall proclaim freedom wherever we go."[27]

The fury of the battle was transferred to the floor of Congress when it convened the next day, July 22, and began considering the confiscation bill. Nearly all the discussion centered on the emancipation amendment. An enraged Trumbull tied his proposal directly to the previous day's military disaster. Referring to reports of slaves used by Confederates on the battlefield, Trumbull demanded a direct up-or-down vote on his emancipation amendment. "[L]et us see who is willing to vote that the traitorous owner of a negro shall employ him to shoot down the Union men of the country," Trumbull declared, "and yet insist upon restoring him to the traitor that owns him." This was hyperbole: Confederates often brought their slaves to the battlefield, especially in the first months of the war, but the slaves themselves were hardly ever armed. For nearly four years slaves were excluded from the Confederate army, and only in the very last weeks of the war were a tiny handful finally accepted. Nevertheless, Trumbull dared the opponents of emancipation to come right out and declare "that negroes who are used to destroy the Union, and to shoot down the Union men by the consent of traitorous masters, ought not to be restored to them." In a pointed reference to the Senate's leading critic of emancipation, John Breckinridge, Trumbull all but equated opposition to emancipation with support for treason. "If the Senator from Kentucky is in favor of restoring them"—that is, returning slaves used in the rebellion to their "traitorous" owners—"let him vote against the amendment." Bull Run thus added an element of emotional urgency to the argument for emancipation. Southerners were using slaves to help their rebel troops shoot down Union soldiers. That's what happened yesterday, Republicans now argued. Are we going to let it happen again tomorrow? Are we going to "disgrace our cause and our country," Massachusetts Senator Henry Wilson asked, "by returning such men to their traitorous masters?"[28] The Union defeat made the argument for military necessity seem less hypothetical, more concrete.

But Bull Run did not really alter the terms of the debate, nor did it change many minds. A few holdouts shifted their votes. On Saturday, the day before the battle, conservative Republican Senator John Ten Eyck of New Jersey had voted in committee against Trumbull's amendment. On Monday, the day after the battle, he announced that he would vote for it. He had not believed that the rebels would actually do it, but having seen slaves used "to shed the blood of the Union-loving men of this country, I shall now vote in favor" of Trumbull's emancipation amendment.[29] But that was it. The sides and the arguments remained the same. Republicans had already voted overwhelmingly in favor of Lovejoy's resolution. In the debates over the Vallandingham and Powell resolutions, not a single Republican would disavow federal attacks on slavery. There was no reason to believe that Bull Run would alter the outcome of the vote on Trumbull's amendment.

Certainly the conservatives were unbowed. Maryland Senator James A. Pearce distinguished the main body of the bill, concerning property confiscation, from the amendment Trumbull offered. The confiscation provisions, Pearce said, were drawn with reasonable care. They targeted persons engaged in rebellion, specified how their property was to be seized, and provided the judicial means for having that property condemned and then confiscated. By contrast, Pearce complained, Trumbull's emancipation amendment merely declared that slaves of rebel masters were to be freed. Pearce then spelled out the arguments against emancipation that would be repeated endlessly during the war. There was no way to enforce the law within the rebellious states. It provided no judicial means for determining whether owners were in fact engaged in rebellion. And it did not specify what was to be done with slaves it claimed to have emancipated. It will "inflame suspicions," add to the "irritations" already dividing Americans, "exasperating the country to far too great an extent."[30] Pearce had no reservations about the confiscation provisions of the bill, but Trumbull's emancipation amendment was something else entirely.

Conservatives were particularly anxious to dispute the claim that the rebellion would force northerners to choose between slavery and the Union. When Senator Browning uttered that standard Republican refrain, Senator Carlile of Virginia immediately denied it. Such a choice, Carlile said, "never can be forced upon the Senator" for the simple reason that the Union was based on the principle that property rights were sacred and inviolable. To uphold the Union was to defend, not repudiate, the right of property in slaves. In Carlile's mind, Browning was posing a false dichotomy. Or as Kentucky's Senator Powell asked, can Senator Browning "uphold constitutional government by putting the Constitution of his country under his feet?" The kind of war Republicans were proposing to wage was outrageous, Powell declared. "[Y]ou have no right to enter with your armies any State of this Union and despoil the people of their property."[31] This made perfect sense—but only to those who believed slaves were constitutionally protected property.

The relentlessness with which conservatives pressed their case only forced the more moderate Republicans to take positions they might have preferred to avoid. Senator John Sherman of Ohio epitomized the dilemma. He desperately reiterated that it was not his purpose to emancipate the slaves. But under the pressure of congressional debate he shifted ground. During the secession crisis he had incurred the wrath of his fellow Republicans by endorsing constitutional changes that would have increased the protection afforded to slavery. That was six months ago, though. "I would not do that now," Sherman admitted. He had struggled to distance himself from radical enthusiasm for emancipation by declaring his fervent wish that such a revolution could be avoided. But neither could he disavow the Republican argument for emancipation as a military necessity. He freely admitted the discomfort he felt. "I do not wish to be placed in that position," Sherman said, but he would not shrink from it either. Quite the contrary: Rather than see "one single foot of this country of ours torn from the national domain by traitors," he declared, "I will myself see slaves set free." If "there is no way of conquering South Carolina, for instance, except by emancipating her slaves, I say emancipate her slaves and conquer her rebellious citizens."[32] Forced to clarify his position, Sherman defended emancipation as a legitimate tool of war.

Trumbull's amendment passed in the Senate, overwhelmingly, by a vote of 33 to 6. The conservatives had now failed three times. They could not block passage of Lovejoy's resolution declaring that Union soldiers had no business returning fugitive slaves. They could not secure passage of the Vallandingham and Powell resolutions renouncing military interference with slavery in the seceded states. Nor could they muster even a slim Senate majority to oppose Trumbull's amendment. The Republicans were now on record unambiguously in favor of emancipating slaves used in support of the rebellion.

THE CRITTENDEN-JOHNSON RESOLUTION

Desperate to slow the march of radicalism, conservatives came back with another resolution. The brainchild of Kentucky Congressman John Crittenden, who introduced it in the House, it was sponsored in the Senate by Andrew Johnson of Tennessee. The Crittenden-Johnson resolution had essentially two parts. The first blamed the war on the South. The "present deplorable civil war," it declared, "has been forced upon the country by the disunionists of the southern States." The second part denied that the war was being "waged upon our part in any spirit of oppression, nor for any purpose of conquest or subjugation, nor purpose of overthrowing or interfering with the rights or established institution of those States." The sole purpose of the war was "to defend and maintain the supremacy of the Constitution and to preserve the Union with all the dignity, equality, and rights of the several States unimpaired."[33] On the surface this seemed no different from the Vallandigham-Powell resolutions Congress had already rejected.

In fact, the Crittenden-Johnson resolution was much more circumscribed. Rather than declare that the Union army had no business interfering with slavery, it declared only that the overthrow of slavery was not the "purpose" of the war. This made the resolution an empty gesture, for even radicals agreed that the Constitution did not allow the federal government to prosecute a war for the "purpose" of abolishing slavery. They argued instead that emancipation would be the *effect*—even the desirable effect—of a war whose *purpose* was to restore the Union. Moderate Republicans likewise embraced military emancipation while freely acknowledging that the purpose of the war remained what it had always been. Up and down the line, Republicans responded to the Crittenden-Johnson resolution by insisting that it was not the "purpose" of the war to interfere with slavery in the seceded states. Lincoln had said it in his inaugural address. Republican editors swore it in their columns. Senator James Lane said it, even as he exulted in the prospect of a slave "insurrection" as the Union forces marched through the South. There was no way to stop emancipation from happening, Lane argued, and yet "I disavow any intent upon the part of the Government or the Army to war against the institution of slavery."

Several Republicans made exactly this point when Johnson introduced the resolution in the Senate. "If slavery shall be abolished, shall be overthrown as a consequence of this war, I shall not shed a tear over that result; but sir, it is not the purpose of the Government to prosecute this war for the purpose of overthrowing slavery. If it comes as a consequence, let it come; but it is not an end of the war." New Hampshire Senator Daniel Clark agreed. He would vote for the resolution, he told his colleagues, secure in the conviction the "we should use all the means which have been put into our power to compel the rebels to submit to the Government." He was "ready" to endorse emancipation, Clark said, but he was also "willing to pass this resolution as it is, without amendment." Senator Hale of New Hampshire reminded his colleagues that antislavery leaders had always understood and acknowledged that the federal government had no authority to abolish slavery in the southern states. Nothing had changed. No opponent of slavery objects to the Crittenden-Johnson resolution, Hale argued. His hatred of slavery, his desire to see it abolished, his belief that the war would lead to its abolition—notwithstanding all of this, Hale still insisted that the "purpose" of the war was not to interfere with slavery, but to restore the Union. Accordingly, Republicans in the House joined in a nearly unanimous vote of 117 to 2 in favor of Crittenden's resolution.[34]

The day after Crittenden introduced his resolution in the House, Republicans in the Senate overwhelmingly endorsed Trumbull's emancipation amendment. Conservatives realized that Republican support for the Crittenden-Johnson resolution was essentially meaningless. In fact, some of them had their own reasons for opposing it. Kentucky Senator John Breckinridge complained that the first part of the resolution blamed the war solely on southern disunionists, when in his view northern antislavery fanatics deserved most of the blame.[35] Accordingly, conservatives asked that the resolution be divided so that they could vote against the first part. They would, of course, support the rest of the resolution stating that the "purpose" of the war was neither the abolition of slavery nor the "subjugation" of the South but merely the restoration of the Union. This stance only succeeded in further inflaming the moderate Republicans.

Senator John Sherman was infuriated by Breckinridge's remarks, and in a stinging rebuke he not only denied that the war was caused by disunionists in the North, but also explained why he had no trouble voting for the resolution after having voted in favor of Trumbull's emancipation amendment. The Crittenden-Johnson resolution, Sherman explained, is a mere statement of "what is literally true." The war was commenced by southern traitors. It "was never commenced, it was never prosecuted, with any idea of interfering with the domestic relations of the southern states. . . . It was prosecuted simply for the purpose of maintaining the Government." As for Trumbull's emancipation amendment, Sherman went on, "I have but this to say: if a slave is used by his master in the actual prosecution of the war, that slave ought to be freed; the master ought to forfeit all right to him." Does Senator Breckinridge deny this? Sherman asked.[36]

One after another, Republicans lined up in agreement. Senator Breckinridge complains that the Trumbull amendment "will accomplish the universal emancipation of the slaves in America," Orville Browning declared. "If it shall be so, if this war results in any such consequence, the responsibility of it is not upon us." The traitors of the South threaten to use their slaves to prosecute their "nefarious" rebellion. "Just let them carry their threats into execution," Browning declared, "and for one I will assail the institution of slavery wherever it exists, through every avenue by which it can be reached, and with every weapon by which I can strike it."[37] A few minutes later Browning cast his vote in favor of the resolution. Thoroughly disgusted, Breckinridge soon resigned from the Senate and defected to the South to become a Confederate general. Conservatives were right; as a barometer of the strength or weakness of Republican support for military emancipation, the vote on the Crittenden-Johnson resolution was meaningless.

"THERE WAS NO NECESSITY"

One of the things Breckinridge most despised about the Republican distinction between the *purpose* and the *consequence* of the war was that it seemingly freed supporters of emancipation from any obligation to justify freeing slaves "upon constitutional grounds." You get up and call us traitors, Breckinridge complained, yet we stand on firm constitutional principles while all you do is declare emancipation a "necessity." Follow the logic of "necessity" to its inevitable conclusion, Breckinridge warned, and you end up at military despotism. There are no limits to "military necessity"; it could be used to justify anything. Even before the fate of slavery came up for debate, Breckinridge was protesting the extraordinary actions Lincoln had taken on his own—calling out a huge army, spending millions of federal dollars, initiating a blockade of southern ports, and suspending habeas corpus in parts of the North. "What is the excuse; what is the justification; what is the plea?" Breckinridge demanded. "Necessity? I answer, first, that there was no necessity. . . . I deny this doctrine of necessity. I deny that the President of the United States may violate the Constitution upon the ground of necessity, and his decision not to be appealed from, the will of one man for a written constitution."[38] Under the doctrine of "necessity," conservatives warned, a tyrant could do whatever he pleased.

A tyrant could free slaves, for example. Breckinridge could not help noticing that congressional Republicans were already invoking the doctrine of military necessity to justify the destruction of slavery. He took particular exception to one of the confiscation bills that had been introduced and sent to the Judiciary Committee for consideration, this one entitled a "Bill to suppress the slaveholders' rebellion." It called for the emancipation of slaves used in the rebellion and for the enlistment of freed slaves into the Union army. "It is not only a congressional act of emancipation," Breckinridge fumed, "but it is intended to arm the slaves against the masters. It is not only to confiscate the whole property, but it is to foment a servile war." When Michigan Senator Kingsley S. Bingham declared that he had no objections to the title of the bill, Breckinridge asked whether he was "in favor of freeing the slaves in the seceded states." Bingham responded without hesitation. "If it be a necessity," he said, "I am."[39]

Republicans responded to charges of tyranny by pointing out that the laws of war were embedded within the Constitution and were therefore subject to its checks and balances. Precisely because the laws of war were unwritten, it was up to Congress to determine their reach as well as their limits. Things that were illegal under the peacetime Constitution were perfectly legal under the laws of war, Senator Edward Baker of Oregon argued, but it was up to Congress to specify what those things were. Emancipation, for example: under the laws of war the government acquired the power to emancipate the slaves of belligerents. Trumbull was adamant on this point. Not only was emancipation justified under the laws of war, he argued, but because these laws were embedded within the Constitution, military emancipation was therefore fully constitutional. In the Senate this discussion was brief. There Republicans were primarily concerned to show that by invoking the laws of war, Congress was ensuring that the military could not become the agent of executive tyranny but was instead legally subordinated to civilians in the legislative branch of government.

A more wide-ranging discussion took place in the House, where the debate over the confiscation bill was bound up with the debate over the laws of war. On August 2, the House Judiciary Committee sent to the floor a confiscation bill that was virtually identical to the Senate's. Everyone understood that Section 4 was an emancipation provision. Burnett interpreted it to mean that the use of any slave "by authority of the owner, in any mode which will tend to aid or promote this insurrection, will entitle that slave to his freedom." Bingham did not dispute this: "Certainly it will."[40] In short, everyone agreed that the legislation before the House was designed to free slaves. The issue was now squarely joined. Did Congress have the power to pass such a law?

Conservatives were emphatic that the answer was *no*. It "has been conceded in all time," Crittenden pointed out, that no branch of the federal government had the power "to legislate upon the subject of slavery in the States." If this is true in peacetime, he insisted, so must it be true in war. But was Crittenden right? Republicans believed that although the seceded states remained under the Constitution, they had nevertheless forfeited the protection of the Constitution when they rebelled. Was this not precisely the condition prescribed by the laws of war? In the face of insistent Republican questioning, Crittenden evaded the issue of what the government could do under the laws of war. Finally, he admitted what was really bothering him. The "laws of war," he suggested, were merely a pretext being used by Congress "to insinuate our jurisdiction" over slavery in the southern states. Trumbull's amendment had nothing to do with property confiscation upon conviction of treason, Crittenden noted. It was designed to emancipate slaves, and its supporters were using the laws of war as an excuse.[41]

Crittenden had a point. It requires very little digging in the corpus of Republican speeches and editorials to come up with a treasure trove of hatred for slavery. But at that point no Republican senator or representative—not even Charles Sumner—was going to stand up in Congress and declare that the federal government could abolish slavery simply because slavery was despicable, no matter how despicable he thought slavery was. Antislavery activists had devoted decades to the formulation of careful constitutional arguments about precisely where and under what circumstances the federal government could attack slavery. The doctrine of "military necessity" was crucial to the legitimacy of their politics. That much every Republican understood.

Yet their opponents raised a serious issue when they wondered if there were any limits to the war powers Republicans were invoking. The most respected legal authorities—Joseph Story, for example, and now Lyman Trumbull—had always been careful to insist that the war powers clause brought the law of nations into the Constitution. But this created the legal anomaly of extra-constitutional powers that were somehow constitutional. During the debate in the House, Thaddeus Stevens insisted that the laws of war allowed the government to do things that would otherwise be considered unconstitutional, and that "constitutions, if they stood in the way of the laws of war in dealing with the enemy, had no right to intervene." In the face of sharp criticism from several of his congressional colleagues, Stevens stood his ground. He was not saying the Constitution be damned in time of war; he was merely noting that in wartime the government was allowed to do things it could not constitutionally do during peacetime. This has been true from "the days of Cicero . . . down to the present time." Stevens freely admitted "that if you were in a state of peace you could not confiscate the property of any citizen. You have no right to do it in time of peace, but in time of war you have the right to confiscate the property of every rebel." Stevens also believed that under the Constitution the executive and legislative branches shared the power to invoke the laws of war. The president could not do it alone, Stevens believed; he needed congressional authorization to do so.[42]

Most important, Stevens offered a justification for emancipation implied by Emmerich de Vattel in his classic study, *The Law of Nations*. "[T]o deliver an oppressed people is a noble fruit of victory," Vattel had written, but it was also "a valuable advantage gained, thus to acquire a faithful friend." Stevens interpreted Vattel's words as sanctioning the emancipation of slaves held by an enemy. "If it be a just war, and there be a people who have been oppressed by the enemy and that enemy be conquered," Stevens explained, "the victorious party cannot return that oppressed people to bondage from which they have rescued them." Accordingly, Stevens argued, "one of the most glorious consequences of victory is giving freedom to those who are oppressed." And once the slaves had been "rescued" from their oppression, they could never be returned to slavery. "God forbid," he declared, "that I should ever agree that they should be returned to their masters!"[43]

Stevens made the strongest case for emancipation under the laws of war, yet even for him this did not alter the purpose of the war. "Our object," he explained, was still "to subdue the rebels." If "in order to save this Union from destruction" the North had to free every slave, lay waste to the entire South, make the entire region into a desert, Stevens said, well then "so let it be." Stevens would not say that the war had reached the point where the complete destruction of slavery was absolutely necessary for the restoration of the Union. But if the war continues, he warned, the time will come when the northern people will not sit by and watch their sons and husbands go to their deaths while their government held back and refused to use every means at its disposal to subdue the rebellion.[44]

For all his rhetorical radicalism, Stevens had presented a thoroughly mainstream Republican argument. From the earliest months of the war, Republicans in both the Senate and the House justified emancipation as a "military necessity" under the laws of war. In times of peace the Constitution did not allow the federal government to interfere with slavery in any loyal state, but in wartime a different set of rules came into play, rules based on the law of nations. No one argued that under the laws of war anything was justifiable. However, Republicans did agree that the states that had seceded from the Union had forfeited the Constitution's protection and entered into a state of war. In those states, no Republican doubted, emancipation was justified as a "military necessity." This was the premise of the First Confiscation Act.

EMANCIPATION, IMMEDIATE AND UNCOMPENSATED

The most consequential criticism to emerge from the House debate was that Trumbull's amendment looked like legislative rather than military emancipation. Conservatives such as Henry Burnett noted that because slaves were "discharged from service" as they ran to Union lines, the confiscation bill "amounts to a wholesale emancipation of the slaves in the seceding or rebellious states." Some representatives thought it did not clearly specify that only slaves used by the Confederate military were emancipated. Lincoln was likewise concerned that the confiscation bill would be interpreted as a general rather than a strictly military emancipation. That was not what Trumbull or anyone else had in mind. Bingham argued that although the bill would emancipate slaves owned by traitors, it was neither written as nor intended to be read as a general emancipation of the slaves. "By the express words of the act it is limited," he said. Even in the midst of his reverie about universal freedom, Thaddeus Stevens had been quick to check himself: under the laws of war he would emancipate any slave "belonging to a rebel, recollect; I confine it to them."[45]

A number of Republicans believed that because it could be constitutionally justified only as a "military necessity," emancipation had to be the work of the president, acting in his capacity as commander in chief. Congress could specify the "persons" whose labor would be "forfeited," but once the federal government had taken control of the "persons" so forfeited, only the president could take the additional step of "discharging" slaves from any further service to their masters. If emancipation was strictly *military*, it had to be done by the commander in chief. To alleviate such concerns the wording of Trumbull's amendment was changed at the last minute.

In the bill's final form, masters would still "forfeit" their claim to the service of a slave. But instead of declaring that forfeited slaves were henceforth "discharged" from service, the revised version prohibited any master from reclaiming any slave who "had been employed in hostile service against the Government of the United States." On August 3, the House passed this version of the bill by a vote of 60 to 48. Of the 60 favorable votes, 59 came from Republicans. Only 7 Republicans voted against the bill, along with nearly every Democrat and representative from the Border States. The bill went back to the Senate that same day.

Later that afternoon, Senator Trumbull reintroduced the revised confiscation bill in the Senate. He did not think the new wording altered the meaning of his amendment. The only thing the House version does, he said, is clarify what the bill always assumed: that Congress could specify which masters had forfeited the labor of their slaves, that it could permanently deny masters the right to reclaim the slave's labor, but that it could not emancipate the slaves. "I think the section as we passed it meant substantially the same thing," Trumbull explained, "but this makes it more definite." Trumbull and everybody else still believed it was an emancipation bill because they all assumed that the commander in chief would execute the law by "discharging" the "forfeited" slaves.[46]

As it was late in the day, the Senate held over the final consideration of the bill until the following Monday, August 5, at which point the amended fourth section was overwhelmingly approved by a 44 to 11 vote. A single conservative Republican—Edgar Cowan of Pennsylvania—voted against it. As in the House, every senator from the Border States and all but one Democrat voted against it. The bill went to the president the next day, and Lincoln signed it. On August 6, 1861, "[a]n act to confiscate property used for insurrectionary purposes," known as the First Confiscation Act, passed into law.[47]

Two days later, on August 8, the War Department restored Trumbull's original wording in the instructions it issued for implementing Section 4. Under the terms of the First Confiscation Act, Simon Cameron explained, masters whose slaves were "employed in hostility to the United States" would forfeit the services of those slaves "*and such persons shall be discharged therefrom.*" The slaves of disloyal masters were emancipated.[48] It was crucial that the instructions came from the War Department rather than the attorney general. This was military emancipation; no judicial proceedings were required. Hence the instructions were issued by the secretary of war in the form of an answer to General Benjamin Butler's letter of July 30 asking for clarification on the status of slaves who ran to Union lines. The immediate circumstances of their composition could not disguise their broader significance.

The War Department's August 8 instructions, in conjunction with its May 30 endorsement of Butler's contraband policy, initiated emancipation and established the basic Union policy regarding slavery in the seceded states that would remain in place for more than a year. Once again, Union soldiers were prohibited from enticing slaves away from their farms and plantations, and the soldiers could not prevent any slave from returning voluntarily to his or her owner. There could be no "interference" with the ordinary workings of slavery. On the other hand, slaves voluntarily entering Union lines from any state that had seceded from the Union were emancipated.

Most of the contrabands at Fortress Monroe had not been working for the Confederates. Was it practical, or even possible, Butler had asked, for commanders on the ground to distinguish the slaves of loyal and disloyal masters? The secretary of war answered by instructing Butler to retain *all* fugitives but to keep careful records of the loyalties of their owners. "Upon the return of peace," Cameron explained, "Congress will doubtless properly provide for all the persons thus received into the service of the Union and for just compensation to loyal masters."[49] This was compensated emancipation, and it effectively extended the reach of the First Confiscation Act far beyond its technical limits. Strictly speaking, the statute freed only slaves used to support the rebellion. But under the War Department's instruction, *all* slaves voluntarily coming to Union lines from disloyal states were emancipated. Owners who had been loyal might someday be compensated, but the freed people would never be re-enslaved.

On August 9, the day after the War Department sent its instructions, Butler informed one of his colleagues that numerous slaves were still coming into his lines at Fortress Monroe and that "as their masters had deserted their homes and slaves he should consider the latter free." That was certainly Edward Pierce's understanding. As a Free Soiler who had grown up within the circles of New England reform, Pierce accepted the abolitionist theory that in the act of running away, slaves had restored themselves to their natural condition of freedom. Pierce was also in a position to act on that belief, for General Butler put him in charge of the contrabands at Fortress Monroe when their numbers had climbed to two hundred. In the November 1861 issue of the *Atlantic Monthly* Pierce explained why, under the principles of the law of nations, the contrabands were now free. Southern state laws regarded them as property to be "used by the rebels for purposes of the rebellion." Under "the strict law of nations" such slave "property" could be legitimately seized. But secession had nullified state laws, leaving escaped slaves under the purview of a natural-law Constitution that recognized slaves only as persons. "Regarded as persons," Pierce wrote, "they had escaped from communities where a triumphant rebellion had trampled on the laws, and only the rights of human nature remained." When the slaveholders of Hampton fled in panic before the advancing Union army, they abandoned not only their slaves but the rule of law as well. Where there is no human law, there is only the law of nature, and by its decrees, Pierce reasoned, the contrabands at Fortress Monroe were persons restored to their natural condition of freedom. He reminded his readers that Hampton Roads was the place where the first African slaves had arrived in Virginia in 1619. "It is fitting," Pierce noted, "that the system which from that slave ship had been spreading over the continent for nearly two centuries and a half should yield, for the first time, to the logic of military law almost upon the spot of its origins."[50]

Between them, Butler, Pierce, and the War Department established two of the basic criteria for emancipation that prevailed during 1861 and 1862—criteria that went beyond the limits of the First

Confiscation Act. The first was labor in service of the Union. Slaves who ran to Union lines and volunteered their services as wage laborers for the Union military, whether male or female, were entitled to their freedom. Having thus served the Union cause, black workers neither could nor would be returned to slavery. The second criterion was abandonment by their owners. Masters who ran from advancing Union occupation troops were presumed to be traitors, whose property was thereby subject to confiscation and who forfeited any further claim to the labor of their slaves, and those slaves were thence discharged from service. Slaves who had refused to run with their masters had, in effect, voluntarily come into Union lines and were thereby emancipated. In the coming months these criteria would confirm the emancipation of thousands of slaves along the southern Atlantic coast, from Virginia to Florida.

There is no reason to doubt that this was the result the Lincoln administration intended. Even before he was elected president, Lincoln had warned that if the slave states seceded, the federal government would stop enforcing the fugitive slave clause, and he had repeated that warning in his first inaugural address. In early July, the House of Representatives, expressing the common sentiment of Republicans, resolved that "it is no part of the duty of the soldiers of the United States to capture and return fugitive slaves." Lincoln himself had said substantially the same thing to Orville Browning. The War Department's instructions to Butler thus reflected Lincoln's conviction that no fugitive slaves voluntarily coming into Union lines from the seceded states would be returned to slavery. If Lincoln had objected to Cameron's interpretation of the Confiscation Act, he almost certainly would have said so. As the secretary of war himself would soon discover, Lincoln was perfectly willing to disavow Cameron's words when he disapproved of them, either for legal or for political reasons. But he did nothing to countermand Cameron's expansive instructions for implementing Congress's emancipation act. And they were hardly secret. Cameron's exchange with Butler was published in the *New York Tribune*, the most popular Republican newspaper in America. The exchange was subsequently reprinted in Frank Moore's influential *Rebellion Record*. The secretary of the navy, Gideon Welles, issued similar instructions, and Welles later recalled that Lincoln was informed of "every step" he took regarding emancipation. The Navy Department's "instructions, and its policy, were reported to the President," Welles recalled, and Lincoln "approved of them without reserve, modification, or qualification. The course of the Secretary of War," he added, "was very similar."[51]

The War Department repeatedly sent copies of its May 30 and August 8 instructions to generals in the field to clarify the status of slaves running to Union lines from the seceded states. When Union General John A. Dix argued that all runaways from Virginia should be treated as fugitive slaves, the War Department corrected him by forwarding copies of the May 30 and August 8 instructions. Union officers in Kentucky were likewise instructed to emancipate slaves escaping from the seceded state of Tennessee. Just before General Thomas W. Sherman embarked on the expedition that would result in Union occupation of the Sea Islands off South Carolina in early November, the secretary of war instructed the commanding officer that his treatment of any slaves coming into his lines should be governed "by the principles of the letters addressed by me to Major-General Butler on the 30th of May and 8th of August, copies of which are herewith furnished to you." No slaves escaping to Union lines were to be returned to their owners, whether they were loyal or not. All slaves escaping from areas in rebellion were to be "discharged" from service—emancipated. General Sherman in turn gave copies of the same War Department instructions to General David Hunter, who, following the policies of his predecessors, declared the emancipation of all the slaves at Fort Pulaski and the surrounding islands his Union troops occupied in the spring of 1862. Even General George

McClellan, who made no secret of his objection to an antislavery war, implemented the War Department policy during the Peninsula Campaign in the spring of 1862. Slaves coming into his lines were not returned to their owners, whether their owners happened to be loyal or not. Within a year of its passage, tens of thousands of slaves had been freed by the First Confiscation Act.[52]

NOBODY INTENDED THE FIRST Confiscation Act to be a general emancipation law. It was still unclear whether it applied to loyal masters in the Border States or the District of Columbia. It depended on the voluntary action of fugitive slaves; it could not extend to slaves unable to reach Union lines. It depended on the army, which meant that despite the resounding support for Owen Lovejoy's resolution, emancipation could be thwarted or advanced by individual soldiers and officers who were not always willing to accept runaways into their lines. Nevertheless, military emancipation became official Union policy when Congress passed the First Confiscation Act. As of August 8, 1861, the federal government was emancipating slaves, not just slaves who had been used by the Confederate military but all slaves voluntarily coming within Union lines from the seceded states. Over the next year the scope of "military emancipation" expanded still further to include all slaves abandoned by their masters in the face of an invading Union army and ultimately all slaves in any part of the Confederacy occupied by Union troops.

As federal policy pushed closer to universal emancipation in the seceded states, Republican radicals occasionally looked back with dismay on the limitations of the First Confiscation Act, and some even expressed regret for having supported the Crittenden-Johnson resolution. But there was no need for them to apologize. The Republicans had endorsed Lovejoy's resolution declaring that it was not the army's "duty" to return runaway slaves to their masters. By resoundingly rejecting the Vallandingham-Powell resolutions, Republicans effectively announced their intention to "interfere" with slavery in the seceded states. They had with remarkable speed begun freeing slaves. Congress had come into session five months ahead of schedule; in less than three weeks the Senate Judiciary Committee reported a confiscation bill to the floor and endorsed Trumbull's emancipation amendment, and within another couple of weeks both houses revised and passed the final bill. Lincoln signed it one day later, and two days after that, on August 8, 1861, the War Department issued its instructions. It's hard to imagine how emancipation could have begun any sooner.

No doubt the Republicans were naive in believing that if the rebellion persisted, emancipation would happen almost automatically as slaves ran to the Union forces marching through the South. But they knew the slaves wanted to be free, and they knew the slaves needed the army to secure their freedom. What the Republicans underestimated was slavery's ability to withstand the rigors of war. The First Confiscation Act turned out to be no match for slavery's size and strength. But it did free thousands of slaves, immediately and without compensation, just as it was supposed to do.

5 THE BORDER STATES

THE FEDERAL GOVERNMENT SETTLED quickly on a policy of emancipating slaves who came "voluntarily" within Union lines from the seceded states, but it took more time—and a good deal more confusion—to settle on an approach to slavery in the four slave states that remained loyal to the Union—Delaware, Maryland, Kentucky, and Missouri. These were the Border States, and for decades they were key to the peacetime scenario of gradual state abolition by means of containment. If slavery was intrinsically weak, it was thought to be weakest in the Border States. Political abolitionists believed that once slavery was effectively contained within the South, the Border States would be the first to abolish slavery. They had fewer slaves than the cotton states, in both absolute and proportional terms. Their economies were more diversified. They had stronger ties to the North. And unlike the cotton states, it was still possible for Border State politicians to advocate the abolition of slavery. For those very reasons the Border States ultimately sided with the Union rather than the Confederacy, and for those same reasons Republicans believed those states would be the first to respond to the combination of federal pressure and federal incentives by abolishing slavery on their own.[1]

But was it possible to implement a peacetime policy of containment in states that remained loyal but were severely disrupted by war? Military emancipation was justified by the laws of war; its purpose was to subdue an enemy or suppress an insurrection. There was no question—at least not among Republicans—that the eleven states of the Confederacy were in rebellion and therefore subject to military emancipation. But what about the Border States where secessionists failed? Could slaves who ran to Union lines in Maryland be retained as "contraband of war"? Did the First Confiscation Act apply to Kentucky? Were the War Department's August 8 instructions applicable in Missouri? The state laws treating slaves as property had been nullified by secession, but were slaves still "property" under the laws of states that remained loyal?

Massive political disruption within three of the four Border States—the civil wars within the Civil War—made it difficult for the federal government to settle quickly on *any* antislavery policy. The fact that the Border States were loyal suggested that a peacetime policy of gradual abolition was appropriate; the fact that they were disrupted by war suggested that military emancipation could be imposed within those states. Further complicating this already difficult problem was the question of fugitive slaves. It was a well-established principle among antislavery politicians that the fugitive slave clause should be enforced by the states, not the federal government, and by July of 1861 Lincoln and congressional Republicans made it clear that the U.S. military should not involve itself in the capture and return of fugitive slaves. Yet Union troops were a powerful magnet to runaway slaves, and by the fall of 1861 there were thousands of northern soldiers in Maryland, Kentucky, and Missouri, and therefore thousands of runaway slaves. It was one thing for General Butler to retain runaways in Virginia on the ground that the state had seceded from the Union, but what was the Union army in the loyal states supposed to do when slaves ran to their lines for freedom?

These questions would have been hard enough to answer if Lincoln and the Republicans had been concerned only with keeping the Border States from leaving the Union. But they wanted to maintain the Union *and* abolish slavery, and they expected abolition to begin in the Border States. The problem policymakers faced was not merely keeping those states in the Union, but keeping them in the Union while at the same time pressuring them to abolish slavery. Not surprisingly, nearly all of the controversial orders and contentious disputes over the implementation of federal antislavery policy during the first year of the war—disputes within the Union army, between the army and Congress, and between Lincoln and the Border States— concerned Delaware, Maryland, Missouri, or Kentucky.

UPHEAVAL IN THE BORDER STATES

When the war began, secessionists were a potent political force in three of the four Border States. Supporters of the Confederacy initially dominated the legislatures in Maryland and Missouri. In two states—Kentucky and Missouri—defeated secessionists established rump legislatures, both of which were immediately recognized by the Confederate States of America. Beyond the legislative halls, secessionists often flexed their muscle through their control of local police and militia companies—bulwarks of southern slave society and, in effect, the military arm of the slaveholding class. Pro-Confederate police rioted in the streets of Baltimore and St. Louis. Police and local militias became centers for the recruitment of Confederate regiments from the loyal slave states. Until these secessionists were politically vanquished and militarily suppressed, neither Congress nor the administration could formulate a coherent policy for attacking slavery in these three states and Delaware.

Brute military force was indispensible to the triumph of unionism in most of the Border States. Delaware alone lacked a viable secessionist faction at the outset of the war, and it remained distinctive because it was never really disrupted by the presence of Union or Confederate troops. In Maryland, by contrast, the Union army was everywhere from the earliest days of the war, and it disrupted slavery wherever it went. Heavy military thumbs also tipped the scales in favor of Maryland unionists. Yankee troops threatened to shut down the legislature, and Union soldiers were stationed at polling places where they intimidated secessionist voters. Kentucky offered still another variation. Having declared its neutrality at the outset, Kentucky had neither Union nor Confederate troops within its borders for the first five months of the war. But an ill-starred Confederate invasion in September led to a series of battles that ended in the expulsion of Confederate forces from Kentucky in early 1862. The military threat persisted, but the threat of secession was over. The most violent struggles between unionists and secessionists took place in Missouri. By midsummer of 1861 political conflict gave way to open warfare that lasted until March of 1862. After their defeat at Pea Ridge, however, Confederate troops did not launch a significant invasion of Missouri until the fall of 1864. The military defeat of the secessionists in the Border States provided ample proof, if such proof were needed, that war was politics by other means.

Political struggles in turn reflected basic social divisions within each of the Border States. In Maryland a sectional divide, pitting north against south, appeared on that state's map with nearly as much clarity as it did on the map of the United States. The southern counties hugging the eastern and especially the western shores of Chesapeake Bay were the most rural, the most committed to slavery, and the most deeply engaged in the production of staple crops

cultivated from the labor of slaves. The more economically diversified counties with few slaves stretched northward from Baltimore to
form a straight edge along the Pennsylvania border, the famous
Mason-Dixon Line.[2]

When the war began in April of 1861, pro-southern Democrats
dominated the Maryland state legislature. Secession sympathizers
also controlled the Baltimore police, who sat on a cache of arms and
ammunition so large it "resembled a concealed arsenal." A week after
the capture of Fort Sumter, a Baltimore mob attacked Union soldiers
on their way to Washington. Anxious to stir up disunion sentiment,
the Baltimore police chief wired the state's attorney that the city
streets were running "red with Maryland blood." He invited "rifle-
men" from "over the mountains of Maryland and Virginia" to head
for Baltimore "without delay" and join the struggle against the invading Yankees. "Fresh hordes will be down on us tomorrow. We will
fight them and whip them or die."[3] Frightened by the Baltimore riot,
Maryland's timorous Governor Thomas H. Hicks tried to assuage the
secessionist mob by ordering the destruction of bridges and rail lines
and the obstruction of waterways, all to prevent the further passage of
any Union troops rushing from the North to protect Washington.
Hicks pleaded with federal officials to recognize the secession of the
southern states and suggested British mediation of the dispute.

But Hicks was not a secessionist, and neither were most Mary-
landers. Within days of the Baltimore riot, the state's unionist majority launched a counterattack. "A great reaction has set in," Henry
Winter Davis wrote to William Seward. "If we act promptly the day
is ours and the city is safe."[4] Lincoln did act promptly, suspending the
writ of habeas corpus along the rail lines running through the state.
Benjamin Butler arrived a few weeks later and made an impressive
show of force in Baltimore. By the end of April, the pro-southern legislature was reduced to issuing defiant *pronunciamentos*, but it didn't
dare pass an ordinance of secession. A potent combination of forces—

a unionist governor backed by a unionist electorate backed by a firm federal first—had effectively thwarted Maryland's secessionists.

On June 13, unionists scored major victories in Maryland's special congressional elections. They did even better in the November balloting, when a unionist candidate for governor overwhelmed his pro-southern opponent while unionists won control of the lower House of Delegates by a landslide. Even in the state Senate—grossly malapportioned to favor the most conservative slaveholding districts—a slight unionist majority took control. The state bureaucracy was quickly cleansed of secessionists as loyalty to the Union became the de facto requirement for all patronage appointments. Reinforcing the electoral victory of the unionists was the departure of many of the state's most ardent secessionists. Thousands went south, offering their services to the Confederacy. The state's attorney, Bradley T. Johnson, would shortly defect and become a Confederate general. Colonel Isaac R. Trimble, who had come rapidly to the assistance of the Baltimore mob, also defected to the southern cause. By the end of the year Maryland's secessionists were vanquished.

As in Maryland, Missouri's social and political divisions were etched visibly on the state's map. A potent slaveholding class had colonized the rich bottom lands along the Mississippi and Missouri Rivers. Yet St. Louis was fast becoming an industrial and commercial center, a railroad hub, with a rapidly growing immigrant community—including a large contingent of radical Germans—that helped sustain a politically active working class. Throughout the 1850s the Democratic Party in Missouri was bitterly divided between a proslavery majority and a vocal minority led by Senator Thomas Hart Benton, who, along with Congressman Frank Blair Jr., opposed the expansion of slavery. Both were blackballed by their party for their apostasy, and by 1856 Blair had gone over to the Republicans.

In 1860 the proslavery forces controlled the Democratic Party machinery and nominated the secessionist Claiborne F. Jackson for governor on a proslavery platform endorsing the unlimited expansion of slavery. Jackson won.[5]

In early January of 1861 the new governor called for a secession convention with the announcement that Missouri could best serve its interests "by a timely declaration of her determination to stand by her sister slave-holding states." A majority of Missourians, however, opposed secession, and in the delegate elections held on February 18, the unionists triumphed overwhelmingly, 110,000 to 30,000. Some of that unionism was "conditional," but not a single overt secessionist was chosen. The convention met in St. Louis on March 4, and the proceedings were dominated by the staunch unionist Hamilton R. Gamble; at his urging, the delegates refused to do anything more than recommend a sectional compromise. The convention adjourned without even considering secession as an option. It looked as though the governor and his pro-southern legislature were thwarted.[6]

But Governor Jackson was a most determined secessionist. After the firing on Fort Sumter on April 12, Lincoln asked Missouri to supply four thousand troops to suppress the rebellion, and Jackson ostentatiously refused to comply. Acting swiftly, Frank Blair—relying on his powerful family connections in Washington—instead arranged for Union Captain Nathaniel Lyon to muster the St. Louis Home Guards, thereby fulfilling Missouri's quota. Lyon's troops took control of the federal arsenal just south of the city, snatching the weapons from the secessionist militia loyal to the governor. Undeterred by the loss of the arsenal, Governor Jackson requested a shipment of arms from Confederate President Jefferson Davis, who promptly complied. The arms arrived on May 8, at Camp Jackson, recently established and occupied by seven hundred secessionist militiamen. Two days later, Lyon, with thousands of men now at his disposal, took control of the camp and arrested all seven hundred men. But the march back to St. Louis turned into a fiasco as mobs of angry citizens, shouting, "Hurrah for Jeff Davis," hurled rocks at Lyon's troops. The troops fired into the crowd and twenty-one people were killed. That night secessionists rioted through the streets of St. Louis, just as their counterparts were doing back in Baltimore.

In Jefferson City the governor wasted no time using the attack on Camp Jackson to persuade the state legislature to grant him absolute power over the state militia and the funds to organize them. Jackson pressured the state's mostly pro-Confederate bankers to finance his rebellion. Lyon's attack also converted many conditional unionists into secessionists, among them former governor Sterling Price. Jackson appointed Price to be major general in charge of the State Guard, and hundreds of volunteers streamed into Jefferson City to join up. Like Jackson, Lyon rejected all efforts at conciliation. Rather than concede the right of any Missouri official "to dictate to my government in any manner," Lyon declared, he would see "every man, woman, and child in the State, dead and buried. *This means war.*"[7] And so it did. Lyon invaded Jefferson City, but the governor and legislature had fled the state capital and, along with thousands of volunteers, joined up with the State Guard assembling at Boonville under General Price.

With Missouri's capital abandoned, the secession convention reconvened, deposed both the governor and the secessionist legislature, and became the de facto Provisional Government with Hamilton Gamble as acting governor. Widely respected, even by pro-southern conservatives, Gamble also had influence with the Lincoln administration through his brother-in-law and former law partner, Attorney General Edward Bates. Lincoln immediately recognized the Provisional Government, but five days before Gamble assumed his duties as acting governor, Lincoln's newly appointed commander of the Department of the West, John C. Frémont, arrived in Missouri to assume his duties as well. Missouri now had three competing systems of authority: an insurgent governor and legislature on the loose but backed by a pro-Confederate army, a rickety civilian government headed by Governor Gamble, and a military department commanded by General Frémont. The situation required nothing if not cooperation among unionists.

FRÉMONT AND CIVILIAN RULE

Frémont had never been the cooperative type. A rebellious streak already evident in his youth—he was expelled from the College of Charleston for "continued disregard of discipline"—was magnified by later success.[8] That success was nonetheless splendid for having originated in nepotism. In 1841 Senator Benton had arranged for Frémont, Benton's son-in-law, to lead a government-sponsored expedition to survey and map the Oregon Trail. Two years later Frémont and his wife, the indomitable Jessie Benton Frémont, published a report of their explorations, an account so engaging and popular that Frémont immediately set out on another military expedition—this time through the Southwest, across the Sierra Nevada into California, and back—a thrilling fourteen-month voyage capped by another report that sealed Frémont's heroic reputation as "The Pathfinder."

He was not one to wear his fame with humility. The reckless youth had grown into an irresponsible man with an imperious disposition and penchant for insubordination. During his second western expedition, Frémont had headed for the Southwest, disregarding explicit orders not to do so. Contempt for authority was one thing in a civilian, but Frémont was still an officer in the U.S. Army, and when, on his third expedition, he went up against Stephen Watts Kearny, his commanding general in California, Kearny had Frémont court-martialed. Despite powerful political support and his own immense popularity with the public, Frémont was found guilty and expelled from the army. Two more privately financed expeditions ensued, both disastrous. In 1848 one-third of his party died trapped in the snowy mountains of southern Colorado. Frémont blamed his guide, but many of the survivors blamed Frémont. Five years later the calamity nearly repeated itself. A brilliant topographical engineer with a flair for self-promotion and a gift for dramatic storytelling, Frémont was nevertheless undone by an inflated opinion of his own greatness and a dictatorial style that made him incompetent as a leader of men.

He went into politics. As California's first senator—he took his seat during the tumultuous debates over slavery that led to the Compromise of 1850—Frémont voted for the abolition of the slave trade in the District of Columbia and against stiff penalties for harboring fugitive slaves. Nevertheless by 1856 his political profile was still so obscure that both Democrats and Republicans wooed him as their presidential candidate, chiefly because of his reputation as an explorer. Because his instincts were antislavery, however, Frémont accepted the Republican nomination. Though he gave no speeches and did not campaign, his views on slavery were squarely within the Republican mainstream. He agreed that the Constitution did not allow the federal government to abolish slavery in any state, but he decried the disproportionate power of slaveholders in national politics and argued that the federal government should "avoid giving countenance to the extension of slavery." It was an increasingly popular view among northern voters, and Frémont's immense personal reputation fired up a constituency to support the new Republican Party. Alas, the traits that would prove so disastrous for Missouri during the Civil War were already on full display during the 1856 campaign. Frémont was an inept candidate, secretive, suspicious, and overly sensitive to the slightest criticism. Nevertheless, although he lost his bid for the presidency in 1856, his impressive showing helped establish the legitimacy of the new antislavery party and paved the way for Abraham Lincoln's victory four years later.[9]

Frémont was in France when the war broke out. He quickly returned to the United States and accepted President Lincoln's appointment as the commanding general of the newly created Department of the West. Lincoln made the appointment on July 1, 1861, but despite the chaos into which Missouri was rapidly descending, Frémont dawdled in New York and did not arrive in St. Louis until the end of the month. His orders were vague, though he was expected to clear the rebels from the state.

Back in Missouri, General Lyon and Governor Gamble were trying to do the same thing. By mid-July Lyon had chased the secessionist army down to Springfield, in the southwest corner of the state. The rebels, however, would soon be joined by Confederate troops invading from Arkansas, and Lyon was desperately short of the men and material he needed to face his enemies in battle. He appealed for help, but Frémont was still back in New York spinning dreams of military glory—dreams that did not include repelling the impending Confederate invasion. Instead, Frémont wanted to send Union troops down the Mississippi River, splitting the Confederacy in two and wrecking its hopes for independence. It wasn't a bad idea, but it occupied Frémont's mind to the exclusion of everything else. Focused completely on eastern Missouri, Frémont scarcely noticed that the western half of the state was being overrun by Confederates and rapidly collapsing into guerilla warfare.

Once installed in the St. Louis mansion that he made his headquarters, Frémont surrounded himself with a protective coterie of sycophants sporting elaborate costumes and bearing pompous titles like "adletus to the chief of staff"—affectations that won few friends among down-to-earth westerners. Lyon's increasingly desperate cries for help rarely got through Frémont's phalanx, and even when they did, the general ignored them. Frémont was more attentive, one Missourian complained, to the California speculators "who surround him like summer pigs."[10] Gamble tried to intercede to get Lyon the men and supplies he needed, but Frémont ignored the governor as well.

Finally on August 9, Frémont wrote Lyon that no reinforcements were available, and urged him to retreat from Springfield to the railhead at Rolla if Lyon felt he could not hold his position. Lyon—as impulsive as Frémont was oblivious—decided instead to launch an attack. The next day, August 10, Lyon and Franz Sigel advanced on Wilson's Creek, where Confederate General Ben McCulloch, moving up from Arkansas, combined his forces with Missouri troops under Sterling Price to turn back Lyon's reckless assault. Lyon was fatally shot while riding around the battlefield on his horse trying to rally his outnumbered men. His death instantly demoralized the already overwhelmed Union troops, and they promptly fled the field in panic. Lyon may have been reckless, but he had undoubtedly been courageous, and for that he was widely proclaimed a hero in the North. Frémont, meanwhile, was criticized for not having given Lyon the support he needed.

Frémont didn't do much to help Missouri's governor either. Hamilton Gamble was struggling to organize and arm a state militia made up of Missouri men who could subdue pro-secession guerillas more effectively than the hostile Union troops from out of state. (Yankee regiments had a tendency to encourage slaves to run away, which Missouri masters found obnoxious.) But rather than sustain the governor's efforts, Frémont went out of his way to undermine them. Indeed, he was so contemptuous of civilian authorities that by early August, reports were already filtering back to Washington detailing Frémont's political ineptitude, military incompetence, high-handed behavior, and reclusiveness. "Save us," John Howe begged Postmaster General Montgomery Blair, "and remove Frémont."[11] The Pathfinder was turning out to be a disaster.

In what looked like a desperate bid to save his collapsing command from the rising chorus of criticism—even from antislavery politicians who had recently been his strongest supporters—Frémont issued a proclamation on August 30 overturning civilian authority, declaring martial law, confiscating the property of disloyal owners, and emancipating their slaves. To Gamble and his allies who were scrambling to construct a legitimate government in Missouri, Frémont's order amounted to a calculated assault on the principle of civilian rule. The general would "assume the administrative powers of the State." The "object" of his proclamation, Frémont admitted, was "to place in the hands of the military authorities the power to give instantaneous effect to existing laws." In the parts of Missouri occupied by secessionist forces—a line extending from Cape Girardeau on the Mississippi River all the way to Leavenworth—Frémont declared that anyone "taken with arms" would be tried by court-martial "and if found guilty will be shot." This was martial law, and though there were few who doubted that it was legal or that the crisis in Missouri justified the imposition of a firm federal hand, there were many—not least the president—who thought it imprudent to go around executing Confederate prisoners.[12]

Frémont also ordered the emancipation of all slaves owned by rebellious masters. The Confiscation Act signed by the president a few weeks earlier applied only to those slaves used in support of the rebellion, although the War Department's implementation instructions freed all slaves coming voluntarily within Union lines. Frémont's order would have emancipated the slaves of "all persons in the state of Missouri who shall take up arms against the United States"—whether or not they had allowed their slaves to be used in support of the rebellion and regardless of whether the slaves were inside Union lines. In theory Frémont's edict would have freed more slaves than the Confiscation Act, but fewer perhaps than the War Department's August 8 instructions implementing the law.[13]

On September 3, four days after Frémont declared martial law in Missouri, Lincoln wrote him a brief, private note urging the general to "modify" his order to conform to the Confiscation Act. That should have been the end of it. Instead, Frémont arrogantly refused to do what Lincoln asked unless directly ordered to do so. On September 11, Lincoln bowed to Frémont's wishes and ordered him to modify his proclamation. The president "perceived no general objection" to martial law, property confiscation, or emancipation. He did worry, however, that if Union generals began shooting Confederate prisoners, the Confederates would retaliate by shooting Union prisoners, "and so, man for man, indefinitely." Accordingly, Lincoln told Frémont not to order any executions "without first having my approbation or consent." Nor was Lincoln opposed, in principle, to confiscating the property and emancipating the slaves of "traitorous" owners. But Frémont's order did not establish the judicial procedures that Congress had established for the confiscation of rebel property as spelled out in the first section of the Confiscation Act, nor did it specify the scope of emancipation called for in the fourth section of the Confiscation Act. Frémont's order "appeared to me objectionable," Lincoln explained, "in its non-conformity to the Act of Congress passed the 6th of last August." Lincoln therefore ordered Frémont to "modify" his order "so as to conform to the *first* and *fourth* sections" of the Confiscation Act passed by Congress a few weeks earlier.[14]

It was a relatively modest request, but it was based on objections far more substantive than Lincoln was prepared to spell out to the general himself. Most seriously, Frémont was making political decisions that were not properly the province of the military—or as the president put it, the general's order was "not within the range of *military* law, or necessity." This was true of both the property confiscation and the emancipation orders. Lincoln understood that under the laws of war a commander could, if he "finds a necessity," seize enemy property and use it for "as long as the necessity lasts." But military law did not allow a general to determine the ultimate disposition of property once the necessity ended. It was a well-established constitutional principle that property confiscated for treason could not be withheld from the traitor's heirs, for that would work "corruption of blood." In other words, Frémont's order violated the constitutional ban on attainder. Similarly, under the laws of war, army officers could impress slaves as a military necessity, but they had no authority to determine the ultimate status of the slaves they impressed. That was a political question, Lincoln pointed out, one that "must be settled according to laws made by law-makers, and not by military proclamations." Frémont's order was therefore not military but *purely political* and as such beyond his authority. Congress was perfectly within its right to pass a law confiscating the slaves of all disloyal masters, Lincoln explained, and if he were a member of Congress he might well vote for it. But it was for lawmakers not generals to decide the "permanent future condition" of the slaves. Generals cannot make such decisions. Frémont's proclamation "is simply 'dictatorship,'" Lincoln added. "It assumes that the general may do *anything* he pleases." As a legal issue, the dispute between Frémont and the president was not about slavery; it was about civilian rule.[15]

Lincoln's gravest concerns, however, had less to do with the sanctity of civilian rule in Missouri than with the integrity of the Union in Kentucky.

THE INVASION OF KENTUCKY

On September 1, two days after Frémont issued his decree, Joshua Speed wrote to his old friend Lincoln warning of the dire consequences Frémont's order would have in Kentucky. Speed's letter could not have reached Washington by the time Lincoln wrote his first note to Frémont on September 3. But when the president wrote his second letter to the general, on September 11, things had changed considerably. The southern army, hoping to rally popular support that would bring the state into the Confederacy, had invaded Kentucky on September 3. Under the circumstances, Kentucky unionists became alarmed that news of Frémont's emancipation edict would dampen support for the North. The danger of Frémont's order was not that it would free slaves in Missouri, but that it would bolster secessionists in Kentucky.

Kentucky voters had been divided over secession, and as in Maryland and Missouri, geography told some of the story. Not all of Kentucky was slave country. The mountainous eastern counties had few slaves and many devoted unionists, as did Louisville—a prosperous Ohio River city with a growing immigrant population and strong economic ties to the North. Unlike Maryland and Missouri, however, Kentucky slaves were not concentrated in certain counties or along the river bottoms but were instead spread broadly over the countryside on farms that were relatively small by the standards of the cotton belt. To be sure, there was little opposition to slavery in Kentucky and considerable sympathy with the southern cause. As in Maryland, the most ardent southern sympathizers, like John Breckinridge, ended up defecting to the Confederacy, and thirty-five thousand Kentuckians eventually did the same. But unionism—even if it was proslavery unionism—was stronger than secessionism. Seventy thousand Kentuckians would fight for the North. The ingredients for a Missouri-style internal collapse were there—a secessionist legislature flew the Confederate flag at Russellville—but the mixture wasn't nearly as combustible. The Union commander, Major General Robert Anderson (of Fort Sumter fame), was patient where Nathaniel Lyon had been aggressive. Kentucky's Governor Beriah Magoffin was a southern sympathizer, but he was no Claiborne Jackson. And far from preparing for war, Kentucky's legislature was determined to maintain the state's neutrality.[16]

For five months northern and southern troops had fitfully respected Kentucky's neutral status. Kentucky families were torn apart by divided loyalties, Confederate armies brutally suppressed unionists in the eastern mountains, but Kentuckians did not make war on each other the way Missourians did. No Union troops marched provocatively through Kentucky as they had through Maryland. General Anderson had been careful to keep his Yankee regiments across the Ohio River in Cincinnati, safely removed from Kentucky soil. In June of 1861, Kentucky voters went to the polls and elected a slate of unionists to represent their state in the special session of Congress scheduled to convene in July. But if Kentuckians thought they had succeeded in avoiding the war, they were soon disabused. By late August the signs were everywhere that the state's neutrality was untenable. Union forces were converging on Cairo, Illinois, in preparation for an assault on Columbus, Kentucky. In Tennessee a large Confederate army was amassing for the same purpose. Kentucky was about to be invaded, and everybody knew it.[17]

Imagine what the Border States must have looked like to Lincoln in late August and early September as he watched anxiously from Washington. In Missouri, Confederate General Sterling Price, flush with his victory over Union forces at Wilson's Creek a few weeks earlier, was hurtling northward unimpeded with his fifteen thousand troops preparing to lay siege to Lexington. Huddled inside his mansion fortress in St. Louis, Frémont was paralyzed even as Missouri seemed on the verge of collapse. In Maryland it took the heavy hand of Union troops to check the secessionist sympathizers in the state legislature. Meanwhile, Confederate forces were preparing to march into Kentucky from Tennessee. If any one of the Border States fell into the Confederacy, the rest might topple out of the Union like dominoes, and the war would be lost. That's when the South invaded Kentucky. In early September Confederate General Leonidas Polk moved his troops into the state and occupied Columbus, strategically situated on the Mississippi River at a terminus of the Mobile & Ohio Railroad. Polk and Confederate leaders in Richmond, including President Jefferson Davis, were confident that with its 225,000 slaves, Kentucky's interest lay with the Confederacy.

It was the imminent Confederate invasion that prompted the letters from Kentucky condemning Frémont's order in Missouri. Frémont's "foolish" proclamation "will hurt us in Ky.," Speed wrote to Lincoln. With the Confederates preparing to attack, Kentucky was already in a state of high military alert; at the very moment Union commanders were trying to organize Kentucky regiments to fight for the North, Frémont's order threatened to "crush out every vestige of a union party in the state." More dire warnings followed. Frémont's order "will be condemned by a large majority of Legislature & people of Kentucky." "We are much troubled about Frémont's proclamation," came another complaint from Frankfort. The "power and fervor of the loyalty of Kentucky" might "at this moment be abated or killed" by Frémont's proclamation, warned Joseph Holt. But the most disturbing message of all was the one General Anderson sent. While busily raising troops to repel the Confederate invasion, Anderson became alarmed by reports that an entire company of soldiers "threw down their arms and disbanded" upon learning of Frémont's proclamation. Anderson predicted that if the emancipation order was not "immediately disavowed and annulled, Kentucky will be lost to the Union." Here was the thing that most concerned Lincoln—that Kentucky would be "lost to the Union."[18]

In Lincoln's mind the issue was this simple: if Kentucky secedes, the North cannot win the war. The president was therefore especially alarmed by Anderson's report. Arms sent to Kentucky for the defense of the Union "would be turned against us," Lincoln concluded, if Frémont's orders were allowed to stand. Lincoln did not doubt that many northerners supported Frémont despite the illegality of his edict. But what good would that do if it led to the complete dissolution of the Union, which was bound to happen if Kentucky seceded? "I think to lose Kentucky is nearly the same as to lose the whole game," Lincoln explained. "Kentucky gone, we can not hold Missouri, nor, as I think, Maryland. These all against us, and the job on our hands is too large for us. We may as well consent to separation at once, including the surrender of this capitol."[19]

As it turned out, there was less cause for alarm than Lincoln feared. The half dozen or so Kentucky protests against Frémont were mere squawks compared to the howls Kentuckians aimed at Confederate authorities in Richmond. Jefferson Davis had badly miscalculated. Far from welcoming the southern troops as liberators, "the people of Kentucky are profoundly astonished that such an act should have been committed by the Confederate States." Both houses of the Kentucky legislature endorsed resolutions "requiring [the] governor of Kentucky to issue [a] proclamation ordering off Confederate troops." Southern leaders were stunned. General Polk felt compelled to draft a defensive response justifying the Confederate action. Tennessee's governor warned that the invasion of Kentucky was a disaster for the Confederate cause, and urged "immediate withdrawal." Authorities in Richmond scrambled to undo the damage. Confederate troops under General Gideon Pillow were ordered to withdraw from Kentucky on the grounds that the movement was "wholly unauthorized" by Richmond. Davis explained that the invasion was a purely "defensive measure" prompted by military necessity and would be "limited by the existence of such necessity." Politically, the Confederate invasion had backfired.[20]

But so did Lincoln's order modifying Frémont's proclamation. When Illinois Senator Orville Browning saw what the president had done, he shot off a blistering rebuke. A week earlier Browning had scribbled a telegram to Lincoln saying that "Fremont's proclamation was necessary, and will do good." Excitable by nature, Browning grew more heated as the days passed. It was true, he wrote, that there was "no express, written law, authorizing" what Frémont had done. But "war is never carried on, and can never be, in strict accordance with previously adjusted constitutional and legal provisions." Why, he asked, are you willing to shoot disloyal masters but not free their slaves? "Is a traitor's negro more sacred than his life?" Whatever the order had done to calm down the slaveholders in Missouri and Kentucky, it had done much to upset the loyal men and women of Illinois.[21]

Browning's notes were but early warnings of the blizzard of protests provoked by Lincoln's order to Frémont. Even before word of the president's action was made public, an Iowa citizen warned Lincoln that the rumor that Frémont's proclamation "is not to be sustained . . . causes *extreme* dissatisfaction—If true it will suspend volunteering." Caleb Smith, Lincoln's interior secretary, got the same warning: If Frémont "is abandoned by the administration the people will take him up & will abandon the war. The feeling is intense in this direction." When the rumors were confirmed with the public release of the president's order to Frémont, the cloud finally burst and a storm of angry letters poured in from across the North, most of the ire directed at Lincoln. Frémont's repudiation "will produce such a shock to the present energy of the western army, as will almost paralyze it," an Indiana man wrote. Frémont's proclamation was "the very thing to save our Government," wrote a Union soldier from Illinois, whereas Lincoln's order "to Countermand a part of his proclamation Seems to be a Death blow to Our freedom and Independence." A group of Michigan citizens "resolved that we fully approve of the recent Proclamation of Major General John C. Frémont confiscating the slave property of rebels in Missouri." Thomas Little swore that he had never been an abolitionist, but he was "one of thousands who have changed views very much," he explained in his letter to the president, "& I just want to say that your letter to Gen Fremont in regard to his proclamation will occasion great dissatisfaction to multitudes of us." J. C. Woods was more blunt: "Either Fremonts proclamation or the South will win. Take your choice." From Kalamazoo, Michigan: "You can heardly imagine the thrill of *pain* that you have sent through many Christian hearts, by *revoking* that *ritcheous proclamation* of Gen. John

C. Fremont. . . . The rebellion can never be put down till slavery is uprooted." From Illinois: "Had you a Brother in Mo. as I have . . . I think you would feel that Freemont was all right—I do earnestly pray God to forgive you." And so on. These were not the complaints of a handful of radicals; they appear to have come from across the Republican spectrum—from church and civic groups, for example, and from conservatives like Browning. As evidence of what Lincoln had done, or of his sentiments regarding emancipation, the letters tell us almost nothing. As testimony of the depth of emancipationist sentiment in the North, however, they are extremely revealing. Whatever else Lincoln was doing about slavery in the first eighteen months of the war, he was not waiting for public opinion to catch up with him.[22]

For all the accolades he won from outside of Missouri, Frémont's support among unionists inside the state continued to plummet. Demands for his ouster had begun arriving weeks before his proclamation, and they did not stop after it. The most devastating attacks came from antislavery Republicans, like Salmon Chase and David Hunter, some of whom had once been among Frémont's staunchest supporters. Frank Blair Jr. had written from Missouri, urging Lincoln to dismiss Frémont as early as September 1. Back in Washington, Postmaster General Montgomery Blair took up the anti-Frémont cause. He singled out Frémont's emancipation edict as "the best thing of the kind that has been issued but should have been issued when he first came when he had the power to enforce it & the enemy no power to retaliate." It was also in Blair's view an exception to Frémont's otherwise disastrous administration. Both Blairs had come to the conclusion that Frémont's administration was so corrupt and incompetent that he had to be fired. When Lincoln sent David Hunter (who would later issue an even broader abolition order of his own) to investigate the charges, he wrote back confirming the worst: Frémont was inaccessible, dictatorial, and surrounded by toadies and corruptionists. "You may be very sure that if Genl F. is recalled from his high command," Salmon Chase wrote to an Ohio friend in early November, "his Proclamn. will not be the cause." However good "in itself," Chase explained, Frémont's order "was an act of insubordination." Chase's antislavery credentials were impeccable, and he was arguably more committed to abolition than anyone else in the cabinet. Yet merely "declaring the slaves of rebels free, frees nobody," Chase argued. In any case, if Frémont were to be fired, it would be for incompetence, not for favoring emancipation. Lincoln waited to give Frémont one more chance to redeem himself by beating back the Confederate military invasion, but when he failed at that, the president finally relieved the Pathfinder of his command.[23]

SOLDIERS AND SLAVES

For as long as there was slavery, there were slaves who took advantage of war and civil strife to break for their freedom in any way they could. The slaves in the Border States were no exception. The political instability and military insecurity caused by the outbreak of the Civil War created ideal conditions for slaves to press for their freedom. Indeed, escaping slaves were not merely responding to disruption—to a large extent they *were* the disruption. Union army commanders had to respond, but it was not clear how. By long-standing federal policy, the government in Washington enforced the fugitive slave clause and the Union army acted accordingly. The Republicans who took power and began making policy in July of 1861 started from a very different premise: even if the federal government was supposed to enforce the fugitive slave clause—which most Republicans doubted—the Union army was not. Veteran officers (and Democratic generals) were sometimes slower than new recruits to appreciate the implications of the Republican takeover of the federal government. Then, too, it took longer for Republicans to formulate an antislavery policy for the Border States that was as clear-cut as the contraband policy they applied early on to the seceded states. As a result, different Union commanders responded differently to the chaotic military and political conditions in the Border States, and slaves who claimed their freedom by running to Union lines often found themselves embroiled in conflicts between soldiers and officers over how to deal with runaways—and the slave owners who came looking for them.[24]

On June 10, 1861, six slaves from Howard County, Maryland, escaped to nearby Washington, where they found a regiment of Union soldiers from Connecticut. Clearly aware of the politics of the sectional crisis, the fugitives declared—or so a Union officer reported— that their masters were "secessionists in sentiment and opinion and members of secret military organizations hostile to the Government." The runaways thereby created a dilemma for Alfred H. Terry, the colonel in charge of the regiment. Maryland was a loyal state, yet many of the state's slaveholders sympathized with the South. If what the fugitives were saying was correct, could Colonel Terry send them back to their traitorous owners? Slaves in Kentucky made the same claim under similar circumstances. In November, shortly after Union troops arrived in the state, ten runaways appeared at Camp Nevin claiming that "there masters are rank Secessionists, in some cases are in the rebel army—and that Slaves of union men are pressed into service" for the Confederates. Like his Maryland counterpart, the Union commander in Kentucky, Brigadier General Alexander McD. McCook, was not sure how to respond. Despite the pro-southern sympathies of many of the state's slaveholders, Kentucky had not seceded from the Union. McCook had "no faith in Kentucky's loyalty" but no particular interest in helping slaves escape, especially if it might weaken the unionists in the states. What, he asked his superiors, was he supposed to do? Slaves often had good reason to believe that their master's disloyalty would justify their emancipation. During the first summer of the war, a black woman who "absconded the premises of her master" was captured and returned to her owner, only to run away a second time. Brought before a provost judge, she "complained of certain bad treatment from her master." Her owner, having refused to swear his loyalty to the Union, was barred from testifying. The slave "was liberated and her master sentenced to be incarcerated."[25]

Denouncing their masters as "secessionists" was only one of the ways escaping slaves tailored their biographies to suit the criteria for freedom established by different Union commanders in different Border States. Where Union troops were under orders to exclude slaves from their camps, fugitives often presented themselves as free blacks. In late 1861, Major George Waring examined the blacks working in a Union army camp in Rolla, Missouri, and found "they all stoutly asserted that they were free." Unable to disprove their claim, though he realized it could not possibly have been true, Waring was unwilling to risk expelling free blacks. By claiming they were already free, the refugees evaded the order to keep "fugitive slaves" from Union camps.[26]

Slaves often provided northern troops with important military intelligence about the location of rebel troops or their supply depots, and Union officers were extremely reluctant to turn over such slaves to their owners. Two slaves in Fulton, Missouri—to give but one example—proved such useful guides and had provided so much "valuable information" to the Union army that General John M. Schofield "permitted them to remain under the protection of our troops. To drive them from the camp," he explained, "would subject them to severe punishment, perhaps death." Beyond the immediate value of slaves who provided military intelligence, there was the increasingly urgent question of the military value of slaves to the rebels. "Every negro returned to these traitors adds strength to their cause," one Missourian explained to the secretary of war in December of 1861. Why, he wondered, would the U.S. Army waste precious resources "hunting up & guarding the slaves of traitors while the secessionists are robbing & plundering loyal men in the western part of the state?"[27]

Union soldiers in the Border States were clearly cooperating with the slaves, refusing to turn them over to their owners and hiding them in camps, sometimes with and sometimes without the support of their immediate superiors. Having come of age during the 1850s, many Yankee soldiers had shared the horror and dismay as "slave-catchers" roamed the streets of northern towns and cities. Recruits came into the Union army in 1861 from a society that had just passed through a decade of protracted debate over slavery and emancipation. Many—if not most—went South assuming that slavery had caused the war, and most were at least familiar with the commonplace Republican prediction that slaves would run for freedom to invading Union troops. So it was hardly surprising that once they got to the South, northern soldiers were enraged by the spectacle of slaveholders and their agents prowling through Union army camps in search of runaways.[28]

From the earliest weeks of the war, there were reports that owners looking for fugitives felt "menaced" by Union troops, especially in Maryland. Slaveholders repeatedly complained that they were harassed when they entered Union camps in search of their runaway slaves. In November of 1861 a Maryland master showed up at a Union camp near Annapolis in search of a "servant, that had left him." But upon entering the camp, the owner was surrounded, or so he claimed, by "quite a number" of soldiers who threatened him "and applied opprobrious Epithets" such as "Negro stealer" and "Negro catchers," until "he was obliged to leave the ground, without looking for his servant." The same thing happened to A. J. Smoot, another Maryland master who went to Camp Fenton looking for a teenage boy who had escaped to the Union army camp. Smoot said that when his mission became "general known" among the soldiers, "a large crowd collected and followed me crying shoot him, bayonet him, kill him, pitch him out, the nigger Stealer the nigger driver." The verbal taunts were supplemented by "a continued shower of stones." Richard Green likewise went looking for a runaway slave at a Union camp in Montgomery County, Maryland, "but was driven out and was not permitted to look for him." Two months later Green went back and found his runaway, but when he "attempted to take him out," Green declared, "a large crowd got around him and knocked him about throwing small stones and dirt at him and otherwise ill treating him and finally driving him out of the camp without allowing him to take his Negro." In Fulton, Missouri, a "gentleman" who tried to retrieve a slave from a Union camp was "repulsed by an *officer* who threatened to shoot him if he persisted."[29] Nor was antislavery intransigence restricted to enlisted men. There were numerous complaints against Union officers who were at best indifferent to masters who came looking for their slaves. The Maryland owner who had been subjected to a "shower of stones" gave up his search when he realized that the Union officer accompanying him "took no notice of what was going on." A Missouri master who asked "for permission to recover his negro" claimed he was "rudely refused" by a Union colonel. When another master was surrounded by a "large crowd of Soldiers" shouting, "Bayonet him, Drum him out," the colonel in charge of the outfit calmly told the owner that "the best thing he could do would be to get on his horse & leave the camp," which he did—"and did not get his negro."[30]

Just as slaves developed strategies for evading the rules excluding them from Union military camps in the Border States, northern soldiers proved ingenious at thwarting slave-catchers. Some of these strategies were clearly holdovers from the fugitive slave crises of the previous decade. Many northern states had passed "personal liberty laws" ensuring the rights of due process for all accused runaways. Northern officers sometimes brought the same standard with them into southern army camps. Colonel Henry Briggs informed masters "that I shall neither give nor permit those in my command to give *aid* in the rendition of slaves beyond that required under due process of law." Union officers often demanded proof of ownership before they would release blacks to anyone coming into a camp claiming a slave. Slave-catchers were likewise required to prove that they were legally authorized to act as "agents" of masters who sent them.[31]

Union soldiers had moral as well as mundane objections to sending fugitives back to their owners. Commanded "to turn out from my camp any colored servant that may be claimed as a slave," Colonel Briggs asked "to be relieved from the order" on the grounds that it would "violate my conscience" to follow it. Under similar orders in Missouri, Major Waring announced to his commanding officer "my private feelings revolt" at the practice. Besides, Waring added, there were very real practical considerations to keep in mind. Blacks working as teamsters for the Union army or as personal servants to individual soldiers needed those jobs; without them they "would be homeless and helpless." Moreover, the loss of "our servants" would be a great "personal inconvenience" to the officers and soldiers who employed them.[32]

Fugitives who arrived accusing their masters of treason, or claiming they were free blacks; common soldiers repelled by the spectacle of slave-catchers scouring their camps; local officers unwilling to turn away slaves who provided the Union army with valuable intelligence—how could Union generals formulate a policy that would not "interfere" with slavery in the Border States when it was clear that slaves would keep running to Union lines and that soldiers within those lines could not be counted on to send the slaves back?

FORMULATING FEDERAL POLICY IN THE BORDER STATES

Because slavery was still formally protected by the Constitution in the Border States, Republican policymakers claimed that the federal government could not emancipate slaves escaping to Union lines from loyal owners in loyal states. On the other hand, as of July in 1861, Republican policymakers made it clear that they did not want the Union army to be involved in the capture and return of fugitive slaves in any states, whether loyal or disloyal. Likewise, slaves used to support the rebellion were emancipated, no matter where they came from—a rule that specifically included slaves escaping into the Border States from seceded states. Faced with a plethora of different, often complicated policies dribbling out of Washington, Union commanders found it difficult to issue consistent orders. Nevertheless, the war was not only disrupting slavery on the ground in the Border States but also allowing Republican policymakers to take a more aggressive approach to slavery than they could have taken in peacetime.

For a short while at the outset of the war, administration officials in Washington and Union commanders in the field tried to protect slavery in the Border States. In May of 1861 General William S. Harney, Frémont's predecessor in the West, had "no doubt whatever" that the government's policy was to protect slave property in Missouri. In one extraordinary case, even Lincoln, responding to intense pressure from Maryland Congressman Charles Calvert, quietly suggested to General in Chief Winfield Scott that owners of slaves escaping from Maryland should be allowed "to bring back those which have crossed" the Potomac with Union troops. Orders followed swiftly, first from the assistant adjutant general to the commander of the Department of Washington and then, one day later, from the commander himself: "Fugitive slaves will under no pretext whatever be permitted to reside or be in any way harbored in the quarters and camps of troops serving in this department." Embarrassed by his own request, Lincoln instructed Scott to ensure that it could not be traced back to the president. Never before, and never again thereafter, did Lincoln order anyone in the U.S. military to return escaped slaves to their owners. Indeed, the order was an anomaly, as well as a violation of his own stated principles. By early July Lincoln and his fellow Republicans in Congress made it clear that as a matter of principle, Union soldiers should not participate in the capture and return of runaway slaves.[33]

But even after July, escaping slaves were sent back to their owners in Kentucky. There General William Tecumseh Sherman returned even slaves whose masters were "rank Secessionists." In mid-October, when two slaves escaped to a Union army camp near Louisville and the owner appealed for help, Sherman declared that the laws of the United States and of Kentucky "compel us to surrender a runaway negro on application of the negro's owner or agent." Sherman's orders were unambiguous: "All negroes shall be delivered up on claim of the owner or agent." As a general rule, Sherman added, it is "better to keep the negroes out of your camp altogether." He repeated his order a few weeks later after learning that ten slaves had escaped to Camp Nevin. Because Kentucky had not seceded, the laws of the state of Kentucky "are in full force," Sherman explained. Therefore, "negroes must be surrendered on application of their masters or agents or delivered over to the sheriff of the County." In one sense Sherman was correct: the civil authorities in Kentucky were functioning, and it was a loyal state so its slave laws were still in force. But was it the business of the Union army to enforce those laws?[34]

In July of 1861, Attorney General Edward Bates emphatically declared that because Missouri remained a state within the Union, the fugitive slave law—like every other law—was still applicable. "The insurrectory disorders in Missouri are but individual crimes and do not change the legal status of the State nor change its rights and obligations as a member of the Union."[35] Bates, at least, believed that the Fugitive Slave Act of 1850 should be enforced in the Border States. However, the clarity of Bates's assertion masked the complexity of the issue. Who was responsible for enforcing the Fugitive Slave Act? On the principle that freedom was national, most Republicans believed that laws relating to slavery should be enforced not by the federal government but by local civil and judicial authorities. Technically, the fugitive slave clause of the Constitution did nothing more than allow owners to reclaim runaway slaves who had crossed state lines. It did not specify who was responsible for reclaiming runaways, nor did it apply at all to slaves escaping *within* a state. The Fugitive Slave Act of 1850 transferred enforcement to a cadre of federal commissioners, and for that very reason most Republicans wanted the law revised, and many wanted it repealed. But even under the 1850 statute, federal commissioners were civilian rather than military officials, and by the time Bates scribbled that entry in his diary, Republicans had already agreed that capturing and returning fugitive slaves was, in the words of Owen Lovejoy's House resolution of July 9, not the "duty" of the Union army or navy—not even in the Border States.

As of August 8, 1861, federal policy was to leave enforcement of the fugitive slave clause in the Border States entirely to the local government. According to Secretary of War Simon Cameron, this is precisely what distinguished the Union's fugitive slave policy in the loyal states from that in the seceded states. In the disloyal states the federal government was officially emancipating slaves who voluntarily escaped to Union lines; in the Border States, slavery still operated within the Constitution, and for Republicans that restricted the federal government's power to emancipate fugitives. In Cameron's words, "[N]o question can arise as to fugitives from service within States and Territories in which the authority of the Union is fully acknowledged." But Cameron was not saying that the federal government was responsible for enforcing the fugitive slave clause. On the contrary, where local "civil authorities" were still functioning, he explained, the problem of fugitive slaves could be dealt with by "the ordinary forms of judicial proceedings." Those civilian authorities "must be respected" by Union officers and soldiers. In short, Cameron's August 8 instructions implied that enforcement of the fugitive slave clause in the Border States was the responsibility of those same states rather than the federal government, and of civilian authorities rather than the Union army. Union officers and soldiers who violated this policy by returning fugitive slaves to their owners were excoriated by Republican editors and politicians and often rebuked by their commanders.[36]

Did Cameron's August 8 instructions mean that the First Confiscation Act, including its emancipation provisions, applied to the Border States? Nothing in the congressional debates or in the text of the statute indicates that Republican congressmen were thinking about the Border States when they passed the law. They had instituted military emancipation under the laws of war, but the Union was not at war with the Border States. At that point Missouri was the only Border State in which Confederate troops had engaged in battle with the Union army. The August 8 instructions were designed to clarify the status of fugitive slaves "in States in insurrection against the Federal Government."[37] On the other hand, the instructions had exempted only those areas in which federal authority was "fully acknowledged." Given the state of military and political affairs in Maryland, Kentucky, and Missouri, it would be hard to claim that federal authority in the Border States was "fully acknowledged." When, decades earlier, John Quincy Adams first declared that under some circumstances the federal government could "interfere" with slavery in the states, what he had in mind was not full-scale civil war but the suppression of domestic insurrections. At various points in 1861, Union troops were actively engaged in suppressing domestic insurrections within three of the four Border States. So the question remained: Did the First Confiscation Act apply to the slave states that had remained loyal to the Union?

Whether deliberately or inadvertently, Lincoln settled the issue when he instructed General Frémont to rewrite his order to comply with the First Confiscation Act. The president thereby left no room for doubt that as far as he was concerned, the laws of war did apply to Missouri. That much was settled. But precisely what did Lincoln expect Frémont to do? Under Section 4 of the First Confiscation Act, slave owners merely forfeited the services of slaves used in the rebellion. Is that all Lincoln intended? Or did the president mean to apply the much broader August 8 War Department instructions, thereby emancipating all slaves who came voluntarily within Union lines in the Border States? Republicans justified military emancipation on the grounds that the disloyal states forfeited all constitutional protection of slavery when they seceded. The August 8 instructions held out the prospect of compensation for loyal masters whose slaves had been freed. Were Union officers in the Border States expected to recognize the distinction between loyalty and disloyalty, whether of states or individuals? Lincoln did not expressly say. For the time being, the Union army was on its own.

"NEITHER NEGRO CATCHERS NOR NEGRO THIEVES"

Northern generals in the Border States interpreted Lincoln's policy to mean two different things. First, when slaves came into Union lines, soldiers would distinguish between those who had been put to work for the Confederates and those who had not. Even General McClellan, who had so ostentatiously vowed to uphold the property rights of slaveholders, now ordered his men to inquire into the origins of slaves arriving at their camps. Union officers should "ascertain the nature of the employment of the negroes in question while amongst the enemy," McClellan explained. "If they or any of them have been employed for military purposes, those so employed will be detained by you for such labor as the public policy may offer."[38] This was the standard established by the First Confiscation Act: slaves used in support of the rebellion would not be returned to their owners. It quickly came to mean distinguishing between the slaves of loyal and disloyal owners.

This left unanswered the question of what Union soldiers should do with the slaves of loyal owners in the loyal slave states. Policymakers in Washington were clear that the Union army should not involve itself in the capture and return of fugitive slaves under any circumstances. In response Union generals devised a second approach to slavery in the Border States. In the vernacular of the times, Union soldiers would be "neither negro catchers, nor negro thieves." The Union army would not enforce the Fugitive Slave Act anywhere in the Border States, but soldiers would never be put in the position of having to enforce it because fugitive slaves would not be allowed into Union camps. The soldiers would not serve as "slave-catchers" for southern masters, but neither could they become "slave thieves" by admitting fugitives into the protection of Union camps. This formula was sufficiently vague that both proslavery and antislavery generals could embrace it with enthusiasm. On August 8, 1861, Major General John Dix, one of the northern commanders most determined to defend the slaveholders' rights of property, nevertheless declared that Union soldiers in Maryland would be "neither negro-stealers nor negro catchers." Two months later in Missouri, James Lane, the ferociously antislavery senator who now commanded the "Kansas Brigade," echoed Dix's sentiment. The men of his unit, Lane vowed, "shall not become negro thieves nor shall they be prostituted into negro catchers."[39]

The first and most obvious of the many problems arising from these two policies was that they contradicted one another. What was the point of ascertaining whether slaves coming to Union camps had been used in the rebellion if all slaves were to be excluded anyway? Conversely, what was the point of a general rule excluding slaves if those used in support of the rebellion had to be admitted to Union camps? "Neither slave catchers nor slave thieves" seemed a simple rule of thumb, but in practice it provoked all sorts of conflicts. If exclusion relieved Union soldiers of any obligation to return fugitives to their owners, it also meant the expulsion of slaves who had escaped to Union camps.

Not surprisingly, more than a few of the officers and soldiers objected to the idea of turning away fugitives, while some willingly assisted slaveholders in their attempts to recover fugitive slaves. Either way, Union commanders had trouble implementing the neither/nor policy. Dix wrote one letter after another ordering his officers to stop admitting slaves into their lines. Slaves who "came to us," he wrote, should always be sent away.[40] When his officers complained that they found the idea of returning slaves to their owners objectionable, Dix repeatedly answered that if runaway slaves were denied admission to begin with, no soldier would ever be asked to return fugitives to their owners. The whole point of the policy, Dix explained, was to prevent the issue of fugitive rendition from arising. In Missouri, General Ulysses S. Grant could not enforce the rule because his own troops, treating official orders "with contempt," continued to hide slaves running to their lines. Sometimes commanders issued orders to assist in the recapture of fugitives, knowing full well that the orders were unenforceable. It did not take long for Union commanders to realize that without the cooperation of rankand-file soldiers there was little they could do to control the flow of slaves into their camps, no matter what policy was announced from on high.[41]

The generals themselves were divided over what to do. In late November of 1861, General Joseph Hooker "accepted sixty or seventy run away negroes" in his camp. Hooker wrote asking for instructions from General McClellan. In compliance with the Confiscation Act, McClellan instructed Hooker to inquire into the background of the fugitives and exclude all those who had not been used in support of the rebellion. But Hooker did not bother to wait for McClellan's reply. Rather than turn away any slaves, he sent the women to Washington and put the men to work. Though he agreed to comply with McClellan's instructions in the future, Hooker was clearly unwilling to do so because the fugitives had furnished him with "information concerning the rebels I had not before learned." General William Tecumseh Sherman gravitated toward the opposite extreme, insisting well into the second year of the war that under both U.S. and Kentucky law, Union soldiers were obliged to return fugitive slaves to their owners. Sherman's views were clearly different from those of General Henry W. Halleck, who insisted that Union soldiers should never be used to enforce state laws protecting slavery. In one case, acting on the constitutional presumption of universal freedom, Halleck ordered the release of sixteen slaves held in the St. Louis city jail by the sheriff, who had planned to sell them. Still other generals, like Grant, made inconsistent rulings based on their shifting understanding of official policy.[42]

Given the inconsistency within the Union army in the Border States, it was inevitable that disputed cases would make their way up the chain of command to officials in Washington. When they did, the antislavery bias of federal policymakers became clear. One of Secretary of War Cameron's favorite tactics—the dodge of many a determined bureaucrat—was to ignore requests for assistance from officers inclined to protect slavery. This drove General Dix to distraction. On August 8, he wrote to the secretary asking for clarification of the administration's policy regarding fugitives who were successfully escaping onto Union ships docked in Maryland. "To this letter I have received no answer," Dix grumbled to his superiors nearly two weeks later. Meanwhile, the captain of a Union navy vessel continued to accept the fugitives. After repeatedly ordering the ship's captain to turn the fugitives away, Dix soon discovered that his instructions were being countermanded by the secretary of the Treasury, Salmon Chase. In frustration Dix appealed instead to General McClellan, who likewise declined to respond. By the end of 1861, Dix's repeated orders were becoming pointless. In November he instructed Colonel H. E. Paine of the Fourth Wisconsin Volunteers to "do all in your power to correct the misapprehension" that this was a war against slavery. Dix insisted that the sole "mission" of the army was to "uphold the Government" against treason. "Multitudes are laboring under delusions—the fruits of misrepresentations and falsehood"—that this was also a war against slavery. "You will take especial care not to interfere in any manner with persons held to servitude, and in order that there may be no cause for misrepresentation or cavil you will not receive or allow any negro to come within your lines."[43]

The secretary of war's reluctance to do anything to sustain slavery was clear in his response to the demands made by Congressman Calvert. In July of 1861, the congressman wrote to Cameron informing him that Union soldiers in Maryland were making "tempting offers" to slaves, encouraging their escape. "I know it is not the desire of the Government to encourage the escapes of this Species of property from the lawful owner," Calvert wrote. The congressman "most respectfully" requested that Cameron order all Union commanders in Maryland to stop enticing slaves into their camps. Although enticement was prohibited by his own policy, Cameron tried to put the senator off. The "pressure of business," he wrote, "has prevented any definite action in the premises." Calvert persisted. In mid-July he wrote another letter to Cameron asking that blacks attempting to board railway cars in Maryland be checked by the Union army, and for assistance in the recapture of one of his own slaves as well as a neighbor's runaway. Under such intense pressure from an aggressive member of Congress, Cameron relented and issued the orders Calvert asked for. But this was a classic case of an exception proving the rule.[44]

In most cases Cameron responded to pressure by tilting in favor of emancipation, if only because so much of that pressure came from the opponents of slavery. If Calvert demanded that the army respect the complaints of slaveholders, Republicans politicians were often quick to denounce the army for being too solicitous of the masters' interests. It was Cameron, for example, who had declined to block the ruling of a provost judge in Alexandria, Virginia, after he freed a slave who had testified that her master was abusive. When Union General W. R. Montgomery wrote Cameron to ask if such proceedings were proper, the secretary replied that he was "not disposed to interfere with the decisions of the Provost Judge" and that he had "no desire to set aside his action" in the case. Cameron's successor, Edwin M. Stanton, if anything was even less responsive than Cameron had been. In March of 1862, Maryland lawmakers were still complaining that the "loyal citizens" of the state, attempting to recover their runaway slaves from Union camps, "have been violently contravened in the legitimate pursuit of their property." The complaints of Maryland slaveholders "will receive his attention," Stanton wrote, "as soon as he is relieved from more pressing and important duties." By then, however, Congress had stepped in to clarify Union policy in the Border States.[45]

GENERAL ORDERS NO. 3

In November of 1861, General Halleck, who replaced Frémont as commander of the Department of the West, attempted to codify the new policy by issuing General Orders No. 3. His "intent" was a familiar one: Halleck wanted "to prevent any person in the Army from acting in the capacity of negro catcher, or negro stealer." The order was brief—a mere two paragraphs—but hopelessly ambiguous. In the first paragraph Halleck explained that a number of "fugitive slaves" who had been admitted to Union lines were subsequently providing information to the Confederates regarding the "numbers and condition of our forces." Hereafter "no such person" should be admitted into the camps of "any forces on the march." The second paragraph was more general. It instructed all Union officers to prevent "unauthorized persons of every description from entering and leaving our lines." A close reading of the order raises a host of questions. Who was being "excluded" from Union camps—"fugitive slaves" or "unauthorized persons"? And what were they excluded from—all Union lines, or the camps of Union forces "on the march"? However unclear the order was, it was immediately and widely read as a blanket exclusion of all slaves coming to Union lines. Union officers in the Border States began expelling blacks from their camps.[46]

In early November, Colonel G. M. Dodge, in command of a post at Rolla, had ordered the confiscation of the property and slaves of anyone whose whereabouts could not be ascertained, on the assumption that if they were not at home they must be away supporting the rebellion. "Be sure they are aiding the enemy," Dodge had written, "and then take all they have got." He qualified the order by warning his men to "[b]e careful in taking contraband negroes that their owners are aiding the enemy." Dodge was enforcing the Confiscation Act in Missouri. But a week after Halleck issued his General Orders No. 3, Dodge revised his own orders and told his officers to "immediately deliver to these Head Quarters, All fugitive slaves," and to forbid any more slaves "to enter and remain, within the Lines." Dodge did not turn any fugitive slaves over to their owners, but he did expel them from his camp.[47]

This was a violation of federal policy. In September, Lincoln had ordered Frémont to enforce the First Confiscation Act in the Border State of Missouri. At the very least, slaves used in rebellion were to be emancipated, not excluded from Union lines. That same month the War Department instructed General Dix to accept slaves escaping to the Border State of Maryland from the seceded state of Virginia. Similar orders were sent to Kentucky, where fugitives escaping from disloyal masters in Tennessee were making their way to Union camps.

On December 22, 1861, the adjutant general directed "that exceptions be made in regard to fugitives in such cases."[48]

Halleck understood that the First Confiscation Act applied to the Border States, and when he realized that his own officers were reading General Orders No. 3 as a blanket exclusion of all escaping slaves, he had to issue a series of clarifications. On December 4, 1861, he released General Orders No. 13, declaring martial law and spelling out the procedures for confiscating rebel property and emancipating slaves. "The laws of the United States confiscate the property of any master in a slave used for insurrectionary purposes."[49] Halleck believed he was enforcing the law as Congress had passed it. "Military officers do not make laws," he explained, "but they should obey and enforce them when made." As a legal scholar who had written an entire book on the laws of war, Halleck had no doubt that military emancipation was a legitimate wartime practice. "These orders may by some be regarded as severe, but they are certainly justified by the laws of war, and it is believed they are not only right, but necessary." He emphasized the point in a letter to Missouri Congressman Frank Blair Jr., which Blair read on the floor of the House of Representatives in December. General Orders No. 3, Halleck explained, was an attempt to comply with Congress's wishes, not to evade them. He was merely trying to implement the policy as best he could understand it, and was ready at any moment to draft a different set of orders should the policy change.[50] Halleck claimed that General Orders No. 3 excluded only "unauthorized persons" from Union camps, whether such persons were white or black, slave or free. Among those authorized to enter Union lines were free blacks working as wage laborers for the army and slaves emancipated under the terms of the First Confiscation Act. None of this was clear from his original order, however.

According to Halleck's clarification, masters who tried to retrieve their runaway slaves were "unauthorized" to enter Union camps. Major George Waring discovered this in December after reluctantly implementing what he believed was Halleck's general exclusion of fugitive slaves. Upon surveying the blacks working in his camp, Waring discovered that the mess cook was a slave claimed by one Captain Holland, who came into the camp waving a copy of Halleck's Orders No. 3. "In compliance with your order," Waring wrote, "she was given up to him." Waring was writing to explain why, for moral as well as practical reasons, he did not want to expel any of the others. But in his response Halleck actually upbraided Waring for allowing a slaveholder to enter a Union camp and retrieve a fugitive. "This is contrary to the intent of General Orders No. 3," Halleck explained. He had never suggested that blacks could not work inside Union army camps, nor were Union soldiers to participate in any way in the capture and return of fugitive slaves.[51]

Perhaps because they were in close contact, General Grant seemed to understand what Halleck was doing. Like most Union officers, Grant believed in civilian rule and was prepared to implement federal policy regardless of his personal feelings. His own position on slavery and the war was a familiar one. "If it is necessary that slavery should fall that the Republic may continue its existence," he wrote to his father, "let slavery go." But he did not believe he had any authority to make policy on slavery, and so his own treatment of fugitives moved with the movement of his superiors. After Frémont issued his emancipation edict in Missouri, Grant issued his own orders to enforce it, but once Lincoln rebuked Frémont, Grant reversed himself. He prohibited his men from interfering with slavery and at one point ordered the return of a fugitive slave to his master. With Halleck's Orders No. 3, Grant instructed his officers to send disloyal masters to local courts for assistance in securing their "civil right" to slave property. Such slaves, Grant ordered, were "not to be *restored* to the master by military authority." The general thereby sustained the decision of Colonel Leonard F. Ross, at Cape Girardeau, Missouri, who claimed it was his "duty as an officer" *not* to return a young black man to his owner, who was then serving in the Confederate army.[52]

Halleck likewise professed himself ready to enforce whatever policy came out of Washington. "I am ready to carry out any lawful instructions in regard to fugitive slaves, which my superiors may give me," he said. As he understood that policy, however, slaves escaping from loyal masters in the Border States would still be legally excluded from Union camps. Like Lincoln, Halleck hinted that he was ready to enforce a much broader emancipation policy if Congress implemented one, but until then he would remain within the confines of the First Confiscation Act. "I cannot make law," Halleck said, "and will not violate it."[53] Until Congress acted, fugitive slaves of loyal masters in the Border States were to be excluded, except those who had been legally emancipated under the statute Congress had passed. That wasn't good enough for congressional Republicans.

When Congress came back into session in early December of 1861, Republicans were in an uproar over stories of Union soldiers turning away fugitive slaves. Outraged congressmen told of slaves who had risked their lives crossing the Ohio River to reach the "flag of liberty" waving on the northern shore, only to be seized by northern soldiers and returned to their owners. In late 1861, Brigadier General Charles P. Stone, a Union officer in Poolesville, Maryland, ordered some Massachusetts soldiers to arrest and return several slaves to their owners. The slaves had come to the camp "for the purpose of selling cake, pies, &c to the Soldiers." Seeing that the blacks were themselves "almost famished," a German American company treated them to breakfast. The soldiers were clearly upset when they later discovered that the blacks had been seized and returned to their owners, and one of them wrote a letter of protest to the antislavery governor of Massachusetts, John Andrew, who had been responsible for organizing the regiments to begin with. Andrew in turn wrote his own letter of protest to the secretary of war, Simon Cameron. "Massachusetts does not send her citizens forth to become the hunters of men," Andrew complained, "or to engage in the seizure and return to captivity of persons claimed to be fugitive slaves." The controversy escalated still further when Andrew demanded an explanation from the officer who had ordered the arrest. The officer in turn protested the governor's interference to General McClellan, who proceeded to make matters worse. Rather than discipline Stone for violating Union policy, McClellan instead chastised Governor Andrew for improper civilian interference in the military chain of command. Cameron in the meantime had written to Stone's commanding officer, General Nathaniel Banks, urging him to prevent such abuses in the future. By then Andrew had alerted his friends in Congress, who made a conspicuous example of Stone by hauling him before the newly formed Committee on the Conduct of the War and destroying his career.[54]

Republicans blamed these violations on Halleck's Orders No. 3. On December 9, the House of Representatives formally requested the president to have Halleck withdraw his order.[55] They introduced legislation designed to overturn it. In the House, Owen Lovejoy proposed a law making it a crime for anyone in the army or navy "to capture or return, or aid in the capture or return, of fugitive slaves." In the Senate, Henry Wilson of Massachusetts introduced a similar bill making it a misdemeanor for any officer to assist in the recovery of fugitive slaves, punishable by dishonorable discharge and permanent exclusion from service in the army or navy. These bills assumed that Halleck had ordered Union soldiers to return fugitive slaves to their owners. In fact, Halleck actually agreed with congressional Republicans that enforcing the fugitive slave clause was none of the army's business.

The real problem with General Orders No. 3 lay elsewhere. Halleck's order required soldiers to determine the status of blacks coming to Union lines. Free blacks along with slaves emancipated by the First Confiscation Act were admitted; slaves of loyal masters in loyal states were excluded. Republicans, however, did not believe soldiers were competent to determine anyone's legal status. On the contrary, as agents of a federal government based on the principle of freedom national, Union soldiers could only presume that all persons coming into their lines were free. By late 1861 a consensus had emerged among Republicans that if an African American arrived at a Union military installation offering to work, and if there was work to be done, the military commander had to assume universal freedom and was therefore within his rights to employ that person. If someone later showed up claiming the black employee as a slave, and if the employee preferred to stay, the putative master was to be turned away and told to seek redress with local civil and judicial authorities. Congressional Republicans repudiated Orders No. 3 for the same basic reason Lincoln had repudiated Frémont: the status of anyone coming to Union lines was a political, not a military question. Union soldiers were not competent to determine whether anyone was legally free or legally enslaved.

Imagine this scenario, Senator Edgar Cowan of Pennsylvania suggested: I'm a Union general and someone shows up at my camp and says to me, "Sir, here is my negro; I want him." What am I supposed to say? "It may be that this is your negro; but I cannot determine that question; I cannot try the title to him; I am not a court; I am not a jury." For me to hand over the alleged slave "presumes that I decide the very question which I am incompetent to decide." A military officer who presumes "to exercise the functions of civil magistracy, and undertakes to sit upon the right of any human being born within the limits of this Republic . . . is worse than a kidnapper. He has no right to do it," Ohio Congressman John Bingham declared, "and by doing so commits a crime, a great crime." It amounted to "military despotism" for the U.S. Army to exercise that kind of power. Slavery was a strictly local institution and could only be enforced by local authorities.[56]

Republicans argued that the bills criminalizing military enforcement of the fugitive slave clause did not "interfere" with slavery in the states where it existed, because slaveholders were still entitled to pursue the return of runaway slaves through the proper legal channels within their own states. "The return of fugitive slaves," a leading Republican radical explained, "is a civil question, a judicial one, not a military one." Another Republican senator understood the bill "as simply prohibiting military men from disgracing the uniform" of the United States "by engaging in the business of slave-catching, and delivering slaves to their owners,—a disreputable business, in which no gentleman, North or South, military or civil, I undertake to say, will willingly engage." Under the legislation the Republicans were pushing through Congress, U.S. soldiers not only were forbidden to enforce state and local fugitive slave laws, but also would actually be punished for doing so.[57]

Democrats and Border State congressman objected. Responding to the Lovejoy bill criminalizing the return of fugitives by military personnel, Delaware Senator Willard Saulsbury wanted to make it a crime for any soldier to deprive a loyal master of his rightful claim to a slave. His goal was consistent with the Democratic Party's position that the war had nothing to do with slavery: he would separate the military completely from slavery, punishing those who interfered with it *either* by returning fugitives to their owners *or* by refusing to respect the legitimate property claims of owners. But Saulsbury's proposal demanded a degree of federal neutrality that was incompatible with the doctrine of freedom national. As Senator Wilson explained, any legislation "protecting, covering, or justifying slavery for *loyal or disloyal* masters" was a violation of the Constitution. The southern states already had laws regulating the capture and return of fugitives, and those laws were still in force in the slave states that remained in the Union. But U.S. soldiers, agents of the federal government, who returned fugitives to their masters did so without legal sanction. A new law was necessary, Wilson said, to stop the practice by punishing soldiers who returned slaves when they had no legal authority to do so.[58]

In early March of 1862, the House passed, by a vote of 83 to 42, the bill prohibiting the U.S. military from enforcing the fugitive slave clause. Six days later, Wilson brought the House bill up for consideration in the Senate. Once again Democrats did what they could to stall passage, but this time Republicans whisked away every effort to amend the legislation. On March 10, the Senate passed the bill by a vote of 29 to 9. In both houses, Republicans gave the bill their nearly unanimous support while almost every Democrat opposed it. Lincoln signed it on March 13, 1862.

By then Halleck had already rewritten his orders yet again, this time to take his Republican critics into account. "It does not belong to the military to decide upon the relation of master and slave," Halleck decreed. "Such questions must be settled by the civil courts." This effectively destroyed General Orders No. 3 as the army's policy in the Border States. By April of 1862, a month after Lincoln signed the bill into law, not even Halleck was willing to enforce his original order. When a Missouri slaveholder claimed that he was chased down and stoned by northern soldiers as he tried to recapture his runaway slave, Halleck claimed there was nothing he could do. The frustrated master sent his complaint to Secretary of War Stanton, who likewise ignored the slaveholder.[59]

STRUGGLE ON THE GROUND

In most places, restricting enforcement of the fugitive slave clause to local authorities effectively inhibited the capture of runaways, but in Washington it created a loophole that enabled the city marshal, Ward Lamon, to jail runaways from loyal states and Union-occupied parts of Virginia for much of the war. In December of 1861, Secretary of State William Seward instructed General McClellan that Union troops were not empowered to enforce the fugitive slave clause. As a result, fugitives entering the city who found their way to Union army or "contraband" camps were emancipated, whereas those captured by the city marshal were often jailed and returned to their owners. Frustrated Republicans tried to stop Lamon, but by their own legal logic there was nothing they could do; enforcement of the fugitive slave clause was strictly up to local civil and judicial authorities.

By the spring of 1862 a disproportionate number of the complaints about slaves being returned to their owners involved local police officials. Slaveholders in the Border States learned quickly that if they wanted to recover their slaves from a Union camp, they would have to bring the sheriff with them, preferably with a court order in hand. Traveling with Union troops in Maryland in late 1861, a black reporter named George Stephens complained of "a man who is dignified with the title of sheriff" who "rode into camp with a posse of five persons, and seized a little boy about 15 years of age, a fugitive from *slavery*." So hostile were the Union soldiers that the sheriff and his posse required the assistance of "a sergeant and a guard to escort them over the lines." To prevent such incidents in the future, Stephens and others began urging Maryland fugitives to enter federal lines from the Virginia side of the camp because not even a sheriff and his posse could secure the return of a fugitive from a seceded state. Over time fewer and fewer sheriffs succeeded, especially after Lincoln issued the Emancipation Proclamation. In one incident in late 1863, slaveholders in Eastville, Maryland, arrived at a Union gunboat, sheriff and official papers in tow, claiming their slaves who had escaped the night before. Rather than obey the sheriff, the Union troops roughed him up and sailed away with the fugitives untouched.[60]

The new federal policy put enormous pressure on the Border States, which was probably the point. The December 9, 1861, congressional resolution asking Lincoln to overturn General Orders No. 3 noted that Halleck's policy was inconsistent with military practice in the seceded states, where fugitive slaves were being admitted to

Union lines. Republicans were implicitly demanding that the anti-slavery policy already in place in disloyal states be applied as well to the loyal slave states. Senator Wilson implied the same thing when he said that Union soldiers could not legally protect slavery "for loyal or disloyal masters." By the spring of 1862, Republicans from the president on down were becoming more and more frustrated by the resistance to abolition in states like Delaware and Kentucky. By making it all but impossible for the army to enforce the fugitive slave clause even in the loyal slave states, Republicans were ensuring that "the incidents of war" would be felt within the loyal slave states.

6 "SELF-EMANCIPATION"

Whether the Cotton States are permitted to secede, or whether they return to their allegiance, the doom of Slavery will be equally sure. If they insist upon independence . . . Slaves by the scores and the hundreds, from Georgia and Alabama, would soon tread a highway through the vallies, in their exodus. Not to speak of the terrible danger of Slave Insurrections, and of "Mean White" rebellions, the destiny of Slave Institutions in the "Confederate States" would be quickly settled by the process of self-emancipation.[1]

Success in war was the jubilee of emancipation, and the captives returned to their normal state of freedom. And no divine ordinance was enacted covering the assumed right of the master to recover his fugitive slave in such a case. Self-emancipation by such recognized means was the right of the slave.[2]

I N   EARLY   AUGUST   OF   1861, three Virginia slaves who lived
on the shore of Chesapeake Bay escaped by canoe, hoping to make
their way to freedom in Baltimore. Intercepted by Union soldiers in
Maryland, the slaves came to the attention of General John Dix. "I
take it for granted they are fugitives," Dix wrote. As such he proposed
to treat them like other escaping slaves in Maryland. "We would not
meddle with the slaves even of secessionists," the general explained in
a letter to the Secretary of War, "we are neither negro-stealers nor
negro-catchers." It made no difference to Dix that the slaves had run
from a state that had seceded from the Union. "[W]e should send
them away if they came to us," he wrote. But on September 3, the
War Department corrected General Dix. The fact that the fugitives
had escaped from a disloyal state made all the difference. The secretary of war referred Dix to his August 8 instructions to General Benjamin Butler at Fortress Monroe, also in Virginia. Citing the First
Confiscation Act, the War Department had authorized Butler to treat
as free all slaves voluntarily entering Union lines. The secretary forwarded a copy of his instructions along with his reply to Dix, effectively ordering him to apply the same standard to the three Virginia
slaves who had rowed their way to Maryland. Whatever rules applied
to the Border States, they did not alter the fate of slaves escaping from
seceded states. The three refugees would not be turned away but
allowed to remain within Union lines, where they could work for
wages. Dix's fugitives were to be treated as free.[3]

The War Department's instructions also specified the limits that
defined the contours of the Union's initial emancipation policy.
Although they were to treat as free all fugitives from rebel states voluntarily entering Union lines, U.S. soldiers could not go onto farms
and plantations and "disturb" the normal workings of slavery, nor
could they "entice" slaves into their lines, even from states that had
seceded from the Union. This restriction remained in place until Lin-

coln issued the Emancipation Proclamation on January 1, 1863. Until then the Union army was a paradoxically passive agent of emancipation. Because enticement was prohibited, the slaves themselves would have to take action—they would have to run away from their owners or refuse to accompany their owners in flight from invading Union troops.[4] This was known as "self-emancipation."

For decades after the American Revolution, "self-emancipation" almost always referred to slaves who managed to purchase their own freedom from their masters. Sometime around 1840, however, abolitionists began referring to a second type of self-emancipation in which slaves freed themselves by claiming their liberty in areas where slavery had no legal existence. In the absence of "positive" or "municipal" laws creating slavery, the natural right of freedom prevailed. Slaves who escaped to "free soil" or who rebelled against their captors on the high seas were said to have "recovered" their natural right to freedom. An antislavery sermon from 1846 described the annual escape of hundreds of slaves to the North as "a very harmless way of self-emancipation."[5]

The slave rebellions on board the *Creole* and the *Amistad* inspired opponents of slavery to develop the case for this new form of self-emancipation. The abolitionist William Jay repeatedly described the rebels on the *Creole* as "self-emancipated slaves." Arguing before the Supreme Court on behalf of the Africans who had rebelled on the *Amistad*, John Quincy Adams referred to his clients as "self-emancipated." In his published analysis of the case, the abolitionist Samuel May likewise referred to the *Amistad* rebels as "self-emancipated." The terminology was neither an accident nor a coincidence. In his own response to the *Amistad* rebellion, Representative Joshua Giddings explained the concept of self-emancipation on the floor of Congress. Before the revolution, he said, the thirteen colonies adhered to the common-law rule that "if a slave should *escape* to a free state, he would thereby gain his freedom." But the slaveholders,

suspicious of what Giddings called "this species of self-emancipation," demanded the insertion of a fugitive slave clause into the Constitution. This made the status of fugitives in the North legally
anomalous: the natural right of freedom prevailed in the absence of
"positive" local laws creating slavery, yet the Constitution gave masters the right to recapture slaves who escaped to the northern states
where slavery had been abolished.[6] Slaves who made their way to
"free soil" were self-emancipated, but was the North truly free soil?

The question became urgent in the wake of the Fugitive Slave
Act of 1850. Opponents of slavery not only objected to the law but
also claimed that growing numbers of northerners were revolted by
the thought of "returning self-emancipated slaves into bondage." In
a Thanksgiving sermon delivered in late November of 1850, the
Reverend William Marsh declared that "the man who would deliberately, with his eyes open to the character of slavery, send back the
self-emancipated slave, would underbid Judas in selling his Lord."
When southerners responded to northern complaints by threatening
to withdraw from the Union, Congressman Horace Mann of Massachusetts dismissed the likelihood of secession for the simple reason that the "dissolution of the Union repeals the accursed act of
1850." As of 1852, Mann argued, Canada was "the only free soil . . .
on the northeastern part of this continent." But if the South seceded,
the Canadian border would move "down to Mason and Dixon's line,"
instantly transforming the northern states into free soil. "The knowledge of a North star is penetrating further and further into the southern interior," Mann declared, "and arousing new hearts to the effort
of self-emancipation." Secession dramatically increased the prospects
for self-emancipation because, in effect, it *did* move the Canadian
border down to the Ohio River. The Confederate nation created a
new "strategic line" that runaway slaves could cross and thereby
emancipate themselves merely by coming into the North. Under

these circumstances, the radical William Channing asked, "[H]ow long can the 'Confederates' retain their cherished institution? There will be no 'Fugitive-Slave Law' then, no 'Dred Scott' Judges of the Supreme Court, no District Marshals and pliant Commissioners ready to intercept the followers of the North Star." Slavery's destruction would then proceed quickly, Channing explained, "by the process of self-emancipation."[7]

Even more than secession, the Civil War opened the door to self-emancipation on a massive scale. Rather than escape all the way to the North, slaves could free themselves simply by running to the "free soil" within Union lines. Radicals like Senator James Lane of Kansas could scarcely contain their enthusiasm. What will happen, he asked, when "the armies of the Union march into the slave States, and the slaves themselves should get up an insurrection, as I believe will be the case, and flee to the armies of the Union, or march out by the roads that the Union armies march in?" Under such circumstances, he wondered, could any senator "expect the people of the North, or the armies of the North, to become the servants of the traitors, and return those slaves to their traitorous masters?"[8] Not all of Lane's fellow Republicans were so sanguine about the prospect of slave rebellion, but they all assumed that the First Confiscation Act cleared the path for self-emancipation. Under the terms of the statute, the president would order troops into areas in rebellion, slaves would escape into Union lines, and Union commanders would accept the fugitives— legally, because secession freed the North from any obligation to enforce the fugitive slave clause, and practically, because the northern people would not tolerate returning slaves to traitors.

As a policy, self-emancipation was formulated in Virginia, at Fortress Monroe, in the summer of 1861, but it was first applied on a large scale later that same year when the Union launched a successful invasion of coastal South Carolina.

THE SEA ISLANDS

Within days of the fall of Fort Sumter, Lincoln proclaimed an ambitious naval blockade of the entire South—from northern Virginia all the way down the Atlantic coast to Key West, back up the western edge of the Florida peninsula and around the wide arc of the Gulf Coast embracing Pensacola, Mobile, and New Orleans, until it finally reached the Mexican border at Brownsville, Texas. It soon became clear, however, that for the Union to make the blockade effective, it would have to establish naval bases as refueling stations along the southern Atlantic coast. By October, plans for a joint army-navy operation had been devised for the capture of Port Royal in the Sea Islands off South Carolina. Captain Samuel Francis Du Pont commanded the naval operation. The ground forces were placed under the command of General Thomas W. Sherman. The army and navy converged on Hampton Roads in late October and from there moved south for the attack on the Confederate fort on Hilton Head, the most formidable of the three forts guarding Port Royal Sound. A storm at sea scattered the fleet and nearly scuttled the operation. Sherman's troops were in no condition to participate as planned. Instead, they watched from their transport on the morning of November 7, by which time the water was "as smooth as glass," as Du Pont's squadron delivered an intense pounding that reduced the fortress on Hilton Head and sent its defenders scurrying in retreat. Within hours Union troops were in control of Port Royal, scoring one of the first important northern victories of the war and giving the Union a crucial foothold on the southern Atlantic coast. It also brought thousands of slaves within Union lines.[9]

The Sea Islands south of Charleston were home to some of the wealthiest and most impressive plantations in the South. They produced an especially fine and valuable fiber from the long-staple cotton plants that could not be grown on the farms of the southern interior. The islands around Port Royal were also home to eleven thousand slaves—more than eight out of ten Sea Island inhabitants were black—who had developed over the centuries a subculture of their own, different not merely from the culture of their masters but from that of most southern slaves as well. Planter families and slave lives—largely untouched by the great inland cotton boom—were uncharacteristically stable on the Sea Islands. But on the morning of November 7, 1861, the sound of bursting shells and Union cannon fire turned that old way of life upside down in a matter of hours. Slaves dropped their hoes and ran from the fields as their owners scampered to gather their belongings and escape from the islands before the Yankee invaders arrived. When a young slave named Sam Mitchell heard the cannons roar, he thought it was thunder. "Son," his mother explained, "dat ain't no t'under, dat Yankee come to gib you Freedom."[10] And so the Yankees had.

Just before Sherman embarked on the expedition in early November, the assistant secretary of war instructed the general that his treatment of slavery should be governed "by the principles of the letters addressed by [the secretary of war] to Major-General Butler on the 30th of May and 8th of August, copies of which are herewith furnished to you." As was true for Butler, Sherman was not to entice slaves from plantations that were functioning peaceably; however, slaves who voluntarily came under Union army control were to be treated as free. Sherman was instructed to avail himself of the services of any person, "whether fugitives from labor or not, who may offer them to the National Government." Once again, labor in service of the Union secured emancipation. In keeping with these instructions, on November 8, Sherman issued a proclamation promising Sea Island planters that the army's policy was not to "interfere with any of your lawful rights or your social and local institutions" beyond what the circumstances of war and rebellion make "unavoidable." But the owners were in no position to take comfort from Sherman's promises—by the time he arrived, they were gone.[11]

"The effect of the victory is startling," Sherman reported to his superiors on November 11. "Every white inhabitant has left the island." The "beautiful estates of the planters" had been abandoned in panic and "left to the pillage of hordes of apparently disaffected blacks." The panic was general. Hilton Head, St. Helena, Lady's, and Port Royal Islands—every one had been abandoned by the white inhabitants. Retreating Confederates passing through the town of Beaufort found it "deserted by the white population." Shortly after the fort on Hilton Head surrendered, U.S. reconnaissance troops scouted the island "without encountering any of the enemy or any white person whatever." Not only had the whites fled, but also they had tried, and largely failed, to force their slaves to flee with them. Young black men, the most valuable and productive workers, were the ones most likely to be taken. On island after island, however, there were reports of slaves who hid in the fields and swamps to avoid being carried off to the mainland. By refusing to leave with their masters, by welcoming the invading Yankees, the slaves of Port Royal had effectively "volunteered" to come into Union lines, even though they never left their plantations. If the War Department instructions prevailed, the Sea Island contrabands would be treated as free.[12]

But it was not up to the War Department. Shortly after the Union victory, the administration of the Sea Islands was transferred to the Treasury Department. The Sea Island plantations had been abandoned, and it was the Treasury that disposed of abandoned property. Treasury Secretary Salmon Chase was reputed to be the member of Lincoln's cabinet most congenial to emancipation. By late 1861, the more radical Republicans in Congress regularly consulted with Chase, either at his office or at his home, where they frequently dined together. Yet Chase's views on slavery and emancipation did not differ significantly from the other members of Lincoln's cabinet, or from

those of most Republicans. Here again it was hard to discern a dis-
tinctively "radical" position on slavery and abolition. As of September
in 1861, for example, Chase continued to insist that neither he nor
any member of the administration "has any desire to convert this War
for the Union . . . into a War upon any State Institution whatever,
whether that institution be slavery or another." For Chase this meant
that the federal government had no constitutional authority to prosecute the war for any purpose other than the restoration of the Union.
Like all Republicans, however, Chase understood that the war had
been caused by slavery and that slavery would be a casualty of the
war. "We all see," he wrote, "that the madness of disunion" was
endangering "the system of slavery." It was "impossible" for civil war
to go on "without harm to slavery," and should the war be prolonged,
"a fatal result to Slavery will be well nigh inevitable." Frémont's order
emancipating the slaves of Missouri rebels was essentially meaningless, Chase explained, because the civil authorities of the state were
still functioning and the federal government had no constitutional
power to overrule them. But in seceded states, like South Carolina,
"the State organization was forfeited and it lapsed into the condition
of a Territory with which we could do what we pleased." In territories
the Constitution was sovereign, and under the Constitution the slaves
"are not recognized as the property of rebels." By Chase's reasoning,
when the slaves on the Sea Islands came within Union lines, they
came under the protection of a Constitution that did not recognize
slavery within its sovereign jurisdiction. The Sea Island slaves were
therefore free.[13]

Administration officials used a distinctive linguistic construction
to indicate that slaves were already being emancipated. They declared
that it was "impossible" or "inconceivable" that slaves, having been
freed, could ever be returned to bondage. As early as July of 1861,
Lincoln had told his friend Orville Browning that the federal government "neither should, nor would send back to bondage such as came

to our armies." A year later he was more emphatic: slaves whose labor had been "forfeited" by their owners and who were subsequently emancipated by the government could never be re-enslaved. "I do not believe it would be physically possible, for the General government, to return persons so circumstanced, to actual slavery," Lincoln explained. "I believe there would be physical resistance to it, which could neither be turned aside by argument, nor driven away by force." Labor in service to the Union remained a crucial guarantor of emancipation. Chase would "never consent," he declared, "to the involuntary reduction to Slavery of one of the negroes who had been in the service of the Government."[14]

In December of 1861, Lincoln himself affirmed emancipation in a statement that almost certainly referred to the slaves on the Sea Islands that had been occupied by the federal forces a few weeks earlier. In his first annual message to Congress, Lincoln noted that numerous contrabands had recently come into Union lines and, under the terms of the First Confiscation Act, were "thus liberated."[15] Chase followed the same policy from the moment the Treasury assumed authority over the Sea Islands. Indeed, everyone in a position of authority at Port Royal, beginning with those in charge of the cotton, agreed that the slaves had been freed.

When the whites fled the islands, most of that year's cotton had been harvested but had yet to be ginned and sold. General Sherman appointed a number of cotton agents to supervise the collection and sale of the cotton, but the army wanted to hand the business off to the Treasury. In early December, acting on the advice of Rhode Island Governor William Sprague, Chase appointed William Reynolds as the Treasury agent to oversee the disposition of the cotton under a system of free labor. That the freedom of the slaves was already presupposed by New England cotton interests was clear from the title of a pamphlet they published in mid-December: *Proposition to Employ Liberated Negroes*. Before the month was out, Reynolds was reporting back to Chase on how the new wage labor system was designed to get the "liberated Negroes" back to work. Because he found it "impossible to hire the Negroes by the day," Reynolds explained, he had authorized his clerks to "allow them a dollar for every four hundred pounds of stone cotton which they deliver at the steamboat landing, paying them partly in money & the balance in clothing and Provisions." That would dispose of the current year's crop. But for the longer term, Reynolds suggested leasing the abandoned plantations to "loyal citizens," with "the Negroes to be paid a fair compensation for their services." This was an opportune moment, he added, "to try the experiment of producing cotton in one of the oldest slaveholding states with paid labor."[16] However, Reynolds and his Treasury agents soon found themselves in competition with an influential group of northern philanthropists, who likewise assumed that the Sea Island slaves had been "liberated."

On December 21, Chase telegraphed Edward L. Pierce, the Massachusetts abolitionist who had served as Chase's secretary some years back and had recently worked for General Butler supervising the contrabands at Fortress Monroe. "If you incline to visit Beaufort in connection with the contraband and cotton," Chase wrote his protégé, "come to Washington at once."[17] The Treasury secretary offered Pierce an appointment as a special Treasury agent in charge of supervising the transition to freedom among the Sea Island blacks. Pierce quickly accepted the assignment and, after stopping in Washington to meet with Chase, arrived at Port Royal on January 13, 1862. Before the month was out, he had produced his first report, titled *The Negroes of Port Royal*, written for Chase but quickly published, first in the *Boston Transcript* and a week or so later in the *New York Tribune*. Pierce estimated that as of late January there were between ten and twelve thousands blacks within Union lines on the islands, although the number was "rapidly increasing" as more and more slaves escaped from the mainland.

In his report Pierce took care to demonstrate that the contrabands met the criteria for self-emancipation. Their "former masters" were almost uniformly rebels who had "offered their slaves to the Governor of South Carolina, to aid in building earth works, and calling on him for guns to mount upon them." This would suggest that the blacks at Port Royal were not unlike those at Fortress Monroe—with whom Pierce was quite familiar—who had escaped to Union lines rather than face the *prospect* of being forced to support the Confederate war effort. In both cases the owners had thereby "forfeited" the labor of their slaves, and the slaves themselves were "discharged" from service. Moreover, Pierce insisted that the Union army had done nothing to interfere with the ordinary workings of slavery on the Sea Islands, nor had the soldiers enticed slaves to leave their plantations. The "negroes within our lines," Pierce reported, "are there by the invitation of no one; but they were on our soil when our army began its occupation and could not have been excluded except by violent transportation." In short, the slaves had chosen to stay within Union lines, thereby satisfying the standard of the War Department's instructions of May 30 and August 8, 1861: the army could not entice slaves off working plantations but all slaves coming voluntarily were emancipated.[18]

Still other blacks on the Sea Islands were fugitives from the mainland who had risked the wrath of Confederate pickets to reach the Union camps at Port Royal. "In March," a local planter reported in his diary, "15 of my negroes including 3 women and 1 child left the plantation and went over to the enemy on the Islands." Forty-eight slaves had recently escaped from a single plantation under rebel control near Grahamville. "[L]ed by the driver," Pierce reported, "and after four days of trial and peril, hidden by day and threading the waters with their boats by night, evading the enemy's pickets," they "joy fully entered our camp at Hilton Head." Pierce wanted to leave no room for doubt in his readers' minds that the "contrabands" had emancipated themselves by voluntarily embracing the Union army occupying the Sea Islands.[19]

Pierce told the contrabands that if they remained on their plantations, worked hard, and behaved themselves, they would be paid wages, their families would be secure, and their children would be educated. But he disagreed with Reynolds's plan to lease the plantations to private investors. Instead, Pierce proposed that the government hire "superintendents" at salaries high enough to attract the most qualified men to take charge of the plantations and oversee the transition from slavery to freedom. The superintendents would put the former slaves back to work as free laborers raising cotton, but they would do so with the specific needs of the freed people in mind. There was to be no more whipping, for example. "The lash, let us give thanks, is banished at last." The freed people would have to work, but they would be "assured at the outset that parental and conjugal relations among them are to be protected and enforced; that children, and all others desiring, are to be taught; that they will receive wages." Pierce imagined his system of superintendents as temporary, a stepping stone designed to "fit" the freed people "for all the privileges of citizenship." Once "fitted," they should be "dismissed from the system" and allowed to take any jobs they pleased, save their earnings, and buy land of their own. The laborers were "no longer slaves of their former masters, or of the Government," Pierce explained, but having been acculturated to the vices of slavery, they needed the "paternal" guidance of employers whose "interests" did not conflict with the dictates of "humanity." Pierce thus raised the question that would continually arise in the immediate aftermath of emancipation: If blacks were no longer slaves, what were the boundaries of their freedom? Yet notwithstanding the need for some form of guidance, Pierce insisted, the blacks on the Sea Islands were "entitled to be recognized as freemen."[20]

Pierce's alternative to Reynolds's leasing system would require a cadre of teachers, ministers, and superintendents, none of whom could be paid for by the U.S. government. Instead, Pierce negotiated what today would be called a "public/private partnership" in which volunteers recruited by Pierce would be paid for their services by northern philanthropists but would be provided with transportation, living accommodations, and supplies by the government. The abolitionist communities of the North, particularly in Boston and New York, responded to Pierce's call for volunteers for the great "social experiment" at Port Royal. Like Pierce himself, the volunteers assumed that they would be working with people who had been emancipated, an assumption emblazoned in the names of the organizations that sponsored the effort: the "Educational Commission for Freedmen" out of Boston, the "National Freedmen's Aid Society" out of New York. Edward Philbrick—who arrived with the first boatload of volunteers in early March of 1862—made it clear that he and his fellow volunteers would not leave for South Carolina until they had assurances from Washington that blacks on the Sea Islands were in fact free. Those assurances were forthcoming, Philbrick wrote on February 19, two weeks before his departure. Treasury and War Department officials "ridicule the idea that these blacks can ever be claimed by their runaway masters." To Philbrick this was "satisfactory foundation for our exertions in overseeing their labor and general deportment."[21]

Nor would the freed people themselves go back to work without knowing if their freedom was secure. They needed to be certain that they would be "protected against their rebel masters." Pierce sympathized with their concerns. It would be "wasted toil" to continue the social experiment "without such assurances," he said. If the North could not promise the freed people that their emancipation was secure, none of the volunteers could honorably continue with their work. Pierce thought re-enslavement was simply inconceivable, if only because the freed people on the plantations were technically employed by the federal government. As at Fortress Monroe, labor for the Union government was considered a guarantor of emancipation. It was not "possible to imagine any rulers now or in the future," Pierce wrote, "who will ever turn their backs on the laborers who have been received, as these have been, into the service of the United States."[22]

If the lengths to which Pierce and others went to insist upon the freedom of the Sea Island blacks seemed a bit too strenuous, it was not because they doubted that the slaves had in fact been emancipated. Rather, the tone of uncertainty in their words suggested a vaguely dawning awareness of a weakness built into military emancipation: the possibility that it was not permanent. What if the masters *did* come back? What if they reasserted their claims to their property in slaves? What if the rebellion ended and the southern states re-enslaved those freed by the war? Eventually such questions would drive Union policymakers to move beyond emancipation to support a constitutional amendment permanently abolishing slavery everywhere. But in early 1862, no one expressed any doubts about the status of the contrabands at Port Royal. Those people were presumed to be free.

Blacks were treated as free laborers, for example. Adults worked for wages, either on the plantations or in the Union army camps. Pierce's superintendents were actually frustrated by the mobility of black workers, who presumed the right to move about in search of better or at least steadier wages. Army camps competed with plantations. Mansfield French, sent by Lewis Tappan to head the New York contingent, complained that the "Coffin place"—once one of the largest slave plantations in the islands—was in a "miserable, demoralized condition" because he could not get the young men to stay. There was a Union camp at Bay Point, a few miles away, "so the temptation to leave is very pressing, for smart fellows can get money there."[23] The women likewise preferred housework to laundering, Laura Towne reported, "because the Northerners can't help giving extra pay for service that is done them."[24] Meanwhile several thousand of the children of the free black laborers were in school, learning to read and write.

And their parents were getting married so that their families were at least legally secure.[25] Free labor, schools for children, and legally recognized marriages—all were prohibited under slavery, and all ranked among the basic attributes of freedom as Americans understood it in the middle of the nineteenth century.

In March of 1862 the Reverend Richard Fuller, the pastor of Baltimore's Seventh Baptist Church, called on Treasury Secretary Chase, seeking "advice as to the course he should pursue in regard to his plantations and slaves at Port Royal." Fuller wanted to know what, if any, rights he still had "in respect to them." He was a South Carolina slaveholder, but because he was loyal to the Union he believed he was entitled to retain ownership of his slaves on the Sea Islands. Chase told Fuller that "as a loyal man, he was the Proprietor of the *land*." That answer did not satisfy Fuller. "How about the negroes?" he asked the Treasury secretary. Chase was straightforward: "They were free, I replied."[26]

By the spring of 1862, more than ten thousand former slaves on the Sea Islands had been emancipated under the authority of the First Confiscation Act as it was implemented by the Lincoln administration. Yet by 1896 the memory of slaves freed prior to the Emancipation Proclamation was so thoroughly obliterated that when a compilation of Edward Pierce's papers was prepared for publication, the editor was at a loss to explain why the reports, which Pierce published as articles in February and June of 1862, were written as though the slaves on the Sea Islands were already emancipated. It "should be observed," A. W. Stevens wrote, that Pierce's reports "preceded by several months President Lincoln's proclamations of emancipation." Pierce's articles had appeared at a time when, according to Stevens, "there was as yet no definite policy or public opinion as to the fate of the Southern negroes." Yet the articles assumed otherwise. What could possibly explain the way Pierce had written them? He must have "deemed it wise," Stevens guessed, given "the sensitive state of the public mind, to avoid argument on the vexed question of their *status*, and thought it better to assume their freedom as already established by events."[27] It would be better to assume that Pierce was right to begin with, that the contrabands at Port Royal were already emancipated when he published his reports in 1862.

NORTH CAROLINA AND THE PENINSULA

When the Civil War broke out, Allen Parker was working as a slave in Chowan, in the northeastern part of North Carolina. He was born sometime between 1835 and 1840. "I do not know exactly when I was born," he recalled, "for slaves keep no family records." But "in common with all the Negroes" Parker had developed a "very strong yearning for freedom." That yearning was strengthened by the outbreak of Civil War. The more Parker and his fellow slaves heard about the "Yankees," the more anxious he became. Some of the slaves on nearby plantations had escaped to Union lines; others had been "refugeed" to Richmond to prevent their escape. In their attempt to keep any more slaves from running away, the slave owners had beefed up the patrols. "[E]very effort was made to keep the slaves on the plantations at night," Parker remembered, "and it was very hard to get a pass." But in August of 1862—several months after Union forces had captured Roanoke Island and established bases in eastern North Carolina—Parker and a number of slaves on adjoining plantations began to plan their escape. Union gunboats had appeared on the Chowan River, providing the slaves with an opportunity. One night Parker and three of his friends "stole our way down to the river bank, where we knew there was a boat." As they approached the Union vessel, they were hailed by a Yankee sailor.[28]

"Who are you?" the Yankee asked.

"Friends," the slaves answered.

"Advance, friends, and come alongside."

When the escaping slaves reached the boat, a Union officer "inquired if our owners were Union people or not, and we replied that they were not." The slaves asked to be taken on board immediately; otherwise they would have to get back home by morning before their escape was discovered. The officer excused himself and returned a few minutes later with "orders from the captain" to let the slaves come aboard. At daybreak a party of armed men and dogs appeared on the riverbank searching for the runaway slaves. "The captain watched them for a while," Parker recalled some years later, "then ordered a gun loaded with a shell fired in that direction." That night the Union sailors went ashore and, with one of the fugitives as their guide, made their way to the plantation, where they "got quite a lot of chickens, ducks, and geese." A few days later, on one of the foraging expeditions, the Yankees arrested the slave's owner and took him to New Bern as a prisoner. Allen Parker joined the U.S. Navy and served for one year on the *Knockum*, an ammunition boat captured from the Confederates.[29]

Parker's experience demonstrates how federal emancipation policy was implemented in coastal North Carolina, despite the fact that the Union commanders in charge of the expedition objected to the policy. In early 1862, George McClellan, then general in chief of the army and a vocal opponent of a war against slavery, gave extremely conservative instructions regarding military emancipation to General Ambrose Burnside as he was about to embark on another joint army-navy operation aimed at capturing Roanoke Island. "I would urge great caution in regard to proclamation," McClellan wrote. "[S]ay as little as possible about politics or the negro. Merely state that the true issue for which we are fighting is the preservation of the Union and upholding the laws of the General Government, and stating that all who conduct themselves properly will as far as possible be protected in their persons and property." Upon capturing Roanoke Island in early February, Burnside issued a proclamation that was more guarded than the one General Sherman had issued on the Sea Islands a few months earlier: We have not come "to liberate your slaves," Burnside declared, and would "inflict no injury unless forced to do so by your own acts."[30] McClellan's instructions, like Burnside's proclamation, were technically correct: the "purpose" of the Union invasion was the restoration of the Union, not the liberation of the slaves. The policy of the federal government, however, was to emancipate all slaves coming within Union lines. In North Carolina, as elsewhere along the southern Atlantic coast, Union occupation forces would not actively interfere with the peaceful operation of slavery among loyal farmers and planters, they would not entice slaves away from their owners, but slaves escaping to Union lines were emancipated and employed as wage laborers.

McClellan and Burnside could no more overrule federal policy than could John C. Frémont. On March 12, a few weeks after Burnside vowed to leave slavery untouched, his headquarters on Roanoke Island issued instructions for the payment of wages—ten dollars per month plus rations for men; four dollars per month plus rations for women—for the "contrabands at this post." On March 27, Burnside reported to Edwin Stanton, who had recently replaced Simon Cameron as secretary of war, that the "negroes continue to come in, and I am employing them to the best possible advantage."[31] Slavery deteriorated rapidly in the occupied parts of North Carolina thanks to the policy instructing Union forces to employ fugitives entering their lines, coupled with the prohibition against military enforcement of the fugitive slave clause.

On March 13, 1862, just as Burnside's troops were about to capture New Bern, Lincoln signed the articles of war making it a crime for Union soldiers to participate in any way in the capture or return of fugitive slaves. L. R. Ferebee, for example, was still only thirteen years old when he ran to Burnside's army a few months later. "I reached Yankee lines about (30) minutes before my master overtook me on the road," Ferebee recalled. Eventually the Union troops evacuated the area and moved to New Bern, "carrying as many colored people with them as wanted to go." There Ferebee attended his first school, set up by northern missionaries. Burnside occupied New Bern on March 14. Two months later, W. H. Doherty, the principal of the Newbern Academy, wrote somewhat ruefully that the Union invasion has "overthrown the whole fabric of society, founded as it was, on the Institution of negro Slavery." It was "perfectly futile to hope," Doherty added, "that the slaves now practically emancipated, will ever return to their former condition." Union troops were "prohibited from assisting, or aiding in the restoration of fugitive slaves," not only by the recent act of Congress but also "by the prevailing sentiment of the North." In what he believed was a spirit of fairness, Doherty wrote to President Lincoln suggesting that the burden of emancipation be borne equally by each of the three parties concerned—the owners, the former slaves, and the federal government. He wanted the federal government to compensate North Carolina masters for one-third of the value of their slaves, and the freed people to pay off another third by working for their former owners for five more years. Lincoln ignored the request.[32]

But the generals could not ignore Lincoln and the Republican lawmakers. The clearest example was McClellan. No Union commander was more strongly committed to separating the war for the Union from a war against slavery. Early on McClellan announced to the people of western Virginia that his Union troops would protect civilian property and suppress servile insurrection. Yet on March 17, 1862, when the Army of the Potomac embarked from Alexandria, Virginia, to begin the Peninsula Campaign, McClellan was constrained by the law Congress had passed a few days before as well as the War Department's instructions of the previous August. By then it was illegal under the March 13 statute for anyone in the Union army to turn away slaves coming into its lines. Once they were within Union lines, neither McClellan nor any other military officer had any legal authority to determine the status of the contrabands. That was a *political* decision, made by civilian rather than military officials, and both Congress and the Lincoln administration had already determined that slaves coming into Union lines in the seceded states were free.

McClellan conceded the point. "Slaves contraband under the Act of Congress, seeking military protection, should receive it," he wrote. The Union army could not exclude slaves from its lines. "The right of the Government to appropriate *permanently* to its own service claims to slave labor should be asserted." Civilian authorities had the right to emancipate contraband slaves. Indeed, it could go further. The confiscation of slaves "might be extended upon grounds of military necessity and security *to all slaves within a particular state; thus working manumission in such a state.*" Following the War Department's August 8 instructions, McClellan held out the possibility that loyal owners might eventually be compensated for their freed slaves. This policy might even apply to the loyal slave states of Missouri, western Virginia, and even Maryland, where "the expediency of such a military measure is only a question of time." McClellan was a reluctant emancipator, but he wasn't a criminal. He was not going to break the law.[33]

McClellan's armies had no choice but to implement Union emancipation policy during the Peninsula Campaign. When his troops arrived, slaves on nearby farms and plantations predictably flocked to Union lines, and they were not turned away. The "negroes all running helter skelter," Hill Carter complained on June 30, 1862, "owing to the Yankee army occupying the plantation." Two weeks later Carter's plantation diary noted the first of the many escapes that would frustrate the master for the next several years: "15 negro men & boys ran off at different times." Unlike what occurred in the Border States in 1861, Union commanders in Virginia in the spring of 1862 issued no orders to exclude slaves from Union lines. In the *Official Records* there are no requests from Union commanders asking for clarification of Union policy regarding slaves and no complaints from soldiers objecting to their orders. Instead, the evidence indicates that McClellan was emancipating slaves in accordance with the policies laid down by Congress and the Lincoln administration. The most conspicuous records left behind document the numerous instances in which escaping slaves provided McClellan and his commanders with valuable military intelligence. Meanwhile contrabands were being ferried in large numbers from the peninsula to Fortress Monroe and elsewhere. Plantation letters and diaries reveal that slaves were running in large numbers to Union lines all along the peninsula as McClellan's troops approached, and they were not coming back. And when McClellan spelled out his own views to Lincoln, the general made it clear that he was adhering to the emancipation policy established by Congress and the War Department. Against everything he believed the war should be about, George McClellan oversaw the emancipation of more slaves than any other Union commander in the first year of fighting.[34]

GENERAL HUNTER'S TWO PROCLAMATIONS

Slaves were also being emancipated farther down the Atlantic coast. On April 13, 1862, two weeks after he was given command of the Department of the South, General David Hunter issued an emancipation edict covering Fort Pulaski and Cockspur Island, Georgia, the coastal areas most recently occupied by the Union forces under his command. "All persons of color lately held to involuntary service by enemies of the United States," Hunter's proclamation read, "are hereby confiscated and declared free." At the approach of the Yankees, Susie King Taylor, a slave living in Savannah, was rushed into the countryside by her mother. "Two days after the taking of Fort Pulaski," King recalled, "my uncle took his family of seven and myself to St. Catherine Island. We landed under the protection of the Union fleet." They stayed for two weeks before being transferred to St. Simons Island. Because King could read and write, she was quickly enlisted as a teacher at one of the recently established schools for the freed people on the Sea Islands. All of these educational activities provoked the ire of a Union soldier named William Lilley, who complained on April 16 that "the abolition feeling" was too widespread in the Sea Islands. "Is it right," Lilley asked, "to detail the soldiers to perform laboring work while the blacks go to school?"[35] Apparently it was, for by mid-April of 1862, tens of thousands slaves had been emancipated along the southern Atlantic coast. Because Hunter's order was, as the general himself put it, "in conformity with law," not to mention prevailing practice, it did not cause so much as a ripple.[36]

The same was not true of the proclamation that Hunter issued less than a month later, on May 9. In this second proclamation, Hunter declared the abolition of slavery in three entire states—South Carolina, Georgia, and Florida—only small portions of which were actually under Union control. "Slavery and martial law in a free country are altogether incompatible," Hunter declared—though it is not entirely clear what he meant by this. Martial law is the suspension of civil and judicial authority in times of emergency. If Hunter was assuming the *Somerset* principle, he may have reasoned that slavery could be sustained only by the local civil and judicial authorities that had been suspended by martial law. The Union military authorities that replaced them operated under the Constitution, which did not recognize slavery wherever it was sovereign. By that reasoning, slavery and martial law were incompatible.[37]

No one in the Lincoln administration would have disputed the broad principles Hunter was enunciating; Lincoln frequently used the terminology of martial law when he declared that the civil and judicial authorities in the rebellious states had ceased to function. But Hunter had already emancipated slaves in areas where his troops had imposed martial law. The War Department instructions under which Union officers operated allowed them to emancipate slaves who came into their lines from seceded areas. Hunter's first proclamation conformed to those guidelines; the second one did not.

Once again, the president felt compelled to reassert the essential principle of civilian rule: generals do not make policy. When Chase urged Lincoln to sustain Hunter's order, the president lost his temper. "No commanding general shall do such a thing, upon *my* responsibility," Lincoln snapped, at least not "without consulting me." Chase had defended Hunter's order on the grounds that it was "made as military measure to meet a military exigency." Precisely for that reason, Chase believed, the decision to emancipate was best left to local commanders on the ground. Let them issue such proclamations as the "military necessity" arose, Chase argued. Carl Schurz, another prominent Republican with radical leanings, made a similar point: don't say anything in public about Hunter's general abolition edict, he urged the president. Like Chase, Schurz still believed that the complete destruction of slavery would inevitably accompany the Union army as its invasions penetrated deeper and deeper into the South. Hunter's troops, however, occupied almost none of the ground covered by his second proclamation. Schurz acknowledged that Hunter may have been a bit "premature," nevertheless federal policy "will come to this all over the Cotton states during the summer." If you simply let it happen, "the people will readily acquiesce if you see fit to sustain Hunter."[38]

But for Lincoln all of that was beside the point. The law governing Hunter and all other Union commanders was still the First Confiscation Act and the War Department instructions for implementing it.

By them the general was empowered to free all slaves coming voluntarily within his own lines. That's what Hunter's first proclamation did, and nobody in the administration objected to it. Hunter's second proclamation stepped beyond those legal boundaries by pronouncing the emancipation of slaves in three entire states. By no conceivable standard could it be said that the slaves in those states had come voluntarily within Union lines. Lincoln certainly understood that Congress was at that moment considering a second confiscation act that would empower the president to proclaim a general emancipation in the seceded states. But that was months away. Until then, "neither General Hunter, nor any other commander, or person, has been authorized by the Government to make proclamations declaring the slaves of any State free." That kind of proclamation "I reserve to myself," Lincoln declared, "and which I can not feel justified in leaving to the decision of commanders in the field."[39] Generals don't make policy—not Frémont, not McClellan, and not Hunter. Hunter's second proclamation was therefore illegal, and Lincoln revoked it on May 19, ten days after it was issued.

As with his order to Frémont the previous September, Lincoln was asking only that Hunter comply with the law. Lincoln fully endorsed the policy of emancipating slaves who came within Union lines in the seceded states. Because the general's *first* emancipation proclamation conformed to federal policy, Lincoln had no reason to revoke it. The slaves who had recently come within Union lines at Fort Pulaski and Cockspur Island were still properly emancipated under Hunter's April 13 decree. Thus Lincoln's revocation of Hunter's May 9 proclamation cannot be read as evidence of the president's "reluctance" to embrace emancipation as a policy. Even the way Lincoln framed his revocation suggested this. After pointing out that he alone, as commander in chief, could issue a general emancipation order covering areas not under Union military occupation, Lincoln strongly suggested that he was ready and willing to do so. It was already clear by then that Congress was likely to authorize such a move. Lincoln heightened the threat by devoting most of his revocation order to a strongly worded warning to the Border States that if they did not abolish slavery on their own, they would lose everything as emancipation spread uncontrollably into their states. Another indication of Lincoln's state of mind was the fact that he would not remove Hunter, despite the fact that Lincoln was being bombarded with demands for the general's head.

The reaction to Lincoln's revocation of Hunter's order was surprisingly muted, however. Unlike the previous September, when antislavery northerners briefly but vehemently bombarded the White House with objections to the president's order to Frémont, not a single letter of complaint landed in the president's mailbag after he revoked Hunter's second proclamation. This time only a handful of letters arrived, all of them praising Lincoln. By then there was no longer any doubt where Lincoln stood on the issue of emancipation. For nine months his administration had been instructing the Union troops to free the slaves in areas they occupied, including the areas under Hunter's control. The president had rejected calls to fire Hunter. A month earlier, in a message to Congress, Lincoln had made it clear that he was an avowed supporter of abolition. If he was reticent in public, he was vocal in private, expressing his determination to use all of his constitutional powers to undermine slavery. Even Schurz understood that in revoking Hunter's second proclamation, Lincoln was merely upholding the rule of law. "I do not see how you could have acted otherwise," he wrote. Having spoken with Lincoln at the White House only a week earlier, Schurz was "fully convinced that, in spite of appearances to the contrary, you were determined to use all your constitutional power to deliver the country of the great curse" of slavery.[40]

And yet the Hunter affair suggested that the emancipation policy in place since August of 1861 had reached the limits of its effectiveness. The general's first proclamation was based on familiar premises: slaves who refused to leave when their masters fled the approaching Union army and who then offered their services to the military had, in effect, emancipated themselves by choosing loyalty over rebellion. This policy had worked well enough on the southern Atlantic coast, though even there, kidnapping raids by Confederate troops and southern militia raised questions about whether emancipation was truly secure. But the real test of Union policy came in Louisiana, where dramatic Union advances in early 1862 brought huge numbers of slaves within Union lines, raising both legal and practical questions that neither the First Confiscation Act nor the War Department instructions of May 30 and August 8, 1861, could address.

"WHAT AM I TO DO?"

The successful Union occupation of the southern Atlantic coast beginning in late 1861 was soon followed by even more dramatic advances in the Mississippi Valley, where the number of slaves who ended up inside Union lines dwarfed anything the army had yet encountered. In February, General Ulysses S. Grant seized the military initiative and, in conjunction with the navy, launched serial attacks on Forts Henry and Donelson, on the Cumberland and Tennessee Rivers. Having routed the Confederates, Grant quickly followed up his victories with advances down the Mississippi River nearly to Vicksburg. At almost the same time, yet another joint army-navy operation, this time led by naval commander David Farragut, set off from Ship Island off the Gulf Coast on a spectacular campaign to move up the river and seize the crucial southern city of New Orleans. Once the Crescent City was safely in Union hands, Farragut continued upriver, taking Baton Rouge and moving as far up as he could, until he, too, was stopped by powerful Confederate fortifications at Vicksburg. Though it would take the Union more than a year to finally capture Vicksburg—and with it substantial control of the Mississippi River—the stunning victories of early 1862 provided the northern armies with crucial staging grounds for an ultimately devastating series of attacks on the Confederate armies west of the Appalachian Mountains. At the same time, the occupation of the Mississippi Valley brought vast numbers of slaves within Union-held territory.

Like the plantations along the southern Atlantic coast, those along the Mississippi River were unusually large and wealthy. Rich bottom lands proved exceptionally fertile grounds for cotton production in Tennessee, Mississippi, Missouri, and Louisiana. These plantations sustained some of the wealthiest families in the United States. The sugar parishes of southern Louisiana were larger and wealthier still. They were also deadlier. The same subtropical climate that was so conducive to the cultivation of sugarcane proved lethal to the slaves who did the cultivating. The mortality rates among sugar slaves were the highest in the South. Besides being more lethal, sugar plantations were also larger than cotton farms. Cotton could be baled and stored after harvest, but sugarcane rotted quickly if it was not processed immediately, and sugar processing required expensive machinery for pressing and boiling the cane. Sugar plantations thus demanded a much higher capital investment to operate and were therefore more efficient with larger numbers of slaves. On average, sugar plantations were the largest in the United States. All of this meant that the successful federal occupation of the lower Mississippi Valley in early 1862 brought more than 150,000 slaves into Union lines. These numbers alone put a great deal of pressure on Union emancipation policy.

No one understood these pressures better than Benjamin Butler, the Union general in charge of the occupation of New Orleans and the same man who had formulated the original contraband policy at Fortress Monroe in Virginia a year earlier. Butler's troops arrived in New Orleans on May 1, 1862, and as he had in Baltimore at the beginning of the war, the general made it clear from the start that he would brook no "rebellious" behavior from the city's "sullen and dangerous" residents. On the day he arrived, Butler issued a proclamation making the same promise that Generals Sherman and Burnside had previously made when they occupied portions of the Carolinas: the Union would not interfere with the property rights of those who were loyal to the United States. To disloyal Louisianans, Butler made no promises. Yet for a number of reasons, this otherwise familiar declaration left the status of slavery in Louisiana up in the air. On the one hand, many Louisiana sugar planters declared their loyalty to the Union; on the other hand, the state of Louisiana had seceded and as such had forfeited the protection the Constitution afforded to slavery.[41]

Precisely because Louisiana had left the Union, some northern commanders welcomed contrabands into their lines and treated them as emancipated. General John W. Phelps, a Vermont abolitionist, was the most aggressive advocate of this approach. When he first arrived on Ship Island, Phelps had ostentatiously declared that the very admission of Louisiana as a slave state had been a violation of the Constitution and that slavery therefore had no legal standing. Over the next few months, Phelps, who commanded Camp Parapet above New Orleans, treated Louisiana's slaves as emancipated and welcomed them into his camp. Local planters complained that Phelps was stepping beyond the law by sending his soldiers onto plantations and enticing slaves to leave, but Phelps denied it. "Many of these Negroes have been sent away from one of the neighboring sugar plantations, by their owner," Phelps explained. Owners were rumored to be telling their slaves that "the Yankees are King here now, and that they must go to their King for food and shelter."[42] Butler responded on July 19 with an order declaring that the expulsion of slaves from plantations would be "deemed an act of Voluntary emancipation and slaves sent away by their Masters with such declarations" would "be regarded and treated as manumitted & emancipated."[43]

Yet both generals had the sense that the War Department instructions implementing the First Confiscation Act were no longer adequate. "It is clear that the public good requires slavery to be abolished," Phelps wrote, "but in what manner is it to be done? The mere quiet operation of Congressional law cannot deal with Slavery as in its former status before the war."[44] Notably less self-righteous than Phelps, Butler was in his own lawyerly way equally certain that existing policy could not adequately address the conditions in Louisiana. It was not obvious to Butler, for example, that the slaves in Louisiana met the criteria for self-emancipation. All along the southern Atlantic coast the slaveholders abandoned their farms and plantations, but in southern Louisiana many slaveholders did not leave, some claimed to have opposed secession all along, and still others were willing to proclaim their loyalty to the Union. By one report, Jefferson Parish, just south of New Orleans, had opposed secession by an overwhelming vote of 900 to 200.[45] "The planters and men of property are now tired of the war," Butler reported. Moreover, they were "well-disposed toward the Union, only fearing lest their negroes should not be let alone, would be quite happy to have the Union restored in all things."[46] Under the circumstances it was not clear whether existing emancipation policy was applicable. On what basis, Butler wondered, could the military legally free Louisiana slaves?

The problem arose because the slaves in Louisiana behaved just as the slaves in the Border States and along the southern Atlantic coast behaved: they ran to Union army camps and claimed their freedom. When they got to Camp Parapet, General Phelps welcomed them. But as night follows day, owners followed runaways and demanded their return. Butler had to do something, and what he first tried to do was split the difference. He advised Phelps that if he had any useful employment for a runaway, he should "employ him without any scruple." If there was no such work, the runaway should be treated "like any other vagrant about the Camp." Butler himself "caused as many to be employed as I have use for." He also tried to distinguish the slaves of actively disloyal masters from those who were loyal or who, if not quite loyal, had nevertheless peacefully acquiesced to the authority of the Union. The slaves of disloyal masters "I am hunting out and holding for confiscation under the laws," Butler explained. With these distinctions—between slaves who could be employed and those who could not, between slaves of loyal and those of disloyal owners—Butler was trying to remain within the law. He understood that "a Military Commander has no right to an opinion" on what government "policy" ought to be. Phelps was prepared to proclaim the freedom of all the slaves in Union-occupied Louisiana, but Butler doubted that any Union general had the legal authority to do so. A series of testy exchanges between the two generals ensued.

Butler also faced an urgent practical problem: "*It is a physical impossibility to take all.*" There were upwards of 100,000 slaves in the areas occupied by Union forces in Louisiana in 1862 and perhaps more than 150,000 in the Union-occupied parts of the lower Mississippi Valley. The army could not employ that many workers, nor could its commissary readily supply the provisions to feed and shelter them. For Butler it was not a question of the right or wrong of slavery. "Reared in the full belief that slavery is a curse to the nation," he explained, "further acquaintance with it only deepens and widens" that conviction. But whereas Butler could accommodate a few thousand freed people in Virginia, he felt overwhelmed by the numbers in Louisiana. "Now," Butler asked Secretary of War Stanton on May 25, "what am I to do?"[47]

Here Benjamin Butler proved yet again that however incompetent he was as a military commander, he was a sharp lawyer with a keen sense of the politics of the war. When he wrote his letter to Stanton, he had to know—because anyone who read the papers knew—that

Congress was in the final stages of debate over a second confiscation bill that would address precisely the issue raised by the status of the slaves in the occupied Mississippi Valley. Phelps also knew it. In mid-June he asked Butler to forward their correspondence to Washington in the hopes that Stanton would settle the dispute.[48]

7

"BY THE ACT OF CONGRESS THEY ARE CLEARLY FREE"

A FEW DAYS AFTER the Thirty-Seventh Congress returned to Washington in early December of 1861, Senator Lyman Trumbull introduced "A Bill to Confiscate the Property of Rebels and Free their Slaves." *All* the slaves of *all* the rebels. The bill—now known as the Second Confiscation Act—made its way slowly through both houses until it finally became law on July 17, 1862. A lot happened in those intervening months. Dramatic northern military successes in the Mississippi Valley brought perhaps 150,000 slaves into Union lines. In the East, General McClellan's long-awaited campaign in Virginia lumbered forward and finally stalled within earshot of Richmond, the Confederate capital. Frustrated Republicans began to demand a harder war, and with it a more aggressive approach to slavery. By then they had lost all hope that a submerged unionist sentiment among southern whites would assert itself and overthrow secession. The only truly loyal southerners were the slaves, Republicans concluded. A "general" emancipation would punish the disloyal slaveholders, reward the loyal slaves, and suppress the rebellion. The laws of war, Trumbull explained, gave the federal government the "right to free the slaves of rebels," whether or not their slaves had been used by Confederate forces in direct support of the rebellion.[1]

This was still military emancipation, but dramatically expanded in scope. In truth, emancipation had been expanding for some time. Back in mid-1861, in the First Confiscation Act, Congress deprived masters of any slaves used in the rebellion. Almost immediately the War Department broadened emancipation's reach by freeing all slaves from rebel areas who emancipated themselves by coming into Union lines voluntarily. By 1861 the concept of self-emancipation through voluntary entry into Union lines had ballooned to include all slaves who remained behind when their masters fled from invading Union forces. But this left uncertain the status of large numbers of slaves in places like southern Louisiana, where masters often remained on their plantations when Union troops arrived in early 1862. The Second Confiscation Act freed many of those slaves as well.

As the scope of emancipation expanded, both Congress and the president made bolder claims of authority under the war powers clause of the Constitution. In the First Confiscation Act, Congress declared the forfeiture of slaves used in rebellion, but it ceded to the president, as commander in chief, the power to emancipate forfeited slaves. In the Second Confiscation Act, Congress itself would directly emancipate rebel-owned slaves within Union lines in the seceded states, affecting thousands of slaves in the Union-occupied parts of the Mississippi Valley. But what about the unoccupied parts of the Confederacy? In those areas Republicans once again ceded the power to proclaim a general emancipation to the commander in chief. By clearing two distinct legal paths for the emancipation of slaves in both the occupied and the unoccupied areas of the Confederacy, the Republicans believed they had set in motion the complete destruction of slavery in all the seceded states.

THE SECOND CONFISCATION ACT

The First Confiscation Act zoomed through the legislative process at breakneck speed in July of 1861. Its successor moved at the slowest-possible pace for a single session; having been introduced in the opening days of Congress, it was not passed until the very last day of an unusually long session. Preliminary versions of the Second Confiscation Act were introduced into both houses in December of 1861, disappeared into the dark recesses of congressional committees, reemerged haltingly as winter gave way to spring, but did not occupy the full attention of either house until May and June of 1862. It was not until mid-July, more than six months after the process began, that the Senate and House passed the bill into law, to be signed by the president on July 17, 1862. This Second Confiscation Act was far more complicated, but also more comprehensive, than its predecessor.[2]

Less than a week after Trumbull introduced his bill, Republican Senator Lot Morrill of Maine proposed a resolution "to provide for the confiscation of the property of rebels" nullifying "all claim or right" by traitors and abettors of treason "to the labor of any person under the laws of any State or Territory."[3] Morrill's resolution was referred to Trumbull's Judiciary Committee, which reported it back to the Senate on January 15. It was not until late February, however, that Trumbull moved "consideration" of the resolution. Debate proceeded on and off for weeks, during which time various bills, amendments, and alternatives piled up. On April 29, Pennsylvania Senator Edgar Cowan proposed sorting them all out by referring everything to a select committee. At first a number of Republicans objected to Cowan's motion, but when a substantive disagreement arose between two versions of the bill—one proposed by Senator Jacob Collamer of Vermont and the other by Senator Henry Wilson of Massachusetts—they handed the controversy off to a committee to sort out the differences.

At issue between the two senators was how much latitude to give the president in enforcing the "prospective" clause of the statute, the clause designed to emancipate slaves in unoccupied areas of the Confederacy by means of a presidential proclamation. Collamer's proposal authorized the president, at his discretion, to free the slaves in any state that had been in rebellion for at least six months. Wilson proposed an alternative amendment that "authorized *and required*" the president to proclaim the emancipation of slaves owned by rebels in any area still in "a state of insurrection" within thirty days of the bill's passage. Wilson's amendment would force the president's hand; Collamer's gave the president more leeway.[4] Both versions authorized the emancipation of slaves of any person "engaged in rebellion" in the areas the president proclaimed to be in a state of insurrection. But where Collamer's version empowered the president to issue a proclamation "if he deems it necessary for the suppression of the Rebellion," Wilson's took the decision away from the commander in chief. Collamer believed that "the existence of an actual military necessity in military operations must be judged by those who conduct those operations." If the president finds that "such a necessity has come, he shall issue his proclamation" stating "that after a certain day, if they then continue in arms against the United States, their slaves shall be free."[5] To resolve the difference between Collamer and Wilson, the Senate on May 6 created a special committee, chaired by New Hampshire Senator Daniel Clark, with instructions to report a bill back to the floor.

On May 16, Clark's Select Committee reported a bill that gave the president substantial discretion, thus sustaining Senator Collamer's proposal.[6] At stake, it seems, was the constitutional legitimacy of emancipation in unoccupied areas of the Confederacy. By taking the decision away from the president, Wilson's amendment seemed to make emancipation a legislative rather than a military act, something most Republicans still thought was unconstitutional. Though Wilson was a radical, this was not an issue that clearly divided radicals from moderates. New Hampshire's Senator John Hale aligned himself with the radicals on emancipation, for example, but he worried that by stripping the president of his discretion, Wilson's amendment was "not in accordance with the Constitution." Hale was "as anxious and as earnest as anybody to advance the cause of free principles," he said, "so far as might be done consistently with the rights we owe under the Constitution." On that principle he was in complete agreement with Senator Wilson. The problem was that Wilson's amendment "does not look like a war measure." Instead, it made emancipation seem like punishment for a crime and thereby vested the president with judicial rather than military power. For Hale, that contradicted the Republicans' long-standing declarations of "fidelity to the Constitution."[7] Nor was Hale alone; Wilson could not attract any significant support among his fellow Republicans. From mid-May onward, Senator Clark's committee report—giving the president discretion to issue an emancipation proclamation as a military necessity—was the focus of senatorial debate. But before the Senate got around to voting on the Clark bill, it was forced to consider a somewhat different version that passed the House on June 18.

The legislative history of the Second Confiscation Act was similar in the House, though it resulted in two bills, separating confiscation from emancipation. On December 2, 1861, Republican Congressman Thomas Eliot of Massachusetts introduced a resolution that became the basis of subsequent debate. He began by reaffirming his commitment to the federal consensus. We "disclaim all power under the Constitution to interfere by ordinary legislation with the institutions of the several States," Eliot began. Yet "the war now existing must be conducted according to the ordinary usages and rights of military service." Congress could not legally abolish slavery in any state, but under the laws of war "the commander-in-chief of our Army, and the officers in command under him, have the right to emancipate all persons held as slaves in any military district in a state of insurrection against the national government." Eliot was thus careful to reiterate the military justification of emancipation, as well as the president's prerogative in enforcing it. The Eliot resolution would free not merely the slaves owned by rebels but all slaves "in any military district in a state of insurrection."[8] Congressman Roscoe Conkling, a Republican from New York, immediately moved to amend it to apply instead to the slaves of disloyal owners. Several other resolutions were introduced that day and the next, but consideration of them all was postponed until December 10. Meanwhile, on December 3, Republican Congressman John Bingham of Ohio introduced a bill to "forfeit the property and slaves of persons who shall engage in or aid and abet rebellion against the United States."[9] On December 17 the House voted to refer the Eliot resolution, and all others like it, to the Judiciary Committee. It was not until several months later, on March 20, that the committee finally reported back to the House, recommending against passage of any of the emancipation bills and resolutions. But Bingham, a member of the committee, issued a minority report consisting of a bill freeing the slaves of all persons engaged in or supporting the rebellion.[10] Bingham's minority report became the focus of discussion in the House. Various amendments and alternatives were proposed, and the House decided on April 23 to resolve matters by sending everything to a special select committee of its own, chaired by Congressman Eliot, author of the December 2 resolution.

On April 30, Eliot separated the issues of confiscation and emancipation by putting them into two different pieces of legislation. The first was "[a] bill to confiscate the property of rebels for the payment of the expenses of the present rebellion, and for other purposes." The second was "[a] bill to free from servitude the slaves of rebels engaged in abetting the existing rebellion against the Government of the United States." Rather than confiscate slaves, it emancipated them, not as a military necessity but as punishment for the crime of rebellion. It was legislative rather than military emancipation; hence, no presidential proclamation was required.[11] Eliot reported both bills out of committee on May 14, debate began on May 20, and after six days of heated discussion, the House passed the confiscation bill but narrowly defeated the emancipation bill by a vote of 74 to 78.

It is hardly surprising that the House rejected such a radical emancipation measure; what is truly remarkable is that so many Republican congressmen supported it. Like Wilson in the Senate, a growing number of representatives in the House were coming to believe that the Constitution allowed Congress, as a war measure, to legislatively abolish slavery in a state. This conclusion divided congressional Republicans. Eliot led off the ensuing debate. He justified congressional emancipation on the ground that the Constitution vested the war powers in the legislature as well as in the commander in chief. He even claimed that Congress could free all the slaves in a *state* because, in this instance, entire states had committed the crime of treason. When Eliot finished his lengthy address, he was followed to the podium by a long line of Republicans defending the radical emancipation bill. The Constitution no longer applied to the seceded states, they said. And even if it did, surely the Constitution required the federal government to protect the slaves who had proved their loyalty to the Union rather than the slaveholders who had rebelled against it. In a state of war, another Republican declared, we may take the enemy's property, "burn his cities, devastate his fields, deprive him of his life, all of which are great intrinsic evils, but it is said that we may not perform that intrinsically righteous act—emancipate his slaves."[12] The upsurge of radicalism among House Republicans was impressive, but it was not enough to get the Eliot bill passed.

The bill went back to committee with instructions to specify more clearly the classes of persons whose slaves could be confiscated, and to restore the president's discretion—and with it the "military" character of emancipation—by requiring a proclamation from the commander in chief for the law to take effect. The substitute bill was a labyrinth of classifications and jargon, but it did specify six classes of persons whose slaves would be emancipated, including those still in armed rebellion sixty days after a presidential proclamation. It also authorized the president to "appoint commissioners to carry the act into effect." Thus amended, the emancipation bill sailed through the House on June 17 by a vote of 82 to 54.[13]

When the two House bills arrived in the Senate on June 23, they were rejected in favor of the single bill that had been hammered out by Senator Clark as chair of the Senate's Select Committee. On June 28, the Senate approved its own bill by a typically lopsided vote (28 to 13) in which nearly every Republican approved and nearly everyone else opposed. The House, in no mood to be snubbed, took up consideration of the amended Senate bill on July 3 and quickly rejected it by an overwhelming vote of 124 to 8. Eliot and his colleagues clearly preferred to put confiscation and emancipation into two separate bills. Back in the Senate, Clark insisted on a single bill. All of this meant that the legislation would have to go to a conference committee. On July 11, Congressman Eliot caved, and the Conference Committee reported the Senate version to both Houses. As Senator Wilson later put it, the Conference Committee's report "combined confiscation and emancipation in one bill."[14] That same day, the House voted, 82 to 42, to accept the report. The next day, July 12, the Senate approved it by an even more lopsided vote of 27 to 12. Only two Republican senators—Browning and Cowan—voted against it.

The differences among Republicans over emancipation were largely strategic. The most troublesome issue—presidential discretion—did not arise from any fundamental disagreement among Republicans over the desirability of emancipation. To be sure, senators sometimes expressed concerns over the wording of different clauses in the bills under consideration. Senators Samuel Pomeroy and Charles Sumner, for example, wanted Trumbull's bill to make absolutely clear that the U.S. government would in no way be involved in the capture and return of fugitive slaves. Trumbull assured them that it would not. Occasionally an errant conservative, like Republican Senator Cowan of Pennsylvania, complained that an emancipation bill would "extinguish" all hope of sectional reconciliation, but hardly any other Republicans agreed with him. Cowan also took the position, expressed most forcefully by Illinois Senator Orville Browning, that an emancipation statute was superfluous because "the war powers of the Government were fully adequate to the needs of the occasion." Cowan insisted that authorizing the president to emancipate the slaves of rebels was "utterly valueless" since "the President and his generals, under the war power" were already "clothed with ample authority." In the House, Pennsylvania Congressman John Hickman took a similar position and opposed the bill "because the President had all the power now."[15] Senators Sherman and Collamer wanted the bill to specify the "classes of rebels" whose slaves would be freed, as did several Republicans in the House, and the final bill did so. But no Republican denied that emancipation was legally sound, militarily necessarily, or morally just.

Notwithstanding the Senate's decision to combine the two House bills into one, the distinction between emancipation of slaves and the confiscation of other property was clearly understood at the time. Slaves could be emancipated because the constitutional restriction on permanent confiscation—the ban on attainder—applied only to real estate. "It was the realty, and the realty only, that the attainder acted on," Senator Browning explained. The "words of the Constitution," Sumner argued, applied to real estate but "do not forbid the forfeiture of personal estate." The ban on attainder, Lincoln agreed, "applies only in this country, as I understand, to real, or landed estate." This distinction meant, among other things, that court proceedings were unnecessary to emancipate slaves whose owners were "in rebellion." In loyal slave states like Kentucky and Missouri, where the courts were functioning but where numerous slaveholders supported the Confederacy, "the property of the traitor" could be forfeited upon conviction, Trumbull explained, "the personalty [slaves] forever, and the real estate, under the Constitution, for life only." For more than a generation, antislavery lawyers had carefully worked out the distinction between slaves and other forms of property, arguing that "property in man" was *not* constitutionally protected. Here, in the careful construction of the Second Confiscation Act—more than anywhere else during the long process of slavery's destruction—the seeds sown by the antislavery movement were bearing fruit. Thanks to abolitionist lawyers and politicians, it was easier for Republicans to free a slave than to confiscate a house.[16]

Lincoln had only a few minor concerns about the emancipation provisions of the bill. It was "startling," he said, to claim "that congress can free a slave within a state." It is unclear what Lincoln was concerned about here. He may have wanted Congress to indicate that it was emancipating slaves not in "states" but in areas "in rebellion." He might have wanted to clarify that Congress could emancipate only in areas occupied by the Union army, thus preserving its military character. Or he may have been thinking of the Border States, where the law specified emancipation as a punishment for rebellion or treason. But whatever Lincoln was referring to, he considered it a minor problem—"an unfortunate form of expression, rather than a substantial objection," Lincoln explained. Lincoln's second minor concern pertained to a technical procedure, which was easily met by the addition of a simple sentence. Under the bill there were six classes of rebels whose slaves could be forfeited, but the bill did not state who had the authority to determine whether the owner of any given slave fell within one of those six classes. Finally, Lincoln wanted to ensure that emancipation as a punishment for crime—as opposed to military emancipation—could apply only prospectively, to activities that were deemed criminal *after* the bill's passage.

Lincoln's major objection to the Second Confiscation Act had nothing to do with emancipation. He was worried that the provisions for confiscating real estate in rebellious areas violated the constitutional ban on attainder. When he introduced the bill in December, Senator Trumbull had proposed "the absolute and complete forfeiture forever to the United States of every species of property, real and personal" owned by rebels in any areas that were "beyond the reach of civil process in the ordinary mode of judicial proceeding in consequence of the present rebellion." That is, in the seceded states there was no distinction between real estate and slaves—all the property was forfeited "forever," without court proceedings. Only in the loyal states were courts required, and only in those cases was the real estate of convicted traitors protected by the constitutional ban on attainder. Lincoln objected to this. He did not believe real estate *anywhere* could be confiscated "forever." To be sure, under the laws of war, belligerents had the right to occupy territory and confiscate homes for military purposes, but the confiscation of real estate lasted only as long as the war persisted. Lincoln worried that the bill Congress was about to pass did not make this clear enough, that it might therefore violate the Constitution's ban on the confiscation of real estate beyond the life of the convicted traitor. Lincoln asked Congress to remain in session an extra day to remedy the legal defect. His concerns were so serious that he was prepared to veto the entire bill if the problems were not corrected.[17]

To accommodate Lincoln's objections, Senator Clark proposed two amendments. The first declared that "forfeiture of real estate of the offender" could not extend "beyond his natural life." The second clarified the bill's amnesty provision, authorizing the president to restore the property of those he might choose to pardon, thus ensuring that constitutional errors could be corrected by means of executive clemency. There was a flurry of senatorial huffing and puffing about the integrity and independence of the legislative branch. A handful of senators professed to be "astonished" by the "irregularity" of the president dictating the content of legislation to Congress. But calmer heads prevailed once it became known that a number of senators had initiated the contact with the president and had asked Lincoln to explain his objections so that they might be dealt with in Congress.[18]

The disagreement over property confiscation was serious—it had the potential to cause a major rift within the Republican Party—but it did not undermine the consensus in favor of emancipation. Several Republican congressmen made it clear that they doubted whether the property confiscation provisions of the bill would have any real effect, given the constitutional limits on the permanent forfeiture of real estate. By contrast, there was broad agreement on the importance of the provisions emancipating slaves, as well as the clause authorizing the president to employ black men *within* the Union army. (Up until then, the army paid wages to emancipated slaves only as civilian employees.) "I have never from the beginning disguised my conviction that the most important part of the bill relates to emancipation," Charles Sumner explained. He supported Clark's amendment, readily conceding the point on confiscation to secure passage of the more important emancipation provisions. "Whatever may be the difference between the President and Congress" regarding the confiscation of property, Sumner added, "there are two points on which there is no difference. The blacks are to be employed, and the slaves are to be freed. In this proclamation the President and Congress will unite."[19]

WITH THE DIFFERENCES BETWEEN Congress and the president settled, Lincoln signed the Second Confiscation Act—officially known as "An Act to suppress Insurrection, to punish Treason and

Rebellion, to seize and confiscate the Property of Rebels, and for other Purposes"—on July 17, 1862. It was a complicated statute, ambiguous in places, though not the legally incoherent mess historians sometimes pronounce it to be. It was carefully framed by some of the best constitutional lawyers in the Congress, but it was also complicated by the differences among Republicans about how it ought to be framed. The easiest way to understand the statute is to grasp the relative simplicity of its most important goal: it would free the slaves of all disloyal masters. This would extend emancipation far beyond the scope of the First Confiscation Act, which applied only to slaves actually used in the rebellion. It likewise surpassed the reach of the August 8, 1861, War Department instructions, which emancipated all slaves voluntarily entering Union lines. By freeing the slaves of all disloyal masters, the Second Confiscation Act was—by comparison with its predecessors—much broader and at least in principle much simpler.

But the simplicity of the statute's basic goal was obscured at various points by the unstated assumptions upon which it rested. Republicans believed, for example, that the Constitution did not recognize slaves as property, hence the statute's complicated rules governing the confiscation of real estate did not apply to the emancipation of slaves. Republicans made this clear during the congressional debates, but they did not make it clear within the statute itself. Similarly, Republicans assumed that the Constitution did not allow them to treat slavery in the loyal Border States in precisely the same way they could treat slavery in the seceded states. This, too, was clearer in the floor debates than it became in the actual wording of the law. Guided by these invisible premises Republican lawmakers produced a statute that, among other things, created several different procedures by which slaves could be emancipated. Some would be freed when a master was convicted of treason, others upon the master's conviction for a brand new crime: "rebellion." These would seem to apply only to masters in the loyal slave states where the courts were still functioning, but the statute itself is unclear about this. By far the largest number would be freed by presidential proclamation, a purely "military" emancipation requiring no judicial tribunals whatsoever. Military emancipation would seem to apply chiefly to the disloyal states, but once again the statute is not explicit about this. Emancipation by means of presidential proclamation was "prospective"—it would be imposed in the future on those slaveholders still in rebellion after the proclamation's deadline had passed. But the Second Confiscation Act also made it clear that some slaves were already emancipated and specified that others should be emancipated immediately. As a result, a law originally designed—in Lyman Trumbull's deceptively simple words—"to confiscate the property of rebels and free their slaves"— can be maddeningly difficult to unpack.[20]

The truly radical scope of the statute emerges only in Section 6, where courts and treason convictions give way to direct military seizures of all rebel property upon orders from the commander in chief. It was in this section that Congress called for a presidential proclamation warning of the consequences for those who persisted "in armed rebellion" against the Union. Persons still "aiding or abetting such rebellion" sixty days after the proclamation (Lincoln later stretched it to one hundred days) would have their property seized and sold by the government. Section 2 had already established "rebellion" as a crime punishable by the "liberation" of the convicted rebel's slaves. Section 6, however, allowed the commander in chief to punish "rebels" under the laws of war without resort to courts, after a fair warning by means of a presidential proclamation. Implicitly but unmistakably, Congress thereby cleared the way for an emancipation proclamation freeing the slaves of all disloyal masters. Lincoln seems to have understood it this way. Within days of signing the bill into law, he drafted the first version of an emancipation proclamation that began by citing Section 6 and closed by promising to free all the slaves in areas still in rebellion the following January 1. This was "prospective" emancipation.[21]

Unlike Section 6, Section 9 specified and affirmed the immediate emancipation of rebel-owned slaves in areas already occupied by the Union army. Three distinct classes of slaves were covered here. The first were slaves who had run to Union lines from rebellious owners, including those who escaped into a loyal state or onto "free soil" from seceded states such as Virginia. This applied to slaves who ran to places like Fortress Monroe, to Maryland from Virginia, or to Kentucky from Tennessee. The second were slaves deserted by their owners "and coming under the control of the government of the United States." This included slaves in Hampton, Virginia, the Sea Islands, and indeed most of the southern Atlantic Coast. The third and by far the largest group encompassed rebel-owned slaves living in places previously "occupied by rebel forces" but "afterwards occupied by the forces of the United States." Here Congress meant to emancipate slaves of all disloyal owners, immediately, throughout much of the Mississippi Valley, most importantly in Louisiana.[22]

Three other sections pushed emancipation still further, albeit indirectly. Section 10 overruled without quite repealing the Fugitive Slave Act of 1850. It declared that "no slave escaping into any State, Territory, or the District of Columbia, from any other State, shall be delivered up, or in any way hindered of his liberty." The entire burden of proof was shifted to the owners of runaway slaves, who were now required to go to court, prove their ownership, and swear under oath that they had never given aid or comfort to the rebellion. Once again Congress affirmed that no Union military personnel could participate in any way in the capture and return of fugitive slaves, "on pain of being dismissed from the service." Section 11 codified in statute the practice that General Benjamin Butler had established at Fortress Monroe at the beginning of the war—that the restoration of the

Union was better served by employing fugitives rather than by returning them to their owners, where their labor would support the rebellion. Here again, paid labor in support of the Union validated
emancipation. Section 12 authorized the president to assist any slaves
"made free by the provisions of this act, as may be willing to emigrate" to a colony "beyond the limits of the United States" in which
they would be guaranteed "all the rights and privileges of freemen."
This was subsidized, voluntary emigration—the form of "colonization" most often advocated by Lincoln and the Republicans.[23]

It was an extraordinary statute—meticulously crafted yet sweeping in scope, respectful of the constitutional limits of property confiscation yet bold and comprehensive in its attack on slavery. It reaffirmed
the most important antislavery policies Republicans had embraced up
to that point—the emancipation of slaves who came within Union
lines from the seceded states, the neutralization of the fugitive slave
clause, and the repeal of the ban on black enlistment in the Union
army—but it pushed much further, to the prospective emancipation
of virtually all slaves in the rebellious states. Though it has come to be
known as the Second Confiscation Act, in the months after its passage
it was frequently referred to as "the emancipation bill" and was understood to have freed significant numbers of slaves immediately. As one
Boston paper explained, "Certain classes of slaves enumerated in the
act are declared free 'hereafter,'—that is from the moment when the
act took effect. . . . No proclamation is required to give these provisions effect." The "Confiscation-Emancipation Act" required court
orders to confiscate property, but not to free slaves, the *Springfield
Republican* noted. Union generals may "safely take it for granted that
they are to consider the classes declared free by the bill as free at once,
to all intents and purposes." By the time Lincoln signed the Second
Confiscation Act on July 17, 1862, Republicans in Congress had made
it clear that in passing the law, they intended to destroy slavery completely in the seceded states.[24]

"LET SLAVERY FEEL THE WAR"

Democrats and Border State congressmen were scandalized by the vast implications of the Second Confiscation Act. Though stridently opposed to the emancipation provisions of the proposed law, most of their objections were familiar, and the debates they managed to provoke fell out along predictable lines. It was "the unnecessary agitation of the slavery question [that] was the cause of the war," Democratic Congressman John B. Steele of New York declared. No, Republicans answered, slavery itself was the cause of the war, and only by destroying slavery could the rebellion be thoroughly crushed. The large-scale emancipation Republicans were proposing was "fanaticism," Representative William Holman, a Democrat from Indiana, declared, and would "destroy the hopes of restoring the Union." But Republicans had given up waiting for the phantom unionists to rise up and overthrow secession. The slaveholders were the heart and soul of the rebellion, Republicans argued, and the only way to suppress their insurrection was to destroy the slave society that spawned the insurrectionists to begin with. Democrats denounced "military necessity"— the "wild, heated, and monstrous" brainchild of John Quincy Adams—as a spurious rationale for abolitionist radicalism and an outrageous violation of the Constitution. "Pass these acts," Indiana Democrat John Law warned, "emancipate their negroes; place arms in the hands of these human gorillas to murder their masters and violate their wives and daughters, and you will have a war such as was never witnessed in the worst days of the French Revolution, and horrors never exceeded in St. Domingo." The Republicans went ahead and did it anyway.[25]

Throughout the spring of 1862, denunciations of the impending legislation were heard far beyond the halls of Congress. Less than a week before the House passed the final version of the bill, none other than General George McClellan jumped into the debate by telling the president what he thought of the shift in emancipation policy. Lincoln inadvertently gave the general the opportunity when, disturbed by McClellan's disappointing performance, he decided to visit the general at the headquarters of the Army of the Potomac at Harrison's Landing in Virginia. There McClellan handed the president a letter decrying the expansion of the military conflict into a full-scale assault on slavery. This should be a limited war, not one aimed at the "subjugation of the people of any state," the general explained. "Neither confiscation of property, political executions of persons, territorial organization of states or forcible abolition of slavery should be contemplated for a moment." Where Congress was about to confiscate the slaves of anyone supporting the rebellion, McClellan insisted that "all private property and unarmed persons should be strictly protected." He accepted the military rationale for a limited emancipation but believed that in general "[m]ilitary power should not be allowed to interfere with the relation of servitude." McClellan understood what Congress and the administration had decreed, and he did not dispute the policy already in place of emancipating slaves who came into Union lines after escaping from rebellious owners. But the Second Confiscation Act would do something far more radical, McClellan complained. Under the guise of "military necessity" Congress was about to pass a law aimed at the complete destruction of slavery in the seceded states. That, the general argued, would completely alter the character of the war.[26]

Any civilian who read the papers could also see that the Second Confiscation Act represented an important shift in federal emancipation policy. On the day the Senate passed the bill, Anna Ella Carroll—who had read nothing but a synopsis of it—wrote an urgent letter to Lincoln asking him to veto it. "This bill will inaugurate a new policy, and change the whole morale of the war," Carroll warned. "It will no longer be regarded, as a war for the maintenance of the

American Constitution, but as one, for the subjugation of the Southern States, and the destruction of their social system." If you sign the bill into law, she warned Lincoln, "you will no longer be considered by the American people, as the President of the mighty republic of the United States; but, as the head of the Abolition faction, warring for the destruction of slavery."[27] It was as clear to critics as it was to supporters that with the Second Confiscation Act federal policy had shifted from limited to universal emancipation in the seceded states.

Although Republicans always insisted that the war for Union was inseparable from the issue of slavery, by early 1862 there were novel elements in the way they defended emancipation. It was not simply that military policy had become more aggressive. There was a new emphasis on the *slaveholders* as the source of the rebellion and with it the abandonment of any hope that there might exist somewhere in the South a significant unionist element within the slave-owning class. As more and more Republicans zeroed in on the slaveholders, the suppression of the rebellion became synonymous with the destruction of the slaveholders as a class.

Limited emancipation had been a feature of limited war. Hoping to provoke unionist slaveholders to give up their rebellion, and convinced that the tide of escaping contrabands would sweep slavery away, Republicans had initially restricted emancipation to slaves who came within Union lines in the seceded states. But by the spring of 1862, having lost their faith in southern unionism, and no longer persuaded that self-emancipation would be enough to destroy slavery, Republicans began calling for a harder war that included universal emancipation in the seceded states. "Who does not know that treason has gained strength by the leniency with which it has been treated?" Senator Lyman Trumbull asked as he recommended emancipating the slaves of all rebels in the seceded states. "Surely we have dealt gently with our enemies" by not emancipating all of their slaves, Republican Representative Samuel Blair of Pennsylvania declared. "We have held back these powerful engines of military policy in the hope that the enemies of the nation would return to reason and repentance." But as the slaveholders had shown neither "reason" nor "repentance," it was time for the North to demonstrate "downright earnestness of purpose" by passing the Second Confiscation Act. What should the government do with slavery now, another Republican congressman asked in the spring of 1862. "What policy, if any, should the loyal men of the country adopt respecting the future treatment of this cancer upon the body politic? The reply which ought, in my judgment, to be made to these questions, is this: '*Since slavery made the war, let slavery feel the war.*'"[28]

The problem was not merely slaveholders who rebelled; the problem was that the institution of slavery bred rebellion within the slaveholding class. Republicans therefore spoke as if the Second Confiscation Act was designed to free *all* the slaves in the seceded states. "*I am for destroying this hostile institution in every State that has made war upon this Government,*" Republican Congressman Charles D. Sedgwick of New York put it. "I propose to leave not one slave in the wake of our advancing armies; not one." Congressman James M. Ashley, Republican of Ohio, agreed. "My purpose," he declared, is "to destroy the institution of slavery, if it became necessary to save the country . . . in every State which had rebelled." "By the laws of peace [slavery] was entitled to protection, and had it," Republican Congressman John Rice of Maine declared. "By the laws of war it is entitled to annihilation."[29]

The "vast majority of slaveholders within the territory now held by the rebels," one Republican newspaper explained, "—probably nineteen-twentieths at the least—have overtly identified themselves with the rebellion." A second confiscation law freeing the slaves of rebels was therefore tantamount to universal emancipation in the rebellious states. "As most of the owners of slaves are engaged in the rebellion, and will probably continue so for some time," Senator Trumbull explained, "the effect" of the Second Confiscation Act "would be, if this bill were speedily enacted into a law, that they would by their own act give freedom to most of the slaves in the country."[30]

As Republicans were coming to see emancipation as a punishment of rebellious masters, another novel element entered into their discussions of emancipation. Republican congressmen, editors, government officials, and private citizens—all noticed that whenever Union soldiers or sailors arrived in the South, the slaves made their allegiance to the United States clear. Everywhere along the Atlantic coast, rebellious masters fled from advancing Union forces, but their slaves stayed behind. On the streets of New Orleans, sullen whites, men and women alike, averted their eyes, spat in contempt, and stood on their balconies emptying chamber pots onto Union soldiers below. In contrast, the slaves in the South welcomed U.S. troops, risked their lives to make their way to Union camps, and provided crucial intelligence on the size and location of nearby Confederate forces. Impressed by the allegiance of the slaves, Republicans began to argue that the United States was obliged not only to suppress the rebels but also to protect the four million loyal blacks in the southern states. Emancipation was not merely a punishment for treason; it was also a just reward for the loyalty of the slaves. That the slaves hated slavery, that they would take advantage of the war by claiming their freedom—these had always been the premises of Republican emancipation policy. By 1862, however, countless Union soldiers and officers had sent word back home, and to Washington, that the slaves were the only people they could trust when they got to the South. This was a new theme in the wartime debate over slavery and emancipation.

There is no such thing as a disloyal slave, Frederick Douglass declared in what became a standard feature of Republican rhetoric. Salmon Chase called for "liberation of the loyal population of the South from slavery to the rebels." One version of the confiscation act would have authorized Union commanders in the South "to invite all *loyal* persons to come within his lines and be enrolled in the service of the United States." Slaves themselves raised the issue when they came to Union lines claiming their masters were "rank secessionists." This made the slaves' loyalty to the Union all the more compelling. "The slave of a rebel is placed in a somewhat peculiar position," one Republican congressman explained. The master demands the slave's allegiance, but so does the government. "In my opinion the Government's claim to allegiance is paramount to all others, and in order to prevent the slave being forced to aid in rebellion, it has the unquestionable right to break the bonds by which the master holds him."[31]

Another line was being crossed. If the Constitution prevented the federal government from interfering with slavery in the states, it just as surely required the federal government to protect those who resisted the claims of their disloyal masters and instead kept faith with their government. The implications of the new policy were felt most clearly, and immediately, in Louisiana.

LOUISIANA EMANCIPATED

Sometime in the spring of 1862 a number of Babbillard Lablanche's slaves walked off his plantation and made their way to the Union army at Camp Parapet, with their clothes and furniture in tow. The Lablanche place was located twelve miles above New Orleans, and he himself was one of the most prominent planters in the area. As General John Phelps, the commander at Camp Parapet, told the story, Lablanche threw the slaves off his plantation, telling them that "Yankees are king here now, and that they must go to their king for food and shelter." Lablanche told a somewhat different story. He claimed to have been loyal to the Union and "to have taken no part in the war," though his son was off fighting for the Confederacy. When the Union occupied the area the previous month, Lablanche told his slaves "that they were free" if they left and went to nearby Camp Parapet, where Phelps was welcoming runaways as emancipated. Led by "Jack," a number of Lablanche's slaves decided to leave, whereupon their owner provided them with a boat that would take them safely across the river to the Union camp. As of June 16, the slaves were living outside of Camp Parapet, excluded from entering by the orders of General Benjamin Butler. Butler was unsure what the actual policy regarding such slaves was. Phelps wanted to admit the slaves and to have them—along with all the slaves in the seceded states—declared free by the commander in chief as an act of military necessity. He was using the Lablanche slaves to force the issue. Phelps "intends making this a test case for the policy of the Government," Butler explained to the secretary of war on June 18. "I wish it might be so."[32]

As the Second Confiscation Act was making its way through Congress, the status of slaves in Union-occupied areas of the Mississippi Valley remained unclear. Unlike Fortress Monroe and the Sea Islands, Butler noted, many of the sugar planters of southern Louisiana had been reluctant secessionists, and many stayed on the plantations when the Union occupied the area in early 1862. Should Louisiana be treated like the loyal Border States, or should it be treated like the abandoned plantations along the southern Atlantic coast, where all the slaves were emancipated and put to work as free laborers? As he struggled to formulate a policy in May of 1862, Butler issued carefully worded instructions that combined elements of the two policies. He never referred to *slaves*, and he did not so much as hint at the status of those employed or excluded. Instead, Butler wrote his instructions as if the people arriving at the Union camps were vagrants. Those who could be usefully employed, black or white, were welcome to stay. Those who could not work, black or white, were to be excluded.[33]

This was a holding pattern, a temporary solution that Butler devised while he awaited policy instructions from his superiors in

Washington. It could not last for long. As the weeks passed and the number of escaping slaves increased, even Phelps realized that he could not provide for all the runaways with the resources at his disposal. "In spite of indirect discouragements," Captain John W. DeForest wrote, the slaves "are continually quitting the plantations and swarming to us for protection and support." When DeForest asked Phelps what to do with the most recent arrivals, the exasperated general replied, "*I* don't know,' as much bothered by the 'inevitable nigger' as if he were not an abolitionist." It was in the hopes of some resolution that Phelps had insisted that the exchange of letters between himself and Butler be forwarded to Washington, so that administration officials could determine what to do. Nobody wanted clarification more than Butler, and he happily complied with Phelps's request by forwarding the exchanges to the War Department along with a characteristically astute letter explaining the situation. But Secretary of War Edwin Stanton kept Butler waiting. "It has not yet been deemed necessary or wise to fetter your judgment by any specific instructions," Stanton told Butler on June 29.[34]

By then it was clear that the Republican policymakers in Washington were about to revise emancipation policy. Treasury Secretary Chase explained this in a letter to Butler in late June. Before the war began, Chase wrote, he had hoped that the rebellion would be quickly suppressed and the abolition of slavery "would be gradually effected" by the slave states themselves, "without shock or disturbance or injury, but peacefully & beneficially." But as the war persisted, Chase concluded that "the restoration of the old Union, with slavery untouched except by the mere weakening effects of the war, was impossible." Like "the great majority of the people of the United States," Chase concluded that to suppress the rebellion and restore the Union, "slavery must go." He had never doubted that "the war power" could be used to "destroy slavery," but he initially "doubted the expediency of its exercise." As the months passed, however, Chase's doubts dissipated until he realized that it was foolish "to abstain from military interference with slavery," that it would merely perpetuate "the subjugation of some four millions of loyal people [the slaves] to some three hundred thousand disloyal rebels." The letter also indicated that the president was changing his mind as well. In the meantime, the secretary urged Butler to let everyone in Louisiana know that "you are no proslavery man."[35]

A few days later Lincoln weighed in on the side of slaves who ran to Union lines, effectively endorsing Phelps's policy. The president, Stanton wrote Butler, "is of the opinion" that fugitive slaves coming into Union lines "cannot be sent back to their masters; that in common humanity they must not be permitted to suffer for want of food, shelter, or other necessaries of life: that, to this end, they should be provided for by the Quartermaster's and Commissary's Departments; and that those who are capable of labor should be set to work and paid reasonable wages."[36] As he had done with the Sea Islands, Lincoln gave Chase—the most fervent opponent of slavery in his cabinet—effective control of emancipation in Louisiana. And as *he* had done with the Sea Islands, Chase appointed a dedicated abolitionist—George Denison—as the special Treasury agent in Louisiana. Denison soon began sending Chase glowing reports of General Butler's enthusiastic support for emancipation.

On July 22, Secretary of War Stanton, acting under instruction from Lincoln, issued General Orders No. 109 implementing Section 11 of the Second Confiscation Act, which authorized the president to employ as many of the former slaves as was consistent with the "public welfare." Stanton directed all military commanders in the seceded states, including Louisiana, to "employ as laborers . . . so many persons of African descent as can be advantageously used," and enjoined the commanders to pay the black workers "reasonable wages for their labor." Butler clearly understood what all of this meant. "The Government have sustained Phelps about the Negroes," Butler wrote his wife, "and we shall have a Negro insurrection here I fancy." Blacks in the area were becoming "saucy and troublesome," Butler added, "and who blames them?" Though a longtime Democrat, Butler had come to agree with the Republicans that the war would undermine southern slave society—"This people are doomed to destruction," he said—and that as it did so, the slaves might well take advantage and rise in rebellion. For more than a year Butler had been among the most aggressive of antislavery generals, yet like so many other northerners in mid-1862, he felt a new determination to destroy slavery completely. "I am changing my opinions," he wrote in late July. Fed up with recalcitrant rebels, he concluded that there was "nothing of the people worth saving. I am inclined to give it all up to the blacks." He likened the fate of southern rebels to the rain of fire and brimstone that fell upon Sodom and Gomorrah, except that in this instance "the Lord will do so in the shape of the negroes."[37]

The timing could scarcely be more revealing. The two houses of Congress had passed the Second Confiscation Act on July 11 and 12. Lincoln signed the bill on July 17, drafted the implementation orders a few days later, and presented them to his cabinet on July 21 and 22. Stanton issued the orders that same day, July 22. Three days later, on July 25, Butler was explaining the new policy to his wife and preparing to implement it in Louisiana.

If Lincoln's endorsement of Phelps indicated the direction the government was taking, an even clearer indication was Lincoln's response to the Maryland unionist Reverdy Johnson. Back in June, acting on diplomatic complaints about Butler's treatment of foreign consuls in New Orleans, the State Department had dispatched Johnson to Louisiana to investigate the matter.[38] Overstepping his mission, Johnson reported back to Lincoln on July 16 that Louisiana unionists were becoming alienated by the drift toward emancipation, especially by the policies of General Phelps—which Lincoln had already effectively endorsed. Loyal Louisianans were beginning to worry that it was the "*purpose* of the Govt to force the Emancipation of the slaves." Johnson warned Lincoln that if Phelps was allowed to proceed unchecked, "this State cannot be, for years, if ever, re-instated in the Union." Lincoln's answer to Johnson was uncharacteristically blunt. He dismissed Johnson's claim that unionist sentiment in Louisiana was being "crushed out" by Phelp's policy. All they had to do to stop Phelps was stop the rebellion, Lincoln noted. "If they will not do this," he wondered, "should they not receive harder blows rather than lighter ones"? Like his fellow Republicans in Congress, Lincoln had given up waiting for southern unionists to rise up against secession. They have "paralyzed me in this struggle more than any other one thing," Lincoln declared. Then he made it unmistakably clear that the time for a more concerted assault on slavery had come. "I am a patient man," Lincoln told Johnson, "but it may as well be understood, once for all, that I shall not surrender this game leaving any available card unplayed."[39]

Two days later Lincoln wrote another letter, this time to a prominent lawyer in New Orleans, indicating once again that he had no more patience for Louisiana unionists who claimed to represent the majority but who did nothing to stop their state from seceding. Now they were complaining "that in various ways the relation of master and slave is disturbed by the presence of our Army," and that Congress was claiming "military necessity" as a spurious justification for suspending "constitutional guaranties." But as long as the secessionists were prepared to "hazard all for the sake of destroying the government," Lincoln wrote, he was willing to let them lose all. "What would you do in my position?" he asked. "Would you drop the war where it is? Or, would you prosecute it in future, with elder-stalk squirts, charged with rose water?" Rather than deal more lightly with slavery, the president warned, he was prepared to deal with it more heavily than before.[40] Ensuring that his words would have an immediate impact, Lincoln authorized Chase to send copies of the letters to General Butler in New Orleans.

In his own cover letter, Chase underscored the president's point: either we abandon all hope of bringing the Gulf States back into the Union, "or we must give freedom to every slave within our limits." As far as Chase was concerned, the recent "acts of Congress" did not leave "much room for choice." Universal emancipation was effectively the law of the land, and the new policy was to have "practical application in Louisiana." Butler was to use whatever authority he had to shift the plantations to a system of free labor. "[I]f I were in your place," Chase told Butler, I would "respectfully notify the slaveholders of Louisiana that henceforth they must be content to pay their laborers wages." Before the month of July was out, the various new laws forbidding military enforcement of the fugitive slave clause and establishing universal emancipation were being implemented in Louisiana. "How these acts can be enacted and slavery maintained," Chase wondered, "I am at a loss to conceive."[41]

If anything remained unclear in August, it was settled beyond doubt on September 22 when Lincoln issued a "Preliminary Emancipation Proclamation" in which he quoted verbatim the entire Section 9 of the Second Confiscation Act. All rebel-owned slaves "within any place occupied by rebel forces and afterwards occupied by the forces of the United States, shall be deemed captives of war, and shall be forever free of their servitude and not again held as slaves." Chase rushed a letter off the very next day urging Butler to "anticipate a little the operation of the Proclamation" in southern Louisiana. "The law," Chase pointed out, "frees all slaves of rebels in any city occupied by our union troops and previously occupied by rebels. This is the condition of New Orleans." Only "clear proof of *continuous* loyalty" could thereafter overcome the "presumption of freedom" in Louisiana.[42]

Butler declared himself "satisfied that Slavery must be abolished," and promised to "do his part at such time as he thinks proper." By late September he was instructing one of his generals that slaves voluntarily entering their lines could not be returned to their owners.

When another Union general complained of the number of slaves running into his lines, Butler insisted that "[b]y the Act of Congress they are clearly free." In a follow-up note, Butler stressed that the slaves were freed "[b]y the Act of Congress, independent of the president's proclamation." On November 1, Butler ordered all police and prison officials to release "from confinement" all the slaves of disloyal owners. No other Union officer, as George Denison reported in mid-October, "appreciates, like Gen. Butler, the importance of freeing and arming the colored people—and he is not afraid to do it. All the pro-slavery influence in this State cannot change him in this matter."[43]

Wherever plantations were abandoned, Butler reorganized them on the basis of free, wage labor. In one case, the general put his brother in charge of a sugar plantation where he "hired negroes at a fair rate per day." Butler's brother—known as "Colonel," though he was a civilian—was involved in a number of shady financial deals that caused endless trouble for the general, but in his dealings with the former slaves the Colonel "deserves credit," Denison reported to Chase. Butler was "the first man bold and enterprising enough to undertake the raising of a large crop of sugar by free labor." As Chase's agent in Louisiana and a devoted opponent of slavery, Denison was inclined to look favorably on the "experiment" of sugar produced by free labor. Not surprisingly his observations on various plantations in late 1862 persuaded him that blacks worked "with more energy and industry" once they were freed and paid wages. Denison noted that several plantations in the area had switched over to free labor and "met with the same success" as Colonel Butler's.[44]

Although the Second Confiscation Act distinguished between loyal and disloyal masters, the distinction broke down almost immediately under the free labor system Butler instituted. Plantations owned by disloyal planters were to be confiscated by the U.S. government, and the freed people would be paid wages to continue working, but the same terms were effectively imposed on loyal owners who remained on their plantations. The model contract Butler drew up required plantation owners to pay their black workers wages of ten dollars per month, with three dollars deducted for food, clothing, medicine, and care of the sick and elderly. "No cruel or corporal punishment" was allowed, and the United States promised to enforce the contracts and protect the black workers. If any planter "refuses to entertain this arrangement," Butler's contract stipulated, "his slaves may hire themselves to any other loyal planter, or any person whom the United States may elect."[45] In this way, de facto free labor was being established on plantations owned by loyal whites in southern Louisiana.

Lincoln was fascinated by these developments. Chase had been keeping the president fully informed about what Butler was doing. Lincoln even read the enthusiastic reports on emancipation that Denison sent back to Washington. In early November of 1862, Lincoln wrote Butler personally. He had learned from one of Denison's letters "that some of the planters were making arrangements with their negroes to pay them wages. Please write to me," Lincoln asked Butler, "to what extent, so far as you know, this is being done."[46] This was more than mere curiosity on the president's part. He was close to issuing the Emancipation Proclamation, and Louisiana was about to hold elections for a loyal government that would exempt it from the proclamation's reach. It would be better if slavery were substantially destroyed in Louisiana before then.

Butler reassured the president. He was "happy to report" that "our experiment in attempting the cultivation of sugar by free labor" was "succeeding admirably." He claimed that the same workers on the same plantations were proving far more productive as free laborers than they had been as slaves. As evidence, Butler forwarded to the White House a barrel of "the first sugar ever made by *free black labor* in Louisiana." To be sure, Butler reported, some of the local planters had refused to endorse the free labor contract he had drawn up "because they would not relinquish the right to use the whip." In those cases, Butler refused to return black workers to their former plantations and instead employed them in Union army camps, where they were paid wages and where corporal punishment was prohibited. In Lafourche, Butler reported, Union troops had taken over "the richest sugar-planting part of Louisiana" and with it "a very large number of slaves all of whom under the act are free." They, too, were in the process of making sugar under a free labor system. Of course, there were problems, Butler explained to the president. For the time being, the profits from government-run sugar plantations were helping to defray the cost of a massive relief program to feed and house thirty-two thousand desperate whites and ten thousand blacks, mostly women and children, who otherwise faced starvation. Butler was not sure how much longer he could pay for such provisions without requesting drafts from the Treasury. In addition, Butler was worried that many planters were signing wage contracts for the current season but only with the hope that in the future the "Institution" of slavery "can be spared them." Such problems were to be expected, Butler observed, and he was doing all he could to manage them. "It cannot be supposed that this great change in a social and political system can be made without shock," the general explained, adding that the only real surprise was "that it can be made at all." Butler was optimistic, in part he told Lincoln, because of "the almost universal sentiment and opinion of my Officers that Slavery is doomed."[47]

As LINCOLN MADE HIS INQUIRIES about the free labor system that Butler was establishing in Louisiana, he also asked about the upcoming elections for a new unionist government slated for early December. Butler and Denison assured the president that, although free elections were possible in only two of the state's districts, the candidates were sound Union men, some of them firm supporters of emancipation. Before the year was out, Louisiana was able to send two new congressmen to Washington, Benjamin Flanders and Michael Hahn, both of whom pledged to support the policies of the Lincoln administration. With "duly elected" representatives of a unionist government serving in Congress, Louisiana met the standard of "loyalty" that Lincoln had established in the September proclamation. On January 1, 1863, he therefore exempted occupied Louisiana from the Emancipation Proclamation, but only after having made sure that its slaves were already being freed.

8

"A CORDON OF FREEDOM"

BACK IN THE LATE 1840S during the heated congressional debate over the Wilmot Proviso—which would have excluded slavery from all the territories acquired from the war with Mexico— Ohio Congressman Columbus Delano warned the South that the North intended to "establish a cordon of free states that shall surround you." For Delano, containment was not an end in itself. By surrounding the slave states "we will light up the fires of liberty on every side," he explained, "until they melt your present chains and render all your people free."[1] The federal government could not abolish slavery in the states, but it could restrict slavery to the states where it already existed, surround those states, and squeeze slavery to death. Containment was never the goal of abolitionism; it was a way to achieve the goal. When William Lloyd Garrison said that the North should secede from the Union, for example, it wasn't merely because he wanted to free the North from the moral taint of association with slavery; he also wanted to surround the South with a "cordon of free-dom" that would hem the slave states in and eventually force them to abandon slavery on their own.[2] Once surrounded, abolitionists believed, the first to succumb to the pressure of the cordon would be the Border States. Unlike Garrison, most abolitionists believed this could be done within the Union thanks to a Constitution that made freedom national and slavery merely local. Peacetime containment—the cordon of freedom—was designed to bring about the "ultimate extinction" of slavery by the slave states themselves.

It's hard to imagine that Republicans could have contained slav-ery without the Civil War, and it's even harder to imagine that con-tainment could have ended slavery even if it had been implemented in peacetime. But the secession of eleven slave states gave Republi-cans the congressional majorities that allowed them to ban slavery from the territories, abolish slavery in the District of Columbia, and withdraw federal protection of slavery on the high seas—long the basic elements of antislavery politics. But war also made it possible for the Republicans to construct a cordon of freedom stronger than anyone had previously imagined, and to construct it much more rap-idly than would have been possible in peacetime. As Yankee squad-rons moved into the South, generating a flood of runaways, the Congress—with its eyes chiefly on the Border States—prohibited the Union army from participating in the capture and return of fugitive slaves. By early 1862, Republicans decided for the first time to require a state, West Virginia, to abolish slavery as a condition for admission to the Union, setting a precedent that they would later apply to all states that applied for *re*admission to the Union. By these means, Republican policymakers put pressure on the loyal slave states—states that were beyond the constitutional reach of full-scale military emancipation—to abolish slavery on their own.

THE THEORY OF CONTAINMENT

In the early 1830s, when abolitionists first proposed a cordon around the slave states, they meant something like a moral quarantine. By persuading more and more people of the evil of slavery, the abolitionists would "lay the slaveholders under an embargo, surround them, as the moral invalids of the universe, with a *cordon sanitaire*. It will confine the contagion to the spot of its origin, as the pest house of human nature." At other times abolitionists spoke of the cordon as the slave South's self-imposed isolation from "the literature and philosophy and religion of all the rest of mankind." But as abolitionists moved into politics, the cordon became less spiritual and more material, not so much a moral quarantine as a physical one. The federal government would implement a number of policies that would surround the South, cordoning off slavery, forcing the states to abolish slavery on their own. Senator Henry Wilson, the Massachusetts radical, mentioned some of those policies in 1851. "We shall arrest the extension of slavery, and rescue the Government from the grasp of the Slave Power. We shall blot out slavery in the National Capital. We shall surround the slave States with a cordon of free States." But preventing slavery's extension into the territories was only one piece of the cordon the opponents of slavery proposed to build.[3]

Containing slavery also meant transforming the North into truly "free soil" by the federal government's refusal to enforce the fugitive slave clause. "What will be accomplished by a dissolution of the Union?" Massachusetts abolitionists asked as early as 1837, already responding to southern threats of secession. "The line of Virginia will be blackened with fugitive slaves fleeing into the free States. Gone is your guarantee to restore the fugitives, which now alone restrains them; gone is the *whole* compact of the Constitution to uphold slavery, for the alleged *partial* infraction of which the Republic is to be torn asunder. Your slave States will be depopulated, and how will you prevent it? Will you do it with a cordon of soldiers, covering the whole extent of Mason and Dixon's line?" This argument for why the South would never secede became a standard theme in antislavery circles. As James Gillespie Birney the Ohio abolitionist, explained, one of the reasons "the South will not dissolve [the Union] is, that the slaves would leave their masters and take refuge in the free states. The South would not be able to establish a *cordon* along her wide frontier sufficiently strong to prevent it."⁴

Most Republicans objected to the Fugitive Slave Act of 1850 because it transferred enforcement of the fugitive slave clause from the states to the federal government, a violation of the premise that freedom was national and slavery merely local. It soon became difficult, not to say dangerous, for the slaveholders to capture and bring home with any degree of regularity runaways found in the northern states. "We ought not to deceive Southern men," the veteran antislavery Congressman Joshua Giddings declared as Congress enacted the 1850 statute. "We should say to them, in all frankness and sincerity, that the day for arresting fugitive slaves has gone by forever."⁵ Lincoln similarly warned on more than one occasion that if the slave states left the Union, the free states would no longer be under any obligation to return fugitive slaves. When slaves began running to Union lines early in the war, Republicans in both Congress and the administration responded predictably. Beginning with the decision to withhold "contraband" slaves from their owners in the first weeks of the war, Republican policymakers would eventually make it a crime for anyone in the armed forces to participate in the capture and return of fugitive slaves. Congress went a step further when, in the Second Confiscation Act, it restricted enforcement of the fugitive slave clause to local civil and judicial authorities. Under the principle of freedom national, the slave states alone were responsible for enforcement of the fugitive slave clause. The free states would thus become another part of the cordon of freedom surrounding the South.

Ideally all of the slave states would eventually succumb to the pressure of the cordon and begin to abolish slavery on their own. As Pennsylvania Congressman Thaddeus Stevens explained in 1850, slavery should not be allowed to expand, "because confining it within its present limits will bring the States themselves to its gradual abolition." Like most northern opponents of slavery, Stevens assumed that slavery was too weak to survive the pressure of a cordon. "Confine it, and like the cancer that is tending to the heart, it must be eradicated, or it will eat out the vitals," he explained. But it was up to the slave states themselves to reach that conclusion. "The sooner the patient is convinced of this, the sooner he will procure the healing operation. . . . Confine this malady within its present limits. Surround it by a cordon of freedom so that it cannot spread, and in less than twenty-five years every slaveholding State in this Union will have on its statute books a law for the gradual and final extinction of slavery."[6]

This is undoubtedly what Lincoln meant when he said that confining slavery within its existing limits would lead to its "natural death." The genius of this approach, as antislavery politicians saw it, was that it did not violate the constitutional ban on direct federal interference with slavery in the states. "The North has no desire to oppress the South," one New York congressman insisted. "They will leave it untouched by any national legislation in those States, but will surround it by a cordon of free States." A popular metaphor likened slavery, trapped within the cordon, to a scorpion that kills itself once it realizes that it is surrounded. "The Republican Party does not wish to interfere in the internal government or social institutions of the slave States, but merely to place around them a cordon of free States," Republican Congressman Anson Burlingame explained in 1856. "Then this *horrible* system will die of inanition; or, *like the scorpion,*

FREEDOM NATIONAL; SLAVERY SECTIONAL.

SPEECH

OF

HON. CHARLES SUMNER,

OF MASSACHUSETTS,

ON HIS MOTION TO

REPEAL THE FUGITIVE SLAVE BILL,

IN THE SENATE OF THE UNITED STATES, AUGUST 26, 1852.

If any man thinks that the interest of these Nations and the interest of
Christianity are two separate and distinct things, I wish my soul may never
enter into his secret.   OLIVER CROMWELL.

BOSTON:

TICKNOR, REED, AND FIELDS.

M DCCC LII.

The published version of Charles Sumner's first important speech after his election
to the U.S. Senate in 1851. In it the senator spelled out a number of antislavery
policies the federal government could pursue despite the constitutional prohibition
of direct federal abolition in any state where slavery was legal.

After a slave rebellion in 1839 aboard *La Amistad* led by Joseph Cinqué (top right), the rebels ended up in New England, where federal authorities tried to have the slaves returned to their Cuban owners. Abolitionists took up the cause of the rebels, arguing that slavery had no legal standing on the high seas. Massachusetts congressman and former president John Quincy Adams (top left) defended the slave rebels when the case reached the Supreme Court in 1841 (bottom; *The Granger Collection, New York*). The justices voted against the slave owners, though for technical rather than abolitionist reasons, and the rebels were ultimately able to return to their homes in West Africa.

In one of the first legal moves against slavery during the Civil War, Union General Benjamin F. Butler (top left) refused to return fugitive slaves who escaped from their owners to Fortress Monroe, Virginia (bottom). The fugitives arrived in such large numbers that Butler appointed a New England abolitionist, Edward L. Pierce (top right), as supervisor of "contrabands"—as the fugitives were popularly known. Pierce later assumed a similar position in the Sea Islands, where he organized the first important wartime experiment in free labor.

Lyman Trumbull. Republican senator from Illinois and chairman of the powerful Senate Judiciary Committee.

Thaddeus Stevens. Republican congressman from Pennsylvania, a leading radical and skillful parliamentarian.

Charles Sumner, senator from Massachusetts, a leading voice of radical Republican principles.

Salmon P. Chase. secretary of the Treasury, the most radical member of Lincoln's cabinet.

General in chief of the Union army in the first years of the war, George B. McClellan objected to a war whose purpose extended beyond the restoration of the Union. (*The Granger Collection, New York*)

John J. Crittenden, senator from Kentucky, advocated a proslavery compromise during the secession crisis and spoke out against all Republican efforts to undermine slavery during the war.

Willard Saulsbury, senator from Delaware, a pugnacious defender of slavery and a leading congressional critic of Republican antislavery policies.

Fernando Wood, Democratic congressman from New York, led the successful move to block passage of the Thirteenth Amendment in June 1864. (*The Granger Collection, New York*)

Republicans based the policy of military emancipation on the assumption that slaves would escape to Union lines if given the chance.

Escaping slaves increasingly ran to one of the many contraband camps set up by the Union army.

Camp Nelson, Kentucky (top and bottom), one of the largest contraband camps in the South and the major recruiting center for black troops.

Lincoln brought a draft of the Emancipation Proclamation with him to the cabinet meeting of July 22, 1862. On the advice of Secretary of State William H. Seward (seated, third from right), however, Lincoln decided to wait for a military victory to make the announcement.

In January 1863 *Harper's Weekly* published an "Emancipation" drawing by Thomas Nast (top). After the war and Lincoln's assassination, an adulterated version of Nast's drawing that dramatically enhanced Lincoln's role in emancipation was widely circulated (bottom).

Lincoln drafted the Emancipation Proclamation himself, meticulously editing and reediting it before allowing it to be published.

All SLAVES were made FREEMEN.

BY ABRAHAM LINCOLN,

PRESIDENT OF THE UNITED STATES,

JANUARY 1st, 1863.

Come, then, able-bodied COLORED MEN, to the nearest United States Camp, and fight for the

STARS AND STRIPES.

ORIGINAL VERSION
OF THE
JOHN BROWN SONG.

The author of the original John Brown Song is H. H. Brownell, of Hartford, a nephew of Bishop Brownell.

Words that can be sung to the "Hallelujah Chorus."

Old John Brown lies a-mouldering in the grave,
Old John Brown lies slumbering in his grave—
But John Brown's soul is marching with the brave,
    His soul is marching on,
    Glory, Glory, hallelujah!
    Glory, Glory, hallelujah!
    His soul is marching on.

He has gone to be a soldier in the Army of the Lord,
He is sworn as a private in the ranks of the Lord—
He shall stand at Armageddon with his brave old sword,
    When Heaven is marching on.
    Glory, etc.
    For Heaven is marching on.

He shall file in front where the lines of battle form,
He shall face to the front when the squares of battle form,

Time with the column, and charge in the storm,
    When men are marching on.
    Glory, etc.
    True men are marching on.

Ah, foul tyrants! do you hear him when he comes?
Ah, black traitors! do ye know him as he comes?
In thunder of the cannon and roll of the drums,
    As we go marching on.
    Glory, etc.
    We all are marching on.

Men may die and moulder in the dust—
Men may die, and arise again from dust,
Shoulder to shoulder, in the ranks of the Just,
    When God is marching on.
    Glory, etc.
    The Lord is marching on.

"All Slaves were made Freemen." Handbills like this, distributed by Union agents in the Confederate states, were designed to entice slaves to leave their plantation homes and escape to Union lines.

TO COLORED MEN!

FREEDOM,

Protection, Pay, and a Call to Military Duty!

On the 1st day of January, 1863, the President of the United States proclaimed FREE-DOM to over THREE MILLIONS OF SLAVES. This decree is to be enforced by all the power of the Nation. On the 21st of July last he issued the following order:

PROTECTION OF COLORED TROOPS.

"WAR DEPARTMENT, ADJUTANT GENERAL'S OFFICE,
WASHINGTON, July 21.

"*General Order,* No. 233.

"The following order of the President is published for the information and government of all concerned:—

EXECUTIVE MANSION, WASHINGTON, July 30.

"'It is the duty of every Government to give protection to its citizens, of whatever class, color, or condition, and especially to those wh are duly organized as soldiers in the public service. The law of nations, and the usages and customs of war, as carried on by civilized powers, permit no distinction as to color in the treatment of prisoners of war as public enemies. To sell or enslave any captured person on account of his color, is a relapse into barbarism, and a crime against the civilization of the age.

"'The Government of the United States will give the same protection to all its soldiers, and if the enemy shall sell or enslave any one because of his color, the offense shall be punished by retaliation upon the enemy's prisoners in our possession. It is, therefore, ordered, for every soldier of the United States, killed in violation of the laws of war, a rebel soldier shall be executed; and for every one enslaved by the enemy, or sold into slavery, a rebel soldier shall be placed at hard labor on the public works, and continued at such labor until the other shall be released and receive the treatment due to prisoners of war.

'"ABRAHAM LINCOLN."'

'"By order of the Secretary of War.

'"E. D. TOWNSEND, Assistant Adjutant General."'

That the President is in earnest the rebels soon began to find out, as witness the following order from his Secretary of War:

"WAR DEPARTMENT, WASHINGTON CITY, August 8, 1863.

"SIR: Your letter of the 3d inst., calling the attention of this Department to the cases of Orin H. Brown, William H. Johnston, and Wm. Wilson, three colored men captured on the gunboat Isaac Smith, has received consideration. This Department has directed that three rebel prisoners of South Carolina, if there be any such in our possession, and if not, three others, be confined in close custody and held as hostages for Brown, Johnston and Wilson, and that the fact be communicated to the rebel authorities at Richmond.

"Very respectfully your obedient servant,

"EDWIN M. STANTON, Secretary of War.

"The Hon. GIDEON WELLES, Secretary of the Navy."

And retaliation will be our practice now—man for man—to the bitter end.

LETTER OF CHARLES SUMNER,

Written with reference to the Convention held at Poughkeepsie, July 15th and 16th, 1863, to promote Colored Enlistments.

BOSTON, July 13th, 1863.

"I doubt if, in times past, our country could have expected from colored men any patriotic service. Such service is the return for protection. But now that protection has begun, the service should begin also. Nor should relative rights and duties be weighed with nicety. It is enough that our country, aroused at last to a sense of justice, seeks to enrol colored men among its defenders.

"If my counsels should reach such persons, I would say: enlist at once. Now is the day and now is the hour. Help to overcome your cruel enemies now battling against your country, and in this way you will surely overcome those other enemies hardly less cruel, here at home, who will still seek to degrade you. This is not the time to hesitate or to higgle. Do your duty to our country, and you will set an example of generous self-sacrifice which will conquer prejudice and open all hearts.

"Very faithfully yours,

"CHARLES SUMNER."

A recruitment poster, probably from late 1863, urging black men to enlist in the Union army. The recruitment agents, among them the prominent black activist Martin Delany, besides promising substantial bounties and good pay, also boasted of the bravery and indispensability of black troops in engagements as far afield as Honey Springs, Arkansas, and James Island, South Carolina.

On June 7, 1863, six months after Lincoln formally lifted the ban on black troops in the Union army, African American soldiers at Milliken's Bend, Louisiana, stood their ground against superior numbers of Confederate soldiers, even as white Union troops fled the battlefield. News of the event swept the nation and helped turn the tide of northern public opinion strongly in favor of black troops. Lincoln came to think of black troops as indispensable to Union victory, and therefore to slavery's destruction.

UNION AND LIBERTY!   AND   UNION AND SLAVERY!

Lincoln's conduct of the war was the central issue in the 1864 presidential election. But as this cartoon demonstrates, the issues of slavery and the war could not be separated. Lincoln and his fellow Republicans stood for "Union and Liberty." His Democratic opponent, George McClellan, stood for the swiftest possible restoration of the Union, even if that meant the survival of slavery.

𝔗𝔥𝔦𝔯𝔱𝔶-𝓔𝓲𝓰𝓱𝓽𝓱   ℭ𝔬𝔫𝔤𝔯𝔢𝔰𝔰 𝔬𝔣 𝔱𝔥𝔢 𝔘𝔫𝔦𝔱𝔢𝔡 𝔖𝔱𝔞𝔱𝔢𝔰 𝔬𝔣 𝔄𝔪𝔢𝔯𝔦𝔠𝔞;

𝔄𝔱 𝔱𝔥𝔢 *Second* 𝔖𝔢𝔰𝔰𝔦𝔬𝔫,

Begun and held at the City of Washington, on Monday, the *fifth* day of December, one thousand eight hundred and sixty-*four*

A RESOLUTION

Submitting to the legislatures of the several States a proposition to amend the Constitution of the United States.

𝔚𝔢𝔰𝔬𝔩𝔳𝔢𝔡 by the Senate and House of Representatives of the United States of America in Congress assembled,

(two-thirds of both Houses concurring), that the following article be proposed to the legislatures of the several States as an amendment to the Constitution of the United States, which, when ratified by three-fourths of said Legislatures shall be valid, to all intents and purposes, as a part of the said Constitution, namely: Article XIII. Section 1. Neither slavery nor involuntary servitude, except as a punishment for crime whereof the party shall have been duly convicted, shall exist within the United States, or any place subject to their jurisdiction. Section 2. Congress shall have power to enforce this article by appropriate legislation.

Schuyler Colfax
Speaker of the House of Representatives

H. Hamlin
Vice President of the United States
and President of the Senate

Abraham Lincoln

Approved. February 1. 1865.

After his decisive reelection in November 1864, Lincoln threw himself into an intense campaign to secure the handful of Democratic votes needed to pass the Thirteenth Amendment. As evidence of his commitment to the cause, Lincoln affixed his signature to the congressional resolution sending the amendment to the states for ratification. That signature provoked some controversy because under the Constitution the president has no formal role in the amendment process. (*The Granger Collection, New York*)

HARPER'S WEEKLY.
A JOURNAL OF CIVILIZATION

VOL. IX.—No. 425.]   NEW YORK, SATURDAY, FEBRUARY 18, 1865.   [SINGLE COPIES TEN CENTS. $4.00 PER YEAR IN ADVANCE.

Entered according to Act of Congress, in the Year 1865, by Harper & Brothers, in the Clerk's Office of the District Court for the Southern District of New York.

Until the final vote was taken on January 30, 1865, no one could be certain that there were enough votes in the House of Representatives to pass the Thirteenth Amendment. When the result was announced, the House erupted in chaos and celebration.

seeing no means of escape, sting itself to death." In principle, containment did not merely isolate slavery; it destroyed it.[7]

Free territories and free states would go a long way toward making freedom national within the United States, but keeping slavery *local* also had implications for foreign policy. Freedom was not merely national, it was also international. Because slavery was a purely state institution, it had no "extraterritorial" reach whatsoever. On the high seas, where the law of nations ruled, the natural right of freedom prevailed. The destruction of slavery would require free oceans along with free soil.

FREE OCEANS

When in 1860 opponents of slavery looked back over the course of American diplomatic history, they saw an unbroken record of support for slavery. The very treaty recognizing America's independence included a provision, demanded by the Americans, requiring British compensation for the slaves England had freed during the War of Independence. The Americans demanded a similar provision in the Treaty of Ghent, which concluded the War of 1812. And in the treaty that transferred French Louisiana to the United States, the Jefferson administration made explicit promises to protect slavery. Jefferson and his successors squashed all moves to grant diplomatic recognition to the independent black republics of Haiti and Liberia. In a series of incidents during the 1820s and 1830s, the federal government repeatedly protested when British officials in the Bahamas enforced their own nation's law by emancipating slaves on U.S. ships that made their way into British ports. When slaves rebelled on the high seas, the U.S. government consistently supported slaveholders in their attempts to return the rebels to slavery. With the annexation of Texas and the war with Mexico in the 1840s, the United States dramatically extended the territorial reach of slavery and increased the number of slave states in the Union. And during the 1850s the federal government sent bellicose proslavery southerners on diplomatic missions to Europe, where they issued not-so-veiled threats to take Cuba by force if the Spanish government refused to sell the island to the United States. To abolitionists this was a sordid record that tarnished America's image in the world.[8]

Nothing so clearly exposed the slaveholders' sway in foreign affairs, abolitionists believed, as the refusal of the United States to join with Great Britain in its attempts to suppress the Atlantic slave trade. The issue was not the illegal importation of African slaves into the United States. The federal government had made slave trading a crime in 1790, banned the importation of slaves in 1808, and went further in 1820 when it branded the slave trade a form of piracy. Thereafter very few slaves were smuggled into the country. The real problem was the participation of American ships and captains in the business of purchasing slaves in Africa and selling them in Cuba and Brazil. Americans became active in the Cuban slave trade in the 1830s, but in the 1840s the focus of their business shifted to Brazil. After 1850, when Brazilian authorities began suppressing the slave trade, American slavers turned their attention once again to Cuba. All of this commercial activity was illegal under U.S. law, but it was impossible to suppress so long as the American government refused to allow British patrols to search American ships. With the Webster-Ashburton Treaty of 1842, the United States committed itself to the deployment of a squadron that would patrol the African coast in cooperation with British ships, but it was not until the very end of the 1850s that the Buchanan administration finally commissioned enough ships to make the slave-trade patrols effective.[9]

In the spring of 1861, within weeks of taking office, Secretary of State William Seward approached Britain's foreign ministry indicating that at long last the United States was willing to sign a slave-trade treaty. The British were initially suspicious of American intentions. Seward had come into office making provocative proposals to stave off secession by uniting the country in a war against England. Anglo-American relations were further hampered by mutual misunderstandings. The British never understood that the Constitution did not allow the federal government to prosecute a war whose "purpose" was to abolish slavery in the southern states. The Lincoln administration, on the other hand, never understood that Britain's formal declaration of neutrality benefited the North because it meant that English ships would respect the Union blockade of the Confederacy. In late 1861, relations between Britain and the United States reached a low point when an impetuous American naval commander illegally boarded a British ship, the *Trent*, near Havana and removed two Confederate diplomats on their way to Europe. The peaceful resolution of the *Trent* affair, however, opened the way to renewed negotiations for a slave-trade treaty in early 1862.[10]

For once, Seward's penchant for intrigue proved advantageous. Anxious to disarm any anti-British sentiment that might undermine ratification, Seward suggested a diplomatic shuffle between himself and the British ambassador in Washington. The Americans would insist on a meaningless sunset provision in the treaty; the British would publicly protest but then back down, making it seem as if they had succumbed to the demands of the United States. The ruse worked.[11] The Senate approved the slave-trade treaty by a unanimous vote on April 24, 1862. After decades of reluctance the Americans finally signed a slave-trade treaty that would allow the British to search American ships suspected of engaging in the illegal transatlantic slave trade. The number of African slaves sold to Cuba dropped from fourteen thousand in 1861 to ten thousand in 1862 to under four thousand in 1863. Within another few years, four centuries of Atlantic slave trading came to an end.

The slave-trade treaty was not the only indication that decades of proslavery diplomacy had come to a sudden halt. Under the Republicans there would be no more moves to annex Cuba for slavery, no more demands for compensation of slaves freed in British ports, and no more official endorsements of the property rights of masters whose slaves rebelled on the high seas. Some changes were symbolic, though telling. In the wake of the *Dred Scott* decision in 1857, the State Department had stopped issuing passports to African Americans on the grounds that they were not citizens. Under the Lincoln administration the policy was reversed and blacks were once again issued passports.

Abolitionists had long decried the refusal of successive administrations to recognize the independent black republics of Haiti and Liberia. Though black and white abolitionists alike generally shied away from celebrations of the Haitian Revolution, once France recognized Haiti's independence in 1825, antislavery activists pressed for the United States to follow suit. In the late 1830s, abolitionists sent hundreds of petitions to Congress demanding diplomatic recognition of Haiti. But nothing came of this effort until December of 1861, when Lincoln urged Congress to reverse the long-standing U.S. policy. He wondered if there was "any good reason" for the United States to "persevere longer in withholding our recognition of the independence and sovereignty of Hayti and Liberia." That was all Lincoln said about it, but several months later in Congress, Massachusetts Republican Thomas Eliot declared that diplomatic recognition of Haiti was—like emancipation—a matter of both "justice" and sound "policy." As in the abolitionist petitions decades earlier, the "policy" Eliot endorsed promised the reciprocal benefits of free trade between Haiti and the United States. Congress endorsed Lincoln's proposal, and within a few months the first black ambassador from Haiti arrived in Washington.[12]

By then U.S. foreign policy had been dramatically altered. The federal government was allied with Great Britain in the suppression of the Atlantic slave trade, it was aggressively prosecuting slave traders, it was issuing passports to African Americans, and it was inviting black diplomats from Haiti and Liberia to Washington. Southern slave ships were no longer safe in the coastal waters of the United States. Slavery in the seceded states no longer reached beyond the water's edge, and the slave South was effectively surrounded by free oceans.

FREE TERRITORIES

As the Lincoln administration was finalizing the details of the slave-trade treaty, Congress was moving to plant free territories all along the Confederacy's western border. This was the terrifying scenario that had long alarmed so many southern defenders of slavery. "Will you suffer yourselves to be surrounded by a cordon of free States?" asked one southern pamphleteer in 1848.[13] That same year a Florida senator denounced the Wilmot Proviso for striking "at the security of property in the southern States, by aiming to surround them with a cordon of States having antagonist institutions." Two years later Jefferson Davis objected to northern claims that because "the South held the African race in bondage . . . [it] should be restricted from future growth—that around her should be drawn, as it were, a sanitary cordon to prevent the extension of a moral leprosy." Legitimate southern suspicions that the incoming Republicans would construct their "cordon of fire" drove the secession movement ten years later. "A cordon of Free States must never be permitted to surround the God-given institution of Slavery," Senator Clement C. Clay of Alabama declared in 1860. "[T]he beautiful tree must not be thus girdled that it may wither and die."[14]

Forcing slavery to "wither and die" was precisely the point. When Republican Congressman Isaac Arnold introduced his bill "to render freedom national, and slavery sectional" on March 16, 1862, he made it clear that excluding slavery from the territories was but one part of a much larger project. As Arnold originally drafted it, the law would have banned slavery from all federal installations—forts, arsenals, dockyards, and the like—and freed American slaves on the high seas. It would, in short, establish the presumption of freedom "in all places whatsoever where the National Government is supreme."[15] As it made its way through the legislative process, Arnold's bill was simplified and ended up as the law prohibiting slavery in all the territories of the United States, but the principle it embodied—establishing a cordon of freedom around the South—remained.

The problem of slavery in the territories had beleaguered American politics since the founding days of the republic. Even before the Constitution was drafted, the Congress, meeting under the Articles of Confederation, had passed the "Ordinance of 1787," known as the Northwest Ordinance, indicating its desire to keep slavery out of the northwestern territories. Antislavery congressmen later tried to implement similar restrictions on slavery's expansion into the southwestern territories, but they were defeated by the united opposition of the southern states. The first great sectional crisis in 1820 was provoked by the admission of Missouri as a slave state. The next came in the 1840s, when antislavery northerners tried to prevent the annexation of Texas, opposed the war with Mexico, and having failed in both quests, nevertheless came close to banning slavery from all the territories acquired during the war. Out of the struggle to ban slavery from the territories came the Free Soil Party in 1848 and the Republican Party a few years later. By the late 1850s the same struggle over slavery in the territories split the Democratic Party in two, leading in 1860 to the stunning electoral victory of a Republican president whose party promised to ban slavery in all the western territories. Once secession gave the Republicans control of Congress, it was only a matter of time before they set about fulfilling their promise.[16]

On May 8, 1862, Owen Lovejoy reported Arnold's "freedom

national" bill out of the House Committee on Territories. It would abolish slavery not only in the federal territories but also in all "forts, magazines, arsenals, dock-yards, and other needful buildings" under the jurisdiction of the United States. It would abolish slavery "on the high seas, beyond the territory and jurisdiction of each of the several States." In short, the bill abolished slavery "in all places whatsoever where the national Government has exclusive jurisdiction." This was freedom national carried to one of its logical conclusions.[17]

"I denounce this bill," one Maryland congressman declared, "as a palpable violation of the rights of States, and an unwarrantable interference with the rights of private property." Another Democrat declared that the bill banning slavery in the territories was utterly superfluous because "nothing but positive law can carry slavery there; and we might as well here undertake to re-enact the Decalogue as to enact this law." As they had for nearly forty years, Democrats insisted that slavery was none of the federal government's business. Having struggled to keep slavery out of national politics from the 1820s through the 1850s, Democrats continued struggling to keep slavery out of the war. "The conservative men of the House," Democratic Congressman Samuel Cox of Ohio insisted, "ought to 'squelch' out the whole negro business." Instead, he complained, Republicans kept dragging the issue of slavery up. "They are responsible for this continuous agitation. From the very commencement of the session, we have had these bills before us in one shape or another."[18]

No less consistently Republicans insisted that slavery could never be separated from the war. "The Rebellion is the result of slavery," Republican Congressman William D. Kelley of Pennsylvania shouted. Yet even as he denounced slavery for having drenched American soil in blood, Kelley denied that the territorial bill violated the federal consensus. The Constitution neither creates nor even recognizes slavery, he explained, "it only tolerates it" in the states that have created it. The "freedom national" bill "does not interfere with that toleration. It does not propose to abolish slavery anywhere. It only proposes to say to the slave-owner: 'Keep your slaves out of these places.'" But if Republicans freely acknowledged that the federal government could not directly abolish slavery in any state, they nonetheless pressed for Congress "to exhaust the last power it has over this institution, whenever and wherever it can be done." Roscoe Conkling would have Congress "march up to the line of constitutional power wherever we possess that power, and to that extent prohibit this institution." But where was "the line of constitutional power"? Exactly how much authority to regulate slavery did Congress possess?[19]

For a minority of Republicans the presence of slavery on federal installations *within a slave state* created a legal ambiguity that they would just as soon avoid. All Republicans agreed that Congress had the power to abolish slavery in federal territories and Washington, and all were committed to maintaining freedom on the high seas. But not all Republicans agreed that Congress had the power to abolish slavery on federal installations inside a state where slavery was legal, largely because the federal government occupied such spaces only with the consent of the state. Fearing that some of his fellow Republicans might hesitate to support the bill, Lovejoy amended his own committee's report by stripping it down to its most important component—the abolition of slavery in the territories. As was often the case, the flexibility of the radicals sustained the Republican consensus in favor of emancipation. The final House vote of 85 to 50 broke down along familiar lines. Nearly all Republicans voted for it; almost every non-Republican voted against it. To emphasize the partisan nature of the bill, Congressman Cox proposed a tongue-in-cheek amendment declaring that the purpose of the law was "to carry out the Chicago platform, and to dissolve the Union."[20] There was a half truth in Cox's gesture: abolition in the territories was the one item on their agenda over which the Republicans had always refused to compromise.

The Senate took up the bill on June 9, rearranged some of the wording, and with very little debate, endorsed it by an overwhelming vote of 28 to 10. The House accepted the rewording and sent it off to the president on June 17. Two days later Abraham Lincoln signed "An Act to secure Freedom to all Persons within the Territories of the United States." Unlike the Second Confiscation Act, which was long and complicated, the territorial bill was simplicity itself. A mere seventy-six words, it recalled the phrasing of the Northwest Ordinance and foreshadowed that of the Thirteenth Amendment. "[N]either slavery nor involuntary servitude" would thereafter exist in any U.S. territories, "otherwise than in punishment of crimes whereof the party shall have been duly convicted."[21]

With that single sentence, Congress excised a source of tension that had torn at the nation since its founding. And notwithstanding the fate of the broader legislation originally proposed by Isaac Arnold and Owen Lovejoy, it was nonetheless true that banning slavery in the western territories, and the suppression of slavery on the high seas, were parts of a larger project whose ultimate purpose was the abolition of slavery in the states. One indication of that project was Congress's determination to establish an oasis of free labor in between two slave states by abolishing slavery in Washington.

FREEDOM IN WASHINGTON

Sliced from a chunk of land alongside the Potomac River at the border of Maryland and Virginia, the District of Columbia had slavery inscribed in its very origins. In 1801 Congress was formally charged with governing the cities of Washington and Georgetown, and it chose to exercise its authority by importing wholesale the laws of the state of Maryland, including its slave codes and its statutes discriminating against free blacks. From the moment of its creation, slaves were conspicuous in Washington. They helped construct the Capitol, laid out the city's impossibly complicated street grid, and worked as servants in the homes of senators, congressmen, cabinet members, and a succession of slaveholding presidents. The number of slaves declined steadily over the decades, yet for half a century slave traders plied their human property through the streets, within sight of the White House and earshot of the Capitol, until slave trading was finally banned as part of the Compromise of 1850. Ending the slave trade, however, did not end slavery. In 1860 the U.S. census still counted 3,185 slaves in the District.

For abolitionists the political significance of slaves working in the nation's capital far outweighed their numbers, and for generations opponents of slavery made abolition in the District of Columbia a priority. In their first attempt to force slavery back into national politics in the 1830s abolitionists bombarded Congress with mass petitions demanding the abolition of slavery in the nation's capital. In the 1840s, during his one term as a Whig congressman and long before he had committed himself to antislavery politics, Abraham Lincoln had drafted a bill for the gradual abolition of slavery in Washington, provided district voters gave it their approval in a referendum. Lincoln's was only one of a number of such bills introduced by antislavery congressmen over the years. Their authors believed that slavery in the nation's capital was an ongoing scandal in the land that called itself the freest on earth. Critics denounced it as an affront to the nation's founding values, a disgrace to America's reputation in the world. "Nobody can hear that slaves are now sold in the markets of Washington," Charles Sumner declared, "without confessing the scandal to liberal institutions. For the sake of our good name, if not for the sake of justice, let the scandal disappear."[22]

Beginning in the 1830s the abolition of slavery in Washington took on a broader constitutional significance: it became a test of competing views of congressional power over slavery in areas where federal rather than state government was sovereign. The great abolitionist

Theodore Dwight Weld is most often remembered for his antislavery pamphlet, *American Slavery as It Is*, but he may have been more important for another pamphlet he published at the same time, *The Power of Congress over the District of Columbia*, which argued for the federal government's right to abolish slavery in Washington. Much depended on the outcome of this legal debate. If proslavery constitutionalism prevailed in Washington, it would prevail on the high seas. It meant that slavery was a national—and international—rather than a merely local institution. But if Weld's antislavery constitutionalism succeeded, the freedom of the seas could be presumed, slavery could be excluded from the territories, it could be abolished in Washington, and the federal government could build a cordon of freedom around the slave states. By the late 1850s virtually all Republicans had embraced Weld's principle, but not until the Civil War did they have the power to act on it.

Surrounded on all sides by slave states, but with tens of thousands of Union troops protecting the city from a possible Confederate invasion, Washington quickly became a magnet for slaves escaping to freedom, whether from loyal Maryland or from disloyal Virginia. One measure of the radicalizing effect of the war was the fact that some opponents of emancipation in the District tried to thwart Republican plans by introducing a bill nearly identical to the one Lincoln had drafted in the late 1840s, calling for gradual abolition only after a referendum. By the time the District emancipation bill was debated in early 1862, war had made Republicans far more aggressive. Repeatedly and by overwhelming margins they rejected every amendment that would have made abolition in the capital gradual, and they barely considered a referendum. Gradual emancipation was something Republicans offered as an incentive for abolition in the loyal states, where Congress was not allowed to "interfere" with slavery. Because no such restriction applied to Washington, Congress was free to abolish slavery immediately.

Republicans began introducing bills for the emancipation of all slaves in the District of Columbia within a few weeks after the Thirty-Seventh Congress convened for its second session, in early December of 1861. The Senate Committee on the District of Columbia reported an abolition bill to the floor in February, and on March 12 the Senate began its formal deliberations. Various senators introduced amendments to ensure that slaves could not be secreted out of the District to be sold rather than emancipated. Another amendment repealed the original statutes that had adopted Maryland slave law within the District. To many advocates of freedom national, those original statutes were illegitimate because the Constitution was sovereign in the District, and where the Constitution was sovereign freedom, not slavery, was supposed to prevail. Repealing the original slave statutes would effectively end slavery while at the same time reaffirming that freedom was national. Ohio Republican Congressman Harrison Blake went further. Reiterating the position staked out by Weld decades earlier, Blake declared that the power to abolish slavery implied a moral obligation to do so. "It is our duty to abolish slavery here," he argued, "because Congress, by the Constitution, has the power to do it; and, slavery being a great wrong and outrage upon humanity, we should at once do right, and pass this bill."

Not surprisingly, much of the debate over abolition in the capital centered on constitutional questions. Opponents insisted that Congress had no power to abolish slavery in Washington or anywhere else. Senator Garrett Davis of Kentucky denounced the "unconstitutional legislation" by which Congress would "liberate" slaves "without the intervention of the courts."[23] By Davis's reasoning, the federal government could never abolish slavery and could only authorize the emancipation of individual slaves as punishment if an owner was found guilty in a trial for treason. Republicans believed that Congress had all the authority it needed to abolish slavery in the District. "The fundamental law of the land is broad and clear," Maine's Republican

Senator William Pitt Fessenden explained. "Congress, under the Constitution, is gifted with all power of legislation over this District, and may do any thing in it that any legislature can do in any State of the Union."[24]

Radicals took the lead in the debate on District abolition, just as they took the lead in nearly every emancipation debate during the war. They were instrumental in drafting legislation and guiding it through committee; they set the terms of debate on the floor. Yet in pursuit of party unity, radicals sometimes sent their own bills back to committee, accepted friendly amendments, and even amended their own bills, thus ensuring Republican unanimity when the votes were cast. The District emancipation bill, for example, was not as radical as Congressman James Ashley of Ohio would have liked, but "I am a practical man," he explained, "and shall support this bill as the best we can get at this time."[25] Conservative Republicans responded in kind. During the debate it became clear that Senator Orville Browning was prepared to endorse forced colonization, and that Senator John Ten Eyck of New Jersey preferred gradual to immediate abolition, but both supported the final bill because their primary goal was neither colonization nor gradualism but abolition of slavery in the nation's capital. In the House, Republican Congressman John T. Nixon, also from New Jersey, admitted that gradual emancipation was "more in accordance" with his own views. "But if immediate emancipation with just compensation, shall prove to be the sentiment of the House, I am prepared to exercise an express constitutional power, and vote to remove for ever the blot of slavery from the national capital."[26] Agreeing on the ends, Republicans readily negotiated among themselves over the means. This in turn allowed Republicans to remain steadfast in their resistance to the opposition of Democrats and Border State congressmen.

The Washington abolition bill passed the Senate on April 3, 1862, by a vote of 29 to 14. One week later, Pennsylvania Republican Congressman Thaddeus Stevens introduced the same bill to the House. To speed its passage, Stevens moved its immediate consideration by the entire House meeting as a Committee of the Whole. He skillfully turned back all efforts to amend the bill, at one point moving to limit debate to one hour. Democrats and Border State congressmen failed to stall consideration of the bill and to table it once it came up, but they did win enough Republican votes to extend the debate. Several days of protracted wrangling ensued. Even after Stevens called for a vote on the bill, opponents kept coming up with desperate amendments designed to derail it. In the end, the House approved the Senate version of the bill by another overwhelming vote of 92 to 38. President Lincoln signed it into law on April 16, 1862.

The statute followed the language of the Constitution by referring to slavery as a servile status rather than a right of property. But for the first time Republicans were specific that they were abolishing *racial* slavery. "All persons held to service or labor within the District of Columbia *by reason of African descent* are hereby discharged and freed." Also for the first—and only—time in the war, the bill provided for compensation at an average of three hundred dollars for each emancipated slave, though it restricted payments to "loyal" slaveholders. Owners had ninety days to apply for compensation to a three-man commission charged with examining the owners' claims. An oath was insufficient as proof of loyalty; there had to be witnesses, and often the only competent witness was a former slave. The commissioners were free to subpoena testimony "without the exclusion of any witness on account of color." Former slaves were thereby empowered to testify as to the loyalty of their former owners. The law made it a felony for any former owner to remove emancipated slaves from the District in an attempt to sell or re-enslave them, and anyone convicted of the felony could be sentenced to between five and twenty years in prison. Finally, Congress appropriated one hundred thousand dollars "to aid in the colonization and settlement of such free persons of African descent . . . as may desire to emigrate." Lincoln appointed the three men on the commission, and they set about their work quickly, issuing a notice on April 28 that all masters wishing compensation had ninety days to document their claims. By mid-June the commission published a list of all those claiming compensation and inviting testimony from anyone with knowledge of their loyalty. The commissioners completed their work and submitted a final report on August 16, 1862.[27]

A few days after the bill was passed, District blacks, many of them newly emancipated, met at an African American Presbyterian church to celebrate. They passed a series of resolutions, praising God for having brought to the District "that dearest of all earthly treasures—Freedom." They also resolved to "prove ourselves worthy" of freedom and to remain "orderly and law abiding." Finally, they expressed "heartfelt and enduring thanks to Congress, to President Lincoln and to our friends generally."[28] But as free blacks celebrated, Maryland masters complained that the abolition bill had turned Washington into "free soil," making it more than ever a refuge for their escaping slaves.

Like the existence of slavery on federal military installations within the southern states, slavery in the District presented Republicans with a legal anomaly. Committed to the proposition that slavery was purely local, they could not agree on the status of slavery in areas where state and local law created it. Wasn't slavery in the District of Columbia *local*? Though Republicans were generally loath to compensate masters on the principle that slaves were not "property" under the Constitution, they held their noses and compensated District masters because local law did recognize slave property. A similar anomaly arose over the legal status of slaves of loyal Maryland masters escaping into the District. Republicans generally believed that the fugitive slave clause should be enforced by state and local authorities only, and they were adamant that the Union army should not enforce the clause at all. In Washington, therefore, slaves escaping to Union military camps were generally emancipated, whereas local police and judges continued to enforce the Fugitive Slave Act. Republicans were frustrated with the continued capture of fugitive slaves by the District's city marshal, but by their own legal logic there was not much they could do about it. The contradiction became acute after the District abolition bill all but invited Maryland slaves into the capital to claim their freedom.[29]

Even before the statute took effect, Washington newspapers reported that slaves were "running away in numbers, the most of them making their way to the City of Washington, having got the idea that they will be free here." There were reports that between "100 and 200 slaves crossed the Eastern Branch Bridge every week." Owners watched helplessly, "knowing that they could not stop the stampede." The *Evening Star* predicted that once the law was passed, it would "bring hither within the next year a population of between 50,000 and 100,000 negroes liberated by the natural contingencies of the war."[30] This was pretty much what the Republicans had in mind: the destruction of slavery in one area would weaken it elsewhere, thanks to "the natural contingencies"—or, in Lincoln's phrase, the "friction and abrasion" of war.

More than a decade had passed since Senator Henry Wilson vowed to "blot out slavery in the National Capital" as part of a larger effort to "surround the slave States with a cordon of free States." Opponents were not wrong to see District abolition as "part of a series of measures already initiated, all looking to the same ultimate result,—the universal abolition of slavery by Congress." Clement Vallandingham of Ohio pronounced the abolition of slavery in Washington "the beginning of a grand scheme of emancipation; and there is no calculation where that scheme is to end." Republicans made no attempt to deny the charge, and radicals freely admitted it. The abolition of slavery in Washington was, in Charles Sumner's words, "the first installment of that great debt which we all owe to an enslaved race. . . . At the national capital, slavery will give way to freedom: but the good work will not stop here; it must proceed." Debate over slavery "will go on," one Republican congressman declared, and "should go on, till slavery is extinct."[31]

COLONIZATION

In 1860, writing "as an Abolitionist and a Republican," James Redpath proposed the construction of a colony of former slaves on the Caribbean island-nation of Haiti. Colonization would do two things, Redpath argued. It would demonstrate "the capacity of the race for self-government," and it would also "carry out the programme of the ablest intellects of the Republican Party,—of surrounding the Southern States with a cordon of free labor, within which, like a scorpion girded by fire, Slavery must inevitably die."[32] Colonies of freed people in Central America and the Caribbean would block the southward expansion of slavery, further tightening the cordon around the slave states and hastening the ultimate extinction of slavery in the South. Redpath had his own reasons for supporting a colony of freed slaves in Haiti, and though they were compatible with the reasons most Republicans would have given, they were not the same.

Colonization—the idea that blacks should be colonized somewhere outside the United States—always meant different things to different people. Cotton planters objected to colonization because it presupposed emancipation. Upper South slaveholders initially embraced it as a means of ridding the country of a despised class of free blacks. Moderate antislavery politicians endorsed colonization as a respectably conservative path to gradual abolition, but radical abolitionists denounced colonization because it delayed emancipation indefinitely and because it assumed that blacks and whites could never live together as equals. In the 1780s Thomas Jefferson argued that while the principles of universal freedom necessarily implied that the slaves should be emancipated, the indelible fact of black racial inferiority also demanded that emancipated slaves be deported to some other country. But abolitionists generally disliked the idea. In their campaigns to abolish slavery in the northern states in the late eighteenth century, they insisted that through diligence and education emancipated slaves and their descendants would overcome the degradation of slavery and eventually take their place as equal citizens. Not surprisingly, abolitionists were shocked by the emergence of the American Colonization Society (ACS) after the War of 1812, precisely because it seemed to deny the possibility of eventual racial equality.[33] To be sure, many sincere abolitionists were initially attracted to the society when it was first formed in 1817, but most of them departed within a few years as the organization put more and more emphasis on racial exclusion. By the late 1820s a new, more militant abolitionism defined itself in opposition to colonization.

The colonization movement waxed with the buildup of the Missouri crisis in 1821 and then quickly waned with the departure of the abolitionists. By the 1830s and 1840s the American Colonization Society was essentially moribund. Abolitionists had repudiated it, and meanwhile the Whigs and Democrats had excluded all forms of antislavery from national politics. Colonization revived alongside antislavery politics during the 1850s. In 1859 and 1860 the ACS sponsored more emigrants to Liberia—some four thousand—than at any period in its history. The war itself brought forth a new wave of colonization schemes and proposals, peaking in the same year—1862—that Republicans adopted a policy of universal military emancipation in the seceded states and put unprecedented pressure on the loyal slave states to abolish slavery on their own. But once the Republicans committed themselves to the complete destruction of slavery—which they had by the end of 1862—the colonization movement sputtered and for all practical purposes died. The Civil War brought colonization back to life, and then killed it. It's easy to see why. Among Republicans, support for colonization served two purposes: it would make it easier for northern racists to accept the emerging policy of universal emancipation, and it was part of a broader package of incentives designed to encourage the Border States to abolish slavery on their own. By the end of 1863, colonization no longer served those purposes, and though individual Republicans continued to endorse it, it all but disappeared as a serious policy. But which policy?

Historians generally use a single word—*colonization*—to describe two very different proposals. The first was deportation, the forced expulsion of free and emancipated blacks from the United States. During the war this was a policy advocated primarily by northern Democrats, and it went nowhere. Not a single freed slave was deported from the United States during or after the war. Only a few of the most conservative Republicans—Orville Browning in the Senate and Edward Bates, the attorney general—even hinted that they would support deportation. Most Republicans who supported colonization—and a substantial minority did not—endorsed a very different policy: federal subsidies for the voluntary emigration of blacks who chose to leave the United States. Though both policies are referred to as "colonization," the advocates of each were sharply critical of the other, and both were at some level disingenuous. Democrats insisted that they would support emancipation only if it was accompanied by deportation, when in truth they opposed emancipation under almost any circumstances. Republicans appropriated funds for voluntary emigration, knowing full well that hardly any blacks were likely to accept the offer. These rather sharp divisions became clear in the congressional debate over the colonization provision of the District emancipation bill.

Democrats and Border State congressmen belittled the very idea of voluntary emigration. You "will never find one slave in a hundred that will consent to be colonized, when liberated," Senator Davis of Kentucky insisted.[34] Indeed, widespread black reluctance to emigrate was one of the reasons Democrats gave for demanding involuntary deportation as a condition of emancipation. If blacks were allowed to remain in the United States after they were freed, Democrats predicted, either the states would re-enslave blacks as soon as they could, or else a race war would erupt across the South, ending in the complete extermination of all blacks. Border State representatives took a very different position. Delaware Democrat Willard Saulsbury opposed the appropriation of any funds for colonization on the grounds that Congress had no business offering states incentives to abolish slavery—at the taxpayers' expense, no less.

Despite such criticism, voluntary emigration was the only policy Republicans were willing to pursue. President Lincoln endorsed this type of colonization in his first annual message to Congress in December of 1861. By then his administration, led by Postmaster General Montgomery Blair—an avid colonizationist—was energetically pursing the possibility of building a colony for African American emigrants at Chiriquí, in Central America. Meanwhile Congress, having already included an appropriation for voluntary emigration in the District abolition statute, attached another appropriation to the Second Confiscation Act and authorized Lincoln to implement the colonization clause. By late 1862 the Chiriquí scheme fell apart, but the administration instead turned its attention to a different colony, at Île à Vache, a Caribbean island off the coast of Haiti. In December of 1862, Lincoln once again endorsed voluntary colonization in his second annual message to Congress.[35]

But by then much of the Republican support for voluntary emigration had already dissipated. Lincoln never mentioned it publicly again. In 1863 the colony at Île à Vache collapsed. Only about five hundred blacks, mostly former slaves from Virginia, had volunteered to go, yet within months they were dying from exposure and malnutrition. Less than a year after it was initiated, the only experiment in colonization came to an end when Lincoln, hearing of the disaster, sent a ship to the island to return the remaining colonists to the United States. Here and there a Republican could be heard to utter words in support of colonization, but as a policy it was finished.

It is not hard to understand the flurry of support for colonization during the Civil War. Notwithstanding the opposition of radical abolitionists, colonization presupposed emancipation, and whenever talk of emancipation rose, so too did talk of colonization. The more difficult question to answer is why it came to so little. In the modern world, wars of national unification, especially civil wars inflamed by ethnic nationalism, commonly lead to forced population transfers and sometimes genocide. The Civil War in the United States was certainly a war of national unification, and the Republicans exhibited more than their fair share of ethnic nationalism. Nor was the idea of forced expulsion unheard of in the United States. Most Republican policymakers were old enough to remember the brutal "removal" of the southeastern Indians during Andrew Jackson's administration. And during the Civil War itself the Union army forcibly expelled some ten thousand whites from their homes in Missouri. The same army systematically uprooted tens of thousands of slaves from their plantations to relocate them in areas safe from the reach of their former masters. And yet not a single emancipated slave was involuntarily "removed" from the United States in the wake of emancipation. Why was there so much talk of colonization and so little of it?

The most likely explanation is that colonization interfered with Republican efforts to get the former slaves back to work as free laborers. However much Republicans supported voluntary emigration, it paled beside their overwhelming desire to demonstrate the superiority of free labor on the farms and plantations of the post-emancipation South. If Republican emancipation policy is to be faulted, it is not for the relatively inconsequential efforts to colonize the former slaves, but for the far more substantial efforts to keep them in place, to put them back to work as soon as possible—often on their old farms and often for their former masters. Union officers in the South filled their reports with news of their efforts to get former slaves back to work, often boasting of their allegedly successful experiments in free labor. When they began moving large numbers of freed people, Union officials transplanted blacks not to Central America or Liberia, but to Memphis and Cincinnati, or to new plantations on Island No. 10 in the Mississippi River. Colonization was incompatible with the central thrust of Union policy—which was to retain black laborers, not to remove them.[36]

Colonization proposals flourished from late 1861 to late 1862 as Republicans were developing and coordinating their various programs of military emancipation and state abolition. Subsidies for voluntary emigration might appease the racists, particularly in the northwestern states, who were reluctant to accept emancipation on any other terms. More important, voluntary colonization proposals were offered to the loyal slave states as part of the Republican effort to encourage those states to abolish slavery on their own. But the racists were not appeased, and the Border States were not impressed. By the end of 1862, most Republicans gave up on the idea of colonization altogether, and once Lincoln issued the Emancipation Proclamation on January 1, 1863, he stopped advocating it as well. Colonization had served whatever purpose it ever had. Frustrated Republicans instead put their faith in the "friction and abrasion" of war, which, they concluded, was far more likely than colonization to push the Border States into abolishing slavery on their own.

ABOLITION IN THE BORDER STATES

An Irishman walks into a drugstore in Maine, where liquor can be sold only for medicinal purposes, and orders a shot of whiskey. The druggist sees that the man is clearly healthy and will sell him only soda. Well, asks the Irishman, can't you "slip" a little of the stuff into my soda, "unbeknownst to yourself"? That's what I'm doing, Lincoln told Wendell Phillips in early 1862. I have "put a good deal of Anti-slavery" into my policies, "unbeknown" to most people. A short while later Lincoln told the same joke to another abolitionist, Moncure Conway. Both Phillips and Conway had been critical of what they believed was Lincoln's slow pace toward emancipation, and on both occasions Lincoln's response was the same. I'm not as slow as you think; you're just not noticing.[37]

During the first year of his administration, Lincoln was discreet about his approach to slavery, but there was no mistaking the substance of his policies. Within days of General Benjamin Butler's decision not to return fugitive slaves to their owners, Lincoln met with his cabinet and endorsed the general's "contraband" policy. Lincoln not only signed the First Confiscation Act, his War Department implemented it more aggressively than the statute itself required. Lincoln had put the decidedly antislavery Salmon Chase in charge of the transition to freedom in both the Sea Islands and southern Louisiana, and Chase in turn had appointed committed abolitionists to oversee both processes. Lincoln had also made it clear to friends and visitors in private that he supported the antislavery policies of his fellow Republicans. Yet despite all of this, Lincoln remained almost completely silent in public. In his December 1861 message to Congress, he mentioned, just barely, that slaves were being "liberated" under the First Confiscation Act. But his most conspicuous public acts—the revocation of the edicts by Generals Frémont and Hunter—made him seem far more reluctant to attack slavery than his actual policies indicated. In fact Lincoln had embraced military emancipation from the earliest months of the war, and before the first year of the war was out, he began pressuring the Border States to abolish slavery on their own.

In November of 1861, Lincoln quietly drafted two proposals for the abolition of slavery in Delaware, proposals he considered a model for the Border States generally. Both versions promised federal compensation to the state government in return for the gradual abolition of slavery. The versions differed chiefly in the timelines each proposed for the completion of abolition, though Lincoln indicated a preference for ten years. It was important to Lincoln and most Republicans that, however gradual the timeline, abolition must begin immediately. As soon as any state began abolishing slavery, Republicans believed, they began voting like free states. In Lincoln's ideal world, this is how slavery would disappear: the states themselves would abolish it; the process would begin immediately; it would be completed in about a decade; and above all it would be peaceful. Lincoln added federal compensation to the mix not because he believed the slaveholders deserved to be paid for their property, but as an incentive to the states to get abolition under way and to speed it up. Under his proposals, the states, not the slaveholders, would be compensated. Moreover, the federal government would dole out the money to the states in proportion to the number of years it took to abolish slavery. The sooner slavery was abolished, the sooner the state would be compensated.[38] It was an astonishing proposal. No president had ever so much as suggested federally funded incentives for abolition in the states. Almost all of his predecessors—like nearly all Democrats at the time—would have viewed Lincoln's plan as unwarranted federal "interference" with slavery in the states, a blatant violation of the federal consensus.

Lincoln never mentioned his proposal in public. He had drafted it in November, and through the early months of 1862 he maintained virtual silence on all matters related to slavery. Whatever his reasons for lying low, however, Lincoln's failure to publicly acknowledge his own support for both military emancipation and state abolition was becoming counterproductive. The radicals who were closest to Lincoln—Owen Lovejoy and Charles Sumner, for example—repeatedly assured their fellow Republicans that Lincoln was sound on slavery. Carl Schurz, another Lincoln ally with strong ties to the radicals, warned the president in May of 1862 that he was not making his position clear to the most ardently antislavery Republican voters in the North. Having spoken with Lincoln at some length, Schurz wrote that he was "perfectly happy and contented, fully convinced that, in spite of appearances to the contrary, you were determined to use all your constitutional power to deliver this country of the great curse. But there are many who do not understand your policy as I do, or rather, there are probably few who do. The majority want to be confirmed in their faith from time to time."[39] By then Lincoln was coming to understand that his antislavery supporters needed clearer evidence of his stand.

Democrats in the Delaware legislature denounced Lincoln's proposal on all possible grounds: the federal government had no business taxing citizens to pay for such a thing; Lincoln was trampling the Constitution by interfering with slavery in a state; abolition was the entering wedge of racial equality. As soon as the Republicans freed the slaves, Democrats warned, they would give black men the vote, and they would vote for Republicans. The proposal died without even coming up for a vote in the state legislature.[40]

Frustrated by Delaware's angry rejection, and meanwhile under pressure to be more outspoken about his antislavery policies, Lincoln decided to go public. On March 6, 1862, he sent a special "Message to Congress" proposing a package of federal incentives that would encourage the Border States to abolish slavery on their own. Unlike the Delaware abolition proposals, the March 6 address was general rather than specific. Lincoln asked for a joint congressional resolution vowing federal cooperation "with any state which may adopt gradual abolishment of slavery" and promising compensation—to the *state* rather than to individual masters—for any "inconveniences" caused by "such a change of system."[41]

Though Lincoln's effort to promote abolition in the Border States had long been a familiar feature of antislavery politics, the war enabled him to cloak that agenda with an urgency it could not have worn in peacetime. Abolition in the Border States was, he said, "an efficient means of self-preservation" for the federal government. If any seceded state returned to the Union and accepted the offer of compensation, the leaders of the "insurrection" would lose all hope of maintaining the Confederacy. "To deprive them of this hope," Lincoln said, "substantially ends the rebellion." Not that Lincoln expected any Confederate state to abandon the insurrection and initiate a gradual abolition. But what if "the more Northern" slave states—the Border States—would, "by such initiation, make it certain to the more Southern that in no event, will the former ever join the latter, in their proposed confederacy?" That would surely demoralize the Confederacy and shorten the war, Lincoln argued, and thereby reduce the cost to taxpayers. Hence federally compensated abolition would prove a more "efficient" means of suppressing the rebellion.[42]

Lincoln contended that his proposal did not violate the federal consensus because it "sets up no claim of a right, by federal authority, to interfere with slavery within state limits." As was generally the case among Republicans, the president interpreted the word *interfere* narrowly; it meant "abolish." The federal government could not *abolish* slavery in a state. No less predictably, Democrats and Border State congressmen drew the line of interference more widely, and emphatically, and Lincoln's proposal went well beyond it. Border State representatives did not want to sell their slaves to the federal government, and northern Democrats did not think the government should ask taxpayers to buy them. The "people were not prepared," one Illinois Democrat explained, "to enter upon the proposed work of purchasing the slaves of other people, and turning them loose in their midst." For Democrats it was a matter of strictly limited powers. The *Boston Post* insisted that Congress had "no authority" to appropriate public funds for "the purchase and emancipation of slaves." The *Albany Argus* denounced it as a step toward the development of a "consolidated government." Border State officials insisted that the president's proposal violated the constitutional consensus barring federal interference with slavery in the states. Charles A. Wickliffe of Kentucky wondered "what clause of the Constitution" gave Congress the power "to appropriate the treasure of the United States to buy negroes, or to set them free." Opponents were also disturbed by the larger political purpose of the president's proposal. Lincoln understood that for his plan to work, antislavery parties would have to emerge and triumph in the loyal slave states. His proposal was designed to promote that process. John Crittenden grasped this most clearly. Though Lincoln himself may not intend it, his proposal would "stir up an emancipation party in Missouri, in Maryland, and in Delaware," not to mention Crittenden's home state of Kentucky.[43]

Republicans countered that Lincoln's proposal did nothing unconstitutional since it left entirely to the states the decision to sell slaves to the federal government. Indeed, the Republicans professed astonishment that the constitutional issue should even be raised. All the president's proposal says, Representative Abram B. Olin of New York declared, is that "if you gentlemen of the slave States are willing to get rid of slavery, the General Government will aid you to do it by giving you a compensation for any loss that you may sustain. . . . God knows, I would divide my last crust of bread to aid our southern friends to get rid of slavery." Thaddeus Stevens of Pennsylvania wondered what all the fuss was about. "I think," he said of Lincoln's message, "it is about the most diluted, milk and water gruel proposition that was ever given to the American nation." Such skepticism was aimed at the efficacy rather than the legitimacy of Lincoln's proposal. By early 1862 few Republicans believed that there was any meaningful sentiment against slavery to "stir up" in the Border States. Wherever there were "men whose interests are identified with slavery," one Republican congressman explained, there was "no great diversity of opinion" on the subject. "I have never been able to discover a difference in views or feelings between a man from Maryland and a man from South Carolina or Alabama." Skepticism notwithstanding, congressional Republicans overwhelmingly endorsed the president's joint resolution. The House supported it by a vote of 89 to 31, with nearly every Republican favoring it and nearly everyone else opposed. The same thing happened in the Senate, where the vote was 32 to 20.[44]

The Republican press was no less supportive. Henry J. Raymond, the reliably conservative editor of the *New York Times*, praised Lincoln's proposal as a "master-piece of practical wisdom and sound policy." The more radical—and influential—Horace Greeley was equally effusive, if only because Lincoln's plan for Border State abolition seemed to have been modeled on the one Greeley had first proposed a year earlier, as Lincoln himself acknowledged: "you have advocated it from the first," he wrote to Greeley, "so that I need to say little to you on the subject." Greeley's *New York Tribune* "never printed a State paper with more satisfaction." The president's message "constitutes of itself an epoch in the history of our country." Yet there was skepticism in the Republican press, just as there was in Congress. The *Springfield Republican* approved of Lincoln's proposal but doubted whether any of the Border States would immediately take the president up on his offer. Still, the editors noted that the proposal itself necessarily implies "that slavery is an evil and that the slave states have good reason to wish to be rid of it." And however limited its immediate effects, surely "a standing offer from the general government" would have a beneficial "moral effect," helping to promote the growth of "an emancipation party" in those states."[45]

"BY MERE FRICTION AND ABRASION"

Curiously, most observers—whether skeptical, critical, or enthusiastic—ignored one of the crucial elements of Lincoln's March 6, 1862, message: its unambiguous threat that if the Border States did not quickly adopt abolition on their own, slavery would be destroyed anyway, and the loyal slave states would end up without slavery and without compensation. In his earlier December message, Lincoln had said that if necessary he was prepared to use "all indispensable means" to suppress the rebellion, implying a more aggressive attack on slavery, though he hoped that would not be necessary. The March 6 message was more forthright. Lincoln reiterated his readiness to use "all indispensable means" to suppress the rebellion, but now he was talking directly to the Border States and warning that if the rebellion continued, "it is impossible to foresee all the incidents, which may attend and all the ruin which may follow it." Lincoln was using the threat of military emancipation in the seceded states to promote the abolition of slavery in the Border States.[46]

It was radical abolitionists who most appreciated the militant undertone of Lincoln's March 6 address. Not all of them, to be sure. After years of denouncing the Constitution as hopelessly proslavery, William Lloyd Garrison had recently discovered its tremendous antislavery potential and now dismissed Lincoln for *failing* to invoke his constitutional war powers to declare universal emancipation everywhere, even in the states with which the Union was not at war. But readers of Garrison's paper, *The Liberator*, were more discerning. Take another look at the message, Lucius Holmes advised Garrison. "Is it not stated that there is to be no yielding to rebels? Is it not more than intimated," he asked, "that, if they persist in their rebellion, the most efficient course—Emancipation—may be resorted to?" Wendell Phillips read Lincoln's message the same way—as a threat. He praised the president for telling the Border States, "Gentlemen, if you do not take this, we will take your negroes anyhow."[47]

Over the next few months, as Lincoln's frustration with the Border States mounted, his threats became bolder. In his May 19 proclamation revoking General David Hunter's abolition edict, Lincoln devoted most his time to warning the Border States to accept compensation in return for abolition before it was too late. "You can not if you would, be blind to the signs of the times," he said. The end of slavery was coming. God has given you the opportunity to do more good "by one effort" than has ever been possible "in all past time." "May the vast future not have to lament that you have neglected it."[48]

Still the Border States resisted, and in early summer Lincoln invited their congressmen and senators to the White House, where he made one last pitch for support. The timing—July 12, 1862—was scarcely accidental. On that day the Senate adopted the final version of the Second Confiscation Act, establishing universal emancipation as federal policy in the seceded states and reaffirming the ban on military enforcement of the fugitive slave clause, no matter what state the fugitives escaped from. The Border State congressmen knew this when they arrived at the White House and heard the president tell them, apparently with a straight face, that if they had only taken up his proposal of the previous March, the rebellion would be over by now. The Confederacy's greatest hope was that the shared interests of all slave states would ultimately bring the Border States into the southern nation. The slavery interest is "the lever of their power," Lincoln argued, urging his guests to "[b]reak that lever before their faces." With the Second Confiscation Act clearly in mind, Lincoln warned the congressmen that the only alternative to gradual, compensated abolition was immediate and uncompensated military emancipation. "The incidents of the war can not be avoided," he said, slavery "in your states will be extinguished by mere friction and abrasion—by the mere incidents of war. It will be gone, and you will have nothing valuable in lieu of it." Take the money and run, Lincoln told the Border State representatives, before the money is wasted "in cutting one another's throats."[49]

David Strother, a Virginia unionist, was stunned by Lincoln's remarks. Strother had nothing but contempt for the slaveholders who had pushed for secession; he had enlisted in the Union army at the beginning of the war. Yet he was "shocked" by the "tone" the president had taken with the Border State representatives. Lincoln seemed to be caving in to the abolitionists. His message, Strother complained, "supposes that slavery is the cause of the war and proposes that slavery be abolished in the Border States because a certain party thinks so and will not support the war unless this cause is abolished." In Strother's mind, the cause of the war was not slavery but "party spirit."[50] But slavery and party spirit were complementary rather than competing explanations. A proslavery "party" had led the South out of the Union after the electoral victory of an antislavery "party." It is possible to read Lincoln's remarks as a capitulation to the abolitionists, but it's also possible to read them as a legitimate appeal to his party's base, not to mention a reflection of Lincoln's antislavery convictions.

Although they were separate policies, gradual abolition in the loyal slave states and military emancipation in the seceded states became linked in Republican minds by early 1862. When the war started, Republicans believed that abolition would begin in the Border States, where they supposed slavery was the weakest, and would eventually spread southward into the cotton belt. That was one of the things Lincoln assumed when he argued that the destruction of slavery in the Border States would demolish the hopes of the Confederates and set in motion the ultimate extinction of slavery everywhere. Even gradual abolition, if begun immediately, would destroy "the slavery interest" of the Border States. Their representatives in Congress, speaking and voting with the free states, would join the "cordon of freedom" surrounding the South, hastening slavery's destruction everywhere.

That premise, however, turned upside down as the dogged resistance of the Border States to Lincoln's abolition proposal became clear in early 1862. By then Republicans were shifting to a much more aggressive policy of universal military emancipation in the Confederacy, with potent implications for the loyal slave states. The

Republicans began to argue that military emancipation in the disloyal states would inexorably spread into loyal parts of the South. The dominoes were still going to fall, only now they were likely to tumble from south to north. Abolition would still begin in the loyal slave states because only a state could abolish slavery within its limits, but the catalyst for abolition in the Border States would now be military emancipation in the seceded states. For decades the opponents of slavery saw abolition in the Border States as the initial goal of the "cordon of freedom" they planned to build around the South. Secession and war did not alter the goal but it radically altered the way Republicans went about achieving it. They came to see military emancipation in the seceded states as an additional "lever" they could use to pressure the Border States to abandon slavery.

The Union's wartime policy on slavery is sometimes described as a shift from gradual to immediate emancipation, but this misses the distinction between the two policies as well as the critical relationship that developed between them. The Republican Congress had endorsed immediate, uncompensated military emancipation in the First Confiscation Act, which Lincoln signed on August 6, 1861, and began implementing two days later, on August 8. It was several more months before Lincoln formulated his first proposal for gradual abolition in the Border States. Immediate military emancipation came first, and it targeted the disloyal states. Gradual abolition came later and was aimed at the loyal slave states. Indeed, by early 1862 Republicans argued that military emancipation, spreading northward from the cotton states, would force the Border States to abolish slavery on their own. Until 1861 no one had ever imagined such a scenario. But the war changed everything. It enabled Lincoln and the Republicans to put more rather than less pressure on the Border States.

It is often said that Lincoln's embrace of emancipation was impeded by his overriding concern to keep the Border States from leaving the Union. But something closer to the opposite may be true.

Oblivious to the cries of outrage from the Border States, Lincoln and the Republicans began emancipating slaves very early in the war. It wasn't the Border States that made emancipation more difficult; it was emancipation that made keeping the Border States from seceding more difficult. If Lincoln's sole concern had been to prevent their secession, he would have had a much easier job. What made the Border States such a ticklish problem was that Lincoln was struggling to keep them in the Union while *at the same time* he was pressuring them to abolish slavery. Lincoln was not alone. By early 1862 Republicans in Congress were also dreaming up new ways to stimulate abolition in the Border States, ways that would have been inconceivable to antislavery radicals only a year earlier. The Republicans even decided that if the Border States would not abolish slavery on their own, they would create a brand new Border State and force it to abandon slavery as a condition for admission to the Union.

THE FREE STATE OF WEST VIRGINIA

For centuries settlers in western Virginia chafed under the rule of aristocratic eastern planters. Throughout the colonial era the sectional antagonism between east and west remained a struggle within the slaveholding class, pitting the parvenu planters of the inland Piedmont against the more established families of the eastern tidewater regions. These conflicts most often centered on the disproportionate power the eastern planters exercised in the colonial legislature, the House of Burgesses. Piedmont masters—like Thomas Jefferson— emerged from these struggles as the foes of aristocracy, demanding equal representation and a more democratic state constitution. But Jefferson's personal hatred of slavery notwithstanding, the early advocates of legislative reapportionment were anything but abolitionists. They were, instead, the exponents of a slaveholders' democracy. Not

until the 1820s, after settlement had pushed farther into the mountainous western counties where plantation slavery did not take root,
did western democrats express their frustration with anti-democratic
easterners by denouncing slavery itself.[51]

There was an economic component to western demands for more
equitable representation. Yeoman farmers complained that the state's
tax structure was biased in favor of the slaveholders, that slave property was taxed at a lower rate than land, and that the tobacco and
wheat that slaves produced were exempted from taxes while the cattle, sheep, and hogs raised by small farmers were not. Cut off from
ready access to markets, small farmers in western Virginia clamored
for roads, canals, and rail lines that would boost the prosperity of
their region. Throughout the antebellum decades, right up to the
Civil War, the stubborn resistance of eastern planters to support
democratic reform and state funding for "internal improvements"
transformed a simple struggle over political representation into a
simmering class conflict between slaveholders in the east and yeoman farmers in the west. By 1860 democratic politics in western Virginia was anti-slaveholder politics—but it still wasn't abolitionism.[52]

As soon as Virginia joined the Confederacy, the western counties
voted overwhelmingly against secession and quickly declared their
independence from the rest of the state. They formed their own government and pronounced it the legitimate sovereign for the entire
state of Virginia, sending unionist senators and representatives to
Congress and organizing a loyal legislature that granted the western
counties permission to secede and form their own state. In late 1861
those counties sent delegates to a constitutional convention where
they drew up a new state charter that was approved by an overwhelming vote in a referendum held in early 1862. Having thus observed the
formalities, West Virginia applied to Congress for statehood.[53]

If they had their way, West Virginians would have entered the
Union as a slave state. At the constitutional convention in December

of 1861, the delegates overwhelmingly defeated a proposal for gradual abolition. Despite the long history of animosity between east and west, despite the fact that there were relatively few slaves and hardly any plantations in western Virginia, there was still enough deference to the property rights of slaveholders to block the adoption of a gradual emancipation clause in the new state constitution. Instead, all the convention managed to endorse was a resolution banning the further importation of slaves into the new state of West Virginia.[54]

When the statehood request got to Congress, however, Republicans forced the issue by requiring West Virginia to abolish slavery as a condition for admission to the Union. Virginia Senator John Carlile claimed that Congress had no right to impose such demands on a state. Senator Waitman T. Willey of the same state was more cooperative, though he tried to dilute the effects of the abolition requirement by proposing the gradual emancipation of all slaves born after July 4, 1863, once those slaves reached adulthood. But Senator Benjamin Wade, who was in charge of the bill, substituted the more aggressive schedule for gradual emancipation that antislavery delegates had proposed in West Virginia's constitutional convention the previous December. Under the terms of the bill, West Virginia could not enter the Union until President Lincoln issued a proclamation certifying that the state had complied with the abolition requirement imposed by Congress. Sixty days after the president issued his proclamation, West Virginia would become a state.[55]

The slaves themselves would help ensure this outcome—or so some Republicans believed. At one point in the congressional debate, Senator Willey suggested that the slaveholders would evade the gradual abolition law by moving their slaves out of the affected counties and selling them before they reached the age of emancipation. In reply, Senator James Lane cited the example of the slaves in Kansas, who were waiting to be freed on July 4, 1856. As the date of emancipation approached, some Kansas masters attempted "to spirit their slaves out of the State." According to Lane the slaves themselves thwarted their owners' plans. "They said to their masters, 'we are to be freed on the 4th day of July, and you shall not take us from the borders of Kansas.' They remained there and were freed." Lane supposed that "the slaves of Virginia have about as much sense as the slaves of Kansas had in 1856." Wade seconded Lane's sentiments. West Virginia was "essentially a free State," he noted. Of course there were still a "few" who remained in the "anomalous condition" of slavery, but many others had already "nobly emancipated themselves." The slaves, Wade believed, were the final guarantors of abolition in the free state of West Virginia.[56]

As soon as Wade reported the statehood bill out of the Senate Committee on the Territories, Charles Sumner objected to the gradual-abolition clause on the grounds that it amounted to the admission of a new slave state into the Union. It may be "but a few slaves only," Sumner explained, "and for a generation only, but nevertheless a new slave State." As of 1860 there were twelve thousand slaves in the proposed state of West Virginia, and Sumner would not "consent that there shall be two additional slaveholding Senators for another generation in this body." The radicals on the committee rejected Sumner's logic. John Hale thought it would be "a singular fact" if, after years of admitting states with constitutions that made slavery "perpetual and eternal," the Congress should suddenly refuse to admit "the first one that came to our doors with gradual emancipation inscribed on her constitution." Slavery is "an evil," Hale declared, and he was determined "to get rid of it in some practical form, in some practical way." As far as Hale was concerned, the West Virginia bill did that. Benjamin Wade, who did more than anyone to force the incoming state to abolish slavery, likewise disputed Sumner's argument. He would certainly have preferred to see West Virginia emancipate its slaves immediately, but Wade believed it was a fundamental mistake for Sumner to say that the mere presence of slaves made a state into a "slave state." On the contrary, Wade insisted, the historical record of northern abolition demonstrated conclusively that once a state placed slavery under a sentence of death by gradual emancipation, its representatives ceased to vote as slave states. Delaware, by its obstreperous rejection of gradual abolition, continued to behave like a slave state. West Virginia, on the other hand, with far more slaves than Delaware, had embraced abolition and would come into the Union committed to slavery's destruction. It was a stretch, Wade suggested, to call that a "slave state." Senator Fessenden agreed. Once it is "fixed in such a manner as to be irrevocable that slavery is to terminate in a given time," he observed, "it becomes a free State in point of fact." This was the same reasoning that led Lincoln to insist that gradual abolition commence immediately: once a state had committed itself to abolition, it behaved like a free state, further weakening the power of the remaining slave states.[57]

On July 14 the Senate voted down Sumner's amendment, 24 to 11, but several key radicals supported Sumner. Concerned by this split within the party ranks, Wade tried to assuage Sumner by strengthening the gradual-emancipation provision of the bill, freeing more slaves more quickly. When Sumner tried to reintroduce his amendment, even his radical allies abandoned him. Hale wanted a "practical" bill that would ensure slavery's destruction. Wade pleaded with his colleagues for "a little compromise." Lane of Kansas, another dependable radical, agreed. He had originally supported Sumner's amendment, but he wanted "to legislate upon the subject of slavery as upon all other subjects, practically." As they had from the start of the war, Republican radicals pushed for as much as they could get, but compromised when necessary to get as much as they could. Lane would vote for the West Virginia statehood bill, he explained, "being willing to take from a slave State slavery in twenty-one years, if we cannot get rid of it earlier." Congressman John Bingham said the same thing in the House debate later that year. "God knows, I would have preferred that this House had the courage to have said that every human being should be free now and forevermore within the proposed State." If he could "give liberty" to every slave in Virginia, he would. But as the statehood bill gives freedom to "nine-tenths" of them, with the ultimate promise of freedom to all, "I choose," Bingham concluded, "to follow the express will of a majority in that respect." Unwilling to sacrifice goodness on the altar of perfection, radicals took the measure of their colleagues and pressed for the broadest, quickest abolition possible. Sumner voted against the final bill, but most of his fellow radicals—Clark, Wade, Pomeroy, Lane, and Wilson of Massachusetts—supported it.[58]

The dispute over Sumner's amendment was an early indication that Republicans were giving up on voluntary abolition by the Border States as they drew closer to universal military emancipation in the seceded states. Lyman Trumbull drew the connection explicitly. He pointed out that only two days before the Senate was set to vote on the West Virginia statehood bill, it had passed the Second Confiscation Act, thereby freeing all the slaves in the rebel states. Virginia was a rebel state, so wouldn't the emancipation of the slaves in western Virginia be accomplished more rapidly if the area was left within the seceded state? Trumbull asked. But most Republicans understood that state abolition was a far more secure method of destroying slavery than military emancipation. Besides, Wade argued, slavery was already effectively dead in West Virginia, and separate statehood was as much as anything a well-deserved reward for the loyal people, black and white, of those counties that had suffered for generations under the domination of eastern planters. Having watched the Border States reject all proposals for gradual abolition, Republicans had decided to create a Border State of their own—determined to get slavery abolished in at least one state South of the Ohio River.

With Congress ready to adjourn, the House held back on consideration of the statehood bill until it returned in December. There the debate took an entirely different turn. In contrast with the Senate, the House debate scarcely touched on the relative merits of immediate *versus* gradual abolition—most likely because by December of 1862, few Republicans still thought emancipation was likely to happen gradually, no matter what the constitution of West Virginia said.[59] House opponents instead denounced the constitutional irregularity of the process. The "loyal" government of Virginia was essentially indistinguishable from the western counties, yet it was that skeletal entity to which those same counties formally applied for permission to secede from the state. Needless to say, the "loyal" government granted its permission. Democrats, and even a few Republicans, questioned the legitimacy of the western counties' secession and even Lincoln's attorney general, Edward Bates, concluded that the procedure was unconstitutional. But Lincoln disagreed and signed the statehood bill, with the abolition requirement, on December 31, 1862.

The following day he issued the Emancipation Proclamation, excluding from its reach the forty-eight counties of western Virginia. As with Louisiana, West Virginia was excluded not because its slaves would not be freed, but because it was loyal and because slavery in those counties was already slated for abolition by other means. Those means—a federal requirement that slavery be abolished by a state as a condition for admission to the Union—became a crucial precedent. Less than six months after Lincoln certified that West Virginia had met the congressional requirement for the abolition of slavery, the president imposed a similar condition on Louisiana, requiring the state to endorse the Emancipation Proclamation as a condition for *readmission* to the Union. Eventually the federal government would impose the same requirement on every one of the defeated Confederate states.

DURING THE SENATE DEBATE over the West Virginia bill, Lyman Trumbull wondered whether this was the right time to organize a new state, given the turbulence of the war. "Sir," Ben Wade replied, "amidst that turbulence is the very time to organize" a new free state. The admission of West Virginia is "one of those things that the exigencies of the times most eminently demand," Wade argued. "You can do justice now easier than you can begin to contemplate in earlier times." By then it had become a commonplace among Republicans that the "friction and abrasion" of war, spreading northward from the seceded states, would eventually overwhelm and destroy slavery in the loyal states—including West Virginia. The opponents of emancipation were making the same point. In the spring of 1862, as Congress was debating the bill to abolish slavery in Washington, Ohio's Clement Vallandingham pointed out that in the previous Congress "there were not ten men" who would have recorded their votes "in favor of the abolition of slavery in the District of Columbia." Now, only a year later, he complained, Republicans were "availing themselves of the troubles of the times" to do something they could never have done in peacetime.[60]

For at least a generation, antislavery politicians had been struggling to abolish slavery in the District of Columbia, exclude slavery from the western territories, require the slave states to enforce the fugitive slave clause on their own, and reverse the proslavery bias of American foreign policy. The Civil War made it possible to implement these antislavery policies. The war also enabled Republicans to go further, to impose new pressures on the Border States that would have been inconceivable in peacetime—pressures unabashedly designed to get the loyal slave states to abolish slavery on their own. It remained to be seen whether a "cordon of freedom" would be enough to destroy slavery everywhere in the United States.

9

THE "PRELIMINARY" PROCLAMATION

ABRAHAM LINCOLN OFTEN USED comedy to make a serious point, but sometimes he liked to tell stories just because they were funny. When he met with his cabinet on September 22, 1862, he began by reading aloud from a tale by the popular humorist Artemus Ward. There was no fable with a message; it was just a good story. But if Lincoln told the tale for the sheer fun of it, he had called his cabinet together to discuss a serious subject. He wanted to tell everyone that he had decided to issue "A Proclamation" affirming the emancipation of rebel-owned slaves in the Union-occupied parts of the Confederacy and promising to emancipate the slaves in the unoccupied areas of seceded states one hundred days later. Lincoln had sent word that morning to convene at the White House at midday, and by noon all the cabinet secretaries had arrived. After reading the story and chuckling along with most of the cabinet members—Stanton didn't laugh but everybody else did—the president "then took a graver tone." He had "thought a great deal about the relation of this war to

Slavery," he said. Indeed he had intended to issue the proclamation the previous July but withheld it "on account of objections made by some of you." Back then the military situation was so bleak that issuing a proclamation would have seemed like an act of desperation. But on September 17, Union troops defeated Robert E. Lee's Confederate army in a brutal battle at Sharpsburg, Maryland, beside Antietam Creek. Lincoln told the cabinet that he had made a promise to himself and—he hesitated—"to my Maker," that if the "rebel invasion" were turned back, he would release the proclamation. "I think the time has come now."[1] That evening, news of the so-called Preliminary Proclamation began appearing in newspapers all across the nation.

PROCLAMATIONS PROSAIC AND POSTPONED

In the spring of 1862, those closest to Lincoln noticed that, like most Republicans, he was coming to the conclusion that federal antislavery policy would have to become much more aggressive. In late May, as Congress was debating the bill that would become the Second Confiscation Act, Secretary Stanton assured Senator Charles Sumner that "*a decree of Emancipation would be issued within two months.*"[2] In June, Treasury Secretary Salmon Chase sensed that although Lincoln's "mind is not finally decided," the president recognized that the "contingency" of a general emancipation was rapidly becoming a "necessity."[3] Lincoln was hardly alone. During late spring and early summer of 1862, Republicans everywhere were declaring themselves converts to universal emancipation.

On July 11, the House of Representatives approved the joint committee report of the final version of the Second Confiscation Act, freeing the slaves of all rebels in the seceded states pending a proclamation by the president. On July 12, the Senate adopted the same report. The next day, during a carriage ride on the way to the funeral of Stanton's son, Lincoln told two other cabinet members—Gideon Welles and William Seward—that he would issue the proclamation called for in the bill. "It was on this occasion and on this ride," Welles recalled some years later, that Lincoln "first mentioned to Mr. Seward and myself the subject of emancipating slaves by Proclamation."[4] It was in many ways a momentous announcement. "I scarcely know what to make of it," Welles wrote to his wife that evening.[5]

Yet if Welles and Seward appreciated the implications of what Lincoln told them, they could hardly have been surprised. Certainly the president's reasoning would have been familiar to both of them. Lincoln had "come to the conclusion," he said, that a proclamation "was a military necessity absolutely essential for the salvation of the Union, that we must free the slaves or be ourselves subdued."[6] At the other end of Pennsylvania Avenue, on the floor of Congress, most Republicans were saying the same thing. Moreover, during the preceding months of congressional debate, the only serious division among Republicans regarding the prospective emancipation provision of the Second Confiscation Act—and it wasn't all that serious—was whether it should require a presidential proclamation within sixty days of passage or whether the president should be given more discretion about when to issue it. It scarcely occurred to Republican lawmakers that Lincoln would sign the law and then *not* issue the proclamation. There was never any reason to doubt that Lincoln would do so.

Years later, after the war was over, the carriage ride to the funeral entered into the folklore of the Emancipation Proclamation, along with several other belated recollections by less reliable witnesses who maintained that Lincoln had told them even earlier that he had decided to issue it. Some claimed that Lincoln showed them his earliest draft of the proclamation, and still others remembered being in the room when he drafted it. These dubious recollections often suggest a Pauline-style conversion—a sudden, "momentous decision" by Lincoln to "free the slaves"—that nobody at the time seemed to notice.[7] In fact, Lincoln had long supported the emancipation of slaves escaping to Union lines, and he was hardly alone in concluding that a general emancipation was necessary to suppress the rebellion. If there was a decisive moment, it was determined by Congress. When Lincoln signed the Second Confiscation Act on July 17, he would surely issue the proclamation shortly thereafter, but he didn't.

In July of 1862, Congress went out of session the way it usually goes out of session, with a flurry of legislation requiring presidential signatures and authorizations. There was nothing new about passing laws that would be activated by presidential proclamations. They were often required for emergencies when Congress was in recess, so it was hardly surprising that during the Civil War several congressional statutes required presidential proclamations before they could take effect. After the loss of Fort Sumter, Lincoln borrowed the wording of the 1792 Militia Act, which authorized the president to issue a proclamation calling for troops if they were needed to suppress a domestic insurrection. In June of 1862, a month before Congress passed the Second Confiscation Act, Republicans enacted a law allowing the seizure of real estate in areas where the rebellion made it impossible for federal authorities to collect direct taxes. It would take effect as soon as the president "by his proclamation, shall declare in what States and parts of States said insurrection exists." Lincoln issued the proclamation a few weeks later. Shortly thereafter, the Senate passed the West Virginia bill requiring a presidential proclamation to certify when the new state met the congressional requirement for gradual abolition and could therefore be admitted to the Union. The First Confiscation Act required a presidential proclamation to determine which areas were in rebellion and were thereby subject to the law's provisions. By the time Congress passed the Second Confiscation Act, it must have seemed fairly ordinary to link emancipation to a presidential proclamation.[8]

On July 21, a few days after Congress adjourned, Lincoln arrived at the next cabinet meeting with a stack of proclamations and authorizations implementing the laws that Congress had enacted the previous week in the closing days of the session. Most of them concerned the shift to a more aggressive policy of "hard war" against the Confederacy, and universal emancipation was part of that shift. The cabinet discussions continued into the next day, at which time Lincoln read aloud his first draft of an emancipation proclamation. It was a mere two paragraphs. First Lincoln cited Section 6 of the Second Confiscation Act, which required a proclamation warning the rebels of the consequences of their continued insurrection. The second paragraph reiterated the two antislavery policies Republicans had developed over the previous year: federal compensation for loyal states that implemented gradual emancipation, and immediate, uncompensated military emancipation in the disloyal states. By yoking the two policies together in a single paragraph, Lincoln was once again using the threat of military emancipation to encourage abolition by the states, but in this case the threat was aimed at the seceded states rather than the Border States. End your rebellion and return to the Union, Lincoln was suggesting, and you might still be able to abolish slavery gradually, with compensation and federal subsidies for voluntary colonization. When Congress comes back into session at the end of the year, Lincoln vowed, he would urge it to pass a law funding his compensation proposal. This was the first of many indications that Lincoln did not expect the seceded states to return to the Union unless they abolished slavery. As for the states still in rebellion on January 1, 1863, Lincoln's draft declared that "all persons held as slaves . . . shall then, and thenceforward, and forever, be free."[9] Once again compensation was offered as an inducement to loyal states that abolished slavery gradually on their own, whereas immediate and uncompensated military emancipation would be imposed on disloyal states. To all appearances, then, Lincoln was fully prepared to proclaim the emancipation of all slaves in rebel states when he came to the cabinet meeting on July 21.

Although no one in the cabinet objected in principle to the new emancipation policy, there was a good deal of discussion about the details. Only Secretary of War Stanton supported Lincoln without reservation. Attorney General Edward Bates endorsed the proclamation but wanted emancipation tied to compulsory colonization, a proposal Lincoln quickly and predictably rejected. Some wondered whether a presidential proclamation was the best way to implement the new policy, at least at that moment. Montgomery Blair, the postmaster general, proclaimed himself a supporter of emancipation but thought it inexpedient to issue the proclamation at that time. Navy Secretary Gideon Welles likewise approved of the policy, endorsed Lincoln's draft, and supported its immediate promulgation, but he was skeptical of its military rationale; he doubted emancipation would end the rebellion more quickly. "Something more than a Proclamation will be necessary," Welles explained, because it was just as likely to "make opponents of some who are now friends," particularly in the Border States. Chase gave his "cordial support" to the new emancipation policy but thought that, rather than one all-encompassing presidential proclamation, individual generals should issue proclamations as they occupied new areas of the South. Emancipation "could be much better and more quietly accomplished," Chase explained, by "directing the Commanders of Departments to proclaim emancipation within their districts as soon as practical."[10]

None of these qualifications deterred the president, but William Seward's did. The secretary of state was an unwavering opponent of slavery and an ardent supporter of emancipation, but he was so convinced that the destruction of slavery was inevitable that he saw no reason to issue a superfluous proclamation saying so—at least not in July of 1862. The Union army had only recently been humiliated by the failure of General McClellan's Peninsula Campaign to achieve its objective: the capture of the Confederate capital of Richmond, Virginia. Release the proclamation now, Seward warned, and it will seem

like an act of desperation. Better to wait for a Union victory so that
the proclamation appears more like an expression of triumph. "I
approve the measure," Lincoln later recalled Seward telling him, but
"I suggest, sir, that you postpone its issue, until you can give it to the
country supported by military success." Lincoln was persuaded. "The
wisdom of the view of the Secretary of State struck me with great
force," Lincoln recalled. "The result was that I put the proclamation
aside."[11] It turned out to be a fateful decision.

WAITING FOR THE PROCLAMATION

Even before he signed the Second Confiscation Act on July 17, Lincoln was being pressured to proclaim universal emancipation based
on his war powers alone. More and more northerners were coming to
the conclusion that only the complete destruction of slavery would
end the rebellion. Protestant congregations and synods mobilized to
urge the president's endorsement of universal emancipation in the
spring of 1862. Let "liberty be proclaimed throughout the land," their
petitions and resolutions declared, "to all the inhabitants thereof."
Freedom *throughout the land* had become a common theme among
antislavery Christians. A Methodist minister in Pennsylvania forwarded a "Petition for emancipation" to President Lincoln, urging
him to exercise his power as commander in chief to "proclaim 'liberty
through all the land.'" In June a Quaker petition arrived at the White
House urging Lincoln "not to allow the present golden opportunity
to pass without decreeing the entire abolition of slavery throughout
the land." Calls for presidential decrees and proclamations were pouring into the White House even before Congress authorized the president to free the slaves of rebels.[12]

The Lincoln legend tells of a president who waited patiently for
public opinion to catch up with him. In fact, as soon as Lincoln

signed the Second Confiscation Act, he was bombarded with calls to issue the proclamation immediately. When the announcement failed to emerge from the cabinet meeting of July 22, newspapers published misleading reports claiming that Seward and Blair objected so strenuously to emancipation that they dissuaded the president from issuing it. Only a day after the cabinet met, the radical reformer Robert Dale Owen wrote to Lincoln warning him that in times of national emergency "it may be as dangerous to disappoint, as to conciliate, public opinion. And I confess my fears for the result, if decisive measures are much longer delayed." Warning that "every day's delay" strengthens the rebels, one group after another began petitioning the president "to act in his capacity as Commander in Chief" by issuing "the Proclamation of Emancipation." By the middle of August, Sydney Howard Gay, the managing editor of the influential *New York Tribune*, explained to Lincoln that there were many people in the North "who are anxiously awaiting that movement on your part which they believe will end the rebellion by removing its cause." The pressure on the president was mounting.[13]

Gay's letter may have been prompted by reports appearing in that day's papers of a meeting Lincoln had held the day before with a delegation of black leaders from Washington. This was not the first time Lincoln had met with black leaders, but it was an extraordinary encounter all the same. Hoping to build support for the voluntary emigration of freed slaves, Lincoln asked his commissioner of colonization, the Reverend James Mitchell, to arrange for a group of black leaders from the District area to meet with him in the White House on August 14, 1862.

Lincoln's behavior was shocking. Normally a good listener, on this occasion he instead read his guests a high-handed statement that was insulting in both its tone and its substance. He claimed that "a broader difference" separated blacks from whites "than exists between almost any other two races," though he did not specify what those differences were. Lincoln also claimed that both blacks and whites "suffer" from each other's presence. To be sure, slavery was "the greatest wrong inflicted on any people," Lincoln admitted, but look at the "present condition" of the country, he added. "[O]ur white men cutting each other's throats" over slavery. "But for your race among us," Lincoln claimed, "there could not be war." It sounded as if Lincoln was blaming the war not on slavery but on blacks. "It is better for us both," he argued, "to be separated." That was how Lincoln set up his most sustained argument for voluntary colonization.[14]

At that moment Lincoln was actively pursuing plans to establish a colony—Chiriquí—in Central America for expatriated African Americans. Although the Liberian president had recently visited Lincoln and suggested that his country could absorb several hundred thousand American blacks, Lincoln believed a colony in Central America or the Caribbean was more practical. He hoped Chiriquí would serve that purpose. It had a tropical climate that he believed was naturally attractive to blacks, and it was endowed with natural resources—"very rich coal mines"—that could ensure their future prosperity and "self-reliance." In such a colony, blacks would be treated as "the equals of the best."[15] Given the reluctance of so many African Americans to emigrate, however, Lincoln was asking his guests to set an example. As the most intelligent and accomplished members of their community, they could get the colony off and running by leading the exodus.

There was something calculated, not to say demagogic, about Lincoln's performance. In many ways his behavior was out of character. Black leaders who met with Lincoln at other times came away feeling that he had treated them as his equals and had respected what they had to say even when they disagreed. But on this occasion Lincoln's attitude was preachy; there was little or no dialogue, and he seemed uninterested in discovering the views of his guests. In the past Lincoln had had little to say about race, but when he raised the topic, he often dismissed, even ridiculed, the supposed racial differences between whites and blacks. At this meeting, though, he claimed the "differences"—whatever they were—were vast and unbridgeable. Both the nature and the timing of the meeting suggest that Lincoln had another agenda besides the overt one of persuading a handful of accomplished blacks to lead the way on voluntary emigration. If the president seemed to be talking past his guests, it may be because he was. He had invited a reporter into the room to record a transcript of his remarks—something Lincoln never did—thus making sure they would be published in the newspapers the next day. Why? Possibly to appease the contingent of western racists in the Republican Party. Possibly because Lincoln was still trying to persuade the Border States and war Democrats to at least tolerate the emancipation policy he was soon to announce. For those people a strong statement of support for colonization—especially if framed as a condescending lecture to a group of black leaders—might make emancipation more palatable. It would be a mistake to say that Lincoln's meeting with the black delegation was "purely" or "merely" strategic—he really did believe that the voluntary emigration of blacks was the best thing for everybody—but it would be equally mistaken to ignore the strong element of political calculation that haunted the meeting.

Whatever his motives for ensuring that his remarks to the black delegation were widely publicized, Lincoln succeeded only in heightening the speculation as to whether he intended to issue an emancipation proclamation. No doubt Lincoln's proposal tapped into currents of support for emigration among African Americans, but most black leaders reacted with outrage at news of the meeting.[16] No one was more upset than Frederick Douglass, who had been waiting more impatiently than most for Lincoln to issue an emancipation proclamation. Douglass wrote that the president's address to the delegation of blacks "leaves us less ground to hope for anti-slavery action at his hands than any of his previous utterances."[17]

Less than a week later, Douglass's suspicions mounted when he read the exchange between Lincoln and Horace Greeley, the influential publisher of the arch-Republican *New York Tribune*. Waiting for the proclamation that had yet to be issued, Greeley had exploded in frustration on August 20 with a lengthy public appeal called "The Prayer of Twenty Millions." The title was meant to suggest that the entire northern population, for which Greeley presumed to speak, was on the edge of its seat waiting for Lincoln to make his move. The people were exasperated by the president's refusal to "EXECUTE THE LAWS," Greeley declared. Lincoln was "strangely and disastrously remiss" in failing to implement "the emancipating provisions of the new Confiscation Act."[18] Greeley then launched into a protracted series of inferences suggesting that Lincoln's four-week delay was part of a broader pattern of reluctance to emancipate.

Lincoln's famous response to Greeley did little to silence the speculation. To be sure, Lincoln insisted that Greeley's "assumptions" were "erroneous" and that his "inferences" were "falsely drawn," implicitly denying that his delay in issuing the proclamation was grounded in reluctance to emancipate slaves. Rather, Lincoln repeated what he had claimed from the beginning—that the purpose of the war was the restoration of the Union—a position Greeley himself had endorsed and from which Lincoln would never deviate. "I would save the Union," Lincoln explained, in "the shortest way under the Constitution. . . . If I could save the Union without freeing *any* slave I would do it, and if I could save it by freeing *all* the slaves I would do it; and if I could save it by freeing some and leaving others alone I would also do that."[19] Like all Republicans and growing numbers of northern Democrats, Lincoln believed that he could constitutionally emancipate slaves in order to restore the Union. Yet hardly anybody believed that "under the Constitution" the federal government could wage a war whose "purpose" was the overthrow of slavery. Lincoln was careful to explain that this was his understanding of his responsibility as president, but that it in no way diminished his long-standing personal desire to see slavery abolished everywhere.

Lincoln's reply to Greeley fascinated readers at the time and has mystified scholars ever since. What did the letter reveal about Lincoln's intentions? The radical abolitionist Wendell Phillips denounced it as "the most disgraceful document that ever came from the head of a free people."[20] Not all abolitionists agreed. Gerrit Smith, who always believed that legislative emancipation—by Congress—was constitutional, agreed with Lincoln that the only constitutional justification for the war was the restoration of the Union. Smith then scolded his fellow abolitionists who "found great fault with the tenor of the president's Reply to Horace Greeley." Smith, by contrast, thought Lincoln's letter was "sound in doctrine and argument and admirable in style."[21] But opponents of emancipation also approved of the Greeley letter. A Missouri unionist congratulated the president for standing firm against pressure from Greeley. "Emancipation proclamations can only serve to make things worse," he wrote. "Your course is correct."[22] Still others read the Greeley letter in exactly the opposite way, as the first public indication that Lincoln thought universal emancipation was a reasonable possibility. The "general impression," Sydney Howard Gay wrote, is that Lincoln was about to declare that the "destruction of slavery" was necessary to suppress the rebellion.[23]

In some ways the Greeley letter was perfectly straightforward. Lincoln had always hated slavery, but he never believed his personal feelings allowed him to override the Constitution, which protected slavery in the states. Unless the Constitution was rewritten, the federal government could not constitutionally wage a war for the purpose of destroying slavery. Only the "military necessity" of suppressing the rebellion could legally justify emancipation. That, at least, was the standard Republican Party position all through the war, and Lincoln's answer to Greeley merely restated it.

On the other hand, Lincoln's reply to Greeley had a Delphic quality that allowed different people to read very different messages into it. On the face of it, for example, Lincoln seemed to be reciting his three straightforward options regarding emancipation: he could free all the slaves, some of the slaves, or none of the slaves. If that's what Lincoln meant to suggest, it was deliberately misleading because two of those three "options" were already foreclosed. Slavery had already been abolished in the territories and in Washington, thousands of slaves had already been emancipated in various parts of the South, and Lincoln had said more than once that slaves freed by the war could never be re-enslaved. So restoring the Union without freeing any slaves was simply not an option. Lincoln did not actually believe he had the power to restore the Union by freeing *all* the slaves. Under the Constitution, as he and most people understood it, the federal government had no power to *abolish* slavery anywhere, nor did Lincoln believe that universal military emancipation could be imposed in areas that were loyal to the Union. Lincoln, then, did not have the option of restoring the Union by freeing all of the slaves. Of all the ways of reading the Greeley letter, a straightforward description of Lincoln's three options is among the least compelling. No doubt speculation as to the president's true meaning would have gone on indefinitely had Lincoln not made his intentions clear a few weeks later after the battle of Antietam.

SEPTEMBER 22, 1862

The military conditions that delayed Lincoln's announcement in late July only worsened in late August. At a second battle at Bull Run, Union forces under the command of General John Pope were defeated by the skillful maneuvering of the Confederates led by Generals Robert E. Lee and "Stonewall" Jackson. Lee had daringly violated one of the basic rules of warfare when he divided his own troops, sending

Jackson on a bold ride around Pope's army into the Union rear. This set Pope on a fruitless chase in search of the rapidly moving Stonewall brigade until, on August 29, the two armies confronted one another along an unfinished rail line near the site of the previous year's battle at Manassas Junction. Jackson held the Union troops at bay and Pope, with his superior numbers, prepared to counterattack the next morning. When morning came, however, it was Lee who countered Pope's assault. Reinforced by troops under Confederate General James Longstreet, Lee's army crushed Pope at this second battle at Bull Run, sending the northern troops back to the safety of the Washington defenses in another ignominious Union defeat. If Lincoln was waiting for a military success to release his proclamation, he was going to have to wait longer.[24]

Flush with victory, Lee turned his mighty army northward for the first Confederate invasion of the North. Meanwhile Lincoln brought back General George McClellan to lick the wounds of a Union army demoralized by the a second loss at Bull Run. McClellan quickly did what he always did best: he got the Union army into fighting shape. However, when it came time to repel Lee's invasion on September 17, at the battle of Antietam, McClellan did what he did worst. He managed the battle disastrously, launching consecutive rather than concurrent attacks against enemy lines and holding back fresh Union troops when their presence in the field might have proved decisive. Still, the Confederates were badly mauled at Antietam, which turned out to be the bloodiest single day of the war. Unable to keep up the fight, much less sustain his invasion of the North, Lee retreated across the Potomac back into Virginia. With fresh troops still at his disposal, McClellan nevertheless refused to chase Lee down and, in effect, allowed the Confederate armies to escape. For all that, Antietam was a Union victory, the one Lincoln was waiting for.[25]

By then rumors were circulating wildly throughout the capital. Delano Smith, a clerk in the auditor's office, "eagerly looked at the newspaper" in hopes that the talk of an impending emancipation proclamation would be confirmed.[26]

On Monday morning, September 22, a State Department messenger notified all the cabinet members that the president would meet with them at noon, at which time Lincoln told them the funny story by Artemus Ward, followed by his reading of the proclamation. Lincoln had not invited the cabinet to offer advice about the policy—he already knew what everyone's opinion was—but to consider any suggestions about the precise wording of the document. Seward recommended a few changes to make it clear that slaves emancipated by the proclamation were freed forever and that emigration by the former slaves would be strictly voluntary and only at the invitation of the host country. All agreed to Seward's suggestions. Chase gave the proclamation his full support, though he continued to believe it would be more effective to have individual generals issue local proclamations as they moved through the South. Blair said that while he agreed to the policy of emancipation in the seceded states per se, he still thought it was a bad time to issue it, that it would alienate the Border States and disturb the army. With a few changes in wording, Lincoln released the document that same day.[27]

The Preliminary Proclamation began by declaring once again that the "object" of the war had always been and would always be "restoring the constitutional relation" between the states and the national government. Lincoln would accomplish this object by attacking slavery in several different ways. First, he would once again urge Congress to endorse federal incentives encouraging the loyal states to abolish slavery on their own—gradual emancipation, federal compensation, and subsidies for former slaves who chose to emigrate. He reserved more radical assaults on slavery for the disloyal states. Taking his cue from the Second Confiscation Act on which it was based, Lincoln distinguished between military emancipation in the occupied and unoccupied areas of the Confederacy. Universal emancipation would commence in the parts of the South not occupied by the Union but still in rebellion on January 1, 1863. "Thenceforward," Lincoln declared, slaves in rebel areas would be "forever free," their freedom recognized and maintained by the federal government. The army and navy of the United States would do nothing, Lincoln declared, "to repress" the slaves "in any efforts they make for their actual freedom." This was the "preliminary" element of the proclamation.[28]

The remainder of the proclamation was designed to be implemented immediately in areas already occupied by Union forces. Lincoln quoted the March 13 articles of war strictly prohibiting anyone in the army or navy from "returning fugitives" to their owners, making it clear that U.S. soldiers and sailors were not the enforcement agents for the fugitive slave clause of the Constitution. Lincoln then quoted two entire sections of the Second Confiscation Act that he had signed on July 17. The first, Section 9, freed the slaves of all rebels who came within Union lines or those in areas formerly occupied by the Confederates. The second, Section 10, created the presumption of freedom for any slave escaping into Washington, even those coming from the loyal state of Maryland. Having quoted the statutes, Lincoln then ordered "all persons engaged in the military and naval service of the United States to observe, obey, and enforce, within their respective spheres of service the act, and sections above recited."[29] This was more than a "preliminary" proclamation.

After two months of increasingly anxious anticipation, Lincoln's announcement struck like a thunderbolt. Enthusiastic crowds serenaded the president outside the White House. A delegation of loyal governors meeting in Altoona, Pennsylvania, sped to Washington to congratulate the president "upon his proclamation, believing it will do good as a measure of justice and sound policy."[30] Letters of support, some brief and ecstatic, others long and sober, poured into the White House from all parts of the North. The response, Lincoln said, was all that a vain man could hope for.

If there was an overarching theme to the expressions of support, it was that the restoration of the Union and the destruction of slavery were irrevocably joined. "We now have 'Liberty and Union,' one and inseparable, now and forever," declared three citizens from Erie, Pennsylvania. "Slavery has declared the Union its enemy," another wrote, and "all the friends of the Union must labor for the overthrow of Slavery." A second, related theme noted the proclamation's dual character "as a measure alike Military & Philanthropic," a "sublime act of justice & humanity," both "right" *and* "politic." Gerrit Smith did not doubt that "as a man, [Lincoln] weeps over the wrongs of the Africans in this land," but only the war power gives him the right, as commander in chief, to emancipate slaves. Smith fully endorsed the logic of military emancipation. "We cannot put down the Rebels and save the country," he declared, "if we continue to let them have their slaves to help them carry on the Rebellion." Lincoln was gratified by these shows of support in part because he hoped the proclamation would stiffen the North's commitment to universal emancipation. But he also expected it to have a more immediate impact on a group of generals in the Mississippi Valley.[31]

THE MISSISSIPPI VALLEY

By expressly enjoining the army and navy to begin enforcing the emancipation clauses of the Second Confiscation Act, Lincoln intended his proclamation to be read as a military order, to be implemented at once. The transformation was literal and unambiguous. The War Department quickly printed fifteen thousand copies and began distributing them two days later to commanders in the field. Within the U.S. Army the Preliminary Proclamation became "General Orders No. 139."[32]

The orders had their most dramatic effect on the generals who had most consistently resisted emancipation. On October 7, still resting near Antietam, McClellan issued his own cover letter to be distributed along with the president's proclamation. In the United States, McClellan pointed out, civilians make policy; the military merely carries it out. There was to be no caviling about the emancipation orders beyond the respectful expression of a dissenting opinion. Disobedience was not the appropriate response to an order with which a soldier disagreed. "The proper remedy for political errors, if any are committed, is to be found only in the action of the people at the polls."[33] McClellan was all but inviting his troops to vote against Republicans in the upcoming elections. As an acknowledgment of the president's emancipation order, this could scarcely have been more grudging, but it was an acknowledgment all the same.

The full impact of the Preliminary Proclamation was felt in the West, in Tennessee and Mississippi. Union occupation of the Mississippi Valley had begun in earnest with Grant's victories at Forts Henry and Donelson in February of 1862. As with the occupation of Louisiana, Union military success in western Tennessee and northern Mississippi brought the federal armies into some of the richest plantation districts of the South, densely populated with slaves. If the Gulf States were a cotton kingdom, the Mississippi Valley was its throne. The cotton plantations lining the great river were among the most profitable in the South; measured by per capita wealth, the river counties were the richest in America. As Union troops arrived, planters began "refugeeing" their slaves, sometimes moving them short distances to plantations farther inland, sometimes as far away as Texas, in a determined effort to keep their slaves away from Yankee troops. By then everyone knew that runaway slaves and Union armies formed a nearly irresistible magnetic attraction.

When Grant invaded Tennessee in February of 1862, there was a great deal of confusion about what federal policy toward slavery actually was. On February 22, General Henry Halleck tried to reiterate

General Orders No. 3 in a way that incorporated Republican criticism, but a few weeks later, on March 13, Lincoln signed the law banning Halleck's policy.[34] What replaced it was unclear, in part because Congress was well on its way to revising federal antislavery policy. Geography added another layer of ambiguity. Northern armies frequently moved back and forth between loyal and disloyal slave states. However impractical Halleck's earlier approach to dealing with slavery in the Border States, it was supposed to be distinct from federal policy in the seceded states where slaves voluntarily coming within Union lines were accepted and emancipated. Union generals moving back and forth across the borders between the loyal slave state of Kentucky and the disloyal slave state of Tennessee could not conform consistently to either policy. Tennessee's political situation compounded the uncertainty, for although the state had formally joined the Confederacy, it had a unionist military governor reporting directly to the president. By Lincoln's standard a loyal government made Tennessee a loyal state.

The geographical and political vagaries facing the Union forces in the West meant that different commanding generals dealt with slavery in different ways. General Ulysses S. Grant tried to enforce the rules set by Washington policymakers as interpreted by General Halleck, but Grant could never be sure which policy applied and the policy itself was continually evolving. Sometimes he turned away fugitives, more often he protected them, depending on what he thought his commanding officers were asking him to do. In Louisiana, General Benjamin Butler responded the same way. Unsure of what federal policy applied, he excluded some slaves from Union lines while emancipating others. In April of 1862, one Union officer issued orders to expel all slaves "improperly retained or harbored" within his camps, while at the same time offering employment to "fugitive slaves who have become free under the laws of Congress."[35] Another Union general, William Tecumseh Sherman, had no sympathy at all for emancipation. He sprinkled letters with racial epithets, though in truth he was nearly as contemptuous of reporters, secessionists, politicians, and "the people" as he was of blacks. But Sherman was also a professional soldier who, like Grant, believed that civilians made policy and that the army merely implemented it. It's just that he was no more certain about which policy applied than Grant and Butler were. As Sherman's troops moved deeper into the plantation belt of the Mississippi Valley, as more and more slaves came into his lines claiming their freedom, Sherman studied the congressional statutes, presidential proclamations, and military orders flying out of Washington, in an effort to discern official policy and adjust his treatment of slavery accordingly—though generally with a bias against emancipation. Among western commanding generals, however, it was Don Carlos Buell who displayed the most consistent hostility to emancipation. If the Union army was at war with itself over emancipation, ground zero for the infighting was central and eastern Tennessee, where Buell's obnoxious orders protecting slavery provoked flagrant insubordination among his antislavery officers.

Throughout the summer of 1862, concerns about the incoming flood of runaway slaves filled Grant's letters to his wife, Sherman's letters to his brother, and Buell's orders to his subordinates. As was true everywhere else in the Union-occupied South, soldiers frequently encouraged slaves to escape to the protection of Union lines in direct violation of prohibitions against enticement. In June, Grant noted "instances of negro stealing" by individual Union soldiers who went onto the farms of unionist slaveholders "and before their eyes perswaid their blacks to mount up behind them and go off." It was one thing to accept slaves who came into Union lines voluntarily; it was another thing to "perswaid" them. Persuasion was not always necessary. In July, Brigadier General Alvin P. Hovey reported that hundreds of runaway slaves had fled to his lines in Memphis. "Many of the negroes no doubt are from rank rebels in the army," Hovey reported, "and are coming in here in hopes that their masters Treason will liberate them." Hovey put the fugitives to work on the city's fortifications.[36]

In July, Halleck was called to Washington to take up a new post as general in chief. Shortly thereafter—on the same day Lincoln signed the Second Confiscation Act—Grant took Halleck's place in command of the western armies. Within days, Grant's patron, Illinois Republican Elihu Washburne, made it clear that Halleck's earlier orders were dead. "This matter of guarding rebel property, of protecting secessionists and of enforcing 'order No. 3,' is 'played out' in public estimation," Washburne wrote Grant on July 25. "The negroes must now be made our auxiliaries in every possible way they can be, whether by working or fighting. That General who takes the most decided step in this respect will be held in the highest estimation by the loyal and true men in the country." Washburne had just sat through the lengthy congressional debates over various antislavery measures and had voted with his fellow Republicans in support of the Second Confiscation Act. Barely a week after the new policy became law, the congressman was carefully instructing Grant in familiar Republican doctrine. "The idea that a man can be in the rebel army, leaving his negroes and property behind him to be protected by our troops, is to me shocking," Washburne wrote. "If the constitution or slavery must perish," he told Grant, "let slavery go to the wall."[37]

Grant immediately began employing significant numbers of fugitives to work on Union fortifications. It is not clear, however, that Grant paid the "contrabands" wages or that he thought they were emancipated. He spelled out his policy in orders he issued on August 11 through his adjutant general, Lieutenant Colonel John Rawlins. "Recent Acts of Congress prohibit the Army from returning fugitives from labor to their claimants," Grant's order declared, "and authorize the employment of such persons in the service of the Government." That was all. Grant would not return fugitives to their masters and would employ able-bodied fugitives, but he did not so much as hint that any of the fugitives had been freed.[38]

William Tecumseh Sherman had a lot more to say about slavery and emancipation than did Grant, but his policy through the summer of 1862 was essentially the same. And just as Grant was instructed by a Republican congressman on the need to destroy slavery, Sherman was similarly urged by his brother—Ohio Senator John Sherman—to follow a policy of universal emancipation. When slaves enter your lines, the senator explained, "You ought to presume their freedom until the contrary is shown & pay them accordingly." Like Grant, Sherman abandoned Halleck's policy shortly after Congress passed the Second Confiscation Act in mid-July. "My orders," he explained to his wife, "are to take all who come in." But he complied with his new orders in the most limited way possible. On July 22, Sherman instructed that blacks be put to work and given provisions but not be paid wages, and he employed only able-bodied men. "We never harbor women or children," Sherman wrote in late August. Even after reading the Second Confiscation Act and clarifying his orders, Sherman refused to pay the blacks he put to work. "[N]o wages will be paid," he ordered, "until the courts determined whether the negro be slave or free." It was in response to this order that Senator Sherman told his brother to "presume" that the blacks had been freed and to pay them wages. The general resisted. "I think you are wrong in saying that Negros are free & entitled to be treated accordingly," he told his brother in early September. General Sherman had no objection, in principle, to punishing rebels by taking their slaves, but he did not believe the law had made them free and he did object, in principle, to army officers deciding what the law was. Apparently not even lawmakers like his brother were competent to decide what their own laws said.[39]

Grant was indifferent rather than hostile to emancipation, and Sherman resisted emancipation for legal and practical reasons. General Buell was closer in spirit to McClellan. Both men hated the idea that a war to restore the Union had to be a war against slavery as well. During 1862, Buell's orders regarding slaves were, if anything, even more restrictive than Sherman's or Grant's. Oblivious to the shift in federal policy, Buell continued to enforce a rigid exclusion policy that both Grant and Sherman had abandoned. There were even reports that acting on Buell's instructions, Union soldiers were being ordered to hunt down and return fugitives to their masters. By the summer and fall of 1862, Buell's policy had provoked widespread resentment, even outright defiance, among his own officers. Some threatened to resign rather than obey the general's orders.[40]

Lincoln's Preliminary Proclamation bolstered slavery's opponents in Buell's army. When Brigadier General Quincy Gilmore ordered Colonel William Utley to return "four contrabands . . . known to belong to loyal citizens," Utley refused. "You are no doubt conversant with the Proclamation issued Sept. 23d 1862, and the law of Congress on the subject," Utley told Gilmore. The colonel recognized General Gilmore's authority "to command me in all matters pertaining to the Military and movements of the army," he explained. "But I do not look upon this as belonging to that department. I recognize no authority on the subject of delivering up contrabands save that of the President of the United States."[41]

Lincoln's Preliminary Proclamation had indeed made it clear that slaves coming within Union lines were emancipated. By quoting directly from the March 13 statute making it a crime for anyone in the U.S. military to participate in the capture and return of fugitive slaves, Lincoln emphatically repudiated Buell and sided with soldiers like Colonel Utley who had refused to hunt down runaways and return them to their former masters. Under "the express requirement of the President's Proclamation," the *Cleveland Plain Dealer* pointed out, "[n]o more will traitors hunt their human chattels in and drag them forth from Union camps."[42] By highlighting the immediate emancipation clauses of the Second Confiscation Act, Lincoln affirmed the freedom of the tens of thousands of slaves in the parts of the Mississippi Valley recently occupied by the Union army and "formerly occupied" by the Confederates. And by circulating the Preliminary Proclamation as General Orders No. 139, the War Department turned Republican policy into an unambiguous military order.

Grant got the message. In August he had begun employing contrabands as military laborers, but without pay. In early September he appointed Chaplain J. B. Rogers to "superintend the contrabands" at Corinth, Mississippi. On November 11, he appointed another chaplain, John Eaton, to "take charge of the contrabands" who were flocking to Grant's camp near LaGrange, Tennessee. Eaton proceeded directly to Grant's headquarters. As in Louisiana, the Union army in the Mississippi Valley confronted a massive logistical and humanitarian problem once it found itself in control of vast tracts populated by large numbers of freed people. The slaveholders were abandoning their plantations "and negroes [are] coming in by wagon loads," Grant wrote to Halleck. "What will I do with them?" Unwilling to make any decision on his own, Halleck asked the secretary of war for instructions. Stanton directed Grant to employ as many fugitives as he had use for, to provide food and clothing from the quartermaster's supplies, and to put as many people as possible back to work cultivating cotton. Grant in turn ordered Eaton to oversee the operation of a large contraband camp at Grand Junction.[43]

In recognition of their freedom, the former slaves would now be paid wages. By the late fall of 1862, Eaton recalled many years later, "the notion that the Negro was a free agent had penetrated with the advance of our armies into the South." In the areas controlled by Union forces "it became our policy," Eaton added, "whenever possible to put the Negro on the basis of a paid laborer." The adoption of a wage labor system by the Union army forced a general transformation of the entire labor system in the surrounding area. Masters who remained on their plantations were forced to shift from slavery to free labor; otherwise blacks would leave to work for wages on Union-controlled farms. In December, Grant issued orders spelling out the terms under which the former slaves would work. As "Superintendent of Contrabands," Eaton was charged with providing food, clothing, and shelter for the workers, to be paid for "out of their earnings." Eaton in turn would keep accounts "of all earnings and expenditures," subject to examination by the inspector general. By the end of December in 1862, Grant had responded to Lincoln's Preliminary Proclamation by establishing the rudiments of a free labor system in the Mississippi Valley.[44]

Sherman did the same thing. As late as September 23—the day after Lincoln issued his proclamation—Sherman still believed that only a court, never a general, could free a confiscated slave. His brother, Senator John Sherman, had repeatedly told him that no courts were required for military emancipation in areas that were "in rebellion." When the enemy "has destroyed the Court, rendering the Law inoperative," Senator Sherman explained, "the military power may supply the defect." But General Sherman continued to insist that he had "no power under any possible combination of circumstances to 'free a negro.'" That was technically true but beside the point: the law required General Sherman to open his lines to all escaping slaves; once within Union lines the contrabands were "discharged from service," *not by General Sherman* but by congressional statute as implemented by the commander in chief. A week later, however, having read Lincoln's Preliminary Proclamation, Sherman began to shift his position. "They are free," he wrote on October 1, although he wondered whether the government was ready to feed, clothe, and shelter the former slaves. "The President declares the negros free," he added, "but makes no machinery by which such freedom is assured." By early November, however, he had begun paying black workers wages of ten dollars per month, though he still complained that "no provision thus far has been made for the payment."[45]

As always with General Sherman it was a matter of law and order. He viewed secession as a flagrant criminal act—in this case a violation of the Constitution—and believed the rebels deserved to be punished as criminals. In his own peculiar way, Sherman applied the same strict standards to himself. As a military man he believed it was his job to enforce the law as decreed by Congress, the president, and courts. In the Preliminary Proclamation, Lincoln decreed that under the terms of the Second Confiscation Act the slaves within Sherman's lines were emancipated. The law was the law, and Sherman would obey it. "The only safety in the Country now is in Union, and we must be governed by the President," he explained in late November, adding that "we have no right to dispute his acts or instructions and must leave him to manage the war in his own way."[46] He would thereafter assume that the slaves within his lines were legally emancipated.

Sherman's mind gravitated instinctively toward hierarchy and obedience. For him that meant not only that he would do what he was ordered to do, but also that federal statutes and the laws of war took precedence over the laws of the states. A few weeks after Lincoln issued his Preliminary Proclamation, Sherman got into a dispute with a Tennessee lawyer named John Swayne, who, in a charge to a local grand jury, quoted several state statutes that protected slavery "while utterly ignoring," Sherman complained, "the Laws of Congress and the State of war." Sherman accepted the general view that under the laws of war, armies were free to confiscate enemy slaves as a "military necessity" without regard to state and local statutes. It was for lawmakers in Washington to determine the status of confiscated slaves, Sherman told Swayne, and Congress had settled that issue definitively in favor of emancipation. A state could not nullify a congressional statute. Sherman then proceeded to quote at length from the emancipation clauses of the Second Confiscation Act—the same Sections 9 and 10 that Lincoln reproduced in the

Preliminary Proclamation. If you have a problem with that federal law, Sherman instructed the Tennessee lawyer, "a county court is not the place to adjudicate it." Take your case to the Supreme Court and let it decide. In the meantime, Sherman concluded, "I Shall obey the plain Law of Congress and the order of the *President* of the United States under, and my army Shall be used to *enforce* it."[47] The law was the law. Congress and the president had determined that the slaves in the Union-occupied Confederacy were emancipated, and Sherman would obey their commands.

Whether General Buell would have done the same cannot be known, for on October 24—a month after the Preliminary Proclamation was announced—Lincoln relieved Buell of his command. A few weeks later Lincoln likewise relieved McClellan of his command. Neither general lost his job for opposing emancipation but for their persistent failures to pursue the war aggressively. Their dismissals meant, however, that within weeks after release of the Preliminary Proclamation the two highest-ranking Union generals who most consistently opposed emancipation were removed from command.

With the transition to free labor systems among the former slaves in the Mississippi Valley, the antislavery policy initiated by the Republicans in the first summer of the war reached its logical conclusion. Emancipation had begun on August 8, 1861, when General Benjamin Butler was instructed to free the slaves at Fortress Monroe in Virginia. A few months later Edward Pierce was authorized to supervise the transition from slavery to freedom on the Sea Islands. The slaves in coastal North Carolina were emancipated in the wake of General Ambrose Burnside's successful invasion in early 1862, as were those who flocked to McClellan's lines during the Peninsula Campaign. Further south, the slaves at Fort Pulaski and the surrounding area were freed by General Hunter's proclamation, which was never rescinded. In Louisiana, Lincoln tilted Union policy in favor of emancipation in July of 1862, setting in motion a vast experiment in free labor in the densely populated sugar parishes around New Orleans. And with his Preliminary Proclamation, Lincoln forced reluctant generals in the Mississippi Valley to acknowledge that the slaves within their lines had in fact been freed.

This was clearly understood by Union generals and policymakers. As Benjamin Butler explained in August of 1861, because the masters in Hampton, Virginia, had deserted both their homes and slaves, Union generals "should consider the latter free." In March 1862, when a Sea Island planter asked Treasury Secretary Salmon Chase about the status of slaves, Chase's response was straightforward: *"They were free."* A few weeks after Lincoln issued his Preliminary Proclamation, General Sherman wrote about the slaves to his brother and freely admitted the same thing: *"They are free."* In late October, Butler was even more emphatic with his own subordinates: *"By the act of Congress they are clearly free."*

By January 1, 1863, tens of thousands of slaves were already emancipated in those parts of the Confederacy occupied by the Union army, freed not by accident but by an accumulating series of policy decisions made by Congress and the Lincoln administration as they responded to the shifting course of the war, the tide of public opinion, and the steady arrival of slaves coming within Union lines. Moreover, emancipation was only one part of a broader Republican assault on slavery. The federal government had stopped enforcing the fugitive slave clause of the Constitution. Slavery had been banned from the western territories, suppressed on the high seas, and abolished in the nation's capital. West Virginia would be admitted to the Union after vowing to abolish slavery.

Only in historical mythology did the purpose of the war shift on January 1, 1863, from the restoration of the Union to the abolition of slavery. Yet even as the first phase of emancipation policy was reaching its climax in the Mississippi Valley, the mythology of the Emancipation Proclamation was already being constructed.

MYTHMAKING

Several decades after the Civil War ended, when John Eaton sat down to write about his experience superintending contrabands in the Mississippi Valley, he was bemused by the recollection that slaves had somehow been emancipated prior to January 1, 1863. He apparently had no memory of the Second Confiscation Act, Lincoln's Preliminary Proclamation, or the military orders that prompted Grant's appointment of Eaton to supervise the transition from slavery to freedom in the area. Writing in 1907, Eaton viewed the introduction of free labor in late 1862 as a curious local practice that had somehow developed as if spontaneously in the area around LaGrange, Tennessee. Nor was Eaton the only one who could not remember clearly. By 1900 virtually all memory of emancipation policy before January 1, 1863, was lost, and it has remained lost. The memory lapse is etched in the labels historians now attach to the policies that preceded the Emancipation Proclamation. What contemporaries often referred to as the "Confiscation-Emancipation Act" of July 17, 1862, is now referred to as the Second Confiscation Act, a title that effectively obscures the broad emancipation policy it initiated. The Preliminary Proclamation—which Lincoln issued as "A Proclamation" and Republican papers sometimes called the "Emancipation Proclamation"—was dubbed the "Preliminary Emancipation Proclamation" by Lincoln's secretaries in the late nineteenth century, and part of it was indeed "preliminary." But by labeling it the "Preliminary Proclamation" they further obscured the immediate impact Lincoln expected it to have.[48]

But the forgetting began long before John Eaton sat down to write his memoirs in 1907. It was already under way when Grant appointed him in November of 1862. In the preceding months, as Americans waited for Lincoln to enforce the Second Confiscation Act, the mythology of the Emancipation Proclamation was born. The waiting itself led people to wonder whether Lincoln would issue a proclamation at all, and they began to speculate about what was taking him so long. Already in August of 1862, the *Springfield Republican* noted the "insinuation . . . so persistently reiterated in some quarters, that the president will not enforce the confiscation-emancipation act."[49] Everything Lincoln said was scrutinized, like tea leaves, for signs of his intention. The suspense built up all through the summer.

Despite the elation with which the opponents of slavery greeted the Preliminary Proclamation, it did not end the anxiety of anticipation. Universal emancipation had still not been proclaimed, and the prospect of another hundred days of waiting quickly overshadowed the immediate impact of Lincoln's September announcement. During the closing months of 1862 the speculation became more intense than ever. Republicans lost heavily in the November elections. Would that make Lincoln shrink from issuing the final proclamation? "We have every reason to believe that President Lincoln will never issue his Emancipation Proclamation," one Ohio paper declared shortly after the election returns came in. In December, the Union army suffered a disastrous defeat at Fredericksburg. Would the president have second thoughts about his proclamation? Supporters of emancipation tried to discount the "lingering apprehensions that the policy of Emancipation may not be sternly enforced and persisted in." By the time Lincoln issued the Emancipation Proclamation, the feverish anticipation of it, the shear suspense of the wait, had elevated its significance to mythic proportions and begun to erase the memory of the thousands of slaves already emancipated in the Union-occupied areas of the Confederacy.[50]

The collective memory lapse seems to have begun with the shift to a much more aggressive policy of universal emancipation during the early months of 1862. On March 6, Lincoln sent his special message to Congress, proposing federal expenditures to promote abolition in the Border States. A week later Congress made it a criminal offense for anyone in the U.S. military to enforce the fugitive slave clause. Over the next few months the federal government abolished slavery in Washington, banned it from the western territories, endorsed the slave-trade treaty, required West Virginia to abolish slavery as a condition for admission to the Union, emancipated all the slaves in Union-occupied territory, and authorized the president to proclaim universal emancipation in the seceded states. Unable to stop the antislavery juggernaut, Democrats charged that these policies, both individually and collectively, proved that hatred for slavery was and had always been the driving force of the Republican Party. What the Republicans were doing in the first half of 1862, Democrats charged, is exactly what they had always intended to do. We told you so, Democrats shouted.

But you were wrong when you said so, Republicans answered. A year ago we could never have imagined that an attack on slavery could have proceeded this far. By the middle of 1862, Republicans commonly claimed to be astonished by the extraordinary transformation of the public mind, as well as their own minds, regarding slavery. "Gradually, very gradually, as this contest proceeded," Robert Dale Owen wrote, he had come to the conclusion that the only way to guarantee the security of the Union was by "the emancipation of negro slaves throughout this continent." Nor was he alone. With each passing month, Owen noticed, the war was "converting hundreds of thousands of moderate and conservative and peace-loving men" to support for a "General Emancipation."[51] From all across the North—in newspapers and magazines, public speeches and private letters—came similar expressions of astonishment at the dramatic change of heart supposedly taking place among northerners on the subject of emancipation.

Curiously, even those who had been predicting the downfall of slavery since the secession crisis now claimed to have undergone a remarkable conversion. In mid-1862 Benjamin Wade stood up in Congress and declared that universal emancipation had been unimaginable to him a year earlier—even though a year earlier just about every radical Republican had predicted it. Shortly after Lincoln was elected, Salmon Chase declared that the Slave Power had been overthrown, fulfilling the dream of his lifetime. A month later, when the slave states began to secede, Chase bluntly declared that disunion meant "abolition, and abolition through civil and servile war." Charged with overseeing the occupied areas along the southern Atlantic coast and later the lower Mississippi Valley, Chase had made sure that emancipation accompanied the invading Union forces beginning in late 1861. Yet only six months later, as Congress was putting the finishing touches on its universal emancipation bill, Chase seemingly forgot all that he had recently said and done about slavery. "Until long after Sumter," he wrote, "I clung to my old ideas of non-interference with Slavery. . . . It was my hope and belief that the rebellion might be suppressed & Slavery left to the free disposition of the States within which it existed." The states, Chase claimed to have believed, would gradually abolish slavery, "without shock or disturbance or injury, but peacefully and beneficially." Forgotten were all those secession winter predictions of slavery's violent and bloody death.[52]

As they waited impatiently for the president to issue an emancipation proclamation, anxious observers began asking the question, *What was taking Lincoln so long?* When Horace Greeley took it upon himself to answer that question in his "Prayer of Twenty Millions," he was trying to explain something fairly specific—a one-month delay, since the passage of the Second Confiscation Act, in the release of the proclamation required to enforce it. To explain the delay, Greeley went back over Lincoln's year-and-a-half-old presidency and discerned a pattern of reluctance when it came to emancipation: Lincoln should have threatened the rebels with emancipation in his inaugural address. He was "unduly influenced" by the Border States. He had "annulled" Frémont's proclamation and Hunter's order while he let stand Halleck's "unmilitary" and "inhuman" Orders No. 3.

Lincoln "seems never to interfere" with soldiers who return escaping slaves to their owners.[53]

This was the myth of Lincoln the "Reluctant Emancipator." He took so long to issue the Emancipation Proclamation because he never wanted to issue it, and when he finally did issue it, he did so *not* for lofty moral reasons, *not* because slavery was wrong, but because the destruction of slavery had become what Lincoln called a "military necessity." To this day skeptics recite the same litany Greeley recited, use the same reasoning, and come to the same conclusion. It took twenty months to issue the proclamation because Lincoln, like the North he represented, was reluctant to make emancipation a legitimate goal of the war, and finally did so only when it became clear that there was no other choice.

On September 22, one month after Greeley published his "Prayer of Twenty Millions," Lincoln issued the orders to "execute the law" and announced that he would publish the Emancipation Proclamation one hundred days later. The Preliminary Proclamation provoked a rush of commentary, including an extraordinary debate among some of the most prominent constitutional scholars in the United States, disagreeing over whether Lincoln had *any* constitutional authority to free slaves by means of a presidential proclamation. One of the more remarkable commentaries on the Preliminary Proclamation appeared in the November issue of the *Atlantic Monthly* magazine, written by none other than Ralph Waldo Emerson. Think of Emerson's essay as another answer to Greeley's "Prayer of Twenty Millions." Emerson offered an alternative explanation for the timing of the president's proclamation, an explanation that reflected glory rather than disgrace on Lincoln. Where Greeley gave us the myth of the Reluctant Emancipator, Emerson gave us the myth of Lincoln the "Great Emancipator."

"Liberty is a slow fruit," Emerson wrote near the beginning, gearing up for an explanation of why it took Lincoln some time to issue his proclamation: the fruit of liberty does not ripen quickly. The public was not yet ready, Emerson explained, the audience for the proclamation had to be created—"an audience hitherto passive and unconcerned," now at last so "kindled that they come forward." Public indifference to slavery had been so ingrained, hostility to emancipation so deep, that Lincoln had to wait, to educate the people up to the justice of the cause, before he could act. And so Lincoln waited, with infinite patience, until the "public sentiment of the country" was at last "unmistakably pronounced." When we consider "the immense opposition" to emancipation that Lincoln faced, Emerson declared, "one can hardly say the deliberation took too long. Against all timorous counsels he had the courage to seize the moment." This was greatness, and since it's Emerson talking, we might as well call it transcendental greatness. Lincoln was so fair-minded, so patient, and yet so modest—that we can only marvel at that "capacity and virtue which Divine Providence has made an instrument of benefit so vast." In the grand scheme of things, Lincoln really had "no choice" but to issue his proclamation. It was his destiny. He was put here, at this time and in this place, to do what had to be done, to fulfill the momentous task ordained for him. Lincoln, Emerson wrote, "has been permitted to do more for America than any other American man." And just what was it that Lincoln did? He removed the "blot" of slavery "from our national honor," lifted the "heavy load . . . of the national heart." He freed the slaves, but he also redeemed the nation.[54]

Here were two competing explanations for the timing of Lincoln's Emancipation Proclamation, both of them more or less fully formed even before the Proclamation was issued on January 1, 1863. Greeley's Lincoln was the Reluctant Emancipator; Emerson's was the Great Emancipator. They can't both be right, but they can both be wrong. Though Emerson's effusions were more ethereal than Greeley's bill of particulars, both displayed a less-than-firm grip on reality. If Greeley seemed unaware that the Lincoln administration had been emancipating slaves for over a year, Emerson was oblivious to the pressure Lincoln had long felt to move more aggressively against slavery. But these differences of detail hardly matter because the real problem—with both Greeley and Emerson—was the false premise of the question both of them were asking: *What took Lincoln so long?* That question assumes that emancipation could not begin in earnest until the day Lincoln issued the Emancipation Proclamation, January 1, 1863. Both answers erased the history of emancipation before the proclamation.

And both fed the emerging mythology that the freedom of all the slaves depended on the singular act of a single man. In demanding that Lincoln "execute the law," Greeley at least acknowledged that Congress had passed an important statute, but it hardly seemed to matter because Greeley went on to declare that Lincoln should have emancipated all the slaves in the rebel states on the day he was inaugurated, without so much as a nod of approval from Congress. By further insisting that Lincoln had repeatedly and single-handedly thwarted emancipation at every turn, Greeley made Lincoln and Lincoln alone responsible for the success or failure of emancipation. Emerson made the same mistake in reverse. The Emancipation Proclamation was called for in the law Congress had passed in July, and the Preliminary Proclamation included extensive quotations from that law. But in Emerson's analysis there is no one but Abraham Lincoln, acting out the destiny assigned to him not by Congress but by "Divine Providence." The myth of the Great Emancipator had no room in it for the Senate Judiciary Committee or the Republican Party, never mind the escaping slaves.

Some of this singular focus on Lincoln was unavoidable. Because emancipation had to be "military emancipation," because only the commander in chief could legitimately proclaim emancipation in areas not yet occupied by the Union army, the focus of public attention naturally gravitated almost exclusively to the president. This was clear by the end of July in 1862, when people were already telling Lincoln that by proclaiming freedom "throughout the land" he would go down in history as the Great Emancipator. A Pennsylvania editor wrote to Lincoln reassuring him that "a decree of general Emancipation by you now would be hailed as the greatest stroke of policy that any Government ever practiced."[55] "You can give freedom to 4.000.000 of human Beings," one Illinoisan wrote. "You can make yourself the greatest benefactor, of the human race, that God ever permitted to walk the earth."[56] It did not take much for such sentiments to blossom into the myth that in affixing his signature to the Emancipation Proclamation, Lincoln freed all the slaves "with the stroke of his pen."

Myths beget countermyths, and in the months before January 1, 1863, skeptics were already declaring that an emancipation proclamation would be an empty gesture. "The negro can not be emancipated by proclamation," James Speed wrote his friend Lincoln in late July.[57] It was widely understood that the proclamation would extend emancipation into unoccupied areas of the Confederacy where, almost by definition, Union authorities would be helpless to enforce it. The president promises, one New York paper remarked, "that on the first of next January he will issue still another proclamation" freeing the slaves "in territory of which a powerful foe disputes the jurisdiction" of the federal government. That promise, contained in the Preliminary Proclamation, "really amounts to very little," for how could it possibly free any slaves? "The whole world will laugh at the impotence of this mere Paper Thunder," declared the *New York Express*. An emancipation proclamation can have "no *practical* effects," the *Journal of Commerce* predicted. Mr. Lincoln might just as well "order the north wind to blow continuously over the Southern fields."[58] Call this the anti-myth of the Emancipation Proclamation—the claim that it did not free a single slave.

No one contributed more to the mythology of Lincoln's proclamation than Lincoln himself. "When the war began, three years ago," he wrote in April of 1864, nobody expected the fighting to last so long. "Neither did any anticipate that domestic slavery would be much affected by the war." Lincoln repeated the claim on several occasions, most famously in his second inaugural address. Despite the fact that the North and the South had gone to war over slavery, he said, neither "anticipated that the *cause* of the conflict might cease with, or even before, the conflict itself should cease." This was nonsense. When Lincoln was inaugurated, it was hard to find anyone who did *not* anticipate that slavery would be very much "affected" by the war. Lincoln's own actions belie his memory. Within weeks of the South's capture of Fort Sumter, his cabinet approved the policy of refusing to return fugitive slaves in the seceded states, and by early July, Lincoln was already saying—what he would repeat on several occasions—that slaves who escaped to Union lines would never be returned to slavery. He signed the First Confiscation Act in full awareness of its emancipation clause, and two days later his War Department issued the instructions for implementing it, thus initiating military emancipation on August 8, 1861. Before the year was out, Lincoln was publicly announcing, in his first annual message to Congress, that under the terms of the First Confiscation Act "numerous slaves" had already been "liberated." In 1862, Lincoln personally ordered the transition to a free labor system in Louisiana, and by means of his Preliminary Proclamation he likewise ordered his generals in the Mississippi Valley to begin emancipating the thousands of slaves already within their lines. All of this and more had happened prior to his issuing the Emancipation Proclamation, yet by 1864 Lincoln had forgotten that history and instead offered his own explanation of why he had taken so long to begin freeing slaves. When General Frémont "attempted military emancipation," Lincoln wrote more than two years later, "I forbade it." In fact, he had ordered Frémont to implement the First Confiscation Act. "When, still later, General Hunter attempted military emancipation, I again forbade it." In fact, he had allowed Hunter's military emancipation order to stand, revoking only the general's edict abolishing slavery in three states.[59]

Lincoln's memory lapse—like the collective amnesia that overcame Republicans in mid-1862—was likely driven by the partisan atmosphere of the moment. It was April in 1864. After several contentious months the Republicans had finally settled on a new antislavery policy: a constitutional amendment abolishing slavery, which was soon to become the central plank in the party platform. Once again Democrats were shouting, *We told you so. This is what Republicans had in mind all along. They will keep the country at war until they get what they always wanted, the complete abolition of slavery.* And because he was running for reelection, Lincoln responded the same way his fellow Republicans had been responding for two years: *Who could ever have imagined the destruction of slavery four years ago when this war started!* This was the moment when Lincoln made his famous, and famously misleading, declaration of passivity. "I claim not to have controlled events," Lincoln said, "but confess plainly that events have controlled me."[60] Eventually the political conditions that led him to disavow his earlier role in implementing military emancipation would be forgotten, leaving us instead with Lincoln's own mythic account of why he waited so long to begin freeing slaves.

By taking such retrospective accounts at face value, by continuing to ask what took Lincoln so long, generations of writers have perpetuated the myth that there was no emancipation prior to the Emancipation Proclamation. By formulating such extreme answers—that Lincoln was either the Great Emancipator or the Reluctant Emancipator—the long and complex history of emancipation was reduced to a singular act by a single individual. Extravagant predictions of what an emancipation proclamation would do, paired off against cynical claims that it would do nothing at all, made it all but impossible to evaluate its actual significance. By the time the Emancipation Proclamation was issued on January 1, 1863, it was already difficult to cut through the mythology to understand what it was supposed to do, what it actually did, and what it could not do. Lincoln's assassination in 1865 only made things worse. He was instantly proclaimed a martyr, not only to the cause of the Union but also to the cause of emancipation. Ever since then we have careered back and forth between extreme interpretations—of Lincoln the Reluctant Emancipator whose proclamation did nothing and of Lincoln the Great Emancipator who freed all the slaves on a single day. One hundred and fifty years after it was issued, we still can't answer the basic question: What did the Emancipation Proclamation actually do?

10 THE EMANCIPATION PROCLAMATION

N O ONE WAS MORE SKEPTICAL of the Emancipation Proclamation than the president who issued it. On several occasions over the second half of 1862, Lincoln made his doubts clear. "If a decree of emancipation could abolish Slavery," he told a group of visitors on June 20, "John Brown would have done the work effectually." As it is, the federal government cannot even enforce the Constitution in the Confederate states, Lincoln explained. "Would a proclamation of freedom be any more effective?" A few months later, replying to a delegation of Christians who argued that an emancipation proclamation was the will of God, Lincoln expressed even deeper skepticism. "What good would a proclamation of emancipation from me do?" Lincoln asked. It was one thing to emancipate slaves in areas under Union occupation; that could be done and was being done. But the proclamation the visitors were asking for would apply to areas over which the Union army had no control. "I do not want to issue a document that the whole world will see must necessarily be inoperative," Lincoln added. It would be "like the Pope's bull against the comet!" Even after he issued the Preliminary Proclamation in September, Lincoln remained skeptical. Responding to a congratulatory note from Vice President Hannibal Hamlin, Lincoln again admitted that "my expectations are not as sanguine as are those of some friends." It would no doubt bolster support for the administration in the North, he said, but "the time for its effect southward has not come."[1] Lincoln had no doubts about the wisdom and justice of emancipation itself. He speculated that proclaiming emancipation might reinvigorate northern support for the war, help forestall European recognition of the Confederacy, and further undermine the rebellion by attracting more slaves to Union lines. But he was not sure that proclaiming emancipation in the unoccupied areas of the Confederacy would free all that many slaves. And yet, on January 1, 1863, Lincoln issued the Emancipation Proclamation.

One day earlier—December 31, 1862—the same day he signed the West Virginia statehood bill, Lincoln met with his cabinet to go over the draft of the proclamation one last time. The cabinet review had begun on December 29, when Lincoln read a draft aloud, invited criticism, and ordered copies made so that each of the secretaries could make further suggestions when they met again. When the cabinet reconvened at ten o'clock on the thirty-first, Secretary of Treasury Salmon Chase made a few suggestions, most of which were by then familiar. Rather than a single emancipation proclamation, he would have preferred to have individual Union army officers proclaim freedom as they marched through the slave states. Lincoln's final draft lifted the long-standing ban on black troops in the Union army, but Chase thought that announcement should be made separately. Lincoln accepted neither of these recommendations, but he did adopt Chase's suggestion that the final proclamation include a more inspiring coda. Otherwise, the cabinet endorsed Lincoln's proclamation more or less unchanged.[2]

The following morning, Lincoln prepared the final draft before sending it off to the State Department to be engrossed, but when the document came back at ten forty-five, Lincoln noticed an error and returned it for correction. It was New Year's Day, and by tradition the president hosted a reception at the Executive Mansion beginning at eleven. The release of the proclamation would have to wait. Official Washington arrived during the first hour, and at noon the doors were opened to the public until two o'clock. When the reception ended, Lincoln went upstairs to affix his signature to the corrected document. Presidential signatures were not necessary for proclamations, but Lincoln, conscious of the significance of what he was about to do, broke with tradition and signed it anyway. He even used his full name, "Abraham Lincoln," rather than his more usual "A. Lincoln." As he lifted his pen, his hand began to tremble. "I could not for a moment control my arm," Lincoln later recalled. "I paused, and a superstitious feeling came over me which made me hesitate." Then he remembered. "I had been shaking hands for hours with several hundred people, and hence a very simple explanation of the trembling and shaking of my arm." After smiling at himself for a moment, Lincoln proceeded to sign the Emancipation Proclamation. "I never, in my life, felt more certain that I was doing right than I do in signing this paper."[3]

THE DOCUMENT

It's a deceptively straightforward document. Clocking in at under seven hundred words, the Emancipation Proclamation is in many ways more interesting for what it assumed than for what it declared. The most important things about it—the ways it transformed the federal government's approach to slavery—are barely mentioned or not referred to at all. It was the skeleton, but not the flesh, of a sweeping revision of Union emancipation policy.

The first two substantive paragraphs were direct quotations taken from the Preliminary Proclamation of the previous September. They reminded readers of Lincoln's promise to emancipate all slaves in areas still in rebellion as of January 1, 1863, and of his corresponding promise to deploy Union armed forces to "maintain the freedom of such persons." Neither the army nor the navy would do anything "to repress such persons . . . in any efforts they may make for their actual freedom." Critics had denounced this passage as an incitement to slave insurrection, but a better word for it is *enticement*, for Lincoln almost certainly intended the passage as an invitation for slaves to secure their own freedom by running to the safety of Union lines.[4]

Having reaffirmed his vow to free the slaves in all areas "in rebellion," Lincoln explained once more the criteria for distinguishing the loyal from the disloyal areas of the South. His standard was simple: any state, or portion of any state, that was represented in Congress by members chosen by a majority of qualified voters would be deemed loyal and would be exempted from the proclamation. All of the exempted areas had unionist representatives in Congress: northern and western Virginia, southern Louisiana, and the four Border States.[5] Tennessee had a unionist governor cooperating with the administration.

The preliminaries completed, Lincoln's proclamation moved on to the legal justification for his action. It was strictly military emancipation. Lincoln was freeing slaves by virtue of the power vested in the president as commander in chief of the army and navy "in time of actual armed rebellion against the authority and government of the United States, and as a fit and necessary war measure for suppressing said rebellion." His reasoning was by now familiar. Except in time of war or insurrection the Constitution forbade the federal government from directly interfering with slavery in the states where it existed. Military necessity was the only constitutional ground on which Lincoln could justify federal "interference" with a state institution.[6]

Finally Lincoln turned to the business at hand: "I do order and declare," his proclamation read, "that all persons held as slaves within said designated areas . . . are, and henceforward shall be free." He reiterated his promise that the army and navy would "recognize and maintain the freedom of said persons." He urged those emancipated by the proclamation "to abstain from all violence, unless in necessary self-defence" and further recommended that they "labor faithfully for reasonable wages." At first glance, these seem mere reiterations of the criteria for "self-emancipation" by which the federal government had been freeing slaves for nearly sixteen months. Slaves voluntarily entering Union lines from disloyal areas were emancipated, and their freedom was validated by their willingness to work in return for wages. However, by inviting slaves to come within Union lines, by *enticing* them with the promise of freedom, Lincoln was actually initiating a major shift in federal emancipation policy. Up to that point the government had abolished slavery in Washington and had emancipated rebel-owned slaves in the occupied areas of the seceded states, areas that included perhaps two hundred thousand enslaved blacks. If enticement worked, the Emancipation Proclamation could free millions.[7]

In the next paragraph Lincoln announced a second major shift in Union emancipation policy. Emancipated slaves "of suitable condition, will be received into the armed services of the United States." Black men had been excluded from the Union army ever since the nation was founded. With the Emancipation Proclamation, the long-standing ban on black enlistment was lifted.[8]

Together the two new policies announced in the Emancipation Proclamation—enticement and black enlistment—transformed Union soldiers into an army of liberation in the seceded states. They were the means by which the Lincoln administration would enforce the proclamation, making it much more than a papal bull against the comet.

Lincoln closed the proclamation with a slightly edited version of the elegant coda Chase had recommended the day before. With this act, Lincoln said, "sincerely believed to be an act of justice, warranted by the Constitution, upon military necessity, I invoke the considerate judgment of mankind, and the gracious favor of Almighty God." The theme was hardly a new one among Republicans. For months they had been proclaiming the dual character of emancipation: it was a military necessity, but it was also the right thing to do. The coda also sounded an echo of the "decent respect for the opinions of mankind" that Jefferson had invoked in his Declaration of Independence—the ideological touchstone for Lincoln's hostility to slavery. Military necessity and antislavery idealism were not mutually exclusive.[9]

That was it—a no-nonsense document that appeared to do little more than remind readers that Lincoln had promised to proclaim emancipation, and then did it. Its two major policy shifts were mentioned obliquely or in passing, calling no attention to themselves. In one sense the proclamation's modesty was becoming: the brevity and simplicity of its prose belied its staggering scope. By saying very little, however, the Emancipation Proclamation also explained very little. It was full of assumptions that knowledgeable readers would have recognized but which are no longer obvious to us. On what basis, for example, did Lincoln confidently declare that slaves emancipated by the proclamation were "henceforward" and "forever free," that they could never be returned to slavery? What was the theory of military emancipation? And how did Lincoln expect to overcome the problem he himself had repeatedly pointed out: his inability to enforce the proclamation in the very areas it covered? On paper Lincoln had created an army of liberation. But what did that mean on the ground, in the rebellious areas of the South?

A THEORY OF MILITARY EMANCIPATION

Across America the Emancipation Proclamation was praised and denounced for the same reason: Lincoln had issued an abolitionist edict. The Democratic *New York Herald* assailed it as "the last card of the abolition Jacobins." Jefferson Davis called Lincoln's proclamation "the most execrable measure recorded in the history of guilty man." It vindicated secession, Davis said, by demonstrating that Lincoln and the Republicans were the very antislavery fanatics white southerners had long said they were. Abolitionists in the North were not inclined to dispute the point. Wendell Phillips declared that Lincoln had bound the United States "to the throne of the Almighty, proclaiming Liberty as an act of justice, and abolishing a system found inconsistent with the perpetuity of the Republic." In cities across the North— in New York, Brooklyn, and Boston, in Albany, Pittsburgh, and Chicago—African Americans filled churches, meeting halls, and vast auditoriums, celebrating the proclamation. Frederick Douglass called it "the first step on the part of the nation in its departure from the thralldom of ages."[10] Yet the abolitionism that contemporaries often attributed to the Emancipation Proclamation can be difficult for modern readers to discern, in part because of the way it was written.

Lincoln composed the proclamation in prose so dull that readers began objecting as soon as it was issued. It was loaded down with lawyerish language. *Whereas*, and *by virtue of the power*, Lincoln *hereby enjoins*, and *further declares, in witness whereof he hereunto sets his hand*. Karl Marx had dismissed the prose of the Preliminary Proclamation as "mean pettifogging," the kind of language "one lawyer puts to his opposing lawyer," and no doubt the same could be said of the Emancipation Proclamation itself.[11] Where was the call to high ideals, to justice and equality, to basic human decency? Chase's brief coda was too meager. Why none of the exalted rhetoric Lincoln could conjure up on other occasions? Would Harriet Beecher Stowe or Wendell Phillips have produced such a document, so empty of emotion, so devoid of principle? Certainly not.

Other abolitionists, however—William Jay perhaps, or Samuel May, or Gerrit Smith—might well have written the proclamation as

Lincoln did. There was much more to abolitionism than red-hot rhetoric. The literature of the movement included sober treatises on constitutional law, legal tracts, and appellate court briefs reproduced as antislavery pamphlets. Theodore Dwight Weld published a scorching indictment in *American Slavery as It Is*, but in 1840 he also published *Persons Held to Service, Fugitives Slaves, &c.*, specifying the legal distinction between slavery as a servile status and slavery as "property in man"—a distinction that went on to become crucial to the legal process of emancipation. Frederick Douglass wrote the impassioned *What to the Slave Is the Fourth of July?* But in 1861 he went to Scotland and delivered a long and learned lecture on the legal status of slavery under the Constitution. William Jay's *View of the Action of the Federal Government in Behalf of Slavery* ranks as one of the unappreciated classics of abolitionist literature. John Quincy Adams spent two days presenting his oral argument before the Supreme Court in the *Amistad* case and in so doing produced an influential summation of abolitionist legal doctrine. Joshua Giddings's famous congressional "resolutions" were the work of an abolitionist who was also a lawmaker. Abolitionists stressed the inhumanity and injustice of slavery, yet they also formulated antislavery principles based on common law, case law, statute law, and constitutional law. Lincoln may not have been an abolitionist, but the fact that he chose to write the Emancipation Proclamation as a legal document hardly distinguished it from one of the central rhetorical traditions of abolitionism.

Ironically, what most indelibly stamped the proclamation with the influence of the antislavery movement was the very thing that critics have always been quickest to condemn—its reliance on "military necessity." Though a handful of abolitionists later complained about the military rationale for emancipation, most Americans at the time associated military emancipation with antislavery radicalism, and rightly so. To Democrats, "military necessity" was doubly dubious: not only was there no actual "military necessity" for emancipation, they charged, the very idea that the federal government could free a slave on such grounds was sheer abolitionist dogma. The critics had a point. Though the practice of military emancipation was ancient, the claim that the Constitution empowered the federal government to emancipate slaves as a military necessity was most heartily embraced by abolitionists and antislavery politicians. In the earliest months of the war, some antislavery radicals—including Frederick Douglass and William Lloyd Garrison—denounced Lincoln not because he invoked his war powers to free slaves but because he did not invoke them soon enough. Within the antislavery movement it was widely understood that the war powers were the sole constitutional means by which the federal government could emancipate slaves in the states where slavery already existed. "According to our political system," Lincoln explained, "as a matter of civil administration, the general government had no lawful power to effect emancipation in any State." But "as a military measure," he noted, the federal government could free slaves so "that the rebellion could be suppressed."[12] It was a familiar argument within the antislavery movement.

What was new in 1863 was the theory antislavery lawyers put forward to justify military emancipation. When during the debates in the 1830s over the "gag rule" John Quincy Adams first asserted that in times of war or rebellion the federal government was empowered to emancipate slaves, he drew almost exclusively on historical precedent to make his case. None of the classic treatises on the laws of war addressed the issue of slave emancipation. As antislavery lawyers and politicians embraced this idea, however, they fused basic abolitionist principles to familiar historical practice. By the time they finished their intellectual spadework they were justifying military emancipation on the natural-law principle of fundamental human equality.[13]

The antislavery premises of military emancipation were thoroughly aired in the sharp debate that erupted among legal scholars soon after Lincoln issued his Preliminary Proclamation. In late 1862,

Benjamin Curtis, a conservative Whig and former justice of the U.S. Supreme Court, published a lengthy critique of the legal reasoning behind the impending proclamation. Curtis worried that Lincoln was careering downward on a very slippery slope. "If the President, as commander-in-chief of the army and navy in time of war, may, by an executive decree, exercise this power to abolish slavery in the States," Curtis wondered, "what other power, reserved to the States or to the people, may not be exercised by the President, for the same reason, that he is of opinion he may thus best subdue the enemy?"[14] Everyone understood the principle Curtis was invoking: the Constitution did not empower the federal government to abolish slavery in the states where it already existed. Lincoln's proclamation, Curtis charged, would overturn the federal consensus.

But emancipation was not abolition, and by conflating the two, Curtis forced antislavery lawyers to clarify a distinction that had been implicit in federal antislavery policy from the start. Neither the Emancipation Proclamation that Lincoln proposed to issue nor the Second Confiscation Act on which it was based "abolished" slavery anywhere. In a lengthy rebuttal to Curtis, the New York lawyer Grosvenor P. Lowrey made precisely this point. Even universal emancipation "does not abolish slavery; it only abolishes the slave." When the war is over, "when the martial law is removed," Lowrey explained, a master in Georgia whose slaves had been emancipated "may purchase another slave in Maryland, or wherever he can procure a legal title, and hold him afterward, in Georgia, under the same law as before." The "military power, acting through emancipation, does not pretend to destroy the legal right to own slaves."[15] The Emancipation Proclamation, however sweeping, would not violate the federal consensus against abolishing slavery in the states.

Nor was military emancipation an invasion of property rights, because slaves were not "property" under the Constitution. Here again the abolitionist premises of Lincoln's proclamation were clarified in the legal debate it provoked. In the United States slaves were "property" only under state or "municipal" laws. By contrast, the Massachusetts Republican William Whiting explained in his 1863 justification for emancipation, the Constitution "recognizes slaves as 'persons held to labor or service.'" Legally this made "slaves" no different from apprentices or children, for they too were "persons held to labor or service." Whatever the property claims that slave states might conjure up, Whiting argued, "the constitution recognizes only the claim of individuals to the labor and service of other individuals." Because there was no property right at stake none of the legal safeguards against property confiscation applied to military emancipation and the slaveholders had no legitimate claim to compensation for their emancipated slaves.[16] All of this would have been familiar to antislavery politicians by 1860.

More startling was the wartime evolution of the theory behind the practice of military emancipation. In late 1862, General in Chief Henry Halleck and Secretary of War Edwin Stanton invited Francis Lieber, a distinguished professor of law at Columbia University, to summarize the "articles of war" that would govern the Union army. A number of issues had to be dealt with—prisoner exchanges, the treatment of prisoners of war, the army's policy regarding enemy civilians—but none was more urgent than the Union army's approach to slaves owned by the enemy. This was clearly a critical issue. Lincoln had announced that he was about to issue an emancipation proclamation covering all rebellious areas of the South. On what legal basis could he do so? The "code" that Lieber drew up in early 1863 provided a theory of military emancipation.[17]

For years abolitionists argued that the Constitution was a natural-law document and that natural law decreed that all men were created equal. Hence slavery was incompatible with the natural-law principles of the Constitution. But Lieber pushed the argument further by reconstructing the dizzying chain of inferences linking military emancipation to the antislavery premises of natural law. Connect the dots: the laws of war were part of the law of nations, the law of nations was based on natural law, slavery was incompatible with natural law, hence in wartime belligerents had the right to restore slaves to their "natural" condition of freedom. In Lieber's elegant hands it all seemed so respectably constitutional. Because the law of nations was inscribed in the treaty-making provisions and treaty-like character of the Constitution, and because the laws of war were embedded in the war powers clause of the Constitution, military emancipation was strictly within the Constitution. And not only that. Because both the law of nations and the laws of war were based on natural law, military emancipation was ultimately justified by the natural-law principle of fundamental human equality.

More than a dozen of the 157 articles in Lieber's code dealt with slavery, but two in particular, Nos. 42 and 43, summarized the philosophical principles on which military emancipation was based. Lieber began from the crucial abolitionist premise that slaves were "property" under local law but not under the Constitution. Slavery thus complicated and confounded ideas of property and personalty, Lieber wrote, for the slave was legally both a "thing" and a "human" at the same time. This made slavery unnatural, and for that reason the "law of nature and nations has never acknowledged it." Citing the Justinian Code, Lieber declared that "so far as the law of nature is concerned, all men are equal." Because the Constitution was based on natural law, slave property therefore "exists according to municipal or local law only." For this reason fugitive slaves escaping into another country "have, for centuries past, been held free and acknowledged free by judicial decisions in European countries." That being the case, Lieber concluded, "in a war between the United States and a belligerent which admits of slavery," any fugitive who runs for protection into the lines of the U.S. military "is immediately entitled to the rights and privileges of a freeman."[18]

With the Lieber Code the *Somerset* principle became the law of the land. In 1772, Lord Mansfield, speaking from the Court of King's Bench, had ruled that slavery existed only where local or "municipal" law created it, and since no such law existed in England, "slavery" could exist only as a servile status rather than a property right. Mansfield ruled that the master had forfeited his property claim in the slave, Somerset, as soon as the slave set foot on English soil. In England, slaves were legal persons held in service. Under the theory of military emancipation, what had happened to Somerset also happened to slaves in the disloyal states during the Civil War. Secession nullified the state and local laws creating a property right in slaves and federal policy was thereafter guided only by the constitutional definition of slaves as "persons held in service." Because the Union army was the creature of the federal government, fugitive slaves escaping from any belligerent states were immediately emancipated upon entering Union lines.

If Lieber had merely published his conclusions as a contribution to a lawyer's debate over the legality of military emancipation it would remain an interesting curiosity in the history of antislavery thought. But Lieber's code was much more important than that. He was authorized to draft it by two high-ranking officials in the Lincoln administration—the secretary of war and the general in chief. He then submitted his draft to the president, who reviewed and edited the code before approving it. On April 24, 1863, the Lieber Code was issued by the adjutant general's office of the War Department as General Orders No. 100. The abolitionist logic of military emancipation was thereby embedded in the articles of war governing the conduct of the U.S. Army. Lieber's code became, in effect, the Lincoln administration's official legal justification for military emancipation.[19]

CITIZENSHIP AND EMANCIPATION

In his Preliminary Proclamation of September 1862, Lincoln declared
that the slaves, once emancipated, were "forever free." He quoted the
line at the beginning of the final proclamation and reiterated it later
in slightly different wording: the slaves in all rebellious areas of the
South "are, and henceforward shall be free." Once emancipated, the
freed people could never be re-enslaved. The point seems obvious to
us now, but it was not obvious at the time. On the contrary, in defending military emancipation, antislavery lawyers like Lowrey and Lieber
went out of their way to explain why, once they were emancipated,
the freed people could never be legally re-enslaved. Re-enslavement
was impossible, they said, because at the moment they were freed,
blacks became citizens of the United States and a citizen can never be
enslaved.

Lawmakers worried about re-enslavement far more than they
feared a Supreme Court opinion declaring emancipation unconstitutional. Republicans didn't like Chief Justice Roger Taney, but they
weren't especially afraid of him. Whenever he issued a ruling they
disagreed with they simply ignored it. There was a more pervasive fear
that once the war was over, the U.S. courts in general—not merely
Taney's Supreme Court—would limit and possibly even invalidate
the wartime military emancipations. But what frightened Republicans most of all was that the courts would uphold the states in their
attempts to preserve slavery. When the war was over, slavery would
revert to its status as a strictly state institution, and slaves emancipated
during the war might be re-enslaved by the restored state governments. By the spring of 1862, Border State representatives in Congress were openly threatening that once the rebellion was suppressed
the southern states would not only re-enslave the freed people but
would go further and in their righteous anger enslave all blacks, even

those who had been free before the war. Re-enslavement was not merely an abstract threat. Blacks in the Sea Islands had long expressed a legitimate fear that they would be re-enslaved as soon as the Union army left or was driven out by the Confederates. And indeed by the middle of 1862, blacks who had been emancipated by the Union army in other parts of the South were being re-enslaved in areas recaptured by the Confederates. Re-enslavement was, in fact, the official Confederate policy.[20]

The threat of re-enslavement put Republicans in an unusual position. Having defended the constitutionality of the Emancipation Proclamation by pointing out that it did not interfere with a state's right to create or destroy slavery, policymakers had to find some legal means of denying a state's right to enslave, or re-enslave, anyone who was already free. Lowrey and Lieber did this by distinguishing a right to own slaves in a state where slavery was legal—a right the federal government could not interfere with—from the power to enslave someone who was already free—a power they insisted no state could rightfully claim. Slavery might be legal, but enslavement and re-enslavement could never be. Why not? Because blacks were citizens of the United States and enslavement would be a flagrant violation of the "privileges and immunities" to which all citizens were entitled. To ensure that emancipated slaves were "forever free," Republicans adopted the principle of color-blind national citizenship.

In the immediate aftermath of the American Revolution most state courts acknowledged that free blacks were entitled to some, if not all, of the rights of citizenship. As sectional tensions developed, however, northern and southern courts went their separate ways on the citizenship rights of free blacks. Many northern states passed "personal liberty" laws designed to inhibit enforcement of the fugitive slave clause of the Constitution by guaranteeing due process—one of the essential "privileges" of citizenship—to any black man or woman accused of being a fugitive slave. The Fugitive Slave Act of 1850 was

designed to undermine those state laws by making the federal government the enforcement agent of the fugitive slave clause. Undeterred,
several northern states passed a new round of personal liberty laws in
the 1850s, all of them based on the assumption that accused fugitives
were "citizens" of the states.[21]

Like most northerners, Abraham Lincoln had almost nothing to
say about citizenship until the fugitive slave crisis of the 1850s, yet he
repeatedly gestured in the direction of the abolitionist argument by
hinting that free blacks were entitled to at least some of the due-
process rights associated with citizenship. Commenting on the Fugitive Slave Act of 1850, Lincoln said a few years after its passage that
he would have preferred a statute that "did not expose a free negro to
any more danger of being carried into slavery, than our present criminal laws do an innocent person to the danger of being hung."
Acknowledging that the Constitution did contain a fugitive slave
clause, Lincoln urged his fellow Republicans to revise rather than
repeal the 1850 law lest they alienate too many swing voters. He
insisted nonetheless that the law "should have been framed so as to be
free from some of the objections that pertain to it."[22]

Chief Justice Roger Taney's 1857 decision in the *Dred Scott* case
forced Lincoln and many other northerners to think more deeply
about the issue of black citizenship. Taney ruled that blacks were not
and never had been citizens of the United States; because blacks had
not been citizens of the states in either 1776 or 1789, they could not
be citizens of the United States in 1857. States were perfectly free to
extend some of the privileges and immunities of citizenship to whom-
ever they chose, Taney ruled, but no state could ever, under any cir-
cumstance, grant U.S. citizenship to blacks.[23] Taney defined national
citizenship as an inheritance bequeathed only to the descendants of
those who had been citizens at the moment of the nation's founding.

Two weeks after Taney published his decision Lincoln criticized
the chief justice for insisting "at great length that negroes were no

part of the people who made, or for whom was made, the Declaration of Independence, or the Constitution." A year later, Lincoln tied the high court's denial of black citizenship to a conspiracy to make slavery national and perpetual, a conspiracy that began with Taney's claim "that a negro cannot be a citizen." The court's purpose, Lincoln explained, was "to deprive the negro, in every possible event, of the benefit of that provision of the United States Constitution which declares that 'the citizens of each State shall be entitled to all privileges and immunities of citizens in the several States.'" Lincoln's statements on black citizenship were hesitant and inconsistent during the late 1850s, yet it was already clear that in his mind the denial of black citizenship was part of an attempt to make slavery perpetual. By inverse logic, black citizenship would make emancipation perpetual. It would ensure that once they were freed the former slaves were "forever" free—but only if blacks were citizens of the United States, and only if national citizenship trumped state citizenship.[24]

The first indication that Lincoln might be thinking of national black citizenship emerged during the secession crisis shortly after his election in November of 1860. As president-elect, Lincoln was under pressure to offer some substantive compromise proposal that might forestall the secession of the southern states and prevent civil war. Unwilling to bend on the issue of slavery in the territories, Lincoln instead proposed a compromise on the issue of fugitive slaves. Secessionists complained endlessly about the personal liberty laws northern states passed in their efforts to thwart the Fugitive Slave Act of 1850. In response Lincoln was willing to concede that the fugitive slave clause should be enforced by the federal government, but in return for that concession Lincoln wanted two crucial revisions of the Fugitive Slave Act of 1850: first, all private citizens would be absolved from any obligation to help execute the law, and, second, the revised law would have to include "the usual safeguards to liberty, securing free men against being surrendered as slaves." The federal government would thereby guarantee the due-process rights of all accused slaves. In effect, national black citizenship was the price slaveholders would have to pay for national enforcement of the fugitive slave clause.[25] Southern leaders rejected his proposal out of hand and even Lincoln's friends warned him that most Republicans were "unwilling to give up their old opinion that the duty of executing the constitutional provisions concerning fugitives belongs to the States."[26]

A few months later, in his inaugural address, Lincoln once again raised the related issues of citizenship and the rendition of fugitive slaves. Secessionists believed enforcement was a federal responsibility, but most antislavery politicians believed that since slavery was a state institution the states alone should be responsible for the capture and return of fugitive slaves. Lincoln noted that there was "some difference of opinion" about who was responsible for enforcing the fugitive slave clause. "Shall fugitives from labor be surrendered by national or by State authority?" Lincoln asked. "The Constitution does not expressly say." But he still seemed willing to accept federal enforcement in return for federal recognition of citizenship for African Americans. In "any law upon this subject," he said, "might it not be well, at the same time, to provide by law for the enforcement of that clause in the Constitution which guaranties that 'The citizens of each State shall be entitled to all the privileges and immunities of the citizens in the several States'?" Lincoln was once again proposing a revision of the Fugitive Slave Act that explicitly accorded to blacks federal recognition of the "privileges and immunities" of citizenship. What Lincoln hinted at in his inaugural address his administration formally proclaimed a year and a half later.[27]

In late 1862, with the Emancipation Proclamation about to be issued, the citizenship status of the freed people became an urgent question. Treasury Secretary Chase sent a request to Edward Bates, the attorney general, asking whether, as a matter of policy, "colored men [are] citizens of the United States." In reply Bates produced an astonishing document, nearly thirty pages long, repudiating every-thing Chief Justice Taney had to say about black citizenship. Bates made three crucial claims. First, he said, there is no such thing as "partial" citizenship. Anyone entitled to *any* of the privileges and immunities of citizenship was entitled to *all* of them. Second, as far as citizenship was concerned, there was no distinction between blacks and whites. The Constitution "says not one word, and furnishes not one hint, in relation to the color or to the ancestral race" of citizens. Finally, and perhaps most important, Bates declared that national citizenship took precedence over state citizenship. The privileges and immunities granted to citizens of the United States "cannot be destroyed or abridged by the laws of any particular state," Bates reasoned. On this point, he said, the Constitution "is plain beyond cavil." Citizenship in the United States is "an integral thing"; it cannot be "fractionalized," broken down into parts; it cannot mean one thing in one state and something else in another state. In sum, Bates concluded, free blacks were full citizens of the United States, and no state could deprive them of the privileges and immunities attaching to their citizenship. Even blacks born and raised as slaves on American soil became citizens as soon as they were emancipated. Slaves set free by the proclamation or by the war, Bates explained on January 5, 1863, were not partly free but fully free. "In the language of the Constitution they will be 'free persons'" and as such were entitled to all the protections of freedom the Constitution guaranteed to all citizens.[28]

If the attorney general was right—if emancipated slaves were "free persons" as understood by the Constitution—it would mean that freed blacks could never be re-enslaved, for that would amount to a gross deprivation of the privileges and immunities of citizenship. This may have been one of the reasons why Bates issued his opinion. He sent it to Chase on November 29, 1862, one month before Lincoln released the Emancipation Proclamation. The timing may have been fortuitous, but that hardly seems likely. When Lincoln said that slaves once freed could never be re-enslaved he was assuming, like Bates, that no state had the power to deprive any American of the rights and privileges of citizenship. Variations on this theme were repeated in the legal commentaries on the constitutionality of military emancipation. A slave "whom we capture as property" under state law, Lowrey explained, is by the act of emancipation "no longer a chattel, but a man, *insusceptible of recapture.*" As a "man" the emancipated slave is "entitled to all the rights and privileges of such persons." Re-enslavement was impossible because once someone's "status as a slave is suspended," even "for a moment," Lowrey explained, the slave was "remitted to his natural rights as a man." When that happened "there is no power on earth to take away his freedom." Francis Lieber made the same point. Emancipated slaves were "immediately entitled to the rights and privileges of a freeman," he explained. "To return such a person into slavery would amount to enslaving a free person." If the federal government had no such power, Lieber declared, neither did the states.[29]

The Bates ruling was later overshadowed by the Civil Rights Act of 1866, in which Congress legislatively recognized black citizenship, and by the Fourteenth Amendment, which enshrined national, color-blind citizenship in the Constitution. During the war, however, the attorney general's ruling was widely hailed by abolitionists, radical Republicans, and African Americans, as a fundamental repudiation of "Dred Scottism" and a major step toward civic equality for blacks. In August of 1863, a group of black soldiers at Morris Island, South Carolina, drafted a set of resolutions praising three specific actions taken by the federal government: the Emancipation Proclamation, the effort to purchase and free all slaves in the Border States, and "the decision of Attorney-General Bates." In January of 1865, blacks in New Orleans formed the Equal Rights League, whose convention denounced the "difference between 'citizens of the United States' (as we are recognized by Attorney General Bates), and 'citizens of Louisiana' (that we are not according to the laws now in force)." The petitioners demanded that the state adopt Bates's more expansive definition of blacks as "citizens of the United States."[30]

National citizenship for whites and blacks alike is often viewed as one of the most important consequences of emancipation, and there is an important element of truth in that. Bates, though, issued his citizenship opinion before the Emancipation Proclamation was released, and it is reasonable to conclude that he did so to establish the legal basis for the president's claim that once emancipated, slaves were "forever free." National citizenship for blacks may have been less a consequence than a precondition for permanent emancipation.

BATES'S CITIZENSHIP RULING ALSO cleared the way for Lincoln's announcement, toward the end of the Emancipation Proclamation, that as of January 1, 1863, blacks "will be received into the armed service of the United States." Lincoln could not have made that announcement at the beginning of the war, first because Congress had to repeal the racial exclusion that had always reserved enlistment in the Union army to white males, and second because the citizenship of black men had to be established. Since the late eighteenth century, enlistment in the Union army was legally linked to citizenship. If black men were not citizens, they could not enlist.

The Militia Act of 1792 restricted service in the army to "every free able-bodied white male citizen." Northern states generally recognized blacks as citizens but they still often excluded black citizens from their own militias. Because the U.S. Army drew its regimental strength from the state militias the 1792 restrictions meant that from the earliest years of the nation's founding black men were legally barred from enlisting in the army. In the *Dred Scott* decision of 1857

Chief Justice Taney pointed specifically to this long history of racial exclusion in the military to reinforce his claim that blacks were not and never had been citizens. He quoted the 1792 statute as proof that "none but white persons are citizens." He pointed to state laws that likewise restricted the militia to "free white citizens." By Taney's legal reasoning the all-white army demonstrated that blacks were "not permitted to share in one of the highest duties of the citizen." When the Civil War began, both whiteness and citizenship remained conditions for enlistment in the U.S. Army.[31]

The Militia Act of July 17, 1862, removed the words *free* and *white* from the qualifications for enrollment in the militia. Instead of "free able-bodied white male citizens," the new law authorized the president to open enlistment to all "able-bodied male citizens." The racial exclusion was thereby removed along with the ban on enlisting slaves, but citizenship remained a qualification for military service. The statute made no mention of black citizenship, and perhaps for that reason Lincoln's Preliminary Proclamation of September 22 made no corresponding mention of black enlistment. In the hundred-day interim between the preliminary and the final proclamation, however, Bates issued his opinion that blacks were citizens of the United States and that U.S. citizenship took precedence over state citizenship. Emancipated men thereby met the standard of the recent Militia Act and were now eligible for military service. Indeed, citizenship soon made black men available for conscription as well. On March 3, 1863, Congress enacted a national "enrolling" law—a military draft—making "all able-bodied male citizens" eligible for the draft. Within weeks the Union army began sporadically "impressing" slaves directly into the army, for with freedom they became citizens and with citizenship came the obligation to military service. Once again citizenship, often viewed as a reward for black military service during the Civil War, was more likely the necessary precondition for such service. Without the attorney general's citizenship ruling, Lincoln would have had no legal basis for authorizing black enlistment one month later. Like the natural-law principle of fundamental human equality, black citizenship was another of the hidden assumptions embedded in the Emancipation Proclamation.[32]

THE EXEMPTIONS

One full paragraph of the Emancipation Proclamation was devoted to a tedious recitation of the areas exempted from it. In a sense this paragraph was the reason there was any need to issue a proclamation. Congress had already made universal emancipation in the rebellious states the de facto policy of the federal government. In Republican minds the distinction between freeing the slaves of all rebels and freeing slaves in all rebel areas was essentially meaningless, since virtually all slaveholders in the Confederacy were believed to be rebels. Both the First and Second Confiscation Acts called for a presidential proclamation specifying the *areas* in rebellion. Throughout the congressional debates of mid-1862 Republicans sometimes spoke of freeing the slaves of all rebels and sometimes freeing slaves in all rebel areas—as if the two criteria were interchangeable. By proclaiming emancipation in all rebellious areas, Lincoln was not moving beyond what Congress expected, and some Republicans later complained that he had narrowed their intended scope.[33] In any case the Second Confiscation Act required a presidential proclamation distinguishing the loyal areas from those in rebellion. In the closing months, even days, of 1862, Lincoln made concerted efforts to find out exactly which parts of the Confederacy qualified as "loyal" and were therefore exempt.

Exemption meant only that an area was loyal, not that slavery was untouchable. Loyal areas were those that had sent duly elected representatives to Congress, but that was an unreliable guide to the progress of emancipation in any particular area. Slaves were already freed, for example, in several occupied parts of the Confederacy that were nevertheless covered by the proclamation. Emancipation had begun a year earlier in the Sea Islands, and by late 1862 it was already under way in western Mississippi as well as in Arkansas, but none of those areas were exempted because none had held legitimate elections that sent unionist representatives to Congress. On the other hand, slaves were being emancipated in several of the areas that were exempted, such as southern Louisiana and western Tennessee, both of which were represented in Congress by unionists. The day before he issued the Emancipation Proclamation Lincoln signed the West Virginia statehood bill, which required abolition as a condition for admission to the Union. Yet the entire state was exempted. Even in theory the exemptions in the Emancipation Proclamation did not correspond to the areas where slaves were or were not being freed. In practice exempted areas often felt the proclamation most immediately.

Consider one example from Kentucky. There was "great excitement" among the slaves on Charles Hays's plantation, sixteen miles from Louisville, when they "heard the news of Lincoln's emancipation proclamation." Just before the war began Hays had paid eleven hundred dollars for a young slave named Harry Smith, and it was Smith who several decades later recalled the events of January 1863. A number of "Union men" were passing by the Hays plantation and "enquired of the slaves if their master had set them free." Fearing he would be arrested if he failed to let his slaves know of their freedom, Hays appeared one morning as the slaves were eating their breakfast. In a nervous, "uneasy" manner, he made the announcement. "Men and women hear me, I am about to tell you something I never expected to be obliged to tell you in my life, it is this: it becomes my duty to inform you, one and all, woman, men and children, belonging to me, you are free to go where you please." Hays then cursed Lincoln "for taking all you negroes away from me." A "great jubilee" commenced on the plantation, but "Old Massa" got drunk and skulked off to his room while the slaves were "cheering Abraham Lincoln." Bless the Lord, Aunt Bess exclaimed, "my children are all free." The state in which she and Smith lived had been exempted from Lincoln's proclamation, yet as of January in 1863 they were emancipated.[34]

As Charles Hays was letting Harry Smith know that he had been emancipated by the president's proclamation, J. Vance Lewis's master was making a similar announcement farther South, on a sugar plantation in Louisiana. It was a Sunday morning early in 1863, and the master had called all the slaves together "at the big gate." Unlike Hays back in Kentucky, "Mars Dunc" appeared the picture of the southern gentleman—erect, well groomed, wearing a long, gray Prince Albert coat that "added dignity to grace." He spoke in a calm, fatherly voice. "Three days ago Abraham Lincoln, the President of the United States, issued a proclamation whereby you are made free men and women," he explained. Some of the slaves, like Lewis, had been born and raised on the plantation and others had been purchased from different owners. "But now you are free to go anywhere you please," the planter explained. He would not "drive" any of them away; he still needed people to continue the work. "You will be treated as hired servants. You will be paid for what you do and you will have to pay for what you get." I am a poorer man than I have ever been, he admitted, but he was not a pauper and he would not turn his workers "a-loose in the world with nothing." He gave ten dollars to each adult and two to every child, along with a month's supply of food. "I hope you will be honest and industrious and not bring disgrace upon those who have brought you up," he concluded. "Behave yourselves, work hard and trust in God, and you will get along all right. I will not hire anybody today, but tomorrow all who want to go to work will be ready when the bell rings." As Lewis recalled the scene, "there was hardly a dry eye amongst us." The next morning all two hundred of the freed men and women "reported for duty" when the bell rang. The fact that the plantation was located in a part of Louisiana that

had been exempted from the proclamation made no apparent difference to Lewis's owner.[35]

Nor did exemption always make a difference to Union soldiers.
Several months after Harry Smith had been freed in Kentucky and J.
Vance Lewis in Louisiana, Union soldiers in the Eighth New York
Artillery were gleefully helping slaves escape to freedom from another
exempted state, Maryland. Sergeant Edmund Evarts's captain had
given orders for the company to pack up and prepare to leave Eastville for Baltimore. But the area "was full of negroes" and Evarts
suggested to them that if they wanted to leave with the Union troops
they should "run around Eastville, and fall in below the village."
Evarts's suggestion set off a "skedaddling" among the slaves, and
"over the fields they came in all directions." It was a dark night so
Evarts was able to slip the runaways onto the Union gunboat without
the captain noticing. The next morning, when the owners arrived on
the shore demanding the return of their slaves, the Union soldiers
instead treated the whites to "a little mob law." One Union officer
announced that "he was no slave-hunter" and that the masters would
have to recapture the slaves on their own, but only with the help of
local authorities. "Smelling a rat," the "secesh" had brought a sheriff
with them, who proceeded to "make out the papers," but the local
authorities were no match for the Union soldiers. A burly corporal
took hold of the sheriff, cried, "Rally!" and a dozen more Yankees
sprang into action. They tossed the sheriff onto a blanket "and up he
went into the air sprawling in all shapes." Three times, up and down.
Next came Mr. Jarvis, one of the slave owners, whom Evarts
described as "a perfect specimen of a Virginia gentleman, too fine to
look at a laboring man unless he was a black one." Jarvis, too, was
thrown onto the blanket "and up he went." Just think, Evarts wrote,
of a southern aristocrat "being tossed fifteen feet in the air, three
times, by Union soldiers—northern mudsills." Some slaves watched
from nearby fields, "afraid to come." The slave owners who were

there to claim their runaways, however, "got no slaves." Instead the Union gunboat left for "a pleasant ride to Baltimore" with fifteen "free men and women" on board.[36]

It's a familiar precept that things rarely happen in precisely the way law and policy dictate they should happen. The areas where these three incidents took place in 1863—Kentucky, Louisiana, and Maryland—were all exempt from the Emancipation Proclamation. There would always be some Union soldiers and officers, especially troops native to the Border States in which they served, who returned slaves to their owners long after policymakers had banned the practice. Kentucky troops, following the lead of Kentucky politicians, were ferocious in their determination to restrict emancipation to its narrowest possible reach. They captured, arrested, and re-enslaved fugitives from disloyal states until Lincoln's adjutant general, Joseph Holt, declared it illegal, and Secretary of War Stanton ordered Union commanders in Kentucky to put a stop to the practice. Forced to recognize the conscription of their own slaves, Union troops from Kentucky nevertheless expelled the wives and children of black soldiers from their camps, sometimes sending the soldiers' families to their deaths and outraging Republican editors and lawmakers. By 1865 something like legislative warfare pitted the Republican Congress against the Kentucky legislature. The cause of so much tension is clear: it was far more common for slaves to be freed by Union troops in areas that the proclamation explicitly exempted than in the areas it technically covered.

Here was the "friction and abrasion" of war to which Lincoln had referred a year earlier in his warning to the Border States, and his warning suggests that the effect the proclamation had on exempted areas was not mere serendipity. Lincoln and the Republicans were already putting tremendous pressure on the exempted loyal slave states to abolish slavery on their own, and the Emancipation Proclamation dramatically increased that pressure. The policy was in many ways a success. Kentucky would never relent, but by the time the war ended, six states had abolished slavery—West Virginia, Maryland, Tennessee, Missouri, Louisiana, and Arkansas—and five of those six were exempted from the Emancipation Proclamation. Put differently, the exempted states were the *most* likely to abolish slavery before the Civil War ended.

This is surprising only if you assume that by specifying so many exemptions, Lincoln restricted the reach of emancipation. But this ignores all that had happened before the Emancipation Proclamation and thereby obscures its true significance. The federal government had been emancipating slaves since the first summer of the war; for more than a year it had been pressuring the Border States to abolish slavery on their own. The proclamation *increased* the pressure on the Border States and *extended* emancipation into areas previously untouched by federal policy. And this raises the question Lincoln himself asked: How could he enforce a proclamation in areas over which he had no control?

ENTICEMENT

Shortly after issuing the Emancipation Proclamation the Lincoln administration lifted the ban on enticing slaves into Union lines. Unlike the enlistment of black troops, which was clearly announced in the proclamation, the new policy of deliberate enticement was only hinted at in Lincoln's implicit invitation to slaves to run to Union lines where their freedom would be protected and maintained by the federal government. So obscure was this important policy shift within the proclamation itself that is has remained largely invisible. That's why some people still say the Emancipation Proclamation "did not free a single slave." Yet the new policy of enticing slaves was clearly enunciated in the unambiguous instructions flowing from the War

Department to Union officers in the South beginning in early 1863. Whatever else it was, the Emancipation Proclamation was more than a paper threat. After January 1, 1863, military emancipation would be systematically enforced in the disloyal states.

As late as September in 1862, Lincoln's personal secretary could describe the president's emancipation policy in the same terms that had been in place for over a year. The government was "[n]ot to return to slavery those slaves who fall necessarily into our hands in the course of the war," but Union soldiers were "*not to entice them* in, nor to incite them to rise." These were the familiar features of the "self-emancipation" policy. Slaves who came within Union lines were freed, but Union troops would not "entice" slaves away from their farms and plantations. Both elements were already specified in the cabinet's contraband decision forwarded by the secretary of war to General Benjamin Butler in May of 1861. You are to "refrain from surrendering to alleged masters any persons who may come within your lines," the secretary explained, but at the same time "you will permit no interference, by the persons under your command, with the relations of persons held to service under the laws of any state." As northern armies moved down the Atlantic coast, one Union general after another affirmed this distinction and it was reaffirmed in the Mississippi Valley a year and a half after it was first proposed. On December 17, 1862, General Ulysses S. Grant ordered his superintendent of contrabands to employ any "negroes who voluntarily come within the lines of the army." But "in no case," Grant added, "will negroes be forced into the service of the government, or be enticed away from their homes except when it becomes a military necessity." For eighteen months—from August 1861 through December 1862—federal policy remained the same: slaves within Union lines were emancipated, but they were never "enticed."[37]

Beneath the surface continuity of these official orders lay significant changes in the actual practice of self-emancipation. By late 1861 "voluntary" entry into Union lines had come to mean any slave who remained after the masters fled before the arrival of an invading Union army. With the passage of the Second Confiscation Act slaves of all rebels within the lines of Union occupation were emancipated, at least in theory, whether or not their masters had fled. It remained "self-emancipation" however, because Union troops were still technically forbidden to entice slaves away their plantations. To be sure, even that restriction was giving way by late 1862. In Louisiana, General Butler hoped that by offering wages to freed people on abandoned plantations enough slaves on nearby farms would be attracted away from their owners to force a general transition to free labor. Nevertheless as late as February in 1863, Grant was still warning his officers that "the enticing of negroes to leave their homes to come within the lines of the army is positively forbidden." That was the last such order Grant ever issued.[38]

A careful observer might have seen this coming. By the middle of 1862 the advocates of a more aggressive antislavery policy were answering Lincoln's skepticism by arguing that a presidential proclamation would entice slaves into Union lines and thereby undermine the rebellion. "You must weaken the enemy by depriving him of the service of the negro," one citizen advised the president. "This can be easily done, promise them freedom & they will come to you by the 100,000." Aware of the mysterious workings of the "grapevine telegraph" among slaves, many northerners counted on the slaves to spread news of an emancipation proclamation among themselves. Frederick Law Olmsted made the point when, in October of 1862, he urged President Lincoln to print up thousands of copies of his Preliminary Proclamation and let them circulate throughout the South. The "negroes would pass them from plantation to plantation," Olmsted predicted, thereby ensuring that escaping slaves "would come to the hands of the class of men whom it is so desirable, and now so difficult to reach." Benjamin Bannan, editor of a small Pennsylvania newspaper, assured Lincoln that the "Slaves would learn the decree nearly if not quite as soon as their Masters." A presidential proclamation would prompt a mass exodus of slaves, slavery itself would collapse, and with it the rebellion. Enticement was the answer to Lincoln's skepticism.[39]

The Emancipation Proclamation lifted the ban on enticement and instead made it the explicit policy of the Union army in the disloyal states. "Henceforth," Lincoln's secretary explained on January 2, 1863, the slave population will be used to suppress to rebellion "as rapidly as it can be brought within the Union lines." "It is the policy of this Government," General in Chief Halleck explained to Grant in March, "to withdraw from the enemy as much productive labor as possible." Union troops must never "discourage the Negroes from coming under our protection." This "is not only bad policy in itself," Halleck explained, "but is directly opposed to the policy adopted by the Government." The "character" of the war has changed, Halleck added. The "policy now adopted" by the government is "to withdraw from the use of the enemy all the slaves you can."[40]

To promote the new policy, the War Department issued fifteen thousand copies of the Emancipation Proclamation as General Orders No. 1, for distribution throughout the army. Various state and local agencies in the North printed booklet-sized versions of the proclamation for soldiers to carry with them into the South. The State Department printed miniature copies of the proclamation that could be folded away and tucked into a pocket. Various private companies likewise printed different versions of the proclamation in editions ranging in quality from elaborate posters suitable for framing to handbills that could be easily and widely distributed. The point of distributing the proclamation was, at least in part, to get the "grape-vine telegraph" clicking among slaves. Isaac Lane recalled the "studious effort" the slaveholders made to keep word of the Emancipation Proclamation from his fellow slaves. "But it could not be done," Lane wrote. "[T]here were too many Negroes who were able to read and understand the trend of affairs." Yet the various printed editions of the proclamation were intended less for the slaves than for Union soldiers, especially their officers. Union troops were not expected to entice slaves by reading the proclamation aloud. Instead, the War Department organized a cadre of 237 agents specifically authorized to go onto southern farms and plantations, where they announced to slaves that they had been freed by presidential proclamation.[41]

The highest-ranking "agent" of emancipation was Adjutant General Lorenzo Thomas, dispatched by Secretary of War Stanton to the Mississippi Valley in late March with orders to oversee implementation of the new policy. Thomas was assigned several tasks. He was to "secure" the "humane and proper treatment" of "that class of population known as contrabands." He was to meet with General Grant and his officers "and explain to them the importance attached by the Government to the use of the colored population emancipated by the President's proclamation, and particularly for the organization of their labor and military strength." Specifically, Thomas was to warn Union officers and soldiers that "any obstacle thrown in the way" of this policy would be regarded by the president as a violation of the acts of Congress and the purposes of the government. Stanton charged Thomas with recruiting and commissioning white officers who were willing to assume command of black troops.[42]

Thomas proved remarkably diligent and effective in carrying out his instructions. In a speech at Lake Providence, Louisiana, on April 8, 1863, he explained the logic of enticement to Union troops. The Confederates were able to send a large proportion of military-age men into battle because the slaves remained behind "for the raising of subsistence for their armies in the field." To undermine this Confederate advantage, the Lincoln administration "has determined to take from the rebels this source of supply—to take their Negroes, and compel them to send back a portion of their whites to cultivate their deserted plantations." The Confederates "must do this," Thomas added, "or their armies will starve." Accordingly, slaves coming into your lines should not only be welcomed, they "are to be encouraged to come to us." Thomas reiterated the point several weeks later in a letter to General William Rosecrans. By depriving the rebels of their slaves we weaken the enemy while we "add to our own strength. They are to be encouraged to come within our lines," Thomas ordered. Lincoln was so impressed with Thomas's recruitment of black soldiers that by July he concluded that "General Thomas is one of the best, if not the very best, instruments for this service."[43]

On April 11, 1863, less than two weeks after receiving his new instructions from Halleck, Grant reversed his earlier prohibition on enticement and instead directed General Frederick Steele, at Milliken's Bend, Louisiana, to "encourage all negroes, particularly middle-aged males, to come within our lines." For Grant the new policy fit neatly into a broader shift toward "hard war" that began in mid-1862 and was implemented most fully under his command in the western theater. *Hard war* meant several different things, including the widespread resort to foraging to feed Union armies on the march through Confederate territory, as well as the systematic destruction of railroads, factories, and stores that might otherwise be used to sustain the Confederate war effort. In the spring of 1863, Grant began issuing orders that folded enticement of slaves into the practice of hard war. On May 26, for example, he instructed Brigadier General Peter J. Osterhaus to "let" his cavalry "destroy all the railroad bridges as far out as they go" beyond the Black River. "All forage" beyond the river "should be destroyed. All negroes, teams, and cattle," Grant concluded, "should be brought in." In June, Grant ordered Lieutenant Colonel Samuel Nasmith, near Vicksburg, to "bring away all negroes disposed to follow you." Similar orders were issued by other generals. "[B]ring in all able-bodied negroes that choose to come," General Stephen A. Hurlbut instructed one of his own generals in LaGrange,

Tennessee, in mid-May. "It is hard warfare," Hurlbut admitted, "but my orders from General Halleck are to pursue this course."[44]

It is from this point in the war that evidence of truly large numbers of slaves "collected" or "captured" by Union troops begins to appear in official reports as well as in the letters and diaries of individual soldiers. In early June, General Hurlbut reported to Halleck from Memphis that in a recent skirmish his men "killed and wounded 60, captured 150 prisoners, 500 horses and mules, 200 negroes, burned cotton factories. . . ." A few days later a colonel near Holly Springs "brought in 50 negroes" after another skirmish. At almost the same moment but hundreds of miles away on the southern Atlantic coast, Union Colonel Robert Gould Shaw was sent on an expedition to Darien, Georgia, "taking all the negroes to be found, and burning every planter's house" along the way. Some orders maintained the distinction between loyal and disloyal areas. For as long as he remained in Tennessee, Major John Henry was ordered not to disturb private property, "but in Mississippi you will seize all the horses and mules and able-bodied male negroes that you can find."[45]

Slaveholders in the path of the Union army felt the impact of the new enticement policy. From the earliest weeks of the war they had been ruefully recording the escapes of individual slaves who ran away as soon as Union forces approached, but not until the middle of 1863 did southern masters begin noting the wholesale capture of large numbers of slaves. At Greenwood Plantation in South Carolina the overseer's journal traced the approach of the Union army in its campaign to capture Charleston. On June 2, 1863, the Yankees moved up the Combahee River, burning plantation homes, mills, and crops as they went. "Middleton's Place at the Ferry they burned," the overseer wrote. "House and Mills, Carrying off all of the Negroes," 180 from one plantation and 270 from another. Two days later "they landed at Blufton and had it in ashes, they brought Negroes each time with them." There were "750 negroes carried off" as the Yankees continued up the Combahee River. Comparable reports appeared throughout the second half of the war, wherever the Union army approached. "The Yankees lately made a Raid," one Alabama planter wrote in October of 1864. They "committed great destruction of property & carried off over 800 negroes. I begin to fear that we are not safe."[46]

The systematic enticement of slaves reached its peak during General William Tecumseh Sherman's various "marches" through the Deep South. Sherman himself was contemptuous of blacks, had little interest in emancipation beyond its military utility, and resisted constant pressure from Washington to enlist blacks into the army. Yet by the end of the Meridian Campaign, five thousand freed men and women were trailing Sherman's army. Another ten thousand accompanied him on the march to Savannah in late 1864, and seven thousand more joined Sherman's men as they marched through South Carolina. "We burn every thing," one Iowa soldier wrote as Sherman's army pushed from Atlanta to the sea, "& took all the Horses Mules & Niggars that we came acrost." Another of Sherman's men boasted that along the march they "[d]estroyed all we could not eat, stole their niggers, burned their cotton & gins, spilled their sorghum, burned & twisted their R. Roads and raised Hell generally as you know an army can when 'turned loose.'"[47] The numbers of slaves freed by coming within Union lines during Sherman's various marches dwarfed the number of emancipations that had taken place earlier in the war.

The goal of the new emancipation policy was to transfer the productive labor of the slaves from the Confederacy to the Union, but many northerners were aware that enticement would further undermine the rebellion by sowing discontent among slaves who remained on southern farms and plantations. One Republican editor predicted that long before Union troops actually penetrated the Deep South, thousands of slaves would hear about the Emancipation Proclamation and "would refuse to work" and "demand wages." In turn "thousands in the Rebel Armies would go home to protect their families

and to take care of the negroes." The Confederate forces will be deci-
mated, "and as our Armies approached freedom would be declared to
the Slaves." With that "the Power of the Rebels would be broken."
The non-slaveholders "would immediately spring up to support the
Government—and the Rebellion so far as fighting, would be at an
end." Slaves might run away, or they might go on strike, but either
way the Confederacy would be deprived of its main source of labor
and the slaveholders' rebellion would quickly collapse. Union generals sometimes acted on the same assumption. In Louisiana, Butler
believed that if wages were offered to freed people on abandoned
plantations, the slaves on nearby farms would quit their owners
unless they, too, were paid for their labors. Blacks who chose to
return to their homes could help the Union cause, Grant argued, "by
spreading dissatisfaction among the negroes at a distance by telling
that the Yankees set them all free." Enticement was designed to take
advantage of the disruptive potential of slave resistance.[48]

If "spreading dissatisfaction" was one of the goals of enticement,
the new policy seems to have succeeded. Plantation mistresses complained that when the masters and overseers went off to war, the slaves
became insolent and "saucy." The approach of the Union army invariably set off a wave of escapes, especially among young unmarried
men, and the slaves who stayed behind often demanded shorter hours,
improved working conditions, and better rations. House servants
refused to perform menial chores. Some slaves refused to be whipped;
often mistresses dared not use the lash for fear of the reaction it might
now provoke. As conditions on farms and plantations deteriorated,
women wrote desperate letters to their husbands and sons, begging
them to leave the army and return home to restore order—precisely as
antislavery northerners had predicted. Several scholars have attributed
Confederate defeat to the "internal" collapse of southern society, but
the fact that Union policymakers were trying to disrupt the internal
workings of the slave regime suggests that the distinction between

"internal" and "external" causes of Confederate collapse may be artificial. The slaveholders understood as much. Six months after the proclamation was issued, a South Carolina planter explained the new Union policy as well as anyone in the Lincoln administration. We are dealing with an "Enemy," Louis Manigault wrote, "whose only aim is to spread desolation and ruin over our land." He cited the two Union policies designed for that purpose: "to arm our own Negroes against their very Masters; and entice by every means this misguided Race to assist them in their diabolical program."[49]

Lincoln's proclamation had profoundly altered both the nature and the scale of emancipation in the rebellious states. The war on the ground was looking more and more like a revolutionary upheaval, and the clearest indication of the change was Lincoln's announcement, toward the end of the Emancipation Proclamation, that in addition to being freed, enslaved black men were to be armed, uniformed, and sent into battle against their former masters.[50]

BLACK TROOPS

Prominent black leaders and radical abolitionists argued from the earliest months of the war that the surest way to suppress the rebellion was to let blacks join the fight. As Frederick Douglass noted, black men had a powerful interest in the outcome of the war, and slaves had the most powerful interest of all, for they would be fighting for their own freedom. You can let slave laborers work for the Confederates and thus sustain the rebellion, Douglass argued, or you can arm slave men and thus transform them into revolutionary agents for the overthrow of the slaveholders' regime. He was not alone. Free blacks across the North offered their military services as soon as the war began, but for more than a year—long after the federal government had begun emancipating slaves—the Lincoln administration rejected all such offers of black service in the Union army, in part because there were legal obstacles that had to be removed.[51]

Lincoln himself was more willing to emancipate slaves than to enlist blacks in the Union army. Like many Americans Lincoln wondered whether men reared in bondage could become good soldiers. Raised within the terrors of slavery, schooled in fear, slaves—or so many northerners worried—would make for a sullen and cowardly armed force for the same reason they were a sullen and undisciplined labor force. More than that, though, Lincoln feared a white backlash, particularly in the Border States. As late as August of 1862, he told a delegation of visitors that "the nation could not afford to lose Kentucky at this crisis, and gave it as his opinion that to arm the negroes would turn 50,000 bayonets from the loyal Border States against us that were for us."[52] By the time Lincoln wrote those words, however, the connection between military emancipation and military service was already being established. Like wartime emancipation, the history of black enlistment in the Union army is a tale of gradual evolution as much as sudden transformation.

At Fortress Monroe in July of 1861, General Benjamin Butler linked emancipation to the willingness of freed men and women to work for the Union army in return for wages. Wouldn't it be better to emancipate the fugitives and pay them to work for the U.S. military, Butler wondered, than to return them to an enemy who would put them back to work as slaves? Over the ensuing months the connection between emancipation and labor for the army was reinforced as more and more northerners—especially Republican policymakers—interpreted the readiness of blacks to work for the Union as evidence that the slaves were the most reliably "loyal" people in the South. This made the transition from work *for* the army to work *in* the army relatively smooth. Black men who had escaped to Union lines often earned their wages by digging trenches and building fortifications. The first moves to enlist black men into the Union army built on that record. In July of 1862, Congress authorized the president to enlist black men "for the purpose of constructing intrenchments, or performing camp service, or any other labor, or military or naval service, for which they may be competent."[53]

The first authorized black regiments were organized shortly after Congress lifted the ban on blacks in the army. On August 22, General Butler ordered the enlistment of a regiment of free black soldiers known as the Louisiana "Native Guards" only months after he had repudiated a similar effort by General John Phelps. The same thing happened in South Carolina. In May, General David Hunter had tried to organize a unit of black troops in the Sea Islands, but his heavy-handed approach alienated blacks and abolitionists alike, and with no support from the War Department, Hunter was forced to disband the unit. In July, Congress lifted the ban on black enlistment, and by late October, Hunter's successor, General Rufus Saxton, was explicitly authorized by the War Department to begin enlisting freed men into what became the First South Carolina Volunteers. In early November, Saxton invited a prominent northern abolitionist, Thomas Wentworth Higginson, to assume command of the troops. There were similar moves in Kansas during the latter half of 1862. These early initiatives, however, were local and uncoordinated until Lincoln formally authorized the general enlistment and arming of black men on January 1, 1863.[54]

The Emancipation Proclamation went a step beyond the Militia Act of the previous July. The statute mentioned only physical labor—"constructing intrenchments, or performing camp service"—whereas Lincoln authorized the enlistment of black men into the "armed service" of the United States "to garrison forts, positions, stations, and other places, and to man vessels of all sorts in said service." Once the president had authorized the enlistment of blacks into the "armed service" it was but one last step to the deployment of black soldiers in combat. At the end of March, General in Chief Henry Halleck instructed General Grant to use black soldiers "for the defence of forts, depts.,&c," as indicated in the president's proclamation, but then added that "they can also be used as a military force." Within months black troops were proving themselves in battles at Port Hudson and then Milliken's Bend on the Mississippi River and, heroically but catastrophically, at Battery Wagner in South Carolina.[55]

Once authorized by the proclamation, black enlistment began swiftly, accelerated steadily, and became increasingly organized. On January 13, 1863, Secretary of War Stanton authorized General Daniel Ullman "to raise a brigade (of four regiments) of Louisiana volunteer infantry." They would serve three-year enlistments or the duration of the war. Exactly the same order went out, on exactly the same day, to Colonel James Montgomery, instructing him to raise "a regiment of South Carolina volunteer infantry." Two days later the adjutant general authorized the governor of Rhode Island to raise "an infantry regiment of volunteers of African descent." On January 26, Stanton himself authorized Governor John Andrew of Massachusetts to do the same. These last instructions to northern governors would eventually produce a regiment of free blacks from several northern states that became famous as the Massachusetts Fifty-Fourth. By the end of January, General Saxton was reporting the successful organization of the First Regiment of South Carolina Volunteers and urging his superiors in Washington to let the men prove themselves in battle, thus "giving them a chance to strike a blow for the country and their own liberty."[56]

Yet despite the alacrity with which blacks were recruited, the Union army never treated them as the equal of white soldiers. Black regiments were strictly segregated and nearly always commanded by whites. At the outset, black soldiers were paid—when they were paid at all—at a lower rate than white soldiers. Not until June of 1864 did Congress abolish the distinction in pay for black and white soldiers. Even after that, most black soldiers found the traditional avenues to promotion blocked. Long after they had proved themselves in combat, black regiments were often relegated to garrison duty or manual labor. Meanwhile Confederate captors refused to treat black soldiers as legitimate prisoners of war. Former slaves captured in uniform were to be re-enslaved, their officers were to be executed, and though the Confederate government did not officially sanction mass executions it did almost nothing to punish the southern troops who massacred black prisoners.

Hoping to thwart the mistreatment of black prisoners, Lincoln issued an order of retaliation in July of 1863, and subsequently halted all prisoner exchanges until the Confederates agreed to treat black Union soldiers as legitimate prisoners of war. Halleck urged Grant to use his influence and prestige to combat racial "prejudice" within the Union army, and in speech after speech, Lorenzo Thomas warned white soldiers that they would be punished for racial intolerance. Racial prejudice within the ranks did seem to diminish. White soldiers who were initially hostile to black troops often came to admire them.[57]

IN THE LAST CABINET MEETINGS to put the finishing touches on the final proclamation, Treasury Secretary Chase had urged Lincoln to remove the paragraph lifting the ban on enlistment in the Union army. Chase supported black enlistment but didn't think it belonged in the Emancipation Proclamation. Lincoln, however, was already beginning to grasp the connection between emancipation and black troops. He understood that to destroy slavery, the Union had to win the war, and he came to believe that black troops would help make that happen. Indeed, by late 1863 both Lincoln and Grant were convinced that black troops were indispensable to northern victory. Black soldiers were a double blessing to the Union cause, Lincoln said, because every slave recruited added as much strength to the northern armies as he subtracted from the South's productive capacity. Grant told Lincoln that emancipation and black troops had definitively shifted the tide of the war against the Confederacy. Historians generally concur. Approximately 180,000 black men eventually served in the Union army. By the last year of the war there were as many as 100,000 blacks in uniform at one time, accounting for nearly 20 percent of the military's fighting force. To have deprived the Union war effort of that many troops, in 1864, would have been devastating. Indispensable to northern victory, black troops were thus indispensable to slavery's destruction.[58]

AN ARMY OF LIBERATION

On May, 7, 1864, a Union army recruiter named James Ayers rode onto a plantation ten miles outside of Huntsville, Alabama, and into a field where twenty-seven slaves were gathering corn. "Whose farm is this?" Ayers asked.

"Master Eldridges, sir."

"Is that his house yonder?"

"Yes, massa."

"Is he good to you?"

"Not mighty good massa?"

"Is he A union man or secessionist?"

After telling Ayers that their master "swares and cusses the yanks terribly," the slaves hurried back to their work lest their master "flog us [if] he see us idle" and "whip us for talking with you." Ayers reassured them. "I have come to tell you good news," he said. "Father Abraham has declared you all free[;] you have no master now. You are free and I have come to tell you." Getting down from his horse, Ayers began to distribute leaflets depicting on one side Union soldiers freeing slaves and, on the other, announcing that "[a]ll Slaves were made Freemen by Abraham Lincoln" and urging "able-bodied colored men" to come to the nearest Union camp and "fight for the Stars and Stripes!" Ayers made his pitch. The army would pay ten dollars a month, plus food and clothing, "and make you free if you will inlist and be soaldiers. How many of you boys will Turn out?" Ayers asked.

"When do you want us?"

"Want you Rite now."

"Oh massa wont let us go."

"Never mind your master," Ayers protested, "you have none." Ayers then rode up to the house where he understood there were more potential recruits, and there he met the Eldridge family, "Master, Missus and galls."

"How do you do," Ayers said, "fine day this is."

"Yes," Mr. Eldridge answered, "what's all this mean? My niggers say you Come into the field and set them all free, is that so?"

"Yes sir."

"Well I would like to know how you got the authority to do so, Sir."

"By the War Department, sir, I get my Autherity, the verry best of Autherity aint it."

"What do you want with my niggers?" Eldridge demanded.

"Your niggers," Ayers replied, "you've got no niggers my dear sir. These are all free men as you or I am and thease women here that have been your Slaves are all free now as much so as this Lady."

Eldridge then invited Ayers to leave, but the Union recruiter was hardly finished. "Leave," Ayers said, "why sir I will leave when I get Ready. But I am going to take your men or thease men when I go. You may bet you Eyes on that." Ayers then drew his revolver and continued the lecture. "I shall not hurt a hair of your head, sir, if you be quiet, but I have Come for your Darkeys and your Darkeys I'll have."

"Mister," one of Eldridge's daughters asked, "are you going to take dads niggers Away from him wether they are willing or no?"

"Well no mam I aint," Ayers replied. "But I'll tell you what I am going to do." In his experience, Ayers explained, he had found it best to walk off with the young black men a half mile or so and "have a big talk with them" to see if he could persuade them to enlist in the Union army. Those he "cant coax" would be sent back. Eldridge's daughter next suggested that Ayers allow her father to speak with the men before they walk off, but the recruiting agent thought that was a bad idea. Ayers had his solitary chat with the men, and when he left, he had six black recruits with him. Shortly thereafter they enlisted in the Fifteenth Tennessee Colored Regiment, based in Nashville.[59]

Before he joined the army, James Ayers had been an antislavery preacher in Illinois. The new Union policy of black enlistment offered him an opportunity to put both his preaching skills and his convictions to good use. On May, 22, 1863, the War Department issued General Orders Nos. 143 and 144 establishing a Bureau of Colored Troops and spelling out the guidelines for the appointment of "specially authorized" agents to recruit blacks into the Union army. Lorenzo Thomas was the most well known and arguably the most indefatigable of these recruiting agents, but James Ayers— appointed the following February—was no less committed to the task. From his base of operations in Tennessee, Ayers fanned out across the towns and villages of northern Alabama, tacking recruiting posters to trees and buildings and giving speeches to the groups of slaves he gathered to listen. He had two messages. He told all the slaves that they had been freed under the Emancipation Proclamation, and he told black men that it was their special obligation to serve in the Union army, that they had a powerful interest in fighting not simply for the restoration of the Union but for their own freedom. Eventually nearly 250 agents like Ayers were commissioned to spread word of the Emancipation Proclamation into Union-occupied areas of the South and recruit black men to join the army. By the time their work was done, approximately 146,000 blacks enlisted in the Union army from the slave states.[60]

The private chat that garnered Ayers's six recruits reflected official Union policy: blacks were encouraged but not forced to enlist. Not all Union recruiters, however, were as deferential as Ayers was to the preferences of the potential recruits. As the policy of black enlistment was becoming organized in the spring of 1863, there were increasing complaints against Union soldiers who coerced slaves into the army against their will. For some recruiters this was a straightforward application of the conscription policy that was initiated at the same time in the North, but not everyone saw it that way. In April, Captain Alfred Sears complained of the tactics used by Union troops in Florida who were "enlisting and drafting soldiers for the African Regiments." My men, Sears complained, "*have not been drafted. They have been kidnapped by the night.*" In the area around Norfolk, Virginia, one northern missionary complained, Union soldiers were "making arrests of Colored Citizens . . . for the purpose of compelling them to volunteer in the U.S. Service." In June a Louisiana master denounced the "pressgang" of black soldiers who came onto his plantation "and FORCIBLY removed nearly all the male negroes therefrom." The blacks had already been freed and were working for wages, but that may have made them even more vulnerable to conscription. On the streets of New Orleans, free blacks were "being seized and enlisted in the Army."[61]

Impressment was controversial for a number of reasons. The most common complaint was that conscripting able-bodied black men interfered with the various "experiments" in free labor that were a centerpiece of federal antislavery policy. As black enlistment opened another avenue to emancipation, the two policies sometimes collided with one another. The one sought to validate emancipation by demonstrating that blacks would work more efficiently as free laborers than as slaves; the other, by demonstrating that black men would make good soldiers if only because they were fighting for their own freedom. Conflicts of this sort tended to pit antislavery men against one another. That's what happened on the Sea Islands off South Carolina in May of 1862. Abolitionist General David Hunter began forcibly conscripting blacks from the very plantations where another abolitionist, Edward Pierce, was conducting his "social experiment" in free labor. Such conflicts multiplied a year later after black enlistment began in earnest. In Louisiana, General Ullman complained that "the contract system has been a serious impediment" to his efforts to recruit black troops. Benjamin Flanders replied that if the army impressed blacks into service, "we lose the confidence of the negro" and "we shall labor in vain to secure his services in a profitable working of the plantations." Ullman denounced the contract system as "a virtual rendition of the negro to slavery," but Flanders hurled the same accusation back at Union recruiting agents. "If the negroes are to be impressed," Flanders wrote, "they have lost, not gained," by the Emancipation Proclamation. "They are, nominally, free, but in reality, the most unprotected of serfs." Both were exploiting what was by then a widespread fear of re-enslavement. Major George Stearns, who had been one of the first black recruiting agents in Kentucky and Tennessee, was worried about something else. He urged that "the impressments of Colored men be discontinued" because it interfered with the goal of enticing slaves away from their masters. Impressment, Stearns warned, will "prevent the slaves from running to our lines." Some Union officers disputed the claim that black men should be spared conscription because their labor was needed on the plantations. J. G. Foster, the commander of the Department of the South, insisted that he be allowed to "collect all the men that are capable of carrying arms to fill the ranks," because women and children were perfectly capable of cultivating the fields. In Louisiana, Colonel H. N. Frisbie defended the "peremptory draft" of black men. "The same reasons why these men should not be taken from the plantations here," Frisbie argue, "are equally applicable to Northern farms."[62]

Black enlistment also implied a departure from the policy of emancipating men and women alike, so long as they were employed by the Union army. Black men were initially enlisted into the army to do the same work they had been doing as civilian employees, but in opening the enlistment option to men the new policy also opened a distinction between the way black men and women were emancipated—for the simple reason that black women who worked as cooks and laundresses for Union soldiers could never enlist. As compensation of sorts Republican lawmakers introduced a patriarchal criterion for emancipation. The Militia Act of July 1862 explicitly freed any slave who enlisted in the Union army and at the same time freed "his mother and his wife and children."[63] For the first time the freedom of women and children depended on the freedom of their husbands and fathers. Yet like the exemptions in the Emancipation Proclamation, the patriarchal qualification for freedom was part of a broader Republican effort to expand rather than limit the scope of emancipation. It would have been easier if the Constitution had simply allowed Republicans to pass a law directly abolishing slavery in the southern states. Persuaded that such a law would have been unconstitutional, Republican congressmen resorted instead to a series of legislative flanking maneuvers, attacking slavery in a variety of indirect ways. As the number of roundabout assaults piled up, however, they began to interfere with one another.

In the Border States the different approaches to emancipation tended to merge rather than collide. The enlistment of blacks into the Union army, for example, was an especially potent means of undermining slavery in the loyal slave states. By removing the word *free* from the qualifications for enlistment, the Militia Act of 1862 allowed slaves from loyal slave states to be conscripted. Once the army began recruiting slaves from the Border States shortly after the Emancipation Proclamation was issued, Republicans all but abandoned their offers of compensation to states that abolished slavery on their own. Never again would Lincoln publicly mention federal subsidies for voluntary colonization. Instead, beginning in 1863 the War Department pushed military emancipation directly into the Border States by openly encouraging slaves in loyal areas to enlist and promising them freedom in return. On March 26, 1863, Lincoln wrote to Andrew Johnson, the military governor of Tennessee, urging him to help recruit blacks into the Union army. "The colored population is the great *available* and yet *unavailed* of, force for restoring the Union," Lincoln wrote. "The bare sight of fifty-thousand armed, and drilled black soldiers on the banks of the Mississippi, would end the rebellion at once."[64] This letter is generally cited as evidence of how fully Lincoln had changed his mind about black enlistment over the previous year—and it certainly does show that—but it is scarcely noticed that Johnson was the governor of *Tennessee*, a state Lincoln had exempted from the Emancipation Proclamation three months earlier. In urging the recruitment of Tennessee slaves, all of whom would be freed by virtue of their enlistment, Lincoln was directly undermining slavery in a loyal slave state. Not only would slaves recruited from the loyal states be emancipated, so would their wives, mothers, and children.

The emancipation of soldiers and their families was part of a broader Republican effort to undermine slavery in the Border States. In 1863 the War Department opened recruiting offices for blacks in Maryland, Tennessee, and Missouri. The results were dramatic. Of the 146,000 black men recruited from the slave states, nearly 60 percent—as many as 85,000—enlisted from areas exempted from the Emancipation Proclamation. This was partly the inevitable consequence of the fact that the Union army occupied the loyal areas more or less undisturbed from January 1, 1863, until the end of the war. Four exempted slave states—Kentucky, Maryland, Tennessee, and Missouri—had fewer than 20 percent of the slaves yet provided 40 percent of the black soldiers from the South. With the exception of Mississippi—parts of which were continuously occupied by the Union army from the moment the proclamation was issued—the disloyal states of the Deep South generated relatively few black recruits for the Union army. Some of this may have been due to General Sherman's persistent reluctance to enlist black men during his marches through the cotton states. Some of it may have been caused by the active recruitment of blacks by agents from northern states trying to fill their draft quotas with slaves from the nearby Border States. But for whatever reason, the disparity was stark. Some 5,000 Alabama slaves enlisted, compared to more than 20,000 from neighboring Tennessee. Fewer than 3,500 black Georgians enlisted; more than 23,000 Kentucky blacks did. An astonishing 57 percent (23,703) of Kentucky's eligible black men served in the Union army, compared with a mere 8 percent (5,462) of blacks from South Carolina who were eligible for military service. More astonishing still were the Delaware numbers. The state had fewer than 1,800 slaves in 1860, yet by the end of the war more than 900 blacks from Delaware served in the Union army. Approximately 44,000 black soldiers, comprising nearly one-third of the recruits from the South, came from just two exempted states—Tennessee and Kentucky. For enslaved men in loyal parts of the South, military service provided the clearest path to emancipation for themselves and their families.[65]

Black soldiers in exempted areas became especially aggressive liberators of their fellow slaves. Early in the war, for example, Peter Bruner had tried to escape from his Kentucky master, but when he reached Union lines and told the Union soldiers he wanted to join the army, "they said they did not want any darkies, that this was a white man's war." Bruner tried again in July of 1864, by which time Union policy had changed. He rose early one morning and headed for Camp Nelson, Kentucky, a major center for the Union army's recruitment of black troops. It took him nearly twenty-four hours to make the forty-mile trek, but along the way he met up with sixteen other blacks who, like Bruner, "were on their way to Camp Nelson." When he arrived the Union officers asked him what he wanted. "I told them that I

came here to fight the rebels and that I wanted a gun." When enough
recruits had come into camp a new regiment was formed and on July
25, 1864, Bruner was mustered into service in the Twelfth U.S. Heavy
Artillery. Bruner saw little combat, but if emancipation was part of
the broader effort to suppress the southern rebellion, he and his unit
performed an essential service by "recruiting" slaves off the plantations near his own home. As they moved onto their old farms and
plantations some of the slaves resisted, telling Bruner that "they had
no time for war." Bruner's unit conscripted them anyway, and when
their masters came after them Bruner's unit refused to return the con-
scripts, declaring the slaves "prisoners of war." Other slaves, often in
large numbers, ran to Bruner's unit "for protection." "At one time,"
Bruner recalled, "we sent away five hundred men, women and children to Camp Nelson.[66]

Henry Clay Bruce, himself a former slave, recalled that in
Missouri—another state exempted from the proclamation—"any
slave man who desired to be a soldier and fight for freedom, had an
opportunity to do so." By late 1863 "recruiting officers" from Iowa
were pouring into Missouri looking for black men who might serve as
replacements for white men trying to avoid the draft back home. But
Bruce had "trouble" with the black Missourians once they were
enlisted, because "they thought it no more than right to press in every
young man they could find." Urged on, bribed even, by the Iowa
recruiters, the black troops "scoured the county in search of young
men for soldiers."[67]

In most cases, however, black soldiers did not have to be pressured or bribed into recruiting other blacks into the army. In Tennessee, for example, as soon as Lincoln issued the Emancipation
Proclamation, Samuel Hall decided he would be "permanently safe
with the union army and he went to it." William Wallace, who had
recently paid over eleven hundred dollars for Hall, had already been
warned that the slave "knowed too much." Fearing the worst, Wallace

.

tried to "refugee" his slaves—including Hall's wife and children—southward into Alabama beyond the reach of Union forces. Before the slaves were moved, Sam Hall escaped, joined the army, and quickly returned along with several other soldiers to his old plantation, where they exacted "revenge." The soldiers ordered the "ex-master" to "hitch up his mules, load up his wagon with hams and bacon and include in the load Sam's wife and five children and haul them all over into the union lines." Within a few days Hall's family and several other blacks were on a boat heading northward to freedom as the "old master stood by the side of the river watching tearfully at the disappearance of his $1,125.00."[68] The experience of slaves like Peter Bruner, Henry Clay Bruce, and Samuel Hall suggests that, exemptions notwithstanding, the Emancipation Proclamation made slavery more vulnerable than ever in the loyal slave states that were technically beyond its reach.

IT HAS ALWAYS BEEN TEMPTING to read the text of the Emancipation Proclamation and draw inferences from words about what it did or did not do—that it freed all the slaves, or that it freed no slaves at all. But the proclamation did not explain itself. Lincoln issued it at a specific moment in the long history of the struggle against slavery. Read in the context of decades of abolitionist efforts to legitimate "military emancipation," for example, Lincoln's legalistic tone was a culmination, not a rejection, of the antislavery movement. Read on their own terms the proclamation's exemptions can seem like restrictions on the scope of emancipation; read in light of the antislavery policies in place prior to January 1, 1863, the proclamation dramatically expanded military emancipation into the areas that were previously beyond emancipation's reach. It is impossible to tell, from the text alone, how heavily the Emancipation Proclamation rested on the attorney general's earlier declaration that under the Constitution blacks were full citizens of the United States. Even the most careful reading of the proclamation will not fully explain how federal anti-slavery policy changed after January 1, 1863.

What, then, did the Emancipation Proclamation do? It lifted the ban on the enticement of slaves from their farms and plantations. Beginning in early 1863, Union soldiers systematically invited unprecedented numbers of slaves to claim their freedom by coming into Union lines. It opened the Union army to the enlistment of black soldiers who, for obvious reasons, were among the most enthusiastic liberators. By these means the Emancipation Proclamation transformed Union soldiers, especially black Union soldiers, into an army of liberation. The proclamation greatly intensified the pressure on the Border States. Because the Militia Act of 1862 had eliminated the word *free* from the conditions for enlistment, the Emancipation Proclamation empowered federal recruiters to enlist slaves in the Border States, which they proceeded to do with an aggressiveness that outraged loyal slaveholders.

Yet the Emancipation Proclamation did not transform the "purpose" of the war. Like most Republicans, Lincoln had long insisted that the only constitutional justification for the war was the restoration of the Union, and he continued to say the same thing even after he issued the proclamation. Barely a week into 1863, Lincoln told John McClernand—a political general and a Democrat—that his purpose was unchanged: he would restore the states to their proper place under the Constitution. "For this alone have I felt authorized to struggle; and I seek neither more nor less now." Ten days later Lincoln formally thanked the working men of Manchester, England, for their expression of support, telling them that his "paramount" duty was "to maintain at once the Constitution and the integrity of the federal republic."[69] Lincoln never stopped saying this. In saying it, however, neither he nor his fellow Republicans had ever meant to suggest that the war was caused by anything other than slavery or that slavery was in any way shielded from the war's destructive force. It was always a war for the Union and always a war over slavery.

It was the nature, not the purpose, of the Civil War that changed after January 1, 1863. When the fighting started Republicans defended emancipation as a legitimate means of suppressing the southern insurrection. By 1863 they were saying something slightly but significantly different: emancipation—not of some slaves, but of all of the slaves—had become the necessary condition for the restoration of the Union. As this conviction spread it accustomed both the Union army and the majority of northern voters to the idea that Union victory could be accomplished only by means of the complete destruction of slavery. The Emancipation Proclamation thereby created the political will that would become indispensible to the passage of the Thirteenth Amendment—indispensible because by the end of 1863, a year after Lincoln issued it, Republicans realized that the Emancipation Proclamation would not be enough to destroy slavery forever.

11 "THE SYSTEM YET LIVES"

FOR MORE THAN A YEAR, from the spring of 1862 into the summer of 1863, the progress of federal antislavery policy was substantially shaped by the misfortunes of the Union army in the South. After Grant's capture of Forts Henry and Donelson and Farragut's capture of New Orleans in early 1862, there was not much good news for the Union armed forces. The northern victory at Shiloh was widely viewed as a near disaster caused by Grant's presumed incompetence. McClellan's failure to defeat the Confederates during the Peninsula Campaign had propelled the North's shift to a harder war and with it a harder emancipation policy. That same failure led Lincoln to delay issuing the Emancipation Proclamation for several months, during which the Union forces were defeated for a second time at Bull Run. The "victory" at Antietam that finally prompted Lincoln's announcement was bloody, disappointing, and soon followed by disastrous Union defeats at Fredericksburg in late 1862 and Chancellorsville in early 1863. Yet amid these cascading military disappointments, and in part because of them, the federal government abolished slavery in the nation's capital, excluded it from the western territories, adopted universal emancipation in the seceded states, lifted the ban on enticement, and opened enlistment in the Union army to African American men. Federal antislavery policy seemed to progress most rapidly when Union armies fared most poorly.

The irony reversed itself in the summer of 1863, when spectacular Union victories turned the tide of war in the Union's favor. In the West, after a long and brilliant campaign that ended in a prolonged siege, Grant succeeded in capturing the strategically important city of Vicksburg, Mississippi. As long as the Confederates controlled Vicksburg, they held a choke on the Mississippi River, and Grant had been struggling for months to wrench the southern stranglehold from what Lincoln called the "Father of Waters." Union forces pounded Vicksburg's well-fortified defenses, but to no avail. Grant tried to dig a new channel for the river that would allow his army to slip down past the guns aimed at it, but that failed. Instead, a daring series of nighttime flotillas enabled Grant to move his army downriver past the city and then over to the east bank, where he broke loose from his own supply lines to chase one Confederate army all the way to Jackson and beyond, feeding his soldiers by foraging off the land. When a second Confederate force retreated to the security of the Vicksburg defenses Grant promptly closed off their escape and settled in for the siege. Within weeks the Confederate soldiers, desperate and starving, demanded that their officers surrender and in early July the victorious Yankees entered the city. Shortly thereafter the remaining Confederate strongholds along the river, unable to sustain themselves, likewise surrendered. The Mississippi River was now under the more or less complete control of the Union. Never again would Confederate armies west of the Appalachians regain the momentum. It was one of the most spectacular Union triumphs of the war, yet it was nearly eclipsed by an equally dramatic Union victory in the East.[1]

After his stunning triumph at Chancellorsville Confederate General Robert E. Lee came to believe that his remarkable army could do anything he asked of it, so he asked it to do the impossible. In late June of 1863, as Grant was closing in on Vicksburg a thousand miles away, Lee moved his Army of Northern Virginia across the Potomac into Maryland, launching his second invasion of the North. Cut off from his own supply lines and for a time from his own cavalry, Lee pushed into Pennsylvania and bumped into the Union army, led by the newly appointed General George Gordon Meade, at the small crossroads town of Gettysburg. And there, for three successive days, Union and Confederate troops fought the climactic battle of the Civil War. On July 1 Lee instructed his men to get control of the heights just south of the town, but they failed. On July 2 he ordered simultaneous assaults on the Union right and left, and both assaults failed. Undeterred, Lee ordered General George Pickett to launch a direct attack on the Union center the next day, July 3, and "Pickett's Charge" instantly became synonymous with military disaster. If everything went wrong for the hardened Confederate veterans, the Union soldiers and officers did everything right—seizing control of the heights, taking good advantage of interior lines of communication, fighting ferociously to close any gaps that opened in their own lines, bravely and ingeniously holding off one Confederate advance after another. On July 4 Lee and his devastated army retreated back across the Potomac into Virginia. "Peace," Lincoln said, "does not appear so distant as it did."[2]

The prospect of peace, however, raised a disturbing possibility for Lincoln and the Republicans: the war might end without slavery having been destroyed. They believed that slaves actually freed by the war—that is, slaves who had come within Union lines one way or another and been "practically" emancipated—were free forever. But most slaves never left their farms and plantations, and in that sense most were never actually freed. There were a dozen reasons why military emancipation could never reach the majority of slaves, but a few stand out. For one thing, as the Union began freeing slaves the Confederacy took countermeasures that successfully prevented thousands from reaching Union lines and inhibited countless others from making the attempt. Then, too, the Union army was overwhelmed by military emancipation and was never able to care adequately for the huge numbers of freed men and women who ended up within its lines. The slaves themselves had reasons to be cautious about attempting to escape. Beyond the threat of severe Confederate retaliation and the inability of the Union army to provide adequately for the contrabands, escape was often difficult—even lethal—especially for parents with children or the elderly. Many chose to stay, but most never got to choose because the Union army never came close enough to them to make successful escape possible. Here was the last and arguably the most important reason why military emancipation could not free most slaves: slavery itself was simply too big. There were too many slaves on too many farms spread out over too many square miles.

With four million slaves in 1860, the South was by far the largest slave society in the world, possibly the largest in the history of the world. At the height of its strength, ancient Rome never counted more than two million slaves on the Italian peninsula. After the southern United States, the largest slave society in the Americas was Brazil, with fewer than half as many slaves. Cuba was next, with under a million slaves. Not only did the South's slave population dwarf all others, its sheer expanse all but defied military conquest. Spread across two-thirds of the continent, slavery reached all the way from Wilmington, Delaware, to Brownsville, Texas. It took a vast and powerful Union army four years of brutal war to defeat the Confederates—but not even the victorious Yankees could field enough men to physically reach and emancipate more than a fraction of the slaves in the immense southern empire.

At the end of the Civil War fewer than 15 percent of the slaves in the rebellious states had actually been freed. These were military emancipations. What would happen to the others once the fighting stopped? Indeed, could Lincoln or anyone else really be sure that slaves freed by the war would never be re-enslaved? The spectacular successes of the Union armies in the summer of 1863 forced Lincoln and the Republicans to realize the shortcomings of military emancipation. It was brutal. It would not free all the slaves. And it might not free any of them forever.

THE CONFEDERATE COUNTERATTACK

Slavery has been tolerated in all manner of societies throughout human history, Lincoln observed, but the Confederacy was the first nation whose "primary, and fundamental object [is] to maintain, enlarge, and perpetuate human slavery." The slaveholders had sound reasons for creating their own nation. A very real threat to slavery—a revolutionary threat—had emerged when abolitionists built a successful political movement on the proposition that there was no such thing as a constitutional right of property in slaves. When the slaveholders seceded in defense of their rights, the "counter-revolution of property" began. Protecting slavery was the raison d'etre of the Confederate States of America. Even the treaties regulating the relations between the Confederate government and the Indian nations within its borders had to be renegotiated to reflect proslavery ideals: each new treaty declared, in nearly identical language, that "the institution of slavery in the said nation is legal and has existed from time immemorial." The Confederate nation was conceived in slavery and dedicated to the proposition that it would last forever.[3]

The Confederate constitution advertised its proslavery character in a point-by-point repudiation of antislavery constitutionalism. Where Lincoln and the Republicans denied that the U.S Constitution protected slavery as a right of property, the Confederate constitution expressly recognized "the right of property in said slaves." On the principle that the North was "free soil," northern courts and legislatures had severely limited the right of southern masters to "sojourn" in their states. Confederates responded with a constitution protecting the slaveholders' "right of transit and sojourn in any State of this Confederacy, with their slaves and other property." Several northern states had passed personal liberty laws in an attempt to limit the reach of the fugitive slave clause, but the Confederate constitution protected the right to recapture fugitive slaves in any state despite "any law or regulation therein." Republicans argued that the federal government had every right to ban slavery from the territories, so the Confederate constitution not only empowered its government to "acquire new territory" but also declared that "the institution of slavery, as it now exists in the Confederate States, shall be recognized and protected by Congress and the territorial government." It is hardly surprising, then, that from the founding charter of the proslavery nation, down through state constitutions, state laws, and local police regulations, the Confederacy threw all of its legal weight behind a concerted effort to thwart slave rebellion, which the Yankees euphemistically called "emancipation."[4]

The official Confederate view was that there was no meaningful distinction between "emancipation" and "servile insurrection." There was some exaggeration in this—Republicans had no wish to repeat the "horrors" of the Haitian Revolution—but it wasn't all hyperbole. Union antislavery policy depended on the willingness of slaves to claim their own freedom in various ways—by running to Union lines, by offering to work for the Union army, and eventually by taking up arms against their former masters. Maybe this wasn't Haiti, but surely the slaveholders can be excused for calling it slave rebellion and for demanding that their government do what was necessary to suppress it. Throughout the southern war for independence major

Confederate policies were invariably justified as a defense against slave uprisings or denounced for failing to protect white southerners against the atrocities of servile insurrection. It was in the nature of the Confederacy that this should be so.

Southern policymakers observed the evolution of Union antislavery policies with increasing horror and at the same time saw it as proof of what they had always claimed: the Yankees were stirring up slave insurrection. The riotous behavior of blacks on the Sea Islands in the wake of Union occupation in November of 1861 was proof, Jefferson Davis declared, that the purpose of the Union invasion was "to incite a servile insurrection in our midst." The following month when Lincoln's first secretary of war, Simon Cameron, proposed enlisting blacks in the Union army, Virginia's Governor John Letcher saw another effort to "incite them to hostility against their masters and the destruction of their families." North Carolina's Zebulon Vance read Lincoln's Preliminary Emancipation Proclamation of September 1862 as evidence that the South's "[a]bolition foes" were determined "to re-enact the horrors of Santo Domingo"—Haiti, again—"and to let loose the hellish passions of servile insurrection to revel in the desolation of our homes." As always, Jefferson Davis agreed. It was now Union policy to "wrest" the slaves from their owners, he declared, "and thus to inflict on the non-combatant population of the Confederate States all the horrors of servile war." Lincoln's Emancipation Proclamation sealed the case. With "the late proclamation of the tyrant and usurper," announced Confederate General Gideon Pillow in January of 1863, the Union was "proposing to free all our slaves and taking them into his Army, and inciting them to insurrection and massacre of their owners and their families." Rhetoric of this sort strikes modern readers as extreme, but only because the North eventually won the war and successfully abolished slavery. Among slave owners who had been born and raised in the antebellum South, for whom slavery was justified by the annals of history, the laws of nature, and the will of God, for those men and women Lincoln's proclamation was nothing less than a shattering descent into barbarism. The defense of the Confederacy was the defense of civilization itself.[5]

Yet the clarity of the Confederacy's purpose—the defense of slavery—masked the contradictions at its core. The one policy that might have allowed the Confederates to win their independence, for example, was all but foreclosed. Slave societies throughout history have strategically emancipated some slaves to secure military victory and thereby ensure that slavery itself would survive. But the southern Confederacy was created for the purpose of protecting slavery. To emancipate slaves was to violate the fundamental premise of the Confederacy's existence. Not until the closing weeks of the war did the Confederate Congress offer to emancipate a minuscule number of slaves who might fight to ensure southern independence and with it the permanent survival of slavery. Even then the point was not to abolish slavery but to preserve it. What was true of Union policy was no less true of Confederate policy: emancipation was not the same thing as abolition. The would-be southern nation, precisely because it was a proslavery nation, deprived itself of one of the most powerful weapons at its disposal, an army of slaves fighting for their own freedom.[6]

Where Union emancipation policy reinforced the goal of restoring the Union by undermining the Confederacy, the twin impulses that drove the southern war effort—the need to secure independence and the need to protect slavery—never quite meshed. The most famous example was the planter exemption, which immunized one white adult male from conscription in the Confederate army on any plantation with twenty or more slaves. The exemption was deemed necessary to suppress servile insurrection for, as South Carolina's planter-politician James Chesnut argued, "[t]he masters or owners of negroes in this State are, for the most part, now in the Army." Drafting the overseers who remained, Governor Joseph E. Brown of Georgia warned, would leave the plantations—not to mention the "peace and safety of helpless women and children"—to the mercy of "bands of idle slaves, who must be left to roam over the country without restraint." Brown likewise resisted the conscription of those serving in Georgia's militia because they were indispensable to "the suppression of servile insurrection which our insidious foe now proclaims to the world that it is his intention to incite." Yet if the planter exemption was essential to the defense of slavery, it only exacerbated the tensions between slaveholders and non-slaveholders. Small farmers, many of them primed by decades of hostility to the disproportionate political power of the planters, denounced the exemption as evidence that the conflict with the North was a "rich man's war, but a poor man's fight."[7]

The impressment of slaves by the Confederate government had equally ambiguous implications. It was clear from the earliest weeks of the war that the Confederacy could not sustain itself without the impressed labor of thousands of slaves. Yet almost immediately Confederate impressment became the catalyst for the Union's wartime attack on slavery. Benjamin Butler's original contraband policy was prompted by the fact that if he returned the slaves to their owners they would be put to work on Confederate fortifications. From that moment on stories of Confederate troops using impressed slave labor stoked the fires of northern antislavery sentiment. It became a cycle: the more slave labor the Confederates impressed the more determined the Yankees became to free the slaves and instead impress them into service for the Union. Soon enough the Confederates justified mass impressment as a means of keeping slaves away from the emancipating hands of Union troops. "Our able-bodied negro men are now being conscripted into the army of the enemy," one southerner wrote to the Confederate inspector general in August of 1863. To "prevent more of our slaves from being appropriated by the enemy," he suggested, "we should ourselves bring their services into requisition." Slaves would not be enlisted as Confederate soldiers, but they could easily serve the Confederates as "wagoners, pioneers, sappers and miners, &c." The Union army naturally responded in kind. By the end of the war both sides were ruthlessly exploiting the labor of tens of thousands of black men impressed into the dangerous and demoralizing work of draining swamps, digging ditches, and building fortifications.[8]

But Confederate impressments prompted the hostility of slaveholders whose loyalty to the southern cause was driven by their desire to protect their slave property, certainly not to hand it over to government authorities who had no personal stake in taking care of it. Eventually the slaveholders' resistance to impressments forced the Confederate government to compensate southern masters for any loss of slave property, even as those same masters were sending their sons off to die for the Confederacy without so much as a hint of compensation. Of course, sons were family members whose lives could not be measured in dollars and cents. Slaves were personal property; almost by definition they were available for the right price.[9]

Because impressed slaves were most often sent to work on Confederate lines they were particularly susceptible to enticement by nearby Yankee troops. The problem became acute in 1863 when the federal government began actively enlisting able-bodied black men for armed service in the Union army. Thereafter Confederates made concerted efforts to keep such men a safe distance from northern recruiters. As one Confederate general pointed out, "Every sound black male left for the enemy becomes a soldier we have afterward to fight." In August of 1864, Confederate General Joseph E. Johnston ordered his subordinates to "bring off all male negroes of military age in danger of falling into the enemy's hands." In response, the governor of Mississippi warned that Johnston's orders were counterproductive, for rather than keeping slaves from the Yankees' impressment they prompted slaves to "fly to the enemy." The state legislature resolved that Confederate impressments would "hasten the very evil this order is intended to prevent." Johnston could not deny the validity of his critics' claim. "We have never been able to keep the impressed negroes with an army near the enemy," Johnston explained. "They desert." Rather than return control of impressed slaves to their owners, however, Johnston urged the Confederate Congress to overrule the Mississippi legislature by giving his army full power to remove slaves from out of the way of Union troops.[10]

At issue between General Johnston and the Mississippi legislature was the authority of states versus the central government to determine how best to protect the slaveholders' interests. In the broadest sense protecting slavery was the first responsibility of the Confederate government in Richmond; nothing would ensure slavery's survival as effectively as a successful war for southern independence. Yet in many ways individual southern states were better prepared to meet the specific challenge of thwarting emancipation. Policing slavery had always been the responsibility of state and local governments. So in addition to all the peacetime laws and policies aimed at thwarting escape and punishing runaways, southern states administered even stronger doses of repression to meet the contingencies of war. Early in the war the Georgia legislature passed a law prescribing the death penalty for any slave found guilty of sabotaging any part of the state's railroad system. Other state legislatures passed draconian laws authorizing private citizens to shoot-to-kill any slave attempting to escape to Union lines.[11]

Because slavery was ultimately policed locally, towns and counties across the South beefed up their militias, organized Home Guards, and stepped up slave patrols. State officials and private citizens alike often petitioned authorities in Richmond to exempt from conscription particular individuals who had proved themselves indispensable to the policing of slavery. Alfred W. Kidd of Lowndes County, Mississippi, was so diligent "in Police duty amongst the slaves" that his neighbors asked that he be exempted from conscription. Owners of dogs who specialized in capturing runaways were especially valued by the locals. William Hatton, for example, owned "a pack of negro dogs and has heretofore employed himself catching runaways." Hatton's neighbors declared that "his character for firmness and decision in the management of Slaves is so notorious . . . as to exercise a very salutary restraining influence on their conduct." Twenty-seven citizens of Dallas County, Alabama, likewise petitioned to exempt Archibald Berrey from the draft on the grounds that he was "the only one that [has] a pack of dogs any where in reach for the purpose of catching negroes."[12]

Where policing proved inadequate there was always terror. The slaveholders had never been squeamish about suppressing slave insurrection, but with the war they redoubled their efforts. Instances of wartime terror would loom large in the autobiographies freed men and women later wrote about their experience of slavery. Years afterward Harry Smith recalled the fate of twelve of his fellow slaves who were caught "giving information" to the Yankees about the whereabouts of pro-Confederate guerillas. "The men were taken down to salt river, a hole cut in the ice and they were singled out, shot and pushed under the ice." In another case—as Smith remembered it—patrollers caught up with and massacred fifty slaves "on their way to join the Union army." Yet another group of escapees had "their ears cut off" when they were caught trying "to join the Yankees." Fearing no reprisal southern rebels killed slaves caught escaping to Union lines. As a warning to others who might have considered escaping white southerners lined the roadsides with the bodies of slaves suspected of rebellion. Officials in Richmond all but winked at reports of black troops slaughtered by their Confederate captors.[13]

If the slaves learned early on that they could secure their freedom by escaping to Union lines, they just as quickly learned that they could lose their lives in the attempt. "During the years of 1860 and 1861," Henry Clay Bruce recalled, he and his fellow slaves "had to keep very mum and always on their masters' land, because patrols were put out in every township with authority to punish slaves with the lash, if found off their masters' premises after dark without a written pass from them." Levi Branham likewise recalled that the masters beefed up the slave patrols during the war to thwart potential escapes. "In 1862," Branham wrote, "the slave owners had paddle rollers that they used to whip their slaves with when they were caught away from home."[14]

There is no way to fully assess the effect of the Confederate counterrevolution, but it would be foolish to assume that it was ineffective. We have fairly solid estimates for the number of slaves who were emancipated by the war, but cannot even guess at the number of slaves who failed in the attempt, not to mention those who were inhibited from making the attempt. Lincoln launched an aggressive campaign to enforce the Emancipation Proclamation in the seceded states, but the slaveholders did not wilt before the challenge. Throughout the war they commented on the fact that their slaves were "restless" or "unfaithful," but they also claimed that notwithstanding the restlessness of the slaves their plantations remained "secure." The slaveholders had gone to war to protect slavery; they would not give it up without a fight.

MAKING ESCAPE DIFFICULT

The slaveholders themselves were the first line of defense against military emancipation. With or without the support of the local police, state officials, or the Confederate army, most slaveholders managed to hold their plantations together despite the disruptions of wartime. The simplest and most effective way to thwart emancipation was to "refugee" the slaves, moving them away from enemy lines and out of the way of an advancing Union army. For wealthy masters who owned more than one plantation "refugeeing" could be relatively simple, however painful for the slaves. Charles Heyward, a wealthy South

Carolina slaveholder who in 1860 owned three plantations, felt the approach of Union troops in late spring of 1862. "In consequence of the war," he admitted, his plantations were in a "deranged state of affairs." In March, he wrote in his diary, "15 of my negroes including 3 women and 1 child left the plantation and went over to the enemy on the Islands." But Heyward owned 471 slaves when the war began, and he was able to prevent most of them from escaping. A few days after the fifteen slaves escaped, Heyward "considered it necessary to move away." He sent most of his slaves to another of his plantations farther inland, where they remained, largely undisturbed, until the closing months of the war.[15]

Such moves were common in those parts of the Confederacy threatened by Union occupation—areas like the southern Atlantic coast and the Mississippi Valley. After several of John Screven's slaves escaped to the Yankees in September of 1862, the South Carolina planter moved the remaining slaves to another one of his plantations, Brewton Hill, farther inland "where they stand but little chance of running away." Having been safely removed from the coast the slaves "work very cheerfully," Screven wrote his wife, "though I have no confidence in their fidelity."[16] Farther west slaveholders in the Mississippi Valley often refugeed their slaves to Texas, where there were few Union troops to harass them.[17]

Louisa Alexander, a Georgia plantation mistress, was distressed by the reports of slaves near Savannah running to Union lines, but what outraged her even more were reports of slaves who refused to be moved inland beyond the reach of the Yankees. "It seems to me in such a case," she suggested, Confederate troops should be brought onto the plantations to "march" the slaves off "at the point of the bayonet." Meanwhile, "companies of cavalry [should] scour the whole woods about the neighborhood with the understanding that every negro out will be shot down. This seems dreadful doctrine to preach," Alexander admitted, "but it does seem to me it must come to that. It is *we* or *they* must suffer."[18] This was war. And just as Union authorities were coming to the conclusion that the slaves were the only reliably loyal southerners, the slaveholders were coming to the conclusion that the slaves had to be treated like the enemy.

In South Carolina the Manigaults, one of the wealthiest planter families in the South, succeeded in keeping their slaves from escaping to nearby Union troops through four years of war. In January of 1861, three months before the fighting began, the slaves on the various Manigault plantations were already becoming restless. "They have very generally got the idea of being emancipated when 'Lincoln' comes in," Charles Manigault wrote. Reports of runaways were spreading throughout the Georgia and South Carolina low country, and Manigault warned that "no overseer, or Planter should speak on such subjects even before a small house boy, or girl, as they communicate all that they hear to others." Dogs were no longer adequate to track down runaways. "It is absolutely necessary to go armed with a double barreled gun loaded with duck shot," Gabriel Manigault explained, "with the intention of shooting in the leg, or in a vital part if necessary, any negro who attempts to resist or escape after being caught." With those extra precautions in place, the family's Savannah River plantation, Gowrie, remained calm until the Union invasion and occupation of the nearby Sea Islands in November of 1861. "Then at once was a change discerned amongst the Negroes." Throughout the area "great numbers of Negroes were running away."[19] Not surprisingly "great consternation spread" among the planters and their families.

They may have overreacted however. Although the Union occupation advanced down the coast, it did not penetrate into the interior. Charleston proved impregnable to the Yankees and their passage up the Savannah River was blocked. "I think those persons who have, or intend to move their Negroes," Louis Manigault reported in late 1861, "have acted too hastily." And so within six months Charles reported that "we have very much fortified ourselves."[20]

The Manigaults' success in keeping their slaves "Safe" did not mean that their slaves could be trusted. "This war has taught us the perfect impossibility of placing the least confidence in any Negro," Charles admitted in the second year of the war. Rather than remove all of his slaves from areas too close for comfort to Union lines, Manigault and his overseer selected "[t]en of the men . . . we deemed most likely would cause trouble" and moved them to Silk Hope, another of the family plantations farther inland. When Yankee gunboats moved up the Savannah River still more slaves, "a Total of Twenty Three of our primest Savannah River Hands," were sent to Silk Hope, "where they are to remain until Savannah is no longer threatened by the Yankees." In case Union soldiers threatened the slaves who remained behind, "every preparation has been made to decamp at a moment's notice."[21]

Precautions and severe recriminations worked to keep the Manigault slaves in place until the closing months of the war. William Capers, the overseer at Gowrie, reported several failed escape attempts in late 1861. In one case two slaves were caught when they were betrayed by a third. In another case Driver John captured one slave attempting to escape "in the small canoe." When another slave tried to run off "in my presents," he too was captured by Driver John. "I gave him 60 straps," Capers reported, in the "presents" of those who saw him run. One slave, Jack Savage, gave Manigault and Capers a great deal of trouble. Even before the war, Manigault wrote, he suspected Savage was capable of anything, including murder. He was not merely a "bad Negro," Manigault wrote, he was "the worst Negro I have ever known." Even after Savage was moved from Gowrie to Silk Hope he continued to cause trouble, threatening to run, hiding weapons, and the like. Finally, in January of 1862, after three months in "Dark Solitary Confinement" the slave seemed humbled. He expressed "Great Contrition" for his "misconduct," acknowledged that he had "been bad," and promised "never to give offense or trouble again."

How "easy it is to fix a bad Negro," Manigault gloated, somewhat prematurely as it turned out. A short time later Savage ran away, along with another slave, Charles Lucas. Neither of them escaped to freedom, however. In August of 1863, after a year and a half of hiding out in the "dense Carolina Swamp," Jack Savage "returned of his own accord to us . . . looking half starved and wretched in the extreme." Jack let Manigault know where he had been hiding, and Lucas was soon captured. By then the planter had had enough. He sent Savage to the Savannah jail, where he waited to be sold—for eighteen hundred dollars to another slaveholder in Columbus, Georgia.[22]

Having isolated the most troublesome slaves and removed them to a plantation far from Union lines, having sold the "bad Negro" who caused the most trouble, Manigault and his overseer kept Gowrie working more or less smoothly for the remainder of the war. It would appear that not one of the dozens of slaves on the Manigault plantations—not even Jack Savage—ever succeeded in escaping to Union lines. To be sure, the war was hard on the planter and even harder on his slaves. The rice harvests were smaller, supplies were short, the Union blockade of Savannah made the city useless as a commercial port, and the high taxes Manigault had to pay to sustain the Confederate war effort threw his finances into disarray. Meat supplies were reduced because, fearful that the slaves would steal his beef cows, Manigault had all of them butchered and preserved in Savannah. To help support the war effort, the lead weights in the fishing nets were melted down to make bullets, so the slaves no longer had fish from the Savannah River. Reduced to an unvarying diet made up largely of rice, the slaves grew sickly and began to die. Conditions deteriorated even further when the Confederates impressed Manigault's slaves to work on the fortifications around Savannah.

Not until Sherman's army actually occupied the plantation in the closing days of 1864 were the Manigault slaves finally liberated. Through four years of war the Manigault plantation journal recorded the peaceful workings of his slaves at Gowrie, despite the fact that it was located in one of the "rebel" areas covered by Lincoln's Emancipation Proclamation. As "a general thing," Manigault wrote in mid-1863, "the most perfect quietude has reigned upon all of the Plantations in the Savannah River Swamp." As late as December in 1864, Louis Manigault visited Gowrie, where "the Negroes were all working well." The harvest would be a good one, Manigault noted. The war had disrupted plantation routine at Gowrie, but slavery itself had not been undermined. If anything, the master's control over the slaves became more severe than ever. "Suffice it to say we were working upon it to the very last," Manigault later wrote, and "only the Yankee bayonets put a stop to our work." Sherman's troops arrived at Gowrie on Christmas Eve in 1864. They set fire to the mill and the houses, imprisoned the overseer, and freed the slaves.[23]

SLAVES WERE MORE LIKELY to be freed during the war by the arrival of the Union army than by escaping to it. Peter Bruner, the Kentucky slave, repeatedly tried and failed to reach the Union recruiting center at Camp Nelson on his own. Sometimes he simply got lost. "I always made a great mistake every time I ran away," Bruner remembered. "I always took the wrong direction. Instead of going north to the free states I went farther and farther south, just the opposite direction from which I wanted to go." On one occasion Bruner and another slave nearly made it to the Ohio River, having been assisted in their escape attempts by several whites, but were nabbed by a group of "Nigger Catchers," jailed, and reclaimed by their owners. Chained and beaten, Bruner was dragged barefoot back to his owner's place, where he was shackled in the barn. Bruner was freed during the war when, shortly after he had been recaptured, Union troops arrived on the plantation, where they found the slave in chains, ordered him freed, and jailed his master. When Bruner's owner was released, he tried to persuade his former slave to stay on and work for wages, but Bruner instead made his way to Camp Nelson where, in July of 1864, he enlisted in the Union army.[24]

Countless slaves attempted to take advantage of the war but were unable to do so. Louis Hughes, for example, had been trying to escape from slavery for years before the Civil War began. Born in 1832 near Charlottesville, Virginia, Hughes had been separated from his family as a young boy and sold back and forth to several different masters before Edward McGehee bought him and marched the twelve-year-old, along with sixty other slaves, halfway across the continent to a plantation in Mississippi, in 1844. Notwithstanding the special treatment he received at the hands of his owner—or perhaps because of it—Hughes grew discontented with his enslavement and by the time he reached his early twenties he made the first of several attempts to escape. He made his way to the docks in Memphis, hid himself away on a boat headed upriver, and jumped ashore at West Franklin, Indiana, but bounty hunters soon captured and returned him to his master. A few months later Hughes tried again but after three days of hiding in the hull of another boat, "despairing and hungry," Hughes surrendered and was returned once again to his owner. Shortly afterward Hughes fell in love, started a family, and settled down, until the Civil War broke out and his hunger for freedom was revived.[25]

On Edward McGehee's plantation, as on so many in the South, whites spoke so openly and with such violent emotion—about the election of Abraham Lincoln, secession, the formation of the Confederacy, and Fort Sumter—that it was impossible for Louis Hughes and his fellow slaves not to notice that something big was happening in the country, something that had very much to do with them and with the possibility of their freedom. Hughes recalled the slaves whispering, "[W]e will be free," as they spoke among themselves about the likely consequence of a Union victory. "As the war continued," Hughes wrote, the slaves would "now and then, hear of some slave of our neighborhood running away to the Yankees." Hughes watched for opportunities, but it turned out to be harder than he hoped—even with Union forces nearby.

When Yankee troops began moving southward into the Mississippi Valley in the spring of 1862, McGehee moved his slaves out of the way, sending them to his father-in-law's plantation in Panola, Mississippi. Not even the proximity of the Union army could guarantee an easy escape, however, for the simple reason that wherever there were large numbers of Union troops there were bound to be large numbers of Confederate troops. It was just about impossible for most slaves to get to Union lines if they first had to pass through Confederate lines. Hughes recalled one occasion when a Yankee boat made it all the way down the Mississippi River to Carson's Landing, "right at Boss's farm." Immediately rebel soldiers stationed in the vicinity "put out pickets just above our farm, and allowed no one to pass, or stop to communicate with the boat. Every one that sought to pass was held prisoner." No slaves got through. Hughes himself was ordered by Boss to stand on the veranda and keep a lookout for any vessels coming down the river, and the slave had little choice but to comply. "I kept a close watch the next morning until about eight o'clock," Hughes explained, when he saw a boat and "ran into the house and told Boss." When McGehee went to investigate *he* was taken prisoner by the Yankees.

The temptation was too much for Hughes—Boss was in prison, the Yankees were nearby. "I made up my mind that this would be a good chance for me to run away." He went to the Panola farm, where his wife and children were living. From there he would "try to get to the Yankees." He told his wife, Matilda, of his plan to run to the Union camps at Memphis, and they made their tearful good-byes. But Hughes could not get to the Union lines without passing through Confederate lines. He was captured by rebel soldiers who suspected him of spying for the Yankees. Returned to Panola, Hughes got "another flogging to satisfy the madam. I was never so lacerated before," he remembered. "I could hardly walk." It was the third time Hughes had tried to escape, and the third time he failed.

The fourth attempt, a few months later, would be more carefully thought out. It would be a group escape, planned with friends and including family members. It must have been around March in 1862. Union troops had entered Mississippi, beginning a military occupation that would not end until after the war was over. Hoping once again to make it to Union lines, Hughes's group left the plantation one evening and spent the night walking twelve miles until they reached a swamp at daybreak. Traveling only when it was dark, unable to walk along roadways, the slaves had to make their way through briars, cornfields, wet grass, and marshes. By the second day their clothes were soaked and they were running out of food. On the third day they heard the dogs approaching. They tried to save their escape by scattering in all directions, but with fourteen hounds and several men chasing them the slaves had no hope. They were marched back to the plantation where "all of us were whipped."

Meanwhile Hughes's owner, Edward McGehee, was released by the Yankees and, unwilling to take any more chances, he moved one hundred slaves, house servants and field hands alike, to Demopolis, Alabama, where he hired most of them out to a Confederate salt works. McGehee made good money, and it gave him an even better idea. He sold his Mississippi plantation, mortgaged his Memphis home, bought himself an island in Mobile Bay, and began building a salt works of his own. "He was very enthusiastic over this scheme," Hughes recalled, "claiming that he would make far more money by it than he was then receiving from hiring out his slaves." Before he could realize his ambitious plans, though, McGehee contracted pneumonia and died on New Year's Day in 1864. The slaves were hired out for another year, but Louis and Matilda Hughes, along with their newborn child, were sent back to the father-in-law's plantation in

Panola, Mississippi. When the war finally ended in 1865, Louis Hughes and his wife were still enslaved.

Escape was not easy, not even for a slave as knowledgeable and determined as Louis Hughes. Young unattached men were the most likely to escape to freedom during the war, just as they were the most likely to flee before the war. Men with wives and children were more reluctant to leave their families. Women with children, the elderly, and the disabled were least likely to make a run for it. The enticement policy instituted by the Emancipation Proclamation reinforced these demographic biases. Union recruiters went onto southern farms and plantations and announced that all the slaves had been freed, but they most actively recruited the able-bodied young men. After 1863, as large Union forces marched eastward from the Mississippi River, those biases diminished as entire slave families flocked to Union camps in huge numbers. But enticement agents thought their work was done if they left a plantation with a handful of young male recruits.

If it was clear that most slaves wanted to be free, it was not clear that freedom was easily achieved by simply packing up and walking off to the nearest Union camp. Like everybody else, slaves were driven by a complex mixture of incentives and calculations, and different people responded in different ways to the prospect of freedom—even though nearly all slaves found that prospect enticing. Union troops came and went. Who could be sure that the brutal uncertainties of life trailing an army on the march were preferable to the meager securities of life on a plantation? It cannot have been obvious to all slaves that they should quit their families, neighbors, or homes in exchange for a filthy, overcrowded contraband camp.[26]

Not even the offer of enlistment in the Union army—in some ways the most straightforward of all the options available to slaves—was all that straightforward. Masters sometimes threatened reprisals against the families of those young men who volunteered to fight for the Yankees. It was hard enough for any soldier, white or black, to leave behind a family and a community he might never see again, but for an enslaved husband and father there was the added fear that he was leaving his family at the mercy of an enraged master. Then, too, the Union army to which he was fleeing was not uniformly welcoming. Enticement was the official Union policy and so, for that matter, was the suppression of racial "prejudice" within the ranks. Until the last year of the war, however, it was also official Union policy to discriminate against black soldiers with lower pay and limits on promotion, and there were always some Union soldiers who treated slaves with contempt and abused their own black comrades-in-arms. Young black men had a powerful incentive to enlist, but they had plenty of reasons not to.[27]

Union officials sometimes noted the reluctance of slaves to claim their freedom. General Sherman, after accepting the proposition that "universal emancipation" was an effective way to "injure our enemy," nevertheless doubted it would work. "Not one nigger in ten wants to run off," he complained in September of 1862—before enticement began. He estimated that there were twenty-five thousand slaves within twenty miles of his base in Memphis. "[A]ll could escape & would receive protection here," he wrote, "but we have only about 2000." James Ayers had so much trouble recruiting slaves into the Union army that he grew frustrated with his assignment and eventually resigned.[28] "I am heartily sick of coaxing niggers to be Soaldiers Any more," Ayers complained. Some were unwilling to leave their wives; others were too sick for soldiering. "I would rather be A slave all my days than go to war," one man said. Ayers, in turn, was ready to "throw up my papers and resign." But most recruiters never reached most slaves. Adjutant General Lorenzo Thomas reported to Secretary of War Stanton in late 1864 that his men were having trouble recruiting slaves from "the interior counties" of Kentucky. Those areas "abound with Southern sympathizers," Thomas explained, "who adopt every means possible to prevent the negroes from proceeding to the Camps of Reception."[29]

In theory the Union was committed to universal emancipation in the seceded states, but in practice its armies could not possibly emancipate three million slaves in the areas covered by the Emancipation Proclamation. If nothing else the Confederate counterrevolution ensured that untold numbers of slaves would never make it to the freedom they were promised once they entered Union lines. Even without fierce resistance from the slaveholders, though, universal emancipation would have been impossible to achieve in practice. Congress could pass a law freeing the slaves of all rebels, and Lincoln could proclaim emancipation everywhere in the rebel states, but not even the Union army at full strength could make that happen. Most slaves never reached Union lines, and Union troops never reached most of the slaves. If Lincoln was right, if the only guarantee of postwar freedom was actual, physical emancipation during the war, most slaves would still be enslaved when the war was over.

"WHAT SHALL I DO WITH THE NEGROES?"

And yet black men enlisted by the tens of thousands. Families and communities uprooted themselves. For the chance of freedom they risked separation from their loved ones, reprisal by their masters, capture by the Confederates, and indifference or worse from their Union liberators. The Union army was never prepared for them. From the earliest months of the war Union officers were daunted by the numbers of contrabands coming into their lines. A steady stream of pleading letters flew up the military chain of command, all of them asking the same question: What am I to do with them? Many arrived half-starved after strenuous escapes or having borne the brunt of wartime shortages on their own farms and plantations. After complaining that most slaves seemed unwilling to escape to his lines, even General Sherman was soon overwhelmed by those who did come. A year earlier General Frémont had boldly declared the emancipation of all rebel-owned slaves in Missouri, Sherman noted ruefully, but how would he have responded to the vast number of "refugee negros" now streaming into Union camps? "What could he do with them?" They were "free," he admitted, "but freedom don' clothe them, feed them & shelter them."[30] From Louisiana, General Benjamin Butler sent letters to Washington wondering how he could provide food and shelter to the tens of thousands of freed people, even as his own commissary was providing rations for thousands of starving whites. John Eaton, farther up the Mississippi Valley, raised the same issue. Aware of the looming humanitarian disaster, Lincoln administration officials, including Lincoln himself, ordered Union generals to provide the freed people with food and shelter from army supplies. By the second year of the war the military was feeding tens of thousands of freed men and women and desperately trying to find shelter for them. It was the largest program to provide direct aid to individuals the federal government had ever undertaken.

But it was never enough. There was no federal bureaucracy, not even the Union army, equipped to handle the numbers of desperate human beings arriving day after day at Union camps. Even the best medical care was often useless since no one yet understood the germ theory of disease. In September of 1862, General Butler asked one of his officers to explain reports that "some of the negro women and children who have sought protection within your lines, are not sufficiently provided with shelter from the inclemency of the weather." The colonel responded frankly. "The report of a want of protection for the Negroes is correct," he wrote, "and I have been trying to-day to secure suitable shelter for them, but they have come in upon me so fast I have found it very difficult." Butler in turn acknowledged the problem to his superiors and detailed the lengths to which he went to supply desperate whites and blacks alike with food and shelter.[31]

Union authorities, already overwhelmed by the scope of the humanitarian problem, were bedeviled by reports of individual Union soldiers, particularly from the Border States, who resisted federal emancipation policy and abused the contrabands. In one notorious case late in the war, Kentucky-born General Speed Smith Fry at Camp Nelson ordered the expulsion of the families of black soldiers during an especially harsh winter. As a direct result, Joseph Miller's wife and their four children died from exposure and hunger. One of Fry's own officers, Captain T. E. Hall, wrote desperate letters asking that something "be done for these poor women and children." Four days after issuing his notorious edict, Fry was ordered to reverse it, to let those he expelled back into Camp Nelson, and "if necessary to erect buildings for them." When Fry balked, Hall was given exclusive authority over the contrabands. Fry's outrageous behavior caused a national scandal. The army launched an investigation and concluded that the expulsion order was entirely improper. New homes were built, and the families of black soldiers were given rations from the army commissary. Two months later, in the letter appointing General John Palmer as the new commander of the entire Department of the Ohio—which included Kentucky—Secretary Stanton indicated that Lincoln was "grieved" by the reports of "cruel and barbarous treatment" of blacks. "Your hand should be laid heavily upon all outrages of this nature," Stanton wrote. "To the destitute women and children of soldiers in the service of the United States, without regard to color, protection and support should be given." A few weeks later, Republicans in Congress, shocked by the scandal in Kentucky, passed a resolution reaffirming the emancipation of the wives and children of freed men who enlisted in the Union army.[32]

. . .

BY 1862 THE NUMBER OF SLAVES flooding into Union lines was so great that the government was transferring them to "contraband camps" in all parts of the South occupied by the army. Freed people arrived in steady numbers, often in boatloads. On a single day in October of 1862, three hundred and sixty emancipated slaves arrived in Washington from Virginia, "having at different times made their way within our lines. They were immediately sent to the contraband camp." In November there were reportedly more than five hundred contrabands in the camp. In May of 1863, six hundred and fifty more contrabands arrived in Washington from Aquia Creek in a single afternoon. Quickly overwhelmed, the camps soon became notorious for their filth, disease, and criminal violence. Drinking water polluted by the sewage led to outbreaks of dysentery. In December of 1862, the overcrowded contraband camp in Cincinnati, Ohio, was described as "disgraceful to barbarism."[33]

The Emancipation Proclamation only worsened the problems by increasing the numbers. In early 1863, visitors to the camp in the District of Columbia were warned "not to enter because smallpox was prevalent there." By then there were three thousand people living in the camp, with as many as twenty dying each day. As long as the epidemic raged, no one was permitted to leave the camp, and the criminal element began preying on the desperate. Gangs of angry whites sometimes attacked the contraband camps. In June of 1862, the Union cavalry was dispatched to the camp in Washington to put down an assault by "some disorderly whites." Conservatives complained that blacks were living in "idleness" at the expense of the taxpayer. More reliable accounts described the inhabitants of the camps as "suffering intensely, many without bed covering & having to use any bits of carpeting to cover themselves—Many dying of want."[34] By late 1863 and 1864, conditions in some of the camps improved as Union officials became familiar with the problems and as private relief agencies pitched in to help. Federal officials set up "model" camps, notably

Freedman's Village in Arlington, Virginia, on the confiscated estate of Robert E. Lee's wife. It is not clear, however, that there was general improvement over time, if only because the numbers of contrabands grew exponentially and the army remained overwhelmed.[35]

The alternative to the camps—or at least the alternative that came immediately to the minds of antislavery Republicans—was to put the former slaves back to work as free laborers. Though "able-bodied male contrabands" could enlist in the Union army, Lincoln admitted, "the rest are in confusion and destitution." Rather than let them suffer in camps, it would be better for the Union army to locate abandoned plantations and "put as many contrabands on such, as they will hold—that is, as can draw subsistence from them." Loyal owners could employ them "on wages, to be paid to the contrabands them-selves." Responding to Lincoln's suggestion in March of 1863, General Stephen Hurlbut ordered two large contraband camps on the Mississippi River "to be broken up, and all the negroes not in the actual service of the United States will be sent to Island No. 10 and set to work." This, at least, was more consistent with general Republican Party principles. If emancipation meant anything, it meant not contraband camps or colonization but free labor.[36]

Yet even as General Hurlbut was closing down contraband camps and sending the freed people to work for wages on abandoned planta-tions, other Union officers were rounding up unemployed freed people on the streets of New Orleans and Memphis and sending them *to* con-traband camps to earn their own "subsistence."[37] In an attempt to pre-vent the recapture and re-enslavement of freed people, the Union army, especially in the Mississippi Valley, forcibly removed thousands of con-trabands from their farms and plantations to areas at a safe distance from the Confederates—not only onto islands in the Mississippi River but also to Memphis and sometimes as far away as Cincinnati.

· · ·

THE GREAT PARADOX OF military emancipation was that although the Union army was overwhelmed by the numbers of contrabands entering its lines, those numbers were never more than a small fraction of the slaves in the rebel states. The Yankees swept through plantation districts like a tornado, destroying deserted farms and uprooting slavery along the way. Like a tornado, though, the severity of the damage ended abruptly at the edge of the storm's track. Sherman's men cut a ten-mile path of destruction wherever they went, but their marches traced a thin ribbon over Georgia's vast terrain and so swept up only a fraction of the state's slaves. By the time it reached Savannah, Sherman's army had ten thousand freed slaves marching with it, but there were 462,230 slaves in Georgia according to the 1860 census. Another seven thousand slaves joined Sherman's army as it marched through South Carolina, but South Carolina had 402,541 slaves when the war began. In the most concerted attack on slavery during the most deliberately destructive campaign of the war, Sherman had dislodged only about 2 percent of the slaves in Georgia and South Carolina.

Of the nearly four million slaves living in the South in 1860, approximately 525,000—just over 13 percent—were freed by the end of the war and living under the rubric of federal authority in various capacities, as free laborers on farms and plantations, as military laborers or soldiers in the Union army, or as inhabitants of the contraband camps. Of that number, approximately 50,000 were from the four Border States. In 1860 the U.S. census counted 3,520,116 slaves in the eleven states that went on to form the Confederacy, and approximately 474,000 of those were freed by the end of the war. These figures—compiled by the Freedmen and Southern Society Project—are naturally subject to various qualifications, but they are the best, most carefully compiled numbers we have.[38] They are particularly apt because they closely track the criteria Lincoln and many Republicans had set for the freed people whose emancipations were most legally secure: those who were actually freed by the war.

"Those who shall have tasted actual freedom," Lincoln said, "I believe can never be slaves, or quasi-slaves again."[39] When the Civil War ended, however, no more than 14 percent of the slaves in the eleven Confederate states had "tasted actual freedom." Lincoln had proclaimed them "forever free." But were they?

RE-ENSLAVEMENT

On March 11, 1862, during the congressional debate over the Second Confiscation Act, Virginia Senator John Carlile warned that when the war ended, "self-preservation would compel the States within which slavery now exists, if the slaves were emancipated, either to expel them from the State, or re-enslave them." One month later, on April 10, Senator Waitman Willey—also of Virginia—repeated the threat. Emancipation would "increase the free negro population" of the state, Willey declared, and Virginia "will be driven not only to re-enslave those who may be manumitted under the operation of the present bill, but also to re-enslave the sixty-thousand free negroes already there." How would this be possible? Delaware's Senator Willard Saulsbury explained. By 1870 this war will be over, and unless state governments are destroyed in the process, power over slavery will be returned to the states. When that happens, Saulsbury warned, the southern states "will not only re-enslave every person that you attempt to set free, but they will re-enslave the whole race."[40]

It had happened before, elsewhere. During the upheavals of the French Revolution slavery was abolished not only on San Domingue—later Haiti—but also on the Caribbean island Guadeloupe, in 1794. Invoking the revolutionary language of citizenship, black insurgents on Guadeloupe established a republic, allying themselves with the French in their war against Great Britain. From the start, however, the fragile republic was beset by internal divisions between former slaves demanding greater equality and former masters allied with merchants intent on suppressing black discontent. When Napoleon came to power in 1799 he tilted the French state against the former slaves, reasserted its colonial authority, defeated the black rebels, and in 1804 reestablished slavery on Guadeloupe. For another four decades, slavery survived on the island.[41]

Re-enslavement was no abstract threat. Once again Kentucky proved especially zealous in its determination to thwart emancipation. When slaves from Alabama and Tennessee followed the Union army as it retreated into Kentucky, authorities in that state imprisoned them as runaway slaves. Those who were not claimed by their owners in Alabama and Tennessee were instead sold to new owners in Kentucky. This was an obvious violation of the Second Confiscation Act and the Emancipation Proclamation, and soon enough Lincoln's judge advocate general, Joseph Holt, ruled that the re-enslavement of blacks in Kentucky was illegal. Outraged by reports of freed people being re-enslaved, Lincoln instructed Secretary of War Stanton to put a stop to it. Stanton in turn fired off a telegram to General Ambrose Burnside ordering him, on behalf of the president, to "take immediate measures" to prevent any persons freed by the war "from being returned to bondage."[42]

If re-enslavement was possible in the loyal slave state of Kentucky—where federal pressure to free slaves was particularly intense—it was routine in the Confederate states wherever the Union army was pushed back. Among blacks in the rebel states, re-enslavement was a familiar wartime experience. Slaves learned about the threat of re-enslavement as quickly as they learned about the Emancipation Proclamation. Beginning with some of the earliest Union invasions of the Confederacy, southern slaves worried about their fate should their masters return. In the first year of the war, the contrabands on the Sea Islands wanted assurance from Union officials that they would be "protected against their rebel masters." Not even free blacks were safe.

Free blacks who left the state of Georgia were forbidden to return lest they "be sold as a slave."[43]

Slaves had good reason to be concerned. Why would the slaveholders ever acknowledge the legitimacy of a Union-decreed emancipation? To a slaveholder an "emancipated" slave was nothing more than a fugitive slave. As far as military and political leaders of the Confederacy were concerned, there were no emancipated slaves; there were only runaways. Indeed, what northerners called "re-enslavement," the slaveholders called "recapture." Even in the North, Democrats insisted that military emancipation was unconstitutional; under the Confederate constitution it had no meaning whatsoever. Confederate political and military leaders could not recognize captured black soldiers as anything other than runaway slaves, and the first obligation of southern officials—forcefully decreed by the Confederate constitution—was to return runaway slaves to their owners. When Confederate General Leonidas Polk asked Jefferson Davis what to do with captured black Union soldiers, Davis's answer was unambiguous: "If the negro soldiers are escaped slaves they should be held safely for recovery by their owners." Polk wrote back that all of the captured soldiers were "escaped slaves." Should I "inform their owners & deliver them to them?" Polk asked. Once again Davis was clear: "Captured slaves should be returned to their masters." On May 31, 1863, the Confederate Congress passed a law requiring the same thing: black soldiers who had been slaves were to be treated as escaped slaves and returned to their masters.[44]

But to northerners this was re-enslavement, and as outrageous as it was on its own terms, what disturbed Lincoln and the Republicans at least as much were the inescapable implications of re-enslavement for the fate of southern blacks once the war ended. Clearly the southern states never recognized the legality of any emancipations justified by the Union under the laws of war. There was good reason to believe that when peace was restored and federal war powers evaporated, the former Confederate states would re-enslave those who had been emancipated by the Union.

When Union officials first addressed the issue of re-enslavement they were concerned to discount the possibility that the *Union* might renege on its promise of freedom by returning freed blacks to slavery. Writing from the Sea Islands in the first year of the war, Edward Pierce, charged with supervising the contrabands, declared that it would be immoral for the federal government to allow re-enslavement. It was not "possible to imagine any rulers now or in the future," Pierce wrote, "who will ever turn their backs on the laborers who have been received, as these have been, into the service of the United States." Likewise Treasury Secretary Salmon Chase would "never consent," he declared, "to the involuntary reduction to Slavery of one of the negroes who had been in the service of the Government." Eventually Union policymakers took the broader position that slaves actually freed by the war could never be re-enslaved. Lincoln said this repeatedly. Slaves whose labor had been "forfeited" by their owners and subsequently emancipated by the government could never be re-enslaved, he explained in March of, 1862. "I do not believe it would be physically possible, for the General government, to return persons so circumstanced, to actual slavery," he explained. "I believe there would be physical resistance to it, which could neither be turned aside by argument, nor driven away by force." This remained Lincoln's baseline position until the end of the war.[45]

By the middle of 1862, however, it was clear to Union officials that the real threat of re-enslavement came from the southern states bent on restoring slavery, not the federal government reneging on its promises. In September of 1862, Lincoln cited examples of Confederate re-enslavement to a group of Chicagoans visiting him in Washington. In one case rebels captured several black soldiers on a boat on the Tennessee River and promptly enslaved them. After both battles of Bull Run, Lincoln noted, federal authorities dispatched expeditions to the battlefield "under a flag of truce to bury the dead and bring in the wounded, and the rebels seized the blacks who went along to help and sent them into slavery." Suppose the demands of the war forced the Union to "call off our forces from New Orleans to defend some other point," Lincoln wondered. "[W]hat is to prevent the masters from reducing the blacks to slavery again?" Already, black soldiers were routinely re-enslaved by their Confederate captors. "Whenever the rebels take any black prisoners, free or slave," Lincoln complained, "they immediately auction them off!"[46]

As more slaves were emancipated by the Yankees, more of them were re-enslaved by the rebels, and Union officials adopted a number of policies aimed at shielding freed people against both the legal and the physical threat of re-enslavement. By statute and by presidential proclamation they insisted that slaves freed by the war were "forever free." When, weeks before the Emancipation Proclamation was issued, Attorney General Bates ruled that blacks were citizens of the United States, he was motivated in part by the desire to prevent re-enslavement. If slaves became citizens the moment they were emancipated, and if national citizenship took precedence over state citizenship, no state could subsequently deprive freed men and women of the privileges and immunities of citizenship by attempting to re-enslave them. Of course the Bates ruling had no effect on Confederate policy. On the contrary, re-enslavement increased dramatically after the proclamation was issued. In late July of 1863, Lincoln retaliated by ordering that one Confederate prisoner be sentenced to hard labor for every black Union soldier re-enslaved by a Confederate captor. Weeks later, responding to reports of freed people being re-enslaved in Mississippi, Lincoln drafted an order to General Stephen Hurlbut, instructing him to make every effort to find employment for them on secure plantations whose owners would "not let the contrabands be kidnapped, or forcibly carried away." The secretary of war wrote to several Union generals on Lincoln's behalf ordering them to stop the re-enslavement of blacks in the Border States.[48]

AFTER THE CONFEDERATE DEFEATS at Vicksburg and Gettysburg in the summer of 1863, the prospect of an impending Union victory focused the attention of Republican policymakers on the inadequacy of military emancipation as a means of destroying slavery. The slaveholders were throwing too many roadblocks in emancipation's way. From the congress in Richmond through state and local governments, all the way down to local militia units and individual planters, the Confederacy mobilized itself to prevent the slaves from taking advantage of the war to claim their freedom. No doubt plantation routine was disrupted by the war, but sometimes the disruption itself was part of the often successful efforts to keep the Union army away from the slaves. As it was, Union troops could reach only a fraction of the southern slaves, and it could not support those it was able to reach. It is hardly surprising, then, that when the war ended, only one out of seven slaves had actually been emancipated. No one in Washington could say for certain that those still enslaved would be freed, or even that those who had been freed could never be re-enslaved.

Yet military emancipation was not a complete failure. It seriously weakened the Confederacy by depriving the South of the labor of thousands of black workers, in addition to those who fought for the Union. When the Confederates impressed slaves into service, they disrupted plantations, angered slaveholders, and sent countless slaves fleeing to Union lines. By contrast, Union impressment transferred the labor of tens of thousands of African Americans from the South to the North, simultaneously weakening the Confederacy and strengthening the Union—the famous "double" benefit of which

Lincoln and other Republicans spoke. Lincoln and many of his leading generals—not least Ulysses S. Grant—came to believe that emancipation and black enlistment were "indispensable" to Union victory,
and without Union victory there could be no abolition. The Emancipation Proclamation did something else as well, something harder to
measure but perhaps equally important: it created the expectation
among northerners that when the war was over, slavery would be fully
destroyed. The proclamation helped forge the political will to do what
emancipation itself could not do—abolish slavery everywhere in the
United States. Emancipation made the Thirteenth Amendment politically viable.

Yet if military emancipation was in many ways a success, it was a
success that came at a terrible price. By definition *military* emancipation took place amid the chaos and horror of war. The horror began but
did not end with the hundreds of thousands of soldiers who died, and
the generation of maimed veterans who survived. For the slaves themselves, military emancipation could be a terrifying and deadly experience. Tens of thousands were ripped from their communities, families
were physically separated, the contrabands—sometimes frozen, often
starving—got sick and died in the very process that was supposed to
free them. Republicans had warned from the start that military emancipation would be brutal and bloody, though they could scarcely have
imagined the staggering human cost. They had always said that a
peaceful, gradual abolition was the better, more humane alternative to
bloody military emancipation. All through the war Lincoln continued
to offer the disloyal states that option in return for an end to the blood-
letting. But the slaveholders could never accept abolition, on any terms.
That left only two alternatives: either the North accepted perpetual
slavery or the South was subjected to military emancipation.[48]

Having embraced military emancipation, however, Republicans
ultimately concluded that it would not destroy slavery. When Lincoln
and the Republicans expressed fears of a court decision overturning

wartime emancipation, what they mostly worried about was a state court upholding a state's right to enslave those freed by the war. By their own understanding of the Constitution, slavery was a state institution, military emancipation a wartime expedient, and when the war was over, control over slavery would revert to the states. By early 1864, Republicans were pointing anxiously to the shortcomings of military emancipation to justify their new proposal for an antislavery amendment. Congress had passed confiscation laws and the president had issued emancipation proclamations, one Republican congressman explained, but "the world knows" that "none of the laws I have mentioned have gone beyond the fact of making men affected by them free; that no one of them has reached the root of slavery and prepared for the destruction of the system. We have made some men free," he concluded, "but the system yet lives."[49]

12

"OUR FATHERS
WERE MISTAKEN"

"SIR, IS IT NOT MADNESS to act upon the idea that slavery is dead?" Republican Congressman James T. Wilson of Iowa asked in March of 1864. He cited the threats coming from the Border States to "reenslave every person you attempt to set free." Even after three years of war, Wilson said, slavery was a "condemned" but "unexecuted culprit." We "know that it is not dead," he declared. "Why should we not recognize the fact and provide for the execution?" But by what means shall it be executed, Wilson wondered. "How shall we perform it?"[1] That was the question on every Republican mind when the Thirty-Eighth Congress opened its first session in December of 1863. Slavery was not yet dead. How can we kill it? Republicans were more certain than ever that the Union forces would soon win the war, but less certain than ever that slavery would be destroyed in the process. Desperate to abolish slavery and even more desperate to prevent the re-enslavement of those emancipated by the war, Republican lawmakers introduced a raft of bills designed to "enforce" emancipation and make it irreversible. Most of their proposals, however, ran afoul of the federal consensus: for reasons of military necessity the government could *emancipate* slaves as individuals, but the power to abolish slavery resided exclusively in the states. As a result Republicans could not unite around any of the proposals to abolish slavery by means of congressional legislation.

There were only two ways to destroy slavery: the states could abolish on their own, or the Constitution could be amended to abolish slavery everywhere. When the Thirty-Eighth Congress convened, it was not clear whether either of these approaches would succeed. At that point—in December of 1863—not a single state had abolished slavery on its own, notwithstanding intense federal pressure to do so. Only West Virginia had adopted gradual abolition, and only because Congress had demanded it as the price of admission to the Union. It seemed unlikely that every loyal slave state would abolish slavery, and even where it was abolished it could eventually be reestablished. That left only a constitutional amendment, but there was as yet no Republican consensus in favor that strategy, nor was it clear that Republicans had the power to get an amendment through Congress. Over the next several months, as the weaknesses of other approaches became more evident, Republicans settled on a thirteenth amendment as the best way to destroy slavery completely. In so doing they finally repudiated the federal consensus.

"SLAVERY CANNOT BE ABOLISHED BY CONGRESS"

On December 14, 1863, Senator John Hale of New Hampshire introduced a bill to "more effectually suppress the rebellion." It was brief and simple: Hale's bill abolished slavery everywhere in the United States. Hereafter, it read, "all persons within the United States are equal before the law." All "claims of personal service . . . are hereby forever abolished." The only exceptions were parental claims on the labor of minors, state claims on the labor of convicted criminals, and personal claims based on voluntary contract. This was federally mandated abolition, all state laws and constitutions to the contrary notwithstanding. There was no chance that Hale's bill would pass. It was an open rejection of the Republican Party's long-standing acknowledgment that the Constitution recognized slavery as a state institution and that the federal government had no power to abolish slavery in a state where it existed. Hale himself had long proclaimed his allegiance to the federal consensus, as had Massachusetts Senator Charles Sumner. Yet by 1864 both had shifted ground, adopting the position that the Constitution was actually an antislavery document, that it was incompatible with slavery in the states, and that Congress was fully empowered to abolish slavery anywhere within the territorial limits of the United States.[2] It was a desperate move to get slavery abolished, and there were others—less desperate, but each one controversial.

One of the most startling proposals designed to achieve abolition legislatively—it later became the basis of radical reconstruction—was to reduce the seceded states to the status of territories. All Republicans, even those who believed that the federal government had no power to abolish slavery in a state, agreed that Congress could abolish slavery in the territories. Senator John Brooks Henderson, the stanch Missouri unionist, derisively explained the logic of the proposal: "The argument admits that slavery cannot be abolished by Congress in a State, but insists that it can be in a Territory." Thus by treating the seceded states like territories, Congress could abolish it. Henderson favored the complete abolition of slavery, but he dismissed territorialization as yet another attempt by Congress to devise *indirect* "ways and means to cripple slavery." Reducing the states to territories put the Republicans in a legally absurd position of simultaneously declaring the secession ordinances null and void, while on the other hand investing those same ordinances "with sufficient validity to destroy the state."[3] As a means of abolishing slavery, territorialization gained few supporters.

Emancipating the families of Union soldiers was yet another way to expand the scope of emancipation indirectly. Congress had already approved this in the Militia Act of July 1862 as part of the attempt to put added pressure on the Border States. At the time it provoked little comment. The issue came up again in November of 1863, however, when a Kentucky general caused a nationwide scandal by cruelly expelling the wives and children of black soldiers from camp, sending them off into a brutal winter where several of them froze to death. The order was quickly reversed, the general was nearly removed from command, and the surviving families were readmitted to the camp, where they were housed and fed. In Congress the scandal resulted in a resolution reaffirming that the families of freed men who had enlisted in the army were emancipated. By then Democrats and Border State politicians had launched a ferocious legal counterattack, claiming that the federal government had no constitutional authority to free any slaves of any loyal masters in a loyal slave state. Democrats conceded that the federal government might have the power to conscript the slaves of loyal masters into the Union army, but it could not touch their families. Like every other Republican, Senator John Sherman of Ohio was prepared to "guaranty" the freedom of any slave "employed in the military service of the United States," but he did not think Congress had the power to legally emancipate the slave's family members if his master was loyal. The only way to do that was by passing a constitutional amendment abolishing slavery everywhere, which Sherman strongly supported. Lyman Trumbull wondered if it was possible to free the wives of slaves when state laws did not recognize the legality of slave marriages. Nevertheless, frustrated and angered by the intransigence of the Border States, especially Kentucky, Republicans passed the resolution.[4]

Searching for constitutionally viable ways to prevent re-enslavement by the southern states once peace was restored, several Republican lawmakers proposed legislation to "enforce" Lincoln's proclamation. "The decree of emancipation," Senator Henry Wilson argued, "should be enforced and sanctioned by measures of legislation." Isaac Arnold, a Republican congressman from Illinois, introduced a bill to "carry into immediate execution" the Emancipation Proclamation. Arnold's proposal would prohibit "the reenslaving or holding, or attempting to hold, in slavery or involuntary servitude of any person who shall have been made or declared free by said proclamation." On the same day that Arnold introduced his bill another Illinois congressman, the abolitionist Owen Lovejoy, introduced a complementary proposal "to protect freedmen and punish any one for enslaving them." His bill would give congressional sanction to the attorney general's earlier ruling that free or freed blacks were citizens, thereby making re-enslavement a palpably unconstitutional deprivation of the "privileges and immunities" of citizenship. Re-enslavement would become a crime under Lovejoy's bill, punishable by one to five years in prison and a fine of between one and five thousand dollars.[5]

The fear that even black soldiers might be re-enslaved led the Republicans to repeal the Fugitive Slave Act of 1850, even though the statute had been a dead letter for several years, ever since the war began. As early as December in 1861, a Republican congressman warned that if "the rebellion be suppressed to-morrow, the masters of those slaves now coming within our lines, and helping us, would have a claim to their rendition under the fugitive slave law." In March of 1862, Congress made it a crime for anyone in the military to enforce the fugitive slave clause, and a few months later, in the Second Confiscation Act, Republicans went further by restricting enforcement to the states. Nevertheless, by early 1864, Republicans were still concerned by threats to re-enslave even black soldiers recruited from the Border States whose masters had remained loyal to the Union. Democrats and Border State congressmen had always denounced the Emancipation Proclamation as unconstitutional, but some were willing to concede that the Union could legally conscript and emancipate the slaves of disloyal masters. They made no such concession for black enlistees owned by loyal masters in the loyal slave states. When pressed in congressional debate, Democrats refused to disavow their intention to re-enslave those black recruits. Republican Senator Edgar Cowan wondered whether any black soldier freed by the war was secure from re-enslavement by the states. "Is there any authority in this Government," Cowan asked, "to prevent that return to his original status?" Because enlistment was the surest path to freedom for black men in the Border States, tens of thousands of them had abandoned their owners and joined the Union army, and for the same reason, federal authorities made special efforts to recruit blacks from those areas. Hoping to make their re-enslavement difficult, Republicans finally repealed the Fugitive Slave Act on June 28, 1864. States were thereby deprived of any statutory claim to federal assistance in the capture of former slaves who had joined the Union army and left the state.[6]

The repeal of the Fugitive Slave Act was uncontroversial among Republicans because it flowed logically from the principle that freedom was national and slavery merely local. Republicans, though, could not unite around the other legislative measures to expand the scope of emancipation. Sherman questioned the resolution to free the families of Union soldiers not because he opposed abolition, but because he did not think the Constitution in its current form allowed Congress to do such a thing. Like Trumbull, Sherman supported a constitutional amendment abolishing slavery everywhere as a sounder means of achieving universal emancipation. In the Senate, the same position was articulated by a crucial handful of influential unionist Democrats from states that were on the verge of abolishing slavery on their own. Like Henderson of Missouri, Reverdy Johnson of Maryland supported a constitutional amendment after coming to the conclusion that there could be no "prosperous and permanent peace" until slavery was abolished. He also questioned "the legality and effect of the other means by which it is proposed to get right of it." Abolition, Johnson said, was not "within the power of Congress by virtue of its legislative authority." Nor could the president do anything more than emancipate slaves within the actual reach of the Union army. He "has no practical power to effect the manumission of slaves belonging to the enemy where he has not the physical power to attain the result."[7]

It was 1864, and the opponents of slavery still faced the same dilemma that abolitionists had faced since the late eighteenth century: slavery was immoral, but the Constitution protected it. "[A] majority of our people believe slavery to be wrong," Senator Henderson explained, "but a small number, comparatively, believe that Congress possesses the power to abolish it. In other words," he concluded, "the moral law condemns it, but the Constitution tolerates it." Slavery has been a festering sore on the body politic since the republic was founded and "should now be abolished," Henderson said, but "the Constitution as it now stands confers upon Congress no power to abolish it." He dismissed most of the proposals to attack slavery indirectly through congressional legislation. Territorialization was legally incoherent. Guaranteeing states a "republican form of government" would not work, since seceded States "were republican before secession." Enforcing the Emancipation Proclamation would do no good if the proclamation itself was limited in its reach. "We act as though a presidential proclamation against slavery would end the rebellion," he complained. There was really no alternative: there must be "a change of the Constitution."[8]

Even Lyman Trumbull, who had no apologies to make for his own antislavery record, doubted that Congress could enforce emancipation, much less abolish slavery, by mere legislation. "I am as anxious to get rid of slavery as any persons," he declared, "but has Congress authority to pass a law abolishing slavery everywhere?" Not under the terms of the federal consensus. "[I]t has been an admitted axiom from the foundation of this Government, among all parties, that Congress had no authority to interfere with slavery in the States where it existed." The solution was clear. "[T]he only effectual way of ridding the country of slavery, and so that it cannot be resuscitated, is by an amendment to the Constitution, forever prohibiting it within the jurisdiction of the United States."[9] Only a constitutional amendment would abolish slavery and sanction the various congressional efforts to enforce emancipation.

THE END OF THE FEDERAL CONSENSUS

In retrospect it seems obvious that the easiest way to destroy slavery was to add an amendment to the Constitution abolishing it everywhere in the United States. But until 1864 the amendment never struck Republicans—or even abolitionists—as necessary or desirable. The Constitution had not been amended for over half a century. It was almost universally revered as the capstone of the American Revolution—the near-perfect handiwork of the Founders. No one was eager to tamper with it. In the mid-1830s a few abolitionists had proposed amending the Constitution but the addition of several new slave states soon made it impractical. By 1860 an antislavery amendment would have required the unanimous votes of forty-five free states to secure ratification over the opposition of the fifteen slave states then in the Union. That would be impossible, even today. No wonder some abolitionists were more likely to burn the Constitution than propose revising it. A constitutional amendment was scarcely thinkable as an antislavery strategy until after eleven slave states seceded, yet until December in 1863, hardly anybody suggested it.

Why, having moved so swiftly to attack slavery as soon as the war began, did Republicans come so belatedly to such an amendment? In part it was because all of their antislavery politics were based on the assumption that the Constitution was already adequate to destroy slavery. Under sustained assault from southern slaveholders and northern Democrats that they were trampling on the constitutional rights of the southern states, Republicans always responded by insisting that their antislavery policies were not only constitutional but also consistent with the federal consensus. They could put slavery on the course of "ultimate extinction" without directly abolishing it in the states where it was legal. Convinced that slavery was weak, Republicans initially believed that southern slave society would crumble once they pulled the federal props from beneath the unstable foundations of the Slave Power. In the first year of the war they implemented the basic elements of freedom national—abolishing slavery in the territories and Washington, restricting enforcement of the fugitive slave clause to the states, ratifying a treaty with England suppressing slavery on the high seas—all the while emancipating thousands of slaves coming into Union lines from the rebel states. By mid-1862, having realized that slavery was stronger and white unionism weaker than they had previously thought, Republicans committed themselves to a much more aggressive policy of universal military emancipation in the seceded states and with it the expectation that the "friction and abrasion" of war would quickly undermine slavery in the loyal Border States. That policy was fully implemented when Lincoln issued the Emancipation Proclamation on January 1, 1863. A year later, two things seemed clear to Republicans: the North was going to win the war, and neither military emancipation nor state abolition would be enough to destroy slavery. If something wasn't done, the thing that caused the war would survive the war.

The Thirty-Eighth Congress opened for business in early December of 1863, and in less than two weeks Republican Congressman

James Ashley of Ohio proposed a constitutional amendment "prohibiting slavery, or involuntary servitude, in all the States and Territories now owned or which may be hereafter acquired by the United States."[10] A month later a similar amendment was introduced in the Senate. Both the House and the Senate proposals were referred to their respective judiciary committees. At that point a constitutional amendment was but one of several Republican legal strategies for fixing the problems with military emancipation and state abolition. But as the winter months passed, the amendment emerged as the consensus policy. With each passing week, as Republicans considered the various statutory approaches—legislating federal abolition, emancipating the families of black soldiers, criminalizing re-enslavement, reducing the slave states to territories—it became obvious that none of them inspired general support within the party. To be sure, a majority of Republicans seemed ready to abolish slavery by simple congressional legislation, but key party leaders—notably Trumbull and Lincoln—remained convinced that legislative abolition was both unconstitutional and, just as bad, vulnerable to legal challenge by a later Congress, by the courts, or by the southern states. Gradually the conclusion dawned: if the Constitution did not allow the federal government to abolish slavery in states where it was legal, the problem was the Constitution itself. And the problem suggested its own solution.

Once Republicans settled on a constitutional amendment as their preferred strategy for destroying slavery, the powerful antislavery consensus within the party reemerged. In 1864, winning the war and abolishing its cause by means of a thirteenth amendment were the two positions around which all Republicans could unite. In turn the Democrats lined up in opposition and called for a negotiated peace without regard to slavery. The result, especially in the House of Representatives, was a sustained and vituperative debate. Congressmen called each other names—traitors, Jacobins, war-mongers, slave-mongers, and negro-worshippers. And the reason for the bitterness was elementary: everyone understood that slavery was still very much alive and that the outcome of this debate would determine once and for all whether slavery would survive the war or be destroyed by it. The stakes could not have been higher.

The Republicans were in an awkward position. They had always been scrupulous about the constitutional legitimacy of their antislavery policies, stressing their allegiance to the intentions of the framers. How would they now justify rewriting the framers' Constitution? Senator Lyman Trumbull established the terms of the Republican debate when he reported the Thirteenth Amendment out of his Judiciary Committee on March 28, 1864. Indeed, the wording of the amendment was designed to shield the party from the charge of repudiating the Founders' intentions:

> SEC. 1. Neither slavery nor involuntary servitude, except as a punishment for crime whereof the party shall have been duly convicted, shall exist within the United States, or any place subject to their jurisdiction.
>
> ---
>
> SEC. 2. Congress shall have the power to enforce this article by appropriate legislation.[11]

Section 2, the enforcement clause, would give constitutional sanction to the various legislative proposals offered by Republicans to enforce the Emancipation Proclamation.[12] The wording of Section 1, however, came almost verbatim from the Ordinance of 1787, restricting slavery in the Northwest territories. It had been adopted by Congress under the Articles of Confederation and readopted by the very first Congress that met under the new Constitution. By importing the 1787 wording, the Senate Judiciary Committee linked the abolition amendment directly to the Founders and in particular to Thomas Jefferson, its original author.

Invoking the Northwest Ordinance, however, was not a purely instrumental move. Among political abolitionists and antislavery politicians, particularly in the Midwest, the Ordinance of 1787 was the touchstone of antislavery constitutionalism. It was widely believed that thanks to the ordinance there was no slavery in Michigan, Ohio, Indiana, Illinois, or Wisconsin. Eastern abolitionists felt no similar attachments, and Charles Sumner actually complained that the Judiciary Committee's amendment smacked too much of "the Jefferson Ordinance." Looking instead to Europe for a model, Sumner proposed an alternative wording based on the Declaration of the Rights of Man: "Men are born and continue free and equal in rights." This was just too . . . well, *French*, for the Senate. "I would not go to the French Revolution to find the proper words for the constitution," Trumbull declared. "We all know that their constitutions were failures." Michigan's Senator Jacob M. Howard agreed. "I prefer to dismiss all reference to French constitutions or French codes," he explained. Instead Howard would "go back to the good old Anglo-Saxon language employed by our fathers in the Ordinance of 1787." Not only was it domestically produced, not only did it tie the antislavery amendment to the Founders, it was also *popular* language, the familiar language of constitutional politics. The Northwest Ordinance, Howard explained, "is perfectly well understood both by the public and by judicial tribunals." It is "peculiarly near and dear to the people of the Northwest Territory," but it is also "well understood, well comprehended by the people of the United States." Some scholars suggest that the Northwest Ordinance was actually far more ambiguous in its language and effect than the senator believed. Rightly or wrongly, however, by the 1860s the Northwest Ordinance occupied an almost sacred place in the constitutional politics of the antislavery movement. It was a logical, popular choice for the wording of the new amendment. When Howard finished his paean to "the Jefferson Ordinance," Sumner conceded defeat. "My proposition," he said, "is withdrawn."[13]

If the wording alone were not enough to shield Republicans against the charge of shredding the constitutional fabric so carefully woven by the Founders, Trumbull draped himself in the tapestry as he introduced the amendment to his Senate colleagues. The Founders *intended* for slavery to disappear, he declared. "They looked forward to the not distant, nor as they supposed uncertain period when slavery should be abolished, and the Government became in fact, what they made it in name, one securing the blessings of liberty to all." Their intentions, though, were thwarted by a Slave Power that grew year by year more powerful, more belligerent, scuttling the hopes of the Founders. The Thirteenth Amendment merely implements their original intentions.[14] This was a familiar argument, long predating the war. The Founders intended to put slavery "in the course of ultimate extinction," but they were foiled by a Slave Power that dominated the presidency, the Congress, and the courts for seventy-five years. Opponents of slavery had been arguing this way for decades.

But hadn't the Slave Power been overthrown by the Republican ascendancy in 1860? Wasn't slavery doomed by the mere withdrawal of federal support? Wouldn't it crumble under the weight of war? What about all those antislavery laws and presidential proclamations attacking slavery? Weren't they enough? No, Trumbull answered. Slavery was not yet killed, and so long as it lived the Slave Power lived with it. Trumbull cited the conservative critics who claimed that the two confiscation acts had no effect and the Emancipation Proclamation freed no slaves. Trumbull was not prepared to say that the critics were entirely correct, but he was not going to dispute them either. "It is enough for me to show," he admitted, "that any and all of these laws and proclamations, giving to each the largest effect claimed by its friends, are ineffectual to the destruction of slavery." The Democrats may be wrong to claim that Republican antislavery policies had accomplished nothing, for clearly many slaves had been emancipated, but just as clearly, Trumbull acknowledged, emancipation had not been enough to abolish slavery. Full abolition could only be accomplished by rewriting the Constitution.

The Thirteenth Amendment that Trumbull reported out of his Judiciary Committee would do two things that military emancipation alone could not do. "[N]ot only does slavery cease," Trumbull explained, "but it can never be reestablished by State authority." Military emancipation could not free all the slaves; the Thirteenth Amendment would. Emancipation was no guarantee against the reestablishment of slavery; constitutional abolition was. Even "if slavery should be abolished by act of Congress or proclamation of the President," Trumbull warned, "there is nothing in the Constitution to prevent any State from reestablishing it." A constitutional amendment was the *only* way to ensure against re-enslavement.[15]

Thus did Lyman Trumbull spell out the terms on which Republicans would justify the antislavery amendment. Much of his argument was familiar, and over the ensuing months of congressional debate much of it would become repetitive as one Republican after another, in both the House and the Senate, took to the floor to regale his colleagues with yet another recitation of the shocking history of the Slave Power and its decades-long distortion of the true meaning of the Constitution.

It wasn't all familiar, though. There was a new twist in the history Republicans recited, a different lesson to be drawn that spoke directly to the need for a new amendment. In the prewar telling, slavery would be overthrown when the Slave Power was dislodged and the original meaning of the Constitution was restored. In 1864, Republicans wanted to rewrite the Constitution, and to do that the history of the Slave Power required a new concluding chapter. In the revised version the Founders were certainly well intentioned, yet they had made a fatal mistake. In 1787 they looked around and surmised that slavery was dying, and on that faulty assumption they willingly entered into a series of constitutional compromises with slavery. But slavery didn't die—it flourished, and the Slave Power flourished with it, thanks to the fatal concessions the Founders had made to slavery at the Constitutional Convention in Philadelphia. "They were good men and were wise in their day and generation," Congressman William Kelley of Pennsylvania explained, "but all wisdom did not die with them, and we are expiating in blood and agony and death and bereavement one of their errors—the unwise compromise they made with wrong in providing for the toleration and perpetuation of human slavery."[16] Here was the new lesson for 1864: don't make the same mistake the Founders made.

Slavery "still battles for existence," Henry Wilson warned. "[L]et not the anti-slavery men forget that the founders of the Republic believed slavery would wither and die beneath rays of the Christian and democratic institutions they founded." Slavery had "eluded and deceived our fathers." They had shown it mercy in what they hoped were its final days, but "from a feeble mendicant" slavery went on to become "the master of the Government and the people." Indeed so arrogant and powerful did slavery become that it finally plunged the entire nation into a brutal, bloody war. It would be a crime for that war to end without its cause having been eradicated. As in 1787, so in 1864. Congress and the president had done much to weaken slavery, and there was more that Congress could do to enforce the Emancipation Proclamation, Wilson argued, but "the crowning act" in this record of executive and legislative attacks on slavery "is this proposed amendment to the Constitution." Wilson had come to believe that Congress could legislatively abolish slavery, but killing slavery was no longer enough. All possibility of slavery's resurrection had to be destroyed as well. A constitutional amendment would not simply abolish slavery; it would also outlaw the reestablishment of slavery.

"The incorporation of this amendment into the organic law of the nation will make impossible forevermore the reappearing of the discarded slave system, and the returning of the despotism of the slave-masters' domination."[17]

The Founders made another error when they left slavery under the control of the states. "Our fathers were mistaken," California's Republican Congressman Thomas B. Shannon declared, when they compromised with slavery on the assumption that it would become extinct when in reality slavery "was not waning." On the contrary, every year "added strength to the accursed tree. . . . This mistake," Shannon concluded, "leaving to the people of the several States the right and authority to establish and regulate the crime of human slavery, has well-nigh proved a vital one."[18] It was time for the Republican Party to correct the error by abandoning the federal consensus. We abided by it, Shannon explained. "We said to the South, we will not interfere with your pet snake while you keep it in the den you have provided for it." The South, though, was not satisfied. "[E]very pacific overture was rejected, and no alternative was left to freemen of the North but war." The struggle has to be concluded, now and "for all future time." And the only way to do that was "by so amending our organic net that slavery can never again be an element of discord among our people."[19]

By its denial of federal power to interfere with slavery in the states where it existed, the Constitution had made it impossible to restrain the growth and power of slavery. The Thirteenth Amendment would rectify the error. It would allow the federal government to reach directly into the southern states and destroy forever one of their most cherished "domestic" institutions. It was on precisely this point—the deliberate assault on state authority—that Democrats and Border State congressmen launched their counterattack on the "unconstitutional" constitutional amendment.

DEMOCRATS COUNTERATTACK

On February 18, 1864, New York Democratic Congressmen James Brooks declared "the abolition of slavery as a fact accomplished." Brooks may have been sincere, but it's hard to tell because his fellow Democrats expunged his speech from the congressional record. He was not towing the party line. In the presidential election year of 1864, Democratic orthodoxy held that all Republican attempts to destroy slavery had failed. The confiscation acts were legally unenforceable, and both the Preliminary Proclamation and the final Emancipation Proclamation were mere *brutum fulmen*—they hadn't freed a single slave. The Republican war against slavery was not simply a failure; it was much worse than that. The wartime attack on slavery had actually strengthened the resolve of the rebels. Far from hastening the suppression of the rebellion, all those antislavery laws and proclamations had prolonged the "misery, bloodshed, and desolation" of the war. The South would never return to the Union so long as the Republicans maintained their determined opposition to slavery. Why would the seceded states ever negotiate the complete destruction of a social system that had already survived every Republican effort to overthrow it? It's easy to see why the Democrats suppressed James Brooks's speech. In the great congressional debate over the Thirteenth Amendment he was the outlier. Everybody else, Republicans and Democrats alike, were agreed on one crucial premise: the abolition of slavery was *not* "as a fact accomplished."[20]

It has always been too easy to fall into the habit of thinking that the abolition of slavery was inevitable, especially after the Emancipation Proclamation was issued. So it comes as something of a surprise to find Democrats launching a full-scale defense of slavery as late as June in 1864. It's less the substance of their argument that raises eyebrows than the mere fact that the debate over slavery was still raging so late in the game. Why now? Not since the war began had Democrats been able to stop Republicans from passing antislavery legislation. Republican majorities were too solid for that. But to stop a constitutional amendment, all the Democrats needed was one-third of the votes in either the House or the Senate. With crucial unionist Democrats in the Senate endorsing the amendment, it could be stopped only in the House. If Democrats kept their congressmen in line they could prevent slavery from being abolished. That's why they silenced Brooks; that's why Congress was still debating slavery.

The terms of the debate were familiar. Democrats objected to the amendment on the principle of "limited government," at least limited *central* government, for the decision to protect or abolish slavery had always been a state right. Republicans answered that the principle was perfectly sound but that slavery was hardly a worthy example of *limited* government. Wasn't it more like *tyranny*, they asked? Democrats claimed that slave property was indistinguishable from all other constitutionally protected forms of property; Republicans insisted that "property in man" was different, that it was both immoral and inconsistent with the Constitution. Democrats claimed that blacks were racially inferior and uniquely suited to slavery; Republicans insisted that as human beings blacks were equally entitled to their natural rights, to the fruits of their labor, and even to the privileges and immunities of citizenship. Republicans blamed the war on slavery; Democrats, on antislavery.

And yet, as familiar as it was, the debate was also extraordinary in part because it focused so exclusively on slavery itself. In the 1850s, slavery debates were indirect—they were provoked by the repeal of the Missouri Compromise, the protection of fugitive slaves in the North, or the legal propriety of the *Dred Scott* decision. Those debates had raised fundamental questions by means of distracting questions: Was the Lecompton Constitution valid? Were the personal liberty laws constitutional? Did Taney and Buchanan enter into a proslavery conspiracy? But 1864 was different. There were relatively few distract-ing side issues and the terms of the debate were fully understood. All sides agreed that slavery was still very much alive. To kill it, Republi-cans endorsed the Thirteenth Amendment, thereby repudiating the federal consensus that had always left the decision for or against slav-ery to the states. Democrats, content to let slavery survive, opposed the amendment and reiterated their support for the right of states to control their own "domestic institutions." And so in the spring of 1864 the U.S. Congress played host to the last full-scale national debate over the right versus the wrong of "property in man."

The defense of slavery had always rested on two distinct claims. The first was the abstract right of property in human beings, and in mid-1864 northern Democrats were still making the claim on behalf of southern slaveholders. "This proposition strikes at prop-erty," declared Fernando Wood, the New York Democrat, in his spirited denunciation of the Thirteenth Amendment. The Republi-can proposal "is unjust," Wood said, "because it involves a tyranni-cal destruction of individual property." All Democrats and Border State congressmen agreed. "[P]roperty is not regulated and was not intended to be regulated by the Constitution of the United States," Senator Willard Saulsbury of Delaware explained. Only states were constitutionally entitled to say "what shall be property and what shall not be property." He invoked the inevitable slippery slope: once you declare that one species of property—slaves—shall not be property, "you have a right to say that any other subject of property heretofore shall not be property." The proposed amendment, Sauls-bury warned, would "sweep away and blot out hundreds of millions of dollars' worth of property in the States." So fundamental was the right of property to the structure of government and society created by the Constitution, Democrats argued, that the proposed constitu-tional amendment was itself unconstitutional. "I do not deny the right of Congress to amend the Constitution of the United States for the benefit of the people," Pennsylvania's Democratic Congress-man Alexander H. Coffroth explained, "but I do deny the right of Congress to amend the Constitution to the destruction of the right of the people to hold property."[21]

Republicans responded with their familiar repudiation of "prop-erty in man." It was intrinsically immoral, and although some states had legalized it, the Constitution did not; it recognized slaves only as "persons held in service," never as property. Slaves "are property," one Republican explained, "only when we acknowledge the institution as a legal and right one between man and man. But I deny that, in right and justice, such an institution can exist." Democrats complain that the Thirteenth Amendment "strikes at property," Republican Con-gressman John F. Farnsworth noted, "that it interferes with the vested rights of the people of the States in property." But can a statute make property of men? "I deny it," Farnsworth answered. "What vested right has any man or State in property in man?" God gave man dominion over chattels, *things*. "But nowhere did He give dominion to man over another man." As legal "persons," blacks were entitled to the fruits of their labor. It was possible for one person to make a "property" claim, based in contract, on the "services" of another per-son, but it was not legitimate to claim a right of property in the entire person, and certainly not in the "services" of that person's children.[22]

The second enduring element in the proslavery defense—complementing the abstract justification of slavery as an inalienable right of property—was the claim that blacks were racially inferior and as such uniquely suited to slavery. The horrors of emancipation, espe-cially the prospect of a war of racial extermination, loomed as another major theme in the Democratic attacks on the Thirteenth Amend-ment. Abolition, one Democrat warned, would "set free four million ignorant and debased negroes to swarm the country with pestilential effect." Another predicted that Republicans would sweep through the South "with a sword in one hand and a fire-brand in the other, burning and destroying as they went, in order to do—what? To wipe out the white people of the country and supplant them by black free men, whom they are going to make American citizens."[23]

Democrats put the matter in the bluntest terms: blacks weren't worth a war. "If negro emancipation is found to stand in the way of the reestablishment of our free and united Government," Democrats argued, the Republicans were obliged by "high and patriotic duty to *let the negro slide*." Where Democrats wanted to negotiate a swift peace that would let slavery survive, Republicans "would peril the nation with its thirty million Anglo-Saxons for the supposed benefit of three or four million African slaves; they would extirpate slavery at whatever cost of sacrifice of blood and treasure." Republicans, Democrats charged, would foment servile insurrection, starve white women and children, desolate the southern landscape, confiscate property— and for what purpose? To "place the negro as to civil and political rights on an equality with whites."[24]

Here were the twin pillars of proslavery thought, the abstract and the particular: on the one hand, the general right of property in man—a natural right, predating law and society, yet spanning all of human history and sanctioned by the unimpeachable authority of the Bible; and on the other hand, the racial specification of *who* should be enslaved, a limitation decreed by the biological destiny of blacks whose innate inferiority rendered them uniquely suited to be slaves. For decades these had been the core precepts of proslavery thought, the organizing themes of proslavery politics, and they were reiterated freely and without apology by Democrats in both houses of Congress in the spring of 1864.

Republicans countered both arguments, denouncing the morality and the constitutionality of "property in man" and ignoring, sometimes even mocking, the claims for black racial inferiority. They insisted that slavery was immoral because all men were equal in the sight of God, or because it violated the natural-law principle of fundamental human equality. They presupposed the basic humanity of blacks and declared that the promise of universal freedom in the Declaration of Independence applied to whites and blacks alike. They said that all men and women, regardless of their race, were equally entitled to the fruits of their labor. And they claimed that blacks were citizens of the United States and as such were entitled to the privileges and immunities of citizenship. It was their citizenship that ensured that emancipated blacks were "forever free." It was their citizenship that enabled black men to enlist in the Union army. When Senator Garrett Davis of Kentucky proposed a law declaring that "no negro, or person whose mother or grandmother is or was a negro, shall be a citizen of the United States," the overwhelmingly Republican Senate rejected his proposal by a resounding vote of 32 to 5. Sometimes Republicans even denounced racism itself. Senator Timothy O. Howe of Wisconsin heaped contempt on the claim that blacks were suited to slavery because "they as a race are inferior to the whites." In the "whole catalogue" of excuses for the "crime" of slavery, Howe declared, this "one single excuse" was actually "more odious than the crime itself." Even if the racist argument were true, which Howe doubted, it would make the crime only worse, for it would imply the sinful enslavement of the weak by the strong. Howe likewise dismissed the repeated warnings of Democrats and Border State congressmen that abolition would lead to a war of extermination between the races. "This is not to be insisted upon; it is not to be believed," Howe replied, "it is a libel upon humanity, black or white."[25] The Republican commitment to racial equality did not extend into the social spheres of life that were traditionally regulated in states and localities, but their antislavery policies presupposed a basic racial equality and they defended that position more and more openly as the war went on.[26]

Thus did the debate over the Thirteenth Amendment raise the

most fundamental questions at stake in the Civil War: What kind of nation was the United States supposed to be? The supporters of abolition had always believed that freedom should be presupposed everywhere, unless local laws interposed against that premise. In the end the commitment to freedom national led Republicans to support a constitutional amendment imposing freedom even on states that would have preferred to maintain slavery. Democrats presupposed that freedom was intrinsically local, and that it extended even to the paradoxical "freedom" of states and localities to enslave black people. Indeed, precisely because the right of "property in man" was a natural right, it did not require "positive" law to exist. Thus Fernando Wood rejected the *Somerset* principle when he insisted that slavery "is not the creature of law. It existed without law before this Government was established. It is incorporated into the organization of society as part of the existing domestic relations. It cannot be brought within constitutional jurisdiction any more than any or either of the other private and personal interests." For Wood, positive local law was necessary to *abolish* slavery, not to create it.[27]

This implied a fundamentally different view of the nature of the federal Union. For Democrats freedom depended on state rights, and slavery was one of the things states were by right free to have. "Give up our right to have slavery," Congressman Robert Mallory of Kentucky warned, "and in what right are we secure? One after another will be usurped . . . until all State rights will be gone, and perhaps State limits obliterated." In Fernando Wood's words, by "obliterating" the right of states to have slavery, the Thirteenth Amendment would "alter the whole structure and theory of government by changing the basis upon which it rests." The federal consensus had long decreed that only a state could abolish slavery. "The right of Kentucky to continue slavery," Senator Garrett Davis insisted, "was as perfect as was the right of Massachusetts to abolish it." By this reasoning the Thirteenth Amendment would actually violate the fundamental premises of the Constitution.[28]

The debate raged on. Democrats charged that the Republican Party's fanatical commitment to abolition had united white southerners in support of the rebellion. Republicans pointed to the flood of southern whites deserting the Confederacy, abandoning their armies and pouring into Washington. Is that what you call uniting the southern people? Kelley asked. Do so many confederate defectors suggest that we are making the people of the South "a unit"? Democrats claimed that by making the abolition of slavery a precondition for peace, the Republicans had destroyed all possibility of a negotiated settlement. The amendment "means nothing else than eternal disunion and a continuous war." Republicans insisted that "[w]e can have no permanent peace while slavery lives." Democrats claimed that Republican animosity toward slavery had crushed southern unionism. Republicans answered that slaves were the only reliable unionists in the South and that emancipation properly rewarded and protected blacks for their loyalty. Democrats charged that the proposed constitutional amendment proved that for Republicans the "purpose" of the war had never been the restoration of the Union but the overthrow of slavery. They "had this design from the commencement" of the war, Fernando Wood claimed. Republicans, on the other hand, insisted that the "purpose" of the war was no different in 1864 than it had been in 1861. They would suppress the rebellion and restore the Union, and they would do so by undermining slavery, the cause of the rebellion. The means, not the ends, of the war had changed. Among Republicans and Democrats alike "the common end is the maintenance of the Union," Lincoln observed in December of 1864, and "among the means to secure that end" is the constitutional amendment "abolishing slavery throughout the United States." Republicans equated liberty with Union and slavery with disunion. "On the one side is disunion for the sake of slavery," Maryland Congressman John A. J. Creswell declared, "on the other side is freedom for the sake of Union."[29]

THE DEMOCRATS SUCCEEDED; the amendment failed. Not in the Senate, which had approved it by a lopsided vote of 38 to 6,[30] but in the House. On June 15, 1864, the House Democrats maintained their party's discipline and prevented the resolution from garnering the two-thirds vote necessary to send the Thirteenth Amendment to the states for ratification.[31] The votes fell out in what was by then a thoroughly familiar pattern. Seventy-eight Republicans voted yes and one voted no. Four Democrats supported the amendment; fifty-eight opposed it. With ordinary legislation this would have resulted in yet another Republican antislavery victory, but because it was a constitutional amendment, the Democrats won with only one-third of the votes in the House.

Infuriated by the Democratic sabotage of the amendment, Republicans revived the idea of legislative emancipation and passed "[a] bill to guarantee to certain states whose governments have been usurped or overthrown a republican form of government." The Wade-Davis Bill, as it was later called, is best known as an early indication of the disagreement between Lincoln and the radicals over Reconstruction policy, and that was certainly part of it. The timing of the bill, however, suggests that it was at least as much a repudiation of the House Democrats. The title refers to a precept long familiar to a small but ingenious group of radical abolitionists who interpreted the Constitution as an antislavery document. The Constitution guaranteed every state a "republican form of government," which, they argued, was incompatible with slavery. Most abolitionists and nearly all Republicans had resisted that logic, for that would mean that the federal government could legislatively abolish slavery in the states. But by June of

1864, especially in the immediate aftermath of the House vote, a majority of Republicans were prepared to abandon the federal consensus, with or without a constitutional amendment. Lincoln was not prepared to go that far.

The difference between Lincoln and the Republicans in Congress had become substantial. Both would require state abolition as a condition for readmission to the Union. However, because Lincoln continued to believe that only "military emancipation" was strictly constitutional, he believed that only the commander in chief could require a state to endorse the Emancipation Proclamation as a means of suppressing the rebellion. By contrast, Section 12 of the Wade-Davis Bill simply abolished slavery outright, declaring that "all persons held to involuntary servitude" in the rebel states "are hereby emancipated and discharged therefrom, and they and their posterity shall be forever free." Re-enslavement was declared illegal. If any emancipated slaves "shall be restrained of liberty, under pretense of any claim to such service or labor, the courts of the United States shall, on *habeas corpus*, discharge them." Persons convicted of the crime of re-enslavement were liable to a steep fine and a prison sentence of at least five years and as much as twenty years.[32]

This was too much for Lincoln. We were elected on the principle that the Constitution did not allow us to abolish slavery in the states, he said. To repudiate that principle now would discredit every promise the Republican Party ever made. The issue was not really Reconstruction. The Wade-Davis Bill imposed more stringent requirements for reestablishing loyal governments in the rebel states than had Lincoln, but he was not "inflexibly committed to any single plan." Lincoln would not, however, "declare a constitutional competency in congress to abolish slavery in states." He pocketed the bill rather than sign it, a veto because it was passed on the last day of Congress. There was the usual outrage against executive usurpation but no lasting breach within the party, in part because Lincoln himself had already required the rebel states to endorse the Emancipation Proclamation as a condition for readmission to the Union and in part because many Republicans still agreed with Lincoln that Congress could not abolish slavery in a state. Like the more conservative John Sherman and the more radical Lyman Trumbull, Lincoln was "sincerely hoping and expecting that a constitutional amendment abolishing slavery throughout the nation will be adopted."[33]

Lincoln had one more reason for not signing the Wade-Davis Bill. Two states—Louisiana and Arkansas—had already reorganized their state governments and were abolishing slavery. If the president signed the bill, those new state governments would be invalidated and their abolitions thereby undermined. Notwithstanding Lincoln's hopes for a thirteenth amendment, its failure in the House made state abolition more critical than ever.

STATE ABOLITION

Part of the frustration on display during congressional passage of the Wade-Davis Bill stemmed from the fact that by July of 1864 only two states had actually abolished slavery. All along, state abolition had been the major goal of antislavery politics, and this was an unpromising record of success, especially so in light of the increasingly obvious limits of military emancipation. Lincoln had devoted increasing attention to state abolition in the year since he issued the Emancipation Proclamation. In the summer of 1863 his letters to state officials strongly urged them to endorse some form of abolition, whether gradual or immediate. By the fall of that year his tone shifted, and he began to warn state politicians that their efforts to reorganize loyal state governments would come to nothing if they did not abolish slavery along the way. Lincoln had hoped that Louisiana would abolish slavery by the time Congress returned in December of 1863. Antislavery coalitions had formed in

several states, but by July of 1864 none of those coalitions had succeeded. Finally, in September of 1864, Louisiana voters endorsed an
abolition amendment to the state constitution, and in late October,
Maryland voters did so as well, though by an extremely narrow margin. Yet as of Election Day in November of 1864, when the fate of the
Thirteenth Amendment was being decided in the presidential balloting
only three of the fifteen slave states had abolished slavery.

Lincoln had announced his decision to require the rebel states to
emancipate their slaves in his annual message to Congress on December 8, 1863. He began with the reminder that under the Constitution
"the general government had no lawful power to effect emancipation
in any State." It could, however, establish standards for admission to
the Union—and by extension for readmission to the Union. It could,
for example, require all those wishing to participate in state government to swear "an oath of allegiance to the Constitution of the United
States." And if it could require loyalty to the Constitution, Lincoln
wondered, why not "also to the laws and proclamations in regard to
slavery?" After all, those laws and proclamations were justified as measures needed to suppress the rebellion and sustain the Constitution.
Moreover, one hundred thousand blacks had by then enlisted in the
Union army. Together with the confiscation acts and the emancipation proclamations, black troops had proved to be invaluable weapons
in the federal arsenal. "To now abandon them would be not only to
relinquish a lever of power, but would also be a cruel and an astound-
ing breach of faith." He reiterated, emphatically, that he would never
retract the Emancipation Proclamation, "nor shall I return to slavery
any person who is free by the terms of that proclamation, or by any of
the acts of Congress." For all of these reasons, Lincoln concluded, he
would henceforth require two basic things of any seceded states
choosing to "resume their allegiance" to the Union. First, all those
participating in the restored state government would have to swear an
oath of loyalty to the Union. Second, the restored government would

have to endorse the Emancipation Proclamation. At that point there was no Thirteenth Amendment, so abolition would be accomplished by formal state endorsement of the military.[34]

These were the major elements of Lincoln's famous "Proclamation of Amnesty and Reconstruction," which he submitted to Congress along with his annual message. Though often treated like tea leaves that might reveal Lincoln's "plan" for reconstruction, the proclamation was at least as significant for its immediate and relatively unambiguous implications for emancipation. Lincoln required 10 percent of the 1860 voters to take the oaths he prescribed, although he also indicated that he had no particular commitment to this so-called Ten Percent Plan for reconstruction. More telling than the percentage of citizens swearing the oath was the content of the oath itself. Lincoln required Louisianans to avow their allegiance to "the Constitution of the United States, and the union of the States thereunder," but he also required them to "faithfully support all acts of Congress passed during the existing rebellion with reference to slaves" as well as "all proclamations of the President made during the existing rebellion having reference to slaves."[35] Simply put, they had to endorse both liberty *and* Union. Everything else was negotiable.

As of December 8, 1863, then, seceded states had to embrace the Emancipation Proclamation as a condition for readmission to the Union. Whether those states would comply was an open question. It depended on how much power the slaveholders retained. At its core secession was a slaveholders' rebellion, and even in the Border States support for secession was concentrated in the master class. By requiring an oath of loyalty to the Union, President Lincoln therefore helped shift the balance of political power within the loyal slave states away from the master class, making antislavery politics much more viable. Federal authorities had far less leverage in the four Border States that had remained loyal to the Union, but in two of them—Maryland and Missouri—state-imposed loyalty oaths had a similar effect, severely undermining the political influence of the slave-owning class. The slaveholders inadvertently helped as well. In the Border States thousands of secessionist masters defected to the Confederacy, absenting themselves from the wartime politics of their respective states. In Missouri the slaveholding class bankrupted itself by investing heavily in a pro-Confederate government that lost control of the state early in the war.[36] As the power of the slaveholding class waned a new politics of slavery emerged. Proslavery forces were weakened, of course, but antislavery forces divided into factions, with conservatives supporting gradual abolition and radicals favoring immediate.

Lincoln was frustrated by these divisions within the antislavery coalition. For him "the common object"—the abolition of slavery— was more important than the particular means of accomplishing it. "Of all things," he urged General Frederick Steele in Arkansas, "avoid if possible, a dividing into cliques among the friends of the common object." He had initially proposed a system of gradual abolition to begin right away, but when the Arkansans went further, abolishing slavery outright, Lincoln was pleased and urged Steele to back off. "They seem to be doing so well," he wrote, that the best thing to do was "to help them on their own plan."[37] This was one indication that Lincoln's support for gradual abolition was more pragmatic than dogmatic. It never affected his commitment to immediate and uncompensated military emancipation, for example. Gradual abolition was something Lincoln urged on the states acting on their own, and he supported it for different reasons. He worried about the effect immediate emancipation would have on children and the elderly, who might not be able to care for themselves if emancipated immediately. Fully aware of the humanitarian crisis in the South and shocked by its dimensions, Lincoln held to his conviction that gradual abolition was a more humane way to destroy slavery. He also thought a gradual approach would garner the broadest base of support for abolition within the affected states. But Lincoln was never inflexibly committed to gradualism. Indeed, he complained that his "expressions of preference for *gradual* over *immediate* emancipation, are misunderstood." He had thought a gradual approach would be easier for everyone, but if "those who are better acquainted with the subject" preferred immediate emancipation, "most certainly I have no objection." Lincoln's basic "wish," he explained, "is that all who are for emancipation *in any form*, shall co-operate." When in 1864, Arkansas, then Maryland, then Missouri, adopted immediate abolition, Lincoln gave them his enthusiastic endorsement.[38]

ARKANSAS WAS THE FIRST seceded state to abolish slavery. As early as July in 1863, Lincoln was urging General Stephen Hurlbut to promote a plan of gradual abolition in the state. The slaves already freed were free forever, Lincoln explained. For those remaining enslaved, emancipation should "begin at once," even if it proceeded gradually. Commencing abolition immediately would diminish the chances of slavery being reestablished, or so Lincoln hoped. In late 1863 Union forces routed the Confederates and expelled them from the state, setting off an exodus of pro-southern planters who packed up their farms and moved their slaves to Texas. The "loss of the Ark. Valey was disastrous in the extreme," one pro-Confederate Arkansan wrote to Jefferson Davis. The "immense immigration of planters & others flocking there [to Texas] to save their slaves" meant that the only people left in Arkansas were "lukewarm and disloyal" southerners, otherwise known as unionists.[39] Almost immediately the balance of political power shifted to the supporters of abolition.

A state constitutional convention met on January 4, 1864, composed only of delegates who could swear an oath of loyalty to the Union and who had never participated in the rebellion. Since this effectively excluded most of the state's slaveholders, the convention had no trouble meeting Lincoln's requirements. By then the Thirteenth Amendment had been introduced in Congress, and Arkansas chose that route to abolition rather than the endorsement of the Emancipation Proclamation that Lincoln had asked for in early December. Ten days into the convention a committee reported to the floor a proposal to retain the existing state constitution, but with an amendment declaring that "[t]here shall be neither slavery nor involuntary servitude" in Arkansas. In late January a delegation petitioned Lincoln to be allowed to reorganize the state government under a new constitution. When he learned that the convention's own proposal for government reorganization differed slightly from his own, Lincoln instructed General Steele to "harmonize" the two plans, making "sure to retain the free State constitutional provision in some unquestionable form." The amended Arkansas constitution was submitted to the eligible voters for ratification on March 4. Confederates vowed to disrupt the voting process and immediately denounced the results, which were indeed spectacularly lopsided: 12,177 in favor of the new abolition constitution, 266 against. Thus was slavery abolished in Arkansas on March 4, 1864.[40]

Arkansas was a success for Lincoln, but Louisiana was a more important one. In June of 1863, a group of Louisiana planters petitioned Lincoln to allow them to form a loyal state government under the old constitution, with slavery intact. By then, however, Lincoln had already been warned by Michael Hahn, a leader of the emerging Free State movement, that "the more radical or free-soil Union men" of Louisiana favored a new constitution that would abolish slavery. Lincoln rejected the conservatives' petition, noting that "a respectable portion of the Louisiana people desire to amend their State constitution, and contemplate holding a convention for that object."[41] There was no doubt what Lincoln meant by this: he wanted Louisiana to abolish slavery on its own. "I would be glad for her to make a new Constitution recognizing the emancipation proclamation, and adopting emancipation in those parts of the state to which the proclamation does not apply."[42] At that point Lincoln was still willing to suggest but not force Louisiana, or any state, to comply with his wishes.

But the proslavery forces in Louisiana proved obstreperous, and by November, Lincoln was clearly losing patience. "If a few professedly loyal men shall draw the disloyal about them, and colorably set up a State government, repudiating the emancipation proclamation, and re-establishing slavery, I can not recognize or sustain their work." I would be "powerless to do so," Lincoln added, for it would fatally divide "this government"—that is, the Republican-dominated government—which was firmly committed to "general freedom." Louisiana could rejoin the Union only "by acting in harmony with this government." He was less concerned with the specific terms by which the slaves were emancipated, "but my word is out to be *for* and not *against* them on the question of their permanent freedom."[43] As much as anything else it was Lincoln's frustration with Louisiana that led him, in December of 1863, to settle the dispute between radical and conservative unionists by requiring state endorsement of the Emancipation Proclamation as a condition for readmission to the Union.[44] Thereafter, supporters of emancipation in Louisiana split between moderates, led by Hahn, who stopped with abolition, and radicals who hoped to push the revolution further into the realms of civil and political equality for blacks and whites.

Pressed by Lincoln, General Nathaniel Banks called for delegate elections on March 28, 1864, to a constitutional convention that would abolish slavery in Louisiana. Led by now-Governor Hahn, the moderates swept the elections and dominated the convention, which opened on April 6. Planters and the prewar political elite were conspicuously absent, having been effectively disfranchised by the loyalty oath Lincoln required. By then Republicans had embraced the Thirteenth Amendment. Abolition was therefore a foregone conclusion, and most of the convention debate focused instead on the issue of racial equality after abolition—on the establishment of a public school system for African American children, voting rights for black men, and various civil rights. Yet these discussions presupposed universal emancipation, which remained the main business of the convention. The abolition of slavery was debated for two days beginning on May 9, and on May 11 the convention approved a brief amendment to the state constitution. Like that of Arkansas, it was modeled on the Northwest Ordinance, abolishing "slavery or involuntary servitude, except as a punishment for crime." The convention adjourned in late July and submitted the new constitution to eligible voters. On September 5, 1864, Louisiana's anti-slavery constitution was approved by the overwhelming majority of a minuscule electorate. The legislature of Louisiana, the new constitution read, "shall make no law recognizing the right of property in man."[45]

LINCOLN BELIEVED HE COULD REQUIRE seceded states like Arkansas and Louisiana to endorse the Emancipation Proclamation, but he had no such power over slavery in the four Border States, which had never left the Union. Nevertheless, federal authorities resorted to increasingly aggressive tactics to weaken slavery and strengthen its opponents. The most effective, and controversial, of those tactics was the conscription of slaves owned by loyal masters. The Militia Act passed on July 17, 1862, had opened the army to black men by removing the word *white* from the requirements for enlistment, but it had also eliminated the word *free*. That meant that when Lincoln ordered the enlistment of *black* men in the Emancipation Proclamation he was simultaneously endorsing the recruitment of *slaves*. Republicans were aiming at loyal masters, especially in the Border States, since slaves in disloyal areas were already emancipated and therefore eligible for enlistment. By mid-1863 the Union army had opened recruitment centers in all four Border slave states—Maryland, Delaware, Kentucky, and Missouri—setting off a series of feuds between the War Department and proslavery state politicians. In late September of 1863, after months of wrangling, Secretary of War Stanton met with Maryland's

Governor Augustus Bradford and came to an agreement on federal recruitment policy. Because the military situations were similar in Maryland and Tennessee—which had been exempted from the Emancipation Proclamation—Stanton waited to issue a general order until after he had concluded an agreement on the same terms with the military governor of Tennessee, Andrew Johnson. Under the new policy, slaves of disloyal masters as well as free blacks could be recruited without obstruction. Slaves of loyal masters could also be recruited as a military necessity, with a possibility of later compensation to unionist owners. In practice this meant that army recruiters in the Border States could enlist any able-bodied men they chose.[46]

Lincoln endorsed Stanton's proposal in a memo indicating that he had "no objection" to the recruitment of either "free negroes" or "slaves of disloyal owners." Slaves of loyal masters could be recruited if the master consented, or if there was an "urgent" military necessity. Otherwise, Lincoln indicated, the ban on enticement of slaves owned by loyal masters remained in effect in the Border States. That is, all able-bodied males could be recruited into the Union army, but no other slaves should be "enticed" from their owners. Unlike the disloyal states, enticement in the Border States was restricted to able-bodied men willing to serve in the Union army. Slaves of loyal masters who voluntarily came to Union lines—the wives and children of recruits, for example—could not be legally excluded. Once Johnson's agreement was secured Stanton formalized the policy as General Orders No. 329 on October 1, 1863. Union recruiters treated the agreement as carte blanche to enlist all able-bodied black men, regardless of the loyalties of their owners.[47]

Within weeks the War Department opened seventeen black recruitment stations in Maryland, over the renewed protests of Governor Bradford. The Board of Claims, established to determine the loyalty of masters whose slaves had been recruited, was stacked with radicals hostile to slavery. As the federal government engaged in its not-so-veiled assault on slavery in Maryland, state politics shifted in ways that reflected the severely weakened power of the slaveholding class. The victory of the unionists in the 1861 elections had prompted a large number of Maryland slaveholders to defect to the Confederacy. Once in power the unionists imposed loyalty oaths that effectively disfranchised many more slaveholders. Over the course of 1863 long-simmering anti-slaveholder politics mushroomed into antislavery politics. With the hard-core proslavery element effectively squashed, politics in Maryland was no longer a struggle between secessionists and unionists, but between conservative and radical unionists.[48]

In the 1863 state elections conservatives struggled to restrain antislavery radicalism. At first they dismissed all talk of emancipation as "unwise and impolitic." Pressured to go further, conservatives ended up calling for a "sound" and "practical" emancipation," by which they meant gradual abolition with compensation for the owners. With each passing month, though, the radical opponents of slavery grew bolder in their demands. By November the radical unionists had staked out a position in favor of immediate, uncompensated abolition of slavery. In rhetoric that fused hostility to slaveholders with hostility to slavery, Maryland radicals denounced "the domination of an interest over free men; of property over people; of aristocratic privilege over republican equality, of a minority over a majority." It was in these 1863 canvasses that Henry Winter Davis emerged as a leading voice of Maryland radicals, and his own shifting position reflected the general drift of the state's politics. If compensation "can be gotten, let it come," he declared, but "if it can not be gotten, Emancipation will come without it." The radicals, in league with the Union army, did what they could to suppress the conservative vote—test oaths, arbitrary arrests, and voter intimidation—resulting in a lopsided victory for the supporters of abolition. But the conservatives seemed to grasp that even without electoral chicanery the radicals would have won anyway. By December conservative unionists like Governor Bradford were abandoning their support for gradual emancipation and endorsing a constitutional convention that would abolish slavery immediately. Lincoln repeated to Maryland emancipationists the same thing he had told Louisianans the year before—that notwithstanding his preference for gradual abolition, his primary concern was to get slavery abolished by whatever means garnered the most support within the state.[49]

In early February of 1864, Maryland unionists in the legislature endorsed a referendum for a constitutional convention, and the elections for delegates offered the state's voters a straight-up choice between the unionists who supported immediate abolition by means of a new state constitution and Democrats who opposed both. "If you are opposed to free-loveism, communism, agrarianism," Democrats declared, *"vote against a Convention."* Not surprisingly the slaveholding districts in the southern part of the state rejected the convention by two-to-one-margins, but they were swamped by the antislavery votes from Baltimore and the northern counties.[50]

The constitutional convention met at Annapolis on April 27, 1864, but it did not complete its work until September 6, when the delegates sent to the people a new constitution that duplicated the language of the Thirteenth Amendment passed by the U.S. Senate the previous spring: "Hereafter, in this State, there shall be neither slavery nor involuntary servitude, except in punishment of crime, whereof the party shall have been duly convicted; and all persons held to service or labor, as slaves, are hereby declared free." Democrats denounced emancipation as "robbery." They tried to secure compensation but, failing that, tried instead to establish an apprenticeship system. All such halfway measures were easily swept aside by the emboldened antislavery forces.[51]

Their boldness, however, did not command a majority of votes in the constitutional referendum held on October 12. Lincoln made his own position clear two days before the ballot. "[I]t is no secret, that I wish success to this provision," he declared. "I desire it on every consideration. I wish all men to be free." Nevertheless, when they

went to the polls on October 12, it looked as though Maryland voters had defeated the new constitution by a tally of 27,541 to 29,536.
Only the uncounted soldiers' ballots, which split ten to one in favor,
saved the antislavery constitution. On October 29, Governor Bradford announced that Maryland's new constitution had been ratified
by a mere 263 votes. Slavery was finally abolished in Maryland.[52]
When news arrived in Washington, Lincoln congratulated "Maryland, and the nation, and the world, upon the event."[53]

At that point the fate of slavery was still undecided in Tennessee.
As with Arkansas, Lincoln pressed for the organization of a loyal anti-
slavery government as soon as the Confederates were expelled from
the state, months before he issued his Proclamation of Amnesty and
Reconstruction. His strongest ally in the struggle to get slavery abolished in Tennessee was the state's military governor, Andrew Johnson.
"Not a moment should be lost" organizing a loyal government, Lincoln urged in September of 1863. But loyalty would not be enough.
"Get emancipation into your new State government," Lincoln told
Johnson, "and there will be no such word as fail for your case." To
help ensure that Tennessee would remain secure against further Confederate military incursions, Lincoln also urged Johnson to "do your
utmost to get every man you can, black and white, under arms at the
very earliest moment."[54]

Johnson made repeated attempts to organize a loyal government
on the basis of Lincoln's plan. He called for elections to state offices
on March 5, 1864, but almost no "loyal" citizens appeared at the
polls. In May, Johnson made another attempt, this time in Knoxville,
to organize a loyal convention, but the majority opposed abolition
and the movement died. Another convention met in Nashville in September. This time military raids kept numerous delegates from attend-
ing, and those who participated endorsed abolition by means of
amendments to the Tennessee state constitution. To that end, the delegates called for a constitutional convention to assemble in Nashville

on January 9, 1865. As the 1864 elections approached, though, it was not clear what Tennessee would do.[55]

In Missouri, a familiar combination of loyalty oaths and slaveholder defections to the Confederacy might not have been enough to undermine the political power of Missouri's slave owners, but their financial self-beheading finished them off. They had invested heavily in an insecure pro-Confederate state government by borrowing heavily from insecure pro-southern banks. When Union forces expelled the rebels and took over the state they installed unionist bankers who called in the loans and foreclosed on the rebel investors. In an unusual real-world test of land confiscation, the slaveholders' farms were expropriated and sold off in lots. The slaveholding class was thereby destroyed.[56] There had been a current of antislavery politics in antebellum Missouri, but when the war came the subtraction of planter power and the addition of federal pressure gave the opponents of slavery an unusual opportunity.

Federal pressure was already apparent in early September of 1862, when Secretary of War Stanton informed General John M. Schofield that "disloyal persons" in Missouri were "subject to the provisions of the [Second] Confiscation Act." Stanton was effectively ordering Schofield to emancipate all slaves owned by rebel masters, something General John Frémont had tried to do a year earlier, before Congress had authorized it. Schofield issued the appropriate orders, but in the autobiography he published after the war he all but boasted that he had done nothing to implement Stanton's instructions. Schofield's replacement, General Samuel Curtis, had very different views "in regard to the negro question." On November 1, 1862, he distinguished between the slaves of loyal owners—who should be left alone—and "the negroes of men in rebellion or giving encouragement to rebellion that are free." Since the majority of Missouri's slaveholders were probably disloyal, Curtis's policy represented a direct federal threat to slavery in the state.[57]

As in Maryland, Missouri's conservative unionists—led by Governor Hamilton Gamble—initially pushed back against federal antislavery policies. But radical gains in the 1862 elections persuaded Gamble to support gradual abolition as the alternative to the immediate abolition endorsed by the radicals. In July of 1863, the provisional government approved a gradual abolition statute, but it would not be submitted to voters in a referendum until a year and a half later. Meanwhile, as Missouri's slaveholding class was dying, the radicals were gaining ground. In November they elected B. Gratz Brown to the Senate. By 1864 both of Missouri's senators in Washington were avowed supporters of the Thirteenth Amendment. The presidential election in 1864 finally split the unionists apart. The most conservative among them went over to the Democrats and endorsed George McClellan. Gradual and immediate emancipationists sent competing delegations to the National Union (Republican) convention in June. Since the Republicans were by then committed to a thirteenth amendment, the radical delegation was seated. Back in Missouri, however, the fate of the radicals—and with it the future of slavery in the state—depended on the outcome of the November elections for a new governor and legislature, the first such elections to be held in Missouri since before the war began.[58]

LIKE MILITARY EMANCIPATION, state abolition was a limited success rather than an abject failure. No state had abolished slavery in more than half a century until, in 1864 alone, Arkansas, Louisiana, and Maryland did so. By the end of the year there was a good chance that Missouri and Tennessee would do so as well. But— again like military emancipation—state abolition was not enough to destroy slavery. In some states all of the Union efforts to force abolition had failed. In early 1864, Lincoln's representatives in Florida gave up any hope of finding even 10 percent of the 1860 electorate willing to take the loyalty oath. In Delaware, opposition to abolition seemed to strengthen rather than weaken over the course of the war, despite the fact that a substantial number of Delaware blacks enlisted in the Union army. Most disconcerting of all to Republicans was Kentucky, where the slaveholders resisted all federal pressure and instead launched legal challenges that threatened to undermine the basis of Union antislavery policy. In all but one of the most heavily populated slave states of the Deep South, the federal government was in no position whatsoever to force the issue of abolition. And even in those states that had succumbed to federal pressure, wartime abolition was sorely lacking in democratic and constitutional legitimacy. Slavery could be abolished only if secessionist voters—often electoral majorities that included the wealthiest, most powerful men in the state— were somehow disfranchised. But they could not be disfranchised forever, and so the question Republicans began asking in 1862 was more salient than ever in 1864: What will happen to slavery when the war is over, even in the states that had abolished slavery? The answer— which is to say the fate of slavery—depended on the outcome of the election of 1864.

THE ELECTION OF 1864

On June 17, 1864, two days after the proslavery minority in the House blocked passage of the Thirteenth Amendment, the *New York Times* observed that the Democrats had thereby confronted voters with "a first-class civil question, at the coming election." The campaign might otherwise have focused exclusively on the Lincoln administration's conduct of the war, but now the Republican Party had "two momentous objects before it." The first was the reelection of Abraham Lincoln, which, the *Times* said, would "insure that the war shall be prosecuted until the last rebel soldier lays down his arms."

That was always going to be an issue. Now, though, there was a second one: "the election of two-thirds of the members of the next Congress," giving the Republicans the votes they needed to send to the
states "the amendment abolishing all Slavery in the land forever." By
their action the Democrats ensured that the 1864 election would do
the very thing they most objected to: render inseparable the issues of
slavery and the conduct of the war.[59]

Actually, the Republicans had made the amendment a partisan
political issue even before the June 15 vote in the House. Rechristen-
ing themselves the Union Party, Republicans had met in Baltimore
on June 7 and 8 and easily nominated Abraham Lincoln for reelection on a platform forthrightly endorsing the unconditional and
immediate abolition of slavery everywhere in the United States.
Although the party had never before endorsed such a proposal, the
Republicans nonetheless fitted it into their traditional theme of liberty and Union. The primary purpose of the war remained the same.
It is "the highest duty of every American citizen" to maintain the
"integrity of the Union and the paramount authority of the Constitution," the party platform announced. Republicans would accept nothing less than the "unconditional surrender" of the rebels to federal
authority. As they had done from the outset of the war, however,
Republicans linked the fate of the Union directly to slavery. Slavery
"was the cause, and now constitutes the strength of this Rebellion."
Hence all congressional laws and presidential proclamations aimed at
slavery were more than justified. Determined to aim "a deathblow at
this gigantic evil," Republicans endorsed "an amendment to the Constitution" that would "terminate and forever prohibit the existence of
Slavery" in the United States.[60] This was the only plank Lincoln
responded to after his renomination. "I approve the declaration in
favor of so amending the Constitution as to prohibit slavery throughout the nation," he said.[61]

Democrats likewise reiterated their long-standing denial that slavery was the cause of the war and continued to insist that slavery should have been left alone. They most strenuously objected to the Republican policy of making abolition a condition for terminating the war. This meant, of course, that Democrats strongly opposed the Thirteenth Amendment. They would maintain the Constitution "as it is" and restore the Union "as it was." To be sure, the party was divided between War Democrats, who favored the armed struggle for the restoration of the Union, and Peace Democrats, who were willing to negotiate an armistice recognizing Confederate independence. But just as the antislavery consensus prevailed despite the divisions among Republicans, Peace and War Democrats generally agreed that slavery was not the cause of the war and abolition should not be a condition for reunion.

Hoping to overcome the divisions between the factions within the party, the Democrats postponed their convention until late August, nearly three months after the Republicans renominated Lincoln. In those three months a new war weariness spread over the North. The brutal slugfest in Virginia between Grant and Lee— which many northerners hoped would end the war very shortly— had instead ended inconclusively, with Lee's army besieged within the seemingly impregnable defenses at Petersburg. Astounded by huge numbers of casualties that had produced no definitive outcome, more and more northerners began to wonder if the Democrats might be right after all. Maybe holding out for unconditional surrender and the abolition of slavery had prolonged the war unnecessarily. By August some Republicans were wondering if Lincoln was electable, and even Lincoln came to doubt that he would win in November.[62]

Lincoln knew that if he lost to a Democrat—any Democrat— slavery would almost certainly survive the war. All he could do was weaken slavery further by putting added pressure for abolition on the loyal slave states and by increasing the number of slaves actually emancipated by the time he left office. In late August—when he and his fellow Republicans were most pessimistic about his chances for reelection—Lincoln invited the great abolitionist Frederick Douglass to the White House to discuss the matter. They had met a year earlier when Douglass, disturbed by reports of abusive treatment of black soldiers by the Confederates, visited Washington to urge Lincoln to issue a retaliation order. In 1864 the invitation came from Lincoln, and when Douglass arrived he found the president in an "alarmed" state, disturbed by calls for a negotiated peace sounded not only by Democrats but also by moderates within Lincoln's own party. Even Horace Greeley, a strong advocate of emancipation, was calling on Lincoln to broker a speedy end to the war by sending emissaries to Niagara Falls to meet with representatives of the Confederacy. The peace conference was a southern setup, and when it failed the Confederates released a letter Lincoln had written "To Whom it May Concern," making it clear that he would not consider any restoration of the Union that did not also include the complete abolition of slavery. The letter had provoked another wave of Democratic denunciations of Lincoln, but even a few skittish Republican conservatives were urging Lincoln to withdraw the condition. Lincoln would not do that, but he was considering issuing a public statement of clarification. He would reiterate the standard Republican position—that it would be impossible for him to wage a war purely for the purpose of abolishing slavery. Slavery was the cause of the rebellion and abolition was a precondition for its suppression—but abolition could never be the *purpose* of the war. The public would not stand for it, Congress would not authorize it, and the Constitution did not sanction it. He showed Douglass a draft of the statement and asked whether it should be published. No, Douglass said. It would be misconstrued, by friends and enemies alike, as an indication that Lincoln was not as committed to abolition as he actually was. Lincoln never did publish the letter. Nevertheless, the president worried that if the Democrats won, they would swiftly abandon abolition as a condition for reunion. Convinced that slaves actually freed by the war could never be re-enslaved, Lincoln wanted Douglass to help ensure that as many slaves were emancipated as possible.[63]

"The slaves are not coming so rapidly and so numerously to us as I had hoped," Douglass recalled Lincoln as saying.

The masters had ways to keep news of the proclamation away from the slaves, Douglass pointed out.

"Well," Lincoln said, "I want you to set about devising some means of making them acquainted with it, and for bringing them into our lines." Hundreds of Union agents were already at work in the slave South, informing blacks of the Emancipation Proclamation and enlisting men into the Union army. But those agents were white, and though successful, their impact was limited. Lincoln was proposing that Douglass organize a number of black agents who might prove more persuasive in enticing slaves away from their farms and planta-tions. Douglass, stunned by the realization that abolition was any-thing but certain and impressed by the depth of Lincoln's commitment to it, went home and drew up his plan for a cadre of black enticement agents. By then, however, Republican prospects for an electoral vic-tory had brightened considerably.

The Democrats finally held their convention and ended up split-ting the difference between competing factions. They nominated a War Democrat on a platform that fell just short of advocating peace at any price. Though expressing support for a restored federal Union, the Democrats decried virtually *every* measure employed by Republi-cans to suppress the rebellion—military arrests, loyalty oaths, denial of the people's "right to bear arms," and the "open and avowed disre-gard of State rights." This implied that the southern states had a right to secede and that a war for the restoration of the Union was unjusti-fied. The Democrats, however, also nominated George McClellan, the prominent Union general who supported peace only on the basis of reunion. McClellan continued to believe, as he always had, that the war should be prosecuted solely for "the preservation of the Union, its Constitution & its laws." An amendment to the Constitution abolishing slavery was an unacceptable departure from that purpose, McClellan believed. "I think the war has been permitted to take a course which unnecessarily embitters the inimical feeling between the two sections," he wrote shortly after Lincoln was renominated, "& much increases the difficulty of attaining the true objects for which we ought to fight." The "true objects" were the restoration of the Union on the basis of the Constitution as it is.[64]

The Democrats were banking on the war weariness of northern voters, many of whom were indeed tired of the war. But they were tired of slavery as well, and they were most emphatically not tired of the Union. As summer turned to fall, war weariness gave way to renewed optimism. Mobile Bay, one of the last major southern ports still in Confederate hands, fell to the Yankees in August. In September, Sherman's armies finally captured Atlanta, causing Confederate General Joseph Johnston to split his forces in a futile attempt to throw the Yankees off. Instead, Sherman sent one of his own armies, under General George Thomas, to track down those Confederates moving back into Tennessee, while Sherman himself set off on his devastating "march to the sea," from Atlanta to Savannah. Farther north, General Philip Sheridan rampaged through the Shenandoah Valley, clearing the area of guerillas and stripping it of the produce that would otherwise have gone to feed General Lee's men, still besieged in Petersburg.[65]

Democratic appeals to antiwar sentiment and racial animosity fell flat as the Republican war effort seemed to be succeeding. Contrary to what the Democrats were saying, the destruction of slavery seemed to be helping rather than hindering the northern military campaign. Far from arousing racial hatred, the enlistment of black soldiers had proved indispensable to northern victory and had weakened rather than strengthened the hold of racial prejudice. The Democrats had run a campaign of unparalleled racial demagoguery, and voters repudiated it. Lincoln was reelected easily, and Republicans regained many of the seats in the House that they had lost two years earlier. With their support for the Thirteenth Amendment vindicated at the polls, Republicans returned to Washington in December ready to make the final push.

"A KING'S CURE"

The Republican electoral victories in November of 1864 kept the Thirteenth Amendment alive, but they did not ensure its passage or ratification. The Congress that returned to Washington a month later was the same Thirty-Eighth Congress in which House Democrats had thwarted the amendment the previous June. Lincoln freely admitted this in his annual message to Congress on December 6. Although "the present is the same Congress, and nearly the same members," Lincoln noted, the circumstances were nonetheless different. There had been an "intervening election" that had given the Republicans enough votes to secure passage of the amendment in the next Congress, which was not scheduled to meet for another year. The amendment will pass, Lincoln said, it was "only a question of *time* . . . [and] may we not agree that the sooner the better?" The voters had spoken. Democrats had campaigned against abolition and they had been repudiated at the polls. "It is the voice of the people now," Lincoln said.[66]

Lincoln let it be known that if the Thirty-Eighth Congress failed to pass the amendment, he would call the Thirty-Ninth Congress—with its overwhelming Republican majorities—into special session in July of 1865. But he was unwilling to wait that long. A growing number of Republicans freely admitted that the constitutional amendment was a "civil" rather than a "military" measure, but for many the rationale for altering the Constitution was still tied to the suppression of the rebellion. With each passing week the collapse of the rebellion seemed closer at hand, and with it the military justification for the Thirteenth Amendment grew more tenuous. If Republicans waited until July for the Thirty-Ninth Congress to convene the war would probably be over and though they would have the votes to secure passage of the amendment they would have lost the major justification for it. Rather than risk the wait, the Republicans would try again, beginning in December of 1864, to win a handful of War Democrats over to their side.

Shortly after Congress returned to Washington in December, Representative James Ashley of Ohio reintroduced the amendment into the House. The Democrats, however, remained largely unmoved by either the changing circumstances of the war or the results of the November elections. When the debate opened in January, Republicans invoked their electoral victory as evidence of popular support for the amendment, but few Democrats were impressed. Republicans pointed to the recent abolitions of slavery in Missouri and Maryland as further evidence of the breadth of antislavery sentiment; Democrats pointed to those same results as proof that state abolition remained the only constitutionally reputable means of ending slavery. Republicans continued to argue that the Thirteenth Amendment was necessary to suppress the rebellion; Democrats continued to insist that abolition was an obstacle to peace, and they pointed to evidence, real but misleading, that the Confederates were willing to pursue a negotiated settlement. By the middle of January it was clear to Ashley that he did not have the votes he needed to secure passage and that the debate was not changing anyone's mind. The votes would have to be gotten by other means, and those means were already in play.[67]

The 1864 election did shift a few votes from Border States where the supporters of abolition scored important victories. The Missouri elections had taken place against a backdrop of resurgent guerilla war in the western and northern counties. Confederate troops in Arkansas, still led by Sterling Price, fomented the guerillas in an attempt to prepare the ground for a military invasion, but the violence had the opposite effect. When Price invaded in September, loyal Missourians rallied not to the Confederate standard but to Union General William Rosecrans, who organized the various militias to repel the Confederate advance. Shoved all the way to the western border and then southward back into Arkansas, the Confederates suffered a stinging defeat. Leading radicals such as Thomas Fletcher, a candidate for governor, had played a conspicuous role in the military counterattack against the Confederate invasion, and for this they were rewarded at the polls in November. On the same day Lincoln was reelected, Fletcher also won handily. Radicals took control of both houses of the General Assembly, and the referendum calling for a constitutional convention to abolish slavery was approved by a margin of twenty-nine thousand votes. In early 1865, just as Congress was taking up the debate on the Thirteenth Amendment, a radical-dominated convention met at the Mercantile Library in St. Louis, and on January 11 a special committee reported an ordinance declaring the immediate, unconditional emancipation of all slaves in Missouri. Back in July of 1864, several congressmen from Missouri and Maryland, voting as representatives of slave states, had opposed the Thirteenth Amendment. By January those states had abolished slavery on their own, and their representatives now voted as representatives of free states in favor of the Thirteenth Amendment.

Lincoln, however, was not willing to take those votes for granted. Shortly after his reelection he embarked on an unusually intense lobbying campaign to secure the support of Border State congressmen for the Thirteenth Amendment. The president was only one participant in this broad lobbying effort. In the preceding months, Congressman Ashley—who had reintroduced the amendment resolution in December and managed the floor fight in January—had written more than one hundred letters urging his fellow Republicans, particularly in Ohio, to promote the amendment in their home states in hopes of increasing the pressure on the few Democrats who might be vulnerable to such appeals. Former postmaster general Montgomery Blair lent a hand as well. But the most important of the lobbying efforts, along with Lincoln's, were those of his secretary of state, William Seward, who gathered influential politicians and financiers into what came to be known as the Seward Lobby. Where Lincoln's lobbying efforts focused on the Border States, Seward's focused on his home state of New York. They did everything lobbyists are known for: twisted arms, promised patronage, and scuttled bills in exchange for votes. There is little question that money for bribes was made available, but no hard evidence that it was ever paid out.[68]

The lobbyists singled out representatives who had not been reelected in November and therefore had less to lose—and in the end all but two of the Democrats who voted for the Thirteenth Amendment were lame ducks. They also focused on representatives from Border States where slavery had recently been abolished, and in the final vote nineteen Border State congressmen voted yes. The Seward Lobby paid off as well. Six of the sixteen Democratic votes for the amendment came from New York. The previous year the amendment had fallen twelve votes short of the two-thirds required for passage in the House of Representatives. Had the lobbyists corralled enough congressmen to secure passage? Until the final vote was taken, nobody knew for sure.

Ashley scheduled the vote for January 31, and on that day the galleries filled with eager spectators—newly installed Chief Justice Salmon Chase, feminists who a year earlier had organized a massive petition campaign in favor of the amendment, and African Americans anxious for the result, including Frederick Douglass's son. Half-a-dozen Republicans had been absent when the June vote had been taken; this time every Republican was present and every single one of them voted yea. It was the Democratic votes that would matter, however. Only four Democrats had supported the amendment in the previous session; at least a dozen would be needed this time. With each Democratic vote cast in favor of the amendment the House fell into an uproar as fellow Democrats expressed their vocal disapproval and Republicans and spectators broke into applause. In the final vote—119 in favor, 56 against—fifteen Democrats had voted yes, along with all eighty-six Republicans.[69] A shift of three votes would have changed the result. When the final tally was announced, it took a moment for everyone to realize what had happened. Then the House erupted. Republicans threw their hats in the air; spectators wept and danced. Democrats tried to prevent adjournment but to no avail. The chamber emptied in an atmosphere of jubilation.

The next day, in response to a congratulatory serenade outside the White House, Lincoln spoke about the significance of the amendment. He had always said that slavery was the only thing that ever threatened to destroy the Union; the amendment would "remove all causes of disturbance in the future." He had "never shrunk," he said, from doing all that he could to eradicate slavery. That was why he had issued the Emancipation Proclamation. "But that proclamation falls far short of what the amendment will be when fully consummated." There were those who believed the proclamation was not "legally valid." It freed only those "who came into our lines" but was "inoperative as to those who did not give themselves up." Nor could the proclamation definitively secure the freedom "of the slaves born hereafter." But the Thirteenth Amendment does all of this, Lincoln said. It frees all slaves, everywhere, for all future time. It was "a King's cure for all the evils" that had not been cured by the Emancipation Proclamation.[70]

"BUT FREEDOM IS NATIONAL"

Across the North and throughout the West legislatures took the King's cure with remarkable ease. There were thirty-six states in the Union and three-fourths of them—twenty-seven states in total—had to ratify an amendment for it to become part of the Constitution. Here and there Democrats raised the usual objections—that the Thirteenth Amendment was a racial and constitutional nightmare—but to no avail. In several northern states the amendment was adopted unanimously. In New York, after the Senate had approved the amendment easily, Democratic holdouts in the Assembly lined up against it, but it passed by a vote of 72 to 40. That was February 3, only days after Congress had sent the amendment to the states for ratification. By then the legislatures of Illinois, Rhode Island, Michigan, Maryland, and West Virginia had already ratified it. Before the month was out eleven more state legislatures did the same. After this initial burst of support in which seventeen states endorsed the amendment, ratification slowed down but without ever coming to a halt. Two legislatures ratified the amendment in March, two more in April. Connecticut endorsed it on May 4 and New Hampshire on July 1. These twenty-three legislatures, composed overwhelmingly of northern states and loyal slave states that had already abolished slavery, brought the first round of ratification to a close. It would be more than four months before the second round began, composed primarily of western states—Oregon and California—which were delayed by the slow mails, and seceded states coming back into the Union under President Andrew Johnson's direction. Not until December did the necessary twenty-seven states finally ratify the amendment. This meant that for almost the whole year of 1865, slavery was still legal in most of the southern states.[71]

Until ratification was secured the two existing antislavery

policies—military emancipation and state abolition—remained in operation. Indeed, they were more potent than ever. Since the start of the war slaves had found their way to freedom by a variety of different means with countless individual variations. Between December of 1864 and December of 1865 the emancipation process accelerated dramatically. It began with Sherman's ferocious march through the Carolinas, where his troops tore up slavery in some of the oldest, wealthiest plantation districts of the South. In January, Missouri, still plagued by a civil war within the Civil War, finally abolished slavery. Shortly thereafter Tennessee did the same, bringing to six the number of states that abolished slavery by the time Lee surrendered to Grant at Appomattox Court House on April 9, 1865, barely a week short of the fourth anniversary of the firing on Fort Sumter.

Across the South many slaveholders took the news of Lee's surrender as the signal to acknowledge the end of slavery, calling their slaves together to inform them that the Yankees had won and they were now free. But many others said nothing, and throughout the spring and summer of 1865, Yankee soldiers were still going onto farms and plantations across the South emancipating slaves whose masters would not relent. Still other slaveholders were stoic, noting little more than that they were in the process of reconstructing the labor system on their farms because the workers now had to be paid. "Have lost my negro property by universal emancipation," Everard Green Baker recorded on May 31, 1865, "in common with all the South." His cotton "was burnt by the Confederates," but "[m]y negroes are still with me & I can hire them." On November 27, Hill Carter noted in his diary, simply, that "Betty, Julia, Nancy, Lucy began work at 25 cts a day." Augustin L. Taveau of Charleston, South Carolina, was more contemplative than most. "The conduct of the Negro in the late crisis of our affairs has convinced me that we were all laboring under a delusion," he wrote.

I believed that these people were content, happy, and attached
to their masters. But events and reflection have caused me to
change these opinions. . . . If they were content, happy, and
attached to their masters why did they desert him in the
moment of his need and flock to an enemy whom they did not
know; and thus left their, perhaps, really good masters whom
they had known from infancy?

In Texas, "Juneteenth" is still celebrated as the day slavery ended,
commemorating the announcement on June 19, 1865, by Union General Gordon Granger that "all slaves are free."[72]

The last great wave of emancipations came in 1865, in summer
and fall, when the new governments organized under President Johnson's direction began to function. Abraham Lincoln had been assassinated on April 14, and though Johnson's accession to the presidency
would decisively alter the history of Reconstruction, his initial
instincts were to continue the antislavery policies of his predecessor.
Specifically, Johnson would require the defeated southern states to
abolish slavery as a condition for readmission to the Union. By the
time Johnson made this clear, the Thirteenth Amendment was working its way through the state legislatures, and though it was likely to
be ratified, the new president was taking no chances.

On May 29, Johnson issued a proclamation of amnesty restoring
the property, "except as to slaves," of those rebels who had taken no
part in the leadership of the rebellion and who swore an oath of future
loyalty to the Union. That same day Johnson appointed a series of
provisional governors to organize constitutional conventions in the
seceded states and required that those conventions provide the people
with "a republican form of government," which by then had become
code among antislavery politicians for governments without slavery.
In yet another proclamation issued a few weeks later, on June 13,

Johnson affirmed that all congressional statutes and presidential proc-lamations "abolishing slavery" were "in full force." His formal guide-lines were far less direct about abolition than Lincoln's had been, but in August he wrote to William Sharkey, the provisional governor of Mississippi, expressing the hope that the state would amend its own constitution "abolishing slavery and denying to all future legislatures the power to legislate that there is property in man."[73]

It is not clear whether Johnson ever formally required the recon-structed states to ratify the Thirteenth Amendment as a condition for readmission, but as those states were becoming organized in late 1865 Secretary of State Seward made clear that ratification was what the president preferred. The first state to get this message was South Car-olina. Its newly organized legislature, meeting on September 19, declared that "the slaves in South Carolina have been emancipated by the action of the United States authorities." This would not do. Speak-ing on behalf of Johnson, Seward let it be known that there was "a deep interest felt as to what course the Legislature will take in regard to the adoption of the amendment to the Constitution of the United States abolishing slavery." Growing bolder with each new communi-cation, Seward finally told South Carolina's provisional governor that the president "considers the acceptance of the amendment indispens-able" to the state's restoration. "Let writers say what they will," a Ten-nessee correspondent wrote for the *Chicago Tribune*. "The South never gave up the hope of re-establishing slavery, until President Johnson informed South Carolina that she must adopt the constitutional amendment before she could retake her position in the Union."[74]

On November 13 the South Carolina legislature complied by rati-fying the Thirteenth Amendment. Johnson's message got through to other states. North Carolina ratified it on December 1, Alabama on December 2, and Georgia two days later, on December 4. Some states refused to ratify the amendment and instead did nothing more than concede that the federal government had, as a matter of inescapable

fact, destroyed slavery in their states. The "institution of slavery having been destroyed in the State of Mississippi," its constitutional convention declared, it was thereby abolished. Florida's constitutional
convention ignored Johnson's wishes and declared only that slavery
had been "destroyed in the State by the Government of the United
States." Under intense pressure from Washington, the new state legislature relented, and in late December, Florida finally ratified the
Thirteenth Amendment. For all their reluctance, most of the former
Confederate states complied, and as a result, more slaves may have
been emancipated in a single month—December in 1865—than had
been freed in the four preceding years of war.[75]

The extraordinary resistance to abolition in two of the four Border
States brought the antislavery movement to an ironic conclusion. On
October 7, 1865, Florida's Provisional Governor William Marvin
informed Secretary of State Seward that there was "some reluctance"
among Florida legislators to ratify the amendment because it would
"impose abolition on Kentucky and Delaware, which have not yet
abolished slavery."[76] For decades abolitionists had assumed that slavery would eventually disappear first in the states where, as things
turned out, it disappeared last. They thought slavery was intrinsically
weak, especially in the Border States. Dislodge the Slave Power, surround the South with a "cordon of freedom," and the deterioration of
slavery would commence first in the slave states bordering on the free
states. By early 1862, barely a year after the Civil War began, that
fantasy was dead.

Delaware was a particular object lesson in this regard. Lincoln
assumed that Delaware, with fewer than two thousand slaves and no
secessionist movement to speak of, was the ripest fruit ready to fall
from slavery's decrepit tree. The mere offer of federal compensation
would do the trick. Instead, Delaware clung tenaciously to slavery and
through four years of war its representatives in Congress were among
the institution's most unswerving defenders. When Charles Sumner

worried that the admission of West Virginia would bring another slave state into the Union, Benjamin Wade argued that the new state was formally committed to gradual abolition and would therefore vote as a free state. Contrast this with Delaware, Wade said: with far fewer slaves than West Virginia but with no comparable commitment to abolition, Delaware consistently voted like a slave state.

The graveyard of antislavery hopes for the Border States was not Delaware, however, but Kentucky. In Kentucky every escalation of federal pressure to abolish slavery produced an equal and opposite proslavery backlash. Kentucky's civil and military leaders did everything they could to thwart the Union antislavery policy. In no other state was the civil war over slavery *within* the Union army so visceral. Soldiers and officers from northern states simply refused to obey orders from a handful of proslavery commanders from Kentucky. Troops from Kentucky nearly went into battle against troops from the Midwest. A proslavery justice of the Kentucky supreme court, George Robertson, brought fifteen lawsuits—including one of his own—against Union soldiers who refused to return escaped slaves to their owners. In his annual message to the legislature in January of 1863, Governor James Robinson denounced Lincoln for issuing the Emancipation Proclamation, "a manifesto from which nothing but evil" could flow. As politics in Maryland and Missouri were resolving into a dispute between immediate and gradual abolitionists, politics in Kentucky hardened into a contest between two proslavery factions, the Peace Democrats, who all but endorsed secession, and the Union Democrats, who merely denounced Lincoln and vowed eternal vigilance in defense of slavery.

The Lincoln administration did what it could to clamp down on proslavery elements in Kentucky, especially those within the Union army. In late 1862, Secretary of War Stanton dismissed a proslavery colonel in the Kentucky infantry, John McHenry, for ordering his troops to return escaped slaves to their owners in deliberate violation of Lincoln's Preliminary Proclamation. The final Emancipation Proclamation prompted "an epidemic of resignations" among Kentucky officers, resignations that the War Department refused to accept. In 1863, Kentucky officials began arresting and re-enslaving fugitives from seceded states, only to be thwarted by Lincoln's judge advocate general, who ruled the re-enslavements were illegal, and Stanton, who ordered them stopped. In late 1864, Kentucky General Speed Smith Fry was nearly removed from his command after he ordered the brutal expulsion of the wives and children of black soldiers from his camp.[77]

Union officers responded to Kentucky's recalcitrance by stepping up the pressure on slavery. After the Republican victory in the 1864 national election, General John Palmer began issuing "passes" by the thousands to Kentucky slaves so that they could cross the Ohio River without obstruction. Instead of succumbing to the pressure, white Kentuckians only stiffened their resistance. In August of 1865, months after Congress passed the Thirteenth Amendment and sent it to the states for ratification, Kentucky voters elected a proslavery legislature that not only refused to ratify the amendment but also vowed to nullify it. In November a Kentucky grand jury indicted General Palmer on a charge of "enticing" slaves away from their owners, in violation of Kentucky law. By December of 1865, Kentucky had become a national spectacle. The *Chicago Tribune* observed that Kentucky's behavior was driven by the "insane hope" of reestablishing slavery. "Kentucky alone remains a slave state," commented the bemused correspondent for the *Manchester Guardian*.[78]

On December 18, 1865, Secretary of State Seward officially certified that the requisite twenty-seven states had ratified the Thirteenth Amendment. On that same day slavery was finally abolished in Kentucky and Delaware. There were loose ends still to be tied up. The treaties between the Confederate States of America and various

Indian nations—treaties recognizing the perpetual existence of slavery—would have to be renegotiated with the triumphant Union government. Texas had yet to reorganize its government in the wake of the Confederacy's collapse. On February 10, 1866, a constitutional convention meeting in Austin finally acknowledged the facts. Slavery had been abolished "by force of arms," the new state constitution read, and "its re-establishment . . . prohibited, by the Amendment to the Constitution.

In EARLY DECEMBER OF 1865, two weeks before Seward announced the ratification of the Thirteenth Amendment, Kentucky's Governor Thomas Bramlette pleaded with his state's intransigent legislature to accept what had at long last become inevitable. Speaking to those who objected that the amendment was an "inroad upon *State rights*," the governor conceded that "the *regulation* and *government* of *slave property* is the right of the State; but *freedom* is national," Bramlette insisted, "and is, therefore, more appropriately declared so to be through the Federal Constitution than by local or State action."[79]

EPILOGUE: WAS FREEDOM ENOUGH?

IN DECEMBER OF 1865, just as the defeated Confederate states were ratifying the Thirteenth Amendment, a "Christmas Insurrection Scare" swept across much of the South. Having just been emancipated, the former slaves made their first attempts to test the meaning and limits of their hard-won freedom. Hoping for land of their own—believing themselves entitled to it after years of unrequited toil—freed people across the rural South resisted the terms of the labor contracts offered to them by their former masters. Emancipated men and women defied new vagrancy statutes by moving about—sometimes in search of relatives from whom they had been separated, sometimes bargaining for better terms of employment, or sometimes just to get away from the man who had long claimed them as his personal property. Infuriated in defeat, the former masters responded with an extraordinary spasm of anti-black violence that shocked northerners and provoked a backlash against the Johnson governments among Republicans in Congress.[1] Already a new kind of struggle was beginning to take shape.

Southern leaders feared nothing so much as federal intervention on behalf of the freed people. The enforcement clause of the Thirteenth Amendment was particularly troubling. Alabama had ratified it only "with the understanding that it does not confer upon Congress the power to legislate upon the political status of freedmen in this State." South Carolina's provisional governor, B. F. Perry, noted that the delegates to that state's constitutional convention had no objection to Section 1 of the amendment, abolishing slavery, "but they fear that the second section may be construed to give Congress power of local legislation over negroes, and white men, too, after the abolishment of slavery."[2]

The kind of "local legislation" southern lawmakers had in mind was already clear by late 1865, as they busily enacted a series of notoriously repressive "Black Codes" designed to sharply restrict the freedom of the former slaves. In Mississippi, the same convention that reluctantly acknowledged that the federal government had destroyed slavery enacted apprenticeship, vagrancy, and "civil rights" statutes that, among other things, allowed the state to take children from parents said to be unable to care for them, defined as a "vagrant" any black person who had not signed a labor contract, prohibited blacks from renting or leasing land in rural areas, and outlawed gun ownership by black civilians. Georgia prohibited interracial marriage and denied blacks the right to testify against whites. Alabama banned blacks from the state militia, replaced "whipping" with "hard labor" as a legal punishment, and made it a crime for employers to "entice" black workers away from their present employers by offering better wages. Florida retained whipping—"thirty-nine stripes"—as punishment for any black man found guilty of "fornication" with a white woman; the white woman could be imprisoned for up to three months for the same offense. These Black Codes were passed by the same state legislatures that abolished slavery, often at the same time, sometimes in the abolition statute itself. In Florida, the "same ordinance" that grudgingly conceded the destruction of slavery "denies them the right to testify where the interest of the white class are involved."[3]

African Americans had very different expectations of what freedom should mean for them. On September 29, the eve of the convention that would reorganize the state's government for the benefit of whites, North Carolina blacks called their own convention, where they "petitioned for legislation to secure compensation for labor, and enable them to educate their children, and asking for protection for the family relation, and for repeal of oppressive laws making unjust discriminations on account of race or color." In January of 1866, "[a] convention of colored persons in Augusta advocated a proposition to give those who would write and read well, and possessed a certain property qualification, the right of suffrage." A petition signed by the "educated colored persons" of Louisville, Kentucky, asked the legislature to grant blacks equal access to the courts, to legitimize marriages, and to "aid in the education of colored children" by the establishment of a public school system "to be controlled by the colored people" and funded by "a fair proportion of the public school fund."[4]

DECENT WAGES, SCHOOLS FOR CHILDREN, legally secure marriages, equal justice under law, land for the freed people. These were demands that did not—could not—arise under slavery. Such things were incompatible with a system in which slave laborers were forbidden to own land and their labor was uncompensated, in which it was a crime to teach a slave to read, where slave marriages had no legal standing, and where the privileges and immunities of citizenship did not apply. No one ever debated whether slaves should vote, because slaves were understood to be outside of the "political" community. There was no discussion of slave citizenship because, in a tradition dating back to antiquity, slaves were "non-citizens" by definition. Before any of these issues could arise, slavery had to be destroyed. Only then could the fight for abolition give way to the struggle over the meaning of freedom. "Reconstruction is impossible," the *New York Times* observed, "so long as Slavery exists in the land."[5] It made sense that in late 1865, African Americans were asking for farms of their own and demanding decent wages, school for their children, civil rights, and the vote. The long and difficult struggle to abolish slavery had been fought and won. Four million African Americans had been freed. A new question, and with it a new struggle, suddenly loomed: Was freedom enough?

ACKNOWLEDGMENTS

This was a hard book for me to write. I called on an unusual number of friends and colleagues for advice, and I'm anxious to acknowledge their help.

Two generous grants were indispensable: the first from the Dorothy and Lewis B. Cullman Center for Scholars & Writers at the New York Public Library at the outset of my research; the second from the American Council of Learned Societies, at the outset of my writing. My home base, the Graduate Center of the City University of New York, could not have been more supportive; its president, Bill Kelly, and its provost, Chase Robinson, gave me all the time and encouragement I needed.

To my great benefit, I was able to try out some of my ideas by presenting them, twice, to colleagues at the Gilder Lehrman Center for the Study of Slavery, Resistance, and Abolition at Yale University, as well as the history departments at the University of Texas at Austin, Rice University, and the University of Delaware. I gave an earlier version of chapter 2 at a historical society meeting; my thanks to Chandra Manning and Alex Lichtenstein for their criticisms and suggestions. Josh Brown, besides helping me locate some of the images, gave me the opportunity to shock several listeners with some of my heresies at a conference he organized on new approaches to the Civil War. Individually and collectively, Tom Hafner, Anthony Zacchino, Joe Murphy, and Lawrence Cappello have been outstanding research assistants.

Jim Livingston, Jim Goodman, Steve Hahn, and Sean Wilentz read parts of the manuscript, raised their eyebrows at certain points, but were consistently encouraging. George Forgie and Jim McPherson read the final manuscript; Jim caught several embarrassing errors, and George demanded more evidence and greater clarity for some of the arguments I make. Matt Pinsker gave me free reign to try out my ideas during two consecutive summer seminars we co-taught; his probing questions forced me to clarify my analysis at several critical points. Three friends stand out. In numerous conversations over several years, as well as in his careful reading of most of the text, Eric Foner has been a source of invaluable criticism, good advice, and generous support. I talked the ears off Greg Downs, but he listened patiently and carefully as I shared my discoveries and tried out my ideas. Finally, I could not ask for a better editor than Steve Forman. Enthusiastic from the start, he read each chapter as it came in, raised questions, offered helpful advice, and pressed me to meet my deadlines. I might have finished without Steve, but not for several more years.

NOTES

ABBREVIATIONS

ALP-LC   Papers of Abraham Lincoln, Library of Congress

CW   Roy P. Basler, ed., *The Collected Works of Abraham Lincoln* (New Brunswick, NJ: Rutgers University Press, 1953–1955).

FSSP   Ira Berlin et al., eds., *Freedom: A Documentary History of Emancipation, 1861–1867* (Cambridge: Cambridge University Press, 1983–1995). Published under the auspices of the Freedmen and Southern Society Project.

NES   Howard Cecil Perkins, ed., *Northern Editorials on Secession* (American Historical Association, 1942).

OR   *The War of the Rebellion: A Compilation of the Official Records of the War of the Union and Confederate Armies* (Washington, DC: Government Printing Office, 1880–1901).

SES   Dwight Lowell Dumond, ed., *Southern Editorials on Secession* (American Historical Association, 1931).

PREFACE

1 *Cong. Globe*, 37th Cong., 2d Sess., p. 1340.

2 Charles Sumner, *Recent Speeches and Addresses* (Boston: Ticknor & Fields, 1856), pp. 69–171.

3 Seymour Drescher, *Abolition: A History of Slavery and Antislavery* (New York: Cambridge University Press, 2009).

4 Stanley Engerman, *Slavery, Emancipation, and Freedom: Comparative Perspectives* (Baton Rouge: Louisiana State University Press, 2007); Robin Blackburn, *The American Crucible: Slavery, Emancipation and Human Rights* (New York: Verso, 2011); Robin Blackburn, *The Overthrow of Colonial Slavery* (New York:

Verso, 1998). On the theme of slavery and progress, see David Brion Davis, *Slavery and Human Progress* (New York: Oxford University Press, 1984).

5 *Cong. Globe*, 37th Cong., 2d Sess., p. 1641.

6 Ari Helo and Peter Onuf, "Jefferson, Morality, and the Problem of Slavery," *William and Mary Quarterly*, 3d ser., 60, no. 3 (July 2003), pp. 583–614.

7 For evidence of popular antislavery, see Blackburn, *Overthrow of Colonial Slavery*, and Christopher Leslie Brown, *Moral Capital: Foundations of British Abolitionism* (Chapel Hill: University of North Carolina Press, 2006).

8 J. David Hacker, "A Census-Based Count of the Civil War Dead," *Civil War History* 57, no. 4 (Dec. 2011), pp. 307–348. An accurate count of Civil War dead is probably impossible. Hacker's "preferred estimate" of 752,000 deaths is the best one available.

9 Gilbert Hobbes Barnes, *The Antislavery Impulse, 1830–1844* (1933; New York: Harcourt, Brace & World, 1964); Kenneth M. Stampp, *And the War Came: The North and the Secession Crisis* (Westport, CT: Greenwood Press, 1980); Dwight Lowell Dumond, *Antislavery Origins of the Civil War in the United States* (1939; Ann Arbor: University of Michigan Press, 1959); Eric Foner, *Free Soil, Free Labor, Free Men* (New York: Oxford University Press, 1970); William M. Wiecek, *The Sources of Antislavery Constitutionalism in America, 1760–1848* (Ithaca: Cornell University Press, 1977); Richard H. Sewell, *Ballots for Freedom: Antislavery Politics in the United States, 1837–1860* (New York: W. W. Norton, 1980).

10 "Four years of warfare *inadvertently* enabled Republicans to accomplish something about which radicals such as Frederick Douglass and William Lloyd Garrison had only dreamed in early 1860: the end of slavery in their lifetimes." Shearer Davis Bowman, *At the Precipice: Americans North and South during the Secession Crisis* (Chapel Hill: University of North Carolina Press, 2010), pp. 34–35 (emphasis added). "No one is arguing—no one beyond what would have been considered the abolitionist fringe—is arguing for emancipation in 1860. What the Civil War is a pluperfect example of is how wars rage out of control and bring consequences no one could have anticipated. The end of slavery in four years? No one could have anticipated that. Absolutely no one." Transcription of Gary Gallagher speaking at Gilder Lehrman Center for the Study of Slavery, Resistance, and Abolition Yale University, New Haven, CT, March 29, 2012.

11 John W. Blassingame and John R. McKivigan, eds., *The Frederick Douglass Papers, Series One: Speeches, Debates, and Interviews*, vol. 4: *1854–1880* (New Haven: Yale University Press, 1991), p. 434.

12 *New York Times*, Oct. 26, 1880.

13 *CW*, vol. 2, p. 126.

14 Charles M. Segal, ed., *Conversations with Lincoln*, introduction by David Donald (New Brunswick, NJ: Transaction, 2002), quotation on pp. 62–63, but see also pp. 41, 43.

15 Michael Burlingame, ed., *Lincoln Observed: Civil War Dispatches of Noah Brooks* (Baltimore: Johns Hopkins University Press, 1998), p. 22.

16 *CW*, vol. 8, p. 332.

17 During the secession crisis the question *What is to be done with the Negro?* was pro forma in Democratic newspapers across the North. It was a form of race-baiting designed to put Republicans on the spot. Only a handful of the most conservative Republican editors, like Henry J. Raymond of the *New York Times*, raised the question at that point. A few radical papers picked up the question, mostly to belittle it.

CHAPTER 1: "ULTIMATE EXTINCTION"

1 *CW*, vol. 4, pp. 263, 270.

2 Pinckney quoted in Richard R. Beeman, *Plain, Honest Men: The Making of the American Constitution* (New York: Random House, 2009), p. 269.

The scholarship on slavery and the Constitution is vast. See especially Staughton Lynd, "The Compromise of 1787," *Political Science Quarterly* 81 (1966), pp. 225–250; William M. Wiecek, *The Sources of Antislavery Constitutionalism in America, 1760–1848* (Ithaca: Cornell University Press, 1977), pp. 62–83; Don E. Fehrenbacher, *The Dred Scott Case: Its Significance in American Law and Politics* (New York: Oxford University Press, 1978), pp. 19–27; Paul Finkelman, *An Imperfect Union: Slavery, Federalism, and Comity* (Chapel Hill: University of North Carolina Press, 1981), pp. 20–45; Finkelman, "Slavery and the Constitutional Convention: Making a Covenant with Death," in Richard Beeman et al., eds., *Beyond Confederation: Origins of the Constitution and American National Identity* (Chapel Hill: University of North Carolina Press, 1987), pp. 188–225; Don E. Fehrenbacher, *The Slaveholding Republic: An Account of the United States Government's Relations to Slavery*, completed and edited by Ward M. McAfee (New York: Oxford University Press, 2001), pp. 15–47; George William Van Cleve, *A Slaveholders' Union: Slavery, Politics, and the Constitution in the Early American Republic* (Chicago: University of Chicago Press, 2010), pp. 101–183. On slavery in the ratification debates, see James Oakes, "The Compromising Expedient: Justifying a Proslavery Constitution," *Cardozo Law Review* 17, no. 6 (May 1996), pp. 2023–2056; David Waldstreicher, *Slavery's Constitution: From Revolution to Ratification* (New York: Hill & Wang, 2009); Pauline Maier,

Ratification: The People Debate the Constitution, 1787–1788 (New York: Simon & Schuster, 2010), passim.

3 John P. Kaminski et al., eds., *The Documentary History of the Ratification of the Constitution*, vol. 6: *Ratification of the Constitution by the States: Massachusetts*, No. 3 (Madison: Wisconsin Historical Society Press, 2000), p. 1371; Max Farrand, ed., *The Records of the Federal Convention of 1787* (New Haven: Yale University Press, 1911), vol. 2, pp. 364, 372; William J. Cooper Jr., *Liberty and Slavery: Southern Politics to 1860* (New York: Knopf, 1983), pp. 67, 97–98.

4 On the federal consensus, see Wiecek, *Sources of Antislavery Constitutionalism*, pp. 15–19; Herman Belz, "The Constitution, the Amendment Process, and the Abolition of Slavery," in Harold Holzer and Sara Vaughn Gabbard, eds., *Lincoln and Freedom: Slavery, Emancipation, and the Thirteenth Amendment* (Carbondale: Southern Illinois University Press, 2007), pp. 161–162; Stephen C. Neff, *Justice in Blue and Gray: A Legal History of the Civil War* (Cambridge: Harvard University Press, 2010), pp. 128–130.

5 *The Declaration of Sentiments and Constitution of the American Anti-Slavery Society* (New York: American Anti-Slavery Society, 1835), p. 8; Benjamin Franklin Morris, *The Life of Thomas Morris: Pioneer and Long a Legislator of Ohio, and U.S. Senator from 1833 to 1839* (Cincinnati: Printed by Moore, Wilstach, Keys, & Overend, 1856), p. 147; Joshua Giddings, *Pacificus, The Rights and Privileges of the Several States in Regard to Slavery....* [Warren, OH?] [1842?], p. 6; Reinhard O. Johnson, *The Liberty Party, 1840–1848: Antislavery Third Party Politics in the United States* (Baton Rouge: Louisiana State University Press, 2009), p. 317; Arthur Schlesinger Jr., ed., *History of American Presidential Elections, 1789–1968* (New York: Chelsea House, 1971), vol. 2, p. 903.

6 *Groves v. Slaughter*, 15 Peters (U.S.) 449 (1841) (emphasis added); John P. Niven, *Salmon P. Chase: A Biography* (New York: Oxford University Press, 1995), p. 53; Charles Sumner, *Freedom National; Slavery Sectional: Speech of Hon. Charles Sumner, of Massachusetts, on His Motion to Repeal the Fugitive Slave Bill, in the Senate of the United States, August 26, 1852* (Washington, DC: Buell & Buckner, 1853), p. 21.

The "main body" of the antislavery movement "never deviated from the position that Congress could not, by *direct* legislation, constitutionally abolish slavery in the southern states." Jacobus tenBroek, *Equal under Law* (New York: Collier Books, 1965), p. 91.

7 *Cong. Globe*, 37th Cong., 1st Sess., p. 260; tenBroek, *Equal under Law*, pp. 42–110; Wiecek, *Sources of Antislavery Constitutionalism*, pp. 16–18, 249–275; James Oakes, *The Radical and the Republican: Frederick Douglass, Abraham Lincoln, and the Triumph of Antislavery Politics* (New York: W. W. Norton, 2007), p. 27. But see chapter 12 in this text for the number of Republicans—

including Sumner—who between 1862 and 1864 adopted the view that the Constitution was an antislavery document.

8 Many historians argue that the key difference between abolitionists and Republicans was that abolitionists advocated "immediate" abolition. But most abolitionists understood that slavery could not be abolished immediately under the Constitution. They generally advocated immediate *implementation* of policies that would eventually lead to the *gradual* extinction of slavery. Republicans advocated the same thing. On the antislavery origins of Republican Party policies, see Gilbert Hobbs Barnes, *The Antislavery Impulse, 1830–1844* (1933; New York: Harcourt, Brace & World, 1964), pp. 48–50; Dwight Lowell Dumond, *Antislavery Origins of the Civil War in the United States* (1939; Ann Arbor: University of Michigan Press, 1959), p. 27. On the ambiguities of "immediatism," see David Brion Davis, "The Emergence of Immediatism in British and American Antislavery Thought," *Mississippi Valley Historical Review* 49 (Sept. 1962), pp. 209–230; Bertram Wyatt-Brown, *Lewis Tappan and the Evangelical War against Slavery* (New York: Atheneum, 1971), pp. 81–82; James Brewer Stewart, *Holy Warriors: The Abolitionists and American Slavery*, rev. ed. (New York: Hill & Wang, 1996), pp. 35–50. As William Lloyd Garrison explained it, "Urge immediate abolition as earnestly as we may, it will, alas! be gradual abolition in the end. We have never said that slavery would be overthrown by a single blow; that it ought to be, we shall always contend." Quoted in Louis Filler, *Crusade against Slavery: Friends, Foes, and Reforms, 1820–1860* (Algonac, MI: Reference Publications, 1986), pp. 81–82.

9 David Armitage, *The Declaration of Independence: A Global History* (Cambridge: Harvard University Press, 2008); Peter Onuf and Nicholas Onuf, *Federal Union, Modern World: The Law of Nations in an Age of Revolutions, 1776–1814* (Madison: Madison House, 1994); David M. Golove and Daniel J. Hulsebosch, "A Civilized Nation: The Early American Constitution, the Law of Nations, and the Pursuit of International Recognition," *New York University Law Review* 932 (Oct. 2010).

10 M. I. Finley, in *Ancient Slavery and Modern Ideology* (New York: Viking Press, 1980), highlighted the "chattel" principle as central to the definition of slavery. Orlando Patterson, in *Slavery and Social Death* (Cambridge: Harvard University Press, 1982), pp. 17–21, disputes the property element; but David Brion Davis, in *Inhuman Bondage: The Rise and Fall of Slavery in the New World* (New York: Oxford University Press, 2006), pp. 32 and 337 n. 13, reaffirms it.

Property as the most important defining feature of a slave's status is most thoroughly documented in Thomas Morris, *Slavery and American Law, 1619–1860* (Chapel Hill: University of North Carolina Press, 1997). Gavin Wright, in *Slavery and American Economic Development* (Baton Rouge: Louisiana State

University Press, 2006), puts the slave's legal status as property at the center of his analysis of the slave economy. See also James Oakes, *The Ruling Race: A History of American Slaveholders* (New York: Knopf, 1982); James L. Hutson, *Calculating the Value of the Union: Slavery, Property Rights, and the Economic Origins of the Civil War* (Chapel Hill: University of North Carolina Press, 2003); Walter Johnson, ed., *The Chattel Principle: Internal Slave Trades in the Americas* (New Haven: Yale University Press, 2005).

11 On the "freedom principle" in Western Europe, see Seymour Drescher, *Abolition: A History of Slavery and Antislavery* (New York: Cambridge University Press, 2009), pp. 23–24, 66–67, 93–96. The standard account of the complicated history of the *Somerset* case is Wiecek, *Sources of Antislavery Constitutionalism*. See also "Forum: Somerset's Case Revisited," *Law and History Review* 24 (Fall 2006), pp. 601–671; Van Cleve, *Slaveholders' Union*, esp. pp. 31–40. The popular origins of the freedom principle are examined in Robin Blackburn, *The Overthrow of Colonial Slavery, 1776–1848* (New York: Verso, 1988), pp. 36–47.

12 Quoted in Paul Polgar, "Standard Bearers of Liberty and Equality: Reinterpreting the Origins of American Abolitionism," PhD dissertation, CUNY Graduate Center, New York (forthcoming), chap. 2.

13 In Massachusetts and New Hampshire, emancipation was accomplished by a series of freedom suits initiated by slaves who cited the declarations of universal rights contained in both states' revolutionary constitutions. More and more judges ruled in favor of freedom, and as the cases and precedents piled up, slavery in Massachusetts and New Hampshire gradually died away.

14 David Gellman, *Emancipating New York: The Politics of Slavery and Freedom, 1777–1827* (Baton Rouge: Louisiana State University Press, 2006), p. 167: John P. Kaminski, ed., *A Necessary Evil? Slavery and the Debate over the Constitution* (Madison: Madison House, 1995), p. 237.

15 Gellman, *Emancipating New York*. On the "First Emancipation" more generally, there are several older but still valuable studies: Benjamin Quarles, *The Negro in the American Revolution* (Chapel Hill: University of North Carolina Press, 1961); Arthur Zilversmit, *The First Emancipation: The Abolition of Slavery in the North* (Chicago: University of Chicago Press, 1967); Donald Robinson, *Slavery in the Structure of American Politics* (New York: W. W. Norton, 1971, 1979); Duncan McLeod, *Slavery, Race and the American Revolution* (Cambridge: Cambridge University Press, 1974); David Brion Davis, *The Problem of Slavery in the Age of Revolution* (Ithaca: Cornell University Press, 1975). On the important debate Davis inspired, see Thomas Bender, ed., *The Antislavery Debate: Capitalism and Abolitionism as a Problem in Historical Interpretation* (Berkeley: University of California Press, 1992). Subsequent

studies have tended to view abolition in the northern states as a question of *race* rather than *slavery*. See, for example, Joanne Pope Melish, *Disowning Slavery: Gradual Emancipation and "Race" in New England, 1780–1860* (Ithaca: Cornell University Press, 1998); Ira Berlin, *Many Thousands Gone: The First Two Centuries of Slavery in North America* (Cambridge: Harvard University Press, 1998), pp. 228–255.

16 On the Northwest Ordinance, see Peter Onuf, *Statehood and Union: A History of the Northwest Ordinance* (Bloomington: Indiana University Press, 1987); Paul Finkelman, *Slavery and the Founders: Race and Liberty in the Age of Jefferson*, 2nd ed. (Armonk, NY: M. E. Sharpe, 2001), pp. 37–80; Fehrenbacher, *Slaveholding Republic*, pp. 135–172. The British anti–slave trade movement had strong ties to the movement in America and was strongly influenced by the American Revolution. See Christopher Leslie Brown, *Moral Capital: Foundations of British Abolitionism* (Chapel Hill: University of North Carolina Press, 2006).

17 Rufus King's precedent was not forgotten. On March 6, 1862, President Lincoln sent a message to Congress urging it to compensate any state that chose to abolish slavery. Two days later, retired General Winfield Scott sent Lincoln's Secretary of State, William H. Seward, a note reminding him of King's anti-slavery record. "My dear Mr. Secretary: If, perchance, this historical reminescence has escaped the notice of the President & yourself, I may do you a service by recalling it, viz;— Mr. Rufus King ceased to be a U. States' Senator, March 3, 1825. In the act of leaving that body, he laid upon the table a resolution pledging the public domain, after the discharge of the national debt, to aid such states as might adopt a system of slave emancipation —— entertaining the pardonable belief that his resolution might, in generations more or less, be dug up for consideration, when his name would add weight to the measure. Living in the same Hotel with him (now Willard's) I called to thank him, as a Southern man, the same night, & added that altho' the Southern prejudice against him, on account of the Missouri question, could not be overcome in his time, yet after generations would venerate him as a great benefactor, &c. My gratitude to the President, for his late message, on the same subject, is equally great." Winfield Scott to William Seward, Mar. 8, 1862, ALP-LC.

18 *Annals of Cong.*, House of Representatives, 16th Cong., 1st Sess., pp. 956–957. For a similar argument in the Senate, see *Annals of Cong.*, Senate, 16th Cong., 1st Sess., p. 183.

On the Missouri Crisis generally, see Glover Moore, *The Missouri Controversy, 1819–1821* (Lexington: University of Kentucky Press, 1953); Richard H. Brown, "The Missouri Crisis, Slavery, and the Politics of Jacksonianism," *South Atlantic Quarterly* 65 (1966), pp. 55–72; William W. Freehling, *The*

Road to Disunion, vol. 1: *Secessionists at Bay, 1776–1854* (New York: Oxford University Press, 1990), pp. 144–161; Sean Wilentz, *The Rise of American Democracy* (New York: W. W. Norton, 2005), pp. 218–240; Wilentz, "Jeffersonian Democracy and the Origins of Political Antislavery in the United States: The Missouri Crisis Revisited," *Journal of the Historical Society* 4 (Fall 2004), pp. 375–401; Wiecek, *Sources of Antislavery Constitutionalism*, pp. 106–125; Robert Pierce Forbes, *The Missouri Crisis and Its Aftermath: Slavery and the Meaning of America* (Chapel Hill: University of North Carolina Press, 2007); Van Cleve, *Slaveholders' Union*, pp. 225–266.

19 *Commonwealth v. Aves* 18 Pick. 193 (Mass., 1836). See also Finkelman, *Imperfect Union*, pp. 103–114.

20 William Birney, *James G. Birney and His Times: The Genesis of the Republican Party with Some Account of the Abolition Movements in the South before 1828* (New York: D. Appleton, 1890), pp. 261ff.

21 Ibid., pp. 262–263.

22 Niven, *Salmon P. Chase*, pp. 50–54. For the legal context of the *Matilda* case, see Betty Fladeland, *James Gillespie Birney: Slaveholder to Abolitionist* (Ithaca: Cornell University Press, 1955), pp. 148–149, 152; tenBroek, *Equal under Law*, pp. 38–39; Thomas Morris, *Free Men All: The Personal Liberty Laws of the North, 1780–1861* (Baltimore: Johns Hopkins University Press, 1974), pp. 88–90; Robert Cover, *Justice Accused: Antislavery and the Judicial Process* (New Haven: Yale University Press, 1975), pp. 162–174; Wiecek, *Sources of Antislavery Constitutionalism*, pp. 191–192; Finkelman, *Imperfect Union*, pp. 160–162.

23 These quotations come from the two cases arising from the escape, the first against Matilda Lawrence herself and the second against Birney. Both Lawrence and Birney were defended by Salmon P. Chase, and the quotes are all his. See *In re Matilda*, from *Speech of Salmon P. Chase in the Case of the Colored Woman Matilda* (Cincinnati: Pugh & Dodd, 1837); and *Birney v. The State of Ohio*, 8 Ohio 230, 232 (1837). For the legal context of *Ohio v. Birney*, see Finkelman, *Imperfect Union*, pp. 162–163.

24 Finkelman, *Imperfect Union*, pp. 162–163.

25 [Theodore Dwight Weld], *The Power of Congress over the District of Columbia* (New York: J. F. Trow, 1838), p. 39. For political context, see tenBroek, *Equal under Law*, pp. 21–23; Wiecek, *Sources of Antislavery Constitutionalism*, pp. 189–191; Helen Knowles, "Slavery and the Constitution: A Special Relationship," *Slavery & Abolition* 28 (2007), pp. 309–328. On Weld's role in the antislavery movement, see Barnes, *Antislavery Impulse*; Benjamin P. Thomas, *Theodore Weld, Crusader for Freedom* (New Brunswick: Rutgers University Press, 1950); James M. McPherson, "The Fight against the Gag Rule: Joshua

Leavitt and Antislavery Insurgency in the Whig Party, 1839–1842," *Journal of Negro History* 48 (July 1963), pp. 188–195.

26 Weld, *Power of Congress*, pp. 13, 41–43.

27 *New York Plaindealer*, Sept. 22, 1838, quoted in Sean Wilentz, "Slavery, Anti-slavery, and Jacksonian Democracy," in Melvyn Stokes and Stephen Conway, eds., *The Market Revolution in America* (Charlottesville: University of Virginia Press, 1996), p. 216; Morris, *Life of Thomas Morris*, p. 155. See also Jonathan Earle, *Jacksonian Antislavery and the Politics of Free Soil, 1824–1854* (Chapel Hill: University of North Carolina Press, 2004), pp. 17–48.

28 Farrand, ed., *Records of the Federal Convention*, vol. 2, pp. 374, 416–417; *Argument of John Quincy Adams, Before the Supreme Court of the United States, In the Case of the United States, Appellants, vs. Cinque, and Others, Africans, Captured on the Schooner Amistad . . .* (New York: S. W. Benedict, 1841), p. 39.

29 *Groves v. Slaughter*, 15 Peters (U.S.) 449 (1841). On the *Groves* case, see Paul Finkelman, "John McLean: Moderate Abolitionists and Supreme Court Politician," *Vanderbilt Law Review* 62 (2009), pp. 552–554; Harold Melvin Hyman and William M. Wiecek, *Equal Justice under Law: Constitutional Development, 1835–1875* (New York: Harper & Row, 1982), pp. 101–102.

30 *Philanthropist* (Cincinnati), Nov. 3, 1841. See also David L. Lightner, *Slavery and the Commerce Power: How the Struggle against the Interstate Slave Trade Led to the Civil War* (New Haven: Yale University Press, 2006).

31 Glyndon G. Van Deusen, *William Henry Seward* (New York: Oxford University Press, 1967), p. 67; George E. Baker, ed., *The Works of William H. Seward* (New York: Redfield, 1853), vol. 1, p. 71; *CW*, vol. 2, p. 245.

32 Daniel Webster to Edward Everett, Jan. 29, 1842, reprinted in William Jay, *The Creole Case and Mr. Webster's Dispatch . . .* (New York: Redfield, 1842). Details of the insurrection are taken from Webster's account, on pp. 5–6. Quotation is from p. 6. For background, see Edward Rugemeyer, *The Problem of Emancipation: The Caribbean Roots of the American Civil War* (Baton Rouge: Louisiana State University Press, 2009), pp. 176ff.

33 *Speech of Salmon P. Chase*, p. 8.

34 Jay, *Creole Case*, p. 12; Charles Sumner to Jacob Harvey, Jan. 14, 1842, in Edward L. Pierce, ed., *Memoir and Letters of Charles Sumner* (Boston: Roberts Brothers, 1893), vol. 2, p. 200.

35 Pierce, ed., *Memoir and Letters of Charles Sumner*, vol. 2, p. 200; Jay, *Creole Case*, pp. 18–19.

36 *Journal of the House of Representatives*, vol. 37, p. 567. See also James Brewer Stewart, *Joshua R. Giddings and the Tactics of Radical Politics* (Cleveland: Press of Case Western Reserve University, 1970), esp. pp. 62–78.

37 Barnes, *Antislavery Impulse*, pp. 161–170; Aileen S. Kraditor, *Means and Ends*

in American Abolitionism: Garrison and His Critics on Strategy and Tactics,
1834–1850 (New York: Pantheon Books, 1970), pp. 118–136; Richard H.
Sewell, *Ballots for Freedom: Antislavery Politics in the United States, 1837–1860*
(New York: Oxford University Press, 1974), pp. 24–79; Louis S. Gerteis,
Morality and Utility in American Antislavery Reform (Chapel Hill: University
of North Carolina Press, 1987), pp. 37ff.

38   The 1844 platform appears as Appendix C in Johnson, *Liberty Party*, pp.
315–322.

39   Ibid., pp. 56–61.

40   Quotations from the 1848 Free Soil Party platform, reprinted in Schlesinger,
ed., *History of American Presidential Elections*, vol. 2, pp. 902–905. On the
antislavery critique of the "Slave Power," see Eric Foner, *Free Soil, Free Labor,*
Free Men (New York: Oxford University Press, 1970), pp. 73–102. On the
Slave Power as a political reality, see Leonard L. Richards, *The Slave Power:*
The Free North and Southern Domination, 1780–1860 (Baton Rouge: Louisiana State University Press, 2000). For a different but complementary
approach to the influence of slaveholders on American politics, see Robin L.
Einhorn, *American Taxation, American Slavery* (Chicago: University of Chi-
cago Press, 2006).

41   On the Free Soil Party, see Sewell, *Ballots for Freedom*, pp. 170–253; Frederick
J. Blue, *The Free Soilers: Third Party Politics, 1848–1854* (Urbana: University
of Illinois Press, 1973); John Mayfield, *Rehearsal for Republicanism: Free Soil*
and the Politics of Antislavery (Port Washington, NY: Kennikat Press, 1980);
Earle, *Jacksonian Antislavery*, pp. 163–192. On the determination of the Whigs
and Democrats to exclude antislavery from national politics, see David Potter,
The Impending Crisis, 1848–1861 (New York: Harper & Row, 1976), pp.
121ff.; Donald J. Ratcliffe, "The Decline of Antislavery Politics, 1815–1840,"
in John Craig Hammond and Matthew Mason, eds., *Contesting Slavery: The*
Politics of Bondage and Freedom in the New American Nation (Charlottesville:
University of Virginia Press, 2011), pp. 267–290.

42   Baker, ed., *Works of William H. Seward*, vol. 1, pp. 73–74. The 1844 Liberty
Party platform explicitly declared that the antislavery principles of natural and
common law were embedded in the Constitution—exactly the point Seward
would make in his 1850 "higher law" speech.

43   Ibid., pp. 78, 60–62.

44   Sewell, *Ballots for Freedom*, pp. 190ff.; Johnson, *Liberty Party*, p. 57; Wilentz,
"Slavery, Antislavery, and Jacksonian Democracy," pp. 216–217.

45   Baker, ed., *Works of William Seward*, vol. 1, pp. 86–87.

46   Ibid., p. 87.

47   Sumner, *Freedom National; Slavery Sectional*, p. 31.

48 On the legal issues prompted by the Fugitive Slave Act of 1850, see Morris, *Free Men All*; Steven Lubet, *Fugitive Justice: Runaways, Rescuers, and Slavery on Trial* (Cambridge: Harvard University Press, 2010).

49 Howard Jones, *Mutiny on the Amistad*, rev. ed. (New York: Oxford University Press, 1987); Davis, *Inhuman Bondage*, pp. 12–26.

50 *Argument of John Quincy Adams*, pp. 6, 8–9.

51 On the relationship of slavery to the diplomatic history of the early republic, see Fehrenbacher, *Slaveholding Republic*.

52 Quotations in Burrus M. Carnahan, *Act of Justice: Lincoln's Emancipation Proclamation and the Laws of War* (Lexington: University Press of Kentucky, 2007), pp. 8–9. See also William Lee Miller, *Arguing about Slavery: John Quincy Adams and the Great Battle in the United States Congress* (New York: Knopf, 1996).

53 Carnahan, *Act of Justice*, pp. 10–18. On the military use of slaves, see Christopher Leslie Brown and Philip D. Morgan, *Arming Slaves: From Classical Times to the Modern Age* (New Haven: Yale University Press, 2006); Patterson, *Slavery and Social Death*, pp. 289–293; Blackburn, *Overthrow of Colonial Slavery*, pp. 331–380; Laird W. Bergad, *The Comparative Histories of Slavery in Brazil, Cuba, and the United States* (Cambridge: Cambridge University Press, 2007), pp. 251–290.

54 Carnahan, *Act of Justice*, p. 14.

55 Weld, *Power of Congress*, pp. 45–47; Johnson, *Liberty Party*, p. 321; Baker, ed., *Works of William H. Seward*, vol. 1, pp. 85, 86, 88.

56 Joseph Story, *The Conflict of Laws* (Boston: Redfield, 834), pp. 92–93; David Herbert Donald, *Charles Sumner and the Coming of the Civil War* (New York: Alfred A. Knopf, 1960), p. 388.

57 Schlesinger, ed., *History of American Presidential Elections*, vol. 2, pp. 1037, 1125. On the Republicans in the 1850s, see Foner, *Free Soil, Free Labor, Free Men*; William E. Gienapp, *The Origins of the Republican Party, 1852–1856* (New York: Oxford University Press, 1987); Wilentz, *Rise of American Democracy*, pp. 521–796. On the Democrats, see Joel Silbey, *A Respectable Minority: The Democratic Party in the Civil War Era, 1860–1868* (New York: Hill & Wang, 1977); Jean H. Baker, *Affairs of Party: The Political Culture of Northern Democrats in the Mid-Nineteenth Century* (Ithaca: Cornell University Press, 1983).

There are many surveys of the "crisis" of the 1850s. See, for example, Potter, *Impending Crisis*; Michael Holt, *The Political Crisis of the 1850s* (New York: W. W. Norton, 1978); Bruce Levine, *Half Slave and Half Free: The Roots of the Civil War* (New York: Hill & Wang, 1992); John Ashworth, *The Republic in Crisis, 1848–1861* (Cambridge: Cambridge University Press, 2012). On the origins of secession, see Avery O. Craven, *The Growth of Southern Nationalism, 1841–1861* (Baton Rouge: Louisiana State University Press, 1953); William L. Barney, *The Road to Secession: A New Perspective on the Old South* (New York: Praeger, 1972); William J. Cooper Jr., *The South and the Politics of Slavery* (Baton Rouge: Louisiana State University Press, 1978); William W. Freehling, *The Road to Disunion*, vol. 2: *Secessionists Triumphant, 1854–1861* (New York: Oxford University Press, 2007).

58 *Cong. Globe*, 36th Cong., 2d Sess., pp. 1038, 1040. The Liberty platform insisted that it was "not a Sectional party, but a National party," the "party of 1776" representing "the true spirit of the Constitution." Johnson, *Liberty Party*, p. 316.

59 Lynda Lasswell Crist et al., eds., *The Papers of Jefferson Davis* (Baton Rouge: Louisiana State University Press, 1989), vol. 6, pp. 140, 122, 274. See also p. 158. The now-standard biography of Davis is William J. Cooper Jr., *Jefferson Davis, American* (New York: Knopf, 2000). Cf. Huston, *Calculating the Value of the Union*, pp. 127–128.

60 *Dred Scott v. Sandford*. 60 U.S. 393 (Howard). Fehrenbacher, in *The Dred Scott Case*, argues that the case was wrongly decided. Mark A. Graber, in *Dred Scott and the Problem of Constitutional Evil* (New York: Cambridge University Press, 2006), argues that the case was correctly decided.

61 *CW*, vol. 3, pp. 80, 257.

62 Rodney O. Davis and Douglas L. Wilson, eds., *The Lincoln-Douglas Debates* (Urbana and Chicago: Knox College Lincoln Studies Center and University of Illinois Press, 2008), pp. 31, 115, 198, 286.

63 *CW*, vol. 3, p. 545. For the background and significance of the Cooper Union speech, see Harold Holzer, *Lincoln at Cooper Union: The Speech That Made Abraham Lincoln President* (New York: Simon & Schuster, 2004); Michael Burlingame, *Abraham Lincoln: A Life* (Baltimore: Johns Hopkins University Press, 2008), vol. 1, pp. 582ff. On the evolution of Lincoln's views on slavery, see Eric Foner, *The Fiery Trial: Abraham Lincoln and American Slavery* (New York: W. W. Norton, 2010).

64 *CW*, vol. 3, pp. 542 n. 31, 543–545.

65 Schlesinger, ed., *History of American Presidential Elections*, vol. 2, pp. 1124–1125.

66 *Cong. Globe*, 37th Cong., 2d Sess. p. 2043. Alexander Diven's reference to antislavery constitutionalism as the "corner-stone" of the Republican Party may have been a deliberate response to the famous speech in which Confederate Vice President Alexander Stephens declared that the subordination of blacks to whites was the "cornerstone" of the Confederacy. Donald G. Nieman, in *Promises to Keep: African Americans and the Constitutional Order, 1776*

to the Present (New York: 1991), pp. 30–49, traces the evolution of antislavery constitutionalism as it moved from radical abolitionism to the political mainstream. Wigfall is quoted in Shearer Davis Bowman, *At the Precipice: Americans North and South during the Secession Crisis* (Chapel Hill: University of North Carolina Press, 2010), p. 267.

CHAPTER 2: "DISUNION IS ABOLITION"

1 *Springfield (MA) Daily Republican*, Dec. 22, 1860, in *NES*, vol. 1, p. 483.

2 Herman Belz, *Emancipation and Equal Rights: Politics and Constitutionalism in the Civil War Era* (New York: W. W. Norton, 1978), pp. 26–28.

3 Eric Foner, *Free Soil, Free Labor, Free Men* (New York: Oxford University Press, 1970), pp. 115–123, 207–211.

4 Rodney O. Davis and Douglas L. Wilson, eds., *The Lincoln-Douglas Debates* (Urbana and Chicago: Knox College Lincoln Studies Center and University of Illinois Press, 2008), p. 166.

5 *Chicago Daily Democrat*, Oct. 31, 1860, in *NES*, vol. 1, pp. 77, 509.

6 Gunja Sengupta, *For God and Mammon: Evangelicals and Entrepreneurs, Masters and Slaves in Territorial Kansas, 1854–1860* (Athens: University of Georgia Press, 1996), p. 129; Shearer Davis Bowman, *At the Precipice: Americans North and South during the Secession Crisis* (Chapel Hill: University of North Carolina Press, 2010), p. 241; Salmon P. Chase to Charles A. Dana, Nov. 10, 1860, in John Niven, ed., *The Salmon P. Chase Papers*, vol. 3: Correspondence, *1858–March 1864* (Kent, OH: Kent State University Press, 1996), p. 32; Seward quoted in *Morning Pennsylvanian*, Feb. 9, 1861, in *NES*, vol. 1, p. 447.

7 *New York Tribune*, Jan. 19 and Feb. 27, 1861, in *NES*, vol. 1, pp. 288, 300–302. Seward had made a similar proposal in his "higher law" speech of 1850. Horace Greeley's version has gone largely unnoticed, though it helps to explain his willingness to let the cotton states secede. Like William Lloyd Garrison, Greeley assumed that if the slave and free states separated, it would be easier for the North to surround the South and squeeze slavery to death. For Greeley's views on slavery, see Mitchell Snay, *Horace Greeley and the Politics of Reform in Nineteenth-Century America* (Lanham, MD: Rowman & Littlefield, 2011), pp. 117–121. For his thoughts during the secession crisis, see Glyndon G. Van Deusen, *Horace Greeley, Nineteenth Century Crusader* (Philadelphia: University of Pennsylvania Press, 1953), pp. 255–270.

8 *Columbus Crisis*, Feb. 7, 1861, in *NES*, vol. 1, p. 444; Edward McPherson, *The Political History of the United States of America, during the Great Rebellion . . .* (Washington, DC: Philip & Solomons, 1865), p. 209. See also Jon L. Wake-

lyn, ed., *Southern Pamphlets on Secession* (Chapel Hill: University of North Carolina Press, 1996), p. 289.

9 *Hartford Evening Press*, Oct. 25 and 26, 1860; *Chicago Daily Democrat*, Oct. 31, 1860; *Cincinnati Daily Commercial*, Nov. 3, 1860, in *NES*, vol. 1, pp. 62, 75, 109.

10 *Iowa State Register* (Des Moines), Dec. 12, 1860, in *NES*, vol. 1, p. 156, and in general pp. 125–157; *Morning Pennsylvanian* (Philadelphia), Feb. 18, 1861, in *NES*, vol. 2, p. 610. See also *Philadelphia Public Ledger*, June 7, 1861, in *NES*, vol. 2, p. 845.

11 *OR*, ser. 4, vol. 1, pp. 5–7, 34, 36, 40–41.

12 *Cong. Globe*, 36th Cong., 1st Sess., pp. 1155ff. Quote on p. 1158.

13 Message of Jefferson Davis to the Confederate Congress, Apr. 29, 1861, in Frank Moore, ed., *The Rebellion Record: A Diary of American Events* (New York: Putnam, 1861), vol. 1, "Documents and Narratives," pp. 4, 168; *New Orleans Daily Crescent*, Nov. 13, 1860; *Daily Constitutionalist* (Augusta, GA), Dec. 1, 1860; *Examiner* (Gallatin, TN), Dec. 1, 1860, in *SES*, pp. 237, 283, 287.

14 *Kentucky Statesman* (Lexington), Jan. 6, 1860, in *SES*, p. 4.

15 *New Orleans Daily Crescent*, Dec. 14, 1860; *Richmond Enquirer*, July 10, 1860, in *SES*, pp. 141, 333; *Cong. Globe*, 36th Cong., 1st Sess., p. 1162.

16 *Daily Illinois State Register* (Springfield), Sept. 28, 1860; *Philadelphia Press*, Dec. 21, 1860; *New York Daily News*, Jan. 9, 1861, in *NES*, vol. 1, pp. 43, 124, 299.

17 *Charleston Mercury*, Oct. 11 and Nov. 3, 1860; *Daily True Delta* (New Orleans), Oct. 12, 1860, in *SES*, pp. 179, 185–186, 204.

 Northern Democrats agreed that the Republicans in power would try to abolish slavery. If they are victorious, one Washington editor predicted, the Republicans will "push their aggressive policy to its legitimate conclusion" by attempting to "expel slavery from the Union." The influential Springfield *Daily Illinois State Register*, the editorial voice of Democratic Senator Stephen Douglas, warned that Lincoln "proposes to legislate so that slavery must soon be extinguished." Another Douglas paper declared, on the eve of the election, that the Republicans were "making war upon the Southern people" so as to "make them ultimately forego that system of labor which they prefer." See *Constitution* (Washington, DC), Sept. 6, 1860; *Daily Illinois State Register* (Springfield), Sept. 28, 1860; *Daily Ohio Statesman* (Columbus), Nov. 2, 1860, in *NES*, vol. 1, pp. 33, 43, 68.

18 In some ways the best brief narrative of secession remains Dwight Lowell Dumond, *The Secession Movement, 1860–1861* (New York: Macmillan, 1931).

See also David Potter, *The Impending Crisis, 1848–1861* (New York: Harper & Row, 1976); William W. Freehling, *The Road to Disunion*, vol. 2: *Secessionists Triumphant, 1854–1861* (New York: Oxford University Press, 2007).

19 For a comprehensive narrative of Lincoln during the interregnum, see Harold Holzer, *President-Elect Lincoln* (New York: Simon & Schuster, 2008). For an older but still useful account, see William E. Baringer, *A House Dividing: Lincoln as President Elect* (Springfield, IL: Abraham Lincoln Association, 1945).

20 John Gilmer to Abraham Lincoln, Dec. 10, 1860, ALP–LC, Lincoln to John Gilmer, Dec. 15, 1860, in *CW*, vol. 4, pp. 151–153.

21 David Potter, in *Lincoln and His Party in the Secession Crisis* (New Haven: Yale University Press, 1942), was critical of Lincoln for derailing the compromise "movement" led by William H. Seward. Van Deusen, *William Henry Seward*, p. 246; Kenneth M. Stampp, in *And the War Came: The North and the Secession Crisis, 1860–1861* (Baton Rouge: Louisiana state University Press, 1950), doubted there was any meaningful support for compromise among the Republicans.

In late 1860 the influential New York Republican Thurlow Weed published an editorial proposing the extension of the Missouri Compromise line as a resolution to the sectional crisis, a proposal at odds with the Republican Party platform and stoutly rejected by most Republicans. Because Weed was close to Seward, historians often read this as evidence of Seward's willingness to compromise, but Seward's leading biographer says that there is "no real evidence" for this. Glyndon G. Van Deusen, *William Henry Seward* (New York: Oxford University Press, 1967), p. 242. Daniel Crofts, in *Reluctant Confederates: Upper South Unionists in the Secession Crisis* (Chapel Hill: University of North Carolina Press, 1989), believes Seward represented a significant movement for compromise among leading Republicans. For similar interpretations, see Holzer, *Lincon President-Elect*; William J. Cooper, *We Have the War upon Us: The Onset of the Civil War, November 1860–April 1861* (New York: Knopf, 2012). See also Russell McClintock, *Lincoln and the Decision for War: The Northern Response to Secession* (Chapel Hill: University of North Carolina Press, 2008).

There is no doubt that Seward and other leading Republicans initially suggested a conciliatory posture, believing that a war was unnecessary to destroy slavery. The question is whether that posture indicated a willingness to make substantive compromises on slavery. The evidence for conciliation is strong; the evidence for substantive compromise is much weaker.

22 Salmon P. Chase to John Greenleaf Whittier, Nov. 23, 1860, in Niven, ed., *Chase Papers*, vol. 3, p. 35. William Howard Russell reported that in late March of 1861, Charles Sumner felt the same way. "I walked home with Mr. Sumner

to his rooms and heard some of his views which were not so sanguine as those of Mr. Seward, and I thought I detected a desire to let the Southern States go out with their slavery if they so desired it. Mr. Chase, by the way, expressed sentiments of the same kind more decidedly the other day." Quoted in William Howard Russell, *My Diary North and South*, ed. Eugene H. Berwanger (New York, 1863; Baton Rouge: Louisiana State University Press, 2001), entry for Mar. 31, 1861. Charles Francis Adams, *An Autobiography, 1835–1915* (Boston: Houghton Mifflin, 1916), pp. 73–75. In retrospect, Adams concluded, the "conciliators" underestimated the South's determination to secede.

23 Van Duesen, *William Henry Seward*, p. 246.

24 *Cong. Globe*, 36th Cong., 2nd Sess., pp. 343–344.

25 Ibid., p. 342.

26 Ibid.

27 *Indianapolis Daily Journal*, Dec. 14, 1860; *Iowa State Register* (Des Moines), Jan. 23, 1861, in *NES*, vol. 1, pp. 117, 439–441; Salmon P. Chase to Ruhama Ludlow Hunt, Nov. 30, 1860, in Niven, ed., *Chase Papers*, vol. 3, p. 38.

28 *Boston Daily Atlas and Bee*, Nov. 12, 1860; *Indianapolis Daily Journal*, Dec. 14, 1860; *Daily Illinois State Journal* (Springfield), Mar. 6, 1861, in *NES*, vol. 1, pp. 117, 90, and *NES*, vol. 2, p. 640; *Weekly Pantagraph* (Bloomington, IL), Jan. 9, 1861, in Don Munson, ed., *It is Begun!* The Pantagraph *Reports the Civil War* (Bloomington, IL: McLean County Historical Society, 2001), p. 2.

29 *CW*, vol. 3, p. 454.

30 *Springfield (MA) Daily Republican*, Dec. 22, 1860; *Iowa State Register* (Des Moines), Jan. 23, 1861, in *NES*, vol. 1, pp. 482, 440, 118.

31 *Indianapolis Daily Journal*, Dec. 14, 1860.

32 *Indiana American* (Indianapolis), Nov. 21, 1860; *Worcester Palladium*, Jan. 16, 1861; *Western Kansas Express* (Manhattan City), May 11, 1861, in *NES*, vol. 1, pp. 97, 222, and *NES*, vol. 2, p.834; Stampp, *And the War Came*, pp. 250–252; *Weekly Pantagraph* (Bloomington, IL), Jan. 6, 1861, in Munson, ed., *It is Begun!* p. 2.

33 John Sherman to William T. Sherman, Nov. 26, 1860, in Rachel Sherman Thorndike, ed., *The Sherman Letters: Correspondence between General and Senator Sherman from 1837 to 1891* (New York: Charles Scribner's Sons, 1894), p. 87; Howard Kennedy Beale, ed., *The Diary of Edward Bates, 1859–1866* (Washington, DC: Government Printing Office, 1933), entry for Mar. 16, 1861, p. 179; Allan Nevins, ed., *Diary of George Templeton Strong*, vol. 3: *1860–1865* (New York: Macmillan, 1952), entry for Apr. 18, 1861, p. 124.

34 *Kentucky Statesman* (Lexington), Nov. 20, 1860, in *SES*, p. 255.

35 *Louisville Daily Journal*, Jan. 26, 1861; *Republican Banner* (Nashville), Jan. 26, 1861, in *SES*, pp. 422–423, 425–426.

36 On the first inaugural address, see Harry V. Jaffa, *A New Birth of Freedom: Abraham Lincoln and the Coming of the Civil War* (Lanham, MD: Rowman & Littlefield, 2000), pp. 237–355; Ronald C. White, *The Eloquent President: A Portrait of Lincoln through His Words* (New York: Random House, 2005), pp. 62–97; Douglas L. Wilson, *Lincoln's Sword: The Presidency and the Power of Words* (New York: Knopf, 2006), pp. 42–70; Michael Burlingame, *Abraham Lincoln: A Life* (Baltimore: Johns Hopkins University Press, 2008), vol. 2, pp. 45–68.

37 *CW*, vol. 4, pp. 263–264.

38 Ibid., pp. 156–157, 264.

39 Ibid., p. 267.

40 Ibid., pp. 268–269 (emphasis added). Lincoln seems to have accepted the premises of William Jay, Samuel May, and other abolitionists who argued—most famously in the *Amistad* case—that the U.S. government should not capture and return fugitive slaves from foreign countries. Once the slave states declared their independence, Lincoln seemed to be arguing, the federal government would no longer be obliged to enforce the fugitive slave clause. This was precisely the same logic General Benjamin F. Butler would use two months later to justify his refusal to return slaves to their owners at Fortress Monroe.

41 *Philadelphia Evening Journal*, Mar. 5, 1861, in *NES*, vol. 2, p. 635.

42 Michael Burlingame and John R. Turner Ettlinger, eds., *Inside Lincoln's White House: The Complete Civil War Diary of John Hay* (Carbondale: Southern Illinois University Press, 1997), entry for Apr. 27, 1861, pp. 12–13; George Field to Abraham Lincoln, May 9, 1861; Burt Van Horn to Lincoln, May 1861; "Pennsylvanicus" to Lincoln, May 8, 1861; Orville H. Browning to Lincoln, Apr. 30, 1861, ALP-LC.

43 *Evansville (IN) Daily Journal* [Lincoln], Apr. 20, 1861; *Oxford Democrat* (Paris, ME) [Independent], Apr. 26, 1861; *Norfolk County Journal* (Roxbury, MA), May 4, 1861, in *NES*, vol. 1, pp. 463–464, and *NES*, vol. 2, pp. 812–813, 821.

44 *Madison (WI) Daily Argus and Democrat*, May 4, 1861; *Daily Capital City Fact* (Columbus, OH), May 18, 1861, in *NES*, vol. 2, pp. 824, 839.

45 Russell, *My Diary North and South*, entry for Mar. 28, 1861.

CHAPTER 3: "FULFILLMENT OF THE PROPHECIES"

1 *Cleveland Daily Plain Dealer*, Jan. 12, 1861, in *NES*, vol. 1, p. 481.

2 Orville H. Browning to Abraham Lincoln, Apr. 30, 1861, ALP- LC.

3 William Howard Russell, *My Diary North and South*, ed. Eugene H. Ber-

wanger (London, 1863; Baton Rouge: Louisiana State University Press, 2001), entry for May 23, 1861, pp. 161–162.

4 Ibid., entry for May 15, 1861, p. 151.

5 Ibid., entry for May 13, 1861, p. 142.

6 See, for example, Susan O'Donovan, *Becoming Free in the Cotton South* (Cambridge: Harvard University Press, 2007), p. 65.

7 William H. Freehling, *The Road to Disunion*, vol. 2: *Secessionists Triumphant, 1854–1861* (New York: Oxford University Press, 2007), pp. 333ff.

8 Russell, *My Diary North and South*, entry for Apr. 22, 1861, p. 98.

9 On the policing of slavery in the antebellum South, see John Hope Franklin, *The Militant South, 1800–1861* (Cambridge: Harvard University Press, 1956); John Hope Franklin and Loren Schweninger, *Runaway Slaves: Rebels on the Plantation* (New York: Oxford University Press, 1999), pp. 149–208; Sally E. Hadden, *Slave Patrols: Law and Violence in Virginia and the Carolinas* (Cambridge: Harvard University Press, 2001).

10 Daniel Crofts, ed., *Cobb's Ordeal: The Diaries of a Virginia Farmer, 1842–1872* (Athens: University of Georgia Press, 1997), entries for Jan. 13, Mar. 11, Apr. 7, Apr. 29, and June 9, 1861, pp. 181–198. On the government's impressments of Cobb's slaves, see the entries for Nov. 21, 24, and 25, 1861, p. 207.

11 Charles J. Mitchell to Jefferson Davis, Apr. 27, 1861, in Lynda Lasswell Crist et al., eds., *The Papers of Jefferson Davis* (Baton Rouge: Louisiana State University Press, 1992), vol. 7, p. 134.

12 William H. Lee to Jefferson Davis, May 4, 1861, in ibid., p. 148.

13 George W. Gayle to Jefferson Davis, May 22, 1861, in ibid., p. 175.

14 Quoted in Clarence Mohr, *On the Threshold of Freedom: Masters and Slaves in Civil War Georgia* (Athens: University of Georgia Press, 1986), pp. 36–37.

15 Thomas L. Johnson, *Twenty-Eight Years a Slave in Virginia . . .* (Bournemouth UK: W. Mate & Sons, 1909), p. 27.

16 Rawick, *American Slave*, orig. ser., 13 (pt. 4), p. 192, quoted in Steven V. Ash, *The Black Experience in the Civil War South* (Santa Barbara, CA: Praeger, 2010), p. 2.

17 Russell, *My Diary North and South*, entry for May 4, 1861, p. 117.

18 Quoted in Winthrop D. Jordan, *Tumult and Silence at Second Creek: In Inquiry into a Civil War Slave Conspiracy*, rev. ed. (Baton Rouge: Louisiana State University Press, 1995), p. 11.

19 Levi Branham, *My Life and Travels* (Dalton, GA: A. J. Showalter, 1929), p. 45.

20 Quoted in Anthony E. Kaye, *Joining Places: Slave Neighborhoods in the Old South* (Chapel Hill: University of North Carolina Press, 2007), p. 183.

21 *OR*, ser. 2, vol. 1, pt. 1, p. 750.

22 Ibid.

23 Hans Louis Trefousse, *Ben Butler: The South Called Him Beast!* (New York: Twayne, 1957), pp. 34–41. For a more skeptical view of the Massachusetts Free Soil coalition, see David Herbert Donald, *Charles Sumner and the Coming of the Civil War* (New York: Knopf, 1960), pp. 205–237.

24 Trefousse, *Ben Butler*, pp. 42–64.

25 Benjamin F. Butler, *Butler's Book*, (Boston: A. M. Thayer, 1892), pp. 228–242.

26 The coincidence of slavery beginning to end where it began was widely noted at the time and has been ever since. For a recent example, see Adam Goodheart, *1861: The Civil War Awakening* (New York: Knopf, 2011), pp. 295–296.

27 Edward L. Pierce, *Enfranchisement and Citizenship* (Boston: Roberts Brothers, 1896), p. 3. The private's letter from Fortress Monroe was dated Apr. 26, 1861.

28 *OR*, ser. 1, vol. 2, pt. 1, p. 862.

29 Robert F. Engs, *Freedom's First Generation: Black Hampton, Virginia, 1861–1890* (New York: Fordham University Press, 2004), pp. 5–16.

30 *OR*, ser. 2, vol. 1, p. 752.

31 Pierce, *Enfranchisement and Citizenship*, p. 23.

32 Butler, *Butler's Book*, p. 258. Butler's recollection of his reasoning is consistent with arguments he would put in writing in July of 1861, two months after his interview with Major John Cary.

33 *OR*, ser. 2, vol. 1, p. 753. Cary's account of Butler's reasoning, sketchy though it is, tends to confirm the version Butler himself recalled in his autobiography many years later.

34 *OR*, ser. 2, vol. 1, pp. 752, 754.

35 *Private and Official Correspondence of Gen. Benjamin F. Butler* (Norwood, MA: Plimpton Press, 1917), vol. 1, p. 114.

36 Montgomery Blair to Benjamin Butler, May 29, 1861, in *Private and Official Correspondence of Butler*, vol. 1, pp. 116–117. It is unclear from Blair's letter whether the joke about "Butler's fugitive slave law" was Lincoln's or Scott's.

37 *CW*, vol. 3, p. 454.

38 Ibid., pp. 268–269.

39 The second set of War Department instructions was issued on August 8, 1861. For months thereafter Union commanders moving into the seceded states were routinely issued copies of both the May 30 and August 8 instructions. See chapter 4.

40 *OR*, ser. 2, vol. 1, pp. 754–755.

41 *New York Times*, May 31, 1861, p. 8.

42 FSSP, ser. 1, vol. 1, pp. 75–76, 76n.

43 *OR*, ser. 2, vol. 1, pp. 754–755.

44 *Private and Official Correspondence of Butler*, vol. 1, pp. 111–112.

45 Ibid., pp. 185–188. The absence of any reference to "contraband of war" in Butler's first letters later gave rise to speculation that someone else originated the use of the term. This is unlikely. In press reports from Fortress Monroe dated the same day as Butler's meeting with Major Cary, reporters—who appear to have taken their notes from Butler—called the refugees "contraband of war." Postmaster General Montgomery Blair referred to "contraband of war" in a letter he wrote to Butler in late May informing the general that the cabinet was about to meet to discuss the matter. Butler himself claimed to have used the term from the start, and some years later Cary, in a letter to Butler, recalled that "contraband" was "the term . . . employed by you at a conference held between us on the Hampton side of Mill Creek Bridge, on the evening of May 24th, 1861." John B. Cary to Benjamin F. Butler, Mar. 9, 1891, in *Private and Official Correspondence of Butler*, vol. 1, p. 102. Butler's later reconstruction of the events is in *Butler's Book*, pp. 256ff.

46 *New York Times*, May 31, 1861, p. 1.

47 *OR*, ser. 2, vol. 1, p. 752.

48 Ibid., p. 751.

49 Ibid., p. 753. Russell, *My Diary North and South*, entry for July 7, 1861, p. 234.

50 Allan Nevins, ed., *Diary of George Templeton Strong*, vol. 3: *1860–1865* (New York: Macmillan, 1952), entry for June 4, 1861, p. 156.

51 *New York Times*, May 31, 1861, p. 8.

CHAPTER 4: AUGUST 8, 1861: EMANCIPATION BEGINS

1 Edward L. Pierce, *Enfranchisement and Citizenship* (Boston: Roberts Brothers, 1896), pp. 24–25.

2 *Private and Official Correspondence of Gen. Benjamin F. Butler* (Norwood, MA: Plimpton Press, 1917), vol. 1, pp. 185–188.

3 Ibid.

4 *OR*, ser. 2., vol. 1, pp. 755, 757, 760.

5 Stephen W. Sears, ed., *The Civil War Papers of George B. McClellan* (New York: Da Capo Press, 1992), p. 26. The timing of McClellan's order—May 26—is important. Four days later, on May 30, Lincoln's cabinet met and endorsed Butler's contraband policy. By August, after Congress passed the First Confiscation Act, McClellan's orders changed to reflect the new policy.

6 Theodore Calvin Pease and J. G. Randall, eds., *The Diary of Orville Hickman Browning* (Springfield: Trustees of the Illinois State Historical Library, 1925–

1933), entry for July 8, 1861, p. 478; *Cong. Globe*, 37th Cong., 1st Sess., p. 32. The question of who should be responsible for enforcing the fugitive slave clause is discussed more fully in chapter 6.

7 *Cong. Globe*, 37th Cong., 1st Sess., p. 186.

8 Michael Burlingame and John R. Turner Ettlinger, eds., *Inside Lincoln's White House: The Complete Civil War Diary of John Hay* (Carbondale: Southern Illinois University Press, 1997), p. 20.

9 *Cong. Globe*, 37th Cong., 1st Sess., pp. 151, 153, 77.

10 Ibid., p. 119.

11 Ibid., p. 187.

12 Ibid., pp. 189, 191.

13 Ibid., pp. 187, 189.

14 Ibid., p. 194.

15 The standard accounts of the two confiscation acts passed by Congress in 1861 and 1862 pass over the First Confiscation Act on the assumption that it did nothing and was never enforced. This is the historiographical legacy of James Garfield Randall, a leading "revisionist" historian who—as part of his effort to deny the antislavery origins of the Civil War—dismissed evidence that Republican policymakers were interested in attacking slavery as early as July in 1861. See his *Constitutional Problems under Lincoln* (New York: D. Appleton, 1926), pp. 275–292. One of Randall's most misleading points was that the confiscation acts were so legally incoherent that the attorney general never bothered to issue the instructions for implementing the law. In fact, the two statutes legalized *military* emancipation and were therefore implemented by the secretary of war, not the attorney general. Even scholars unsympathetic to Randall's revisionism repeat the error. The best recent studies devote little attention to the First Confiscation Act. See, for example, Silvana R. Siddali, *From Property to Person: Slavery and the Confiscation Acts, 1861–1862* (Baton Rouge: Louisiana State University Press, 2005); Daniel W. Hamilton, *The Limits of Sovereignty: Property Confiscation in the Union and the Confederacy during the Civil War* (Chicago: University of Chicago Press, 2007); Stephen C. Neff, *Justice in Blue and Gray: A Legal History of the Civil War* (Cambridge: Harvard University Press, 2010). An exception is Robert Fabrikant, "Emancipation and the Proclamation: Of Contrabands, Congress, and Lincoln," *Howard Law Journal* 49, no. 2 (June 2006), pp. 321–329.

16 *Cong. Globe*, 37th Cong., 1st Sess., pp. 216–217.

17 Salmon P. Chase to Green Adams, Sept. 5, 1861, in John Niven, ed., *The Salmon P. Chase Papers*, vol. 3: *Correspondence, 1858–March 1863* (Kent, OH: Kent State University Press, 1996), p. 96.

18 *Cong. Globe*, 37th Cong., 1st Sess., p. 269.

19 Ibid., pp. 411, 190.

20 In February of 1862, the provost marshall for the Department of Missouri asked the U.S. district attorney whether emancipation under the First Confiscation Act required judicial proceedings. The district attorney said no. Although the first three sections of the statute established judicial procedures for confiscating rebel property, he pointed out, Section 4 "makes no provision for the case of slaves whose services have been forfeited by reason of their being employed in hostile services against the government." The "evident intention of the act," the district attorney pointed out, "was to make the slave *eo instant* free." FSSP, ser. 1, vol. 1, pp. 425–426. Neff, in *Justice in Blue and Gray*, pp. 135–136, notes that under the First and Second Confiscation Acts, slaves were emancipated "automatically," without judicial proceedings.

21 *Cong. Globe*, 37th Cong., 1st Sess., pp. 218–219.

22 Samuel S. Cox, *Three Decades of Federal Legislation, 1855–1885* (1885; Providence: Reid, 1888), p. 157.

23 There are numerous accounts of First Manassas, but three of the best brief treatments are Shelby Foote, *The Civil War: A Narrative* (New York: Random House, 1958), vol. 1, pp. 72–86; Bruce Catton, *The Coming Fury* (New York: Doubleday, 1961), pp. 436–473; James M. McPherson, *The Battle Cry of Freedom: The Civil War Era* (New York: Oxford University Press, 1988), pp. 334–350.

24 Cox, *Three Decades of Federal Legislation*, p. 158.

25 William Howard Russell, *My Diary North and South*, ed. Eugene H. Berwanger (New York, 1863; Baton Rouge: Louisiana State University Press, 2001), entry for July 22, 1861.

26 The rumors of slaves at Bull Run, armed but not enlisted in the Confederate army, are dissected in Glenn David Brasher, *The Peninsula Campaign and the Necessity of Emancipation* (Chapel Hill: University of North Carolina Press, 2012).

27 Nevins, *Diary of George Templeton Strong*, entry for July 25, 1861, p. 170; Philip Foner, ed., *The Life and Writings of Frederick Douglass* (New York: International, 1952), vol. 3, p. 128; Siddali, *From Property to Persons*, p. 75.

28 *Cong. Globe*, 37th Cong., 1st Sess., p. 219.

29 Ibid.

30 Ibid.

31 Ibid., pp. 189–190.

32 Ibid.

33 Ibid., p. 209.

34 Ibid., pp. 259, 260. Maine Republican William Pitt Fessenden made the same

point about "subjugation." The resolution also declared that it was not the purpose of the Union to subjugate the South. This is true, Fessenden noted; the "purpose" was to restore the Union. But it may be necessary to achieve that purpose by subjugating the South.

35 Ibid., p. 261.

36 Ibid., p. 262.

37 Ibid., p. 264.

38 Ibid., pp. 262, 139–140.

39 Ibid., p. 142.

40 Ibid., p. 410.

41 Ibid., pp. 411, 412. There was never a single "Republican" position on the legal status of the seceded states. Lincoln thought the seceded states were still legally within the Union; others claimed that those states committed "suicide" by leaving the Union; and still others, that they had reverted to the status of territories. For purposes of antislavery policy, these distinctions did not matter very much. All Republicans agreed that the seceded states were "in rebellion," that the laws of war applied to the situation, and that military emancipation was therefore a constitutionally legitimate means of suppressing the rebellion.

42 Ibid., p. 414.

43 Emmerich de Vattel, *The Law of Nations*, book 3, sect. 203 (J. Chitty trans., 1852), cited in Burrus M. Carnahan, *Act of Justice: Lincoln's Emancipation Proclamation and the Laws of War* (Lexington: University of Kentucky Press, 2007), p. 115, n. 45 (endnote on p. 186); *Cong. Globe*, 37th Cong., 1st Sess., pp. 414–415.

44 *Cong. Globe*, 37th Cong, 1st Sess., p. 415.

45 Salmon P. Chase to Green Adams, Sept. 5, 1861, in Niven, ed., *Chase Papers*, vol. 3, p. 96; *Cong. Globe*, 37th Cong., 1st Sess., pp. 410, 411, 415.

46 *Cong. Globe*, 37th Cong., 1st Sess., pp. 431, 427.

47 *Statutes at Large*, 37th Cong., 1st Sess., p. 319.

48 *OR*, ser. 2., vol. 1, pp. 761–762.

49 Ibid., p. 762.

50 Ibid., p. 763; Pierce, *Enfranchisement and Citizenship*, pp. 23, 20.

51 Gideon Welles, "The History of Emancipation," *Galaxy* 14 (Dec. 1872), reprinted in Albert Mordell, comp., *Civil War and Reconstruction: Selected Essays by Gideon Welles* (New York: Twayne, 1959), p. 231.

52 FSSP, ser. 1, vol. 1, p. 35; *OR*, ser. 2, vol. 1, p. 791; *OR*, ser. 1, vol. 6, pp. 176–177. The impact of the War Department instructions along the southern Atlantic coast is discussed in more detail in chapter 6.

CHAPTER 5: THE BORDER STATES

1 On the distinctive attributes of the Border States, see William W. Freehling, *The Road to Disunion*, vol. 1: *Secessionists at Bay, 1776–1854* (New York: Oxford University Press, 1990); Freehling, *The Road to Disunion*, vol. 2: *Secessionists Triumphant, 1854–1861* (New York: Oxford University Press, 2007). See also Daniel Crofts, *Reluctant Confederates: Upper South Unionists in the Secession Crisis* (Chapel Hill: University of North Carolina Press, 1989); Freehling, *The South vs. the South: How Anti-Confederate Southerners Shaped the Course of the Civil War* (New York: Oxford University Press, 2002); Steven Deyle, *Carry Me Back: The Domestic Slave Trade in American Life* (New York: Oxford University Press, 2005). On the importance abolitionists attached to the Border States, see Stanley Harrold, *The Abolitionists and the South, 1831–1861* (Lexington: University Press of Kentucky, 1995). For Lincoln's policy, see William C. Harris, *Lincoln and the Border States: Preserving the Union* (Lawrence: University Press of Kansas, 2011).

2 This and subsequent paragraphs draw heavily on Charles L. Wagant, *The Mighty Revolution: Negro Emancipation in Maryland, 1862–1864* (Baltimore: Johns Hopkins University Press, 1964); Barbara Jeanne Fields, *Slavery and Freedom on the Middle Ground: Maryland during the Nineteenth Century* (New Haven: Yale University Press, 1985).

3 Fields, *Slavery and Freedom on the Middle Ground*, p. 93.

4 Wagant, *Mighty Revolution*, p. 13.

5 Much of the political background can be found in Louis S. Gerteis, *Civil War St. Louis* (Lawrence: University Press of Kansas, 2001).

6 Quotation from William E. Parrish, *Turbulent Partnership: Missouri and the Union, 1861–1865* (Columbia: University of Missouri Press, 1963), pp. 6–7. Notwithstanding Claiborne Jackson's success in the 1860 gubernatorial election, in the presidential balloting Missourians cast 134,000 votes for Douglas, Bell, and Lincoln, all of them unionists, versus 31,317 votes for the pro-southern John C. Breckinridge. The February vote for convention delegates closely mirrored the presidential results.

7 Parrish, *Turbulent Partnership*, p. 30.

8 John C. Frémont, *Memoirs of My Life*, introduction by Charles M. Robinson III (Chicago, 1887: New York: Rowman & Littlefield, 2001), p. 19.

9 Tom Chaffin, *Pathfinder: John Charles Frémont and the Course of American Empire* (New York: Hill & Wang, 2002), p. 440; William E. Gienapp, *The Origins of the Republican Party, 1852–1856* (New York: Oxford University Press, 1987), pp. 376–377.

10 John Howe to Montgomery Blair, Aug. 4, 1861, ALP-LC.

11 Ibid.

12 *OR*, ser. 1, vol. 3, pp. 466–467.

13 The War Department's implementation instructions freed *all* slaves coming into Union lines in the rebellious states.

14 John C. Frémont to Abraham Lincoln, Sept. 8, 1861, ALP-LC; *CW*, vol. 3, pp. 506–507, 517–518; Joshua Speed to Lincoln, Sept. 3, 1861, ALP-LC.

15 Abraham Lincoln to Orville H. Browning, Sept. 22, 1861, in *CW*, vol. 3, p. 531.

16 On Kentucky, see E. Merton Coulter, *The Civil War and Readjustment in Kentucky* (Chapel Hill: University of North Carolina Press, 1926); Victor B. Howard, *Black Liberation in Kentucky: Emancipation and Freedom, 1862–1884* (Lexington: University Press of Kentucky, 1983); FSSP, ser. 1, vol. 1, pp. 493–518; Kent T. Dollar, Larry H. Whiteaker, and W. Calvin Dickinson, eds., *Sister States, Enemy States: The Civil War in Kentucky and Tennessee* (Lexington: University Press of Kentucky, 2009).

17 On the "geopolitical" importance of the Border States for the Confederacy, see Robert E. Bonner, *Mastering America: Southern Slaveholders and the Crisis of American Nationhood* (New York: Cambridge University Press, 2009), pp. 232ff.

18 Joshua Speed to Abraham Lincoln, Sept. 1 and Sept. 3, 1861; Greene Adams and James Speed to Lincoln, Sept. 2, 1861; Leslie Combs to Lincoln, Sept. 6, 1861; Joseph Holt to Lincoln, Sept. 12, 1861; Robert Anderson to Lincoln, Sept. 13, 1861. Context was crucial. The Confederate invasion, launched only days after Frémont's order, explains why the reaction was so much stronger in Kentucky than it was in Missouri. To be sure, there were complaints of a similar sort from Missourians, but far fewer and they were far less excited. See, for example, John B. Henderson to James O. Broadhead, Sept. 7, 1861. All these letters are from ALP-LC.

19 *CW*, vol. 4, pp. 531–532.

20 *OR*, ser. 1, vol. 4, pp. 185–190.

21 Orville H. Browning to Abraham Lincoln, Sept. 11 and Sept. 17, 1861, ALP-LC.

22 Timothy Davis to William H. Seward, Sept. 16, 1861; Richard M. Corwine and J. P. C. Schanaks to Caleb B. Smith, Sept. 16, 1861; John R. Cannon to Abraham Lincoln, Sept. 17, 1861; Samuel Camp to Lincoln, Sept. 17, 1861; O. B. Clark and John Root, resolutions, Sept. 17, 1861; Thomas H. Little to Lincoln, Sept. 17, 1861; J. C. Woods to Samuel Ward, Sept. 17, 1861; H. Montague to Lincoln, Sept. 17, 1861; Mrs. L. C. Howard to Lincoln, Sept. 17, 1861, ALP-LC.

23 Francis P. Blair to Abraham Lincoln, Sept. 1, 1861, ALP-LC; Niven, ed., *Chase Papers*, vol. 3, pp. 105–106.

24 Chandra Manning, in *What This Cruel War Was Over: Soldiers, Slavery, and the Civil War* (New York: Knopf, 2007), captures the conflicts within the Union army caused by antislavery recruits flooding into the ranks in 1861.

25 FSSP, ser. 1, vol. 1, pp. 167, 519–520, 172.

26 Ibid., pp. 421–422.

27 Ibid., pp. 429, 418. See also p. 416, for a similar incident in which Missouri slaves provided the Union army with "important information" and who sought the protection of the military "from their masters who threaten to kill them."

28 Manning, *What This Cruel War Was Over*, pp. 19–51.

29 FSSP, ser. 1, vol. 1, pp. 352, 361, 177, 427.

30 Ibid., pp. 361–362, 427.

31 Ibid., pp. 344, 345, 349–350.

32 Ibid., pp. 349, 422.

33 Ibid., pp. 413–414; *OR*, ser. 2, vol. 1, p. 760; Charles Calvert to Abraham Lincoln, ALP-LC.

34 *OR*, ser. 2, vol. 1, pp. 774, 776–777.

35 Ibid., p. 761.

36 Ibid., p. 762.

37 Ibid.

38 FSSP ser. 1, vol. 1, p. 174.

39 *OR*, ser. 2, vol. 1, pp. 763, 771.

40 Ibid., pp. 763, 772–723.

41 FSSP ser. 1, vol. 1, pp. 173, 342, 522, 361.

42 Ibid., pp. 174–175, 419–420.

43 *OR*, ser. 2, vol. 1, p. 775.

44 FSSP, ser. 1, vol. 1, pp. 167, 169, 347. This was the very same Congressman Calvert who, at the very same moment, managed to persuade Lincoln to issue his one and only order to return slaves, those taken by the Union army from Maryland into Virginia. See Calvert to Abraham Lincoln, July 10, 1861, ALP-LC.

45 Ibid., ser. 1, vol. 1, pp. 361–362.

46 *OR*, ser. 2, vol. 1, pp. 778, 796. General Henry Halleck had originally issued Orders No. 3 in response to reports that slaves coming into Union camps to sell provisions to soldiers were returning to their own farms, where, according to Congressman Frank Blair Jr., "they fell into the hands of the enemy, who exacted information from them." Blair's claim was supported by other congressmen from the area. *Cong. Globe*, 37th Cong., 2d Sess., p. 58.

47 *OR*, ser. 2, vol. 1, pp. 775–776; FSSP ser. 1, vol. 1, p. 419n.

48 *OR*, ser. 2, vol. 1, p. 791.

49 Ibid., ser. 1, vol. 8, pp. 405–407.

50 Ibid.

51 FSSP, ser. 1, vol. 1, pp. 421–423.

52 Mark Grimsley, *The Hard Hand of War: Union Military Policy toward Southern Civilians, 1861–1865* (Cambridge: Cambridge University Press, 1995), p. 126; FSSP, ser. 1, vol. 1, pp. 424–425, 522–523.

53 Henry Halleck to Frank Blair, Dec. 8, 1861, printed in *Cong. Globe*, 37th Cong., 2d. Sess., p. 76.

54 FSSP, ser. 1, vol. 1, pp. 353–357.

55 Henry Wilson, *History of the Antislavery Measures of the Thirty-Seventh and Thirty-Eighth Congresses, 1861–1864* (Boston: Walker, Wise, 1864), pp. 18, 21; *OR*, ser. 2, vol. 1, p. 784.

56 *Cong. Globe*, 37th Cong., 2d Sess., pp. 130, 956.

57 Ibid., p. 1142.

58 Ibid., pp. 358–359.

59 *OR*, ser. 1, vol. 8, p. 564; FSSP, ser. 1, vol. 1, pp. 429–432.

60 Donald Yacovone, ed., *A Voice of Thunder: A Black Soldier's Civil War* (Urbana: University of Illinois Press, 1998), p. 133; Sgt. Edmund Evarts, 8th New York Artillery, Federal Hill, Baltimore, Sept. 9, 1863, in Lydia Minturn Post, *Soldiers' Letters from Camp, Battle-Field and Prison* (New York: Bunce & Huntington, 1865), p. 192.

CHAPTER 6: "SELF-EMANCIPATION"

1 William Henry Channing, *The Civil War in America, or the Slaveholders' Conspiracy* (Liverpool: W. Vaughn; London: G. Vickers, 1861), pp. 89–90.

2 Rev. William H. Boole, *Antidote to Rev. H. J. Van Dyke's Pro-Slavery Discourse* (New York: E. Jones, 1861), p. 8.

3 *OR*, ser. 2, vol. 1, p. 763; FSSP ser. 1, vol. 1, p. 351.

4 Instructions issued by Union authorities and army officers can seem confusing or even self-contradictory, and often they were. In one sentence soldiers would be ordered to "secure the substantial rights of loyal masters," and in another they would "avail" themselves of the services of "fugitives from labor." One officer might order his men to "assure the white inhabitants . . . in the enjoyment of their private property," while another officer informed slaves that "they were free" once they left their plantations. These seemingly inconsistent instructions reflected different aspects of the "self-emancipation" policy whereby Union soldiers accepted runaway slaves who came voluntarily into their lines, but were forbidden to "entice" slaves from their farms and plantations. As navy Lieutenant Daniel Ammen told a group of fugitives, the Union

forces "had not come for the purposes of taking them from their masters, nor of making them continue in a state of slavery." See the examples in FSSP, ser. 1, vol. 1, pp. 114–116.

5 Rev. Almon Underwood, *A Discourse on the Death of the Late Rev. C. T. Torrey, a Martyr to Human Rights* (Newark: Small & Ackerman, 1846), pp. 9–10.

6 William Jay, *The Creole Case and Mr. Webster's Dispatch* . . . (New York, 1842), pp. 12, 36, 37; *Speech of Mr. Giddings of Ohio, Upon The Proposition of Mr. Johnson, of Tennessee* . . . (Washington, DC: Printed at the National Intelligence Office, 1842), p. 16. For a discussion of the *Creole* and *Amistad* cases, see chapter 1.

7 *The Thirteenth Annual Report of the American and Foreign Antislavery Society* (New York: Lewis J. Bates, 1853), p. 113; Rev. William H. Marsh, *God's Law Supreme: A Sermon, Aiming to Point Out the Duty of a Christian People in Relation to the Fugitive Slave Law* . . . (Worcester, MA: H. J. Howland, 1850), p. 19; *Speech of Hon. Horace Mann, of Massachusetts, on the Institution of Slavery* (Washington, DC: Buell & Blanchard, 1852), p. 22; Channing, *Civil War in America*, pp. 89–90. For an earlier reference to the "self-emancipated" slaves who had escaped to Canada, see *The Annual Report of the American and Foreign Anti-Slavery Society* (New York: A[merican] F[oreign] Anti-Slavery Society, 1849), p. 66. Sometimes abolitionists referred to individuals who escaped from slavery as "self-emancipated." See, for example, William Lloyd Garrison's preface to Frederick Douglass, *Narrative of the Life of Frederick Douglass, An American Slave* (Boston: Anti-Slavery Office, 1846), p. v.

8 *Cong. Globe*, 37th Cong., 1st Sess., p. 189.

9 *OR*, ser. 1, vol. 6, pp. 3–4, 14–16; Craig L. Symonds, *Lincoln and His Admirals: Abraham Lincoln, the U.S. Navy, and the Civil War* (New York: Oxford University Press, 2008), pp. 37–70.

10 Willie Lee Rose, *Rehearsal for Reconstruction: The Port Royal Experiment* (Indianapolis: Bobbs-Merrill, 1964), pp. 3–31; Charles Joyner, *Down by the Riverside: A South Carolina Slave Community* (Urbana: University of Illinois Press, 1986).

11 *OR*, ser. 1, vol. 6, pp. 5, 176–177. Cf. Bell Irvin Wiley, *Southern Negroes, 1861–1865* (New Haven: Yale University Press, 1938), pp. 295–296.

12 *OR*, ser. 1, vol. 6, pp. 6, 25, 31.

13 John Niven, ed., *The Salmon P. Chase Papers*, vol. 3: *Correspondence, 1858–March 1863* (Kent, OH: Kent State University Press, 1996), pp. 95–96; pp. 95-96; vol. 1: *Journals, 1829–1872* (Kent, OH: Kent State University Press, 1993), entry for Dec. 11, 1861, pp. 315–316.

14 Theodore Calvin Pease and J. G. Randall, eds., *The Diary of Orville Hickman*

Browning (Springfield: Trustees of the Illinois State Historical Library, 1925–1933), entry for July 8, 1860, p. 478; *CW*, vol. 5, p. 329; Niven, ed., *Chase Papers*, vol. 1, entry for Mar. 13, 1862, p. 331.

15 *CW*, vol. 5, p. 48.

16 Niven, ed., *Chase Papers*, vol. 3, pp. 116–118; Rose, *Rehearsal for Reconstruction*, p. 33n.

17 Edward L. Pierce, *Enfranchisement and Citizenship* (Boston: Roberts Brothers, 1896), p. 54.

18 Edward L. Pierce, *The Negroes at Port Royal*, Feb. 3, 1862, in Frank Moore, ed., *The Rebellion Record*, vol. 12 (New York: D. Van Nostrand, 1869), vol. 1 (Supplement I), Document 51, pp. 303–304.

19 Charles Heyward Diary, Colleton District and Charleston, SC, South Carolina Library, *Records of Antebellum Southern Plantations*, ser. A, pt. 2, reel 7; Pierce, *Negroes at Port Royal*, in Moore, ed., *Rebellion Records*, pp. 303–304.

20 Pierce, *Negroes at Port Royal*, in Moore, ed., *Rebellion Record*, pp. 306, 311–313.

21 Elizabeth Ware Pearson, ed., *Letters from Port Royal, Written at the Time of the Civil War* (Boston: W. B. Clarke, 1906), pp. 1–2.

22 Pierce, "Second Report," June 2, 1863, in Moore, ed., *Rebellion Record*, p. 322.

23 Pearson, ed., *Letters from Port Royal*, p. 13. Letter from "W. C. G." dated Mar. 24, 1862.

24 Rupert Sargent Holland, ed., *Letters and Diary of Laura M. Towne, Written from the Sea Islands of South Carolina, 1862–1864* (Cambridge, MA: Riverside Press, 1912), pp. 7, 8, 13.

25 Niven, ed., *Chase Papers*, vol. 1, entry for May 1, 1862, pp. 333–334.

26 Ibid., entry for Mar. 13, 1862, p. 331.

27 Pierce, *Enfranchisement and Citizenship*, p. 55.

28 Allen Parker, *Recollections of Slavery Times* (Worcester, MA: Chas. W. Burbank, 1895), pp. 84–91.

29 Ibid. *Knockum* was the name Parker gave; it was more likely *Knockern*.

30 *OR*, ser. 1, vol. 9, pp. 352–353, 363–364.

31 Ibid., pp. 369–370, 373.

32 L. R. Ferebee, *A Brief History of the Slave Life of Rev. L. R. Ferebee . . .* (Raleigh, NC: Edwards, Broughton, 1882), pp. 7–9; W. H. Doherty to Abraham Lincoln, May 13, 1862, ALP-LC.

33 *CW*, vol. 5, July 7, 1862.

34 Entries for June 30, July 14, and Dec. 6, 1862, Shirley Plantation Journal, Library of Congress, *Records of Antebellum Southern Plantations*, ser. C, pt. 1. In June of 1864, when George B. McClellan was running for president, one of

his supporters in Congress pointed out that "while General McClellan was in command he received and protected every negro who came within his lines. He never refused one, never returned one to slavery. But it was not his ideal to employ the armies of the Union for the purpose of destroying their property, liberating slaves." *Cong. Globe*, 38th Cong., 1st Sess., p. 2951. For the importance of the military intelligence provided by slaves, see Glenn David Brasher, *The Peninsula Campaign and the Necessity of Emancipation* (Chapel Hill: University of North Carolina Press, 2012).

35   *OR*, ser. 1, vol. 14, p. 333; Susie King Taylor, *Reminiscences of My Life in Camp with the 33d United States Colored Troops Late 1st S.C. Volunteers* (Boston, 1902), pp. 8–9; William Lilley Memorandum, Apr. 16, 1862 ALP-LC. Lilley had been court-martialed for, among other things, treating "poor defenceless blacks" in such a manner as "to outrage all the common feelings of humanity, characterized by the most cowardly and brutal treatment, and apparently in one or two instances by criminal indecency." Rufus Saxton to Montgomery Meigs, Apr. 19, 1862, ALP-LC.

36   *OR*, ser. 1, vol. 14, p. 333.

37   Ibid., p. 341.

38   *CW*, vol. 5, p. 219; Salmon P. Chase to Abraham Lincoln, May 16, 1862, ALP-LC; Carl Schurz to Lincoln, May 16, 1862, ALP-LC. Chase's point was that emancipation proclamations could be effective only on the ground where they could actually be enforced.

39   *CW*, vol. 5, pp. 222–224.

40   Carl Schurz to Abraham Lincoln, May 19, 1862, ALP-LC. For letters endorsing Lincoln's revocation of Hunter's order, see Alexander T. Stewart to Lincoln, May 21, 1862; Andrew Johnson to Lincoln, May 22, 1862; Carlton Chase to Lincoln, May 22, 1862; Joseph M. Wightman to Lincoln, May 23, 1862, ALP-LC.

41   Butler's "proclamation" is in *Private and Official Correspondence of Gen. Benjamin F. Butler* (Norwood, MA: Plimpton Press, 1917), vol. 1, pp. 433–436. The reference to the "sullen and dangerous" residents is in a letter from Butler's wife, p. 438.

42   FSSP, ser. 1, vol. 1, pp. 208–217, quotation on pp. 210–211.

43   Ibid, p. 218.

44   Ibid., p. 213.

45   W. Mitthoff to Benjamin Butler, May 29, 1862, in *Private and Official Correspondence of Butler*, vol. 1, p. 526.

46   Benjamin Butler to Edwin M. Stanton, June 29, 1862, in ibid., vol. 2, p. 14.

47   The Phelps proclamation, the exchange between General John W. Phelps and

Butler, and Butler's letter to Edwin M. Stanton, are reprinted in FSSP, ser. 1, vol. 1, pp. 199–208.

48 *Private and Official Correspondence of Butler*, vol. 1, pp. 614ff.

CHAPTER 7: "BY THE ACT OF CONGRESS THEY ARE CLEARLY FREE"

1 *Cong. Globe*, 37th Cong., 2d Sess., p. 19.

2 The best study of the Second Confiscation Act is Silvana R. Siddali, *From Property to Person: Slavery and the Confiscation Acts, 1861–1862* (Baton Rouge: Louisiana State University Press, 2005). Daniel W. Hamilton's *Limits of Sovereignty: Property Confiscation in the Union and the Confederacy during the Civil War* (Chicago: University of Chicago Press, 2007), is more concerned with confiscation than emancipation, but is also worthwhile.

3 *Cong. Globe*, 37th Cong., 2d Sess., pp. 49–50; Henry Wilson, *History of Anti-Slavery Measures of the Thirty-Seventh and Thirty-Eighth Congresses, 1861–1865* (Boston: Walker, Wise, 1865), p. 112.

4 *Cong. Globe*, 37th Cong., 2d Sess., p. 1953 (emphasis added).

5 Ibid., p. 1921.

6 Ibid., p. 2163.

7 Ibid., p. 1955.

8 Ibid., p. 5.

9 Ibid., p. 7.

10 Ibid., p. 1303.

11 Ibid., pp. 1886, 2233. Under Thomas Eliot's bill "any person within any State or Territory of the United States shall, after the passage of this act, willfully engage in armed rebellion against the Government of the United States, or shall willfully aid or abet such rebellion, or adhere to those engaged in such rebellion, giving them aid or comfort, every such person shall thereby forfeit all claim to the service or labor of any persons, commonly known as slaves; and all such slaves are hereby declared free and forever discharged from such servitude."

12 Ibid., p. 2274.

13 Ibid., pp. 2792–2793.

14 Wilson, *History of Antislavery Measures*, p. 173.

15 Ibid., pp. 1801, 1916ff. In a testy exchange, Benjamin Wade said that if Senators Orville Browning and Edgar Cowan were right, the Constitution made the president a "despot."

16 Ibid., pp. 18, 2171, 2190; *CW*, vol. 5, p. 331.

17 *Cong. Globe*, 37th Cong., 2d Sess., p. 18; *CW*, vol. 5, pp. 328–331. For similar concerns about the property confiscation provisions of the statute by a Republican congressman who strongly favored military emancipation, see Luther C. Carter to Salmon P. Chase, July 5, 1862, ALP-LC. Like Lincoln, Carter believed the federal government could permanently emancipate slaves but could not permanently confiscate real property. Chase showed Carter's letter to Lincoln.

18 *Cong. Globe*, 37th Cong., 2d Sess., pp. 3373–3374.

19 Ibid., p. 3382. The clause authorizing the enlistment of black troops is discussed in chapter 10.

20 *U.S. Statutes at Large*, 37th Cong., 2d Sess., pp. 589–592.

21 Ibid.; *CW*, vol. 5, pp. 336–337.

22 *U.S. Statutes at Large*, 37th Cong., 2d Sess., pp. 589–592.

23 Ibid., pp. 591–592.

24 *Boston Daily Advertiser*, Aug. 7, 1862; *Springfield Republican*, Aug. 30, 1862.

25 *Cong. Globe*, 37th Cong., 2d Sess., pp. 81, 150–153, 262, and *Appendix*, pp. 68–71, 271.

26 George B. McClellan to Abraham Lincoln, July 7, 1862, in Stephen W. Sears, ed., *The Civil War Papers of George B. McClellan: Selected Correspondence, 1860–1865* (New York: Da Capo Press, 1992), pp. 344–345.

27 Anna Ella Carroll to Abraham Lincoln, July 14, 1862, ALP-LC. For an elaboration of these views, see Anna Ella Carroll, *The Relation of the National Government to Revolted Citizens Defines* . . . (Washington, DC, 1862), reprinted in Frank Freidel, ed., *Union Pamphlets of the Civil War, 1861–1865* (Cambridge: Belknap Press of Harvard University Press, 1967), vol. 1, pp. 357–380.

28 *Cong. Globe*, 37th Cong., 2d Sess., pp. 19, 1797, 2301.

29 Ibid., p. 2327, and *Appendix*, pp. 207, 227.

30 *Farmer's Cabinet* (Amherst, NH), July 31, 1862; *Cong. Globe*, 37th Cong., 2d Sess., p. 1562.

31 Salmon P. Chase to Alexander Sankey Latty, [Sept. 17, 1862?], in John Niven, ed., *The Salmon P. Chase Papers*, vol. 3: *Correspondence, 1858–March 1863* (Kent, OH: Kent State University Press, 1996), p. 273; *Cong. Globe*, 37th Cong., 2d Sess., pp. 2323 (emphasis added), 2246.

32 *OR*, ser. 1, vol. 15, pp. 485–490. Quote on p. 486.

33 Benjamin Butler to Captain Haggerty, May 27, 1862, in ibid., p. 522.

34 John W. DeForest, quoted in Peyton McCrary, *Abraham Lincoln and Reconstruction* (Princeton: Princeton University Press, 1978), p. 84; *OR*, ser. 1, vol. 15, p. 516.

35 Salmon P. Chase to Benjamin Butler, June 24, 1862, in Niven, ed., *Chase Papers*, vol. 3, pp. 218–219.

36 Edwin M. Stanton to Benjamin Butler, July 3, 1862, in *Private and Official Correspondence of Gen. Benjamin F. Butler* (Norwood, MA: Plimpton Press, 1917), vol. 2, pp. 41–42.

37 Benjamin Butler to Mrs. Butler, July 25 and July 28, 1862, in *Private and Official Correspondence of Butler*, vol. 2, pp. 109, 115–117.

38 The secretary of war wrote Butler informing him of Johnson's assignment. E. M. Stanton to Benjamin Butler, June 10, 1862, in ibid., vol. 1, pp. 577–578. Johnson's appointment was controversial. Montgomery Blair, the postmaster general, objected on the grounds that Johnson had spread lies about Butler, claiming he had been drunk while on duty in Baltimore a year earlier.

39 Reverdy Johnson to Abraham Lincoln, July 16, 1862, ALP-LC. Lincoln to Reverdy Johnson, July 26, 1862, in *CW*, vol. 5, pp. 342–344.

40 Abraham Lincoln to Cuthbert Bullitt, July 28, 1862, in *CW*, vol. 5, pp. 344–347.

41 Salmon P. Chase to Benjamin Butler, July 31, 1862, in *Private and Official Correspondence of Butler*, vol. 2, pp. 132–134.

42 "Preliminary Emancipation Proclamation," Sept. 22, 1862, in *CW*, vol. 5, p. 435; Salmon P. Chase to Benjamin Butler, Sept. 23, 1862, in *Private and Official Correspondence of Butler*, vol. 2, p. 324.

43 *Private and Official Correspondence of Butler*, pp. 328–329, 331–332, 379, 430, 437–438, 439.

44 George Denison to Salmon P. Chase, Nov. 14, 1862, in ibid., pp. 426–427. For more sober assessments of the transition to free labor in Louisiana, see C. Peter Ripley, *Slaves and Freedmen in Civil War Louisiana* (Baton Rouge: Louisiana State University Press, 1976); John C. Rodrigue, *Reconstruction in the Cane Fields: From Slavery to Free Labor in Louisiana's Sugar Parishes, 1862–1880* (Baton Rouge: Louisiana State University Press, 2001); Rebecca J. Scott, *Degrees of Freedom: Louisiana and Cuba after Slavery* (Cambridge: Harvard University Press, 2005).

45 Benjamin Butler to General Weitzel, Nov. 2, 1862; Butler to Edwin M. Stanton, Nov. 14, 1862, in *Private and Official Correspondence of Butler*, pp. 439, 474–475.

46 Abraham Lincoln to Benjamin Butler, Nov. 6, 1862, in *CW*, vol. 5, pp. 487–488.

47 Benjamin Butler to Abraham Lincoln, Nov. 28, 1862, in *Private and Official Correspondence of Butler*, vol. 2, pp. 447–450.

CHAPTER 8: "A CORDON OF FREEDOM"

1 Quoted in David Goldfield, *America Aflame: How the Civil War Created a Nation* (New York: Bloomsbury Press, 2011), p. 50. Goldfield's endnote on p. 542 refers readers to David Potter, *The Impending Crisis: 1848–1861* (New York: Harper & Row, 1976), pp. 67–68. Potter's citation for the same Columbus Delano quotation refers to several different pages in the *Congressional Globe*, none of which contain Delano's remarks. Potter also cites Avery Craven, *The Development of Southern Sectionalism: 1848–1861* (Baton Rouge: Louisiana State University Press, 1953), p. 40, which contains the same Delano quotation and refers readers to the *Congressional Globe*, 29th Cong., 2d Sess., Appendix, p. 281, one of the pages Potter cited, and similarly incorrect. A search of surrounding pages of the *Congressional Globe* as well as every citation by Potter and Craven failed to locate the Delano quotation, as did all the index entries for "Columbus Delano" in the *Globe* for the Twenty-Ninth Congress. As a result, I'm not sure *when* Delano made his remark, assuming he is the person who said it. I nevertheless cite Delano's words because, as I hope to demonstrate, they reflect a popular and important strain of antislavery politics.

2 W. Caleb McDaniel, "Repealing Unions: American Abolitionists, Irish Repeal, and the Origins of Garrisonian Disunionism," *Journal of the Early Republic* 28, no. 2 (Summer 2008), pp. 243–269, esp. pp. 251–252. The specific catalyst for William Lloyd Garrison's disunionism, McDaniel argues, was an 1842 speech by Kentucky Representative Joseph Underwood warning that disunion would turn the Mason-Dixon Line into an international border, freeing the northern states from any obligation to protect slavery. With that "slavery was done in Kentucky, Maryland, and a large portion of Virginia." The "dissolution of the Union," Underwood declared, "was the dissolution of slavery."

3 *Third Annual Report of the American Antislavery Society* (New York: William S. Dorr, 1836), p. 87; *Fifth Annual Report of the Board of Managers of the Massachusetts Anti-Slavery Society* . . . (Boston: I. Knapp, 1837), p. 88; quoted in Henry C. Wright, *The Natick Resolution; or, Resistance to Slaveholders: The Right and Duty of Southern Slaves and Northern Freemen* (Boston, 1859), p. 36.

4 *Proceedings of the Fourth New England Antislavery Convention* . . . (Boston: I. Knapp, 1837), p. 104; *Correspondence, between the Hon. F. H. Elmore, One of the South Carolina Delegation in Congress, and James G. Birney, One of the Secretaries of the American Anti-Slavery Society* (New York: American Anti-Slavery Society, 1838), p. 36.

5 Stanley Harrold, *Border War: Fighting over Slavery before the Civil War* (Chapel Hill: University of North Carolina Press, 2010), p. 112 and passim.

6 Speech of Hon. Thaddeus Stevens, of Pennsylvania: In the U.S. House of Representatives, Wednesday, Feb. 20, 1850, in the Committee of the Whole on the State of the Union, on the Reference of the President's Annual message [pamphlet], p. 7.

7 President's Plan: Speech of Hon. E. G. Spaulding, of N. York, in Favor of Gen. Taylor's Plan for Admitting California and New Mexico, and Contrasting the Chicago Convention with the Proposed Nashville Convention: Delivered in the House of Representatives of the United States, April 4, 1850 [pamphlet], p. 13; Andrew Dickson White, *The Doctrines and Policy of the Republican Party: As Given by Its Recognized Leaders, Orators, Presses, and Platforms* (Washington, DC, 1860), p. 3. White's pamphlet was published by the National Democratic Executive Committee.

8 The actual history of slavery and American foreign policy was more complicated than the abolitionists suggested, primarily because territorial expansion was popular in the North as well as in the South. Nevertheless, there was an indisputably proslavery bias to American diplomacy. See Don E. Fehrenbacher, *The Slaveholding Republic: An Account of the United States Government's Relations to Slavery*, completed and edited by Ward M. McAfee (New York: Oxford University Press, 2001), pp. 89–134.

9 Ibid., pp. 135–204.

10 Howard Jones, *Blue and Gray Diplomacy: A History of Union and Confederate Foreign Relations* (Chapel Hill: University of North Carolina Press, 2009).

11 The story is told most recently in Amanda Foreman, *A World on Fire: Britain's Crucial Role in the American Civil War* (New York: Random House, 2010), pp. 277–280.

12 *Cong. Globe*, 37th Cong., 2d Sess. *Appendix*, pp. 252–253, quotation on p. 253. It is possible that Lincoln had colonization in mind when he endorsed diplomatic recognition of Haiti, though he never said so. Thomas Eliot barely mentioned colonization, devoting two sentences to it in a speech that took up ten full columns of small print in the *Congressional Globe*.

13 From the Salem, Ala., *Reporter*, reprinted in Lewis Cass and Zachary Taylor, *Cass and Taylor: Is Either Worthy of a Freeman's Suffrage?* [pamphlet, 1848?], p. 4.

14 Remarks of Mr. Yulee, of Florida, in the Senate of the United States, February 14, 15, and 17, 1848: On the Rights of the People of the United States in Acquired Territory [pamphlet], p. 2; *Cong. Globe*, 31st Cong., 1st Sess., *Appendix*, p. 157; James Ashley Mitchell, *The Rebellion: Its Causes and Consequences: A Speech Delivered by Hon. J.M. Ashley at College Hall in the City of Toledo, Tuesday Evening, November 26, 1861* [pamphlet], p. 14.

15 *Cong. Globe*, 37th Cong., 2d Sess., p. 1340.

16 Fehrenbacher, *Slaveholding Republic*, pp. 253–294.

17 *Cong. Globe*, 37th Cong., 2d Sess., p. 2042.

18 Ibid., pp. 2049, 2051, 2042.

19 Ibid., pp. 2043, 2050.

20 Ibid., p. 2068. The "Chicago platform" refers to the 1860 Republican Party platform, on which Lincoln ran.

21 *U.S. Statutes at Large*, 37th Cong., 2d Sess., p. 432.

22 *Cong. Globe*, 37th Cong., 2d Sess., p. 1446.

23 Ibid., pp. 1191–1192.

24 Ibid., p. 1472.

25 Ibid., *Appendix*, p. 101.

26 Ibid., p. 1629.

27 *U.S. Statutes at Large*, 37th Cong., 2d Sess., pp. 376–378; *Final Report of the Board of Commissioners*, House of Representatives, 38th Cong., 1st Sess., Jan. 14, 1863, Ex. Doc. No. 42.

28 Page Milburn, "The Emancipation of the Slaves in the District of Columbia," *Records of the Columbia Historical Society* (Washington, DC: The Society, 1913), vol. 16, pp. 116–117.

29 Margaret Leech, *Reveille in Washington, 1860–1865* (New York: Harper & Brothers, 1941), pp. 239–241; Benjamin Quarles, *Lincoln and the Negro* (New York: Oxford University Press, 1962), pp. 78ff.

30 Quarles, *Lincoln and the Negro*, pp. 103–105.

31 *Cong. Globe*, 37th Cong., 2d Sess., pp. 1300, 1647, 1446, and *Appendix*, p. 105.

32 James Redpath, *A Guide to Hayti* (Boston: Haytian Bureau of Emigration, 1861), p. 10.

33 Paul J. Polgar, "'To Raise Them to an Equal Participation': Early National Abolitionism, Gradual Emancipation, and the Promise of African American Citizenship," *Journal of the Early Republic* 31, no. 2 (Summer 2011), pp. 229–258.

34 *Cong. Globe*, 37th Cong., 2d Sess., p. 1191.

35 Eric Foner, "Lincoln and Colonization," in Eric Foner, ed., *Our Lincoln: New Perspectives on Lincoln and His World* (New York: W. W. Norton, 2008), pp. 135–166; Foner, "Abraham Lincoln, Colonization, and the Rights of Black Americans," in Richard Follet, et al., *Slavery's Ghost: The Problem of Freedom in the Age of Emancipation* (Baltimore: Johns Hopkins University Press, 2011), pp. 31–49.

36 On the wartime free labor systems, see Eric Foner, *Reconstruction: America's Unfinished Revolution, 1863–1877* (New York: Harper & Row, 1988), pp. 55–56, 165–167.

37 Irving H. Bartlett, ed., *Wendell & Ann Phillips: The Community of Reform, 1840–1880* (New York: W. W. Norton, 1979), p. 52; Moncure Daniel Conway, *Autobiography: Memories and Experiences of Moncure Daniel Conway* (London: Casell, 1904), vol. 1, pp. 346–347.

38 *CW*, vol. 5, pp. 29–31.

39 Carl Schurz to Abraham Lincoln, May 19, 1862, ALP-LC.

40 Patience Essah, *A House Divided: Slavery and Emancipation in Delaware, 1638–1865* (Charlottesville: University Press of Virginia, 1996), pp. 152–185.

41 *CW*, vol. 5, pp. 144–146. On the background and reaction to the March 6 address, see Michael Burlingame, *Abraham Lincoln: A Life* (Baltimore: Johns Hopkins University Press, 2008), vol. 2, pp. 333–347.

42 Ibid.

43 *Cong. Globe*, 37th Cong., 2d Sess., pp. 1149–1150, 1173, *Springfield Republican*, Mar. 15, 1862.

44 *Cong. Globe*, 37th Cong., 2d Sess., pp. 1170, 1154, 1177, 1179.

45 *CW*, vol. 5, pp. 152–153, 169; *Springfield Republican*, Mar. 15, 1862.

46 *CW*, vol. 5, pp. 49, 145–146. In the weeks following the March 6, 1862, message, Lincoln answered skeptics who doubted that his proposal would be cheaper than war. See, for example, his letter of March 9 to Henry J. Raymond, editor of the *New York Times*, in ibid., pp. 152–153. Lincoln's fullest elaboration of the fiscal benefits of compensated emancipation was in a letter to Senator James McDougal, on March 14, in ibid., pp. 160–161.

47 *Liberator*, Mar. 14 and 21, 1862; Henry Wilson, *History of Antislavery Measures of the Thirty-Seventh and Thirty-Eighth Congresses, 1861–1865* (Boston: Walker, Wise, 1865), 89.

48 *CW*, vol. 5, pp. 222–224.

49 Ibid., pp. 317–318.

50 Cecil D. Eby Jr., ed., *The Diaries of David Hunter Strother: A Virginia Yankee in the Civil War* (Chapel Hill: University of North Carolina Press, 1989), entry for July 19, 1862, p. 69.

51 Eva Sheppard Wolf, *Race and Liberty in the New Nation* (Baton Rouge: Louisiana State University Press, 2006). On the sectional divide within Virginia, see also Alison Goodyear Freehling, *Drift toward Dissolution: The Virginia Slavery Debate of 1831–1832* (Baton Rouge: Louisiana State University Press, 1982).

52 Charles Henry Ambler, *Sectionalism in Virginia from 1776 to 1861* (Chicago: University of Chicago Press, 1910), esp. pp. 175–339.

53 George Ellis Moore, *A Banner in the Hills: West Virginia's Statehood* (New York: Appleton-Century-Crofts, 1963), pp. 143–145.

54 Ibid., pp. 195–199.

55 *U.S. Statutes at Large*, 37th Cong., 3rd Sess., pp. 633–634.

56 *Cong. Globe*, 37th Cong., 2d Sess., p. 3309.

57 Ibid., pp. 2942, 3034, 3038.

58 Ibid., pp. 3038, 3316; 3rd Sess., p. 58. The final Senate vote was 23 to 17.

59 For the House debate, see *Cong. Globe*, 37th Cong., 3rd Sess., pp. 37–39, 41–51, 53–59. The House vote in favor of West Virginia statehood bill was 96 to 55. Of the 96 "yes" votes, 86 came from Republicans.

60 *Cong. Globe*, 37th Cong., 2d Sess., p. 3319; Wilson, *Antislavery Measures*, p. 76.

CHAPTER 9: THE "PRELIMINARY" PROCLAMATION

1 There are two accounts of the September 22, 1862, cabinet meeting. My quotations are from John Niven, ed., *The Salmon P. Chase Papers*, vol. 1: *Journals, 1829–1872* (Kent, OH: Kent State University Press, 1993), pp. 393–396. The other account, a bit less detailed, is in Howard K. Beale, ed., *Diary of Gideon Welles: Secretary of the Navy under Lincoln and Johnson* (New York: W. W. Norton, 1960), vol. 1, pp. 142–145. Chase has Lincoln make a vow to "my Maker." Welles has Lincoln making a promise to "God."

2 Charles Sumner to John Andrew, May 28, 1862, in Beverly Wilson Palmer, ed., *The Selected Letters of Charles Sumner* (Boston: Northeastern University Press, 1990), vol. 2, p. 115.

3 Salmon P. Chase to Benjamin Butler, June 24, 1862, in John Niven, ed., *The Salmon P. Chase Papers*, vol. 3: *Correspondence, 1858–March 1863* (Kent, OH: Kent State University Press, 1996), p. 219.

4 Beale, ed., *Welles Diary*, vol. 1, pp. 70, 144. This oft-quoted description is taken from the Beale edition of the Welles diary, but it is in fact a memoir reconstructed some years after the war. Nevertheless, the carriage ride itself is confirmed in a letter Welles wrote that evening to his wife. Two months later, on the day Lincoln issued the Preliminary Proclamation, Welles referred to the announcement in the carriage in an actual diary entry for September 22. In 1872 Welles published a more elaborate description of the carriage-ride conversation in an article, "The History of Emancipation," reprinted in Albert Mordell, ed., *Civil War and Reconstruction: Selected Essays by Gideon Welles* (New York: Twayne, 1959), pp. 237–240. The details in these accounts vary, but not their substance. It seems most likely that on July 13, 1872, Lincoln told Welles and Stanton that he would issue the Emancipation Proclamation called for by the Second Confiscation Act adopted by the Senate the day before.

5 Quoted in Eric Foner, *Fiery Trial: Abraham Lincoln and American Slavery* (New York: W. W. Norton, 2010), p. 217.

6 Beale, ed., *Welles Diary*, vol. 1, p. 70.

7 On the various recollections of Lincoln's "decision" to emancipate, see Matthew Pinsker, "Lincoln's Summer of Emancipation," in Harold Holzer and Sara Vaughn Gabbard, eds., *Lincoln and Freedom: Slavery, Emancipation, and the Thirteenth Amendment* (Carbondale: Southern Illinois University Press, 2007), pp. 79–99.

8 *U.S. Statutes at Large*, 37th Cong., 2nd Sess., p. 422; "Proclamation Concerning Taxes in Rebellious States," in *CW*, vol. 5, pp. 298–299. Lincoln's tax proclamation reads like his later Emancipation Proclamation, with much of it devoted to specifying the areas in rebellion as of the date it was issued.

9 *CW*, vol. 5, pp. 434–436.

10 Beale, ed., *Welles Diary*, vol. 1, entry for Oct. 1, 1862, pp. 159–160; Niven, ed., *Chase Papers*, vol. 1, entry for July 22, 1862, pp. 350–352.

11 Francis B. Carpenter, *Six Months in the White House with Abraham Lincoln* (New York: Hurd & Houghton, 1872), pp. 20–22. Carpenter's account is his recollection of Lincoln's recollection. Aspects of the passage seem to confuse the cabinet discussion of the first draft, on July 22, 1862, with the discussion a few months later of the Preliminary Proclamation. It remains Lincoln's only account of the meeting, however, and most historians accept that Seward's recommendation for postponing release of the proclamation was decisive. Chase's diary entry for July 22 is clearly the most reliable. In his diary entry for October 1, Welles recalled some of the July discussions. There is nothing in Bates's diary about the July 21–22 cabinet meetings. For a detailed account of the meeting, see Michael Burlingame, *Abraham Lincoln: A Life* (Baltimore: Johns Hopkins University Press, 2008), vol. 2, pp. 362–364.

12 John Gregory to Abraham Lincoln, Mar. 12, 1862, ALP-LC. See Fitchburg Massachusetts Citizens to Lincoln, Monday, Mar. 17, 1862 (Petition), ALP-LC, in which the identical wording is used but is printed; and General Synod of Reformed Presbyterian Church to Lincoln, Tuesday, May 20, 1862 (Resolutions); From Religious Society of Progressive Friends to Abraham Lincoln, June 7, 1862, ALP-LC.

13 Robert Dale Owen to Edwin M. Stanton, July 23, 1862; James W. White et al. to Abraham Lincoln, July 24, 1862; Sydney H. Gay to Lincoln, Aug. 15[?], 1862, ALP-LC.

On certain policies—the arming of black troops was one of them—Lincoln made it clear that he was waiting for the people to be "educated up" to support it, but he never made that claim about emancipation. As early as September in 1861, Lincoln noted that General Frémont's emancipation edict was far more popular than his order to revise it, for example. Montgomery Blair claimed that emancipation hurt the Republicans in the November 1862 election, but

Lincoln discounted that explanation and attributed Republican losses to the poor performance of the Union army. There is abundant evidence that emancipation was widely popular among Republicans from the very start of the war. If his incoming mail was any indication, Lincoln was subjected to far more pressure in favor of emancipation than in opposition to it.

For further evidence of pressure on Lincoln, see the petition from the citizens of Quaker Bottom, Ohio, Jesse B. Kimball and James McVey to Lincoln, Aug. 2, 1862; Samuel L. Casey to Lincoln, Aug. 4, 1862; Indiana Methodist Convention to Lincoln, Sept. 12, 1862, ALP-LC.

14 *CW,* vol. 5, pp. 370–375.

15 Ibid., p. 374.

16 On the debate over emigration and evidence of support for it among African Americans, see Kate Masur, "The African American Delegation to Abraham Lincoln: A Reappraisal," *Civil War History* 56, no. 2 (June 2010), pp. 117–144. Stephen Hahn, in *A Nation under Our Feet: Black Political Struggles in the Rural South from Slavery to the Great Migration* (Cambridge: Belknap Press of Harvard University Press, 2003), emphasizes support for emigration among blacks.

17 *Douglass' Monthly,* Sept. 1862.

18 Horace Greeley to Abraham Lincoln, Aug. 1, 1862, ALP-LC.

19 Abraham Lincoln to Horace Greeley, Aug. 22, 1862, in *CW,* vol. 5, pp. 388–389.

20 Wendell Phillips to Sydney Howard Gay, Sept. 2, 1862, Gay Papers, Columbia University, quoted in Foner, *Fiery Trial,* p. 228.

21 Gerrit Smith, *Gerrit Smith to His Townsmen* [flier] (Petersboro, NY, Oct. 6, 1862).

22 John B. Henderson to Abraham Lincoln, Sept. 3, 1862, ALP-LC.

23 Foner, *Fiery Trial,* p. 228.

24 James M. McPherson, *Battle Cry of Freedom: The Civil War Era* (New York: Oxford University Press, 1988), pp. 526–533.

25 Ibid., pp. 538–544. See also Bruce Catton, *The Army of the Potomac: Mr. Lincoln's Army* (New York: Doubleday, 1951), pp. 265–332, a harrowing account of Antietam and a devastating critique of the incompetence of the Union officers.

26 Niven, ed., *Chase Papers,* vol. 1, Sept. 22, 1862, p. 396.

27 Ibid., entry for Sept. 22, 1862, pp. 393–396; Beale, ed., *Welles Diary,* vol. 1, entry for Sept. 22, 1862, pp. 142–145.

28 *CW,* vol. 5, pp. 433–434.

29 Ibid., pp. 434–435.

30 Ibid., p. 441n.

31 W. B. Lowry, H. Catlin, and J. F. Downing to Abraham Lincoln, Sept. 23, 1862; B. S. Hendrick to Lincoln, Sept. 23, 1862; James W. Stone to Lincoln, Sept. 23, 1862; Abiel A. Livermore to Lincoln, Sept. 24, 1862; Henry Asbury to Lincoln, Sept. 29, 1882, ALP-LC; Smith, *Gerrit Smith to His Townsmen*. For a survey of reactions to the Preliminary Proclamation, see John Hope Franklin, *The Emancipation Proclamation* (Wheeling, IL: Harlan Davidson, 1995), pp. 48–65.

32 *OR*, ser. 3, vol. 2, pp. 584–585

33 Ibid., ser. 1, vol. 19, pt. 2, pp. 395–396.

34 See the order issued on February 22, 1862, in which General Halleck reasserts the general policy spelled out in Order No. 3 but incorporates the language of his congressional critics by declaring that the military was not competent to judge the status of fugitives running to Union lines. *OR*, ser. 1, vol. 8, pp. 563–564. The March 13 law was supposed to bury Halleck's policy, but it persisted in parts of the Mississippi Valley.

35 John Y. Simon, ed., *The Papers of Ulysses S. Grant*, vol. 5: *April 1–August 31, 1862* (Carbondale: Southern Illinois University Press, 1973), p. 51n.

36 U. S. Grant to Julia Dent Grant, June 12, 1862; Alvin P. Hovey to Major John A. Rawlins, July 10, 1862, in ibid., pp. 143, 199n.

37 Elihu Washburne to U. S. Grant, July 25, 1862, in ibid., p. 226n. On Grant's use of "contrabands" as workers, see Grant to Gen. William Rosecrans, Aug. 17, 1862, in ibid., p. 272.

38 FSSP, ser. 1, vol. 3, pp. 667–671.

39 John Sherman to William T. Sherman, Aug. 24, 1862, in Brooks D. Simpson and Jean V. Berlin, eds., *Sherman's Civil War: Selected Correspondence of William T. Sherman, 1860–1865* (Chapel Hill: University of North Carolina Press, 1999), pp. 260, 286, 292–294; FSSP. ser. 1, vol. 3, p. 658; *OR*, ser. 1, vol. 17, pt. 2, pp. 113, 158–160.

40 For General Buell's policy and the tensions it provoked within the army, see FSSP ser. 1, vol. 1, pp. 271–289.

41 Quincy A. Gilmore to William L. Utley, Oct. 18, 1862; Utley to Gillmore, Oct. 18, 1862, ALP-LC.

42 *Cleveland Plain Dealer*, Nov. 13, 1862.

43 FSSP, ser. 1, vol. 3, pp. 667–671; John Eaton, *Grant, Lincoln and the Freedmen: Reminiscences of the Civil War* (New York: Longmans, Green, 1907), pp. 5, 12, 20.

44 Eaton, *Lincoln, Grant and the Freedmen*, pp. 24, 27.

45 W. T. Sherman to Thomas Tasker Gantt, Sept. 23, 1862; W. T. Sherman to John Sherman, Oct. 1, 1862 in Simpson and Berlin, eds., *Sherman's Civil War*, pp. 303, 311–312, 320.

46 W. T. Sherman to John Sherman, Nov. 24, 1862, in ibid., p. 337.

47 W. T. Sherman to Hon. Judge [John T.] Swayne, Nov. 12, 1862, in ibid., pp. 324–327.

48 On March 19, 1864, Congressman Wilder praised Lincoln's recent reconstruction proposal in part because it required the rebel states "to corroborate and enforce the proclamation of emancipation which has made the 22d of September, 1862, a date never to be forgotten through the ages." *Cong. Globe*, 38th Cong., 1st Sess., p. 1204.

49 *Springfield Republican*, Aug. 30, 1862.

50 *Cleveland Plain Dealer*, Nov. 13, 1862; *New York Herald Tribune*, Dec. 9, 1862.

51 Robert Dale Owen to Edwin M. Stanton, July 23, 1862, ALP-LC.

52 Niven, ed., *Chase Papers*, vol. 3, pp. 38, 218.

53 *New York Times*, Aug. 20, 1862.

54 R. W. Emerson, "The President's Proclamation," *Atlantic Monthly* 10, no. 61 (Nov. 1862), pp. 638–642.

55 Benjamin Bannan to Abraham Lincoln, July 24, 1862, ALP-LC.

56 Thomas A. Marshall to Abraham Lincoln, July 27, 1862, ALP-LC.

57 James Speed to Abraham Lincoln, July 28, 1862, ALP-LC.

58 All quoted in the *Liberator*, Oct. 3, 1862. Most but not all of this skepticism came from Democrats opposed to emancipation. See, for example, *Boston Daily Advertiser*, July 20 and Sept. 25, 1862; *Wisconsin Daily Patriot*, Aug. 28, 1862.

59 *CW*, vol. 7, pp. 281–282; vol. 8, p. 333.

60 *CW*, vol. 7, pp. 301, 281–228.

CHAPTER 10: THE EMANCIPATION PROCLAMATION

1 *CW*, vol. 5, pp. 278–279, 420–421, 438–439, 444.

2 Ibid., vol. 6, pp. 28–31. Accounts of the final drafting and signing of the proclamation can be found in John Hope Franklin, *The Emancipation Proclamation* (Garden City, NY: Doubleday, 1963); Allen C. Guelzo, *Lincoln's Emancipation Proclamation: The End of Slavery in America* (New York: Simon & Schuster, 2004), pp. 201–210; Douglas L. Wilson, *Lincoln's Sword: The Presidency and the Power of Words* (New York: Knopf, 2006), pp. 105–142; Harold Holzer, *Emancipating Lincoln: The Proclamation in Text, Context, and Memory* (Cambridge: Harvard University Press, 2012); Louis P. Masur, *Lincoln's Hundred Days: The Emancipation Proclamation and the War for the Union* (Cambridge: Harvard University Press, 2012). On the constitutional issues,

see Mark E. Neely Jr., *Lincoln and the Triumph of the Nation: Constitutional Conflict in the American Civil War* (Chapel Hill: University of North Carolina Press, 2011), pp. 113–159.

3 Michael Burlingame, *Abraham Lincoln: A Life* (Baltimore: Johns Hopkins University Press, 2008), vol. 2, pp. 462–473.

4 *CW,* vol. 6, p. 29.

5 Ibid.

6 Ibid.

7 Ibid., pp. 29–30.

8 Ibid., p. 30.

9 Ibid.

10 All quotations are from the survey of reactions to the proclamation in Franklin, *Emancipation Proclamation,* pp. 85ff.

11 Robin Blackburn, *Marx and Lincoln: An Unfinished Revolution* (New York: Verso Books, 2011), p. 199.

12 *CW,* vol. 7, p. 49.

13 Burrus M. Carnahan, *Act of Justice: Lincoln's Emancipation Proclamation and the Laws of War* (Lexington: University of Kentucky Press, 2007), pp. 5–23.

14 Benjamin Robbins Curtis, *Executive Power* (Boston: Little, Brown, 1862), reprinted in Frank Friedel, ed., *Union Pamphlets of the Civil War, 1861–1865* (Cambridge: Belknap Press of Harvard University Press, 1967), vol. 1, p. 461.

15 Grosvenor P. Lowrey, *"The Commander in Chief: A Defense upon Legal Grounds of the Proclamation of Emancipation; and an Answer to Ex-Judge Curtis' Pamphlet . . . ,"* in Friedel, ed., *Union Pamphlets,* vol. 1, pp. 490–491.

16 William Whiting, *War Powers under the Constitution of the United States* (Boston: Little, Brown, 1864), p. 21.

17 On the Lieber Code, see Frank Friedel, "General Orders 100 and Military Government," *Mississippi Valley Historical Review* 32, no. 4 (Mar. 1946), pp. 541–556; pp. 127–130; Matthew J. Mancini, "Francis Lieber, Slavery, and the 'Genesis' of the Laws of War," *Journal of Southern History* 77, no. 2 (May 2011), pp. 325–348; John Fabian Witt, *Lincoln's Code: The Laws of War in American History* (New York: Free Press, 2012).

18 Francis Lieber, *Instructions for the Government of the Armies of the United States in the Field* (New York: D. Van Nostrand, 1863), p. 13.

19 Carnahan, *Act of Justice,* pp. 126ff.

20 The re-enslavement issue is discussed a greater length in chapters 11 and 12.

21 Lowrey, Lieber, and other wartime commentators were undoubtedly relying on a theory of black citizenship that had long since become a staple of antislavery politics. See, for example, the discussion of "paramount citizenship" in Jacobus tenBroek, *Equal under Law* (New York: Collier Books, 1965), pp.

71–93. The best study of the relationship between citizenship and the personal liberty laws is Thomas D. Morris, *Free Men All: The Personal Liberty Laws of the North, 1780–1861* (Baltimore: Johns Hopkins University Press, 1974).

For a more detailed examination of the issue of black citizenship, see James Oakes, "Natural Rights, Citizenship Rights, States' Rights, and Black Rights: Another Look at Lincoln and Race," in Eric Foner, ed., *Our Lincoln: New Perspectives on Lincoln and His World* (New York: W. W. Norton, 2008), pp. 109–134. The literature on citizenship in early America is vast. The analysis in this and subsequent paragraphs derives primarily from the following: James H. Kettner, *The Development of American Citizenship* (Chapel Hill: University of North Carolina Press, 1978); William M. Wiecek, *The Sources of Antislavery Constitutionalism in America, 1760–1848* (Ithaca: Cornell University Press, 1977), pp. 154–171; Rogers M. Smith, *Civic Ideals: Conflicting Visions of Citizenship in U.S. History* (New Haven: Yale University Press, 1997); William J. Novak, "The Legal Transformation of Citizenship in Nineteenth Century America," in Meg Jacobs, William J. Novak, and Julian Zelizer, eds., *The Democratic Experiment: New Directions in American Political History* (Princeton: Princeton University Press, 2003), pp. 85–119. For a recent examination of the importance as well as the limits of citizenship for former slaves, see Kate Masur, *An Example for All the Land: Emancipation and the Struggle over Equality in Washington, D.C.* (Chapel Hill: University of North Carolina Press, 2010).

22 *CW*, vol. 2, p. 233n. Lincoln's concerns about the political wisdom of calling for repeal of the Fugitive Slave Act of 1850 were expressed in an 1859 exchange of letters with Salmon P. Chase of Ohio. See ibid., vol. 3, pp. 41, 384, 386.

23 *Dred Scott v. Sandford*, 60 U.S. 393 (How.)

24 *CW*, vol. 2, pp. 403, 453.

25 Ibid., vol. 4, pp. 156–157.

26 Ibid. Quote from p. 157n.

27 Ibid., p. 264.

28 All quotations of Bates in this and subsequent paragraphs are taken from *Opinion of Attorney General Bates on Citizenship* (Washington, DC: Government Printing Office, 1862) (quotes are from pp. 3, 8, 17); Attorney General Edwards Bates to Robert C. Winthrop [Massachusetts], Jan. 5, 1863, quoted in Bruce Catton, *Never Call Retreat*, vol. 3: *The Centennial History of the Civil War* (London: Phoenix Press, 1965), pp. 56–57.

29 Lowrey, *The Commander in Chief*, in Friedel, ed., *Union Pamphlets*, vol. 1. p. 493–494 (emphasis added); Lieber, *Instructions for the Government*, p. 13.

30 Daniel Yacovone, ed., *A Voice of Thunder: A Black Soldier's Civil War* (Urbana: University of Illinois Press, 1997), p. 254; Stephen Hahn, *A Nation under Our*

Feet: Black Political Struggles in the Rural South from Slavery to the Great Migration (Cambridge: Belknap Press of Harvard University Press, 2003), pp. 108–109.

31 *U.S. Statutes at Large*, 2d Cong., 1st Sess., p. 271; *Dred Scott v. Sandford*, 60 U.S. 19 How. 393 (1856).

32 *U.S. Statutes at Large*, 37th Cong., 2d Sess., pp. 597, 599; *U.S. Statutes at Large*, 37th Cong., 3d Sess., p. 731–737, quotation on p. 731.

33 Lincoln never explained why his proclamation applied to slaves in rebel areas rather than to all slaves owned by rebels. The shift was already in the first version of the proclamation he presented to his cabinet on July 22, 1862, less than a week after signing the Second Confiscation Act. Lincoln cited Section 6 of the statute—the passage calling for a presidential proclamation—and the wording of the law is slightly ambiguous. It refers to "any person within any State or Territory of the United States . . . engaged in armed rebellion." Previous statutes required proclamations specifying *areas* in rebellion, and Lincoln seems to have read the new law that way. For Lincoln's July draft, see *CW*, vol. 5, pp. 336–337.

It is widely assumed that in shifting to a territorial standard Lincoln expanded the scope of emancipation beyond the limits of the Second Confiscation Act, but this is not obviously true. For one thing, Lincoln never made such a claim, and he seemed to be implementing what he took to be the requirements of the statute itself. Then, too, Republicans in Congress made it quite clear that they considered virtually all slaveholders to be rebels and that emancipating their slaves amounted to universal emancipation. Interestingly, two years later, during the debates over the Thirteenth Amendment, Senator Lyman Trumbull criticized Lincoln's shift from "rebels" to "areas in rebellion" on the grounds that it *narrowed* the scope of emancipation. If Lincoln had retained the wording of the statute, Trumbull argued, the slaves of disloyal owners in the Border States would have been emancipated by then.

34 Harry Smith, *Fifty Years of Slavery in the United States of America* (Grand Rapids: West Michigan Printing Co., 1891), pp. 122–124.

35 J. Vance Lewis, *Out of the Ditch: A True Story of an Ex-Slave* (Houston: Rein & Sons, 1910), pp. 12–13.

36 Sgt. Edmund Evarts, Eighth New York Artillery, Federal Hill, Baltimore, Sept. 9, 1863, in Lydia Mintura Post, ed., *Soldiers' Letters, from Camp, Battle-Field and Prison* (New York: Bunce & Huntington, 1865), pp. 191–192.

37 Michael Burlingame, ed., *Lincoln's Journalist: John Hay's Anonymous Writings for the Press, 1861–1864* (Carbondale: Southern Illinois University Press, 1998), p. 309 (emphasis added); *OR*, ser. 2, vol. 1, pp. 754–755; John Eaton,

Grant, Lincoln and the Freedmen: Reminiscences of the Civil War (New York: Longmans, Green, 1907), p. 27.

38 *OR*, ser. 1, vol. 24, pt. 3, p. 46. Historians can tally the number of slaves in the territory covered by Union emancipation policy, but there is no way to know how many of the slaves in those areas were actually emancipated, though it is clear that many were not freed until after the war ended.

39 Thomas A. Marshall to Abraham Lincoln, July 27, 1862; Frederick Law Olmsted to John G. Nicolay, Oct. 10, 1862; Benjamin Bannan to Lincoln, July 24, 1862, ALP-LC.

40 Michael Burlingame, ed., *With Lincoln in the White House: Letters, Memoranda, and Other Writings of John G. Nicolay, 1860–1865* (Carbondale: Southern Illinois University Press, 2000), p. 100; Henry Halleck to U. S. Grant, Mar. 31, 1863, in *OR*, ser. 1, vol. 24, pt. 3, pp. 156–157; G. W. Williams, *A History of Negro Troops in the War of the Rebellion* (New York: Negro Universities Press, 1888), pp. 106–108.

41 On the various editions of the proclamation published up to 1865, see Charles Eberstadt, *Lincoln's Emancipation Proclamation* (New York: Duschness Crawford, 1950). Harold Holzer points out that there was very little iconographic representation of the proclamation before Lincoln's assassination in 1865. See Harold Holzer, Edna Greene Medford, and Frank J. Williams, *The Emancipation Proclamation: Three Views* (Baton Rouge: Louisiana State University Press, 2006), pp. 89–90; Isaac Lane, *Autobiography of Bishop Isaac Lane* (Nashville: Pub. House of the M.E. Church, South, 1916), p. 56.

The history of the agents organized by the War Department remains to be written, but for helpful indications of their work, see the introduction to John Hope Franklin, ed., *The Diary of James T. Ayers: Civil War Recruiter*, new introduction by John David Smith (Baton Rouge: Louisiana State University Press, 1999), pp. xxi–xxxv.

42 *OR*, ser. 3, vol. 3, pp. 100–101. On the white officers Lorenzo Thomas and others recruited, see Joseph T. Glatthaar, *Forged in Battle: The Civil War Alliance of Black Soldiers and White Officers* (Baton Rouge: Louisiana State University Press, 1990).

43 Williams, *History of Negro Troops in the War of the Rebellion*, p. 109; Lorenzo Thomas to W. S. Rosecrans, June 15, 1863, National Archives, Record Group 94, entry 363, Records of the Adjutant Generals office, 1780's 1917, Letters Sent by Lorenzo Thomas, General's Papers and Books; *CW*, vol. 6, p. 342.

44 *OR*, ser. 1, vol. 24, pt. 3, pp. 186–187, 330, 351, 437–438. See also Mark Grimsley, *The Hard Hand of War: Union Military Policy toward Southern Civilians, 1861–1865* (Cambridge: Cambridge University Press, 1995).

45 *OR*, ser. 1, vol. 24, pt. 3, pp. 377, 400, 416–417; Russell Duncan, ed., *Blue-*

Eyed Child of Fortune: The Civil War Letters of Colonel Robert Gould Shaw (Athens: University of Georgia Press, 1992), p. 345. Post, ed., *Soldiers' Letters*, p. 254.

46 Entries for June 2 and June 4, 1863, Greenwood Plantation Journal, Beaufort District, South Carolina, Library of Congress. *Records of Antebellum Southern Plantations*, ser. C, pt. 2, real 1, Oct. 8, 1864. George Washington Allen Papers, Southern Historical Collection, *Records of Antebellum Southern Plantations*, ser. J, pt. 7, reel 4.

47 Quoted in Grimsley, *Hard Hand of War*, pp. 152–169.

48 Benjamin Bannan to Abraham Lincoln, July 24, 1862, ALP-LC; *OR*, ser. 1, vol. 24, pt. 3, p. 479.

49 James M. Clifton, ed., *Life and Labor on Argyle Island: Letters and Documents of a Savannah River Rice Plantation, 1833–1867* (Savannah: Beehive Press, 1978), p. 341.

50 Pioneering works on slave discontent during the Civil War include W. E. B. Du Bois, *Black Reconstruction in American* (New York: Atheneum, 1935); Bell Irvin Wiley, *Southern Negroes, 1861–1865* (New Haven: Yale University Press, 1938); Benjamin Quarles, *The Negro in the Civil War* (Boston: Little, Brown, 1953); James M. McPherson, *The Negro's Civil War* (New York: Random House, 1965).

The theme of wartime disruption on the plantations reemerged in the 1970s. See especially James Roark, *Masters without Slaves* (New York: W. W. Norton, 1977); Leon Litwack, *Been in the Storm So Long* (New York: Knopf, 1979); Ira Berlin et al., *Slaves No More: Three Essays on Emancipation and the Civil War* (New York: Cambridge University Press, 1992). See also Stephen V. Ash, *When the Yankees Came: Conflict and Chaos in the Occupied South, 1861–1865* (Chapel Hill: University of North Carolina Press, 1995); Jacqueline Jones, *Saving Savannah: The City and the Civil War* (New York: Knopf, 2008), for the urban dimension.

For the slaveholders, in addition to the books by Roark and Litwack, see the relevant chapters in Drew Gilpin Faust, *James Henry Hammond and the Old South: A Design for Mastery* (Baton Rouge: Louisiana State University Press, 1982); Edward Ball, *Slaves in the Family* (New York: Ballantine Books, 1988); William Kauffman Scarborough, *Masters of the Big House: Elite Slaveholders of the Mid-Nineteenth Century South* (Baton Rouge: Louisiana State University Press, 2003); Erskine Clark, *Dwelling Place: A Plantation Epic* (New Haven: Yale University Press, 2005).

On the experience of slave women, see Catherine Clinton and Nina Silber, eds., *Divided Houses: Gender and the Civil War* (New York: Oxford University Press, 1992); LeeAnn Whites and Alecia P. Long, *Occupied Women: Gender, Military Occupation, and the American Civil War* (Baton Rouge: Louisiana

State University Press, 2009); Leslie Schwalm, *A Hard Fight for We: Women's Transition from Slavery to Freedom in South Carolina* (Urbana: University of Illinois Press, 1997); Stephanie Camp, *Closer to Freedom: Enslaved Women and Everyday Resistance in the Plantation South* (Chapel Hill: University of North Carolina Press, 2004); Thavolia Glymph, *Out of the House of Bondage: The Transformation of the Plantation Household* (New York: Cambridge University Press, 2008).

Among those arguing that slave resistance contributed to the defeat of the Confederacy, see Armstead Robinson, *Bitter Fruits of Bondage: The Demise of Slavery and the Collapse of the Confederacy, 1861–1865* (Charlottesville: University of Virginia Press, 2004); Steven Hahn, *The Political Worlds of Slavery and Freedom* (Cambridge: Harvard University Press, 2009). Drew Gilpin Faust, in *Mothers of Invention: Women of the Slaveholding South in the American Civil War* (Chapel Hill: University of North Carolina Press, 1996), attributes southern defeat to the plantation mistresses who turned against the Confederacy under the hardships of war. Stephanie McCurry, in *Confederate Reckoning: Power and Politics in the Civil War South* (Cambridge: Harvard University Press, 2010), stresses the resistance of both women and slaves.

Several state studies are cited elsewhere, but see also John Cimprich, *Slavery's End in Tennessee, 1861–1865* (Tuscaloosa: University of Alabama Press, 1985); Larry Eugene Rivers, *Slavery in Florida: Territorial Days to Emancipation* (Gainesville: University Press of Florida, 2000), pp. 229–249.

51 For examples of free blacks offering to take up arms in defense of the Union, see FSSP, ser. 2, pp. 79ff.

52 *CW*, vol. 5, p. 357.

53 *U.S. Statutes at Large*, 37th Cong., 3d Sess., p. 599.

54 FSSP, ser. 2, pp. 46–53. General David Hunter believed that emancipation would be validated by black men serving in the Union army, but Edward Pierce believed that a successful "experiment" in free labor would vindicate emancipation. It was Pierce's letter of complaint to the Treasury Department that undermined Hunter's precocious attempt to enlist black men. When Thomas Wentworth Higginson arrived in early December of 1862, he was struck by "the legacy of bitter distrust" among Sea Island blacks caused by General Hunter's ruthless approach to recruitment. See Higginson, *Army Life in a Black Regiment* (New York: W. W. Norton, 1984), p. 40.

The various moves toward black enlistment prior to January 1, 1863, are surveyed in Dudley Taylor Cornish, *The Sable Arm: Negro Troops in the Union Army, 1861–1865* (New York: W. W. Norton, 1966), pp. 29–103. For documentation of such efforts in Louisiana and Kansas, see FSSP, ser. 2, pp. 62–73.

55 *CW*, vol. 6, p. 30; FSSP, ser. 2, p. 143.

56 *OR*, ser. 3, vol. 3, pp. 14–15, 20–21.

57 *CW*, vol. 6, p. 357; James M. McPherson, *Battle Cry of Freedom: The Civil War Era* (New York: Oxford University Press, 1988), pp. 566–567, 792–793, 798–800; McPherson, *For Cause and Comrades: Why Men Fought in the Civil War* (New York: Oxford University Press, 1997); Chandra Manning, *What This Cruel War Was Over: Soldiers, Slavery, and the Civil War* (New York: Knopf, 2007).

58 Joseph Glatthaar, "Black Glory: The African American Role in Union Victory," in Gabor S. Boritt, ed., *Why the Confederacy Lost* (New York: Oxford University Press, 1992), pp. 133–162; William W. Freehling, *The South versus the South: How Anti-Confederate Southerners Shaped the Course of the Civil War* (New York: Oxford University Press, 2001), pp. 188–196. For a more skeptical view of the significance of black troops, see Gary W. Gallagher, *The Union War* (Cambridge: Harvard University Press, 2011).

59 Franklin, ed., *Diary of James T. Ayers*, pp. 24–33.

60 *OR*, ser. 3, vol. 3, pp. 215–216; Michael T. Meier, "Lorenzo Thomas and the Recruitment of Blacks in the Mississippi Valley, 1863–1865," in John David Smith, ed., *Black Soldiers in Blue: African American Troops in the Civil War Era* (Chapel Hill: University of North Carolina Press, 2002), pp. 249–275; Franklin, ed., *Diary of James T. Ayers*, pp. xxi–xxxv. See also Glatthaar, *Forged in Battle*.

61 FSSP, ser. 2, pp. 55–56, 139, 146, 164, 101.

62 Ibid., pp. 46–53, 61, 101, 145, 158, 168.

63 *U.S. Statutes at Large*, 37th Cong., 2d Sess., p. 599.

64 *CW*, vol. 6, pp. 149–150.

65 The figures were compiled by the Freedmen and Southern Society Project and are summarized in a chart at FSSP, ser. 2, p. 12. The Project estimates that a total of 178,975 blacks served in the Union army during the war. Of these, 146,304 blacks were recruited from the slave states. Six of those states—Delaware, Maryland, Kentucky, Missouri, Tennessee, and large portions of Louisiana—were technically exempt from the Emancipation Proclamation but accounted for 85,904. These figures are only approximations because not all of Louisiana was exempted. Slaves were also recruited from the portions of northern and western Virginia that were exempt.

66 Peter Bruner, *A Slave's Adventures toward Freedom: Not Fiction, but the True Story of a Struggle* (Oxford, OH, [1919?]), pp. 42–46.

67 H. C. Bruce, *The New Man: Twenty-Nine Years a Slave. Twenty-Nine Years a Free Man* (York, PA: P. Anstadt, 1895), p. 107.

68 Samuel Hall, *Forty-Seven Years a Slave: A Brief History of His Life before and after Freedom Came to Him* (Washington, IA, 1912), pp. 22–25.

69 *CW*, vol. 6, pp. 48, 63.

CHAPTER 11: "THE SYSTEM YET LIVES"

1 Abraham Lincoln to James C. Conkling, in *CW*, vol. 6, p. 409; James M. McPherson, *Battle Cry of Freedom: The Civil War Era* (New York: Oxford University Press, 1988), pp. 627–636.

2 McPherson, *Battle Cry of Freedom*, pp. 308–388; *CW*, vol. 6, p. 410.

3 *CW*, vol. 6, p. 176. On the Confederacy as a proslavery nation, see Stephanie McCurry, *Confederate Reckoning: Power and Politics in the Civil War South* (Cambridge: Harvard University Press, 2010); Bruce Levine, *The Fall of the House of Dixie: How the Civil War Remade the American South* (New York: Random House, 2013).

   I borrow the term "counter-revolution of property" from W. E. B. Du Bois, *Black Reconstruction in America* (New York: Russell & Russell, 1956), pp. 580–636. See also McPherson, *Battle Cry of Freedom*, pp. 202–275, who describes the electoral victory of Lincoln and the Republicans as the "Revolution of 1860," and secession as "The Counter-Revolution of 1861."

   The Confederate treaties with Native Americans are in *OR*, ser. 4, vol. 1, p. 433. See also pp. 520 (Seminoles), 643 (Osage), 653 (Seneca and Shawnee), 663 (Quapaw), and 678 (Cherokee). Two older studies explore this history: Annie Heloise Abel, *The American Indian as Slaveholder and Secessionist* (Cleveland: Arthur H. Clark, 1915; repr. Lincoln: University of Nebraska Press, 1992); Abel, *The American Indian and the End of the Confederacy: 1863–1866* (Cleveland: Arthur H. Clark, 1925; repr. Lincoln: University of Nebraska Press, 1992).

4 *OR*, ser. 4, vol. 1, p. 145.

5 Lynda Lasswell Crist et al., eds., *The Papers of Jefferson Davis* (Baton Rouge: Louisiana State University Press, 1992), vol. 7, p. 417; *OR*, ser. 4, vol. 1, p. 848; *OR*, ser. 4, vol. 2, pp. 190, 211, 362.

6 Bruce Levine, *Confederate Emancipation: Southern Plans to Free and Arm Slaves during the War* (New York: Oxford University Press, 2006).

7 *OR*, ser. 4, vol. 1, pp. 1084, 1106; ser. 4, vol. 2, p. 128; also vol. 3, p. 385.

8 Ibid., ser. 1, vol. 24, pt. 3, p. 1044.

9 In early 1864 the Confederate Congress passed a supplemental appropriation to compensate masters "[f]or the loss of slaves which have been impressed by Confederate authorities, or under State laws for the use of the Confederate Government, and while engaged in laboring on the public defenses, have

escaped to the enemy, or died, or contracted diseases which have, after their discharge, resulted fatally, three million one hundred and eight thousand dollars." *OR*, ser. 4, vol. 3, p. 139.

10 *OR*, ser. 1, vol. 22, pt. 2, p. 990; Crist et al., eds., *Papers of Jefferson Davis*, vol. 10, pp. 125–126, n. 3.

11 *Acts of the General Assembly of the State of Georgia* (Milledgeville, GA: Boughton, Nisbet & Barnes, 1862), pp. 68–69.

12 Crist et al., eds., *Papers of Jefferson Davis*, vol. 9, pp. 359, 384; vol. 10, p. 19; Sally E. Hadden, *Slave Patrols: Law and Violence in Virginia and the Carolinas* (Cambridge: Harvard University Press, 2001), pp. 167–202.

13 Harry Smith, *Fifty Years of Slavery in the United States of America* (Grand Rapids: West Michigan Printing, 1891), p. 121. See Winthrop Jordan, *Tumult and Silence at Second Creek: An Inquiry into a Civil War Slave Conspiracy* (Baton Rouge: Louisiana University Press, 1993); John Cimprich, *Fort Pillow: A Civil War Massacre and Public Memory* (Baton Rouge: Louisiana State University Press, 2005); Andrew Ward, *River Run Red: The Fort Pillow Massacre in the American Civil War* (New York: Viking Press, 2005); George S. Burkhardt, *Confederate Rage, Yankee Wrath: No Quarter in the Civil War* (Carbondale: Southern Illinois University Press, 2007).

14 H. C. Bruce *The New Man: Twenty-Nine Years a Slave. Twenty-Nine Years a Free Man* (York, PA: Anstadt & Sons, 1895), p. 96; Levi Branham, *My Life and Travels* (Dalton, GA: A. J. Showalter, 1929), p. 22.

15 Charles Heyward Diaries, Colleton District and Charleston; Rose Hill Plantation diary, June 1, 1861; Lewisburg and Amsterdam diary, entry for 1862; Charleston diary, entries for Dec. 1861, Feb. 1862, and June 1862, South Carolina Library, *Records of Antebellum Southern Plantations*, ser. A, pt. 2, reel 7.

16 John Screven to Mary Screven, Sept. 12, 1862, Arnold and Screven Family Papers, Southern Historical Collection, *Records of Antebellum Southern Plantations*, ser. J, pt. 4, reel 9.

17 In February of 1862 even Jefferson Davis urged his brother, Joseph, to "be ready to move your negroes" should the Union invasion penetrate much farther South. See Crist et al., eds., *Papers of Jefferson Davis*, vol. 8, p. 53. On "refugeeing" of slaves during the war, see James Roark, *Masters without Slaves* (New York: W. W. Norton, 1977); Leon Litwack, *Been in the Storm So Long* (New York: Knopf, 1979); Clarence Mohr, *On the Threshold of Freedom: Masters and Slaves in Civil War Georgia* (Athens: University of Georgia Press, 1986).

18 Louisa Alexander to Adam Leopold Alexander, Nov. 17, 1861, Alexander and Hillhouse Family Papers, Southern Historical Collection, *Records of Antebellum Southern Plantations*, ser. J, pt. 4, reel 13.

19 James M. Clifton, ed., *Life and Labor on Argyle Island: Letters and Documents*

of a Savannah River Rice Plantation, 1833–1867 (Savannah: Beehive Press, 1978), pp. 313, 314, 319–320. On the antebellum history of Gowrie, see William Dusinberre, *Them Dark Days: Slavery in the American Rice Swamps* (Athens: University of Georgia Press, 1996).

20 Clifton, ed., *Life and Labor on Argyle Island*, pp. 327, 320.

21 Ibid., pp. 320–323.

22 Ibid., pp. 325, 328, 331, 337, 339, 324.

23 Ibid., pp. 340, 343, 348, 350.

24 Peter Bruner, *A Slave's Adventures toward Freedom* (Oxford, OH, [1919?]), pp. 32–33, 35ff. See also David Blight, *A Slave No More: Two Men Who Escaped to Freedom, Including Their Own Narratives of Emancipation* (Orlando, FL: Harcourt, 2007).

25 The information on Hughes in this and subsequent paragraphs comes primarily from Louis Hughes, *Thirty Years a Slave: From Bondage to Freedom* (Milwaukee: South Side Publishing, 1897). Hughes made a few minor errors of spelling and dating, but documentary evidence supports the basic outlines of his own account. Throughout his autobiography, Hughes spells his owner's name "McGee," for example, but the U.S. census records indicate that the planter spelled his name "McGehee." Particularly helpful in clarifying the details of Hughes's movements during the Civil War is Stephen V. Ash, *A Year in the South: Four Lives in 1865* (New York: Palgrave Macmillan, 2002). I would like to thank Professor Ash for generously sharing his research notes with me.

26 Litwack, *Been in the Storm So Long*.

27 On the experience of blacks in the Union army, see Dudley Taylor Cornish, *The Sable Arm: Negro Troops in the Union Army, 1861–1865* (New York: W. W. Norton, 1966); Joseph Glatthaar, *Forged in Battle: The Civil War Alliance of Black Soldiers and White Officers* (Baton Rouge: Louisiana State University Press 2000); Ira Berlin, Joseph Patrick Reidy, and Leslie Rowland, eds., *Freedom's Soldiers: The Black Military Experience in the Civil War* (Cambridge: Cambridge University Press, 1998); John David Smith, ed., *Black Soldiers in Blue: African American Troops in the Civil War Era* (Chapel Hill: University of North Carolina Press, 2002).

28 Brooks D. Simpson and Jean V. Berlin, eds., *Sherman's Civil War: Selected Correspondence of William T. Sherman, 1860–1865* (Chapel Hill: University of North Carolina Press, 1999), p. 293.

29 John Hope Franklin, ed., *The Diary of James T. Ayers: Civil War Recruiter* (Baton Rouge, Louisiana State University Press, 1999), p. 46; Richard Sears, ed., *Camp Nelson, Kentucky: A Civil War History* (Lexington: University Press of Kentucky, 2002), pp. 156–157.

30 Simpson and Berlin, eds., *Sherman's Civil War*, p. 311.

31 *Private and Official Correspondence of Gen. Benjamin F. Butler* (Norwood, MA: Plimpton Press, 1917), vol. pp. 244–245, 447–450.

32 Sears, *Camp Nelson, Kentucky*, pp. 134–181.

33 *Philadelphia Inquirer*, Oct. 25, 1862; *Baltimore Sun*, May 18, 1863.

34 *New York Herald*, Jan. 4, 1863; *Baltimore Sun*, May 18 and June 3, 1863; *Boston Herald*, June 3, 1863; *Louisville Daily Journal*, June 2, 1863; Mary Todd Lincoln to Abraham Lincoln, [Nov. 3, 1862], ALP-LC. Cf. Elizabeth Keckley, *Behind the Scenes, or, Thirty Years a Slave and Four Years in the White House* (New York: G. W. Carlton, 1868); *Philadelphia Inquirer*, Aug. 9, 1865.

35 Jim Downs, *Sick from Freedom: African-American Illness and Suffering during the Civil War and Reconstruction* (New York: Oxford University Press, 2012).

36 *CW*, vol. 6, p. 387; *Boston Herald*, Mar. 31, 1863. The editors of *CW* estimate the date of General Hurlbut's memo as August 15, 1863, but if Hurlbut's order was a response to Lincoln's instructions, the president's memo may have been written several months earlier.

37 See, for example, the report in the *Philadelphia Inquirer*, Oct. 17, 1863, of a provost marshal in Cairo, Illinois, who issued an order "requiring all negroes who are not in possession of a certificate that they are in employment adequate for the support of themselves and families, to be placed in the contraband camp and provided for."

38 The Freedmen and Southern Society Project tabulations are in FSSP, ser. 1, vol. 3, pp. 77–80. The Project estimates that at war's end, 271,000 blacks "lived in the plantation regions of the Lower South that came under Union control." Another 203,000 worked under similar circumstances in the Upper South, which includes northern Alabama, eastern North Carolina, middle and eastern Tennessee, and parts of Virginia. Earlier estimates by Louis Gerteis, in *From Contraband to Freedman: Federal Policy toward Southern Blacks, 1861–1865* (Westport, CT: Greenwood Press, 1973), pp. 193–194, were compiled differently and yielded a somewhat lower number. Of the 1,001,300 blacks living within Union lines, 237,800 were under the "organized control" of Union authorities by the end of the war. More recently Stephen V. Ash, in *The Black Experience in the Civil War South* (Santa Barbara, CA: Praeger, 2010), pp. 74–75, arrived at a much higher overall estimate of one million southern slaves who "became free before the Civil War ended." Ash's figure assumes that all slaves in the Border States had been freed.

39 *CW*, vol. 6, p. 358.

40 Henry Wilson, *History of the Antislavery Measures of the Thirty-Seventh and Thirty-Eighth Congresses, 1861–1864* (Boston: Walker, Wise, 1864), pp. 116–117, 130.

41 Laurent Dubois, *A Colony of Citizens: Revolution and Slave Emancipation in the*

French Caribbean, 1787–1804 (Chapel Hill: University of North Carolina Press, 2004).

42 FSSP, ser. 1, vol. 1, p. 259; *OR*, ser. 1, vol. 23, pt. 2, p. 291; Victor B. Howard, *Black Liberation in Kentucky: Emancipation and Freedom, 1862–1884* (Lexington: University Press of Kentucky, 1983), pp. 42–44. Cf. Elizabeth Leonard, *Lincoln's Forgotten Ally: Judge Advocate General Joseph Holt of Kentucky* (Chapel Hill: University of North Carolina Press, 2011).

43 *Acts of the General Assembly of the State of Georgia*, p. 72.

44 See the exchange between Confederate Secretary of War John Seddon and President Jefferson Davis, in which Davis argues that captured blacks should *not* "be regarded as regular prisoners of war." Crist et al., eds., *Papers of Jefferson Davis*, vol. 9, p. 355; vol. 10, pp. 359, 375; Jack Hurst, *Born to Battle: Grant and Forrest: Shiloh, Vicksburg, and Chattanooga* (New York: Basic Books, 2012), p. 326.

45 Edward L. Pierce, "Second Report," June 2, 1863, in Frank Moore, ed., *The Rebellion Record* (New York: D. Van Nostrand, 1869), vol. 12, p. 322; John Niven, ed., *The Salmon P. Chase Papers*, vol. 1: *Journals, 1829–1872* (Kent, OH: Kent State University Press, 1993); entry for Mar. 13, 1862, p. 331; *CW*, vol. 5, p. 329.

46 *CW*, vol. 5, pp. 421–422.

47 *CW*, vol. 6, p. 357; *OR*, ser. 1, vol. 23, pt. 2, p. 291.

48 The horror of the war is a familiar theme in the scholarship on the Civil War, most recently and vividly in Drew Gilpin Faust, *This Republic of Suffering: Death and the American Civil War* (New York: Knopf, 2008).

49 *Cong. Globe*, 38th Cong., 1st Sess., p. 1203; Henry Wilson, *History of the Rise and Fall of the Slave Power in America* (Boston: James R. Osgood and Company, 1877), vol. 3, p. 406.

CHAPTER 12: "OUR FATHERS WERE MISTAKEN"

1 *Cong. Globe.*, 38th Cong., 1st Sess., p. 1203.

2 Ibid., p. 17.

3 Ibid., p. 1463.

4 Richard Sears, ed., *Camp Nelson, Kentucky: A Civil War History* (Lexington: University Press of Kentucky, 2002), pp. 135–181; *Cong. Globe*, 38th Cong., 1st Sess., p. 1317.

5 *Cong. Globe*, 38th Cong., 1st Sess., p. 1324, 20.

6 *Cong. Globe.* 38th Cong., 1st Sess., pp. 83, 1421, 2978. Illinois Republican John Farnsworth accused Democrats of being willing to re-enslave black sol-

diers. The Democrats voted against black troops, wanted to strip black troops of their uniforms, and voted "universally" against the repeal of the Fugitive Slave Act. Indiana Democrat William S. Holman denied that he would re-enslave those owned by *disloyal* masters, thus indirectly admitting that he approved of the re-enslavement of blacks owned by *loyal* masters—the tens of thousands who enlisted from the Border States.

7 *Cong. Globe*, 38th Cong., 1st Sess., p. 1420.

8 Ibid., pp. 1461–1463.

9 Ibid., p. 1314.

10 Ibid., p. 19.

11 Ibid., p. 1313.

12 Legal scholars studying the Thirteenth Amendment have focused almost exclusively on this second, "enforcement" clause, hoping to find there a justification for federal activism on behalf of civil rights. See, for example, the symposium on the Thirteenth Amendment in *Maryland Law Review* 71, no. 1 (2011). Cf. Michael Kent Curtis, *No State Shall Abridge: The Fourteenth Amendment and the Bill of Rights* (Durham, NC: Duke University Press, 1986), pp. 48ff.

13 *Cong. Globe*, 38th Cong., 1st Sess., pp. 1482–1483, 1488, 1489.

14 Ibid., p. 1313.

15 Ibid., pp. 1313–1314.

16 Ibid., p. 2983.

17 Ibid., pp. 1323–1324. Charles Sumner, who in 1852 explicitly denied that Congress could constitutionally abolish slavery in a state, had by 1864 become a most indefatigable advocate for the view that the Constitution was an anti-slavery document. Congress and the president already had the power to abolish slavery; hence for Sumner, the Thirteenth Amendment was largely superfluous because "*nothing against slavery can be unconstitutional.*" Yet in the end he supported the amendment because, he claimed, it did what Congress and the president refused to do. Ibid., pp. 1479–1481. Quote on p. 1481.

18 Ibid., p. 2983.

19 Ibid., p. 2949.

20 Michael Vorenberg, *Final Freedom: The Civil War, the Abolition of Slavery, and the Thirteenth Amendment* (Cambridge: Cambridge University Press, 2001), p. 71. One reason we know about James Brooks's speech, even though it is missing from the *Congressional Globe*, is that several Republicans responded to it, most notably Isaac Arnold in a speech entitled "Is Slavery Dead?" Arnold's emphatic answer to his own question was no. "I am not yet willing to admit the fact that slavery is dead." He accused Brooks of "playing '*possum*," pretending slavery was dead so that Republicans would leave it alone and abandon their proposed constitutional amendment. Republican Congressman Wilson of Iowa likewise claimed that

Brooks was being disingenuous. *Cong. Globe*, 38th Cong., 1st Sess., pp. 1197, 1203. Vorenberg, however, believes Brooks was sincere, which may explain why his fellow Democrats were so anxious to disavow the speech. On the other hand, he voted against the Thirteenth Amendment the following January.

21 *Cong. Globe*, 38th Cong., 1st Sess., pp. 2940–2941, 2952, 1366.

22 Ibid., pp. 2978, 2944, 1437ff.

23 Ibid., p. 2952, 2982.

24 Ibid., pp. 2616, 2957.

25 Ibid., *Appendix*, p. 113.

26 Ibid., pp. 1424, 5.

27 Ibid., p. 2940.

28 Ibid., pp. 2981, 2940; *Appendix*, p. 105.

29 Ibid., pp. 2942, 2983, 2988, 2615; *CW*, vol. 8, p. 149; Henry Wilson, *History of the Rise and Fall of the Slave Power in America* (Boston: James R. Osgood and Company, 1877), vol. 3, p. 387.

30 *Cong. Globe*, 38th Cong., 1st Sess., p. 1490.

31 Ibid., p. 2995. The final vote was 93 yeas, 65 nays, and 23 abstentions. James Ashley, the antislavery radical, changed his vote to no so that he could move for a reconsideration of the resolution when Congress returned after the November elections.

32 Edward McPherson, *The Political History of the United States of America during the Great Rebellion*, 4th ed. (Washington, DC: James J. Chapman, 1882), p. 318. On the same day the Senate passed the Wade-Davis Bill, it rejected Charles Sumner's bill, which would have made the Emancipation Proclamation a statute, thus legislatively emancipating all the slaves in all the areas in rebellion.

33 *CW*, vol. 7, p. 433.

34 Ibid., Annual Message to Congress, Dec. 8, 1863, vol. 7, pp. 49–52.

35 Ibid., "Proclamation of Amnesty and Reconstruction," Dec. 8, 1863, vol. 7, pp. 53–56.

36 West Virginia had also abolished slavery as a condition for admission to the Union. Technically, the "loyal" state government of Virginia did so as well, but nobody took that vote seriously since it represented only twelve of the northernmost counties, near Washington. In 1866 the restored Virginia government rejected the Thirteenth Amendment after the "loyal" wartime legislature had abolished slavery.

37 *CW*, vol. 7, Jan. 30, 1864, p. 161.

38 Ibid., [Abraham Lincoln to John A. J. Creswell], vol. 7, p. 226.

39 Lynda Lasswell Crist et al., eds., *The Papers of Jefferson Davis* (Baton Rouge: Louisiana State University Press, 1992), vol. 10, p. 129.

40 *CW*, vol. 6, p. 358; vol. 7, pp. 145, 155; Francis Newton Thorpe, *The Federal*

and State Constitutions, Colonial Charters, and Other Organic Laws of the States, Territories, and Colonies . . . (Washington, DC: Government Printing Office, 1909), vol. 1, pp. 295–296.

41 *CW*, Abraham Lincoln to E. E. Malhiot et al., June 19, 1863, vol. 6, pp. 287–289.

42 Ibid., Abraham Lincoln to Nathaniel Banks, Aug. 5, 1863, vol. 6, p. 365.

43 Ibid., Abraham Lincoln to Nathaniel Banks, Nov. 5, 1863, vol. 7, p. 1.

44 Peyton McCrary, *Abraham Lincoln and Reconstruction* (Princeton: Princeton University Press, 1978), pp. 186–270; LaWanda Cox, *Lincoln and Black Freedom: A Study in Presidential Leadership* (Columbia: University of South Carolina Press, 1981).

45 Thorpe, *Federal and State Constitution*, vol. 3, p. 1429.

46 *OR*, ser. 3, vol. 3, pp. 855–856.

47 Lincoln's memo appears in the *Official Records* as his response to Stanton's explanation of the policy, dated October 1, 1863. The editors of Lincoln's *Collected Works* guessed incorrectly that the memo was dated from July 22, 1862. See *CW*, vol. 5, p. 338.

48 Charles L. Wagant, *The Mighty Revolution: Negro Emancipation in Maryland, 1862–1864* (Baltimore: Johns Hopkins University Press, 1964), p. 131.

49 Ibid., pp. 133–196. Quotations on pp. 135, 142, 143, 147.

50 Lew Wallace, *An Autobiography* (New York: Harper & Brothers, 1906), vol. 2, pp. 670ff. Wallace was the Union commander in charge of Maryland during the delegate elections for the constitutional convention. The "problem," as Wallace remembered it, was "to get a majority of delegates in the convention friendly to the abolition amendment without subjecting the national administration to a charge of military intervention." Quotation on p. 680.

51 Wagant, *Mighty Revolution*, pp. 221–230, quotation on p. 223.

52 Ibid., pp. 231–268.

53 *CW*, vol. 8, pp. 41, 52.

54 *CW*, Abraham Lincoln to Andrew Johnson, Sept. 11, 1863, vol. 6, p. 440; Sept. 18, 1863, vol. 6, p. 462.

55 Hans L. Trefousse, *Andrew Johnson: A Biography* (New York: W. W. Norton, 1989), pp. 152–175; FSSP, ser. 1, vol. 1, pp. 262ff.

56 Mark W. Geiger, *Financial Fraud and Guerilla Violence in Missouri's Civil War, 1861–1865* (New Haven: Yale University Press, 2010); Dennis K. Boman, "All Politics Are Local: Emancipation in Missouri," in Brian R. Dirck, ed., *Lincoln Emancipated: The President and the Politics of Race* (DeKalb: Northern Illinois University Press, 2007), pp. 130–154.

57 John M. Schofield, *Forty-Six Years in the Army* (New York: Century Company, 1897), p. 57; *OR*, ser. 1, vol. 13, pp. 772–773.

58 William E. Parrish, *Turbulent Partnership: Missouri and the Union, 1861–1865* (Columbia: University of Missouri Press, 1963), pp. 123–207.

59 *New York Times*, July 17, 1864.

60 Arthur M. Schlesinger Jr., ed., *History of American Presidential Elections, 1789–1968* (New York: Chelsea House, 1971), vol. 2, p. 1180.

61 *CW*, vol. 7, p. 380. Years later, in retrospective accounts, Noah Brooks and Isaac Arnold claimed that Lincoln urged the convention ahead of time to endorse the Thirteenth Amendment, but there is no contemporary evidence to support them. On the contrary, on the day before the convention opened, Lincoln's secretary recorded in his diary that "[t]he President positively refuses to give even a confidential suggestion in regard to Vice. Prest. Platform or organization." Michael Burlingame and John R. Turner Ettlinger, eds., *Inside Lincoln's White House: The Complete Civil War Diary of John Hay* (Carbondale: Southern Illinois University Press, 1997), p. 200. The Republicans hardly needed Lincoln's urging, and nobody needed to tell Lincoln that his party was already committed to the Thirteenth Amendment.

62 James M. McPherson, *Battle Cry of Freedom: The Civil War Era* (New York: Oxford University Press, 1988), pp. 718–750; Michael Burlingame, *Abraham Lincoln: A Life* (Baltimore: Johns Hopkins University Press, 2008), vol. 2, pp. 665–680.

63 This account is from James Oakes, *The Radical and the Republican: Frederick Douglass, Abraham Lincoln, and the Triumph of Antislavery Politics* (New York: W. W. Norton, 2007), pp. 229–232. See footnotes 18–21 for the sources on which it is based.

64 Schlesinger, ed., *History of American Presidential Elections*, vol. 2, pp. 1179–1180; Stephen W. Sears, ed., *The Civil War Papers of George B. McClellan* (New York: Da Capo Press, 1992), p. 584.

65 David Alan Johnson, *Decided on the Battlefield: Grant, Sherman, and the Election of 1864* (Amherst, NY: Prometheus Books, 2012).

66 *CW*, vol. 8, p. 149.

67 Michael Vorenberg, "The Thirteenth Amendment Enacted," in Harold Holzer and Sara Vaughn Gabbard, eds., *Lincoln and Freedom: Slavery, Emancipation, and the Thirteenth Amendment* (Carbondale: Southern Illinois University Press, 2007), pp. 180–194.

68 Lincoln's lobbying efforts are detailed in Burlingame, *Abraham Lincoln*, vol. 2, pp. 745–751. The classic reconstruction of "The Seward Lobby" is LaWanda Cox and John H. Cox, *Politics, Principle, and Prejudice, 1865–1866* (Glencoe, IL: Free Press, 1963), pp. 1–30. The lobbying campaign is summarized in Vorenberg, *Final Freedom*, pp. 176–197.

69 The remaining 18 votes in favor of the amendment came from "Unionists" (4 votes) and "Unconditional Unionists" (14 votes). There were 56 "nay" votes: 50 from Democrats and 6 from "Unionists." Eight Democrats abstained.

70 *CW*, vol. 8, p. 254.

71 *Journal of the Assembly of the State of New York*, 88th Sess., 1865, pp. 225–226; *A Documentary History of the Constitution of the United States of America* (Washington, DC: Department of State, 1894), pp. 522–637.

72 E. G. Baker Diary, May 31, 1865, Southern Historical Collection, *Records of Antebellum Southern Plantations*, ser. J, p. 6, reel 16; Shirley Plantation Journal, Library of Congress, ser. C., p. 1, *Records of Antebellum Southern Plantations; New York Tribune*, June 10, 1865; *OR*, ser. 1, vol. 48, p. 2, p. 929. One gauge of emancipation during the summer of 1865 is the spate of labor contracts signed and new labor regulations posted between June and September. See Steven Hahn et al., *Freedom: A Documentary History of Emancipation, 1861–1867*, ser. 3, vol. 1: *Land and Labor, 1865* (Chapel Hill: University of North Carolina Press, 2008), pp. 332–391.

73 Edward McPherson, ed., *The Political History of the United States of America during the Period of Reconstruction* (Washington, DC: Philip & Solomons, 1871), pp. 9ff., 19.

74 Ibid., pp. 22–23; *Chicago Tribune*, Dec. 12, 1865.
   Legal scholars disagree among themselves about the legitimacy of the process by which the Thirteenth and Fourteenth Amendments were ratified. See the critique of the process by Bruce Ackerman, *We the People*, vol. 2: *Transformations* (Cambridge: Harvard University Press, 2000), pp. 99–119, 207–234. For a defense, see Akhil Reed Amar, *America's Constitution: A Biography* (New York: Random House, 2005), pp. 364–380.

75 McPherson, ed., *Political History of the United States of America*, pp. 20, 24.

76 Ibid., p. 25.

77 Quoted in Victor B. Howard, *Black Liberation in Kentucky: Emancipation and Freedom, 1862–1884* (Lexington: University Press of Kentucky, 1983), p. 74.

78 *Chicago Tribune*, Dec. 12, 1865; *Manchester Guardian* (UK), Jan. 2, 1866.

79 *Louisville Daily Journal*, Dec. 6, 1865.

EPILOGUE: WAS FREEDOM ENOUGH?

1 Stephen Hahn, *A Nation under Our Feet: Black Political Struggles in the Rural South from Slavery to the Great Migration* (Cambridge: Belknap Press of Harvard University Press, 2003), pp. 146–154.

2 Edward McPherson, ed., *The Political History of the United States of America during the Period of Reconstruction* (Washington, DC: Philip & Solomons, 1871), pp. 22–23, 25.

3 Ibid., pp. 24, 29ff.

4 Ibid., pp. 18, 21.

5 *New York Times*, July 17, 1864.

CREDITS

INSERT

Page 1: National Archives and Records Administration.

Page 2, top left: Brady-Handy Collection, Prints & Photographs Division, Library of Congress, LC-BH82-5159.

Page 2, top right: The New Haven Museum & Historical Society.

Page 2, bottom: The Granger Collection, New York.

Page 3, top left: Prints & Photographs Division, Library of Congress, LC-DIG-cwpb-04894.

Page 3, top right: Brady-Handy Collection, Prints & Photographs Division, Library of Congress, LC-DIG-cwpbh-03901.

Page 3, bottom: Prints & Photographs Division, Library of Congress, LC-USZ62-31165.

Page 4, top left: Brady-Handy Collection, Prints & Photographs Division, Library of Congress, LC-DIG-cwpbh-00210.

Page 4, top right: Prints & Photographs Division, Library of Congress, LC-USZ62-63460.

Page 4, bottom left: Prints & Photographs Division, Library of Congress, LC-USZ62-128709.

Page 4, bottom right: Prints & Photographs Division, Library of Congress, LC-DIG-cwpb-05620.

Page 5, top left: The Granger Collection, New York.

Page 5, top right: Prints & Photographs Division, Library of Congress, LC-DIG-ppmsca-26755.

Page 5, bottom left: Brady-Handy Collection, Prints & Photographs Division, Library of Congress, LC-DIG-cwpbh-00652.

Page 5, bottom right: The Granger Collection, New York.

Page 6, top: Graphic Arts Collection, Department of Rare Books and Special Collections, Princeton University Library.

Page 6, bottom: Yale Collection of American Literature, Beinecke Rare Book and Manuscript Library, Bibliographic Record Number 2111696.

Page 7, top: National Archives and Records Administration, Still Picture Branch.

Page 7, bottom: National Archives and Records Administration, photo no. 525135.

Page 8: Prints & Photographs Division, Library of Congress, LC-DIG-pga-02502.

Page 9, top: Prints & Photographs Division, Library of Congress, LC-USZ62-130778.

Page 9, bottom: Prints & Photographs Division, Library of Congress, LC-DIG-pga-03898.

Page 10: Library of Congress, Rare Book and Special Collections Division, Alfred Whital Stern Collection of Lincolniana.

Page 11: Library of Congress, Rare Book and Special Collections Division, Alfred Whital Stern Collection of Lincolniana.

Page 12: National Archives and Records Administration, ARC identifier 1497351.

Page 13: Prints & Photographs Division, Library of Congress, LC-USZ62-131137.

Page 14: Prints & Photographs Division, Library of Congress, LC-USZ62-945.

Page 15: The Granger Collection, New York.

Page 16: Prints & Photographs Division, Library of Congress, LC-USZ62-127599.

INDEX

Page numbers beginning with 495 refer to endnotes.

ABOUT THE AUTHOR

James Oakes is Distinguished Professor of History and Graduate School Humanities Professor at the City University of New York Graduate Center. He is the author of several acclaimed works on the South and the Civil War, including *The Ruling Race: A History of American Slaveholders, Slavery and Freedom: An Interpretation of the Old South*, and, most recently, *The Radical and the Republican: Frederick Douglass, Abraham Lincoln, and the Triumph of Antislavery Politics*, winner of the Lincoln Prize.

WITHDRAWN

29.95   1/3/13.

LONGWOOD PUBLIC LIBRARY
800 Middle Country Road
Middle Island, NY 11953
(631) 924-6400
mylpl.net

LIBRARY HOURS

Monday-Friday	9:30 a.m. - 9:00 p.m.
Saturday	9:30 a.m. - 5:00 p.m.
Sunday (Sept-June)	1:00 p.m. - 5:00 p.m.